MARKETING
An Introductory Text

Other books by Michael J. Baker include

MARKETING: THEORY AND PRACTICE
MARKETING STRATEGY AND MANAGEMENT
RESEARCH FOR MARKETING

MARKETING
An Introductory Text

Fifth Edition

Michael J. Baker

First edition 1971
Reprinted 1972, 1973
Second edition 1974
Reprinted 1976, 1977, 1978
Third edition 1979
Reprinted 1980, 1981 (twice), 1982, 1983
Fourth edition 1985
Reprinted 1986, 1987, 1988, 1990
Fifth edition 1991

Published by
MACMILLAN EDUCATION LTD
Houndmills, Basingstoke, Hampshire RG21 2XS
and London
Companies and representatives
throughout the world

ISBN 0–333–55685–2 hardcover
ISBN 0–333–55686–0 paperback

A catalogue record for this book
is available from the British Library.

Copy-edited and typeset by Povey/Edmondson
Okehampton and Rochdale, England

Printed in Great Britain by
Billing & Sons Ltd, Worcester

To Sheila

Contents

PART III THE MARKETING MIX

List of figures

List of tables

Preface

In the six years which have elapsed since the publication of the fourth edition there has been a continuing surge of interest in the subject of marketing. In retrospect the 1980s will undoubtedly come to be regarded as the era when belief in the power of market forces finally prevailed, symbolised indelibly in our consciousness by the tearing down of the Berlin Wall and the re-unification of the two Germanies. But the 1980s will also be remembered as symbolising the onset of a transition from conspicuous to caring consumption with the growing recognition of our responsibility to preserve and improve the fragile eco-system which is the world in which we live.

Despite these dramatic changes it is the detail rather than the substance of the book which has called for most revision and updating. Given its publishing history (reprinted almost every year since its first appearance 20 years ago) it would be a foolhardy product manager (author) who attempted a radical change in a proven and successful formula. It is still my experience that the great majority of students new to marketing have had some experience, formal or informal, of economic theory while it is much less common to find them familiar with theories drawn from other behavioural sciences such as psychology or sociology. Accordingly, the treatment of the subject seeks to build upon economic concepts if for no other reason that it was the economist Adam Smith who first drew our attention to the operation of the 'invisible hand' in the market place. That said, the fifth edition preserves the original view that an introductory text should provide a synoptic overview of the whole subject, that it should seek to build upon prior knowledge and experience, and that it should make clear how it relates to other disciplines and managerial functions, and provide a bridge between these rather than seek to perpetuate a myth of disciplinary independence. Above all else marketing, like medicine and engineering, is a *synthetic* discipline which seeks to pull together theories and ideas from a variety of more theoretically based 'single' disciplines and integrate them into a holistic approach capable of implementation through practice.

The major changes in the current edition are the result of *user feedback* from both students and colleagues and a content analysis of other basic textbooks. In summary the major changes are:

1. A new chapter on Marketing Strategy and Management.
2. A new chapter on the Marketing Environment.
3. A separate chapter on the Marketing of Services.

4. The combination of three separate chapters on aspects of distribution into a single chapter, Patterns of Distribution.

In addition to these major changes a number of smaller changes, e.g. discussion of database marketing, teleshopping, the role of branding etc., have been included to keep pace with recent developments in the practice of marketing. (In passing it should be noted that many of the theoretical foundations have changed little if at all in the last decade. Perhaps it is an indication of the onset of maturity in the discipline that while marketing scholars have dotted many i's and crossed many t's in recent years they have done remarkably little to modify basic theories and concepts.) Strenuous efforts have also been made to update the factual content – mainly by my research assistant Jennifer Skene to whom I offer my grateful thanks.

This revised edition is part of a trio of books intended to provide a firm foundation in the subject of marketing. Companion volumes are *Research for Marketing* (1991) and *Marketing Strategy and Management* (1985, but in course of revision) to which may also be added *The Marketing Book* (2nd edition, 1991) which is a compilation by the author of original contributions by the best of British marketing writers on behalf of the Chartered Institute of Marketing. Reference to these is strongly recommended to those seeking a more advanced treatment than is appropriate to an introductory text.

University of Strathclyde
December 1990

MICHAEL J. BAKER

Acknowledgements

The authors and publishers wish to thank the following who have kindly given permission for the use of copyright material:

The American Marketing Association for use of extracts or figures from the following articles: 'Psychographics: a critical review' by William D. Wells (*Journal of Marketing Research*, vol. 12, May 1975); 'A general model for understanding organisational buying behaviour' by Webster and Wind (*Journal of Marketing*, vol. 36, April 1972, pp. 12–19); 'A model of industrial buyer behaviour' by J. N. Sheth (*Journal of Marketing*, vol. 37, October 1973, pp. 50–6; 'Benefit segmentation – a decision-orientated research tool' by R. Haley (*Journal of Marketing*, vol. 32, July 1968, pp. 30–5).

Audit Bureau of Circulation for data on national newspapers.

The Cinema Advertising Association for data on the numbers of screens and costs by ITV area from the 1990 *AA Marketing Pocket Book*.

The Controller of Her Majesty's Stationery Office for extracts from *Fair Deal: A Shoppers' Guide*; for reproduction of the table 'Gross Domestic Product by industry 1979–1989' from *The UK National Accounts, 1990*; and for the use of statistical data.

Bill Donaldson for table, 'The relative importance of elements of marketing communication' in *Sales Management* (Macmillan, 1990).

European Journal of Marketing for use of figure, 'Scale of Elemental Dominance', by G. L. Shostack (1982).

The *Financial Times* for a chart, 'Distribution of world GNP', published 26 September 1989.

Heinemann for a table from D. Cowell, *The Marketing of Services* (1984).

R. W. Hill and T. J. Hillier for figure, 'The constituent elements of the anatomy of the purchase' from *Organisational Buying Behaviour* (Macmillan, 1977).

The Institute of Marketing for the tables, 'Importance of factors in gaining business related to product category', and 'Methods used to set advertising budgets' from *Marketing in the UK* (1983) by G. J. Hooley, C. J. West and J. E. Lynch; the figure 'Listing of major segmentation variables' from *Market Segmentation* by Michael Thomas in *Quarterly Review of Marketing*, vol. 6, No. 1, 1980.

Marketing Week Magazine for use of tabular material.

A. C. Nielsen Company Ltd for use of the table 'Nielsen Food Index'.

NTC Publications Ltd for table from *Marketing Pocket Book 1990*.

Prentice-Hall, Inc. for an extract from *Marketing Management: Analysis, Planning and Control* by Philip Kotler.

Martin Simmons for use of tables from *The Market Research Society Yearbook* (1978).

The World Bank for population statistics from the *1989 World Bank Atlas*.

Every effort has been made to trace all the copyright-holders, but if any have been inadvertently overlooked the publishers will be pleased to make the necessary arrangement at the first opportunity.

Part 1

INTRODUCTION –
THE CONTEXT OF MARKETING

CHAPTER 1

The marketing concept

Learning Goals

The issues to be addressed in this chapter include:

1. What is marketing?
2. How has the marketing concept evolved?
3. Is marketing a science or an art?
4. What are the origins of marketing theory?
5. Is there an overall theory of marketing?
6. What is the scope of marketing?

After reading this chapter you will be able to:

1. State the basic principles underlying the concept and practice of marketing.
2. Trace the development of the marketing concept to its present stage of development and explain why marketing was 're-discovered' in the second half of the twentieth century.
3. Review the theoretical foundations on which the practice is based and determine the extent to which the subject may be considered a synthetic discipline.
4. Offer an opinion on the existence of a genuine theory of marketing in its own right.
5. Assess the relevance and extent to which marketing theory may be usefully applied to practical problems.

■ What is 'marketing'?

In Britain recent years have seen a remarkable growth of interest, both public and private, in 'marketing'. The classified columns of the quality papers come out in a daily rash of advertisements seeking to secure the services of 'experienced marketing men', while the editorial columns exhort the industrialist to export more through the adoption of modern marketing practices.

Despite the interest and publicity a cursory sampling of opinion reveals considerable confusion, and not a little scepticism, as to the exact nature of the subject of marketing. The purpose of this chapter is to try and clarify the nature and scope of marketing.

■ Problems of definition

On first acquaintance with a new subject most of us like to be given a definition which summarises its subject matter as succinctly as possible. Further, we expect this definition to be generally agreed upon by those who profess knowledge of the subject so that whatever personal idiosyncrasies may be demonstrated in the subsequent exposition there will be a common starting-point to which the student can return, and against which he may measure the expositor's interpretation. Herein lies the would-be student of marketing's predicament – virtually every text on marketing starts with a different definition. A selection of the better-known ones in circulation quickly demonstrates this point.

■ Marketing definitions

1. Marketing is the process of determining consumer demand for a product or service, motivating its sale and distributing it into ultimate consumption at a profit. (E. F. L. Brech, *Principles of Management*, Longmans, 1953)
2. Marketing is selling goods that don't come back to people who do.
3. Marketing is not only much broader than selling, it is not a specialised activity at all. It encompasses the entire business. It is the whole business seen from the point of view of its final result, that is, from the customer's point of view. Concern and responsibility for marketing must therefore permeate all areas of the enterprise.
4. Marketing is the distinguishing, the unique function of the business. ((3) and (4) Peter F. Drucker, *The Practice of Management*, Harper and Row, 1954).
5. Marketing – The performance of business activities that direct the flow of goods and services from producer to consumer or user.

   - Marketing is the creation of time, place and possession utilities.
   - Marketing moves goods from place to place, stores them, and effects changes in ownership by buying and selling them.
   - Marketing consists of the activities of buying, selling, transporting and storing goods.
   - Marketing includes those business activities involved in the flow of goods and services between producers and consumers.

   (Converse, Huegy and Mitchell, *Elements of Marketing*: 7th edn, Prentice-Hall, 1965.)
6. Marketing is the set of human activities directed at facilitating and consummating exchanges (Kotler, *Marketing Management*, 2nd edn, Prentice-Hall, 1972).

7. Marketing is the business function that identifies current unfilled needs and wants, defines and measures their magnitude, determines which target markets the organisation can best serve, and decides on appropriate products, services, and programs to serve these markets. Thus marketing serves as the link between a society's needs and its pattern of industrial response (Kotler, *Marketing Management*, 5th edn, Prentice-Hall, 1984).
8. The delivery of a standard of living.
9. Marketing is – the process whereby society, to supply its consumption needs, evolves distributive systems composed of participants, who, interacting under constraints – technical (economic) and ethical (social) – create the transactions or flows which resolve market separations and result in exchange and consumption (Robert Bartels, 'The General Theory of Marketing', *Journal of Marketing*, XXXII (Jan 1968) 29–33).
10. The function of marketing is the establishment of contact (Paul T. Cherington, *The Elements of Marketing*, Macmillan, 1920).
11. Marketing is both a set of activities performed by organisations and a social process. In other words, marketing exists at both the micro and macro levels. Micro marketing is the performance of activities which seek to accomplish an organisation's objectives by anticipating customer or client needs and directing a flow of need-satisfying goods and services from producer to customer or client.
    Macro marketing is a social process which directs an economy's flow of goods and services from producers to consumers in a way which effectively matches supply and demand and accomplishes the objectives of society (E. Jerome McCarthy and William D. Perreault Jr., *Basic Marketing*, 8th edn, Richard D. Irwin Inc., 1984).
12. The purpose of a business is to create and keep a customer. (T. Levitt, *The Marketing Imagination*, Free Press, 1983).

The proliferation of definitions was the subject of an article entitled 'What Exactly is Marketing' (*Quarterly Review of Marketing*, Winter 1975) in which Keith Crosier reviewed over fifty definitions and which he classified into three major groups:

1. Definitions which conceive of marketing as a *process* 'enacted via the marketing channel connecting the producing company with its market', e.g. 'The primary management function which organises and directs the aggregate of business activities involved in converting customer purchasing power into effective demand for a specific product or service and in moving the product or service to the final customer or user, so as to achieve company-set profit or other objectives' (L. W. Rodger, *Marketing in a Competitive Economy*, 3rd rev. edn, Cassell, 1971).
2. Definitions which see marketing as a *concept* or *philosophy of business* – 'the idea that marketing is a social exchange process involving willing consumers and producers', e.g. 'Selling is preoccupied with the seller's need to convert his product into cash; marketing with the idea of satisfying the

needs of the customer by means of the product and the whole cluster of things associated with creating, delivering and finally consuming it' (T. Levitt, 'Marketing Myopia', *Harvard Business Review*, 1960).

3. Definitions which emphasise marketing as an *orientation* – 'present to some degree in both consumers and producer: the phenomenon which makes the concept and the process possible'. Only one example is cited by Crosier (from the philosopher Erich Fromm) and is felt to be an unconvincing argument in favour of a third category beyond the view of marketing as a function or as a concept.

However, one cannot argue with Crosier's final group of definitions, which seem agreed only on the point that marketing is a complex and confusing phenomenon that combines both the philosophy of business and its practice.

There is a general consensus in these definitions but there is no single definition. An explanation of this is to be found in *The Meaning and Sources of Marketing Theory* (M. Halbert, McGraw-Hill, Marketing Science Institute Series, 1965): 'Marketing, however, has no recognised central theoretical basis such as exists for many other disciplines, notably the physical sciences and, in some cases, the behavioural sciences' (p. 9). (Chapter 17 comments further on the development of theory in marketing in recent years.)

◼ Marketing: art or science?

The aim of the book quoted above is 'to explore the possibilities of having a science of marketing. How to put scientific concepts and marketing content together is the subject matter of this report' (Preface, p. xix). Tacitly, the rationale behind the publication of this book is an admission that marketing is *not* a science; it also demonstrates the belief that *it ought to be*.

In examining possible sources of marketing theory Halbert notes that marketing has borrowed heavily from the business disciplines (economics, law, etc), the social and behavioural sciences and the methodological sciences (mathematics, etc.) and that these borrowings have included content, or data, techniques and concepts. As yet this material has not been synthesised into a generally accepted theory and so results in the apparent conflict inherent in the plethora of definitions. However, a closer examination of the definitions reviewed earlier does indicate that in addition to the classification proposed by Crosier one can also detect a clear chronological evolution in the development of marketing thinking. According to Professor Johan Arndt, who was one of the early marketing theorists, marketing thought is developing in precisely the same way as other disciplines, from simple imperatives, 'satisfy your customers', to more complicated notions such as consumer behaviour analysis, to even more complex, ambiguous and sometimes contradictory formulations. In a paper given in 1984 (*The Anthropology of Marketing Systems: Symbols, Shared Meanings, and Ways of Life in Interorganizational Networks*, Proceedings International

Research Seminar on Industrial Marketing, Stockholm School of Economics) he argues that since the Second World War, marketing thought may be classified into three main periods – the Marketing Concept, the Broadened Marketing Concept and the New Institutional Concept.

As Arndt points out, 'the so-called Marketing Concept advocated focus on customers and customer needs and argued for integrated analysis, planning, and control of all elements of the marketing mix, popularised as the 4 P's (Product, Price, Promotion, and Place) by McCarthy (1960). Hence the main avenue to profits went through developing, producing and distributing products satisfying customer wants.' However, by the mid-1960s observers began to inquire about the potential for transferring marketing ideas and thinking into contexts other than regular economic exchanges in the market place, and in 1969 Philip Kotler and Sidney Levy published an article 'Broadening the Concept of Marketing' (*Journal of Marketing*) which argued that marketing techniques 'were used and *should* be used by all organisations needing favourable responses from internal interest groups' (Arndt).

As Arndt observes, 'This development is less a change than may be apparent at first look. As pointed out by Stidsen (1979), this broadening is mostly a widening of *application* rather than theory, transplanting existing theory (mainly relating to promotional activities) into new settings. Another limitation is that the Broadened Marketing Concept, like its predecessors, is mainly a stimulus-response formulation using what Johnston and Bonoma (1977) term the "unit paradigm" focusing on the individual social unit, the firm or the consumer.

Despite these criticisms the Broadened Marketing Concept is still the prevailing model among practitioners, and description and analysis of it will provide the perspective for this introductory text. However, the reader should be aware that marketing thinking and research is moving towards Arndt's third stage of development characterised by 'more complex ambiguous and sometimes contradictory formulations'. This third phase, which Arndt calls 'New Institutionalism', is seen as containing three distinct strands – the notion of marketing as exchange, the transaction cost economics approach, and the political economy approach. While elements of all these approaches will be referred to, detailed consideration and analysis is more appropriate to an advanced text/course in marketing. It is also the case that until a general theory is evolved the practitioners' and academics' view of the subject tends to be coloured by an emphasis of the discipline from which they came to marketing. This is certainly true of this book which is biased towards economics but, it is hoped, for reasons other than that the author was trained as an economist.

As indicated by the title, and in the Preface, this book is intended as an introduction to the subject. In view of the fact that many students have studied some economics it seemed logical to build upon this knowledge rather than give a behavioural or quantitative emphasis. Psychology, Sociology and Mathematics are less often found in the curriculum of 'business' courses at the undergraduate level and a 'Primer of Marketing' is an inappropriate place for an introduction of these disciplines. However, some discussion of concepts from the behavioural science is contained in the chapters on Consumer Behaviour (Chapter 6) and Marketing Communications (Chapter 15) and will be sufficient to indicate the relevance of these disciplines to the newcomer to marketing. The student who intends to progress beyond the elementary and descriptive aspects of marketing contained in this book will find sufficient references in the bibliography and recommended readings from which to launch into an investigation of other disciplines and their relevance to marketing.

From a negative point of view, then, marketing is just a hotchpotch of ideas 'borrowed' from other disciplines. More positively it rests on the simple principle that supply must be a function of demand. In the opinion of marketing men this offers the best approach to the solution of the central economic problem – the allocation of scarce resources so as to maximise satisfaction. However, to say that supply must be a function of demand is an over-simplification. Many economists would add that it is a truism which has been in currency since Adam Smith wrote his *Wealth of Nations* in 1776, in which he states that: 'Consumption is the sole end and purpose of production. . . .'

■ Fundamental problems of an 'economy'

Essentially an economy is a system by which people earn a living and their standard of living is generally accepted as a reliable indication of the efficiency of the economy. Paul Samuelson states succinctly the three fundamental problems which an economy must grapple with in his standard text *Economics – an Introductory Analysis*, 13th revised edn (McGraw-Hill, 1989), namely:

1. *What* commodities shall be produced and in what quantities? That is, how much and which of alternative goods and services shall be produced?
2. *How* shall goods be produced? That is, by whom and with what resources and in what technological manner are they to be produced?
3. *For whom* are goods to be produced? That is, who is to enjoy and get the benefit of the goods and services provided? Or, to put it another way, how is the total of the national product to be distributed among different individuals and families?

Many solutions have been proposed and some at least have proved in part successful; others have merely aggravated this situation. At the same time no commonly agreed on solution has been achieved and there is an apocryphal story of a business tycoon who instructed his personnel director to find and employ a one-armed economist. When asked why he replied: 'I'm fed up of "on the one hand this, on the other hand that"!' In reality most economists agree that maximising satisfaction is the problem, but differ only in how this is to be achieved. Those who have accepted the marketing concept believe the real solution may be expressed something like this: 'If economies are comprised of people, and we are endeavouring to allocate scarce resources in order to maximise satisfaction, then it is the satisfaction of people which we are aiming at. This being so it is essential that we determine first what people want and then allocate our resources accordingly.' In other words, we must determine the nature and strength of demand and create supplies of goods and services to satisfy these demands.

In studying how this concept may be related to the solution of the problem two approaches are possible. Firstly, there is the macro approach which treats national economies as the basic unit and then investigates marketing as a part of a bigger whole. Secondly, there is the micro approach which looks at marketing from the point of view of the business organisation and its functioning within the economy. The latter viewpoint is the one adopted for the purpose of this book in the belief that although all of us are members of large groupings, be they national, ethnic or religious, we are more at home in dealing with smaller sub-groups the operation of which it is easier to evaluate and comprehend. If the role and nature of marketing can be understood in these terms its functions in the economy as a whole will be more easily understood.

If the marketing concept is so simple, how is it that only in this century it has gained any credence and support? The answer is to be found in economic history, in which the evolution of economics may be studied, and no apologies are offered for the summary which follows. The objective underlying the inclusion of this summary is the need to put marketing in perspective – to try and explain why it is only in this century that marketing has emerged as a significant concept which is quickly converting many of its tenets.

■ Economic evolution of a theory of consumption

If one examines the development of an advanced industrial economy such as our own, one can clearly distinguish a number of stages through which it has passed, each of which represents a step forward as compared with the preceding stage.

■ The development of craft industry

From the Norman Conquest to the mid-fourteenth century England's economy was organised on a feudal basis in which the Manor represented the major economic unit of production and consumption. The Manorial system was based on an ideal of self-sufficiency under which each self-contained community endeavoured to meet all its own requirements with regard to both production and consumption. Under such a system the variety of goods available for consumption depended directly on the factors of production possessed by the community, and the skill of the individuals comprising it. The limitations imposed by the size of the unit, coupled with similar limitations with regard to the skill and knowledge of its members, effectively reduced it to a subsistence economy concerned primarily with satisfying the essential requirements of life – food, shelter and clothing.

For a variety of reasons the feudal system broke down far earlier in England than was the case in Europe generally. Among the more important reasons may be distinguished the shortage of labour following the Black Death, and the demand for English wool to trade with Europe to secure supplies of commodities not readily available within the economy. This demand encouraged the Manorial lords to free the serfs from their feudal duties in order that the lords might repossess the land they occupied and rear sheep on it. This dispossession of the serfs in turn led to a migration of population from the country to the urban centres in search of employment in the developing craft industries.

Craft industry leads to specialisation in the production of particular goods, units of which can then be sold, enabling the craftsman to satisfy his needs by purchasing the output of other specialist producers. As a result there is an increase in individual skill which leads to greater productivity and output. At this stage of economic development, however, the volume of production is small, the average income is small, and the market is distinctly local with the exception of a very limited range of goods imported and exported to meet the demand of a gentry with sufficient income to afford them.

■ The division of labour

The next stage of economic development is usually exemplified by Adam Smith's account of the pin-making industry, where an enormous increase in output followed job simplification with the same input of factors of production, excluding raw materials. Smith noted that where men were engaged in all processes involved in the manufacture of pins their average output was twenty pins per day; when the manufacture of pins was broken down into separate processes output for the group rose to nearly five thousand pins per man per day.

Smith's description of this primitive production line identified at least ten separate tasks:

> One man draws out the wire, another straightens it, a third cuts it, a fourth points it, a fifth grinds it at the top for receiving the head; to make the head requires two or three distinct operations; to put it on is a peculiar business, to whiten the pins is another; it is even a trade by itself to put them into the paper.

Two points are of particular significance in this step forward. First, organisation is required to bring together the men, provide a place of work and supply raw materials. Second, the enormous increase in output reduces the price of the commodity, necessitates the development of channels of distribution to make the article available to those with a demand for it, and leads to the exploitation of a much larger market.

■ The industrial revolution

The period when this change occurred coincided with the early stages of the industrial revolution, which was to give impetus to the growth of a factory economy, job specialisation and mass production techniques. The nature of the steam engine as a power unit – large, inefficient and expensive – meant that the installation of such a plant was only justified if its power output was fully utilised in driving several smaller machines as, for example, looms. This in turn required the construction of factories in which a number of machines and operatives could be assembled, while the simplification of process meant that unskilled labour could be readily trained to perform simple operations.

Concurrent with the increase in output of both capital and consumer goods, lines of communication were developed (canals, and later railways), as were distributive channels, to cope with the movement and sale of this output. By 1800 we had already become a 'nation of shopkeepers', a derisory epithet used by Napoleon, who later learned to his cost that only a rich and strong nation can support extensive service industries. It is important to remember that at this stage of development the range of consumer goods offered for sale was limited, and that Britain constituted virtually the sole source of supply for a world market hungry for such manufactures. The disposable income of the home consumer was small but a rapid expansion of population due to advances in medicine and public health created a continually expanding demand. The increase in knowledge of the nature and causes of disease in itself would have been of marginal value had not methods of large-scale production permitted the manufacture of the physical goods required in the creation of adequate sewerage and drainage schemes, and created the wealth with which to pay for them.

■ International trade and industrialisation

Throughout the nineteenth century home industry expanded enormously, as did world demand for our products. In 1850 Britain's exports amounted to nearly 40 per cent of all international trade, which, when it is realised that, by definition, the maximum any single nation could achieve is 50 per cent, is an extremely impressive performance and one which has never been surpassed since. This date marks a watershed, however, for it was to see the birth of the United States of America, and later other Western European countries, as competing industrial powers. At first the trend characteristic of the first half of the century continued; namely, the export of Capital goods to help establish basic industry in overseas countries in exchange for raw materials and food (coupled with a nearly insatiable demand for consumer goods). The development of industry in other countries resulted in a considerable increase in total output so that although our share of world trade declined, its value and volume continued to increase rapidly as the increase in income in other countries created an evergrowing demand for our products.

Initially, the newly emergent industrial nation must pass through the stages noted in respect of the British economy – namely, the development of basic industries such as iron and steel, which provide the raw materials of manufacturing industry, followed by the development of the latter along with lines of communication, and channels of distribution. However, the process is considerably speeded up for the newcomer as it is able to make use of existing knowledge and skill, and unite all the latest design in plant and equipment pioneered by someone else. As a result the new industrial nations are able to achieve rapid economic growth, e.g. the United States 1870–1900, Japan 1900–13 or 1945–65, creating a growing demand for basic consumer goods which can largely be met by the economy itself. In the meantime, however, the original industrial nations are not standing still but are channelling their skill and knowledge into the production of more sophisticated products which the newer industrial nations are eager, and able, to buy. A good current example of this is the demand for electronic equipment, machine tools and transportation equipment by the developing nations like India or Australia, replacing their former demand for basic products like steel or textiles in which they are now largely self-sufficient.

As a result of this economic development an increasing number of people are earning incomes which enable them to translate their latent demand for consumption goods into an effective demand.

■ The creation of 'excess' supply

However, the market, both nationally and internationally, has changed radically for, despite this growth in demand, increased productivity has resulted in a level of supply which is more than sufficient to cater for effective demand in any specific area. No longer is demand for a product chasing a limited supply of that good so that selling is an automatic result of production. Under present conditions large numbers of producers are competing for the privilege of supplying the consumer with their own output while trying to combat the claims of alternative or substitute goods. It is under these conditions that supply becomes directly controlled by demand, as opposed to demand accepting that which is supplied. Marketing must replace the narrower concept of selling in the sense of merely distributing one's output.

The situation with which we are faced, therefore, is one in which consumer demand dictates that which will be produced. In a sense this has always been the case, in that man has concentrated on producing those items in greatest demand. When the consumer has a limited income the majority of this is expended on essential requirements necessary for the maintenance of life, leaving very little for expenditure on desirable, but less essential, goods and services. This situation is to be found in the underdeveloped countries at the present time. For example in India 85–90 per cent of income is expended on basic essentials, leaving only 10–15 per cent for the purchase of medical services, non-essential foodstuffs, etc. The comparative wealth of some national economies is shown in the Table 1.1 and shown graphically in Figure 1.1.

TABLE 1.1 Population and per capita gross national product of some countries, 1988*

Country	Population (thousands)	GNP per capita US$	World rank	Country	Population (thousands)	GNP per capita US$	World rank
Switzerland	6.5	27,260	1	Oman	1.4	5,070	27
Japan	122.4	21,040	2	Greece	10.0	4,790	28
Norway	4.2	20,020	3	Portugal	10.2	3,670	29
United States	245.9	19,780	4	Korea, Rep. of	42.6	3,530	30
Sweden	8.4	19,150	5	Venezuela	18.8	3,170	32
Finland	4.9	18,610	6	Yugoslavia	23.6	2,680	34
Germany, Fed. Rep.	61.0	18,530	7	Argentina	31.5	2,640	35
Denmark	5.1	18,470	8	Hungary	10.6	2,460	37
Canada	26.1	16,760	9	South Africa	33.9	2,290	39
France	55.9	16,080	10	Brazil	144.4	2,280	40
United Arab Emirates	1.5	15,720	11	Malaysia	16.9	1,870	41
Austria	7.6	15,560	12	Poland	37.9	1,850	42
Belgium	9.9	14,550	13	Mexico	83.6	1,820	43
Netherlands	14.8	14,530	14	Turkey	53.8	1,280	49
Kuwait	1.9	13,680	15	Egypt	51.4	650	66 =
Italy	57.5	13,320	16	Philippines	59.7	630	68 =
United Kingdom	57.0	12,800	17	Indonesia	174.8	430	72 =
Australia	16.5	12,390	18	Kenya	23.0	360	79 =
New Zealand	3.3	9,620	19	Pakistan	105.7	350	81 =
Hong Kong	5.7	9,230	20	India	814.0	330	85 =
Singapore	2.6	9,100	21	China	1,083.9	330	85 =
Israel	4.4	8,650	22	Nigeria	110.0	290	89 =
Spain	39.0	7,740	23	Bangladesh	108.9	170	98 =
Ireland	3.6	7,480	24	Ethiopia	46.1	120	105
Saudia Arabia	14.0	6,170	25	Mozambique	15.0	100	106
Libya	4.2	5,410	26				= lowest

* GNP is calculated at market prices.

Source: The World Bank (data to be published in *The World Bank Atlas,* 1989).

Note: The Atlas gives data, sometimes incomplete, for 186 countries. 106 countries have been ranked by per capita GNP. All countries with less than 1 million people and , of necessity, those countries (mostly in the Soviet bloc or at war or civil war) for which GNP fata are not available have been excluded. The above table shows all industrial countries and selected other countries.

14

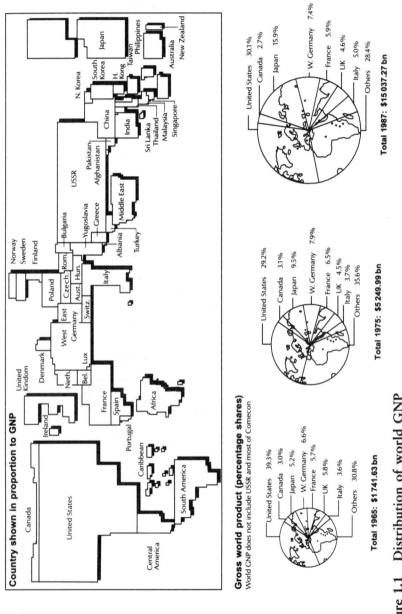

Country shown in proportion to GNP

Canada

United States

Central America

South America

Caribbean

Portugal

Ireland

United Kindom

Denmark

Neth.

Bel.

Lux

France

Spain

Africa

West Germany

East

Switz.

Poland

Czech.

Aust.

Hun.

Rom.

Norway

Sweden

Finland

Italy

Bulgaria

Yugoslavia

Greece

Albania

Turkey

Middle East

USSR

Pakistan

Afghanistan

India

Sri Lanka

Thailand

Malaysia

Singapore

China

N. Korea

South Korea

H. Kong

Taiwan

Philippines

Japan

Australia

New Zealand

Gross world product (percentage shares)
World GNP does not include USSR and most of Comecon

United States	39.3%
Canada	3.0%
Japan	5.2%
W. Germany	6.6%
France	5.7%
UK	5.8%
Italy	3.6%
Others	30.8%

Total 1965: $1741.63 bn

United States	29.2%
Canada	3.1%
Japan	9.5%
W. Germany	7.9%
France	6.5%
UK	4.5%
Italy	3.7%
Others	35.6%

Total 1975: $5249.99 bn

United States	30.1%
Canada	2.7%
Japan	15.9%
W. Germany	7.4%
France	5.9%
UK	4.6%
Italy	5.0%
Others	28.4%

Total 1987: $15037.27 bn

Figure 1.1   Distribution of world GNP

Source: Financial Times, 26 September 1989.

In the eighteenth and nineteenth centuries poverty was prevalent throughout the world for the majority of the population. Production was concentrated in satisfying basic demands, with a limited output of luxury goods for a small market comprising the upper classes.

With the rise in real income which accompanied increased productivity and economic growth the proportion of expenditure absorbed by essential purchases is considerably reduced, despite changes in the nature of the demand for these essentials, e.g. less bread and potatoes, more meat and butter, better houses, clothes, etc., so that in an advanced economy only 50 per cent of disposable income is spent on these items, leaving an equal proportion for the purchase of non-essential goods, services and saving.

Within the realm of essential purchases the nature and volume of demand are relatively simple to predict, and patterns of group behaviour are notably marked. With regard to the balance of expenditure on other products determination of demand for a particular item is far more complex.

The marketing concept in an era of accelerating change

The 'potted history' of the stages through which an advanced economy passes does scant justice to the subject and further reading is essential to a proper and objective understanding of it. As stated initially, the intention underlying its inclusion was to give some perspective to the development of economies to the point at which a need for a new economic concept emerged. A study of economic history develops, above all else, a sense of accelerating change. At the turn of the

TABLE 1.2   Elapsed time, invention to commercial development, of a number of familiar products

Product	Time from invention to commercial exploitation
Electric motor	65 years
TV	52 years
Vacuum tube	33 years
Zip-fastener	30 years
X-ray tube	18 years
Frozen foods	15 years
Nuclear reactors	10 years
Radar	5 years
Solar batteries	3 years

nineteenth century there were no steam engines or steam ships, large-scale steel production had still to be developed, as had the telephone, electricity, the internal combustion engine and innumerable others that were familiar, though not commonplace, by the end of the century. In this century the tempo has quickened and within fifty years of the first manned flight, man had a satellite in space orbiting the earth. By 1969 he had landed on the moon. Table 1.2 indicates the elapsed time between 'invention' and commercial development of a number of familiar 'products' and emphasises the increase in the tempo of technological advance.

Two points need stressing in this context. First, each new development adds momentum to the process, in that it increases our ability to produce. This may be immediately discernible, as in the case when automation is introduced, or less directly so, when a computer is installed to permit the solution of complex problems hitherto considered insoluble. These in turn may provide the key to further technological advance. The second point is that increased wealth results in an overall improvement in the standard of living and, consequently, an increase in population.

Before examining the challenge of the population explosion it should be noted that the foregoing description of the economic evolution on an economy has been criticised as an explanation of the origins of the current marketing era. In an article entitled 'The Development of Marketing – A Compendium of Historical Approaches' (*Quarterly Review of Marketing*, Winter 1990) David Gilbert and Nick Bailey cite this description as 'The Traditional View' of the development of marketing which takes the 'view that modern business practice developed in three stages:

The Production Era – increasing supply/reducing costs
The Sales Era – selling what we can make
The Marketing Era – making what we can sell.

The authors continue to observe:

Such a view infers that a sales orientation did not exist during (or before) the production era but came into being as a result of supply exceeding demand.

Similarly, it suggests that marketing practices were not developed until it became apparent that pushing goods on to the market was not as effective as focusing on the provision of satisfaction.

In order for the two suppositions above to be true, the 'Marketing Era' school of thought makes the following inferences:

- that neither sales nor marketing practices were fully applied in business until towards the end of the production era which lasted from 1870 until the 1930s.
- that sophisticated marketing practices were not incorporated into business operations until the 1950s.
- there was little or no competition in the market place during the production era – and demand exceeded supply.
- firms gave little thought to marketing before and during the production era.

These views are then contrasted with those of a number of other writers who claim that the production era never existed and that the importance of sales and marketing orientations were realised and the practice applied at a time when this supposed era would still have been in its infancy. Gilbert and Bailey then develop a series of arguments to support this view and conclude by offering a dynamic model of change.

This paper is well worth reading for the additional perspectives it offers on the evolution of marketing, many of which will be addressed in the development of this text. However, our purpose in citing it here is to acknowledge that if the inferences and assumptions cited may be deduced from our explanation then it is necessary to say they are incorrect. Our purpose in presenting an economic view of the evolution of marketing as a theory of consumption is simply to emphasise the *dominant* or prevailing theme at varying stages of economic development in Europe and later the USA. Of course, there has always been competition and the most successful suppliers have always been those who have best understood and served their customers using what we would now term marketing and sales practices. Out point simply is that it is only in the nineteenth and twentieth centuries that a fundamental shift in the balance between supply and demand has led to marketing becoming the dominant and prevailing orientation although firms still survive which could be characterised as 'sales' or 'production' orientated. We return to the current view of the marketing metaphor since its 'rediscovery' in the final chapter.

■ The challenge of the population explosion

This increase in population is largely attributable to an extension of the expectation of life, due to medical advance, rather than an increase in the crude birth rate, which, on the contrary, has tended to fall with the increase in affluence. More people represents a greater aggregate demand for goods and services. At the same time it represents an increase in a basic factor of production, labour, and thus provides one resource essential to the increase in supply necessary to satisfy this increase in demand.

Many economists have expressed concern over the population explosion, pointing out that whereas population increases in a geometrical progression increases in output, particularly of foodstuffs, tend to follow an arithmetical scale that will soon reach a point where demand will once again outstrip supply, at least in the areas of basic necessities. It would be foolish to deny that there is an element of truth in this contention, just as it would be foolish to adopt a fatalistic approach and accept the situation as inevitable. A superficial examination of the yield of Dutch farms as compared with those in the American Middle West will soon reveal a disparity of 5:1 in favour of the former in terms of yield. In the present situation there is no point in increasing the yield of the wheat farms of the United States as the present supply/demand situation is such that the increased investment necessary to increase yield would not be recoverable in profits owing to low market prices. On the other hand, if demand increases while supply remains static, prices will rise thus making further investments, necessary to increase yield, a profitable exercise. It is realistic to assume that this increased output will be forthcoming. (For an extended discussion of these issues the reader should consult D. Meadows *et al., Limits to Growth* (London, Earth Island, 1972) and the critique of it in H. S. D. Cole *et al., Thinking about the Future* (Chatto and Windus for Sussex University Press, 1973).)

Over a longer time-scale it is possible to envisage a situation where supply created by conventional farming methods, as we know them today, will be insufficient to meet projected demand based on current world population trends. Marketing has no need for Jeremiahs, still less for fatalists! Recognising that a need exists or is likely to exist, the role of the marketer is to deploy resources to maximise satisfaction by meeting these needs. If we are to predict the nature of demand in the future it also behoves us to undertake courses of action which will enable us to satisfy this demand. To argue that present methods are insufficient to satisfy a predictable future demand ignores the facts. Icarus failed to master the secret of flight because he lacked a high melting point wax: this is a factor which is virtually irrelevant in terms of aerospace research today. Failures, more often than not, result from the narrow inflexible approach which presumes that no further improvement or advance is possible; that the status quo is immutable. The few examples quoted should suffice to show that each breakthrough opens up whole new territories for exploration. During the 1980s, the birth of a baby from a frozen embryo and successful heart-lung transplants were front-page news. When did you last read a front-page newspaper story about an operation for appendicitis? Other than those performed on notable personalities, or under unusual conditions, no reference is made to the thousands of such operations performed annually. Once they were newsworthy, now they are commonplace. This undoubtedly will be the case with test-tube babies, organ transplantation, bionic men and the like in the years to come – always providing that economies continue to grow and increase wealth so that the physical and human resources are available.

■ The role of marketing

Marketing's role is to ensure the continuance in growth of economies, and the individuals' standard of living. In Chapter 5 the nature of demand will be considered in greater detail; at this point it is sufficient to point out that the determination of needs and wants, backed up by purchasing power, must indicate how management is to deploy the resources entrusted to it so as to maximise satisfaction in the total sense. If management succeeds in this, then human welfare will be optimised within the limitations imposed by the then available resources. Not only that; by thinking ahead and predicting the future needs and wants of people, action may be implemented now which will ensure their future satisfaction. (Aspects of welfare economics are largely ignored in this treatment on the basis that if private enterprise concentrates on profit maximisation the State will be able to implement the people's demand for welfare and social services from the taxes levied on these profits, i.e. the bigger the profits the greater the potential revenue from taxation. It is recognised that corporate management frequently abstains from profit maximisation for social and ethical reasons, *inter alia*, but it will be simpler for our purpose here to assume that entrepreneurs seek to maximise consumer satisfaction as a means to maximising profits.)

To conclude this introductory review some reference must be made to the functional aspects of marketing with which the majority of this book is concerned.

■ Marketing functions

If we accept the marketing concept, essentially we are agreeing to a simple proposition that supply is a function of demand and, therefore subservient to it. Demand is the controlling factor, and an analysis and understanding of it must underlie all marketing functions. In their excellent book Business Economics, Bates and Parkinson distinguish four managerial aspects of demand which for brevity and lucidity would be difficult to better, namely:

1. Analysis and forecasting, i.e. market research.
2. Product development and design.
3. Influencing of demand – design, advertising, etc.
4. Service – distribution, after-sales service, etc.

Much that follows is an examination, in greater depth, of these functions in isolation, but before proceeding to such a consideration, it is necessary to understand that marketing depends on co-ordination of these separate ingredients to achieve a 'mix' suitable to the particular situation in hand.

The idea of a 'mix' of marketing functions was conceived by Professor Neil Borden of the Harvard Business School as:

a schematic plan to guide analysis of marketing problems through utilisation of

(a) a list of the important forces emanating from the market which bear upon the marketing operations of an enterprise;
(b) a list of the elements (procedures and policies) of marketing programs.

The marketing mix refers to the apportionment of effort, the combination, the designing, and the integration of the elements of marketing into a program or 'mix' which on the basis of appraisal of the market forces, will best achieve the objectives of an enterprise at a given time.

Each function is a specialisation in its own right and it is unlikely that any single person could acquire full mastery of them all. Even if one could, it is doubtful whether one would then be able to make an objective assessment of the true relative value of each in any given marketing situation. Similarly, although many very successful marketing men have started life as a specialist in a single function, too high a degree of involvement is bound to bias decisions, albeit subconsciously. At such, the marketer, as a strategist and administrator, should aim at an understanding of the specialisations so that he may select the appropriate tactics to achieve his overall objective.

There is no need for a successful general to be a marksman, a ballistic expert, or expert at any other military skill for that matter. On the other hand, if he is not aware of the possibilities and limitations of the resources at his disposal it is unlikely that he will be able to combine them to achieve the maximum effect. As with the general so will the marketer. It is not necessary to be a clinical psychologist to appreciate the value of motivation research, or a statistician to understand the meaning of significance in relation to sampling results.

At the same time it is essential that the various marketing functions be isolated and examined before returning to the question of their co-ordination into an overall managerial concept. In general terms, the chapters which comprise Part III concern functional areas within marketing which are specialisations in their own right. At some time or other the aspiring general manager will come into contact with some, or all of them, just as he will endeavour to acquire knowledge and experience of production and financial management. All of us cannot become chief executive and, for most, a particular functional area such as market research may become a job for life from which great satisfaction can be derived. Whatever our ambitions, or our present occupation, it is of paramount importance that one recognises that the mix variables are interdependent and interacting. To view them as if they existed in isolation and in separate watertight compartments is to ignore the true import of the marketing concept. Everyone in a firm or an economy is making a contribution which in the aggregate will determine the material welfare of us all. Co-ordination of individual effort is critical to the overall standard of performance but this cannot be achieved by direction alone. Co-operation is an essential prerequisite, and this can only come from understanding how the separate parts together make a whole greater than the sum of those parts ('Synergy', q.v., H. Igor Ansoff, *Corporate Strategy*, Pelican, 1968).

Before proceeding to an examination of the mix variables:

Marketing research
Product development
Pricing
Packaging
Distribution
Advertising and sales promotion
Selling and merchandising
After-sales service

some consideration has been given to a review of the basic elements – demand, supply, companies – to provide a broad background against which to relate these more specific areas.

Similarly an extended chapter is devoted to a description of patterns of distribution as they exist; partly to provide background information and partly to contrast the difference, often more real than imagined, in the markets for raw materials, industrial and consumer goods.

CHAPTER 2

Environmental analysis

⎯ Learning Goals ⎯

The issues to be addressed in this chapter include:

1. The sources of major environmental change.
2. The need for the firm to take formal steps to monitor its changing environment.
3. Three broad approaches to environmental analysis – weak signal management, QUEST (Quick Environmental Scanning Technique) and formal environmental scanning systems.

After reading this chapter you will:

1. Know why an understanding of the environment of marketing is an essential prerequisite for competitive success.
2. Be able to identify some of the long-run secular changes which are shaping the future environment.
3. Appreciate why organisations need to plan for uncertainty in order to maximise the opportunities open to them while avoiding potential threats to their continuing success.
4. Recognise the importance of formulating assumptions and developing contingency plans based upon them.
5. Comprehend the importance of environmental analysis and be able to distinguish various methods for monitoring change in the environment.
6. Understand the concept of weak signal management.
7. Be able to define and execute a QUEST (quick environmental scanning technique) analysis.
8. Be aware of the need to establish a formal routine for regular environmental analysis as a key input into the organisation's marketing information system.

■ Introduction

In the preceding chapter it was proposed that marketing is concerned essentially with mutually satisfying exchange relationships. It was further proposed that as our ability to increase the supply of goods and services has grown so it has become possible to pay closer attention to the specific needs of more clearly defined sub-groups of consumers and to cater for these market segments through the provision of differentiated products. In the affluent industrialised economies such as the United States this potential to create an excess supply of any particular good or service led to greatly increased competition between the suppliers of such goods and services and led to what we have termed the rediscovery of marketing. No longer can suppliers be sure that their assumptions about the nature of demand are correct and are unlikely to change. In table 2.1 are listed a number of cherished assumptions which are now thought to be obsolete. To readers brought up in the 1980s it probably seems incredible that anyone could have ever held such assumptions in the first place but for many years it was assumptions such as these that underpinned most of the strategic thinking and planning of many of the world's most successful organisations.

TABLE 2.1   Cherished assumptions now thought obsolete

- Inflation will never exceed 5 per cent per annum
- Energy will always be cheap and abundant
- The price of oil will never exceed $2 a barrel
- Import penetration of home markets will never exceed 15 per cent
- The primary aim of business is to make money
- Strict financial control is the key to good administration
- Market growth of 10 per cent per annum
- Workers do not have an important impact on productivity or product quality
- The consumerist movement does not represent the concerns of a significant portion of the buying public
- Success comes from having the resources to quickly adopt innovations successfully introduced by others
- Frequent styling changes are more important to customers than product quality·

Source: D. Brownlie, *The Marketing Book* (London: Heinemann, 1987) p. 100.

In this chapter we shall examine some of the factors which have resulted in the need not only to revise our former cherished assumptions but to continuously monitor and review those which enjoy currency today. While it has become a cliché to talk of the pace of accelerating change, all the evidence points to the fact that this reflects reality and that, since it is competition which fuels the pace of change, we can look forward to even greater change in the 1990s as international competition intensifies. Accordingly, in this chapter we shall seek to identify some of the major changes which offer both threats and opportunities to the continued existence of an organisation. In order to cope with this change it will be suggested that an organisation must take formal steps to monitor the environment in which it is operating and intends to operate in the future. Three broad approaches will be proposed, namely, weak signal management as developed by Ansoff, Quest (Quick Environmental Scanning Technique) the methodology first proposed by Burt Nanus and, thirdly, a formal environmental scanning activity as an element in the marketing information system.

■ Plotting the future

In recent years it has been frequently suggested that one of the major factors which distinguishes the Japanese approach to business compared with that of the United States or Great Britain, is its willingness to take a long-term view of investment. By contrast it is argued that many British and American companies take a very short-term view on future investment and are unlikely to take on projects where the payback is more than three or at most five years. This reluctance to take decisions which will influence the fortunes of an organisation 10 to 15 years into the future is quite understandable given that the further one attempts to plan for the future the greater the uncertainty one is faced with, the less structured and more complex is the information with which one has to deal the greater the judgement which has to be exercised and the higher the consequences if one commits an organisation to a course of action which cannot easily be changed once it has been embarked upon. Thus, long-term strategic planning is more like the navigation of a supertanker than a sailing dinghy where decisions to change the course of the former may have to be taken up to an hour ahead of any action, whereas one can change the direction of a sailing dinghy instantaneously. It is because environmental analysis possesses these characteristics that it is generally the preserve of senior managers. A survey of top European chief executive officers undertaken in the early 1980s identified eight factors which characterise the environment which they felt faced management up to the millennium. These eight factors were:

1. A demand for quality and advice
2. A move towards a service culture
3. An emphasis upon the specialist
4. Shortening strategic time horizons
5. Scenario planning replacing forecasting
6. A reduction in head office functions
7. A wider international outlook
8. Tighter legislation

The demand for quality and advice is everywhere apparent and closely related towards the move towards a service culture. In advanced industrialised economies service activities now count for almost two thirds of the gross domestic product of countries like the United States and members of the European Community. To a large degree this shift from manufacturing to service industries reflects the application of technology to manufacturing resulting in a greatly increased output of more sophisticated products with a much lesser labour content than previously. Advances in technology have also meant that any new ideas can quickly be imitated or copied by other suppliers. Indeed, it has been estimated that any new technological innovation will be fully diffused through the world within 18 months of its first appearance. Against such a background producers have found it necessary to add value to their core products by providing additional advice and services.

These two trends give rise to the emphasis upon specialisation as suppliers seek to define particular market segments with greater and greater precision in an attempt to exercise monopoly power over a particular market niche rather than compete head on with other suppliers of undifferentiated products in mass markets. However, increased competition and technological change put considerable pressure upon management to plan to recover their investment within a shorter and shorter strategic time horizon. It follows that in seeking to chart the long-term future of an organisation less reliance can be placed upon traditional forecasting methods most of which depend upon an extrapolation of current trends into the long-term future. However, experience shows that technological innovations have resulted in a step change in activity rather than a smooth transition from the current solution to a problem to a new solution. In recognition of this management now has to plan by developing scenarios which represent their best expectations of what the future or futures facing the organisation may be like. The sixth factor identified in the survey, namely the reduction in head office functions recognises that with increased competition organisations need to remain flexible and responsive to changes in the market place. To do this, authority and responsibility need to be decentralised and located in the operating divisions which are close to the customers.

The two remaining trends referred to – a wider international outlook and tighter legislation – reflect the enormous increase in world trade which has taken place in recent years and the efforts of sovereign governments both to ensure that the quality of products and services traded meet the needs of their citizens, whilst also seeking to protect domestic producers from unfair competitive practices by third parties wishing to sell into their markets.

Table 2.2 contains a longer listing of what has been termed the 'new international business realities' which are perceived to be facing companies in the last decade of the twentieth century. These mirror the megatrends identified by John Naisbitt in his book of that name, first published in 1982. In an effort to determine the major trends which were taking place in American society Naisbitt hypothesised that as the relationship between news and advertising in print media remained approximately constant then new news would continuously

TABLE 2.2   New international business realities

- Continued structural unemployment in the OECD countries
- The end of the age of bureaucratic centralism
- Constant struggles with public spending
- Major shift in demographics
- Politics in democratic countries will increasingly become a matter of choice between hard and soft options
- Debt problems in developing countries will become institutionalised and there will be growth in aid dependency
- Gulf separating world's industrial nations from developing countries will remain wide
- Terrorism will continue as a disruptive force
- Investment will be oriented towards the short term
- Proliferation of small businesses
- Disappearance of 'automatic' growth in all major economies
- Heightened competition (including the NICs)
- Common product values
- Erosion of patent protection
- The change in financial services
- Postal services will continue to deteriorate
- Trend towards dichotomy in many areas of business operation – global or national niche
- Continued shortening of product life cycles
- Decline in manufacturing will continue vis-à-vis services
- Economies of scale are disappearing in some industries
- Transportation will increasingly give way to communication
- Changes in technology have made obsolete some human and corporate assets and created new ones
- Extreme and unpredictable currency variations – inhibiting rational decision making in manufacturing sourcing, pricing
- Volatility of basic commodity prices – leading to large changes in national purchasing power
- Merger mania
- Privatisation

displace old news. Accordingly, if one undertook a content analysis of the news contained in print media through the United States it should define the issues of most interest and concern to the American public. As a result of his analysis Naisbitt concluded that the United States was in a state of transition from an industrial society to an information based society. This megatrend has been confirmed in Western Europe and is a trend which may be anticipated to spread to more and more of the advanced industrial economies. The second major trend which he identified was that innovations pursue the path of least resistance. Essentially, this suggests that end users or consumers are more willing to take up major technological innovations than are business or industrial organisations. One explanation of this may be that ultimate customers are concerned with the benefits delivered by high technology and are less concerned how those benefits are delivered. By contrast, people in organisations feel obliged to try and understand the technology before exposing their organisations to the risk which its adoption might expose them to. Given that any new technology must represent significant potential risks it is unsurprising that organisations take longer to make such decisions than do consumers. However, while consumers embrace high technology gladly they have also exhibited a strong wish for greater social involvement with one another and this has created a burgeoning demand for new forms of leisure and recreational activity.

Improvements in information and communication have resulted in a much greater awareness of global issues and recognition that national economies are part of a larger, interdependent world economy. Recognition of this global interdependence has pointed to the need for long-term thinking on development by contrast to the short-term exploitation, such as the destruction of the Amazon rain forests, which have characterised much past decision making. Four closely related megatrends are the move to decentralisation and diversity as opposed to centralisation and homogeneity, from institutional help to self-help, from representative to participative democracy, and to networks in place of hierarchies. All of these trends indicate the wish of individuals to be involved in planning and organising their own lives. In summary, we can see that we are moving towards a post-industrial information era with shifts from standardisation to customisation, from centralisation to decentralisation, from dependence to self-help, from transportation to communication, from autocracy to participation, from hierarchies to networks, and from a state of information scarcity to one of information overload.

Numerous other studies confirm the findings reported above and allow us to state a number of basic propositions which most authorities would agree with. First, without any doubt, the pace of change is accelerating. Second, as a consequence, most aspects of the future are characterised by high levels of risk or uncertainty. Thirdly, while some aspects of their future may be extrapolated from current trends most aspects of it are likely to be both dynamic and discontinuous. Confronted with uncertainty the reaction of many organisations is to seek more and better information. However, because of the pace of change, delays in decision-making in the quest for more and better information is more likely to lead to a loss of competitive leadership than an improvement in competitive performance.

Faced with such scenario it is clear that management must seek to organise its thinking about possible futures in a structured and systematic way. In an analysis undertaken in the 1960s Francis Aguilar identified four main modes of what he termed environmental scanning. These modes are summarised in Figure 2.1 and represent a series of steps which might be termed successive focusing. Thus, undirected viewing is a part of the manager's everyday activity through which he seeks to ensure that he remains aware of information relevant to his responsibilities. As a result of this general awareness, he is likely to identify particular pieces of information which deserve to be followed up. Initially, this follow up will be of a fairly informal kind which is summarised by the phrase 'keeping an eye on things'. If this informal search throws up events or information which could have a direct influence on the firm's actions, then a formal and deliberate search needs to be initiated. To assist management in organising its thinking three complementary approaches may be recommended – weak signal management, QUEST and environmental analysis. However, before reviewing these in more detail it will be helpful to look at the nature of uncertainty and the role of assumptions in helping cope with it.

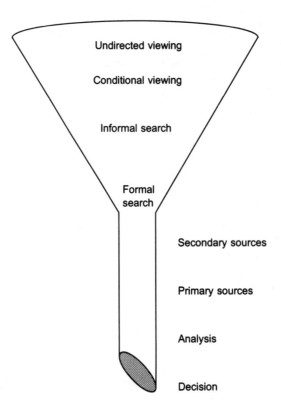

Figure 2.1   Successive focusing

■ Uncertainty and assumptions

In an article entitled 'Planning in a Changing Environment' (*Business Horizons,* September–October, 1988) Dale D. McConkey offered the following observation:

> Effective planning requires managers to plan for *uncertainty* – not for certainty. In the past planning for certainty made sense. Domestic and world economies were more stable. Change occurred less rapidly. The future could be predicted with a greater degree of accuracy. There were fewer uncontrollable variables. Product life cycles were longer; product development cycles were shorter. Planning was easier.
>
> But it is now more and more difficult to predict the future with any degree of accuracy. Thus planning must concentrate on uncertainty – in fact on multiple uncertainties.

In order to cope with such uncertainty McConkey argues that managers will have to subscribe to several practices that may represent dramatic departures from the way they previously planned. Specifically, firms will need to:

1. Place more emphasis on planning for uncertainty.
2. Integrate all planning – strategic, long and short-range – more effectively.
3. Review product performance more rigorously and be prepared to redeploy resources more frequently to optimise total performance.
4. Acquire more and better information.
5. Improve their environmental scanning abilities.
6. Determine their strategy based primarily on external market opportunities rather than internally perceived strengths.
7. Emphasise marketing rather than selling.
8. Review their plans more frequently.
9. Provide better staff support for operating managers.

Faced with uncertainty it is necessary to try and predict or forecast the nature and direction of future events and articulate these as assumptions around which one can construct the strategic plan. McConkey (above) offers a useful definition of assumptions as follows:

> Assumptions are generally defined as best present estimates of the impact of major external factors, over which the manager has little if any control but which may exert a significant impact on performance or the ability to achieve desired results.

In the opening paragraph of this chapter reference was made to assumptions and, in Table 2.1, we listed a number of cherished assumptions which had underpinned much of the strategic thinking and planning of firms in the 1950s and 1960s. While these particular assumptions are obsolete and not held by anyone any longer one should not underestimate the need for relevant assumptions as an essential element in the strategic planning process. The question is 'what are appropriate and relevant assumptions?' Most of the answers are to be found in environmental analysis of the kind discussed in this chapter.

Several clues as to the assumptions which should be built into strategic planning have already been reviewed in the first section of the chapter 'Plotting the future'. To develop formal assumptions, however, one must devise highly specific statements which are much more focused than the broad generalisation of the kind proposed by Naisbitt in *Megatrends*, or derived from surveys of senior executives and the like. For example, one needs to be specific about factors such as interest rates and the rate of inflation and cannot avoid the issue by making vague statements about increases or decreases. However, it is also important to recognise that one does not have to make assumptions about anything or everything which may occur in the future – only those events or issues which are significant and of direct relevance to the organisation developing the plan.

McConkey argues that the formulation of assumptions should proceed in orderly steps and proposes the following sequence:

1. Isolate those future events that are most likely to have a significant effect on the company's business;
2. Evaluate as accurately as possible the probable effects of these events;
3. Determine whether an assumption is necessary; if so, formulate the assumption;
4. Record all assumptions;
5. Continuously track the validity of all assumptions;
6. Revise the assumptions and plans and take corrective action when assumptions prove to be incorrect.

From this it is clear that assumptions represent our best guess as to the future state of affairs at the time we are drawing up or revising our strategic plan. With the passage of time these future events become nearer and the information available to us becomes more certain. It follows, therefore, that we should monitor the accuracy of our assumptions and be prepared to adjust our plans to reflect changes in our original assumptions.

When formulating assumptions it will also be helpful to try and quantify how likely or probable it is that a given assumption will materialise. Initially most people are more willing to express the likelihood of an outcome in qualitative or verbal terms such as 'Very likely', 'Likely', 'Unlikely', or 'Very unlikely'. When pressed, however, it is surprising how wide a discrepancy may exist between two different people's expectations of a given outcome when required to quantify this. Thus one person may consider an event 'likely' when it is just better than an evens (50/50) chance whereas another would only consider it 'likely' if the odds were 3 to 2 on (0.75 or 75 per cent probability). For planning purposes it is vital that all the decision makers share the same scale of values albeit that these values will be subjective, ie particular to each individual decision maker, rather than objective in which case there would be a known or certain outcome for a given event.

In addition to formulating probability estimates McConkey also recommends that one should assign a confidence factor especially when dealing with highly critical assumptions upon which major investment decisions may be made. In this context 'Confidence' refers to the amount of confidence the manager has in the data on which his probability estimate was made so that even though a manager might consider that a given event was very likely (90 per cent chance of occurrence) if he had no facts on which to base this assumption then it would have a low confidence value. Under such circumstances – a strong 'hunch' such and such would happen – the manager would be likely to increase his efforts to secure more and better information to test his belief. As noted earlier, there are several complementary approaches which will help the manager do this and these will be reviewed in the sections which follow.

■ Weak signal management

According to Ansoff most companies depend heavily upon extrapolative techniques in order to forecast sales, the economy and the much wider environmental issues which are of concern to them. In his view, such techniques to not have the ability to capture surprises and discontinuities which, as our earlier analysis has indicated, are more likely to be the norm rather than the exception. Accordingly, he suggests that other types of environmental appraisals are called for and proposes that managers should seek to structure their conditional viewing in such a way that they are more likely to pick up the weak signals which may herald future changes in the environment.

In examining why signals related to future change may appear weak to an organisation, Ansoff suggests that this may be due to at least one or other of four reasons. First, while the signal may have originally been strong, it may have become attenuated because the organisation is not tuned in to the right wavelength. The second explanation is that the original signal strength may have been reduced because of the existence of some filter between the organisation and the source of the signal or, possibly, because of 'jamming' between the receiver and the source of the signal. A third explanation is that the discontinuity or trend which is the source of the signal is a long way off and by the inverse square law the greater the distance between source and receiver the weaker the signal. Finally, it may be that at the very start of the discontinuity a signal is inherently very weak and so only likely to be recognised by those with specialist knowledge and/or paying particular attention to it.

Given that all firms face the same external environment it is obvious that the sooner any given organisation can pick up weak signals that herald future change the more likely it will be able to position itself, either to take advantage of the opportunity which they offer or to avoid any potential threat contained within them. In order to maximise the likelihood that the organisation will be able to do this, it needs to encourage persons who will act as gatekeepers, amplifiers and filters for weak signals in the environment. Gatekeepers, amplifiers and filters (GAFs) are people who are expert in the sector of the environment in which the organisation is scanning for information. In order to accomplish their task they must be positioned on the boundary between the organisation and its circum-scribing environment. GAFs are at the forefront of expertise and are defined as gatekeepers because it is through them that the organisation is able to look out into the surrounding environment. They are amplifiers because they are closest to the source of weak signals, and filters because it is through their expertise that they are able to distinguish the signal and screen out the 'noise' surrounding it.

While the concept of weak signal management is clear, and may be likened to the work of an astronomer or radio enthusiast scanning the heavens or airwaves in search of hitherto undetected signals, the operationalisation of the concept is not without difficulty. One approach which offers a means for reviewing and evaluating the weak signals that may be picked up by the firm's management, is the QUEST methodology proposed by Burt Nanus in an article published in *Long Range Planning* in 1982.

■ QUEST

QUEST is an acronym for quick environmental scanning technique and offers a broad and comprehensive first approximation to environmental trends and events that are critical to strategic decisions.

Nanus defines QUEST as:

> a future research process designed to permit executives and planners in an organisation to share their views about trends and events in future external environments that have critical implications for the organisation's strategies and policies. It is a systematic, intensive, and relatively inexpensive way to develop a shared understanding of high priority issues and to focus management's attention quickly on strategic areas for which more detailed planning and analysis would be beneficial.

Certain key assumptions underline the QUEST technique. First, it is assumed that the individual executives in a firm have a view of the dynamics of the changing environments which face them. It is further assumed that in the aggregate these views represent the organisation's understanding of its environment. However, in the absence of a technique such as QUEST it is unlikely that these separate views (assumptions) are articulated and shared. Thus, while individual executives may programme their future expectations into their decision-making, there is no guarantee that their perceptions and interpretations of the same facts are knows to and/or shared by their managerial colleagues. Only if there is a formal mechanism for enabling the firm's executives to share their different perceptions and interpretations will it be possible to identify any mismatch or disagreement between them. However, if any disagreement or mismatch is made explicit it will then become possible for management to negotiate a consensus on the interpretation of the information available to it and on the desired future towards which the organisation is working.

As with most aspects of decision-making, a systematic approach within an agreed framework is likely to yield better results more quickly than would an unstructured approach. Further, given that the outcome is to be achieved through a negotiated consensus between the key managers then such a process is more likely to instil a sense of ownership in the outcome than would separate independent evaluations.

TABLE 2.3   QUEST: implementation

1. Review current environmental conditions
2. Explain purpose and methodology
3. Review 'futures' literature to stimulate thinking
4. Define scope and boundaries for discussion including stakeholders and performance indicators
5. Identify key issues
6. Select agreed list
7. Assess probability of occurrence
8. Develop a Cross Impact Matrix (CIM)
9. Analyse CIM and develop scenarios

Table 2.3 summarises the steps involved in implementing a QUEST analysis. The purpose of step 1 is to achieve an agreed start point for the scanning exercise. As noted above, the purpose is to help bring out into the open and share the collective wisdom and experience of the participants in terms of their future expectations. The actual methodology for executing a QUEST analysis, is contained in steps 3 to 9 in Table 2.3.

Experience shows that the benefit of a QUEST analysis will be greatly enhanced by a review of other scenarios or projections of likely futures such as those contained in books like *Future Shock, Limits to Growth* or the publications of the Brookings Institution or Hudson Institute. Such speculations by other futurists are both a source of useful ideas to stimulate thinking and an indication of the scope of the exercise. However, as step 4 in the sequence indicates, for a given organisation operating in a particular industry and markets it is important that some limitations be placed upon the exercise so that its scope and boundaries need to be defined as do statements as to the perspective from which the analysis is to be undertaken and what criteria or performance indicators are to be used in assessing the importance and/or relevance of any identified issue.

Step 5 is perhaps the most important step in the sequence as it is the one in which the participants are invited to define what they see as the strategic or key issues facing their organisation. Key issues may be defined as forthcoming developments, either inside or outside the organisation, which are likely to have an important impact on the ability of the organisation to meet its objectives.

More simply put, key issues are those which could either make or break the organisation. Issues which, if well handled, will produce disproportionate benefit but which, if badly handled, could prove to be disastrous for the company. Key issues are often characterised by high opportunity costs for an organisation in that they are likely to foreclose other options. Clearly, there needs to be a limit to the number of key issues and the best way to proceed is to invite each of the participants to construct their own list of say 5 and then circulate these so that the group may proceed to stage 6, which is the agreement of a select list. Once the agreed list has been prepared the participants should then assess the likelihood or probability of occurrence of each of the events contained in the key issue analysis. This, in turn, should be summarised in a cross-impact matrix of the kind illustrated in Figure 2.2 in which the impact of each of the key issues is examined in the context of the other key issues. Finally, analysis of the cross-impact matrix should enable the group to develop scenarios which represent their own best expectation and understanding of the futures which face their own organisation.

From the foregoing description it is clear that QUEST is a broad brush and subjective approach. While its value cannot be over-estimated, it will be greatly enhanced if it is undertaken within the context of a formal environmental analysis activity. Indeed, it is such a formal environmental analysis activity which should provide the information input for both stages 1 and 3 of the QUEST methodology. However, while QUEST provides a means for structuring the knowledge and ideas of the senior managers responsible for strategic direction, environmental analysis is an integral part of the firm's marketing intelligence and information system and, as such, is a staff function which should be manned by professional researchers.

■ Environmental analysis

According to Aguilar environmental analysis seeks to provide 'information about events and relationships in a company's future environment . . . which would assist top management in its tasks of charting the company's future course of actions'. Environmental analysis or scanning is responsible for three major activities. First, it is responsible for generating an up-to-date data-base of information on the changing business scene. Second, it is responsible for alerting management to what is happening in the market place, the industry and beyond. And, third, it is responsible for disseminating important information and analyses to key strategic decision-makers and influencers within the organisation.

In establishing a formal environmental analysis function certain key criteria must be satisfied. First, environmental trends, events and issues must be reviewed on a regular and systematic basis. In order to do this it is important that explicit criteria are established with which one may evaluate the likely impact of the monitored environmental trends. Because it is a formal activity then it should be guided by written procedures and responsibility for the implementation of these procedures must be clearly assigned.

Event	Probability	1	2	3	4	5
1.		▨				
2.			▨			
3.				▨		
4.					▨	
5.						▨

Figure 2.2 Cross-impact matrix

Experience indicates that scanning reports, updates, forecasts and analyses have greater impact when documented in a standardised format and when such documentation is generated on a regular basis and disseminated to predetermined personnel according to a timetable. Finally, successful environmental analysis and scanning systems depend upon the application of formal techniques such as Delphi studies and writing of multiple scenarios.

A survey undertaken in the early 1980s of American corporations indicated that formal environmental analysis resulted in:

1. Increased general awareness by management of environmental change.
2. Better strategic planning and decision-making.
3. Greater effectiveness in government matters.
4. Better industry and market analysis.
5. Better results in foreign businesses.
6. Improvement in diversifications, acquisitions and resource allocation.
7. Better energy planning.

In other words an all-round improvement in performance.

■ Summary

In this chapter it has been argued that competition takes place within an environment which is common to all the competing firms. This environment is becoming more complex and changing more rapidly due to *accelerating technological change* and *increased international competition*. Given this setting it is top management's responsibility to monitor the environment so that it may both anticipate and plan for the future. Such monitoring should be continuous and comprise both *formal environmental analysis* as an input into the marketing information system and informal through *weak signal management* and *environmental scanning* of the kind proposed by the *QUEST* technique. Formal environmental analysis needs to be structured to satisfy the needs of the decision-makers who will use this as an input to their strategic thinking and planning and has become a specialist function with many professional tools and techniques available.

CHAPTER 3

Marketing strategy and management

— Learning Goals —

The issues to be addressed in this chapter include:

1. The nature and definition of strategy and strategic planning.
2. The concept of organisational culture.
3. The concept of the product life cycle.
4. The nature of marketing opportunity and competitive advantage.
5. The fundamental characteristics of the marketing audit and the marketing mix.
6. The idea that there is only a small set of strategic alternatives available to the firm.

After reading this chapter you will:

1. Be able to define strategy and understand the contribution which marketing has to make to the overall strategy of an organisation.
2. Be familiar with the concepts of organisational culture and the product life cycle.
3. Understand the concepts of market opportunity and competitive advantage.
4. Grasp the nature of the marketing audit.
5. Appreciate the need to set out clear objectives.
6. Be able to define the marketing mix.
7. Recognise the basic strategic alternatives open to an organisation.
8. Understand the concept of positioning and its central role in selecting a marketing strategy.

■ Introduction

In the first chapter we examined the substance of the marketing concept and observed how the process of economic development had tended to 'dehumanise' the nature of the exchange process. This dehumanisation through the adoption of task specialisation, the division of labour and the application of technology to the production or supply side of consumption was essential to improve productivity and enhance the standard of living. However, as we have seen, a natural consequence of improved standards of living is an increase in the population – more infants survive, people live longer – which results in a concomitant increase in demand. In other words, the size of the market increases and the supply side has to work even harder to keep up.

One consequence of this struggle to keep pace with an ever growing demand was still further specialisation in production and the emphasis upon what Ricardo was to term 'comparative advantage'. While Ricardo was seeking to explain the benefits of international trade, precisely the same benefits existed within nation states and led to the concentration of particular industries in particular localities. Glass manufacturing at St Helens and St Gobain, iron smelting in South Wales and the Saar, textiles in Lancashire and Lille, ceramics in Staffordshire and Sèvres and so on. Because of the economies of scale and mass production such favoured locations were able to serve evermore distant markets more cost effectively than smaller less well endowed local producers, resulting in a significant physical separation between producer and consumer.

In time this separation was to become psychological too, with producers assuming they knew what consumers wanted and justifying their assumptions by observing that the market was absorbing all their output and was clamouring for more.

So long as the market continued to expand exponentially through population growth there can be little doubt that the emphasis upon the mass production of undifferentiated products resulted in the maximum overall satisfaction. However, with a slowing down in population growth, and a continued acceleration in supply through technological innovation and change, the potential arose for the creation of an excess supply in certain markets. As soon as this occurs the nature of competition changes from so-called perfect competition, under which the product is assumed to be homogeneous, to imperfect competition under which suppliers recognise that if their output is indistinguishable from other suppliers then consumers will have no reason to prefer them to any other supplier with the possible result that they will be left with unsold goods. Given this possibility individual suppliers need to devise specific plans in order to compete with and succeed against other suppliers in the same line of business. In other words they need a strategy, which may be defined broadly as a statement of purpose and the means of achieving it. Why do we need a strategy? Because strategy is concerned with future action and it is a cliché but true that the rest of our lives will be spent in the future.

There are numerous books (including a companion volume to this – *Marketing Strategy and Management*) which are devoted solely to the subject of strategy – its definition, formulation and execution. In this chapter we can only touch on some of the bare essentials but it is felt to be important to introduce them early on as the whole purpose of marketing – both concept and function – is to help structure and improve both the efficiency and effectiveness of exchange relationships with the ultimate goal of maximising satisfaction from the consumption of scarce resources. Accordingly, in this chapter we shall seek to define the nature of strategy and strategic planning as well as the concepts of *organisational culture* and the *product life cycle* for the latter defines the inevitable pattern of change within which the firm must exist and the former the way the organisation chooses to approach and deal with its survival and growth. This consideration leads naturally to the concepts of *market opportunity* and *competitive advantage* which underlie all successful strategies.

In order to formulate a strategy it will be argued that one must carry out a *marketing audit* which will take in both the external threats and opportunities which exist in the competitive environment as well as the firm's own strengths and weaknesses. Based upon such an analysis the firm will wish to articulate clear *objectives* both to provide direction for the firm's efforts as well as milestones to record progress and achievement. In developing such objectives it will be shown that the firm has only a small number of strategic alternatives available to it and techniques for identifying and selecting these will be proposed.

Once a core strategy has been defined its effective execution will depend upon the optimal selection of the elements of the *marketing mix* – the combination of product, price, place and promotion – and this notion will be introduced for extended development in Part III of the book. In selecting the optimal marketing mix it is vital that the firm have a clear view of how it wishes to position itself against its rivals and the idea of 'positioning' will be introduced and described.

■ Strategy and strategic planning

All successful businesses owe their existence to the recognition and existence of a market opportunity. This statement is as true of the technologically driven inventor such as Clive Sinclair or the production orientated Henry Ford as it is of the marketing orientated Anita Roddick. Each of these entrepreneurs succeeded because they brought to the market place a new product which consumers instantly recognised as fulfilling a felt need. Subsequently, one (Sinclair) was to fail badly and another (Ford) was to falter because their initial intuitive success was not supported by a clearly defined strategy for building upon this. In the case of Sinclair the prospect of low cost calculators, personal computers and miniature televisions, were enormously attractive to consumers captivated with the marvels of microelectronics. His products proved the markets existed but poor delivery and, even worse, poor product performance made him an easy victim for those second to the market with more reliable products, guaranteed delivery and after-sales service. Similarly, Henry Ford created the mass automobile market with his Model T but lost out to General Motors because he failed to develop a second generation motor-car to satisfy the increased needs of more sophisticated and demanding buyers.

It was failures of these kinds, but of industries rather than firms, which prompted Ted Levitt to write his seminal article, 'Marketing Myopia' (see below). Using the American railroad system as his examplar Levitt pointed out how the invention of the steam engine revolutionised overland transportation, opened up continents and created an industry which, by 1900, was amongst the richest and most successful in the land. By 1950 this once, all powerful industry was in ruins surviving only with Federal aid and on a greatly reduced basis. What went wrong? Basically the railroad management lacked a strategy based upon clear understanding of the business they were in defined in terms of the needs served. What the railroad moguls failed to appreciate was that the steam locomotive and the railroad were but one step in the evolution of the transportation business. Railways offered significant benefits in speed, comfort and carrying capacity over the stage-coach, ox-train and river/canal barges they largely displaced. Their downfall lay in not appreciating that further technological progress would result in even more convenient, speedy and comfortable means of transportation with the invention of the internal combustion and jet engines. Consumers owe no loyalty to suppliers, only to themselves. If a superior product or service is made available to meet their needs they will have no hesitation in switching to it. Thus, as inner city congestion increases we are seeing an increased demand for improved public transportation systems and growing investment in mass transit/light railways. The question is if you are a motor-car manufacturer or a director of National Car Parks what plans have you for coping with the implications of this change?

To answer this question effectively it is widely agreed that one should undertake a formal and structured analysis along the lines proposed by Kotler and others, namely:

Diagnosis: where is the company now and why?
Prognosis: where is the company headed?
Objectives: where should the company be headed?
Strategy: what is the best way to get there?
Tactics: what specific actions should be undertaken, by whom, and when?
Control: what measures should be watched to indicate whether the company is succeeding?

The first question 'where is the company now?' is frequently couched as 'what business are we in?' Following Levitt's analysis in 'Marketing Myopia' touched on above, it is now accepted that the answer to this question must be in terms of the need served rather than the specific means of serving it. Thus Levitt argued that if the railroad managers had perceived of themselves as being in the transportation business rather than the railroad business then they would have regarded the invention of the internal combustion engine as opening up a whole new range of transportation opportunities. As it was they ignored it initially as unsophisticated and undeveloped (just as steam engines had been 60 years previously) and then sought to compete with it in markets where railroads had little or no competitive advantage. Of course 'the transportation business' is far too broad a definition for operational strategic planning but it is the kind of fundamental assessment necessary to initiate such operational strategic planning.

If one considers an archetypal 'marketing' product such as detergents then we might wish to consider the manufacturers as being in the cleanliness business. If this is the case then there are at least three developments which could seriously threaten the industry out of which Procter & Gamble and Unilever make millions of pounds' profit every year. First, textile manufacturers have developed and are improving soil-resistant treatments which prevent fabrics from becoming dirty so easily and so reduce the incidence of cleaning. Second, there is the potential of disposables – napkins, plates, cups, tablecloths and, above all else so far babies' diapers. (Procter & Gamble saw this coming and market the leading Pampers brand!) Third, there is an ecologically benign technology known as ultrasonics which literally shakes dirt out of fabrics without any need for water or chemicals which pollute the environment. If you are Electrolux or Hoover making cleaning boxes (rather than washing machines) the change in technology is only a limited threat – if you are Procter & Gamble or Unilever it could be fatal. Perhaps Levitt summed it up best of all when he observed 'When a man goes into a hardware store to buy a 1/4″ twist drill he needs a 1/4″ hole'. As soon as someone like Black & Decker develop a hand held-held laser gun which can drill holes with infinite accuracy in any material then the twist-drill business will be dead but the hole making business will continue to flourish.

This continuous cycle of innovation and change is described and analysed in one of marketing's central concepts – the product life cycle.

■ The product life-cycle concept

In *Market Development* (Penguin, 1983) we described the product life cycle concept as follows:

The paradox of the product life cycle (PLC) concept is that it is one of a very small number of original marketing ideas to enjoy a wide currency and yet is largely discredited in terms of practical application and relevance. That it should be discredited reflects a failing on the part of practitioners to understand the role and potential contribution of theory and concepts rather than any intrinsic deficiency in the concept itself – an assertion we will now seek to substantiate.

The analogy of a product life cycle is firmly founded in the biological sciences and the observation that living organisms pass through an inevitable cycle from conception through gestation to growth leading to maturity. In turn, the mature organism begins to decay progressively until its life is terminated in death. This progression is as familiar to us as life itself, and none would deny the inescapable sequence through which the normal organism will pass. That said, it would be a foolhardy bioscientist who would attempt to generalise about the expectations of a particular organism without first establishing its genus, species and sub-species, and even then they would only speculate about any distinct organism in terms of some form of probabilistic statement concerning expected future outcomes.

The validity of this assertion is easily demonstrated by reference to ourselves – human beings. An inspection of life expectancies quickly reveals major disparities between the inhabitants of advanced, affluent economics and their unfortunate brothers and sisters in the developing countries. Thus, while the average British male can look forward to a life-span of 72 years, an Indian has a life expectancy of only 39 years. However, if we were to compare a Briton and an Indian aged 30 years, the discrepancy in their respective life expectancies would be relatively small. The problem is a familiar one in the field of descriptive statistics; means or averages are largely meaningless unless we also possess some measure of dispersion about the mean. In the case of Indians, infant mortality is very high and the age distribution at death is heavily skewed towards young persons. On the other hand, if you survive the dangers of childhood, the probability of a reasonably long life is quite high. A broadly similar pattern also applies to Britons, in that infants and young children are more susceptible to disease and death by accident or genetic defect than are teenagers and adults. On the other hand, by enabling weak specimens to survive childhood one increases the probability of death in middle life, with the result that life expectancies for mature adults are very similar in advanced as well as in developing countries.

Actuaries understand this perfectly and base life insurance premiums upon average probabilities. The impression that your policy is written specifically for you is illusory, for no actuary would presume to predict your personal life expectancy. The irony is that while all of this is entirely commonplace and acceptable to us as insurance risks, as managers, we expect analogous models to possess a level of predictive ability which cannot be achieved with very large populations of essentially homogeneous units.

The level of information which we are likely to possess about a product group such as detergents or industrial fasteners is minuscule by comparison with the demographic data available upon people in general or nationalities in particular. But, despite this, we try to make a generalised statement about the sales history of a successful (unspecified) product into a highly specific predictive device. In fact, PLCs can be used as forecasting tools, but only when one has a considerable amount of information about the product, or one analogous to it, and the market into which the product is to be introduced. In the present context, however, the relevance of the PLC is that it is a constant reminder of the inevitability of change and does mirror the stages through which all successful products pass. These stages and the titles given to them are represented in Figure 3.1.

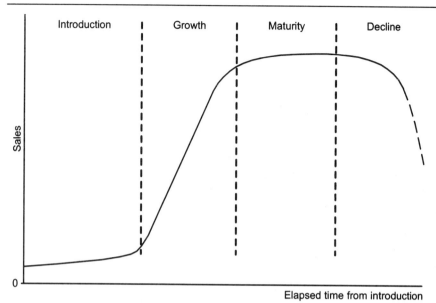

Figure 3.1   The product life cycle

As can be observed, the conventional PLC is seen as comprising four basic stages when sales are plotted against elapsed time from introduction. First, there is a period of very slow growth when the new product or idea is introduced to prospective users. This phase is terminated by a transition to a period of very rapid growth which eventually levels off into a period of maturity followed by a decline culminating in termination of the life cycle.

As noted, this is a conventional representation of a life cycle and must not be taken too literally, for depending upon the product type, the length of the various phases may vary considerably in just the same way as the average length of the mature phase of human beings has a strong correlation with socio-economic status. Similarly, overall life spans will vary enormously, so that fashion goods, like mayflies, are here today and gone tomorrow, while basic materials such as steel have very extended lives analogous to, say, elephants. But, given these caveats, the PLC does contain a number of important messages for us at both a strategic and a tactical level, and we shall return to these frequently in later chapters. At this juncture we merely wish to emphasise the message expressed so eloquently by Ted Levitt in his seminal article, 'Marketing Myopia' (*Harvard Business Review*, July–August 1960), which opens with a sentence which, while tautological, is a requiem for much of UK (and US) industry today: 'Every declining industry was once a growth industry.'

As we have seen earlier, Levitt's thesis is simplicity itself: too many companies and industries are product orientated and so become preoccupied with the manufacture and distribution of a product to the extent that they lose sight of the basic need which the product satisfies. In consequence, such producers become vulnerable to attack by competitors with improved or substitute products, but their myopia usually prevents them from distinguishing this until it is too late to do anything about it.

Myopia or complacency is always well to the fore in preventing the managers of declining industries from remembering the inevitable logic of the PLC: none of us is immortal. Furthermore, many entrepreneurs who rise to fame and riches through an intuitive ability to spot a market opportunity and to develop a product able to satisfy that opportunity overlooked what we have claimed is a marketing maxim: 'the act of consumption changes the consumer'. Railways opened up whole new possibilities for cheap, long-distance travel in comfort and at speed, but cars enabled travellers to plan their journeys to suit their own convenience and not be bound by the tyranny of the timetable while aeroplanes offered such enormous benefits in terms of speed that many services still largely ignore the total satisfaction of their customers.

But the seeds of self-destruction are built into every innovation. General Motors saw that once consumers had become accustomed to the basic benefits of a Model T, many of them aspired to something different and better, just as the Germans saw that economy and reliability would win a significant share of the market, only to be outperformed by the Japanese who added a high level of 'extras' as standard equipment to their own compact cars. Similarly, excess capacity in air transportation has resulted in significant changes in the competitive posture of many airlines.

Levitt's prescription for myopia is that firms think of their business in terms of the basic needs they satisfy, so that railroads, car manufacturers and airlines are all part of the 'transportation business' and thus are concerned with features such as accessibility, convenience, comfort, reliability, speed, frequency and relative cost. Of course, the railways do recognise this, and do attempt to maximise the attractiveness of their product offering within the limitations imposed by technology and their ability of generate finance for investment. It is conceivable that if they had recognised the incipient threat of the internal combustion engine, they would have diversified into an integrated transportation system and so could have shared in the part new, part substitute market for cars and buses. However, it is by no means certain that such a diversification would have proved successful. What is certain is that there is a finite demand for transportation of all kinds and that with the evolution of new forms, so the railroads were bound to mature then decline in the manner predicted by the PLC concept. Furthermore, within the industry, some products (models, brands) and the firms that make them will grow, prosper and decline so that they, too, exhibit the characteristic phases of the life cycle.

In defining product-market structures the key factor to be taken into account is the degree of differentiation recognised by suppliers in seeking to satisfy a market. At the most basic level there is the generic need of the kind described by Levitt in 'Marketing Myopia' such that 'transportation needs' could be satisfied by a myriad of different means ranging from bicycles to supersonic aeroplanes. Next, there is the industry level need in which suppliers of essentially similar products such as motor-car manufacturers or airlines are seen as competing directly with one another. However, experience shows that as soon as the industry's capacity matches or exceeds the demand for its undifferentiated output so individual firms will seek to protect their own market share by catering for a specific segment of demand and developing differentiated products which satisfy that *segment* of demand better than the undifferentiated product. (The concept of segmentation is a particularly important one in marketing and the subject of Chapter 8.)

In addition to product differentiation markets have traditionally been defined also in terms of geography. But, as we shall see in the discussion of globalisation in Chapter 22, the definition of markets on a local area basis is being rapidly eroded by advances in transportation and communication.

The discussion this far has emphasised the fundamental truth that business activity and exchange is based upon the existence of needs and that while these needs are enduring the means of satisfying them are subject to continuous change. While the most basic of all business objectives is survival some organisations succeed while others fail. To a large degree the explanation of this is to be found in another key concept – that of organisational culture.

■ Organisational culture

Irrespective of its stage in the firm's life cycle a major influence, if not *the* major influence upon an organisation's situation, is its culture. Two of the leading authorities on the concept of organisational culture (Deal and Kennedy) have the following to say:

> Every business – in fact every organisation – has a culture. Sometimes it is fragmented and difficult to read from the outside – some people are loyal to their bosses, others are loyal to the unions, still others care only about their colleagues who work in the sales territories of the Northeast. If you ask employees why they work, they will answer 'because we need the money'. On the other hand, sometimes the culture of an organisation is very strong and cohesive; everyone knows the goals of the corporation, and they are working for them. Whether weak or strong, culture has a powerful influence throughout an organisation; it affects practically every-thing, from who gets promoted and what decisions are made, to how employees dress and what sports they play. Because of this impact, we think that culture also has a major effect on the success of the business. (Terrence E. Deal and Allan A. Kennedy, *Corporate Cultures*, Addison-Wesley, Reading, Mass., 1982.)

Deal and Kennedy's belief receives strong support from recent research by the author and Dr Susan Hart (*Marketing & Competitive Success*, Philip Allan, 1989). During the 1980s there was an upsurge of interest in the nature of critical success factors following the publication of Peters and Waterman's path-breaking *In Search of Excellence: lessons from America's best run companies.* Based upon a detailed review of practices and performance in a cross-section of eminently successful American companies the two McKinsey consultants identified eight critical success factors as follows:

1. A bias for action.
2. Close to the customer.
3. Autonomy and entrepreneurship.
4. Productivity through people.
5. Hands-on, value-driven.
6. Stick to the knitting.
7. Simple form, lean staff.
8. Simultaneous loose–tight properties.

Despite the enthusiastic reception and recognition given to Peters and Waterman's analysis and findings, many were critical of the methodology – especially its anecdotal approach, its emphasis solely upon obviously successful companies (although many were experiencing difficulties in the years immediately following the book's publication) without any reference to less successful companies, many of which claimed to possess at least some of the desired attributes, and the absence of specific advice on how one could operationalise the recommendations for action.

To address these criticisms Baker and Hart (*Marketing and Competitive Success*, Philip Allan, 1989) undertook an analysis of a matched sample of both successful and less successful firms within a cross-section of growth (sunrise) industries and declining (sunset) industries. The findings confirmed that many of the attributes of successful firms were also present in less successful firms and so could not be used to differentiate between them. Indeed, one initially surprising result was that managers in sunset industries appeared generally to be more able than most of their counterparts in sunrise industries. On reflection it is clear that when the market is growing rapidly managerial mistakes are compensated for by buoyant demand and generous margins. Conversely in a declining market mistakes or lack of attention to detail lead to loss of market share, pressure on margins and loss of competitive edge.

In the final analysis very few managerial practices emerged which were present in successful firms but absent in less successful firms such that one could recommend the latter to follow the example of the former (e.g. invest in more marketing research). Consequently, we were driven to the conclusion that success is not so much a matter of what you do *but of how well you do it.*

In other words, culture and commitment are vital to organisational performance. However, this is not to say that professional managerial practices and procedures are unimportant and the first step in developing successful competitive strategies must be to play to and exploit the firm's strengths while avoiding and/or improving upon its weaknesses.

The identification and listing of a firm's strengths and weaknesses comprises the internal element of the marketing audit or SWOT analysis (strengths, weaknesses (internal), opportunities and threats (external)). David W. Cravens ('Gaining Strategic Marketing Advantage', *Business Horizons*, September–October 1988, pp. 44–54) suggests that the following information should be used to summarise the firm's strengths and weaknesses in each target market.

- Business scope and objectives;
- Market position;
- Market target(s) and customer base;
- Marketing programme positioning strategy;
- Financial, technical, and operating capabilities;
- Management experience and capabilities; and
- Special capabilities (for example, access to resources, patents).

Once identified and listed the firm's strengths and weaknesses need to be related to the external environment which, as noted above, comprises the product-market, competitive and environmental situations. As we saw in the preceding chapter the external environment represents both the ultimate constraint and opportunity for the organisation's freedom of action. Further, because it is common to all competitors, those who understand it best will be able to use this knowledge as a comparative of competitive advantage.

■ Determining competitive advantage

In a major article in the *Journal of Marketing* ('Assessing Advantage: A Framework for Diagnosing Competitive Superiority', April 1988) George S. Day and Robin Wensley observe:

> The notion that superior performance requires a business to gain and hold an advantage over competitors is central to contemporary strategic thinking. Businesses seeking advantage are exhorted to develop distinctive competences and manage for lowered delivered cost or differentiation through superior customer value.
>
> The promised pay-off is market share dominance and profitability above average for the industry.
>
> The advice is sound, but usually difficult to follow.

In the authors' view the main difficulty arises from deficiencies in available approaches to diagnosing competitive advantage which they analyse with a view to proposing a process which will ensure 'a thorough and balanced assessment of the reasons for the competitive position of a business'.

Two broad approaches to determining competitive advantage may be discerned, one based on customers and the other on competitors. Customer focused assessments best satisfy the marketing concept in that the firm seeks to define precisely the needs of specific market segments and then organise itself to satisfy a segment's needs better than any other supplier. By contrast competitor assessment emphasises an analysis of the strategy and tactics of those firm(s) which are considered to be the major competitors for the segment or segments which the firm is seeking to dominate. Firms which emphasise competitor assessment '... watch costs closely, quickly match the marketing initiatives of competitors, and look to their sustainable edge in technology. Managers keep a close watch on market share and contracts won or lost to detect changes in competitive position'. By contrast customer-focused firms pay relatively little attention to these criteria and emphasise the quality of customer relationships.

Experience and the available evidence indicates that firms tend to one or other of these two perspectives when what is required is a balance between them. However, as Day and Wensley point out such a balance is difficult to achieve because of the lack of any clear agreement as to just what constitutes competitive advantage. In essence Day and Wensley see competitive advantage (or distinctive competence) arising from either superior skills or superior resources which give rise to positional advantages in terms of either superior customer value or lower relative costs with performance outcomes in terms of satisfaction, loyalty, market share and profitability which is then reinvested to sustain and improve the original source of advantage. These elements are summarised in Figure 3.2.

Figure 3.2   **The creation and sustenance of competitive advantage**

Source G. S. Day and R. Wensley, 'Assessing Advantage: A Framework for Diagnosing Competitive Superiority', *Journal of Marketing*, April 1988.

As Day and Wensley point out analysing competitive advantage is but a means to an end – how to improve on one's performance and success. Such analysis frequently leads to the listing of so-called critical success factors – the Peters and Waterman listing of eight attributes of successful firms being a classic example (see p.46). However, as the analysis by Baker and Hart (1989) referred to earlier revealed, critical success factors tend to be highly situation specific, i.e. what works in one industry under one set of circumstances may be entirely inappropriate in another industry or under other circumstances. At best critical success factors (CSF) of the kind listed in Table 3.1 tend to be necessary but hardly ever sufficient reasons for success and little, if anything, is usually said as to how CSF may be converted into actual advantage.

TABLE 3.1   Critical success factors – product factors influencing competitiveness (in rank order)

1. Performance in operation
2. Reliability
3. Sale price
4. Efficient delivery
5. Technical sophistication
6. Quality of after-sales service
7. Durability
8. Ease of use
9. Safety in use
10. Ease of maintenance
11. Parts availability and cost
12. Attractive appearance/shape
13. Flexibility and adaptability in use
14. Advertising and promotion
15. Operator comfort
16. Design

Source: M. J. Baker and S. Hart, *Marketing and Competitive Success* (Philip Allan, 1989).

In the opening quotation from Day and Wensley reference was made to lower delivered cost or differentiation which are two of the three core 'generic' strategies identified by Michael Porter in his seminal work *Competitive Strategy* (Free Press, 1980). The third core strategy 'focus' has been rejected by critics of Porter such as Shiv Mathur of the City Business School on the grounds that 'focus' is concerned with the market scope of differentiation and cost leadership. (In passing it should be noted that Porter's analysis follows closely the much earlier distinction of core marketing strategies into undifferentiated (cost leadership), differentiated and concentrated (focus).) Implicitly Day and Wensley follow this view (although they appear to be singularly unaware of the UK and European literature on marketing strategy) when they stress the importance of the 'drivers' or structural determinants which convert superior skills or resources into positional advantages. Day and Wensley's analysis is more suited to an advanced rather than introductory textbook but, essentially, the point they make is that superior skills and resources are not automatically converted into competitive advantage. This transformation is accomplished by management taking strategic choices and implementing these tactically in accordance with a predetermined timetable. Success will accrue to those organisations most in tune with prevailing customer needs and the determination of these will be best achieved through a combined analysis of consumers themselves and of competitive offerings. Eleven methods of assessing advantage are discussed in detail by Day and Wensley and are summarised in Table 3.2.

TABLE 3.2   Methods of assessing advantage

Competitor-centred	Customer-focused

A. Assessing sources (distinctive competences)
  1. Management judgements of strengths and weaknesses
  2. Comparison of resource commitments and capabilities
  3. Marketing skills audit
B. Indicators of positional advantage
  4. Competitive cost and activity comparisons
    (a) Value chain comparisons of relative costs
    (b) Cross-section experience curves	

	5. Customer comparisons of attributes of firm versus competitors
	    (a) Choice models
	    (b) Conjoint analysis
	    (c) Market maps

C. Identifying key success factors
  6. Comparison of winning versus losing competitors
  7. Identifying high leverage phenomena
    (a) Management estimates of market share elasticities
    (b) Drivers of activities in the value chain
D. Measure of performance	

	8. Customer satisfaction surveys 9. Loyalty (customer franchise)
10a. Market share	
	10b. Relative share of end-user segments
11. Relative profitability (return on assets)	

Source: G.S. Day and R. Wensley, 'Assessing Advantage: A Framework for Diagnosing Competitive Superiority', *Journal of Marketing*, April 1988.

■ The marketing audit

The process of assessing advantage plays a central role in strategic marketing planning and is frequently described as a marketing audit or, particularly in texts dealing with corporate strategy as opposed to marketing strategy (the maintenance of this distinction is becoming increasingly difficult as more and more organisations adopt the marketing concept and accept they should be market led and customer driven) a SWOT analysis. SWOT is an acronym for Strengths and Weaknesses, i.e. the firm's internal status, and Opportunities and Threats which define the external environment.

Probably the most definitive statement of the nature of the marketing audit is to be found in an article by Philip Kotler, William Gregor and William Rogers which appeared in the *Sloan Management Review* (Winter 1977). According to Kotler *et al*. 'The marketing audit as an idea dates back to the early fifties. Rupert Dallmeyer, a former executive of Booz-Allen-Hamilton, remembers conducting marketing audits as early as 1952.' As the term suggests the practice in seen as similar in intention to the accounting audit and Kotler *et al*. offer the following definition.

> A marketing audit is a *comprehensive, systematic, independent,* and *periodic* examination of a company's – or business unit's – marketing environment, objectives, strategies and activities with a view of determining problem areas and opportunities and recommending a plan of action to improve the company's marketing performance.

The author's own view is that the marketing audit should not go so far as recommending a plan of action and prefers to regard it as an activity which will inform and guide the planning process. Indeed, a great deal of a marketing audit can be undertaken by specialist staff (just as an accounting audit is) with the final evaluation and interpretation being left to the company's operating management. The latter is an important part of successful planning.

During the 1960s and 1970s a great deal of planning activity was delegated to specially formed strategic planning departments. Despite the detail and sophistication of the plans developed by such planning units many formerly successful organisations which could afford them got into serious trouble in the late 1970s and early 1980s. In seeking to determine the reasons for their changed fortunes many of these organisations recognised that strategic planning is *the* senior management function and could not be delegated to staff specialists. Where this was done firms were ignoring the wisdom and experience of the senior management who, consequently, felt no ownership of the resulting plans and so were less committed to their implementation.

As stated above, a marketing audit should comprise a comprehensive, systematic and periodic review of all aspects of the organisation's internal operations and external environment. (The other criterion 'independent' is, naturally, one consultants would recommend but its value is regarded as limited unless a firm has seriously lost its way for the reasons touched on in the preceding paragraph.) The importance of the evaluation of the external environment was the subject of Chapter 2 but aspects of reviewing key elements of the firms' internal operations will be dealt with when discussing the elements of the marketing mix in greater detail in Part III.

■ The marketing mix

The concept of the marketing mix and its component elements comprise the content of Part III but, at this juncture, it will be helpful to provide a brief introduction to one of the longest established and most useful concepts in the marketing repertoire.

While the idea of a marketing mix is generally attributed to Neil Borden of the Harvard Business School he freely acknowledges that he picked up the idea from another HBS professor – James Cullinton. Like most ideas that withstand the test of time the concept of the marketing mix is elegant in its simplicity and merely observes that the marketing manager has a limited number of ingredients at his disposal but, like a master chef he can combine these into an almost limitless number of recipes.

Identification and listing of the ingredients of the marketing mix ranges from the very simple to the very complex. At one end of the spectrum there is Eugene McCarthy's 4 P's of Product, Price, Place and Promotion while at the other there is the much longer listing of Borden himself which is reproduced as Table 3.3.

TABLE 3.3   Elements of the marketing mix

1. Merchandising – product planning:
   (a) Determination of product (or service to be sold – qualities, design, etc.).
       To whom when, where and in what quantities?
   (b) Determination of new product programme – research and development merger.
   (c) Determination of marketing research programme.

2. Pricing:
   (a) Determination of level of prices.
   (b) Determination of psychological aspects of price, e.g. odd or even.
   (c) Determination of pricing policy; e.g. one price or varying price, use of price maintenance, etc.
   (d) Determination of margins: freedom in setting?

3. Branding:
   (a) Determination of brand policy, e.g. individual brand or family brand.

4. Channels of distribution:
   (a) Determination of channels to use, direct sale to user, direct sale to retailers or users' sources of purchase, e.g. supply houses.
       Sale through wholesalers.
   (b) Determination of degree of selectivity among dealers.
   (c) Devising of programmes to secure channel cooperation.

5. Personal selling:
   (a) Determination of burden to be placed on personal selling and methods to be employed.
       (1) For manufacturer's organisation.
       (2) For wholesalers.
       (3) For retailers.
   (b) Organisation, selection, training and guidance of sales force at various levels of distribution.

6. Advertising:
   (a) Determination of appropriate burden to be placed on advertising.
   (b) Determination of copy policy.

(c) Determination of mix of advertising:
  to trade
  to consumers.
(d) Determination of media.

7. Promotions:
   (a) Determination of burden to place on special selling plans or devices and formulation of promotions:
      (1) to trade
      (2) to consumers.

8. Packaging:
   (a) Determination of importance of packaging and formulation of packages.

9. Display:
   (a) Determination of importance and devising of procedures.

10. Servicing:
    (a) Determination of importance of service and devising of procedures to meet consumer needs and desires.

11. Physical handling – warehousing – transportation – stock policy.

12. Fact-finding and analysis – marketing research.

While McCarthy's 4 P's still enjoy considerable currency most observers would agree that at the very least they need to be extended to include consideration of People, i.e. the most basic but probably most complex of the mix ingredients, and to acknowledge the importance of research in determining both the nature of the ingredients to be used and the most appropriate recipe.

■ Limited strategic alternatives

Many years before it became fashionable to draw analogies between military and business strategy the author proposed (*Marketing New Industrial Products*, 1975) the view that an organisation has only a limited number of basic strategies available to it. In simple terms these may be listed as:

Peaceful co-existence or 'do nothing'.
Direct assault or price competition.
Indirect or flanking attack using product, place and/or promotion.
By-pass or avoidance of competition through innovation.
Withdrawal – a deliberate and planned decision to disengage.

An even simpler notion of competitive alternatives is contained in Igor Ansoff's 'Growth Vector Matrix' which is reproduced as Figure 3.3. In Ansoff's model only two dimensions are considered. 'Mission', which is equivalent to target market, and 'Technology'. Further, in the interests of simplicity, Ansoff only recognises two states – present and new – giving four basic alternatives which he describes as market penetration, market development, product development and diversification.

Given the present market and present product the organisation will only be able to grow if it can encourage its existing customers to consume more or attract customers away from other current suppliers (market penetration). As we have already seen if the firm is to win new customers then it must offer some advantage *as perceived by potential customers* which, if there is no change in the product, must be based upon price (a cost leadership strategy) or place and/or promotion (which offers differentiation). For reasons which will become clearer in later chapters most organisations avoid price competition (it reduces margins, is highly visible and may be seen as predatory by regulatory agencies) and prefer to use any cost advantage to differentiate their product through other less obvious and less objective advantages such as reputation, availability, after-sales service, etc.

Product Mission	Present	New
Present	Market pentration	Product development
New	Market development	Diversification

Figure 3.3   Ansoff's growth vector matrix

Source: H. Igor Ansoff, *Corporate Strategy*, Penguin Books, 1968, p. 99.

But, given that all consumers may have objective differences drawn to their notice while other, less tangible benefits of the kind listed in the previous sentence often exist largely in the subjective viewpoint of the potential purchasers and vary widely in nature (i.e. the seller cannot control them in the same way as his product specification) most sellers' preferred growth strategy is product development. In the case of a product development strategy it is assumed that one already has detailed knowledge of one's customer base and so is able to utilise this knowledge continuously to update and improve the product (or service) in order to match the increased expectation of one's own customers and offset the claims of one's competitors. (As a working rule of thumb it has been estimated that it costs five times as much to create or win a new customer as to retain an existing one.) Concentration on product development as the preferred strategy (differentiation) has resulted in an acceleration of technological change and shorter and shorter product life cycles. Despite this it is likely to remain a preferred strategy as it enables the seller to exploit his knowledge of particular customer groupings or market segments to the full.

The third strategy suggested by Ansoff's matrix is market development which assumes the firm retains the same technology but finds new customers for it. Basically, it can do this in one of two ways. First, the firm can move into geographically new markets, i.e. it extends the place dimension, or, second, it can find new uses for the existing product. For example, Dow Chemical developed what we now call shrink wrap as a packing material to protect weapons during the Second World War. With the end of the war this market was greatly reduced but Dow saw that the material had considerable potential in the domestic market and, after one or two setbacks, successfully launched it in this new market.

While new uses for existing products offer an opportunity for market development the greater opportunity is undoubtedly that offered by extending the scope of the physical market by expanding into new areas. For the small or start-up company this may simply entail expansion into an adjacent region with no need to modify any of the elements of the marketing mix, i.e. the potential customers in the new region are the same in terms of language, culture, social and economic characteristics, etc. as those in the original market. For the large or highly specialised company, however, extension of the physical market may well require it to cross national boundaries and sell to customers with different languages, customs, etc. Such 'international marketing' is dealt with in greater detail in Chapter 22.

The final option offered by the Ansoff matrix is that of diversification which is closely analogous to the by-pass or innovation strategy mentioned earlier. Clearly, this option carries the greatest risk for, by definition, the firm has no prior experience of either the market or the technology as is the case with all the preceding options. In many cases, indeed the great majority, innovation is introduced to the market by a new entrant as opposed to an existing player as the latter have a vested interest in protecting their current investment in the known and proven technology. That said, a characteristic of the long established multinational corporation is its ability to recognise the inevitable implications of the product life cycle and to switch from old to new technology as the latter begins to take off in the rapidly expanding growth phase of the life cycle. (This is sometimes called 'the strategy of the fast-second' or 'imitative innovation'.)

Clearly, Ansoff's model is about as simple as one can get and, in fact, a more complex 3 × 3 matrix was proposed at virtually the same time, as shown in Figure 3.4. However, this simplicity is seen as a great virtue as the emphasis in this section has been upon reducing the nature of strategy formulation to the bare essentials. Once this has been done the key strategic variable(s) will be easier to identify and, as the later discussion of the mix elements will make obvious, the decision-maker will still be faced with a very wide ranging selection of tactical alternatives. We will touch on this briefly in the final section on Positioning.

PRODUCT EFFECT	No technoligical change Does not require additional laboratory effort.	Improved Technology Requires laboratory effort utilising technology presently employed, known, or related to that used in existing company products.	New Technology Requires laboratory effort utilising technology not presently employed in company products.
No market change Does not affect marketing programmes.		Reformulation	Replacement
Strengthened market Affects marketing programmes to present classes of consumers.	Remerchandising	Improved Product	Product Line Extension
New market Requires marketing programmes for classes of consumers not now served.	New Use	Market Extension	Diversification

KEY:

Research and Development Department

Marketing Department

Joint Responsibility of R & D and Marketing Departments

Figure 3.4   A product development matrix

Source: Samuel C. Johnson and C. Jones, 'How to Organise for New Products', *Harvard Business Review*, vol. 35 (May–June, 1957).

■ Positioning

In common with most of the other basic ideas introduced in this chapter the concept of positioning is both a simple and intuitively appealing one. In essence positioning means the achievement of a unique place in a competitive market for a particular product such that some worthwhile sub-group of consumers perceive you to be different in some meaningful and important respect from all other competitors. In order to determine the position of a product – whether one's own or a competitor's – the first step must be to establish what are the key criteria or attributes which consumers use to judge performance and distinguish between the competitive offerings available to them. Once these key attributes have been defined a survey may be undertaken to find out how consumers perceive each of the different brands in terms of the relevant criteria. This information may then be plotted using pairs of dimensions such as price and performance to determine the position of the ideal product (lowest price/highest performance) and the actual position of the products surveyed as shown in Figure 3.5

Figure 3.5   Product positions in a competitive market

(While the techniques (cluster analysis and perceptual mapping) used in this type of analysis are beyond the scope of an introductory text – a more extended description is to be found in *Research for Marketing*.)

■ Summary

In this chapter we have explored some of the strategic dimensions of marketing in order to provide a framework and perspective for examining the key areas of marketing in greater detail throughout the rest of the book.

It has been argued that marketing is very much about change on the grounds that consumers in the pursuit of their self-interest will always prefer that product or service which offers them the greatest satisfaction. As producers strive to distinguish themselves one from another they will seek to capitalise on this pursuit of self-interest by defining the particular needs of specific customer groups and seeking to satisfy them better than any of their rivals. In doing so they will tend to prefer the creation of objective differences in the physical product or service as these are more readily communicated and evaluated than are more subjective values which relate to aspects such as reputation or aesthetic qualities. Thus, every product has a *life cycle* in which new and better ways of serving basic needs continuously displace older and less satisfactory means of serving the same needs.

In order to succeed in a competitive environment great attention and effort is now given to determining what factors are critical to success. However, as our analysis shows such *critical success factors* (CSF) are a necessary but not sufficient conditions for competitive success. In the real world what distinguishes between more and less successful firms is the quality of management and its implementation of the CSFs – something which may be seen in the *organisational culture* of a firm. It would also seem that successful firms are those which are skilled in identifying the existence of *market opportunities* and developing or exploiting those in which they enjoy a *comparative advantage vis-a-vis* their competitors. This ability to match strengths with opportunities while avoiding threats and making good weaknesses in the firm's performance is greatly enhanced by the conduct of formalised *marketing audits* or *SWOT analyses* and the articulation of clear *objectives*.

In the particular, competitive advantage arises from the manipulation of the ingredients of the *marketing mix* (product, price, place, promotion and people). Such manipulation requires first the selection of one of a very small number of *limited strategic alternatives* most of which may be distinguished in terms of the two dimensions of *Ansoff's growth vector matrix* – mission or markets (people or demand) and technology or product (firms or supply). By definition, for competition to exist two or more suppliers will seek to serve the same market. Their success in doing so will depend very much upon the last concept introduced in this chapter – *positioning*. Positioning requires the supplier to determine the nature of the attributes which consumers use to judge the performance and satisfaction offered by different product offerings and seek to develop a unique combination which will appeal to a sufficiently large sub-group (or *segment*) of users to make the differentiation profitable to the supplier.

In sum, the selection of a successful marketing strategy depends very much upon the firm's ability to interpret the environment in which it is competing and to organise itself in such a way as to exploit those opportunities most in keeping with its own strengths and competences.

CHAPTER 4

Market structure, conduct and performance

Learning Goals

The issues to be addressed in this chapter include:

1. The nature and definition of an industry.
2. An analysis of the factors which underlie the transformation from an agrarian to an industrial to a post-industrial society and their implications for employment and wealth creation.
3. The sources of structural change within industries.
4. The origins, nature and consequence of industrial concentration.
5. Alternative theories of competition and their implications for conduct and performance in the market place.

After reading this chapter you will be able to:

1. Explain what is meant by an 'industry'.
2. Define the terms primary, secondary and tertiary.
3. Describe the changes that have taken place in twentieth-century industrial structure.
4. Identify the causes of structural change.
5. Clarify the concept of industrial concentration.
6. Define the terms supply and demand.
7. Analyse the nature of competition and explain the effect this will have upon interactions between competitors in the market.

In the first chapter we looked briefly at the stages of economic development which led to the emergence of advanced economies with the potential of creating an excess supply of goods and services. To cope with this change in the traditional balance between supply and demand a new approach to resource allocation became necessary and we termed this the marketing concept because of its emphasis upon the market (demand) as the primary basis for investment and production (supply) decisions.

Of course the marketing concept is not new, for producers have always sought to identify those goods in strongest demand and then set out to supply them. However, under conditions of chronic supply deficiency it requires little expertise or sophistication to identify beforehand the most salient demands. Successful entrepreneurs have always been those who have intuitively identified such unsatisfied demands. But in complex, modern markets this is rarely possible without a sound understanding of market structure and market forces and it is these factors which comprise the subject-matter of Part II.

In this chapter we look first at the structure of industry before examining the phenomenon of concentration in some detail. Attention is then turned to theories of competition and the interaction of supply and demand at the macro level, and this is followed by a discussion of competition and market structure. Chapter 5 then explores micro aspects of supply and demand in more detail.

Students of economics may well be familiar with the content of this chapter while others may consider it peripheral to a marketing textbook (a view that has been put to me often!). My own view, and the reason for the chapter's inclusion, is that marketing is all about securing competitive advantage and that competition occurs within markets served by firms which belong to particular industries. As has been argued in the previous two chapters, it follows that the practice of marketing at the level of the individual firm is determined largely by external factors within which the firm has to operate. A knowledge of the structure of markets and competitive behaviour is thus essential to the identification of market opportunity, the development of effective marketing strategies and their efficient and profitable execution. This view has prevailed since the third edition appeared in 1979 and has been greatly reinforced by the fact that industry analysis of the kind advocated here has been central to the highly influential writings of Michael Porter of the Harvard Business School. (*Competitive Strategy: Techniques for Analysing Industries and Competitors*, Free Press, 1989; *Competitive Advantage*, Free Press, 1985; and *The Comparative Advantages of Nations*, Macmillan, 1990.)

■ The structure of industry

Any discussion of the role of industry must perforce commence with some definition of what we understand by the term. In everyday usage we are accustomed to refer to industries such as the textile industry, the motor industry or the chemical industry without specifying the basis on which a given firm may be judged to be a member of a particular industry. Essentially, individual firms are categorised as belonging to particular industries by virtue of the nature of their output. Thus most definitions of an industry tend to rest upon the existence of competition between sellers of similar products. However, as we shall see, changes in the nature of industrial organisation have resulted in many firms becoming members of more than one industry. Similarly, changes in a firm's product mix may well lead to a change in its basic industrial classification. We return to some of these distinctions below but first we must consider a more fundamental distinction between types of industry.

Conventionally all industry is divided into three major groupings, which are frequently referred to as the primary, secondary and tertiary sectors. Primary industry is concerned with the production of raw materials and includes agriculture, forestry and fishing. Secondary industry includes mining and quarrying and incorporates all those firms concerned with changing the nature and form of raw materials through some form of manufacturing process to the point where they are suitable for consumption either by other industrial users or by ultimate consumers. Finally, the tertiary sector embodies all those organisations which provide services, such as wholesaling, retailing, transportation, banking, entertainment, and so on.

In the twentieth century, considerable changes have taken place in the relative importance and size of these three sectors. As can be seen from Table 4.1 employment in the primary sector fell from 8.14 per cent in 1911 to 1.41 per cent in 1988. In fact this downward trend has persisted since the industrial revolution and was apparent even before that. At the time of the industrial revolution alternative employment opportunities in manufacturing industry encouraged a migration from the rural areas to the new factory towns and allowed farmers to substitute capital for labour through the employment of more efficient farming methods. This trend has continued to the present day with the result that mechanisation, advances in plant and animal breeding, and the development of chemical aids have enabled the primary sector to register a significant improvement in output despite a continually declining workforce.

TABLE 4.1   Industrial analysis of occupied population of the
United Kingdom, 1911–88 (per 10 000 occupied persons)

Industry	1911	1951	1973	1982	1988
Service industries	4 541	4 556	5 433	6 299	15 168
Agriculture, forestry and fishing	814	507	191	168	313
Energy and water supply	64	106	152	162	487
Other mineral and ore extraction	712	382	160	154	687
Manufacturing	3 351	3 760	3 455	2 727	4 528
Construction	518	635	609	492	1 043
Total occupied population	18 351	22 610	22 662	21 090	22 226

Source: Annual Abstract of Statistics, various dates.

As can be seen from the table, there has been a decline in numbers employed in the primary and secondary sectors. This has been balanced to some extent by the significant increase in numbers in the tertiary sector.

However, the numbers employed in an industry are only one measure of the level of activity. An equally, if not more significant measure is output, and comparative statistics are given in Table 4.2 (*on the following page*).

Data such as those presented in Tables 4.1 and 4.2 clearly indicate the marked changes which have taken place in industrial structure within a decade. Before examining some of the causes which would seem to account for this change it is important to stress that precise comparisons are difficult due to changes in the definition of industries and in the manner in which data have been collected. It is also important to emphasise that broad categories such as those in the two tables disguise marked changes within the categories themselves. Thus in the engineering industry motor-cars and aircraft have come into existence and exhibited marked growth while more traditional industries such as railway locomotives and shipbuilding have exhibited a decline. Similarly, in the textile industry a chemical revolution has led to the substitution of synthetic fibres for their natural counterparts.

More than anything else change in industrial structure in the twentieth century reflects the application of technology which has led to extensive modification of the traditional craft industries and the birth of completely new industries such as electronics and aviation. The impact of this technological revolution is implicit in the disproportionate increase in productivity *vis-à-vis* employment and other factor inputs. However, technological discovery and advance are only a partial explanation of the radical changes which have taken place during this century.

■ Causes of structural change

As noted in the preceding section, changes in industrial structure are not an invention of the twentieth century and are to be discerned from the industrial revolution onwards. As a very broad generalisation it would seem that the catalyst for change has been on the supply side, but that ultimately the nature and extent of change has been determined by demand. In simple terms the industrial revolution was the joint outcome of a mechanical and an organisational revolution. The mechanical revolution is generally attributed to the harnessing of steam-power, which led to an organisation revolution in the setting up of a factory system to replace the cottage industry which had preceded it. The enormous increase in output which accompanied these changes led to a marked improvement in living standards and set in train widespread changes in demand.

It is difficult to generalise about changes in demand as these arise from a number of different yet inter-related causes. The trend towards greater social equality has led to enormous improvements in education as well as to a redistribution of income and it is clear that both education and income have marked effects upon consumption patterns. In turn the move to greater social

TABLE 4.2 Industrial and sector analysis. Gross Domestic Product by Industry 1979–89 (£m)

	1979	1980	1981	1982	1983	1984	1985	1986	1987	1988	1989
Agriculture, forestry and fishing	3 690	4 197	4 767	5 406	5 214	6 265	5 553	6 026	6 123	5 984	6 561
Energy and water supply	13 864	19 390	23 496	26 104	30 085	29 750	32 659	23 945	24 415	22 394	22 619
Manufacturing	48 835	53 095	54 212	58 729	61 401	66 446	72 615	77 831	82 579	91 196	97 380
Construction	10 637	12 225	13 009	14 076	15 711	16 928	17 748	20 127	23 051	26 953	30 274
Distribution, hotel and catering; repairs	22 855	25 779	27 274	30 135	33 230	36 188	40 497	44 827	48 937	56 561	62 133
Transport and communication	13 210	14 344	15 908	17 201	18 285	19 846	21 243	23 025	24 830	27 614	30 074
Banking, finance, insurance, business services and leasing	20 001	24 355	26 038	29 623	35 553	39 080	46 518	54 209	62 239	74 378	86 628
Ownership of dwellings	10 306	12 147	13 895	15 044	15 945	16 732	17 960	19 583	21 104	23 331	25 482
Public administration, national defence and compulsory social security	11 439	14 518	16 249	17 371	18 821	20 167	21 409	23 019	24 934	27 504	29 571
Education and health service	14 146	18 022	20 616	21 295	23 380	24 649	26 570	29 996	33 237	37 606	42 547
Other services	9 227	10 682	12 004	13 302	15 107	16 557	18 401	20 748	23 250	26 226	29 715

Source: CSO UK National Accounts 1990.

equality is but one manifestation of a marked political change in which large sectors of the economy have come under public control and the purchasing power possessed by such public corporations as coal-mining and the railways must have a marked impact upon the nature of demand.

At the same time industry has not been slow to realise the opportunity which is implicit in increased personal disposable incomes. As personal incomes increase the proportion expended upon purchases essential to life diminishes and even allowing for increased saving the individual is able to increase his consumption. The latent demand represented by unexpended personal incomes is one of the major spurs to new-product development whereby manufacturers compete to translate this latent demand into an effective demand for their own output. In their efforts to communicate the availability of their new and improved products the manufacturer is aided by the evolution and growth of new channels of communication.

Demographic changes, too, have their impact upon demand. With an increased expectation of life Britain now has an ageing population with a concomitant increase in the demand for products suited to the older age groups, for increased medical services, etc.

Further changes in the structure of industry can be attributed to the impact of foreign competition. Until the middle of the nineteenth century Britain had few competitors for manufactured goods. However, since that time many other nations have industrialised and our dependency on imported food and raw materials has required that we open our markets to these foreign manufacturers. Certainly the decline of the traditional textile industries owes much to highly competitive imported textiles from countries with lower labour costs than our own.

Collectively all these changes in demand have resulted in a corresponding change in industrial structure. Some firms will decline and disappear while others will adjust to the changed environment within which they operate and continue their existence. Similarly, new technology will spawn new firms and new industries.

In his book *The Structure of Industry in Britain* (Longmans, 1970) G. C. Allen advances six reasons to explain how firms are persuaded to take up new lines of manufacture, namely:

> the movement may occur as a by-product of efforts to solve some problems of production and distribution, or as the result of growth which leads to plant imbalance, or as the consequence of some technical discovery which may have a wider application than the original context, or simply because firms see enlarged opportunities in pressing their existing marketing organisation into new uses. The spreading of risk may provide the motive, or the pressure of adversity may impel firms to try new fields as their only chance of survival as substantial producers.

The phraseology used by Allen tends to suggest, albeit unintentionally, that firms only embark upon some new form of activity by change or because they are driven to it. As will become clearer later, in dealing with product policy firms may adopt a more purposive attitude than that implied in the above extract.

Without dwelling on the causes of industrial change, many of which are dealt with in greater detail hereafter, it is appropriate at this juncture to examine an apparent consequence of central interest to any discussion on industrial structure, namely the degree of industrial concentration.

■ Industrial concentration

In addition to the changes that have taken place between and within industries in terms of their overall size measured by numbers employed or value of their output there have also been marked changes in the nature of the firms which comprise these industries. A frequently remarked trend has been what J. K. Galbraith in *The New Industrial State* (Penguin, 1974) has termed the rise of the 'super corporation'. In simple terms Galbraith's argument is that an increasing proportion of all output is being concentrated in the hands of a limited number of producers. By virtue of the control which these super corporations exercise over supplies of essential goods and services it is implied that the super corporation may exercise undue influence over the operation of the state. More explicitly it is maintained that supply dominance of this kind eliminates competition to the detriment of the average consumer.

Not all students of industry subscribe to the Galbraithian view, and maintain that the emergence of a limited number of very large firms does not necessarily imply the elimination of competition in the market-place. Clearly, if one is to determine the relative merits of the opposing arguments, some form of measure is required which enables us to make a comparative industry analysis over time. A convenient and widely used measure is the *concentration ratio*.

In fact economists have two concepts of concentration. At the macro, or national level, the concept of concentration is used to define the proportion of total industry output accounted for by some predetermined percentage of all firms. At the micro or industry level the concentration ratio expresses the percentage share of total sales of that industry accounted for by a predetermined percentage of all firms in the industry. It will be noted that both descriptions of concentration ratios state that they are computed by calculating the proportion of all output accounted for by a predetermined number of firms, and it should be noted that there is no universally agreed convention to state what this number should be. Accordingly, when one is interpreting concentration ratios it is most important to ascertain the basis of the computation. In the United Kingdom the most widely used concentration ratios are based on the proportion of all sales in a given product group accounted for by the five largest firms.

As indicated earlier, there is disagreement between economists as to the degree of concentration in UK manufacturing industry and to the extent of change in such concentration over time. Writing in 1969 Allen (in the book referred to earlier) took the view that while the available evidence was fragmentary, such calculations as had been attempted seemed to indicate a stabilisation and possibly a slight decline in the overall concentration in industry since 1930. Further, an examination of the identity of the largest companies shows marked changes in this period, reflecting the changing fortunes of the different industries, with the emergence, of new areas, of activity such as electronics. However , Allen did not have access to the data from the 1968 Census of Production (which was not published until 1974). A summary of these data was presented in an article entitled 'Concentration in U.K. Manufacturing Industry' by David Elliot (*Trade and Industry*, 1 August 1974) and his findings are reproduced in Tables 4.3–4.7. Like Allen, Elliot points out that the data are incomplete for a number of reasons, among which he cites the following:

(a) The Business Statistics Office is bound by disclosure rules and does not publish product groups where individual firms may be identified.
(b) Product groups where total sales are less than £10 million are not generally shown.
(c) No product groups have been selected covering work-done activities.
(d) Products that cannot be identified as being homogeneous have been omitted.

However, despite these deficiencies the evidence contained in the tables clearly contradicts Allen's assertion and confirms the opinions of those who have argued that there has been an increase in concentration over recent years. The overall increase is apparent in Tables 4.3 and 4.7, while the increase in particular industries is shown in Table 4.4.

Increases in concentration arise from two major causes. First, there is the disproportionate growth of certain firms, usually due to the superior nature of their products and management, e.g. Xerox and IBM. Second, there is growth through amalgamation by a process of merger and acquisition. As can be seen from Table 4.5, the data indicate that the increase in industrial concentration in the United Kingdom during the 1960s has been due in some part to the higher levels of merger activity during that period. However, data such as these only indicate the broad nature of change and tell us little if anything of how this was brought about.

TABLE 4.3   Average of five-firm concentration ratios (1958–68)

1963 and 1968: 295 products		*1958, 1963 and 1968:157 products*	
Average	*Change*	*Average*	*Change*
1963 = 62.0%		1958 = 56.2%	
1968 = 66.0%	+ 4.0%	1963 = 59.4%	+ 3.2%
		1968 = 64.5%	+ 5.1%

TABLE 4.4 Average of five-firm sales concentration ratios of products comprising order

S.I.C. order	Description	Number of products for which ratios available	1968 sales (£m.) of products for which ratios available	Average concentration ratio (%)			Coverage of ratios for each order (%)
				1963	1968	Change	
II	Mining and quarrying	5	136.8	57.4	65.0	+7.6	15
III	Food manufactured including tea and coffee, beer, spirits, etc.	33	2 420.1	78.1	78.9	+0.8	85
	Cigarettes, tobacco products	6	1 193.7	74.4	77.1	+2.7	98
IV	Coal and petroleum products	3	1 393.0	99.2	99.4	+0.2	100
V	Chemical and allied industries	6	1 010.5	91.5	93.5	+2.0	87
VI	Metal manufacture	39	1 952.4	74.0	75.5	+1.5	78
VI	Metal manufacture (including steel)	8	975.8	72.9	74.3	+1.4	31
VII	Mechanical engineering	20	2 831.0	70.6	79.8	+9.2	93
		35	1 521.7	60.3	62.4	+2.1	64
VIII	Instrument engineering	5	109.5	60.1	62.3	+2.2	82
IX	Electrical engineering	27	1 546.0	68.1	77.2	+9.1	80
X	Shipbuilding and marine engineering	1	60.1	34.6	57.4	+22.8	14
XI	Vehicles	8	1 724.0	85.2	89.1	+3.9	57
XII	Metal goods nes	21	1 301.0	55.0	57.6	+2.6	78
XIII	Textiles	28	2 040.8	41.5	49.7	+8.2	72
XIV	Leather, leather goods, fur	6	139.0	33.8	37.7	+3.9	90
XV	Clothing and footwear	14	792.1	30.1	37.0	+6.9	91
XVI	Bricks, pottery, glass, cement, etc.	16	662.1	65.6	75.5	+9.9	82
XVII	Timber, furniture, etc.	9	543.5	28.0	28.4	+0.4	87
XVIII	Paper, printing and publishing	10	970.3	54.5	56.2	+1.7	84
XIX	Other manufacturing industries	14	674.7	53.5	57.0	+3.5	88
	Total (excluding steel products)	315	22 908.1				

Note nes = not elsewhere stated.

TABLE 4.5   Concentration change and uses of company funds

Industrial group	Change in concentration 1963–8	Average (1964–8) % of funds used for acquisition of subsidiaries
Food	0.8	12.6
Drink	2.7	17.8
Tobacco	0.2	8.5
Chemical and allied industries	1.6	7.2
Metal manufacture	9.2	8.5
Non-electrical engineering	2.1	9.4
Electrical engineering	9.1	34.7
Shipbuilding and marine	22.8	13.0
Vehicles	3.9	13.5
Metal goods [nes]	2.6	6.8
Textiles	8.2	23.0
Leather, leather goods and fur	3.9	1.7
Clothing and footwear	6.9	20.8
Bricks, pottery, glass, etc.	9.9	16.4
Timber furniture	0.4	5.6
Paper, printing and publishing	1.7	14.0
Other manufacturing	3.5	7.3

Note: [nes] = not elsewhere stated.

TABLE 4.6   Frequency distribution of concentration ratios

Size class of ratio	Number (and %) of product in each class				
	1958	1963	1968	1973	1978
0–19.9	12 (7.6)	8 (5.1)	3 (1.9)	13 (4.4)	7 (2.4)
20–29.9	23 (14.6)	19 (12.1)	12 (7.6)	27 (9.1)	18 (6.1)
30–39.9	21 (13.4)	20 (12.7)	17 (10.8)	34 (11.5)	24 (8.1)
40–49.9	10 (6.4)	13 (8.3)	14 (8.9)	24 (8.1)	28 (9.5)
50–59.9	16 (10.2)	16 (10.2)	23 (14.8)	36 (12.2)	45 (15.8)
60–69.9	18 (11.5)	19 (12.1)	12 (7.6)	37 (12.5)	31 (10.5)
70–79.9	20 (12.7)	19 (12.1)	20 (12.7)	39 (13.2)	35 (11.9)
80–89.9	15 (9.5)	18 (11.5)	22 (14.0)	29 (9.8)	42 (14.2)
90–100	22 (14.0)	25 (15.9)	34 (21.6)	56 (19.0)	65 (22.0)
Totals	157	157	157	295	295

TABLE 4.7   Overall concentration share of manufacturing net output by the largest 100 firms (100%)

Year	Per cent
1958	31
1963	37
1968	42
1970	45

The most recent data available at the time of writing is contained in *Mergers Policy*, a Department of Trade & Industry Paper on the policy and procedures of merger control published by HMSO in 1988. The paper is based upon a review undertaken by the DTI which itself was prompted by the very high level of mergers and acquisition in the mid-1980s particularly in the food, drink and tobacco and distribution industries, with the objective of determining whether this activity was prejudicial to the Government's competition policy. (A review of anti-competitive practices follows at pp. 78–85.) Annex D of the paper summarises recent trends in UK concentration.

The first measure examined is that of aggregate concentration referred to as C100 which measures the percentage share of net output accounted for by the 100 largest private sector enterprises in manufacturing. Table 4.8 shows the results and indicates that aggregate concentration has remained largely stable since 1970 following sharp increases in aggregate concentration in the 1960s.

TABLE 4.8   Percentage share of the 100 largest enterprises in manufacturing net output, 1970–84

Year	1970	1972	1974	1976	1978	1980	1982	1984
C100	39.3	41.0	42.1	41.8	41.1	40.5*	41.1*	38.7*

* Figures after 1978 are not strictly comparable with those coming before; in 1980 there was a definitional change in the Standard Industrial Classification

Source: *Business Monitor*, PA 1002.

TABLE 4.9   Equally-weighted and gross output-weighted mean C5, 1970, 1975 and 1979*

	1970	*per cent* 1975	1979	*Change 1970–79*
Equal weights	46.2	47.9	46.8	+ 0.6
Output weights	46.6	48.1	47.1	+ 0.5

* Sample of 93 comparable industries
Source: *Business Monitor*, PA 1002.

TABLE 4.10   Equally-weighted and gross output-weighted mean C5, 1979, 1981 and 1984*

	1979	1981	1984	1979–84
Equal weights	52.1	51.5	49.9	− 2.2
Output weights	54.2	54.9	52.6	− 1.6

* Sample of 199 comparable industries.
Source: BSO data.

TABLE 4.11   Industry concentration by UK manufacturing sector, 1979, 1981 and 1984

SIC class (2-digit)	Description	No. of industries	Constant (1979) weighted mean C5 (gross output) (%) 1979	1981	1984	Change 1979–84
12/4/5	Fuels, mineral and nuclear	4	76.0	81.5	72.4	− 3.6
21/2/3	Extraction, metal manufacture	8	64.0	61.9	61.4	− 2.6
24	Non-metallic mineral products	12	54.2	53.5	54.4	0.2
25/6	Chemicals	21	64.8	64.0	63.5	− 1.3
31	Metal goods	14	31.6	31.1	30.0	− 1.6
32/3	Mechanical engineering	28	43.9	42.3	42.0	− 1.9
34	Electrical/electronic engineering	15	60.7	61.0	54.4	− 6.3
35/6	Vehicles, transport, equipment	9	73.8	74.9	70.5	− 3.3
37	Instrument engineering	6	42.4	42.3	41.4	− 1.0

(*continued over*)

SIC class (2-digit)	Description	No. of industries	Constant (1979) weighted mean C5 (gross output) (%)			Change 1979–84
			1979	1981	1984	
41/2	Food, drink, tobacco	19	64.0	63.4	60.9	−3.1
43	Textiles	15	39.6	40.3	36.8	−2.8
44/5	Leather, footwear, clothing	16	27.9	29.8	29.0	1.1
46	Timber, wooden furniture	9	19.1	18.2	20.4	1.3
47	Paper, printing	11	36.6	34.3	31.6	−5.0
48/9	Other	12	30.6	30.6	26.7	−3.9
	Total no. of industries	199				

Source: *Business Monitor*, PA 1002.

The second measure of industry concentration is C5 which is the ratio of the output of the five largest firms in the industry to the total industry output. Tables 4.9 and 4.10 show the results. From these tables it is clear that while industry concentration rose slightly between 1970 and 1979 it fell thereafter. Table 4.11 summarises the data by industries and leads to the following conclusions:

- Concentration gives an important indication of levels and changes in the structure of markets but it needs to be examined along with other characteristics of markets before drawing any conclusions on firms' conduct and on policy.
- Aggregate concentration in the manufacturing sector has remained broadly stable since 1970. However, evidence on economic activity as a whole suggests aggregate concentration increased during the early 1970s, but then subsequently declined.
- Industry concentration increased only slightly during the early 1970s. Since the mid-1970s, however, industry concentration has shown a gradual decline, a trend which has continued into the 1980s.
- Foreign trade at the industry level of aggregation has had an increasingly important influence on UK market structure in recent years. This has meant that after adjustment for foreign trade, concentration has shown a steady decline since the early 1970s.
- There remains a small but still appreciable number of persistently highly concentrated domestic industries even after an adjustment for foreign trade is made.
- Since the available data only extends to 1984, it is not yet possible to say what effect the recent mergers boom has had on industry concentration, and the trends outlined above.

■ Concentration and organisational structure

As Channon notes in the introduction to his book (*The Strategy and Structure of British Enterprise* (Macmillan, 1973)) the development of the large business organisation is closely associated with the growth of improved communications, and in the case of the United States, where most research has been undertaken, with the development of the railroad in particular. Improvements in communications extend the firm's ability both to obtain supplies of factor inputs and especially raw materials while simultaneously expanding the market for its output. In the early stage of their evolution most large firms concentrated their efforts upon a single product line or functional activity. Similarly, in the early stages of their development the managers of the more successful firms, who are also usually the owners, focus their attention upon expanding though a process of horizontal integration by means of acquisition and merger with other organisations in direct competition with them. Once a firm has attained a certain degree of dominance over one phase in the productive/distributive process the benefits of vertical integration become increasingly attractive. Thus a firm which has become dominant in the extraction or production of a basic raw material may integrate forward into the process of that raw material into a finished product. Conversely, a manufacturing concern may decide to integrate backwards into primary production in order to achieve control over essential factor inputs. Similarly, firms engaged in primary or secondary industries may perceive advantages through integrating forward into the tertiary sector and achieving control of the distributive function. Clearly, dominant retail and wholesaling organisations may see similar advantages to be gained through integrating backwards into manufacturing and primary production.

With increasing size there developed a need for a more specialised organisational structure and for the delegation of authority and responsibility to subordinates. In the early stages of their development most large corporations adopted a functional form of organisation with professional managers appointed to head each of the various functions, e.g. finance, production, sales, etc.

With the transfer of control from owner-entrepreneurs to professional managers it is possible to discern a change in the primary goal of the firm. Thus, while owner-entrepreneurs tend to pursue a primary objective of profit maximisation, professional managers tend to emphasise survival and a satisfactory level of earnings, to be achieved through sales maximisation rather than profit maximisation.

However, as noted earlier when discussing the six causes of change cited by Allen, this view is essentially a negative one. While it is true that most firms adapt themselves to their environment and react to changes in their market, the really dominant firms in any industry appear to have adopted a more positive approach. Thus Channon cites A. C. Chandler's classic study (*Strategy and Structure*, Anchor Books, 1966) in which two alternative strategies to integration are identified. In essence these two alternative strategies are growth through geographical expansion, and diversification. However, as firms pursued either or both of these alternatives it soon became apparent that the traditional functional form of organisation was inappropriate for multi-product firms operating in a number of different markets. Thus in the 1920s Dupont and General Motors began to develop a divisional structure which has now become the dominant form of organisation.

It is not proposed to dwell on such issues here but it is important to point out that since the 1920s there has been an increasing trend towards diversification. In Channon's study of the 100 largest UK companies between 1950 and 1970 it was found that:

> in 1950 the diversified firm represented approximately 24% of the population of the largest 100 firms. This minority was composed essentially of those enterprises engaged in technological or skill related industries where the technology required to compete, naturally led to the evolution of a wide product line. By 1970 the minority had become the majority and no fewer than 60% of the population was relatively highly diversified. This majority included many industries with a wide variety of technological requirements, such as food, chemicals, paper and packaging, textiles, electrical equipment, and electronics and engineering.

As a result of this diversification many of the larger firms operate in several different industries and one must not assume automatically that the very large firms are necessarily dominant in all markets in which they compete.

Interest in the degree of concentration in industry arises largely because of the light which it throws upon market structure and, as Richard Caves notes, in *American Industry: Structure, Conduct and Performance*, 3rd edn (Englewood Cliffs, N.J.: Prentice-Hall, 1972), 'market structure is important because the structure determines the behaviour of firms in the industry, and that behaviour in turn determines the quality of the industry's performance'. However, as Caves points out, concentration is but one element of market structure, other main elements of which are product differentiation, barriers to the entry of new firms, the growth rate of market demands, the elasticity of market demand, and the ratio of fixed to variable costs in the short run. Collectively all these determine the nature of competition in the market-place and it is to this that we now turn our attention.

■ Theories of competition

Current thinking about competition, like many other economic concepts, owes much to the original contribution of Adam Smith, whose *Wealth of Nations* was first published in 1776. As J. M. Clark (*Competition as a Dynamic Process*, Brookings Institution, 1961) points out, Smith lays the foundation of this thought by defining two competition states – full and free competition, and complete monopoly – and, in a loose fashion, the contrasting outcomes to be expected of each of these states.

Clark offers a useful summary of the evolution of economic thinking about competition from Smith's original and sometimes rather vague specification through to the contribution of Ricardo, Cournot, and Marshall, in the course of which he points out how theory has changed to reflect reality. At the time when Smith first proposed the two basic competitive states monopoly was essentially a local phenomenon which was to be eroded during the nineteenth century with the development of more efficient lines of communication and transportation, while perfect competition mirrored the bargaining power of people engaged in cottage industries such as weaving. Similarly, as we have noted earlier, agriculture was a much more dominant form of economic activity in terms of employment and the markets in agricultural commodities have traditionally approached most nearly to the model of perfect competition.

Just as the impact of the industrial revolution was to lead to improvements in communication and transportation which diminished local monopolies, so the growth of manufacturing industry diminished the importance of agriculture and led to attention being focused upon intermediate competitive states distinguished as being 'imperfect'.

During the nineteenth century the major emphasis of economic activity was upon supply creation or output and its effect upon price. Together these were seen as the crucial competitive variables. In Clark's view it was the addition of the chemical revolution to the preceding mechanical and electrical revolutions which was to give rise to product proliferation and lead to a situation in which 'automatically, the differentiated product has become an economic variable at least as important as price, along with the methods of selling efforts and demand creation that necessarily go with product differentiation.'

The addition of product and selling efforts as variables alongside the traditional inputs of price and output demanded a radical restructuring of the economist's original model and gave rise to the theories of imperfect competition formulated by Edward Chamberlin and Joan Robinson.

Thus we now recognise that between the polar extremes of monopoly and perfect competition there exists an almost infinite variety of states of imperfect competition. For purposes of analysis, understanding and prediction it is important that one should be able to distinguish how certain basic elements influence the development of a particular competitive state. It is also important that one should be able to identify the salient facets of each of these states. To this end we are here concerned primarily with the three basic elements of an economic system, supply, demand, and the market, and their interaction, i.e. the state of competition. (For readers who are pursuing a formal course of study much of the material in this chapter will amount to a review of concepts introduced in a basic course on economics. However, it is anticipated that the treatment here will possibly be more applied than theoretical and its inclusion is predicated on the grounds that it is essential to an understanding of the manner in which real firms behave in the real world.)

Our discussion of supply will concentrate first upon those organisations responsible for its creation, and will then examine the nature of their output.

This consideration will be followed by a summary of some of the more salient factors which go together to make up and influence demand. Next we examine the nature of the mechanism through which supply and demand are brought together – the market – and finally we review the basic competitive states to establish the emergence of product differentiation as a major competitive strategy.

■ Supply: firm and product

Although we deliberately referred to 'organisations' in the previous paragraph, thereby implicitly recognising that there are several distinct types of formal association which might be responsible for supply creation, our main concern here is with the form of business organisation which we call the firm.

In economic theory certain simplifying assumptions are made about the firm. It is assumed that a single person, the entrepreneur, is the owner of the individual firm and that he behaves rationally in that his prime objective is to maximise money profits. Further, it is assumed that entrepreneurs will always minimise costs and that the price of all factor inputs are known and fixed and that each firm produces only one product. Now, no sane economist really believes in these assumptions. He merely adopts them in order to simplify his analysis in order to develop explanations of the ways firms will behave given these conditions. In other words the economist is attempting to develop a bench-mark model so that he can then determine how relaxation of the simplifying assumptions might affect real-world behaviour. Unfortunately many students who have only taken an introductory course in economics never proceed to the stage when real-world considerations are introduced into the model. Accordingly such students find it very difficult to relate observed reality, implicit in the earlier discussion concerning changes in firm structure and organisation, and the simplistic descriptions contained in introductory economic texts.

We have already noted that few, if any, firms regard profit maximisation as their primary goal. The reasons why the unbridled pursuit of profit should not be the sole objective of management is apparent in the role of profit itself. Profit is generally regarded as the reward for the assumption of risk and on the whole it is accepted that the greater the risk, the greater should be the reward. It is also accepted that risk is usually measured in terms of the likelihood of loss. Accordingly professional management tends to try and balance its activities in such a manner so as not to put the whole corporation at risk. Clearly by doing so it forgoes the possibility of maximising profits. It also avoids the possibility of maximising losses!

One area where the firm does make a conscious decision is in terms of its product mix. Fundamentally there is a basic conflict between the relative merits of specialisation and the attractions of diversification. If one pursues a policy of specialisation, one should be able to benefit from the economies of scale in purchasing and production and so reduce costs to the minimum. At the same time it is clear that any diminution of demand for the single-product firm will result in an immediate loss in earnings and, if continued, this could result in the firm operating at a loss.

Diversification offers a firm the opportunity to spread the risk associated with fluctuation in demand for a particular product. At the same time diversification usually requires a firm to duplicate many of the basic business functions, especially in production and marketing, and so increases its cost base. It is clear that if the firm is not operating on a basis of minimum cost, then it will be able to earn less profits than firms which have chosen to specialise in the production of a single product – at least in the short term.

Just as economists make simplifying assumptions about the firm, so too they make simplifying assumptions about the firm's output – its product. The basic assumption which is made is that the output of different firms competing in the same market are viewed as homogeneous by potential consumers. Given this assumption, together with that of a single price, it is clear that users have no rational basis for differentiating between different suppliers of the same product. Accordingly decisions by a consumer to buy a product are perceived as decisions between different categories of products rather than choices between similar products produced by different firms. Thus elementary economic theory proposes that, given a finite disposable income, the consumer will adjust his purchases of different product categories in order to maximise his overall satisfaction. In the sense that all products which the consumer might consider purchasing are competing with one another they are to some degree substitutes for one another.

However, this concept of substitution is too crude to explain the nature of competition between companies like Lever Brothers and Procter & Gamble in the detergent market, Ford and Vauxhall in the motor-car market, Hoover, Electrolux and Goblin in the vacuum-cleaner market, and so on. For this purpose we need a clearer definition of possible degrees of difference between products. That proposed by J. M. Clark (*Competition as a Dynamic Process*) provides a useful basic distinction.

Essentially Clark proposes three categories of products. First there are those which satisfy the same principal want, and in which the producer is free to imitate others as closely as he wishes, using techniques that are not radically different from theirs and differentiating his product only to the extent that it seems advantageous to him to do so, in order to appeal to some subsidiary want more effectively than other variants do, and thus fit into a gap in the array of variant products'. Clark terms this first category 'differentiated competition' and it is clear that different brands of detergent, motor-car and vacuum-cleaner fall into this category.

Clark's second category, which he terms 'substitution', is defined as including 'products that appeal to the same principal want but which are inherently and inescapably different, due either to different materials or basically different techniques'. Into this category, perhaps, we might put the use of a laundry service in place of the purchase of detergents for home washing, the use of public transport or perhaps bicycle or motor-bicycle in place of a motor-car, or a manual carpet-sweeper, or even a brush, in place of an electric vacuum-cleaner. Clearly in all these instances the substitute product is competing directly with that for which it is a substitute, and seeks to satisfy the same basic want.

In Clark's words 'the third category embraces products that serve independent wants and are substitutes only in the mathematic sense that spending more for one leaves less to spend on others'. We return to issues of product differentiation later in this book. Having briefly considered the supply side of the economic equation, it is now necessary to review some basic concepts of demand. However, before turning to these subjects it will be useful to summarise the key aspects of competition policy in the UK under current legislation. A very useful synopsis of this is to be found in the Office of Fair Trading pamphlet *Anti-Competitive Practices* (1986) which provides the following overview, definitions, and examples of 'possible anti-competitive practices':

> The provisions of the Competition Act concerning anti-competitive practices complement those in other statutes giving competition policy functions and powers to the Director General.
>
> Under the Fair Trading Act the Director General can refer cases to the Monopolies and Mergers Commission for investigation if he considers that a monopoly situation exists (normally where 25 per cent or more of the supply in the United Kingdom of the product or service is accounted for by one company or group of inter-connected corporate bodies). The Secretary of State has a similar power to make references.
>
> The Commission must report whether a monopoly situation exists and then whether any behaviour by companies, which can be attributed to the monopoly situation, is against the public interest. The Commission's investigation therefore extends over the whole market in question and over all aspects of the behaviour of any companies which are in a monopoly situation. The investigation can be a time consuming process.
>
> By contrast, the Competition Act allows the investigation of particular practices of individual firms which restrict, distort, or prevent competition, and such an investigation is normally completed more quickly than a Fair Trading Act reference. No specific anti-competitive practice is prohibited and the Act does not specify any which are undesirable. Instead its approach is flexible, allowing each practice to be investigated individually with consideration being given to all the circumstances that may be relevant to the particular case.
>
> The Act adopts a two-stage approach. First, the Director General can carry out a preliminary investigation to establish whether a particular course of conduct amounts to an anti-competitive practice. He is not concerned whether the practice is contrary to the public interest. If an anti-competitive practice is identified he can refer it to the Commission for further investigation. Alternatively, he may accept an undertaking from the firm which has been investigated.
>
> Second, if a reference is made to the Commission they must, within a limited period, establish whether an anti-competitive practice is, or was, being pursued and, if so, whether it is against the public interest. If the Commission's report contains an

adverse finding, the Secretary of State can ask the Director General to seek an undertaking from the firm. Alternatively, the Secretary of State may make an order prohibiting a practice, or remedying or preventing its adverse effects. Only after the Commission have reached an adverse finding is there any possibility of sanctions against any practice.

Although the booklet is concerned only with the anti-competitive practices aspect, the Act has other provisions:

— the Secretary of State can refer to the Commission questions about the efficiency and costs of, the service provided by, or possible abuse of a monopoly situation by, nationalised industries and certain other bodies;

— it amends various provisions of the Fair Trading Act 1973 and the Restrictive Trades Practices Act 1976;

— the Secretary of State can direct the Director General to investigate prices of major public concern.

The Telecommunications Act 1984 extends to the Director General of Telecommunications certain functions which the Director General of Fair Trading has under the Competition Act. The functions are exercisable concurrently by both Directors and relate to practices which have or are intended to have or are likely to have the effect of restricting, distorting or preventing competition in connection with the production, supply or acquisition of telecommunication apparatus, or the supply or securing of telecommunication services.

Finally, although the booklet is a guide to the Competition Act, it has no legal authority and cannot be regarded as a substitute for the Act and the regulations and orders made under it, or as a legal interpretation of them. Those who think they may be affected by the legislation but are in doubt about their position, should seek legal advice.

In the booklet the 'Director General' is the Director General of Fair Trading; the 'Secretary of State' is the Secretary of State for Trade and Industry; the 'Commission' is the Monopolies and Mergers Commission; the 'Act' is the Competition Act 1980.

DEFINITION
An anti-competitive practice is defined in the Act as a course of conduct pursued by a person in the course of business which: 'of itself or when taken together with a course of conduct pursued by persons associated with him, has or is intended or is likely to have the effect of restricting, distorting or preventing competition in connection with the production, supply or acquisition of goods in the United Kingdom or any part of it or the supply or securing of services in the United Kingdom or any part of it'.

Person includes bodies corporate or unincorporate, partnerships and individuals.

EXEMPTIONS
The Act and the Anti-Competitive Practices (Exclusions) Order 1980 (as amended by the Anti-Competitive Practices (Exclusions) (Amendment) Order 1984) allow

certain limited exemptions to the definition. A practice cannot be investigated under the Act if:

— it arises from a relevant restriction in an agreement and by virtue of that restriction, either alone or taken with others, the agreement is subject to registration under the Restrictive Trade Practices Act 1976 (relevant restrictions are presumed to be against the public interest and are subject to the separate jurisdiction of the Restrictive Practices Court);

— it is carried out by a firm with an annual turnover of less than £5 million and which has less than a 25 per cent share of a relevant market and which is not a member of a group with either an annual turnover of £5 million or more or which has a 25 per cent share or more of a relevant market; or

— it is carried out in certain exempted sectors such as international shipping and international civil aviation other than for charter flights.

WHAT COUNTS AS AN ANTI-COMPETITIVE PRACTICE?
The Director General's concern is primarily to promote and maintain competition in markets for goods and services. When his attention has been drawn to particular behaviour or practices, the market is identified and an investigation is started to find what effects they have on competition in that market. The practice may have other commercial and economic effects but, in reaching a conclusion, the Director General will take into account only those effects which concern competition. The wider question of the public interest is a matter for the Commission.

A company will adopt policies and practices with potential or actual adverse effects on competition only if it has strength in a particular market, that is it has market power. Possession of market power depends on a variety of factors including the number of direct competitors, their relative shares of the market, the reputation of their products and the ease or difficulty with which newcomers can enter the market. One company may have a large number of competitors of varying size with a regular flow of firms entering and leaving the market. Another company, possibly in a highly specialised market, may have few, if any, competitors and new entrants may be virtually unknown because of the skill, knowledge and specialised plant needed for the product. In any market, ownership of a leading brand-name can give market power. Because of the wide diversity of types of market the Office does not follow any rigid rules in assessing market power. The prime test is whether a firm is able through its own actions to have a significant impact on prices or on the range and quality of goods or services available. Firms which are insignificant in a market are unlikely to have any such influence whatever practices they may adopt.

Competition can itself result in changes in market shares, or even a reduction in the number of firms in a market. The purpose of the Act is to encourage and protect the process of competition. It is not meant to be used to protect a company whose sales are falling or static or whose market share is being reduced simply because it is less efficient than its competitors or because, for other reasons, it is less able to meet the needs of the market. But if a competitor with market power adopts policies or practices which prevent, exclude or restrict competition from other firms, deter potential new entrants, or distort the process of competition in some other way, the adverse effects on these firms may be evidence of anti-competitive behaviour.

It is the effect on competition rather than the form of the practice that determines whether it is judged anti-competitive. The circumstances of each case have to be considered carefully since a practice which may reduce competition in some circumstances may not do so in others. The Act does not list practices which are to be regarded as anti-competitive in themselves nor does it give guidance on the type of behaviour that the Director General can investigate. Some illustrations of practices that *may* have anti-competitive effects are given below.

The main steps taken when the Director General is considering whether to investigate particular practices are:

IDENTIFYING THE MARKETS
The first step is to identify the market in which the firm in question is operating and the market in which any adverse effects on competition are to be expected. In many cases these two markets will be the same. But this is not necessarily so. For example the distribution policies of a firm may affect not only competition between the firm and its own competitors – for example by making it more difficult for its competitors to expand or for new competitors to enter the market – but also competition between distributors – for example by restricting distributors in their choice of suppliers or in the terms and conditions of their own sales.

In order to be able to identify a market the particular goods or services which are to be regarded as competing in the same market have to be identified. Conventionally, goods are included in the same market only if they are close substitutes for each other in the eyes of the user so that an increase in the price of any one of the items included would lead to a significant loss of sales to other items. Clearly, substitutability has a time dimension; it will be greater in the long term when users have time to adapt their purchasing arrangements. It also has a geographical dimension; where transport costs are significant, the market may have to be defined locally rather than nationally. A market will usually be identified therefore by consideration of the characteristics of the product or service and its uses in relation to any substitutes available to its users (an approach which ties in with that usually followed in marketing in industry and commerce). Sometimes, however, a market may be identified by reference to characteristics of its production; if producers can readily switch their production between different products, this may suggest that a wider – or at least a different – definition of the market is appropriate than one determined according to the characteristics of the product only.

IDENTIFYING THE POSITION OF THE FIRM IN THE MARKET
Where a firm is only one among many in the market, it is unlikely that its behaviour can have any effect on competition. If, for example, it were to attempt to impose restrictive terms on its customers, they could switch to other suppliers; while there would be some effect on market share, there would be no adverse effect on competition in the market. The first step in assessing whether a practice can have anti-competitive effects in a market is therefore to identify the extent and nature of the market power that a firm may hold, or the effect of a firm's practice upon its market power. The main factors that the Director General is likely to consider are the firm's market share, the number of competitors and their market shares, any barriers that may exist to the entry of newcomers, and advantages the firm may

enjoy over its competitors from its scale, brand name, intellectual property rights in the form of copyright, patents, trademarks and such like. In assessing a firm's position in the market, account will always be taken of import penetration, or of potential imports if there are no apparent barriers to trade.

It must be emphasised that there is no minimum level of market share that is required to trigger an investigation. Firms with less than a 25 per cent share of the relevant market are, however, exempt from the Act, if their turnover is also less than £5 million.

IDENTIFYING LIKELY AND INTENDED EFFECTS ON COMPETITION
When considering whether a practice is anti-competitive the Director General may take into account not only the effects which have already occurred, but any that he thinks are likely to occur in the future. An assessment of the way a practice impinges upon other firms in the market or on potential new entrants, is the basic part of any investigation. This assessment will be based upon various kinds of factual information but also upon the statements and views of the affected and interested parties. A firm's plans and motives in adopting a practice are also likely to be a relevant factor.

ILLUSTRATIONS OF POSSIBLE ANTI-COMPETITIVE PRACTICES
An anti-competitive practice is a course of conduct which has, or is intended to have the effect of restricting, distorting or preventing competition in any market in the United Kingdom. Conduct is likely to have this effect only if some degree of market power is present. Market power, however, can be exercised in local markets or in niches of any market and is certainly not the preserve of large firms. The following categories of possible anti-competitive practices can be identified:

— practices which do or could *eliminate* the competition a firm faces in a market in which it is engaged;

— practices which do or could *prevent* the emergence of new competitors or *restrict* competition in a market in which a firm is engaged by making it difficult for existing competitors to expand in the market;

— practices which have such an effect upon the terms and conditions of supply in some market, not necessarily a market in which the firm itself is engaged, that they *distort* competition between firms engaged in that market.

It is the *effect* rather than the *form* of a practice which is relevant and this depends upon the circumstances in which it is operated. An anti-competitive practice is one which in some way frustrates on inhibits the effective working of the competitive process. It should be emphasised that competition may not work effectively for reasons other than that some suppliers have market power, for example, deficiencies in the information available to consumers. But the Act's anti-competitive practice provisions are not intended to deal with all the reasons for market failure. Practices may be adopted for commercial reasons which have nothing to do with their effects upon competition but are intended to increase the firm's efficiency. Where a practice enables a firm more efficiently to meet the needs of its customers competition may be increased to the benefit of everyone. But where a firm has market power it may be able to use that power to the detriment of its own customers even though its own efficiency may be increased by a practice. The Director General would take this into account when deciding whether to exercise his discretionary powers.

ELIMINATION OF COMPETITION

There are many reasons why competitors may withdraw from a market. Predatory behaviour involves the deliberate acceptance of losses in the short term with the intention of eliminating competition so that enhanced profits may be earned in the long term. Diversified and vertically integrated firms may behave in a predatory fashion by subsidising loss-making activities and by reducing the price of output at later stages in a vertically integrated production process. Predatory behaviour is not limited to predatory pricing.

PREVENTING AND RESTRICTING COMPETITION

Prominent in this group of practices are restrictions in the distribution or production chain which make it difficult for competitors to attract the business of customers or suppliers. These restrictions may also make it difficult or, in the extreme, impossible, for new competitors to enter a market. These 'vertical restraints' may, however, serve to improve the efficiency of the firm without causing harmful effects to competition. *In such circumstances the restriction would not amount to an anti-competitive practice.* Examples of vertical restraints, which may have anti-competitive effects according to the structure and other features of the market, include:

Exclusive supply dealing arrangements – A supplier agrees to supply only one customer, usually in a certain geographical area. The customer in turn agrees not to stock or handle products of competitors of his supplier and perhaps not to compete with other customers of his supplier in their exclusive territories.

Exclusive purchasing contracts – A customer agrees to buy his requirements exclusively from a single supplier. Contracts which do not specify exclusivity but require the customer to buy a specified proportion of his requirements or even a specified quantity in a period may also have anti-competitive effects.

Long term supply contracts – Long term contracts which do not contain an exclusivity term can have a similar effect if the customer is faced with onerous termination provisions.

Restrictive terms – These occur in contracts which prevent or restrict the customer from dealing with the supplier's competitors, and in loyalty rebates and discounts which inhibit the customer from switching business to his supplier's competitors.

Selective distribution systems – A supplier will deal with only a certain number of distributors or only those which can satisfy criteria he lays down on such matters as stock holding levels or pre- or post-sales service. Selective distribution systems will restrict competition between distributors, but they may enhance the efficiency with which a product is distributed and users' needs are met. Whether the restrictions of competition between distributors is significant will depend primarily upon the degree of competition between the suppliers of the product (that is, on the degree of inter-brand rather than intra-brand competition). The market power of the supplier is, therefore, again the crucial consideration.

Tie-ins – A second category of practices which can prevent or restrict competition is the tie-in. A tie-in exists when the supplier of one product or service (the tying item) insists that the customer must buy all or part of his requirements of some other product or service (the tied item) from the supplier or someone nominated by him. It may be convenient to customers to buy several items from one supplier and there may be cost savings from tie-ins. But if the supplier has market power competition may be restricted for the tied item. Sometimes the customer is required, as a condition of supply of certain items in the range, to buy all (or more of) the items in the range. This is known as *full-line forcing*. This may restrict competition between the supplier and competitors who offer a more limited number of items.

Restrictions on the supply of parts or other inputs required by competitors – A third category of practice which can prevent or restrict competition can occur if vertically integrated firms refuse to supply items needed by competitors who are not engaged in the complete production process (that is, they are not vertically integrated) or may supply them only at prices which make it difficult for the competitor to sell the end product at a competitive price.

Restrictive licensing policies – These usually arise in relation to the licensing of intellectual property rights, patents, copyright, trade marks and so on but they can occur more generally with the licensing of technology and 'know how'. Some restriction of competition is inherent in the grant of any intellectual property right, the rationale being that invention, innovation and other creative activity will thereby be encouraged. A refusal to license such rights, or the inclusion of restrictive terms in licences of such rights, is therefore fully compatible with the exercise of these rights. Nevertheless the effects of the restriction of competition may, in particular circumstances, and taking account of the market power of the firm enjoying the rights, be such as to suggest that a firm's licensing practices should be regarded as an anti-competitive practice. Similarly with the licensing of technology; while it cannot be suggested that a firm must be prepared to license its technology to all-comers there may be circumstances where a refusal to license so reinforces the market power of a firm that refusal should be regarded as anti-competitive.

DISTORTION OF COMPETITION

Competition may be said to be distorted if firms are not able to compete in a certain market on the same basis for reasons other than differences in their relative efficiency. Many factors can bring about such distortions – differences in the legal, institutional and tax regimes under which firms operate, for example. Distortions can also arise from *subsidies* and other advantages enjoyed by some of the firms competing in a market. The policies and market behaviour of firms may distort competition. *Discriminatory treatment* of customers may distort competition between those customers. Some forms of competition may themselves create distortions. for example, competition between a small number of competing suppliers can result in discriminatory prices to customers (often after discounts or other allowances). It is not possible to say that such behaviour should be regarded as anti-competitive because of the effects on competition between the customers. There has to be a weighing of the competitive effects at the two levels, between the suppliers and between the customers. Behaviour which both *restricts* and *distorts* competition is more likely to have significant anti-competitive effects than behaviour which merely distorts competition; for example a supplier may grant discriminatory terms which, for some customers, include terms restricting their right to buy from other suppliers.

■ Demand

By and large economists tend to be concerned only with what they term *effective* demand, which is defined as demand backed up by purchasing power. However, most managers are also interested in two other types of demand – which we may describe as 'potential' demand and 'latent' demand.

A latent demand may be thought of as one which the consumer is unable to satisfy, usually for lack of purchasing power. For example, many housewives may have a latent demand for automatic dishwashers, but, related to their available disposable income, this want is less strong than their demand for other products and so remains unsatisfied. In other words wants are ranked in order of preference and satisfied to the point where disposable income is exhausted. From the manufacturer's point of view the problem is to translate latent demand into effective demand by increasing the consumer's preference for his particular product *vis-à-vis* all other product offerings.

Latent demand may also be thought of as a vague want in the sense that the consumer feels a need for a product, or service, to fill a particular function but is unable to locate anything suitable. It is clear that latent demand constitutes an important consideration in management planning. In the case of a demand which is latent due to lack of purchasing power a manufacturer may be able to change a consumers' preference through his marketing and promotional activities. Alternatively, if there is a trend towards increasing disposable income, then the producer may be able to project how such increases in purchasing power will enable consumers to translate their latent demand into an effective demand. Given such a forecast he will be able to plan increased production, distribution and sale to keep pace with rising disposable incomes.

In the case of a demand which is latent because the consumer is unaware of the existence of a product or service which would satisfy his ill-defined want, then clearly if the manufacturer produces a product which he feels should satisfy the need, he will wish to bring it to the attention of those with latent demand for it. Alternatively, if a manufacturer does not produce a product which should satisfy a known latent demand but is able to specify what the characteristics of such a product would be, then the latent demand becomes a marketing opportunity which he may wish to exploit.

Potential demand may be said to exist where a consumer possesses purchasing power but is not currently buying. Thus, where a marketer has identified a latent demand and developed a new product to satisfy it, the potential demand consists of all those who can back up their latent want with purchasing power. In another context potential demand may be thought of as that part of the total market or effective demand for an existing product which a firm might anticipate securing through the introduction of a new competitive product.

Once again it must be stressed that while the economists' model serves a useful purpose as a basis for analysing the real world, the assumptions upon which it rests are clearly unrealistic. Thus elementary economic texts usually make assumptions about consumer demand as follows:

1. The consumer's wants remain unchanged throughout.
2. He has a fixed amount of money available.
3. He is one of many buyers.
4. He knows the price of all goods, each of which is homogeneous.
5. He can, if he wishes, spend his money in very small amounts.
6. He acts rationally.

Of these assumptions only 2 and 3 seem likely to be true with any frequency in the real world. For the rest, as managers are only too aware, consumer demand is fickle and changes frequently. Knowledge of the existence of all those goods which the consumer might buy, let alone their prices, seem unlikely. Further, goods are not infinitely divisible and consumers have to pay the price asked for a product, whether it be 10p for a box of matches or £250 for a colour television set. However, these differences between the model and the real world are fairly obvious, but this is not always true with respect to the correct interpretation of what constitutes rational behaviour.

While the economist talks about rationality in terms of consumers maximising their satisfaction, satisfaction is usually defined in terms of solely objective criteria. Using such an interpretation the price–quantity relationship assumes a distorted level of importance and excludes any concept of subjective satisfaction. That consumers do gain subjective satisfaction is apparent from the existence of brand preference for largely undifferentiated physical products, such as flour, baked beans, detergents, and so on. In fact the creation of subjective differentials in the mind of consumers may be just as important in differentiating a product as the development of real physical differences.

Because consumers take cognisance of subjective values this is not to say that they are behaving irrationally, for clearly it would be irrational to ignore such subjective preferences. It is just because consumers do have different preferences and perceptions that producers have found it necessary to develop differentiated products and sophisticated marketing techniques.

If one traces the development of management thought during this century, one can distinguish three main phases. First, there was a production orientation which mirrored a condition which dates back from before recorded history – namely an excess of demand over available supply. However, because of the technological revolution of the eighteenth, nineteenth and twentieth centuries a position was reached by the 1920s where the advanced economies of the Western world were producing more basic goods than they were able to consume or sell elsewhere.

Faced with a situation in which one is producing more than the market is absorbing the immediate reaction is to try and stimulate consumption further. Such efforts gave rise to the second major managerial orientation, which has been termed the 'sales management orientation'. While it is understandable that producers should increase their efforts to sell what they can currently make, it is also clear that this can be but a short-term remedy if there is a basic imbalance between supply and demand. This in fact was the case with the industrialised economies of the West, but the full implications of such a situation were deferred owing to the outbreak of the Second World War. On the conclusion of the war there was a backlog of unsatisfied consumer demand, with the result that most producers found themselves in a sellers' market until the early 1950s. At this time excess supply once again began to develop and producers began to look for a new managerial philosophy to enable them to earn a satisfactory return on the resources under their control.

The philosophy which emerged and which was to give rise to the third major 'managerial orientation' was that of marketing. As we have seen, in its simplest terms the marketing philosophy postulates that supply is a function of demand and therefore must be subservient to it. To this end producers set out to measure the nature of demand in terns of both objective and subjective influences on consumer buying behaviour.

■ Competition and market structure

In essence the nature of competition and of market structure is the outcome of the interaction between supply and demand. As indicated above, it is normal to define two limiting conditions – monopoly and pure competition – and to categorise intermediate forms of competition as 'imperfect'. What, then, are the salient characteristics of these states? Before addressing this issue it is necessary to introduce the concept of *demand elasticity*, for it is this factor which is usually used as the basic indicator of the nature of competition.

Under normal conditions most people anticipate that an increase in the price of a good will result in a decline in the amount demanded, while conversely any fall in price should be accompanied by an increase in the quantity demanded. In simple terms elasticity is a measure of the degree to which a change in price will result in a change in demand. Where a very small change in price is accompanied by a major change in demand, we say that that product has a high elasticity of demand.

Conversely, even where significant price changes have only a limited impact upon the quantity demanded, we say that that product has a low elasticity of demand. Thus in order to determine the elasticity of demand for the given good we need to measure the magnitude of changes in the quantity demanded in relation to changes in the unit price. Such information is termed a demand schedule, and is frequently represented graphically us in Figure 4.1, from which it can be seen that infinitely elastic demand is represented by a horizontal line, infinitely inelastic demand by a vertical line, while varying degrees of elasticity are represented by the angle assumed by the demand curve.

In terms of basic competitive states demand under pure competition is usually represented as being highly, if not infinitely, elastic, while under monopoly conditions demand is considered highly inelastic. However, for a state of pure competition or monopoly to exist certain other conditions must be satisfied.

In the case of pure competition three basic conditions must be satisfied: namely, large numbers of producers, homogeneous output, and freedom of entry. In fact, when talking of a large number of firms it would be more accurate to speak of low levels of concentration, for the basic condition which we are seeking to define is one in which decisions by any single firm have little or no effect upon the output of the industry as a whole. As we have noted earlier, homogeneity in a product depends upon the perception of a prospective buyer. Only in the case of commodities and raw materials is it usual to find agreement that the output of two different producers which meets a given specification can in fact be treated as identical products. The third condition for the existence of pure competition is freedom of entry, by which we mean that there are no barriers or artificial restrictions to prevent any individual or firm from setting up in business to produce supplies of the product in question.

It should be noted that pure competition is not synonymous with perfect competition, for the former only describes the competitive state between suppliers, while the latter makes further assumptions about conditions in the market. Essentially these assumptions are that all buyers and sellers have perfect knowledge of the activities of one another, that there are no transportation costs and that there is perfect mobility of factors of production between industries.

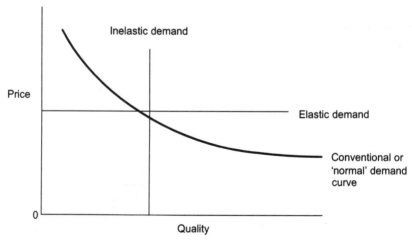

Figure 4.1   Demand curve

Under these conditions the market determines the price of a product and effectively the firm has no control over its destiny whatsoever.

The polar extreme to a situation of perfect competition is one of pure monopoly. By definition a monopolist is the sole supplier of a particular product or service, with the result that firm and industry are synonymous. In economic theory a pure monopolist has no competition at all. Clearly such a position cannot exist, for it presumes that the monopolist commands all of a consumer's income. For practical purposes we consider that a state of monopoly exists when there is no close substitute for the monopolist's output. Applying the concept of concentration a monopolist would have a concentration ratio of 100 per cent. Because the monopolist does not face direct competition from other suppliers, as is the case under conditions of perfect competition, it is frequently held that he has no incentive to maximise his efficiency.

Clearly under conditions of perfect competition the producer must maximise his efficiency, for if he does not his costs will rise above those of his rivals, but he will be unable to recoup these higher costs through increased prices. In the long run, therefore, the inefficient producer under conditions of perfect competition will be forced out of business.

From the foregoing descriptions it is clear that conditions of perfect competition and pure monopoly are exceptions rather than the rule. They are the limiting conditions. Under both sets of conditions the seller reacts solely to external environmental forces. However, in intermediate states between the two extremes the factor which really distinguishes imperfect competition is that the firm has to take account not only of the external environment within which it must operate, but also of the action of other suppliers in the market-place. The need, under conditions of imperfect competition, for firms to take into account the actions of their immediate competitors makes for a much more complex situation, and one demanding a far higher level of managerial skill. Under conditions of imperfect competition sellers are mutually interdependent, and so must allow for each other's actions when formulating their plans.

As noted earlier when discussing different managerial orientations during this present century, the growth of imperfect competition is of relatively recent origin. In fact it was not until the early 1930s that Edward Chamberlin and Joan Robinson first put forward their theories of imperfect competition. In time, therefore, the proposal of a theory of imperfect competition coincided with a change from the production to the sales management orientation and the need for companies to compete with one another along dimensions other than cost and price.

Theories of imperfect competition frequently invite an analogy with games in which choices of courses of action are limited not only by the rules of the game but also by the actions of one's competitors. Thus we find that the study of competition places increasing emphasis upon the strategic choices made by participating firms and the impact which these have upon both the fortunes of their competitors and market structure. In making such choices firms have to operate within the environmental constraints – political, legal and social –

common to them all. Thus in order to develop a distinctive and, it is hoped, successful strategy they have found it beneficial to give much closer attention to microeconomic aspects of supply and demand – especially in the latter. It is these topics with form the subject-matter of the next chapter.

☐ Additional reading

For a wide-ranging but succinct review of the issues raised in this chapter the reader should consult chapter 4, 'Industry and Commerce', in A. R. Prest and D. J. Coppock (eds), *The UK Economy: A Manual of Applied Economies* (Weidenfeld & Nicolson, 1980).

A detailed and extensive analysis of structure, conduct performance and government policy is to be found in *Industrial Structure and Market Conduct* by J. F. Pickering (Martin Robertson, 1974). While the factual content is now somewhat dated, the discussion of the key issues is highly relevant to any student wishing to improve their understanding of how environmental factors (particularly economic and political ones) influence the competitive strategy of the individual firm.

Finally, for a comprehensive review of the implications of market structure, conduct and performance for business management consult Michael E. Porter, *Competitive Strategy* (Free Press, New York, 1980) and *The Competitive Advantages of Nations* (Macmillan, 1990).

Part II
THE THEORETICAL UNDERPINNINGS

CHAPTER 5

Demand and supply

Learning Goals

The issues to be addressed in this chapter include:

1. The nature of demand and the distinction between potential, latent and effective demands.
2. The major determinants of demand – socio-economic and psychological.
3. The nature of supply and its adjustment to market needs.
4. The classification of goods and services.

After reading this chapter you will be able to:

1. Define and describe a demand schedule and a demand curve.
2. Distinguish between needs and wants.
3. List the determinants of demand and distinguish between potential, latent and effective demand.
4. Define a product and list its characteristics.
5. Define supply and explain the concept of diminishing returns.
6. Explain the nature and relevance of Maslow's Hierarchy of Needs.
7. Discuss the origins and importance of branding.
8. Define the various categories of industrial and consumer goods and the distinguishing characteristics of services.

■ Introduction

Most students of marketing have pursued an introductory course in economics and are familiar with the concept of demand as a function of price. According to this concept, the quantity of a good or service which will be purchased is dependent upon its price, such that the higher the price the less will be demanded, and vice versa. This relationship is frequently expressed in tabular form as a demand schedule, and depicted graphically as a demand curve, as shown below.

In the real world it is clear that many factors other than price affect demand, and the exclusion of such factors is often seen as invalidating economic price theory. Such an attitude misses the point that the economist is seeking to define

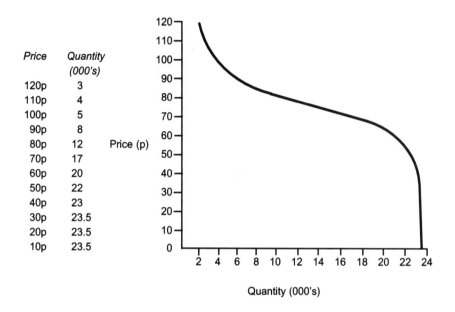

Price	Quantity (000's)
120p	3
110p	4
100p	5
90p	8
80p	12
70p	17
60p	20
50p	22
40p	23
30p	23.5
20p	23.5
10p	23.5

Figure 5.1   Simple demand schedule and curve

an essential functional relationship with which he may then investigate the effect of other independent variables upon the dependent variable, demand. It is not proposed to investigate the sophisticated techniques developed by economists which validate the basic theory, however, and attention here will be concentrated on the nature of these other, independent variables.

■ Needs, wants and choice

Before proceeding to discuss demand variables it will be useful to distinguish between needs, wants and the function of choice.

A *need* is something fundamental to the maintenance of life, such as food, drink, shelter and clothing. Needs are largely physiological in the sense that they are basic and instinctive drives with which we are born. It is clear, however, that a need may be satisfied by any one of a large number of alternatives, e.g. thirst may be assuaged by water, tea, coffee, beer, wine, etc. The availability of alternative means of satisfying a need constitutes *choice*, provision of which is central to the practice of marketing. In the absence of substitute, or alternative, goods there can be no choice, and needs and wants become synonymous.

Where there is more than one way of satisfying a basic need, physiological drives will be modified by economic, sociological and psychological factors. Variations in these factors will predispose individuals to prefer a specific alternative and this preference constitutes a *want*. As will become clear when considering economic and psychological factors in greater detail below, wants are not necessarily synonymous with the concept of demand implicit in a demand schedule. A demand schedule for a specific product may be thought of as expressing effective demand, by which is understood demand backed by the ability to pay a given price. From this it follows that there are two further types of demand – latent and potential.

As noted in the preceding chapter a latent demand may be thought of as a demand which the consumer is unable to satisfy, usually for lack of purchasing power. For example, many housewives may have a latent demand for automatic dishwashers but, related to their available disposable income, this want is less strong than their demand for other products and so remains unsatisfied. In other words, wants are ranked in order of preference and satisfied to the point where disposable income is exhausted. From the manufacturer's point of view the problem is to translate latent demand into effective demand by increasing the consumer's preference for his particular product *vis-à-vis* all other product offerings, As will be seen, marketing is largely concerned with solving this problem.

Latent demand may also be thought of as a vague want in the sense that the consumer feels a need for a product, or service, to fill a particular function but is unable to locate anything suitable. If such a product exists marketing's role is to bring it to his attention; if it does not exist, then marketing should seek to identify the unfilled need and develop new products to satisfy it.

Potential demand exists where the consumer possesses the necessary purchasing power, but is not currently buying the product under consideration. Thus, where a marketer has identified a latent demand and developed a new product to satisfy it, the potential demand consists of all those who can back up their latent want with purchasing power. In another context, potential demand may be thought of as that part of the total market (effective demand) for an existing product which a firm might anticipate securing through the introduction of a new, competitive brand.

■ Determinants of demand

As implied earlier, basic economic theory is concerned largely with price-quantity relationships, and other demand determinants are invariably excluded for more sophisticated treatment. However, corporate success is very closely related to the manufacturer's ability to predict the strength and nature of demand as a basis for deploying the firm's resources and, consequently, management is deeply concerned with all those variables which condition demand. Broadly speaking, demand determinants may be grouped under two headings – socio-economic and psychological – and the next section will be concerned with identifying the more important factors within these groups.

■ Socio-economic factors

■ Population

People constitute the basic raw material from which markets are made, for, ultimately, the demand for any given product or service depends upon the aggregate demand of individual consumers, and can never exceed the sum of their numbers. One of the major arguments behind our attempts to gain membership of the European Economic Community was that this would open the door to a market with a population five times as great as that of the United Kingdom. Clearly, this represents an enormous potential for increasing sales.

Absolute numbers are only one aspect of population, however, three other important aspects being age and sex distribution, geographical distribution and family size.

In the past decade the age distribution of the population of the UK and many other advanced industrial countries has attracted increasing attention. Essentially this attention has arisen from the realisation that, with declining birth rates and longer life expectancies, the population is 'ageing'. Thus, an increasing proportion of people are to be found in the older age groups and a lesser proportion in the younger and 'working' age groups. The implications of these changes in the composition of the population are profound. Consider, for example, the markets for education and health care.

In the case of education many of the readers of this book will be aware that as they grew up in the 1980s many primary and secondary schools were being closed down for lack of 'customers'. In their naivety planners in the Department of Education and Science extrapolated this trend and predicted a decline in the need for places in further and higher education and began to cut back on funding. Fortunately, the educationists were able to point out the difference between potential demand (all young people leaving secondary education) and effective demand (the proportion able and wanting to benefit from higher education). In addition to a growing interest in higher education a closer examination of the population statistics also revealed that although the overall birth rate had declined, in fact it had increased in Social Classes I and II which traditionally have the highest participation rates in higher education. The lesson is clear, while absolute numbers are important in defining market potential it is usage or effective demand which determines market size.

At the other end of the age spectrum the effect of an ageing or 'greying' population has also had a marked effect on consumption patterns. Nowhere is this more evident than in the demand for health care and the provision of sheltered housing, nursing homes and geriatric facilities in hospitals. Here again, careful analysis of trends in the population informed by knowledge of the likely incidence of particular diseases or disabilities such as arthritis can offer considerable insight into future demand and market opportunities. Table 5.1 is based on Government Actuaries projections and indicates how the proportion of those under and over 30 is expected to change from 42.7%:53.6% in 1985 to 38.1%:61.9% by 2006.

TABLE 5.1   Projected population by age to 2006

	Year			
Age	*1985* (%)	*1991* (%)	*1996* (%)	*2006* (%)
0 – 4	6.3	6.8	7.0	6.1
5 – 14	12.8	12.2	12.9	13.5
15 – 29	23.6	22.4	19.8	18.5
30 – 44	20.1	21.1	21.6	21.3
45 – 64	22.0	21.6	22.8	24.9
65 +	15.2	15.8	15.9	15.7

As implied in the preceding paragraphs many products are associated with a particular stage of the human life cycle, as are many other products, and recognition of this has led to the adoption of the life-cycle concept as a useful means of distinguishing the effect of age on consumption patterns. Although it is increasingly recognised that young children influence purchasing decisions, their lack of purchasing power usually excludes them from life-cycle classificatory systems which concentrate on decision-making units (DMUs). A widely accepted system distinguishes the following eight stages:

1. Young, single.
2. Young, married, no children.
3. Young, married, youngest child under six.
4. Young, married, youngest child over six.
5. Older, married, with children.
6. Older, married, no children under eighteen.
7. Older, single.
8. Other.

Although the distinction between Young and Older is not explicit, and category 8 is a meaningless 'catchall', the concept provides a useful basis for breaking down the total population into sub-groups for more detailed analysis. (A useful exercise is to visualise the variations that one would anticipate in consumption patterns as between the different categories in this system.) Life-style analysis is currently enjoying an enormous wave of popularity amongst

TABLE 5.2   Classification of UK households according to alternative
life-cycle structures

Stage	Number of households	Percentage of households
(a) *Murphy and Staples*		
Young single	25 118	1.42
Young (aged under 35):		
(a) married without children	55 018	3.11
(b) divorced without children	—	—
(c) married with children	185 296	10.46
(d) divorced with children	22 271	1.26
Middle aged (aged 35–64):		
(a) marrried without children	21 017	1.19
(b) divorced without children	–	–
(c) married with children	322 970	18.42
(d) divorced with children	34 065	، 1.92
(e) married without dependent children	167 248	9.45
(f) divorced without dependent children	–	–
Older (aged over 65):		
(a) older married	168 308	9.51
(b) older unmarried (divorced and widowed)	250 891	14.14
Total	1 277 787	72.1
(b) *Wells and Gubar*		
Bachelor	25 118	1.42
Newly married couples	55 018	3.11
Full nest 1 (youngest child under 6)	210 888	11.91
Full nest 2 (youngest child over 6) ⎫	300 534	16.97
Full nest 3 (older married with dependent children) ⎭		
Empty nest 1 (in labour force, no children at home)	167 248	9.45
Empty nest 2 (retired, no children at home)	168 308	9.51
Solitary survivor in labour force	47 186	2.66
Solitary survivor retired	250 891	14.17
Total	1 225 191	69.19
(c) *Rodgers*		
Beginning families	55 018	3.11
Pre-school families (oldest child under 6) ⎫	210 888	11.91
School age families (oldest child 6–13) ⎭		
Teenage famiies (oldest child 13–20) ⎫	300 534	16.97
Adult families (oldest over 20) ⎭		
Launching families (with non-dependent children)	111 563	6.30
Middle years (all children launched until retirement)	167 248	9.45
Ageing couples (retired)	168 305	9.51
Widowhood	250 891	14.14
Total	1 264 450	71.41

Source: Household and Family Composition, 1981 Census, 10% sample.

marketers and numerous references to its application are to be found in the management literature. An extended review of the application of the family life-cycle concept appeared in the Summer 1988 issue of the *Journal of Marketing Management* (Rob. W. Lawson, 'The Family Life Cycle: A Demographic Analysis'). Table 5.2 shows the classification of UK households according to alternative life-cycle structures.

The physical distribution of the population has a direct bearing upon the marketer's ability to make his product available to potential customers at an economic cost. The concentration of population in Britain, backed by extensive transportation facilities, make this factor less important than in many other parts of the world, e.g. the United States, Australia, Africa. In the case of bulky materials of low unit value, such as cement, or when considering entry into an export market, it will take on added significance in measuring potential demand. Physical location also has an important bearing upon the existence of regional wants and preferences; porridge, tripe and jellied eels immediately call to mind Scotland, Lancashire and London respectively. Similarly, woollens are in greater demand in the north, and cottons in the south. Overall, however, such differences are less marked than in many larger countries.

For planning and administrative purposes, the marketer will often find it convenient to subdivide the country into areas in some systematic way. An obvious approach is to use the Registrar-General's Standard Regions, namely:

North	Scotland
Yorkshire and Humberside	and the planning sub-regions of Scotland:
North-west	Borders
East Midlands	Central
West Midlands	Dumfries and Galloway
East Anglia	Fife
South-east	Grampian
South-west	Highlands
Wales	Lothian
Ireland:	Strathclyde
Northern	Tayside
Eastern	
Southern	
Western	

The great advantage of using this scheme is that the standard regions are widely used in the collection of Government statistics, and are capable of further subdivision into countries, conurbations, boroughs, etc. On the other hand the standard regions listed above differ from those used prior to the 1971 Census and may be subject to change with Local Government reorganisation. With the ever-growing range of services offered by the independent television companies, many firms now use television areas as a basic unit, although some difficulties arise due to overlap. To some extent this is overcome by the ITV companies distinguishing between primary and secondary areas, i.e. a primary area is unable to receive satisfactory transmissions from adjacent, and competing stations, while a secondary area can.

Several other alternatives are available, including the Nielsen Areas, and 'Geographia's' marketing regions, each of which has its advantages and disadvantages. However, all are to be preferred to a purely arbitrary subdivision which precludes direct use of published data.

Family size has a direct bearing on housing, the size of appliances and cars, container size, etc., etc. In conjunction with income, it also has an important effect on household purchasing patterns for, despite certain economies present in large families, it is clear that for a given income such families will spend more on essentials than small families.

■ Income

This variable is a major demand determinant and is widely used as a measure of potential demand. With the increase in the number of 'working wives', and recognising that the household is the most common decision-making and purchasing unit, it is more useful to think in terms of aggregate household income than to consider the major wage-earner's income alone.

Two concepts are particularly useful in analysing income levels – net disposable income, and discretionary purchasing power. The former consists of income from all sources including wages, interest on savings and investments, health and welfare benefits, etc., less taxes. It is a measure of the amount available for saving and expenditure. Discretionary purchasing power comprises that amount available after all 'essential' expenditures have been met – it is 'uncommitted' income which the consumer may spend, or save, as he pleases. As noted in Chapter 1, increasing income levels are invariably paralleled by an upgrading in what is considered essential but, overall, Engels's Laws seem to hold, namely: As real income increases the proportion spent on food tends to decline, expenditures on rent, heating, etc., remain constant while the proportion spent on clothing, education, recreation and travel, etc., tends to increase.

Most incomes are earned in payment for services rendered, and so depend upon the demand for the services in question (as modified by restrictive labour practices). In broad terms, occupation is determined by education, and there exists a strong correlation between the two and income so that, in the absence of income data, many researchers use education/occupation as a surrogate. Incomes vary considerably across occupational categories and the reader should consult the Department of Employment's *Employment Gazette* for detailed information on wage rates and earnings. One must be careful not to confuse the two, for wage rates do not necessarily bear any resemblance to the actual wages paid in a particular job or area. Further, the incidence of overtime has a marked effect on earnings, and it is the latter with which the demand analyst is primarily concerned.

Effective demand, as defined earlier, implies that consumption is a function of available income, and this relationship has been the subject of extensive research over a long period. Three separate theories have evolved out of this research in an attempt to explain variations in aggregate consumption functions and may be summarised as:

(a) *The absolute income hypothesis*, which holds that expenditures/savings are a function of income.

(b) *The relative income hypothesis*, which holds that expenditures/saving patterns depend upon the relative position of the spending unit on the income scale, and not on the absolute income earned. This hypothesis recognises the 'keeping up with the Joneses' phenomenon.

(c) *The permanent income hypothesis*, which holds that expenditures are based on average income expectations over time. This hypothesis recognises that consumption patterns are relatively stable over time, which suggests that consumers average out their expenditures, i.e. under inflation they anticipate that they will make good current dissaving, due to price increases, out of future wage increases.

An additional, and complicating, factor in recent years has been the increased availability of credit. Although the amount of credit an institution is prepared to extend to an individual is usually related to his income, there are now so many separate sources that the relationship between credit and income has become tenuous. Clearly, the ready availability of credit has done much to enable the consumer to translate latent demand into an effective demand, and has become an important demand determinant.

Collectively, the factors reviewed above are socio-economic variables, and form the basis of a broad but useful classificatory system. Within the United Kingdom, differences in ethnic origin and religion have usually been considered too slight to merit inclusion in such a system, although they may be relevant in foreign markets. (The upsurge of Welsh and Scottish 'nationalism' and the Protestant-Catholic confrontation in Northern Ireland suggest that greater attention may have to be given to these factors in future as does the concentration of ethnic/religious groups in cities such as Bradford or Notting Hill.)

■ Psychological factors

When discussing the distinction between needs and wants it was noted that needs are essentially physiological and instinctive, but that such generalised, basic drives are subject to modification by other factors, resulting in specific wants. To a large degree these 'other factors' are psychological. However, men live in social groups, membership of which modifies behavioural response to the extent that it would be more correct to identify these factors as psycho-sociological and/or socio-psychological. Collectively, the study of these influences has created a whole new field of marketing; usually referred to as 'consumer behaviour'. An extended discussion of the more important concepts follows in Chapter 6, but before turning to this it will be helpful to review the other half of the market equation – supply.

■ Supply: products and services

In the preceding section attention was focused on those factors which determine the precise character of demand for specific goods and services. Here, our objective will be to examine how these demand determinants are reflected in the supply of products designed to satisfy particular wants as identified by the marketer.

■ The 'product' in theory and practice

As a subject, economics is largely concerned with maximising satisfaction through the optimum use of scarce resources. Inherent in this construct is tacit acceptance of the fact that available resources are insufficient to satisfy all conceivable demands of mankind, although it is recognised that conditions of over-supply are perfectly possible in the particular.

In theory, production, or the creation of supply, is a function which expresses the relationship between inputs and outputs. Inputs are referred to generically as 'factors of production', and broadly classified as land, labour, capital and management, while outputs are identified as products. (To avoid endless repetition the term 'products' will be taken to include both physical goods and services, unless stated to the contrary.)

Given that there is a finite limit to the availability of factors of production, whereas demand is infinite, it follows that we need a criterion which will enable us to determine priorities in the use of these factors in order to maximise satisfaction. Such a criterion is provided by the Law of Variable Proportions or, as it is more usually termed, the Law of Diminishing Returns. This law states that incremental units of a given factor of production, other factors being held constant, will yield increasing returns up to a certain point, beyond which diminishing returns will set in. This point is not fixed, and will vary with changes in technology and the other inputs. However, at any given point in time, it is theoretically possible to determine the optimum allocation of inputs which will maximise total output.

In reality, the multi-dimensional complexity of products precludes viable analysis, and economists have found it necessary to suppress such variables in developing theories of competition. Thus, although more sophisticated treatments recognise product differentiation as a competitive variable, in theory the product is usually viewed as a homogeneous entity. In practice, products may be differentiated by any one of a multiplicity of variables as indicated by the following definition: 'Those aspects of the good or service exchanged whether arising from materials, or ingredients, mechanical construction, design durability, taste, peculiarity of package or container or service ... all products beyond the raw material stage are highly variable, for the most part on a continuous scale' (E. Chamberlin, *Towards a More General Theory of Value*: Oxford University Press, New York, 1957).

To further complicate the issue, product differences are determined by the perception of the individual consumer, from which it follows that Daz, Persil Automatic, Bold and Ariel Automatic are all different products, whereas 'detergent' is a generic name for a group of products possessing similar physical characteristics.

In an article entitled 'What is a Product?' (*British Agents Review*, reprinted in *Marketing Forum* (March/April 1968)) C. P. Stephenson emphasised this point by defining a product as 'everything the purchaser gets in exchange for his money', and listed the following 'extras' associated with the physical product:

Advisory services
After-sales service
Replacements
Designing and planning services
Deliveries
Guarantees
Credit terms
Reputation
Experience

The idea that the product is 'everything the purchaser gets for his money' has been developed considerably in recent years through the writings of marketing gurus like Ted Levitt and Philip Kotler and the emergence of the *augmented* product or service. (The growing interest in the marketing of services is reviewed in Chapter 23 but, at this point, it is worth drawing attention to the convergence in thinking which recognises that physical products possess intangible benefits while intangible services usually require physical inputs in their creation and consumption.)

The idea of the augmented product is probably a direct descendant of Levitt's 'Marketing Myopia' in which he argued that one must define market opportunities in terms of the core benefit desired by the potential consumer. Thus, the hungry man wants 'food' but, within the constraints of disposable income and physical availability, will probably have access to literally hundreds of possible solutions to his need. In selecting a particular type of food he will have regard to a wide range of attributes which distinguish one food from another ranging from physical attributes such as animal or vegetable origin, taste and consistency through considerations such as its perceived quality, packaging or presentation and brand name or reputation of the supplier. Finally, the hungry man will have regard for any other benefits associated with different product offerings which will enable him to distinguish between them and select that which most closely meets his needs at the time at which the decision is to be made. For example, is the food prepared or not, can he consume it on the premises or will he have to consume it elsewhere, is it to be served or self-service, etc? The use of increasingly specific criteria to discriminate between goods which pure economists would regard as largely homogeneous or 'generic' products like breakfast cereals, soap, detergent, bread, etc. lies at the very heart of buyer decision making. As a consequence it also lies at the heart of successful product development and the execution of effective marketing strategies. We shall return to this theme many times, especially in the discussions of Consumer Behaviour (Chapter 6), Market Segmentation (Chapter 8) and Product Policy (Chapter 11).

Individually, and collectively, all these factors will lead consumers to distinguish between the product offerings of competing firms in order to best satisfy their particular wants.

■ Competition and the provision of choice

As noted, the ability to create excess supplies of basic goods is of relatively recent origin and is largely responsible for the current emphasis on marketing, as opposed to production. This change of emphasis recognises that the competitive 'ground rules' appropriate to conditions of excess demand must be modified under the threat of excess supply.

Maslow's concept of a need hierarchy (discussed at greater length in Chapter 6, pp. 120–1) is reflected in the nature of consumer demand. At the first level, the consumer's prime concern is to satisfy a basic need such as hunger, thirst or shelter, by whatever means are available. Under conditions where there is an insufficiency of supply to satisfy these basic needs, factor inputs are restricted to those alternatives which offer the maximum output consistent with certain minimum levels of satisfaction. In the last century this objective was achieved by product standardisation, which permitted the division of labour and the adoption of mass production techniques. Such conditions prevailed in the United States during the second half of the nineteenth century and, to a lesser degree, in much of Western Europe. Today they are typical of the developing economy.

Once the basic needs have been satisfied, however, consumers advance to a higher and more sophisticated level of demand. Deficiencies in the 'standard' product become apparent, through possession and consumption, and are expressed in the market-place by a preference for differentiated products which more nearly satisfy specific wants. Moreover, the economic growth associated with mass production, and its attendant economies of scale, increases discretionary purchasing power to the point where consumers can afford to pay more for improved, and differentiated, products.

Product homogeneity is fundamental to the existence of perfect competition, under which price is determined solely by market forces and so is beyond the producer's-control. In these circumstances a firm's profitability is a direct consequence of its cost structure, and the natural emphasis is on production. The realisation that consumers are both willing and able to pay a premium for products with distinctive attributes offers the firm the opportunity to exercise a degree of control over the market, and escape direct competition with its rivals. Such a position is clearly to be preferred and has led to the present concentration on marketing with its emphasis on the provision of choice to meet varied consumer preferences.

■ Branding

Recognising that homogeneity of product offering precluded identification of a given producer's output at the point of sale, manufacturers 'revived' the practice of branding as a means of distinguishing their product from that of their competitors.

Craftsmen have long been accustomed to identifying their work, either by signature or by the use of a distinctive symbol particular to them. In fact this practice was mandatory under the gild system to protect customers and to ensure that shoddy workmanship could be traced back to its originator. An extant example of this is the 'hallmark' used on silver as a guarantee of purity and indicator of its origin. Over time, this practice has enabled consumers to form judgements as to the value of given names and symbols as indicators of the quality of the product, and as a guarantee of satisfactory performance.

Clearly, the identification of a product is two-edged in the sense that although it permits satisfied customers to repeat purchase, it also allows them to avoid repetition of an unsatisfactory purchase. None the less, branding is now standard practice for the majority of goods, although it is most frequently associated with products purchased for personal consumption.

From both the consumer's and producer's point of view the brand serves as a useful shorthand expression for a whole collection of attributes and properties associated with a given product. In part these associations are built up by advertising; in part they are the result of the consumer's perception and past experience. Whatever their origin, the brand enables the purchaser to obtain products which satisfy highly specific wants, without having to resort to a detailed description of them.

Brand names may be given to individual products, e.g. Daz, Bold, Persil Automatic and Ariel Automatic, etc.; or a generic, or family, brand may be used for a firm's complete product line, e.g. Heinz, Black & Decker, St Michael. Individual brand names are expensive to establish, and usually require a large investment in advertising and sales promotion. Their use is usually restricted to situations where:

(a) Potential sales of each product are sufficient to justify the necessary expenditures.
(b) The products vary in price, quality, etc., and are designed to appeal to different market segments.
(c) There is a radical innovation with a high risk of failure and the company does not wish to prejudice the success of existing brands.

The UK detergent market provides an excellent example of brand competition with developments regularly documented in reports published by companies such as the Economist Intelligence Unit (*Retail Business*), Nielsen and Mintel. The following comments are based on Mintel's Market Intelligence report for March 1989 on 'Detergents and Laundry Aids'. This report was the first published by Mintel in which it combined the two sectors which are at different stages of development. The detergent sector is dominated by two major companies, Lever Brothers and Procter & Gamble, and is fairly mature. Recent impetus in this sector has come from the advent of liquid detergent which has had a remarkable effect on the market. Before the launch of Wisk by Lever Brothers in October 1986, the total detergent market was growing by value at about 3.5 per cent a year, whereas in 1988 the market expanded by 21 per cent and was worth £520 million at retail selling prices (rsp). Higher unit costs for liquid detergents have contributed to this value increase. A massive £90 million was added to market size during 1988.

In the detergent market product launches are a vital component for each of the giants to maintain or increase market share. Currently the battle for supremacy is being waged between Wisk and Liquid Ariel launched by Procter and Gamble in January 1987. Interestingly, however, own label brands have managed to secure a strong position *vis-à-vis* the two giants and now account for about 20 per cent by volume. To counteract this the majors have continued to launch more 'new' brands. Lever's major entry has been Persil Liquid Automatic while Procter & Gamble has riposted with Daz Automatic Liquid – its fifth brand introduced between entering the market in 1988 and March 1989. In such a volatile market with a proliferation of new brands market shares were difficult to pin down at the time of writing exhibiting all the characteristics of the rapid growth phase of the product life cycle (see p. 43). By the time you read this it is likely that competition will have settled down in a more mature market under-scoring the need to monitor such markets on a continuous basis by consulting the syndicated market research reports of Mintel, EIU etc.

Family brands tend to be preferred in circumstances where physical differentiation between brands is difficult to establish, the potential market is small, and the firm has an established line of complementary products. Hence a firm like Heinz, Max Factor or Marks & Spencer will usually concentrate its effort on the development of an overall image/reputation and rely on this to introduce new products into the market.

Increased competition at the retail level has prompted many retailers and wholesalers to develop 'own', or 'private', brands which are sold in competition with the manufacturers' brands. (The latter are often termed 'national brands' as they are usually promoted on a national basis.) By avoiding the promotional expenditures necessary to maintain a national brand, private brands can be offered at a lower price, and are widely used in building store 'traffic', i.e. to induce price-conscious shoppers to come into the store in the hope that they will make other purchases.

In many instances private brands are identical with the better-known national brands and, in fact, are produced by the same manufacturers. The use of a second brand allows the manufacturer to sell off his excess production at a lower price than that asked for the major, promoted brand. Naturally, few manufacturers are willing to admit that they are practising this form of price discrimination, and the origin of such private label brands is usually a closely guarded secret. For the price-conscious shopper, private brands offer considerable savings, and are perceived as of equivalent quality to the better-known national brands. However, most consumers prefer the national brands with which they are familiar, and from which they derive additional satisfactions. Whether these arise out of associations built up by advertising, or represent real differences in quality, which is often the case (e.g. washing-up liquids), is largely irrelevant, for the final choice rests with the consumers who will optimise their own choice criterion. The market share of private brands for various product categories is given in Table 5.3.

TABLE 5.3   Private label share by value at December 1987
(TCA product categories)

	%		%
Canned foods	28.0	Beverages	31.4
Frozen foods	37.5	Pet foods	8.1
Packet foods	19.1	Toiletries*	9.5
Dairy products	40.7	Soaps and detergents	9.3
Bakery products	34.0	Cleaners	22.8
Sauces and ketchups	23.1	Paper goods	40.8

*Toilet soap/dentifrice only
Source:AGB/TCA.

More recently supermarkets have upgraded the quality of their own brands and have used them as a means of enhancing their store image. This left a gap in the market which has been filled by the introduction of 'generic' brands – virtually the 'own label' version of supermarkets' own label goods. They have been introduced into the basic food and grocery items market and encompass products such as washing-up liquids, tinned dog meats, flour, sugar and instant coffee. These goods are stripped of expensive packaging and promotion costs and may be of lower quality than branded goods. Their prices can be substantially lower than branded goods. Generic brands are proving to have a widespread appeal to the consumer and already appear to have a significant share (about 5 per cent) of the grocery market.

However, there has been a mixed reaction from both manufacturers and retailers alike. The major manufacturers with strong brands have so far refused to make own label or generic products (e.g. Heinz, Kellogg's and Nescafe, who are even going so far as to advertise the fact). However, manufacturers with weaker brands do produce own label and generic products. The reaction of the supermarkets has also been varied, with Tesco, Presto, Safeway, Gateway and Carrefour all stocking generic goods. Marks & Spencer and Sainsbury's, however, have not yet accepted the concept; this is because both companies have built their reputation on their own label products, Sainsbury's own label goods accounting for approximately 52 per cent of its business and Marks & Spencer's 100 per cent.

The idea of simple packaging was originated by Carrefour Supermarkets in France into the mid 1970s, the idea then spread to America in 1977 and into Britain in 1979. The grocery trade has accepted this concept in its efforts to boost the volume of sales at a time when the rate of food price increases has fallen, leading to a problem for supermarkets, which as a rule have high fixed costs. Although at first they were thought to be a reaction to the world-wide recession, generic brands appear not to be solely a recession concept, as a Fine Fare (now Gateway) spokesman pointed out: 'it appears in the UK as well as the US to have high appeal to relatively high income, affluent and well-educated young shoppers'. A Report published by the Institute of Grocery Distribution entitled 'Grocery Distribution 1982', states that: 'the early sign so far this year suggest a number of major retailers are viewing own label as a more important weapon in the marketing armoury'. The Report also points out that there appears to be a trend of polarisation between supermarkets selling major brands of goods and those selling own label or generic products.

We can conclude by noting that generic products do appear to have gained a foothold in the market and seem likely to be here to stay. However, because of the higher profit margins on own label products, it is predicted that retailers will concentrate more on their development in the future.

■ Classification of products

Given that products may be differentiated in a multiplicity of ways, some form of classification is desirable to simplify discussion and permit the formulation of general principles. Although several bases for classification have been proposed, the most widely adopted system distinguishes two major categories – industrial goods and consumer goods – and is based on the purpose for which the goods are purchased. In the case of industrial goods this same criterion is used to further subdivide the category, but in the case of consumer goods a second criterion, method of purchase, has been found more useful.

It is the author's opinion that little useful purpose can be served by following the example of many writers who attempt to develop their own definitions. Verbal dexterity is rarely mistaken for originality and, in the case of definitions, usually only serves to confuse what it is intended to clarify. Accordingly the definitions used here are those adopted by the American Marketing Association.

■ Consumer goods

Goods destined for use by the ultimate household consumer and in such form that they can be used by him without further commercial processing.

Consumer goods are generally divided into three sub-categories according to the method in which they are purchased following the terminology first proposed by Melvin T. Copeland in 1923 – convenience goods, shopping goods and specialty goods ('Relation of Consumers' Buying Habits to Marketing Methods', *Harvard Business Review* (April 1923)).

■ Convenience goods

Those consumer goods which the customer usually purchases frequently, immediately and with the minimum of effort.

This category encompasses a wide range of household products of low unit value. It is implicit that products in this category have low brand loyalty, as the user is not prepared to go to any effort to secure a supply and will accept a substitute. From this it follows that the producer must secure the widest possible availability if he is to maximise sales.

■ Shopping goods

Those consumer goods which the customer in the process of selection and purchase characteristically compare on such bases as suitability, quality, price and style.

Products in this group are more complex than convenience goods and exhibit a higher degree of differentiation. Usually they are purchased less frequently and are of higher unit value. Many consumer durables fall into this category.

■ Specialty goods

Those consumer goods on which a significant group of buyers characteristically insists and for which they are willing to make a special purchasing effort.

Some critics argue that this is a meaningless category as the 'special purchasing effort' required is due to limited availability and that otherwise such goods would fall into one of the other groups. This argument is rejected on the grounds that brand insistence has a very real bearing on the consumer's patronage of different outlets and therefore on the retailer's stock policy. Thus, although the housewife may be indifferent to the brand of canned peas she buys and will take what is available, she may well change to another store altogether if she cannot find her preferred brand of baby food, cigarette or headache remedy.

■ Industrial goods

Goods which are destined for use in producing other goods or rendering services, as contrasted with goods destined to be sold to ultimate consumers.

Certain goods which fall into this category may also be classified as consumer goods, e.g. paper, typewriters, chairs, fuel oil, etc. Where such an overlap exists, the purpose for which the product is bought determines its classification.

Industrial goods fall into four main categories.

■ Raw materials

Those industrial materials which in part or in whole become a portion of the physical product but which have undergone no more processing than is required for convenience, protection, economy in storage, transportation or handling. Threshed grain, natural rubber and crushed ore fall into this category.

■ Equipment

Those industrial goods which do not become part of the physical product and which are exhausted only after repeated use, such as major installations or installations equipment, and auxiliary accessories or auxiliary equipment. Installations equipment includes such items as boilers, presses, power lathes, bank vaults, etc., while auxiliary equipment includes trucks, office furniture, hand tools and the like.

■ Fabricated materials

Those industrial goods which become a part of the finished product and which have undergone processing beyond that required for raw materials but not so much as finished parts. Steel, plastic moulding powders, cement and flour fit this description.

■ Supplies

Those industrial goods which do not become a part of the physical product or which are continually exhausted in facilitating the operation of an enterprise. Examples of supplies include fuel, stationery and cleaning materials.

Although few producers give much thought to actually classifying their output along the above lines, this is probably due to the fact that their product line falls within a single category, and not because there is no value in developing such a classification. In fact the product category has a fundamental effect on the firm's marketing strategy as a whole, as well as having far-reaching implications for its internal organisation and operation. This point will be examined in greater detail in Chapter 19.

■ Services

As acknowledged at several points in this chapter it is commonplace to speak and write of products – both consumer and industrial – as if the term automatically embraces services. In reality, as the burgeoning literature of services marketing testifies, there are many important differences which demand separate recognition and treatment. Chapter 23 attempts to review the most significant of these differences but, at this juncture, it will be helpful to recognise that services are generally distinguished from physical products in terms of their *intangibility*; the difficulty of separating the service from the supplier of the service and its consumption (*inseparability*); their *heterogeneity* or lack of standardisation, and the problems of matching highly *perishable* outputs with *fluctuating demands*.

CHAPTER 6

Consumer behaviour

Learning Goals

The issues to be addressed in this chapter include:

1. A review of the multiplicity of factors – social, psychological and economic – which form and influence consumer behaviour.
2. The nature of the buyer decision process.
3. The role of perception in determining behaviour.
4. The nature of learning, motivation, personality and attitude and their influence on behaviour.
5. The concepts of culture, social class, reference groups, personal influence and life style as social influences on behaviour.
6. The relevance and explanatory power of composite models of consumer behaviour.

After reading this chapter you will be able to:

1. Explain and justify a simple, generalised model of the buying decision process.
2. Describe the phenomenon of perception and clarify its role in determining how individuals interpret the world around them.
3. Distinguish the salient characteristics and differences between the stimulus–response and cognitive explanations of learning.
4. Elaborate Maslow's theory of motivation.
5. Understand why personality is only one of several major influences on consumer decision making.
6. Explain the essential differences between the CAC and expectancy-value models of attitude and the nature of hierarchy of effects models of decision making.
7. Spell out the influence of culture on buyer behaviour.
8. Describe the concepts of social class, reference groups, personal influence and life style and show how they can be used to help sellers devise effective marketing strategies.
9. Summarise the key features of the best known models of consumer buyer behaviour and their respective strengths and weaknesses.

■ Introduction

In *Consumer Behaviour*, Engel, Blackwell and Miniard (5th edn, The Dryden Press, 1986) define consumer behaviour as 'those acts of individuals directly involved in obtaining and using economic goods and services, including the decision processes that precede and determine these acts'. This definition enjoys a very wide measure of support in the majority of texts concerned primarily with consumer behaviour as a field of study in its own right but, in my opinion, it is important to stress that such an emphasis upon *individuals* tends to ignore largely an equally important area of consumption behaviour – that of organisations.

In the two decades since the first publication of this book there has developed a major interest in organisational buying behaviour as a major sub-field of marketing. This interest was reflected by the inclusion of a separate chapter on the topic in the fourth edition which is continued in this edition.

However, the existence of separate texts dealing with consumer and organisational buying behaviour is symptomatic of a much larger division within marketing of which new students of the subject should be especially sensitive – namely, the dichotomisation of the subject into industrial marketing and consumer marketing. Ever since the first edition of this book appeared in 1971 I have argued that while there are differences between these two branches of marketing they are a matter of degree only and in essence both rest upon the same foundations, as do new branches such as the marketing of services or marketing by non-profit-making organisations. Accordingly it might be more realistic to classify consumption behaviour as 'individual' or 'collective' depending upon whether such behaviour is undertaken solely in pursuit of one's own satisfaction or is engaged on in conjunction with and/or on the behalf of others. Such a classification would require one to include households in the 'collective' category and it is probably preferable to maintain the generally recognised distinction between consumer and industrial or organisational (business) behaviour which exists in the marketing literature.

In this chapter we will accept the traditional approach in which discussions of consumer behaviour are focused upon individuals or ultimate consumers and their consumption behaviour, i. e. what they consume, how they buy, and why. In doing so it will be necessary to review a number of key concepts and ideas which have been borrowed from other behavioural sciences – notably psychology and sociology – before considering how these ideas have become incorporated in composite models of consumer behaviour. To this end we look first at contributions from psychology: namely, perception, learning, personality, motivation and attitude. Attention is then directed to social influences on consumer behaviour with specific reference to culture, social class, reference groups, role and family influence, with that section concluding with a discussion of life-style as an explanation of how and why people consume, which illustrates how the psychological and sociological foundations have been built upon by marketers. This theme is further developed by a survey of some of the major models of consumer behaviour which illustrate the main schools of thought, concluding with my own composite model of buying behaviour in which I seek to justify my earlier claim that differences between different branches of marketing are a matter of degree and not of principle.

■ The buying decision process

Before looking at some of the factors which influence buying decisions it will be helpful first to consider a simple and generalised model of buying as a decision process. In broad terms this may be represented by a flow diagram containing five elements as follows:

PROBLEM RECOGNITION

INFORMATION SEARCH

EVALUATION OF ALTERNATIVES

CHOICE

POST PURCHASE EXPERIENCE

As will become clear later in this chapter the reality is far more complex than implied by this model. As we accumulate experience and learn from past behaviour so this knowledge and the attitudes associated with it will generate feedback loops in the sequence and may short circuit the process so that one moves almost instantaneously from problem recognition to choice. For example, people shopping in a supermarket depend heavily upon the display to stimulate problem recognition – 'I'm short of instant coffee' – and immediately select a preferred brand and size which their past experience has shown to give satisfaction. (Or at least sufficient satisfaction that the opportunity cost in their time and effort to collect new information and evaluate it is not considered worthwhile.) Such behaviour does not invalidate the basic model which emphasises that the consumer purchase decision is sequential and combines both mental and physical activities. As my former colleague Jenny Drayton has explained:

> The sequence can be divided into three basic stages:
>
> (i)   a decision process
> (ii) an act of purchase
> (iii) a period of usage

This sequence of events shows a consumer to be actively involved in the market-place long before the actual buying of goods and to retain such involvement for some time after the purchase has been completed.

(i)   The recognition of a decision process acknowledges the purposive nature of making a purchase, introducing the ideas of pre-purchase deliberation, the willingness to seek information, and the existence of an internal evaluation system to provide the criteria which will guide the choice decision.

   The decision process emphasises that, a consumer prior to buying is *purposive*, *deliberate* and *evaluative*.

(ii) The subsequent act of purchase is inevitably shaped by this preceding decision-making activity. Going out to buy goods is to implement the decision: the buyer is taking a specific course of action bearing upon acquiring a predetermined choice of goods. For example, where household income may be used for *either* domestic appliances *or* for home entertainment equipment, both in themselves deemed desirable, the decision between the two product classes will be made prior to, not at the time of, buying the goods. Equally, when arriving at a choice within a range, pre-purchase thought and evaluation will affect the buying activity by reducing the total number of brands available to a smaller number of brands which the buyer will consider at the time of purchase. Thus the act of purchase becomes simplified, an extension of the pre-purchase consumer activity.

(iii) At the third stage is the gaining of experience through using the goods. Here the consumer can assess all his previous actions in acquiring the goods, to store in the memory to act as reinforcement, or to initiate change. The consumer may consider such things as whether the goods live up to expectation, whether information was readily available and accurate, the nature and surroundings of the shopping situation, and so on. Whatever the answers, this assessment becomes an integral part of the consumer's internal evaluation system, to influence future behaviour in the acquisition of economic goods and services. Thus the consumer learns through experience patterns of behaviour which develop and strengthen.

The 'consumer' then, rather than the 'buyer', implies an active and demanding partner in the economic transaction. In response, the marketer needs to be equally active and aware, employing the tools of marketing in concert with the consumer behaviour sequence to bring together the potential buyer and the company's product.

■ Psychological influences

■ Perception

In psychology an important and fine discrimination is made between the concepts of sensation and perception. Sensation occurs when a sense organ receives a stimulus, while perception is the interpretation of that stimulus. The distinction is particularly important for marketers, for in order to initiate an exchange process we must first establish contact through the generation of a stimulus capable of sensation by the intended recipient. For practical purposes there are five senses – seeing, hearing, touching, smelling and tasting, though experimentation has established eleven sensory mechanisms in all – and it is to one or more of the five basic senses that marketing communications stimuli are directed. However, perception is the critical factor, for this is the interpretation placed upon the stimulus and can vary widely between individuals and even within individuals over time. A frequently used example which makes this point is to compare a photograph – what the eye and the camera physically see – with a painting, which is the receiver's interpretation of that sensation. Clearly Rembrandt and Picasso perceived things rather differently and the critical question must be. 'What factors influence perception?'

In essence, if perception consists of the interpretation of a received stimulus, then, as Sperling (*Psychology*, Made Simple Books, W. H. Allen, 1967) points out, 'What we perceive at any given time, therefore, will depend not only on the nature of the actual stimulus, but also on the background or setting in which it exists – our own previous sensory experiences, our feelings of the moment, our general prejudices, desires, attitudes and goals.' Given that so many forces influence perception it is not surprising that there should frequently occur a mismatch between the interpretation intended by the originator of a stimulus (usually the seller in a marketing context) and the receiver (intended customer). It follows that those responsible for marketing stimuli should pay very careful attention to psychological findings concerning how people perceive things.

A fundamental aspect of perception is that it represents the receiver's effort to organise received stimuli into a meaningful structure. In doing so two major groups of factors are involved – stimulus factors and functional factors. Stimulus factors are neutral in the sense that they are intrinsic to the stimulus and so will be received in exactly the same way by all receivers with normal sensory capabilities. On receipt the brain organises the incoming stimuli into patterns following four basic tendencies: similarity, proximity, continuity and context.

By similarity we understand the tendency of the receiver to group similar things together, while proximity results in the perception that things which are close to one another belong together. In marketing practice similarity is to be seen in the concept of segmentation, while proximity is employed in the use of prominent people to endorse particular products, in the use of generic brands like St Michael, and so on. The need to impose a meaningful structure on stimuli is particularly noticeable in the case of continuity, which is closely associated with closure. The phenomenon of continuity is well illustrated by Sperling with the use of a simple diagram like that below:

In this one see the dots as straight lines rather than as separate dots, and as two continuous lines rather than four short ones. Closure occurs when one completes an otherwise incomplete diagram, picture, sentence, etc. For example, we all know what 'Beans means'.

Finally, context, or the setting in which a stimulus is received, will have a marked effect upon perception (see any basic book for illustrations of the context influencing perception). In this sense context can have a similar 'halo' influence to proximity and is frequently used by marketers when seeking to develop an image of a product by using media or a setting which conveys the overall impression they wish to create, e. g. use of the Sunday colour supplements to convey a feeling of quality allied to value for money, or young people in leisure situations for Coca Cola.

As noted, stimulus factors are neutral and create sensations which are then interpreted in the light of what are generically termed functional factors. Thus individuals have an ability to screen out stimuli which they do not understand or do not wish to recognise, just as they also have an ability to modify stimuli to make them acceptable to us – a phenomenon sometimes termed 'selective perception'.

The classic example of selective perception is that reported by Hastorf and Cantril ('They Saw a Game: A Case History', *Journal of Abnormal and Social Psychology*, vol. 49, 1954) of the perceptions of supporters of two American football teams – Dartmouth and Princeton. The match contained a number of incidents which led to players being injured and penalties being imposed. While most uninvolved viewers felt these were the joint responsibility of both teams, supporters of the two sides were almost unanimous in their view that all the trouble was the fault of the other team.

This tendency to perceive what one wants to 'see' can be traced to several factors. First, there is our ability to screen out or ignore a very large number of stimuli and so enable us to give our full attention to those which have some particular relevance or which strike a discordant note because of the contrast they make with other stimuli. Research has shown that we screen out the vast majority of advertisements to which we are exposed and, in fact, perceive less than 1 per cent of all those we come into contact with. Thus in order to secure our attention advertisers must use contrast, e. g. a colour advertisement in a black-and-white medium, loud noise (or silence) in broadcast media, luxury yacht advertisements in *The Economist*, etc. By the same token we possess perceptual defences which block out stimuli which are offensive, or are otherwise in conflict with our values or attitudes.

The issue of relevance is also important, for clearly we will be more likely to perceive stimuli which cater to our needs, both physiological and emotional, than those which do not. On occasion physical and emotional needs may generate a conflict (termed 'cognitive dissonance') such that acquisition of a physical object to satisfy a need (a car for transportation) may generate uncertainty as to the wisdom of that choice. Under these circumstances it has been shown that purchasers of objects pay more attention to advertising or other stimuli relating to the object than do intending purchasers.

Another perceptual phenomenon of importance to the marketer is that of preparatory set, which, put simply, means that people tend to perceive objects in terms of their expectations (cf. closure, discussed above). A well-known marketing manifestation of the influence of preparatory set is the use of branding and price labelling. Hence, while consumers are unable to distinguish between unbranded products they have no such difficulty when brand names are given. Similarly, Gabor and Granger, Shapiro and others have clearly demonstrated that we use price as an indicator of quality and will select products with a higher price as 'better' when no differences exist with those carrying a lower price and even when the higher-priced items are objectively inferior.

In recent years marketers have made considerable use of psychological explanations of perception in developing their communications strategies and have developed a number of specific applications of their own. Perhaps the most sophisticated of these applications is known as *perceptual mapping*, which is founded on the premise that individuals will seek to relate to new things in terms of their relationship with or similarity to things with which they are already familiar. By collecting information from consumers of their perceptions of existing brands in a product category one can develop a two-dimensional map (usually by making use of a powerful computer program) which shows the relationships between the various brands in terms of the variables used. In Figure 6.1 it can be seen that the various brands are clustered in groups, suggesting that they are perceived as very similar. If one were to develop a new brand in this category, then this knowledge would be very valuable – either one has a product with certain characteristics and can identify the immediate opposition, or one can identify 'gaps' which it may be worth filling with a different type of product (cheap and light?). (The example shown is fictitious but it should be stressed that while Americans prefer lighter whiskies and pay a premium for them, the opposite is largely true in Britain.)

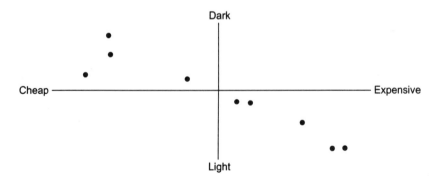

Figure 6.1   Perception of different brands of whisky in US market

■ Learning

Our discussion of perception has made it clear that in every circumstance our perception is conditioned by our prior experience, for it is this which constitutes our preparatory set or expectations and the framework into which we seek to place and organise new stimuli. In other words we have learned from our earlier experience and seek to maintain balance or consistency by relating to and interpreting new stimuli in terms of past or learned stimuli.

Learning may have a number of meanings, depending upon the context in which it is used, and Sperling (in *Psychology*) comments that 'the process of learning can consist of all, or some, or one of three steps: INVENTING an original solution to a problem, or THINKING: COMMITTING a solution to memory, or MEMORISING: BECOMING EFFICIENT at applying the solution to a problem, or FORMING A HABIT'.

In essence there are two schools of thought concerning what is learned – the stimulus – response (S–R) school, and the cognitive school. Although there are some divisions within the S–R camp, the basic theory is that we learn to associate given responses to specific stimuli and these become habitual. One group of S–R theorists subscribe to the view that learning occurs only when there are rewards or punishments to reinforce the correct response, while others believe that learning is the result of an association between a stimulus and response occurring together, i.e. they are contiguous, and that reinforcement is not necessary.

In contrast to the S–R theorists the cognitive school argue that we learn cognitive structures, i. e. more broadly based interpretations of the association between stimuli and alternative courses of action.

In a marketing context there would seem to be support for both theories, in that some consumption behaviour is routinised and habitual (S–R school), while other purchasing decisions are subject to extensive problem-solving generalising from past experience (cognitive school).

The division of opinion about what we learn also exists in the case of how we learn. S–R theorists maintain that learning occurs through a process of trial and error – a view based on extensive experimental evidence using animals. However, some leading members of the cognitive school (notably Wolfgang Kohler) developed what is termed the *Gestalt* explanation of learning as being based on insight.

While it seems likely that the truth is a combination of both schools of thought, in which some actions are learned through direct personal experience based upon trial and error, while others are the product of reasoning, i. e. seeking solutions through symbolic thinking, the S–R explanations tend to dominate in consumer-behaviour research in marketing. In turn the most sophisticated statement of S–R theory which underlies much of this consumer-behaviour research is that developed by Clark Hull, in *Principles of Behavior: An Introduction to Behavior Theory* (New York, Appleton-Century-Crofts, 1943), whose basic model is

$$E = D \times K \times H \times V$$

where E = behaviour and is a multiplicative function of D = drive, K = incentive potential, H = habit strength, and where V = intensity of the cue.

Drives are discussed at greater length in the section on motivation research which follows, where a distinction is made between a drive which is viewed as the initial stimulus and a motive which is a tendency to activity. It is not felt that this distinction is important in the context of Hull's model. The remaining terms are essentially self-explanatory, and it is clear that in a marketing situation two of the variables – the incentive potential, or satisfaction offered by the product, and the intensity of the cue – are controllable to a considerable degree by the seller. It should also be noted that as the equation is multiplicative no reaction will occur if any of the variables has a zero value. At first sight this would seem to suggest that consumers would never try new products, for if they have not consumed them before, then H (or habit) would be expected to have a zero value. However, this possibility is negated by the principle of generalisation, whereby we extrapolate from past experience to a new situation. This potentiality is exploited by companies with generic brand names, where satisfactory experiences with one product group creates a favourable predisposition towards new product groups, e. g. buyers of clothes from Marks & Spencer towards M & S foodstuffs. Of course, generalisation is only potential, and past experience soon teaches us that it is not always true that all the products introduced by a company will automatically yield the same level of satisfaction as the one which we originally approved of. In other words we learn to *discriminate* between very similar cues or stimuli.

Before leaving this brief overview of some learning-theory concepts which have been incorporated into studies of consumer behaviour it should be noted that Howard and Sheth's *Theory of Buyer Behaviour* (Wiley, 1969) is essentially a learning model. It should also be noted that two important areas of research in marketing draw heavily upon learning theory for their conceptual framework – namely, the study of advertising effectiveness and of brand loyalty.

■ Motivation

Reference was made in the last section to the distinction between a drive as an initial stimulus, and motive as a tendency to act, though the terms tend to be used interchangeably in everyday speech. However, perhaps a clearer distinction is apparent if one defines drives as physiological stimuli to action, while motives constitute the intervening variable between the stimulus and response. For example, I have a strong drive to smoke a cigarette but my doctor has told me it is bad for my health and will shorten my life. I wish to live to a ripe old age and am strongly motivated to avoid anything which prejudices that goal – result, I stop smoking and resist drive.

Drives and motives are also often called 'needs' and one of the most enduring and widely used classification of needs is that proposed by Abraham Maslow ('A Theory of Human Motivation', *Psychological Review*, vol. 50, 1943). According to Maslow's basic theory we possess five basic needs which can be placed in a hierarchy such that as lower-order needs are satisfied we lose interest in them and concentrate upon satisfying needs at the next higher level which have become the most pressing. The five steps in the hierarchy in ascending order are:

1. Physiological needs
2. Safety needs
3. Love needs
4. Esteem needs
5. Self-actualisation needs.

Physiological needs or basic drives arise mainly from internal stimuli such as hunger or thirst, though some arise from external sources which threaten the individual with pain, injury or death. It is generally believed that satisfaction of these needs is dominant and overrides all other considerations. It is significant that a marketing function as it has developed in advanced economies in the past fifty to sixty years is irrelevant in countries where basic needs are not satisfied.

Safety needs come next in importance and can themselves be ranked into a rough hierarchy – physical security, stable and routine pattern of living, i.e. avoid the risk of the unknown, acquisition of protection against an uncertain future (religion, insurance):

Love needs include the need for affection and the feeling of belonging to a group – family, social group, work group, etc. Much marketing activity seeks to cater for these needs and includes some approaches most criticised by anti-marketers, e.g. advertising which suggests that failure to use a product (tooth-paste, shampoo, etc.) will lead to ostracism or exclusion from a group which you aspire to join.

Esteem needs include such things as recognition, status, prestige, reputation, etc. In affluent societies achievement of these needs is often reinforced and made public through the acquisition of physical objects which are felt to be appropriate to a person's position in life. (Consider the Sunday colour supplements or *Punch* for a sample of such objects.)

Self-actualisation represents the highest level of need to 'do one's own thing'. Relatively few people would seem to achieve this level and when they do they are unlikely to be much influenced by or interested in the market-place!

Maslow's hierarchy of motives constitutes a general statement of behaviour at the macro level – to understand the behaviour of the individual we need a more comprehensive classificatory scheme such as that provided by the concept of personality.

■ Personality

In his *Introduction to Psychology* (Harcourt Brace, 1967) Ernest Hilgard defines personality as 'The configuration of individual characteristics and ways of behaving which determine an individual's unique adjustment to his environment.' While Hilgard is atypical in offering a definition, as most psychologists fail to do so, his definition reflects the consensus concept of personality as a consistent pattern of response. Because of this overall consistency in an individual's pattern of behaviour it is possible to categorise dominant traits and develop a classification of personality 'types'. In turn such classification provides a valuable working construct for marketers, as it enables them to use personality as a factor in developing marketing strategies and marketing mixes to suit them.

However, if we are to make use of personality as a basis for trying to predict human behaviour, then it follows that we must be able to agree upon what variables we need to measure, and how to measure them, as a basis for classifying individuals. Sperling (in *Psychology*) records that Gordon Allport found 4500 words which designate distinct personal forms of behaviour in the 1925 edition of the unabridged *Webster's New International Dictionary*, and while many of these are no doubt synonyms it underlines the problem of what traits one is to measure to arrive at a personality 'type'. As a result of this extensive range of possibilities, psychologists have devised a battery of personality tests (Allport's being one of the best known and widely used) which reflect different personality theories (Freudian, neo-Freudian, S – R learning theories) and/or the purpose for which the test has been devised. For example, if an employer is looking for persons with a particular and strongly developed personality trait, then they will prefer a test which emphasises identification and measurement of that trait.

Further, although it was stated earlier that personality is a valuable working construct for marketing practitioners, it must be recognised that the research evidence on the relationship between personality variables and consumer behaviour is conflicting. The most widely cited study is that of Franklin B. Evans, 'Psychological and Objective Factors in the Prediction of Brand Choice: Ford versus Chevrolet' (*Journal of Business*, vol. 32, October 1959), in which he used the Edwards Personal Preference Schedule to test for personality differences between owners of the two different makes of car, but concluded that personality is 'of little value in predicting whether an individual owns a Ford or a Chevrolet'. A number of subsequent studies would seem to confirm this conclusion, but at least as many maintain the opposite. Indeed, many writers have criticised Evans's whole approach, but Thomas S. Robertson (*Consumer Behavior*, Glenview, Ill. , Scott Foresman, 1970) probably makes the most useful observation when he points out that while personality data only classified correctly 63 per cent of Evans's sample, this is 'some improvement over chance'. For many marketing problems this is all we can expect, and any approach which can reduce uncertainty is to be welcomed.

However, thirty years after Evans's study we are able to take a more balanced view of the value of personality variables as predictors of specific behaviour such as brand choice, and recognise that it is only one of several major influences upon consumer decision-making. Engel, Blackwell and Miniard (*Consumer Behavior*, p. 252) are of the opinion that personality is unlikely to prove a useful segmentation variable, not least because a homogeneous personality profile does not necessarily imply homogeneity in other respects, and most marketing media and channels of distribution tend to be designed to match other forms of homogeneity. None the less Engel *et al.* indicate several ways in which personality theory has considerable promise for marketing applications, particularly in its role as a moderating variable (i.e. where a personality trait can help explain differences in the behaviour of groups which are homogeneous in other respects), or as an intervening variable where primary segmentation is based upon objective factors such as demographics, but intra-group differences can be best explained in terms of motivational attributes. However, Engel *et al.* also point out that research on personality 'has stimulated the development of broader, more behavioural concepts that are likely to be better targets for market segmentation – namely life-styles'.

In some situations individual attributes or traits may prove sufficient, but in others a more generalised statement of personality may be useful. Sperling (in *Psychology*) gives a list of twelve primary dimensions of personality which is based upon extensive measurement of traits which have a very low correlation with one another but whose defining traits have a very high correlation with one another (see Table 6.1).

TABLE 6.1   Primary dimensions of personality

1. Easy-going, generous, genial, warm, versus cold, inflexible
2. Independent, intelligent, reliable versus foolish, frivolous, unreflective
3. Emotionally stable, realistic, steadfast versus emotionally changeable, evasive, neurotic
4. Ascendant, dominant, self-assertive versus self-effacing, submissive
5. Cheerful, placid, sociable, talkative versus agitated, depressed, seclusive, sorrowful
6. Sensitive, sympathetic, tender-hearted versus frank and hard-boiled, poised, unemotional
7. Cultured, aesthetic versus boorish, uncultured
8. Conscientious, painstaking, responsible versus emotionally dependent, impulsive, irresponsible
9. Adventurous, carefree, kind versus cautious, inhibited, reserved, withdrawn
10. Energetic, persistent, quick, vigorous versus day-dreaming, languid, slack, tired
11. Calm, tolerant versus excitable, high-strung, irritable
12. Friendly, trustful versus suspicious, hostile

Source: Sperling, *Psychology Made Simple* (W. H. Allen, 1967) p. 174.

A more condensed statement of psychographic variables is offered by Kotler and contains the following seven items:

Compulsiveness: compulsive; non-compulsive
Gregariousness: extrovert; introvert
Autonomy: dependent; independent
Conservatism: conservative; liberal; radical
Authoritarianism: authoritarian, democratic
Leadership: leader; follower
Ambitiousness: high achiever; low achiever

■ Attitude

Attitude is one of the most frequently invoked behavioural-science concepts in marketing. While its relationship to behaviour is not entirely clear, the frequent association between attitude and likely future action has resulted in extensive use of attitude surveys in the area of new-product development and in the design and execution of many promotional campaigns. Similarly, public opinion (belief or attitudes) is playing an increasing role in shaping and modifying corporate policy in areas such as consumer protection. It follows that a basic understanding of the current state of knowledge of attitude theory is vital to the student of marketing.

Just as there is no single agreed definition of marketing, so there is a multiplicity of definitions of 'attitude'. In broad terms most of these definitions fall into one of two categories which reflect two basic models in current use, which may be defined as the cognitive–affective–conative (CAC) and expectancy –value (EV) models. The cognitive–affective–conative model has been traced back to Plato's elements of the human soul – reasonable, spirited, appetitive – which in more modern terms may be defined as the realms of thought, emotions and motives, or knowing, feeling and acting. Marketers have developed a number of variants of their own of the CAC model, some of the better known of which are contained in Table 6.2 under the general heading of hierarchy-of-effects models. In all of the marketing versions, starting with Strong's AIDA (1924) and progressing through Lavidge and Steiner (1961), Rogers (1962) to Engel, Kollat and Blackwell (1968), it is assumed that one proceeds from awareness (cognitive) to preference (affective) to action (conative) – an assumption of the direction of cause and effect for which there is little empirical support. In fact it is widely recognised that frequently one or more stages occur simultaneously, e.g. awareness and evaluation, while impulse purchases suggest that the cognitive and affective may occur together, while the conative may, or may not, follow. Despite these deficiencies the CAC model enjoys wide support, and the effectiveness of marketing strategy is often measured in terms of its ability to move consumers up the hierarchy of effects, i.e. from unawareness to awareness, from desire to action – in other words attitude is seen as a predisposition to act.

The expectancy–value model views attitude as comprising two components – beliefs and values – which are broadly equivalent to the cognitive and affective dimensions of the CAC model. It follows that the EV model is lacking a behavioural or action element and so is much more limited in its application.

The EV model is particularly associated with the work of Martin Fishbein, who built upon the work of Rosenberg, which in turn was developed from Fritz Heider's consistency model. In essence Fishbein argues that an attitude comprises two components – beliefs about the attributes of an object and the values ascribed to these beliefs. In order to maintain consistency (or balance, or congruity, as it is sometimes called) consumers need to act in accordance with their beliefs and the *values* associated with them. Thus, while EV models do not seek to establish a link between attitude and behaviour the association between expressed beliefs and action is strong where action occurs, i.e. beliefs experienced about different brands have been found to be good predictors of actual brand preference, where the person expressing a belief about a brand actually consumes an item from that product category. However, there is a world of difference between holding a neutral or positive belief about a product and a willingness to buy it, e.g. 'I believe Romeo and Juliet cigars are of the highest quality, but I would never buy them, because I do not smoke.'

TABLE 6.2   Hierarchy-of-effects models

	Strong (AIDA)	Lavidge and Steiner	Rogers	Engel, Kollat and Blackwell
CONATIVE (motive)	ACTION	PURCHASE CONVICTION	ADOPTION TRIAL	PURCHASE PROCESSES
AFFECTIVE (emotion)	DESIRE	PREFERENCE	EVALUATION AND	EVALUATION
	INTEREST	LIKING	INTEREST	SEARCH
COGNITIVE (thought)	AWARENESS	KNOWLEDGE AWARENESS	AWARENESS	PROBLEM RECONITION
		UNAWARENESS		

This latter caveat is particularly important and explains why the EV model is theoretically more acceptable than the CAC model, which extends the link between an attitude as a *predisposition to act* into *behaviour* without specifying the catalyst which makes action necessary. From a practical point of view it is this missing link which is of crucial importance in converting the results of attitude surveys into realistic sales forecasts. In my own model of buying behaviour I term this motivation to act 'precipitating circumstances', and suggest that the precise nature of these will depend very much upon specific circumstances. Clearly the implication of this is that one must seek to develop one's own check-list of causal factors in the context of one's own marketing problem. In doing so there are a number of other behavioural-science concepts which will prove helpful, including those of change agents, opinion leadership and source credibility. A review of these follows.

While we cannot prove a causal relationship between attitude and behaviour, it is clear that a favourable attitude is more likely to lead to desired action than is an unfavourable attitude. Consequently much marketing activity is devoted to creating a favourable attitude, or climate of opinion, towards an object, or to reinforcing such favourable attitudes if they already exist.

It is generally agreed that attitudes are learned initially from one's family and then from the groups to which one belongs or wishes to belong. From a marketing point of view favourable attitudes to the consumption of particular products and/or services are usually a by-product of more basic group affilia-tions/aspirations. For example, I wish to be accepted as a student, students wear scarves and jeans, therefore I wear a scarf and jeans. The question is, who sets the group norm which specifies scarf and jeans as the accepted dress of the group?

As in most marketing/behavioural-science issues, there is no single universally accepted answer, but the balance of evidence is that certain individuals take it upon themselves to mould and change attitudes and behaviour by setting themselves up as *opinion leaders*.

The opinion leader achieves his satisfaction through his status as the expert adviser on some aspect of importance to a group of which he or she is a member. This status is often highly specific, e.g. the group expert on hi-fi systems, bargain travel, cheap places to eat, etc. , and it is unusual to find an individual who is the opinion leader on all topics of interest to a group. In other words while the existence and role of opinion leaders in influencing attitudes/behaviour is widely accepted, using this idea operationally is restricted, due to the absence, and possibly non-existence, of a profile enabling one to identify the opinion leader.

However, to the extent that opinion leaders act as filters and amplifiers in the communication channel (see Chapter 15, pp. 350–2) their potential role as change agents is particularly significant, as is the concept of source credibility.

Source credibility refers to the confidence we place in the source of informa-tion, and has been shown to have an important influence upon the acceptability of new information as a basis for attitude change (as does the presentation of the message itself). Broadly speaking sources may be divided into two categories – personal and impersonal – and may be 'objective' or marketer-dominated ('objective' only in the sense that the source is not paid for by the marketer in the same way as advertisements and salesmen are). The effectiveness of the different sources in the stages of the consumer decision process, which coincide with the stages in the CAC or EV models, has been the subject of a great deal of research, and an excellent summary table is to be found on pages 248 and 249 in Engel, Blackwell and Kollat's *Consumer Behavior* (1978).

For an extended and rigorous discussion of the issues touched upon in this section on *Attitude* the reader is strongly recommended to consult a companion volume by Gordon R. Foxall entitled *Consumer Choice* (Macmillan, 1983). In this book Foxall argues that researchers have been too ready to conceive of buyer behaviour as a function of 'the black box of the consumer's psyche', and proposes that more attention should be given to situational, especially social, influences on consumer choice.

In a comprehensive review of the extant research Foxall cites the findings of Ajzen and Fishbein whose analysis of 142 studies of attitudes and behaviour indicated that in 107 of these only 16 per cent or less of the observed variance in behaviour could be explained in terms of attitude. Hardly a convincing argument in favour of this model! Because of this weakness Foxall argues cogently that we should pay much closer attention to the 'behaviour modification perspective' according to which 'the proposed sequence is now (i) brand trial, stimulated by the reception and acceptance of some modicum of information but, of necessity, an experiment which occurs in a state of great uncertainty, followed by (ii) the reinforcement of the purchase, partly through advertising and social communication but primarily as a consequence of the user's evaluation of the merits of purchase and consumption outcomes.' (p. 27)

This model corresponds quite closely to that developed by Ehrenberg and Goodhardt which proposes a three-stage buying sequence – awareness – trial – reinforcement, or ATR, that 'is consistent with a "weak theory of advertising" in which marketing communications work primarily through suggestion and reinforcement' (p. 26).

While Ehrenberg and Goodhardt (and Foxall) present some compelling evidence this is also open to objection on the grounds that while it may be a good predictor in low-involvement and low-risk situations where trial is possible and the most economic and cost effective way of determining what one's attitude is or should be is to try it out for oneself, it is much less accurate as a description of behaviour and attitude formation for high-involvement, high-risk decisions where trial is impractical if not impossible.

Clearly the matter is not closed and the present state of knowledge would seem to suggest that both CAC and ATR or behaviouristic models are correct under certain specific conditions. This situation-specific aspect of marketing was well exemplified in a report in *Marketing*: 'How and Why Shoppers Buy' (Hugh Davidson, 28 October 1981).

■ How and why do shoppers buy?

The manner in which housewives shop for frequently purchased consumer goods and the attitudes and motivations which underlie this behaviour are clearly questions of major concern to manufacturers and retailers alike. In consequence the topic is one which has been the subject of considerable research. One recent study which adopted a novel approach, and which largely confirmed the findings of alternative research designs, was that commissioned by *Marketing* magazine and executed by the Schlackman Group.

The method used by Schlackman followed the classic pattern of qualitative research to establish the major dimensions of the research problem followed by a sample survey using a formalised questionnaire in order to quantify the frequency and importance of the behaviour noted in the qualitative phase. Specifically the research technique was summarised as follows:

1. Researchers selected 30 representative housewives who normally did one main shop weekly at a supermarket.
2. Interviewer met housewife at home, accompanied her to the supermarket, and observed a few feet behind.
3. In most cases, the housewife soon became unaware of being observed.
4. Interviewer accompanied housewife home and watched unpacking.
5. In-depth interview, lasting about 45 minutes.
6. Self-completion questionnaire, mailed to 450 housewives on home testing panel.
7. 325 questionnaires returned and analysed. Sample representative by age, class, North/South and family structure.

Of particular note is the combination of both observational techniques and in-depth interviewing in the qualitative stage of the research.

The qualitative research suggested three different 'shopping types' and these were confirmed in the quantitative survey which followed – namely *relaxed*, *controlled*, and *rigid*. Classification was based on several criteria, including:

- degree of pre-planning.
- willingness to experiment and try new products.
- attitude to price and budgeting.
- flexibility in accommodating to different tastes of individual family members.

Based on these and similar criteria Davidson caricatures the three types as:

1. *The Relaxed Shopper* – prepared to experiment with new products, looks carefully at displays, and not especially budget conscious.
2. *The Controlled Shopper* – the majority fall into this category. While not prone to experiment she seeks variety and often buys and cooks for individual family members. Uses a shopping list for basic requirements but most decisions are made instore using the display as a prompt.
3. *The Rigid Shopper* – is very controlled and her behaviour is highly planned and controlled. Shopping is planned in advance, a list is prepared and seldom departed from. Little or no allowance is made for individual family preferences and shopping is performed very quickly. Persons in this category fall in two distinct sub groups – those who are rigid by personality and those who have to be rigid for reasons of economy.

Based on the survey Davidson proposes a typical shopping sequence. While he depicts this as an orthodox ladder or hierarchy it is felt that the process is more circular in nature and so has been recast in this format.

Davidson comments:

The key is that housewives buy meals, not products. Meals, including snack meals, are always the starting point for the shop. The housewife roughly works out the number of meals she has to do before the next main shop, how many people will be present at each, how many will contain 'real meat' and so on. Meal planning is then translated into product needs.

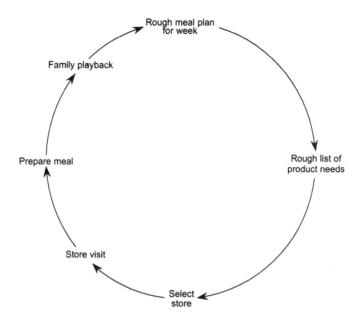

Figure 6.2   Typical shopping sequence

Source: Amended from 'How and Why Shoppers Buy', Hugh Davison, Marketing, 28 October 1981.

In terms of amount of preplanning the following emerged:

Usually make a list of everything to avoid forgetting	23%
Usually make a list and buy nothing else	3%
Usually make a partial list, decide on rest in shop	36%
Don't make list – know exactly what is wanted	26%
Don't make list – decide in shop	12%

Among the other main findings the most striking were:

1. Only 22% enjoyed shopping, 46% disliked it, and the remaining 32% tolerated it.
2. 77% of housewives shop regularly at the same store.
3. 'Value' is more important than price and low prices/value for money was the outstanding reason for choice of store.
4. Shoppers don't distinguish manufacturers' from 'own' brands – they are all 'brands' to shoppers and selected on the basis of price and perceived quality.

In sum, the findings accord well with generalised models of buyer behaviour whilst also demonstrating the significant variations which may occur within the general model.

■ Social influences

The preceding discussion of psychological influences has concentrated largely upon individual characteristics. In this section we are concerned primarily with people as members of groups, for, as will become clear, group membership has a profound influence upon individual behaviour. The approach followed is to start with macro concepts of culture and social class, and then refine the analysis to look at reference groups, role and family influences, and, finally, the concept of life-style.

■ Culture

Bennett and Kassarjian (*Consumer Behavior*, Prentice-Hall, 1972) define culture as 'a set of *learned* beliefs, values, attitudes, habits, and forms of behaviour that are *shared* by a society and are transmitted from generation to generation within that society'.

The emphasis upon learned, shared and transmitted is important, for it reflects attributes common to a vast multiplicity of definitions of culture. Values and beliefs are *learned*; they are not innate or instinctive in the way in which physiological drives are. Because they are *shared* they become a yardstick for behaviour, departure from which is regarded as deviancy and may be punished with considerable severity. Third, while a culture will evolve over time it possesses an enduring quality which enables it to be *transmitted* from generation to generation.

There are many different cultures, and Robertson suggests that a structural framework for classifying these may be developed, using three dimensions – distributive, organisational and normative. In his words:

> The *distributive* dimension summarises demographic characteristics, such as income and education levels, and the distribution of the population ecologically (for example, urban, suburban, or rural) and occupationally. The *organisational* dimension summarises participation patterns within the culture, and the structure of cultural institutions. Social class structure and the rigidity or flexibility of this structure, as well as the nature of family relationships, are organisational topics. The *normative* element treats values and norms, including economic or religious philosophy.

While these three dimensions are very useful in drawing broad distinctions between, say, Eastern and Western cultures, it is obvious that they must be used with caution and as a first broad-brush basis for distinguishing between behavioural patterns. Indeed, for most marketers it is *sub-cultures* which are of more direct and immediate interest because they provide a meaningful way of segmenting a society. Sub-cultures usually develop from a basic dimension of race, religion or nationality, and it is these which tend to have most influence upon consumer behaviour. However, age and ecological sub-cultures are also distinguishable and important.

Bennett and Kassarjian (in *Consumer Behavior*) suggest that culture exerts this influence mainly upon consumption *per se* and media image and has greatest relevance in the sphere of international marketing. In the case of consumption differences food preferences are probably the most obvious case in point, followed by clothing and beverages (e.g. Muslim attitudes to alcohol). Sub-cultures have an important influence upon the acceptability of message content, particularly in terms of the cultural expectancies of the audience, e.g. technical information for men, style information for women for consumer durables, and demands careful attention by advertising strategists. (Robertson gives a number of interesting examples of 'cultural implications for marketing'.)

While it may seem obvious that culture is of most relevance to the international marketer, there is a tendency to exaggerate this. Specifically, the generalisations which are usually cited as dire warnings of the perils of ignoring the cultural differences between different international markets often serve to disguise the fact that there are probably as many different and diverse segments within an overseas market as in the domestic one. Further, given modern communications systems, it is highly likely that very similar segments for particular products may be found in most countries, despite the fact that the commonplace in the United States may be a luxury in Africa or India (or the commonplace in Saudi Arabia a luxury in the United States!). Perhaps the safest policy is to be sensitive to cultural differences but act upon the existence of common sub-cultures. It is for this reason that while the EEC will become a single market in 1992 in economic terms it will still comprise a large number of distinct markets based upon cultural and other regional differences.

■ Social class

A particularly strong and pervasive, indeed universal, sub-cultural division is that of social class, whereby members of a society are stratified into a number of sub-divisions. These sub-divisions or classes are based upon many common characteristics, which usually include income, education, occupation and social status or prestige. These characteristics give rise to similar behavioural patterns and activities which can be differentiated from those of other social classes. This latter point is of particular importance to marketers, for the value of such a classification lies in the ability to discriminate between groupings of people and, it is hoped, to predict their behaviour under given conditions.

Many people find the concept of class offensive, because of the intrinsic implication that people can be ordered according to their worth, and argue that all people are equal. Such an argument would appear to be based largely upon an economic interpretation of equality and leads to attempts to distribute wealth more evenly through society. However, it is clear that the redistribution of wealth has relatively little to do with the value attached to the various roles filled by individuals and it is this which is the essence of social stratification. Thus in most societies teachers and priests are accorded relatively high status and prestige but earn incomes more in keeping with members of a lower class; similarly, pop singers earn more than opera singers but their earnings are probably inversely related to their prestige. Thus, while it is true that the status associated with given roles may change over time, it seems highly improbable that there will ever be a truly classless society.

It follows that if we wish to make use of this universal tendency for societies to 'classify' themselves, then we must identify and measure those factors or criteria upon which such a classification rests. In doing so one must not be surprised if different sets of criteria result in a different number of classes. However, most systems used in Western cultures have a close allegiance to the six-class model proposed by W. Lloyd Warner in his celebrated study of a small New England Town (*Social Class in America*, Harper & Row, 1960).

Social class	*Membership*
Upper-upper	Aristocracy
Lower-upper	New rich
Upper-middle	Successful business and professional
Lower-middle	White-collar worker
Upper-lower	Blue-collar worker
Lower-lower	Unskilled

While this scheme recognises two more classes than did Centers's 1949 division into upper, middle, working and lower classes, Warner himself saw the issue as a false one in that the number of divisions is relatively arbitrary and dependent upon whose opinion you are seeking. It should also be noted that in many instances one is as much concerned with differences within classes as between them.

The most widely used system in the United Kingdom is that developed for use in the *National Readership Survey* (see Table 6.3).

Just as the concept of culture is useful for classifying people into broadly similar grouping, so social-class concepts help refine the classification into smaller and more specific segments with greater operational potential for practitioners. Engel *et al.* cite a large number of studies which illustrate the application of social class in helping to interpret and predict consumer behaviour – social class has been found to be especially useful in predicting preferences for kind, quality and style of clothing, home furnishings, leisure activities, cars, consumer durables, and use of credit cards. Social class has also been shows to be associated with patterns of media usage, language patterns, source credibility and shopping behaviour. This predictive power is considerably enhanced if one is able to add to it knowledge concerning reference groups, role and family influence.

TABLE 6.3   Socio-economic groupings*

Social grade	Social status	Occupation	% of population (approx.)
A	Upper middle class	Higher managerial, administrative or professional	2.4
B	Middle class	Intermediate managerial, administrative or professional	13.3
C$_1$	Lower middle class	Supervisory or clerical and junior managerial, administrative or professional	29.1
C$_2$	Skilled working class	Skilled manual workers	20.4
D	Working class	Semi- and unskilled manual workers	17.4
E	Those at lowest level of subsistence	State pensioners or widows (no other earner), casual or lowest-grade worker, unemployed	17.4
			100.0

* The breakdown in the table is derived from data published by JICNARS (Joint Industry Committee for National Readership Surveys) and is not dependent on income, i.e. it is based on the occupation of the head of household with limited exception – when the chief wage-earner is used instead.

Source: JICNARS National Readership Survey, Jan–Dec 1987.

■ Reference groups, role and family influence

When discussing psychological influences upon behaviour the emphasis was upon the individual. But 'No man is an island', and all of us are subjected to the influence of others with whom we come into contact. This influence is particularly strong in the case of what are termed *reference groups*.

Social psychologists reserve the description 'group' for collections of two or more persons who interact with one another over time. In other words there must be some relationship between the group members which goes beyond collections of persons with common interests such as a theatre audience or passengers in an aeroplane. Bennett and Kassarjian in *Consumer Behaviour* cite Krech, Crutchfield and Ballachey's definition from *Individual in Society* (McGraw-Hill, 1962), namely: 'a group is (1) persons who are interdependent upon each other, such that each member's behaviour potentially influences the behaviour of each of the others, and (2) the sharing of an ideology – a set of beliefs, values, and norms – which regulate their mutual conduct'.

Several different types of reference groups may be distinguished, the most basic distinction being between primary and secondary groups. A primary group is one which is small enough for all of the members to communicate with each other face to face (the family, a seminar group, the area sales team), while a secondary group is one where less continuous interaction takes place (professional societies, trade unions, companies, etc.).

When a group possesses a specified structure and specified functions then it is termed a *formal* group, but where the structure and function are unspecified, as in a circle of friends, we have an *informal* group. Both formal and informal groups have norms which prescribe the pattern of behaviour expected of members and the transmission of these norms to new members is known as *socialisation*. In formal groups the norms are usually much more explicit and readily identified than in informal groups, but the norms of the latter are no less demanding if one wishes to remain in membership of the group. In all cases the influence of the group is towards *conformity*, and the strength of this tendency will depend upon the pressure the group can bring to bear upon the individual, the importance of the group to the individual and the number of groups to which the individual belongs.

In a marketing context perhaps the most important group of all is the family – specifically the *nuclear family* of husband, wife and children (the extended family includes grandparents, aunts, uncles, cousins, etc.). The nuclear family is frequently referred to as 'the household' in consumer studies but such usage is often looser and may include any group of persons occupying the same housing unit, as does the official US Census Bureau definition.

As a primary group the family has great influence upon motives, personality and attitudes and acts as a mediating influence upon external influences which impinge upon it from culture, sub-culture, social class and other reference groups. Because of this mediating influence, and due to the economic inter-dependence of its members, family (household) decision-making has a profound influence upon purchasing and consumption behaviour. All of the basic disciplines upon which marketing is founded have advanced their own explanation of household decision-making and there is no shortage of theories for the marketer to consider. J. L. Drayton (University of Strathclyde Student Note) has traced the basic themes from these disciplines as follows:

Economics: the household has tended to be viewed as an efficiency unit, using an input/output analysis in which input = time and labour (income) and output = goods and services (wealth). This approach uses a unified demand and preference schedule, i.e. each member of the household views each purchase in the same light in terms of utility gains, maximisation of family satisfaction.

One attempt has been made to derive a household preference theory from Hicks' individual preference schedule (drawn from a marginal rate of substitution of one product for another). Empirical testing of this theory caused it to be abandoned – since no apparent relationship existed between the individually stated preference and actual family choice of products.

Psychology: individuals seeking to meet their own needs; finding a balance between power and harmony; suggests a host of separate utility patterns – but little direct contribution to how these combine (given a limited income).

Sociology: with the sophistication of techniques and theory provided by the study of small groups', family sociologists have been the major researchers in the field of how families actually reach a decision. As one would expect, starting from the basis of small group studies, the emphasis has been upon establishing patterns of leadership roles – a dominant partner typology, which might suggest for instance that the UK is basically patriarchal in outlook (therefore husbands will dominate decision making); or that the US is matriarchal! Neither typology has been empirically proven. The idea of producing a typology is that this then becomes the 'Family norm' – anything differing from this norm can be analysed to discover why.

Anthropology: concentrates upon the transfer of cultural values from generation to generation; thus decision making here becomes a factor in the socialisation process, with the roles (or status) within a family (and within a society) determined at birth and learned in childhood.

Thus when marketers require information about household consumption there is no shortage of theories to turn to. The problem confronting us is rather 'which one is the most useful in its application to the marketing of goods and services to families?'

The question may well be raised as to how a greater knowledge of the decision-making processes can assist the marketing practitioner. Three obvious areas spring to mind:

(*a*) Product planning and design
(*b*) Distribution channels
(*c*) Communication strategies

In terms of design factors of household products (e.g. consumer durables) there may be a conflict between the technical perfection the design engineers and production techniques are capable of and the needs of the eventual user. In the trade-off between efficiency and ease of use the marketer needs to know what are the important characteristics of the product as perceived by the product-user/decision-influencer.

A review of empirical studies of family decision-making reveals two major underlying currents:

(*a*) Ideological role theory
(*b*) The resource theory of power

The primary hypothesis in the ideological theory of roles is that household decision-making and activity patterns can be explained in terms of role expectations developed through the pervading culture. Each member of the family, has a meaningful set of chores to perform – meaningful in the sense that such chores contribute to family survival and well-being.

The traditional and best-known exposition of family roles is the goal-orientated husband who 'gets things done', complemented by a supportive wife playing a social emotive role of 'keeping the family together'. Division of roles in this way generalises that husbands are responsible for decisions which are essentially concerned with the interface between the household and the external world, while wives take responsibility for activities within the family.

Although role theory has been useful to sociologists in understanding family survival in periods of social change, research into product decisions utilising role theory has been ambiguous and conflicting.

The alternative explanation of household power structure is resource theory. The main thesis is that authority and activity patterns within the family can be analysed in terms of such variables as income, education and social status. The right to make decisions influencing family welfare is related to the comparative resources brought to the marriage.

A resource in this context is defined as 'any special characteristic, skill or competence of one partner that contributes to family goal attainment' and embraces the following:

(a) Earning capacity (present and potential)
(b) Occupation (both partners)
(c) Education level
(d) Religion
(e) Life-style
(f) Age

From a practical point of view it is useful to try and classify the extent and nature of influence in the household decision-making unit and four basic role-structure categories may be distinguished:

(a) Husband dominant
(b) Wife dominant
(c) Autonomic (an equal number of decisions is made by each partner but without consultation)
(d) Syncratic (most decisions made jointly)

As suggested earlier, an ability to relate role-structure category and purchase of specific products will be of great value in developing new products and the most effective marketing mix to promote and sell them. A very useful review of research in this area is to be found in Engel *et al.* (*Consumer Behavior*, 5th edn (1987) pp. 269–304).

The physical or demographic composition of the family will also have a significant influence upon its consumption behaviour and the concept of the family life-cycle is a particularly useful framework for analysis. The most extensive model contains six stages (as shown in Table 6.4).

For a very extensive analysis of the relationship between these stages and consumption behaviour the book by Reynolds and Wells contains five chapters dealing' specifically with this topic.

TABLE 6.4   Family life-cycles

Age	Developmental level	Stage in the family life-cycle
18–34	Early adulthood	1 The bachelor stage: young, single people 2 Newly married couples: young, no children 3 The Full Nest I: young married couples with dependent children: 　(a) Youngest child under six 　(b) Youngest child over six
35–54	Middle adulthood	4 The Full Nest II: older married couples with dependent children
55 and older	Later adulthood	5 The Empty Nest: older married couples with no children living with them: 　(a) Head in labour force 　(b) Head retired 6 The Solitary Survivors: the older single people 　(a) In labour force 　(b) Retired

Source: Fred D. Reynolds and William D. Wells, *Consumer Behavior* (McGraw-Hill, 1977).

■ Life-style

So far the discussion has focused upon major sociological concepts which have been borrowed and adapted by marketers in seeking to explain and predict consumer behaviour,, We now consider a composite concept which has been developed extensively by consumer-behaviour researchers during the 1970s and early 1980s that seeks to synthesise the economic, psychological and sociological influences, namely 'life-style'.

In essence life-style summarises the way in which we live and is founded upon the observation that people seek consistency or balance in their lives – the old concept of homoeostasis – and so organise their behaviour to try and achieve this state. We have already noticed this tendency in discussing the concepts of perception, personality and motivation and observed how it becomes socialised in cultural traits, norms and values. Given this tendency towards consistency in behavioural response it follows that if we can identify a consumer life-style in one context, then we should be able to extrapolate from that situation and predict how he will behave in different sets of circumstances.

The measurement of life-style in the subject of an area of research known as *psychographics* is discussed at length in Engel *et al.* (*Consumer Behavior*). An excellent overview of the subject is also to be found in an article by William D. Wells, 'Psychographics: A Critical Review' (*Journal of Marketing Research*, vol.

XII, May 1975, pp. 196–213). In this article Wells proposes an operational definition of psychographic research as 'quantitative research intended to place consumers on psychological – as distinguished from demographic – dimensions', a definition which emphasises the distinctive features of the area – it has a quantitative rather than a qualitative orientation and goes beyond demographics. (Engel *et al.* point out that 'psychographics' is often used interchangeably with the mnemonic AIO standing for Activities, Interests and Opinions as a research area.) The use of life-style for segmenting consumer markets is discussed in more detail in Chapter 8.

■ Composite models of consumer behaviour

For many years prominent researchers in the consumer-behaviour field have attempted to develop comprehensive theories of consumer behaviour. In *Marketing: Theory and Practice*, 2nd edn, Michael J. Baker (Macmillan, 1983), my colleague Jennifer Drayton summarises a number of the more important models – those of Nicosia, Andreasen, Engel, Kollat and Blackwell, Clawson, and Howard and Sheth – as follows:

> These models differ in respect to their complexity and orientation but are nevertheless based upon the same strands of thought. Thus similarities are to be found in the isolation and identification of the relevant variables, and in the perspective of a dynamic decision process, with the actions of the consumer viewed as a movement towards some decision point. Although little or no attempt has been made to modify or update these models they still represent an important step in the development of our understanding of consumer behaviour.

■ Nicosia

Nicosia uses as a base for his model a computer flow-chart technique, divided into four distinct areas, or 'fields'. The output from each field becomes the input to the succeeding field.

The model depicts a message (for example, an advertisement for a new product) flowing from its source (in this case the business firm) in the direction of an eventual decision outcome by the consumer. In Field 1 the consumer is exposed to and receives the message, with an outcome of the development of some predisposition, or attitude, towards the product; Field 2 is concerned with the search and evaluation process, which has as its output the arousal of the individual's motivation, leading to Field 3, which is defined as 'possible transformation of the motivation into an act of purchase'. If purchase occurs, Field 4 becomes the area of storage and use of the product, with a related output of experience.

In each of the fields the relevant influences upon the eventual outcome are delineated. As the message flows from the business firm to the formation of a consumer attitude, it will be modified or distorted by internal subjective perceptual elements. During the period of 'search and evaluation' (Field 2) the internal and external forces are differentiated in terms of additional information input. Internally initiated data are concerned with the associations, conscious or unconscious, with the firm, the brand or the product, while external data are culled from the environment in the form of word-of-mouth communication, or an increased receptivity to advertising in the product area.

■ Andreasen

Andreasen has developed the concepts of 'attitude formation' and 'attitude change' contributed by social psychologists to construct a consumer-decision model as an information-processing cycle. This model indicates that attitude change can be achieved via exposure to information. Change of attitude is assumed to be a logical preliminary to a change in behaviour, an assumption which is lacking in verification since the complexity of the attitude – behaviour relationship remains a controversial area in social-psychology studies. It is as yet far from certain that influence in this area is a one-way flow from attitude to behaviour as the model suggests.

Andreasen's model centres upon the individual utilising a message input to reach a decision outcome, with attitude formation and change as the central concepts. The predispositional nature of attitudes (i.e. not based on actual experience) is shown to impinge upon the individual's perceptions, which operate as a filter through which the information must pass to reach the cognitive system. Thus attitudes to message source or 'channel may effectively alter the character of the original communication.

■ Engel, Kollat and Blackwell

These researchers have produced a sequential approach to the purchase decision which has been described as a complete model of buying behaviour. It is a general model which gives a framework for examining the diverse range of influences to which the buyer is subject as the decision process moves from its initial stage of the beginnings of need awareness through its subsequent steps up to the terminal stage of after-the-event evaluation and rationalisation. The contributions of the three basic internal processes – perception, learning and motivation – represent major steps in the model, while personality and attitudes are seen to exert pressure upon the process. The social and cultural aspects of the possible purchase decision are also shown as influencing the individual's movement through the decision stages.

■ Clawson

Clawson has extended the views propounded by Lewin in his behavioural studies, with the contribution of *Gestalt* theories clearly in evidence.

The analysis is concentrated in some depth upon the tension element in a purchase decision as the individual assesses the positive and the negative aspects attached to the decision outcome, producing a situation of psychic conflict. The fact that both the positive and the negative features are perceived subjectively by the consumer is also stressed, indicating that the conflict cannot be resolved on the grounds of objective product characteristics or information. These objective criteria may not penetrate the net of selective perception, or may be distorted on the way.

■ Howard and Sheth

Howard and Sheth have based their approach to the formulation of a general consumer model on the standpoint of the consumer playing an active role in the business transaction. He is not merely exposed to communications but is portrayed as vigorously collecting and processing information.

Fundamentally the model is constructed around a series of stimulus variables passing into the individual's processing system and being acted upon by the internal factors of perception and learning, termed by the researchers 'the hypothetical constructs'. A response variable terminates the process, with the whole being surrounded by the exogenous variables of social class, culture and personality, plus such constraints as time and income availability.

Inputs are separated out into three groups which distinguish source differences. The first group relates to the actual product communications of price, quality, availability, distinctiveness and service. The second group derives from indirect and impersonal sources, such as salesmen or the mass media. The third group of stimulus variables identifies the activity of the consumer collecting data from his social environment via the personal influence of word-of-mouth communication. Thus the interaction between the consumer and his social environment is distinguished and extended, showing the external forces in the decision process not only as a constraint upon behaviour but also as a reference point for the gathering of credible information. Interaction between man and his social environment is seen to be a two-way function.

The hypothetical constructs of perception and learning detail the manipulation of the information gathered from the various sources, affecting the amount and quality of objective information which reaches the system.

Howard and Sheth have acknowledged that these hypothetical constructs and their interrelationships are a consequence of the integration of a number of well-known theories – Hull's learning theory, Osgood's cognitive theory and Berlyne's theory of exploratory behaviour.

■ Paradigms of consumer behaviour

Based upon the above review it is possible to identify two broad paradigms or models of consumer behaviour which may be distinguished respectively as the *cognitive* and *behavioural* explanations.

In essence the cognitive explanation sees consumer behaviour as the consequence of an interpersonal, cognitive, information processing activity which results in choice as the outcome of deliberation and decision-making. By contrast the behavioural paradigm regards choice behaviour as the consequence of prior behaviour and sees choice decisions as the consequence of determined responses to environmental stimuli (G. R. Foxall, *Consumer Choice*, London, Macmillan, 1983).

Most major models such as those of Nicosia, Engel, Kollat and Blackwell, Howard and Sheth fall into the cognitive category and 'depict the consumer advancing along a problem-solving and decision-making sequence, the outcome of which is determined by the buyer's intellectual functioning and rational processing of information. Consumers are credited with the capacity to receive and handle quantities of information as they engage in extensive pre-purchase searches and evaluations. Further, the consumer is viewed as perceiving information critically, using decision rules and evaluative criteria to establish its personal relevance to his goals and purposes, while generally employing mental processes to reach a decision' (Shams, after G. R. Foxall, 'Consumer Choice in Behavioural Perspective', *European Journal of Marketing*, vol. 20, no. 3, 1986, pp. 7–18). Subscribers to cognitive explanations of consumer behaviour regard marketer initiated communications as vital cues or stimuli which make consumers aware of needs and wants and of possible solutions to these felt needs.

Thus, as Foxall ('Radical Behaviourism and Consumer Research: Theoretical Promise and Empirical Problems', *International Journal of Research in Marketing*, vol. 4, 1987, pp. 111–29) has pointed out 'choice is essentially the resolution of conflict, brought about by awareness of a number of options, through cognitive evaluation of the possibilities available and a reasoned consideration of the costs and benefits which each entails'.

In her review of cognitive explanations Shams ('Incremental Consumption and the Purchase of Experiential Products', unpublished PhD dissertation, University of Surrey, 1989) points out that numerous authors have criticised his approach and quotes Markin and Narayana ('Behaviour Control: are Consumers Beyond Freedom and Dignity', *Advances in Consumer Research*, vol. 2, 1976, pp. 222–8) who concluded that most empirical research points to an opposite conclusion. Namely, that consumers:

1. do not seek extensive amounts of information in relation to purchase and consumption problems;
2. do not process large amounts of information when confronted with purchase and consumption problems; and
3. do not appear to engage in extensive problem solving behaviour even in relation to high expenditure purchases.

– all conclusions reached by my colleague Keith Fletcher in his doctoral research 'Social Behaviour: an analysis of information and usage during the decision process' (1986).

As a result of the criticisms of the cognitive school there has developed a renewed interest in behavioural explanations. Two main schools may be distinguished – *classical* conditioning and *operant* conditioning. Classical conditioning was referred to in the section on Learning earlier in the chapter and is usually associated with Ivan Pavlov's experiments with dogs in which he showed that a physiological response – salivation on the presentation of food – could be conditioned by the simultaneous presentation of a second stimulus – the ringing of a bell – such that a dog could be conditioned to salivate on the ringing of the bell alone. Operant conditioning is associated with the work of B. F. Skinner who argued that 'behaviour is shaped by its consequences' and so emphasises actions under the conscious control of the individual by contrast with involuntary responses of the kind studied by Pavlov. Further, operant conditioning is focused on consequences which follow behaviour while classical conditioning emphasises stimuli which precede behaviour. As noted earlier in the chapter, we learn patterns of behaviour based upon the level of satisfaction we derive. Thus satisfactory outcomes reinforce a pattern of behaviour while unsatisfactory outcomes (punishers) dissuade us from repeating such behaviour in future.

It follows that once a consumer has determined a satisfactory pattern of behaviour then he will continue to repeat that behaviour until it either causes dissatisfaction ('familiarity breeds contempt') or he becomes aware of a stimulus which suggests that a modified form of behaviour could lead to even greater satisfaction. In an attempt to accommodate both the cognitive/rational and behavioural explanations of consumer choice – both of which have clear merits and weaknesses – a composite model of buying behaviour is proposed.

■ A composite model of buying behaviour

As noted in the introduction to this chapter there is a tendency to distinguish between individual and organisational buying behaviour by emphasising the qualitative/behavioural nature of the former and the quantitative/rational/economic nature of the latter. In my view this distinction is largely spurious as I believe that all buying decisions are subject to the same economic and behavioural influences and in the majority of cases follow the same basic process. This process is best observed by analysing the purchase of a product of which the user has no prior experience, for otherwise several stages may be omitted, i.e. the purchase of a familiar brand or the automatic re-ordering of an industrial supply.

For a number of years now I have been developing a composite model of buying behaviour which attempts to combine both economic and behavioural factors as well as capturing the essentially sequential nature of buying decisions. The current version of the model may be expressed notationally as follows:

$$P = f[SP(PC, EC, IS, PF, CB, BR)]$$

P = purchase
f = a function (unspecified) of
SP = selective perception
PC = precipitating circumstances
EC = enabling conditions
IS = information search
PF = performance factors
CB = cost-benefit
BR = behavioural response

The first point to be made is that this is a sequential process model very similar to the Buying Decision Process model introduced at p. 138. PC is equivalent to problem recognition, EC to *interest* (i.e. the problem is accepted as a real one deserving further consideration), IS, a new variable corresponds to information search and recognises that if a review of the enabling conditions confirms a continuing interest then one will have to gather additional information on which to make a decision. PF and CB summarise the objective data concerning performance or 'fitness for purpose' and the economic benefits of acquisition and comprise the 'rational' elements of evaluation. BR is a surrogate for the subjective and judgemental factors which will invariably be taken into account when a prospective buyer has more than a Buy–Don't Buy choice, i.e. there are two or more objectively similar products or services which would solve the prospective buyers' consumption problem which initiated the process. Thus BR is composite of one's prior experience and attitudes which may or may not include direct post purchase experience of the object under consideration.

Second, the precise nature of the function is not specified for the simple reason that it is not known and that it is unlikely, to say the least, that any single functional form could capture the interaction between the other variables in the model.

SP or selective perception, is a new variable in the model. in earlier versions, the influence of this factor was subsumed within BR, which occurs at the end of the process. By placing SP at the beginning as a factor mediating the other variables, it is possible to communicate that this is a process model and that selective perception will determine whether or not one will even become aware of a purchase opportunity (EC) besides conditioning the information selected for evaluation and the interpretation placed upon it.

Finally, the behavioural response may be almost automatic, as, for example, when the preceding evaluation indicates that one option is clearly to be preferred. Alternatively, it may be an extremely difficult and protracted stage when the preceding analysis has failed to suggest one choice before all others – a common occurrence in many markets.

Having described the general model, some elaboration of the variables will indicate what sort of factors one would need to take into account to use the model.

In the Pavlovian learning model of buyer behaviour reference is made to the need for some cue or stimulus to activate a drive and initiate action. In our model, this factor is termed a precipitating circumstance – what is it that would make a buyer consider a change in the status quo? Clearly, dissatisfaction with existing alternatives constitutes a marketing opportunity and is one type of precipitating factor. The need to replace or renew a piece of capital equipment or consumer durable is another opportunity, whether the need is caused by breakdown, loss, destruction or a planned replacement policy. Knowing which customers might be in this state would enable the firm to focus its marketing effort to much greater effect, both in terms of the information to be conveyed and the means of conveying it. Similarly, being able to satisfy a known need – to have a faster computer, a more economical car, and so forth – is a claim likely to precipitate active consideration of a new purchase.

Enabling conditions embraces all those factors which make it possible for a prospective purchaser to benefit from the new product. A television is no use if you have no electricity, nor a gas oven if you have no gas. In the same way, many manufacturers try to avoid mixing materials such as steel, aluminium and plastics, since each requires different skills and techniques in use and increases the investment necessary in both plant and labour. In other words, a new product must be compatible with the user's current status and, in many cases, also with their self-image. In the absence of such enabling conditions, interest is likely to be short-lived and unlikely to proceed further to an evaluation.

Technology or performance and the economics or cost-benefit of a purchase are at the very heart of the Marshallian and 'rational' schools of buying behaviour's models – *PF* and *CB* in our model.

Finally, however, it must always be remembered that the majority of buying decisions turn on highly specific characteristics – another reason why a general model cannot' possibly accommodate all conceivable sets of circumstances.

We have already stipulated that the importance of behavioural response will depend heavily upon the objective evaluation of the available facts (albeit that these are perceived subjectively), and 'build a better product at an equivalent price or an equivalent product at a lower price' is clearly the best advice to management. But, in most competitive markets, there is often little to choose objectively between alternative offerings, and the buyer will have to make deliberate recourse to subjective value judgements to assist in distinguishing between the various items available. Because housewives do this daily when preferring Bold to Persil, Sunblest to Mother's Pride and so on and so forth, they are often characterised as choosing irrationally. Nothing could be further from the truth. The important objective decisions about a shopping basket relate to its overall mix and composition *vis-à-vis* the available budget – the choice decision is which detergent, which bread, and soon. It would be a fatal mistake to imagine that the industrial buyer doesn't have just the same problems when deciding between Scania, Mercedes, or Leyland for his lorries or Cincinnati, Kearney and Trecker for his machine tools.

■ Summary

This chapter has ranged over a very wide area that is the subject of many substantial books in their own right. Its purpose has been to sensitise the reader to factors which influence behaviour in the market-place but a full appreciation must depend upon extensive study of the major sources cited.

CHAPTER 7

Organisational buying behaviour

___ Learning Goals ___

The issues to be discussed in this chapter include:

1. The similarities and differences between organisational and consumer buying behaviour.
2. The role and importance of organisational buying behaviour.
3. The nature, functions and practices of organisational buyers and the buying process.

After reading this chapter you will be familiar with:

1. The nature of organisational buying behaviour.
2. The similarities and differences between consumer buying behaviour and organisational buying behaviour.
3. Why organisational buying is important.
4. The key concepts in organisational buying behaviour.
5. The factors which influence organisational buying behaviour.
6. What is meant by 'an interaction approach' to organisational buying behaviour.

In the preceding chapter the emphasis was on individual behaviour and the influence and consequences of this in terms of buying or consumption decisions. In this chapter our attention is focused upon the way the same individuals behave when faced with the responsibility of acting on behalf of an organisation and often as part of a decision making unit (DMU) or buying group.

At the outset it must be stressed that in exactly the same way that it was argued that while one can discern many differences between the marketing of consumer and industrial goods it is important not to overlook the similarities, so in the case of individual and organisational buying behaviour one must be careful not to overlook the fact that the *process* is the same. Thus the generalised model of buying behaviour presented at the end of Chapter 6 is believed to be just as applicable to both individual and group buying decisions, although it is immediately acknowledged that groups may undertake a much more formal and rigorous approach than do most individuals. The purpose of this chapter, therefore, is to identify and describe some of the more salient features of organisational buying behaviour and point out the similarities and differences between it and individual behaviour.

To this end we shall first review the better known models which seek to describe/analyse the nature of the organisational buying process.

Having established a broad framework which defines the general process we shall then look more closely at some of the more important constituent elements beginning with the composition and activities of the buying group, together with the influence of various factors – organisational, environmental and product-related upon these activities. Finally, we shall examine the stages of the purchasing process or 'buyphases' as they are frequently called.

■ Models of organisational buying behaviour

One of the first serious attempts to impose some structure upon the wealth of descriptive material about industrial buying behaviour was provided by Frederick Webster Jr in an article entitled 'Modelling the Industrial Buying Process' (*Journal of Marketing Research*, November 1965). In an effort to distinguish the important variables and the relationships between then, Webster proposed four key areas – *Problem Recognition*, the assignment of *Buying Responsibility*, the nature of the *Search Process* and the nature of the *Choice Process*, with the inference that these are sequential steps in the overall buying process.

According to Webster a buying situation is created by the recognition that there is a difference between an organisation's goals and its performance which may be remedied or solved through a purchase. In that both goal-setting and problem recognition are influenced by personal and impersonal factors, both internal and external to the organisation, it follows that these have to be identified and analysed if we are to understand organisational buying decisions. In terms of the personal factors it has to be remembered that ultimately the organisational decision will be delegated to individuals and the allocation of this responsibility will be influenced by individual, company, product, industry and market factors, so these too must be specified and understood. These same factors will also influence both the search and choice processes.

The next important contribution to the OBB literature was provided by the publication of *Industrial Buying and Creative Marketing* (Allyn & Bacon, 1967) by P. J. Robinson, C. W. Faris and Yoram Wind, which reported the results of a project sponsored by the Marketing Science Institute. Based upon in-depth studies of three companies in the United States over a two-year period, Robinson, Faris and Wind proposed that industrial buying may be conceived of as a process consisting of eight sequential steps or *buyphases*, namely:

1. The anticipation or recognition of a problem or need, including the realisation that a problem exists, and the awareness that a solution may be possible through a purchase of an industrial good.
2. The determination of the quality and characteristics of the needed item.
3. The specific description of the item needed.
4. The search for, and qualification of, potential sources.
5. The examination of the sources, leading to a decision concerning how the item is to be purchased.
6. The evaluation of proposals and the selection of suppliers.
7. Selection of an order routine.
8. Performance feedback and evaluation.

In addition, Robinson, Faris and Wind identified three distinct buyclasses, which may be defined as follows:

1. *New task* – the recognition of a purchasing problem which has not been encountered previously. The buyer will face considerable uncertainty and will seek to reduce this through the acquisition of as much information as he can obtain from both personal and impersonal sources. All the buyphases are likely to receive careful and explicit attention.
2. *Modified rebuy* – the buyer has prior experience of the purchase problem but has reason to re-evaluate this in light of some new information or precipitative circumstance, e.g. a lower bid from another supplier, a change in design or specification, etc. Some of the buyphases may be truncated or omitted.
3. *Straight rebuy* – the buyer is satisfied with an existing source of supply and sees no reason to change. Phases 4–7 are likely to be omitted altogether and only cursory attention given to the others; i.e. purchase has become habitual and routinised.

By combining Buyphases and Buyclasses we obtain the *Buygrid* as depicted in Figure 7.1.

This framework appears simplistic by comparison with the more complex and sophisticated models developed since. However, this is seen as its greatest strength, for it is relatively easy to recall, and by classifying the kind of buying decision and the stage in the process one can quickly focus attention on the key factors which apply to that location in the grid; e.g., for most straight rebuys one can establish routines and procedures for automatic ordering from qualified suppliers provided that previous orders have met the predetermined requirements.

The next important contribution to modelling OBB was published in the *Journal of Marketing* (April 1972) when Frederick Webster Jr and Yoram Wind joined forces to offer 'A General Model for Understanding Organisational Buying Behaviour'. Diagrammatically this model appears as in Figure 7.2 and may be explained as follows.

Organisational buying is a decision-making process carried out by individuals, in interaction with other people, in the context of a formal organisation which is

| | BUY CLASSES | | |
	New Task	Modified Rebuy	Straight Rebuy
B 1. Anticipation or Recognition of a problem (Need) and a General Solution			
U 2. Determination of Characteristics and Quantity of Needed Item			
Y			
P 3. Description of Characteristics and Quantity of Needed Item			
H 4. Search for and Qualification of Potential Sources			
A			
S 5. Acquisition and Analysis of Proposals			
E			
S 6. Evaluation of Proposals and Selection of Supplier(s)			
7. Selection of an Order Routine			
8. Performance Feedback and Evaluation			

Figure 7.1   The buygrid analytic framework for industrial buying situations

Source: Robinson *et al.*, *Industrial Buying and Creative Marketing* (Allyn and Bacon, 1967).

subject to a variety of environmental forces. Thus the factors which impinge on and influence OBB may be classified as individual, social, organisational and environmental. In turn each of these factors may be categorised as comprising task variables, which are directly related to the specific buying problem, and non-task variables which are not.

The earlier work of the authors is readily identified in their joint model which conceives of OBB as a complex process involving many persons, multiple goals and potentially conflicting decision criteria. The process may extend over a considerable period of time, demand large amounts of information from many diverse sources and require numerous inter-organisational relationships. At the heart of the process is the *buying centre* which includes all members of the organisation who may be involved in the various roles of user, influencer,

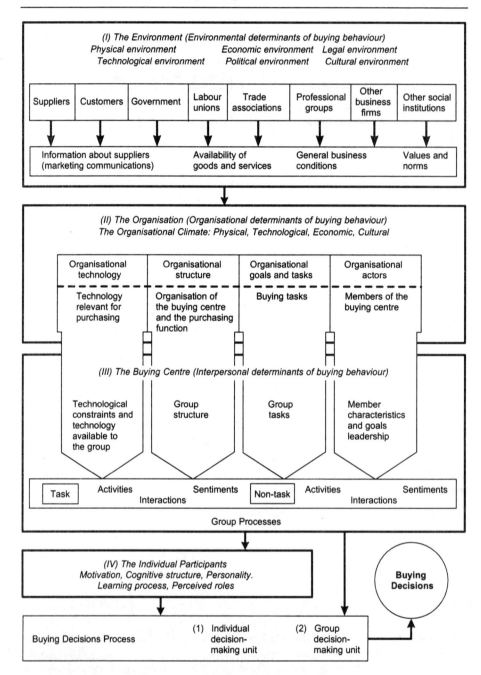

Figure 7.2   **The Webster and Wind model for understanding organisational buying behaviour**

Source: Webster and Wind, 'A General Model for Understanding Organisational Buying Behaviour', *Journal of Marketing*, April 1972.

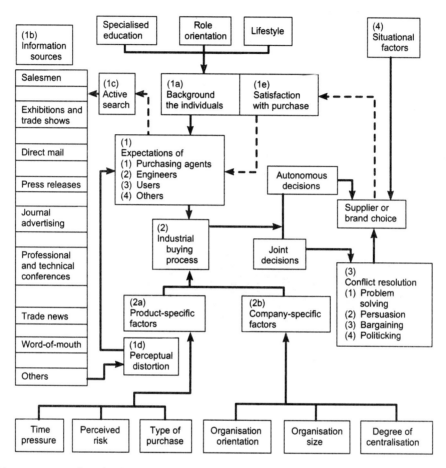

Figure 7.3   The Sheth integrative model of industrial buying behaviour

Source: J. N. Sheth, 'A Model of Industrial Buyer Behaviour', *Journal of Marketing*, October 1983.

decider, buyer and gatekeeper (the person or persons who control the flow of information into the buying centre).

Members of the buying centre are subject to both individual and organisational goals and so their relationships encompass all the complexity of interpersonal interaction which the organisation seeks to structure, influence and control through the subsystems of tasks, structures, technology, and people. Finally, the organisation has to operate within the constraints and opportunities of the environment and the economic, technological, physical, political, legal and cultural forces which comprise it.

As Hill and Hillier point out (*Organisational Buying Behaviour*, Macmillan, 1977), the main deficiency of the actual model is that it conveys a static rather than a dynamic impression, although this is partly compensated for in their description of it. Hill and Hillier also criticise the model as 'a basic skeleton of organisational buying behaviour, without any muscles or nerves', but clearly it is more complex and comprehensive than the Robinson, Faris and Wind model discussed previously. This is even more true of 'A Model of Industrial Buyer Behaviour' proposed by Jagdish N. Sheth (*Journal of Marketing*, October 1983) which is summarised in Figure 7.3.

According to Sheth, OBB comprises three distinct dimensions:

1. The psychological world of the decision-makers.
2. The conditions which determine joint decisions among and between these individuals.
3. The process of joint decision-making and conflict resolution among decision-makers.

In terms of the first dimension it is recognised that most industrial buying decisions are made by a number of people from different backgrounds and performing different roles – Purchasing agents, Engineers, Users and Others in box 1 of the model. The differential expectations of these individuals is seen as the result of their background (1a), information sources (1b), their active search (1c), and perceptual distortion (1d) of these sources and their satisfaction with past purchases (1e). These expectations are modified by product specific factors (2a) such as time pressure, perceived risk and the type of purchase, and company specific factors (2b) such as organisational orientation, organisational size and degree of centralisation in the course of the industrial buying process (1) itself.

The third dimension and central concern of Sheth's model is how the different participants in the buying decision resolve potential conflicts between themselves arising from their different roles, expectations and perceptions. Box 3 suggests four different approaches to conflict resolution – problem solving, persuasion, bargaining, and politicking. However, in the course of arriving at their joint decision a number of *ad hoc* situational factors (4) such as temporary economic conditions, industrial relations problems, production bottlenecks, etc. will play an important part. Recognition of these factors clearly injects the dynamism absent from the Webster and Wind model and so makes it more useful in an operational sense.

Since Sheth's and Webster and Wind's attempts to provide a comprehensive model of OBB the emphasis has shifted to a much more detailed analysis of how actual buying decisions are made and the precise nature of the various forces and influences involved – what Hill and Hillier characterise as 'the anatomy of a purchase', although they use this description in a narrower way than implied here.

The Hill and Hillier model reproduced as Figure 7.4 is intended to analyse purchase decision from the perspective of the buyer and contains three major elements – usage for the purchased item, reasons for the purchase, and the purchase complexity.

The intended use for the proposed purchase is seen as a vital piece of information to the seller, because it will indicate the technical content

Figure 7.4   The constituent elements of the anatomy of the purchase

Source: Hill and Hillier, *Organisational Buying Behaviour*, Macmillan, 1977, p. 25.

involved, the value and essentiality of the item, and therefore the degree of risk involved; the likely timing of the purchase; and whether the product is more likely to be buyer or supplier specified. Hill and Hillier then propose five main categories of use as follows:

1. for incorporation in production output which may be to order or to stock and in the latter case production may be either batch or continuous;
2. for utilisation during the production processes but not incorporated in the product;
3. to provide a production facility in either manufacture, service or resale;
4. for use in maintenance operations;
5. for use in development or engineering work.

Basic reasons for purchase are summarised in the diagram and will have a significant influence upon the criteria used in arriving at a decision. This is also true of the complexity of the purchase which builds upon distinctions made by Lehmann and O'Shaughnessy (D. R. Lehmann and J. O'Shaughnessy, 'Difference in Attribute Importance for Different Industrial Products', *Journal of Marketing*, April 1974) who argued that 'if products could be classified on the basis of problems inherent in their adoption, such a classification might be both predictive of weightings of the relative importance of product/supplier attributes, and predictive of buyer preferences with regard to suppliers'. Four categories are then proposed which Hill and Hillier summarise as:

1. Routine order products which are frequently ordered, and present no significant usage problems because everybody is familiar with them, and it is known that they can 'do the job'.
2. Procedural-problem products, which are known 'to do the job', but problems may arise because personnel must be taught how to use them.
3. Performance-problem products, where the problem concerns the technical outcome of using the products.
4. Political-problem products, where there is likely to be difficulty in reaching agreement among those affected if the purchase is made. This kind of problem arises when large capital outlays are involved, and more frequently when the products are an input to several departments whose needs may not be compatible.

This classification goes beyond Robinson *et al.*'s novelty of purchase buy-classes and also differs in that the four categories are not seen as mutually exclusive but indeed may overlap with one another.

Organisational buying behaviour as an interactive process

Thus far all the models of organisational buying behaviour we have discussed have been uni-dimensional in the sense that they have looked exclusively at behaviour and processes within the customer organisation. Over the past decade (since the mid-1970s) the deficiencies of such an approach have been increasingly recognised, and have led to the development of much more sophisticated models and analyses in which purchasing is seen as an interactive process taking place within a network of suppliers and users. Foremost among the exponents of this approach is the IMP Group, which initially comprised 14 researchers drawn from five European countries (France, Germany, Italy, Sweden and the UK) and later extended to include colleagues in the USA. The major findings of the Group are reported in two major publications: *International Marketing and Purchasing*, by P. Turnbull and M. Cunningham (Macmillan, 1980) and *International Marketing and Purchasing of Industrial Goods*, ed. Håkan Håskansson (John Wiley, 1982). More recently (1990) another member of the Group, David Ford, has edited a collection of the Group's findings in a book entitled *Understanding Business Markets: Interaction of Relationships and Networks* (Academic Press, London). The key concepts and assumptions underlying the interaction approach are described at some length in chapter 2 of the latter book and a synopsis of these is given below.

At the outset it is important to recognise that marketing is a synthetic discipline, in the sense that it seeks to combine insights and ideas from a wide range of other disciplines in the hope that by so doing it will be able to come up with a more powerful explanation of behaviour in the real world. Thus economics, psychology, sociology, anthropology, statistics, law, etc. etc. all provide important contributions to our new discipline of marketing whose own distinctive contribution is to combine and synthesise these in new ways. In the case of the interaction approach the models of OBB described earlier provide an important input, but this has been extended by drawing upon two major theoretical models from outside the marketing, literature – Interorganisational Theory and New Institutional Economic Theory. As Håkansson notes, 'Much of the work in Inter-organisational Theory involves attempts to apply theory and concepts from intra-organisational studies to problems where several organisational units are involved. Here the focus of attention is on relationships between those organisations (hence 'relationship marketing') rather than within each individual organisation.' Three distinct approaches may be distinguished which may be identified as:

1. *Organisation based studies* in which the organisation is studied in terms of the environment within which it has to operate and interact with. The models of OBB described above fit into this category which until now has been the predominant marketing perspective and contains 'two distinct and *separate* approaches to the study of what occurs in industrial markets. On the one hand, there is an analysis of the manipulation of marketing variables by the seller to achieve a desired market response. On the other hand, there is a separate analysis of a single buying process and the factors which affect that process, from which lessons can be drawn for marketing.'
2. *Studies based on several organisations* which are seen as part of a network. In a marketing context this conforms with the 'distribution system perspective' in which the market is seen as 'a system of interconnected institutions performing the economic functions required to bring about exchange of goods or services'.
3. *Studies of the organisation in a societal context* in which 'the organisation is seen as an integrated part in a larger social system'. This approach has been little developed by the IMP Group whose work is mainly focused on approach (2) with a limited recognition of (3).

With regard to the 'New Institutional Economic Theory' the main foundation is to be found in the seminal contribution of O. E. Williamson (*Markets and Hierarchies: Analysis and Antitrust Implications*, Free Press, 1975). Williamson's work constitutes a criticism of perceived deficiencies within traditional microeconomic theory, particularly the view that market exchanges will maximise efficiency.

According to Williamson one must distinguish between situations where exchange efficiency will be maximised through the existence of independent units operating in a market, and those where such efficiency will be achieved through vertical integration within a single unit. Only by examining carefully the factors which influence transaction costs will one be able to determine the most effective institutional structure (including intermediary structures) and such an examination focuses attention on those variables such as bargaining relation-

Figure 7.5   **An illustration of the interaction model**

Source: IMP Group, op. cit.

ships, organisational characteristics, information handling behaviour, etc., which are central to the study of OBB.

In the IMP Group's model, 'the marketing and purchasing of industrial goods is seen as an interaction process between two parties within a certain environment', and comprises four basic elements:

1. The interaction process.
2. The participants in the interaction process.
3. The environment within which interactions take place.
4. The atmosphere affecting and affected by the interaction.

The model is conceptualised as in Figure 7.5 and a full description of the elements is to be found in Håkansson (pp. 16–23). Clearly, the approach proposed above goes a long way towards capturing the dynamic complexity of organisational buying and selling behaviour. In light of this, and not forgetting the composite model proposed in the previous chapter, it will be helpful now to look more closely at some of the constituent elements.

■ The composition of the buying group

All of the models of OBB recognise that buying is a complex process in which purchasing decisions are made by a group or 'buying centre' rather than by an individual. It follows, therefore, that if one is to understand the process then one must be able to define the buying group or centre in terms of its possible composition *vis-à-vis* the various buying situations and phases in the buying process.

As Wind has pointed out ('Organisational Buying Centres: A Research Agenda', in Zalmont and Bonoma (eds), *Organisational Buying Behaviour*, AMA, 1976), 'the basic concept of a buying centre suggests that it is a temporary organisation unit, which may change in components and functions from one purchase to another'. This view has been supported by numerous other studies which confirm that not only do buying groups vary from decision to decision but that their composition varies over the life of a particular purchasing decision.

With regard to who actually is involved, the *Financial Times*/IMR survey, 'How British Industry Buys' (1974), indicated a wide range of participation, including:

1. Collective decisions	– Board
	Management Committee
2. Individual (non-departmental)	– Managing Director
	Other Director
	General Manager
	Company Secretary
3. Department (collective and individual)	– Department Manager
	Operating Manager
	Other
	Design and Engineering
	Production
	Purchasing
	Sales and Marketing
	Research & Development
	Finance/Accounts
	Other
4. External decision	

Several studies which have analysed the composition of the buying group argue that it should be and often is a function of product-related variables. The most frequently cited such variables are:

1. The technical complexity of the product.
2. The value of the item to be purchased.
3. The frequency of purchase.
4. The product's essentiality to the production process.
5. The potential consequences of making a wrong decision.

6. The degree of inherent innovation or novelty in the product.
7. The product's overall complexity.

By analysing and rating the product on these dimensions one should be able to conclude who might be involved and the extent of their involvement in a purchasing decision.

An alternative approach to the study of the composition of buying groups has focused on the roles played by different members, which have been characterised as users, influencers, deciders and gatekeepers (Webster and Wind), or as contributors, participants, responsibles and directors (B. Klass, 'What Factors Affect Industrial Buying Decisions', *Industrial Marketing*, 1961). Another schemata proposed by *Sales Management* in 1963 distinguished those who make major buying decisions, make recommendations, must approve purchases, affect the conditions of use, and conduct the buying negotiations. However, as Anita Kennedy points out in chapter 5 of *Marketing: Theory and Practice* (ed. M. J. Baker, 2nd edn, Macmillan, 1983; this chapter on 'Buyer Behaviour' is strongly recommended for further reading on the subject), 'Operationally, conceptualisation of the buying centre by role definition is of little use to a researcher wishing to study the purchasing decision-making process. Specifically, the notion of generalised role relationships within the buying centre does not accommodate a method for ascertaining the individual membership of the buying task group, nor its decision making potential.'

On the other hand, if one has a model defining the possible roles which members of a buying group may perform, then one is more likely to recognise their existence in an actual buying decision and formulate tactics for overcoming possible resistance while reinforcing and supporting those who are favourably disposed to a sales offer.

Another important contribution of the concept of a buying group is that it reminds us that other people in the organisation are likely to be involved in the purchase decision in addition to the designated purchasing agent or buyer. Thus while most order inquiries are initiated by purchasing agents, and 'the buyer' is the obvious person to approach first with a selling proposition, it is important to recognise that this individual or department may have neither the discretion nor authority to make a decision. How then should one assess the purchasing function's role?

■ The role of the purchasing function

In her review of industrial buying behaviour, Kennedy, in *Marketing: Theory and Practice*, suggests that purchasing's involvement in buying decisions is a function of four sets of factors:

1. The nature and status of purchasing within the organisation.
2. The purchasing agent's perception of his function.

3. Task versus non-task behaviour.
4. Environmental and extraneous market conditions.

With regard to the nature and status of purchasing within an organisation it has been shown that the existence of a separate purchasing function and its size depend very much upon the overall size of the organisation as a whole. However, the size of a purchasing department does not necessarily indicate that it occupies an important place in the organisational hierarchy as it may be charged merely with an order processing-function while all the key decisions are made by R & D or manufacturing. To some extent the status of the purchasing department may be inferred from the status of its senior manager – is he a main Board director, or does he report to the Board, if at all, through a hierarchy of other more senior managers? According to Webster ('Modelling the Industrial Buying Process') the purchasing department's influence on a buying decision will tend to increase as

(*a*) market variables become more important in relation to product variables;
(*b*) the size of firm and spatial separation of activities increase;
(*c*) the organisation formally assigns specific responsibility to the purchasing department.

With regard to the purchasing agent's own perception of his role, most of the evidence suggests that buyers feel their contribution is undervalued. When one reflects on the contribution which efficient buying can make to the firm's overall profitability there would seem to be some justification for this point of view. Consider, for example, a firm with the following sales and cost structure.

	Sales revenue		100
Less	Bought in materials	46	
	Labour and overheads	20	
	Cost of goods sold	68	
			32
Less	Selling, general and		
	administrative expense	20	
	Profit before tax		12

It is clear that any increase or decrease in the price of bought in materials will have a greater effect than a proportionately equivalent change in efficiency of any of the other business functions either separately or together.

Of course, savings on bought in materials may have nothing directly to do with the buyer but result from changes in design or specification initiated by other members of the buying group. None the less, there is good reason to believe that the purchasing agent can play a critical part in the interface between an organisation and existing and potential suppliers, and so should be accorded equal status with senior managers in the other business functions. However, pending such explicit recognition, purchasing agents will no doubt continue to use the tactics described by Strauss in his frequently cited study, 'Tactics of

Lateral Relationships: The Purchasing Agent' (*Administrative Science Quarterly*, 1962) for handling conflicts with other functions:

1. Rule-oriented tactics – the buyer works to the book. In this case a written responsibility to purchase is required.
2. Rule-evading tactics – the buyer revises requisitions and follows a tactic of feigned acceptance.
3. Personal–political tactics – the buyer projects an aura of friendship and willingly exchanges favours.
4. Educational tactics – the buyer attempts to persuade others to think in purchasing terms.
5. Organisation-interaction tactics – the buyer exhibits the willingness to communicate with other organisational departments and to participate in decision-making.
6. Organisational change tactics – in this case, the buyer attempts gradually to evolve change in organisation procedures. One example of these tactics is the materials management idea.

The third factor which influences the purchasing agent's involvement in buying decisions is the emphasis upon task and non-task behaviour. In simple terms, the task elements of buying are those which may be defined and, usually, measured using objective criteria, e.g. supplier identification and qualification, value analysis, price, etc. By contrast the non-task elements tend to be subjective and difficult to quantify – reputation, performance, reliability, etc. As a generalisation, it would seem that the greater the focus upon task elements and the greater the purchasing agent's perceived competence in handling these, then the greater will be the role played by the purchasing department.

The final element which seems likely to influence the importance given to purchasing is the environmental context within which the buying firm has to operate. When the external environment is dynamic and uncertain then the purchasing function is likely to assume more importance as it is called upon to help reduce the uncertainty which these conditions create. Similarly, under conditions of recession more attention is likely to be given to the cost incurring functions and purchasing will assume increased visibility and importance. It is under such conditions that other management functions are forced to consider the relevance of the task elements, with techniques like value analysis calling for close cooperation between purchasing and R & D and manufacturing and inventory control calling for involvement of the finance function.

Another environmental change which is tending to increase the role of the purchasing function is the increasing concentration in many industries which is resulting in the creation of very large and professional buying groups. Indeed, in some consumer goods markets the retail buying groups are much bigger than the manufacturers that supply them and in 1984 the Federation of Food Manufacturers persuaded the Office of Fair Trading to inquire into the impact this was having on profit margins. In its report (*Competition in Retailing*, June 1985) the OFT found that there had been no material change in the facts which led the

MMC (Monopolies and Mergers Commission) to conclude in 1981 that the general effects of multiple buying power had not been harmful to the public interest.

■ Buy-phases

In the earlier review of composite models of OBB we looked at the model proposed by Robinson, Faris and Wind which conceived of buying as a process consisting of eight sequential steps or buy-phases. In evaluating this model it was argued that while it may appear simplistic by comparison with other, later models it possesses the particular strength that it is straightforward, robust and accords well with best practice. The model also draws attention to the sequential nature of buying decisions and invites us to consider whether the different phases are likely to involve different kinds of decisions and different members of the buying group. If so, then clearly one will need to modify one's selling tactics as the process unfolds.

As Kennedy (*Marketing: Theory and Practice*) reports, a number of empirical studies which have analysed industrial buying decisions confirm the existence of such a process which has been characterised by the various authors as follows.

In his doctoral study of over forty capital equipment purchases, T. J. Hillier (see Hill and Hillier, *Organisational Buying Behaviour*) suggested a 4-phase model:

1. The precipitation decision stage – when a definite course of action to solve a problem is confirmed.
2. The product specification stage – when broad solutions to a problem are translated into specific hardware and software requirements.
3. The supplier selection stage – when potential suppliers are identified and one or more selected.
4. The commitment decision stage – when a customer decides to what extent a supplier has fulfilled its expectation.

Such a sequence suggests that each purchase decision commenced *de novo* without prior experience on either side (as do the other buy-phase models). In reality, of course, buyers and sellers tend to interact and build up relationships with each other over time so that a more correct representation of the process is provided by the following diagram (Figure 7.6).

Gordon Brand (*The Industrial Buying Decision*, Cassell, Associated Business Programmes) proposes an 8-step model very similar to the original one of Robinson *et al.*, namely:

1. Problem recognition
2. Determine characteristics of needed items
3. Specific description
4. Search for potential supplier
5. Evaluate sources and products

Figure 7.6   The cycle of industrial-buying decisions

Source: R. W. Hill and T. J. Hillier, *Organisational Buying Behaviour*, Macmillan, 1977, p. 45.

6. Select supplier
7. Establish order routine
8. Evaluate feedback.

With regard to the question of who might be involved in each of these stages, this provided the focus for the *Financial Times* survey mentioned earlier in which the following questions were asked:

1. Who originates the initial decision?
2. Who surveys alternatives and determines the basic characteristics of the product required?
3. Who makes the final decision?
4. Who identifies the potential suppliers?
5. Who collects tenders/information from suppliers?
6. Who evaluates products offered?
7. Who authorises the purchase?
8. Who finally chooses the supplier?
9. Who monitors and evaluates the performance of both the product and the supplier?
10. Who is most likely to initiate the decisions to change supplier?
11. Who finally decides on a change in supplier and selects the new supplier?

As noted earlier, this survey established that a wide range of participants are involved in a purchase decision. During the 1980s, an international group of researchers from six countries (including the author) undertook a series of in-depth case analyses of specific buying decisions in a variety of industries and settings in an attempt to determine more precisely the decision and behavioural routines in the organisational buying process. The findings of this research were published in 1986 (Stephen T. Parkinson and Michael J. Baker, *Organisation Buying Behaviour*, Macmillan) and confirmed that processual interaction models best capture the organisational purchasing decision. The research also confirmed that the composite model presented in the previous chapter is equally applicable to both individual and group buying decisions.

■ Summary

In this chapter we have looked at some of the major dimensions of the rapidly growing field of study known as organisational buying behaviour. With increasing maturity it is both right and proper that such specialised sub-fields should develop, and clearly there are sufficient differences between the way in which organisations and individual consumers make buying decisions to justify such specialisation. However, it must also be remembered that the 'actors' who participate in organisational buying decisions are, in another capacity, the individuals whose motivations, attitudes and behaviour are looked at in Chapter 6, and it would be naive to dismiss or overlook these when analysing corporate buying behaviour. By the same token it would be equally naive to ignore the fact that if groups of people develop procedures, processes and stratagems for making buying decisions which satisfy them, then why should not individuals behave in a broadly similar manner? It is for this reason that I believe the composite model of buying behaviour proposed in the previous chapter is applicable in principle to all buying decisions. This is not to say that each of its elements will receive explicit and conscious attention every time a purchase is made nor that the weighting and emphasis given to the component parts will be the same from product to product, industry to industry or decision-maker to decision-maker. But it does offer a robust and workable conceptualisation or model around which to develop a more detailed analysis of specific purchase decisions.

CHAPTER 8

Market segmentation

Learning Goals

The issues to be addressed in this chapter include:

1. The concept of segmentation.
2. Bases for segmenting markets – geodemographic, preference, benefit, social character, social grading, industrial and international.
3. Methods of segmenting markets.
4. The selection and use of segmentation techniques.

After reading this chapter you will be able to:

1. Distinguish between product differentiation and market segmentation as alternative marketing strategies.
2. Outline the benefits of using a segmentation approach.
3. Summarise the basis for segmenting markets and describe various approaches in some detail, including:

   - geodemographic segmentation;
   - preference segmentation;
   - benefit segmentation;
   - social character segmentation using life style and psychographics;
   - social grading segmentation;
   - industrial segmentation;
   - international segmentation.

4. Describe *how* to segment a market.
5. Determine how to select a segmentation approach.
6. Specify when it is appropriate to use market segmentation.

■ Introduction

From reading Chapter 1 it should be clear that while there are many definitions of marketing there is only one marketing concept. However, it is also true that many criticisms of marketing are prompted by misunderstanding and/or misapplication of this concept. Usually, the 'mistaken marketing concept' is interpreted as 'give the customer what he wants', which, in many cases is a sure road to commercial ruin. In reality the marketing concept advises that we should establish user needs and determine if, how, and to what extent it may be possible to satisfy these given one's existing and potential resources, to the mutual benefit (profit) of both parties to the exchange.

Clearly the 'real' marketing concept requires the marketer to steer a careful course between regarding every individual as a discrete marketing opportunity and considering all customers as being the same. From the preceding chapters on Consumer and Organisational Buying Behaviour it is apparent that one can either disaggregate a population into separate groups or sub-groups or else aggregate individuals into sub-groups, groups or populations through the use of a variety of distinctive features which must be possessed by those within the group but are absent from those excluded from it. In marketing this process is known as *market segmentation*.

In this chapter we shall look first at the concept of market segmentation and the benefits associated with the practice. Next we shall examine the basic approach to segmentation as a preliminary to a more detailed review of segmentation methods in consumer, industrial and international markets. Finally, we will consider how segmentation techniques may be applied and assess their role in marketing planning.

■ The concept of market segmentation

According to Engel (James F. Engel *et al.*, *Marketing Segmentation*, Holt, Rinehart & Winston, 1972), the concept of segmentation is based upon three propositions:

1. That consumers are different.
2. That differences in consumers are related to differences in market demand.
3. That segments of consumers can be isolated within the overall market.

While these three propositions may seem eminently reasonable it has to be appreciated that according to classical economic theory supply and demand are homogeneous. Thus it was not until the 1930s when Chamberlin and Robinson proposed their theories of imperfect competition that explicit recognition was given to the observed reality that in the great majority of markets both supply and demand are heterogeneous. In turn it was not until the mid-1950s that a marketing writer, Wendell Smith, was to point out how recognition of diversity or heterogeneity in demand and supply suggested the existence of two quite different marketing strategies – product differentiation and market segmentation.

In his seminal article ('Product Differentiation and Market Segmentation as Alternative Marketing Strategies', *Journal of Marketing*, July 1956) Smith argued that both planned and uncontrollable differences exist in the products of an industry which result in sellers making quite different appeals in support of their marketing efforts. Among the reasons for this diversity Smith proposed the following:

1. Variations in the production equipment and methods or processes used by different manufacturers of products designed for the same or similar uses.
2. Specialised or superior resources enjoyed by favourably situated manufacturers.
3. Unequal progress among competitors in design, development, and improvement of products.
4. The inability of manufacturers in some industries to eliminate product variations even through the application of quality control techniques.
5. Variations in producers' estimates of the nature of market demand with reference to such matters as price sensitivity, colour, material, or package size.

Three decades later it is revealing to consider the essential production orientation of Smith's analysis with its emphasis upon variations or heterogeneity on the supply side. Even point 5 seems to imply that variations exist in the suppliers' perception of demand rather than in the demand itself. However, given that such differences exist Smith argues that marketing managers could pursue one or other of two alternative strategies. Either they could seek to bring about the *convergence* of individual market demands for a variety of products upon a single or limited offering to the market', which is a strategy of *product differentiation* usually through advertising or promotions. Or, 'In some cases, however, the marketer may determine that is better to accept *divergent* demand as a market characteristic and to adjust product lines and marketing strategy accordingly,' which is a strategy of *marketing segmentation*.

Smith summarises the differences between these two strategies admirably when he writes:

> In its simplest terms *product differentiation* is concerned with the bending of demand to the will of supply. It is an attempt to shift or to change the slope of the demand curve for the market offering of an individual supplier. . . . *Segmentation* is based upon developments on the demand side of the market and represents a rational and more precise adjustment of product and marketing effort to consumer or user requirements.

From this definition it is clear that segmentation is a genuine marketing concept which is intermediate between the polar extremes of the perfectly homogeneous market, which is an underlying assumption of much economic theory, and the completely heterogeneous market perspective, which constitutes the perspective of the behavioural scientist. Enis (*Marketing Principles*, Goodyear Publishing Co., 3rd edn, 1980) illustrates these distinctions in Figure 8.1 reproduced on page 167.

In the opinion of Engel (*Marketing Segmentation*) a segmentation approach offers the marketer the following benefits:

Figure 8.1   A model of market segmentation

Source: B. Enis, *Marketing Principles*, Santa Monica, CA, Goodyear, 3rd edn, 1980.

1. A segmentation perspective leads to a more precise definition of the market in terms of consumer needs. Segmentation thus improves management's understanding of the customer and, more importantly, why he buys.
2. Management, once it understands consumer needs, is in a much better position to direct marketing programmes that will satisfy these needs and hence parallel the demands of the market.
3. A continuous programme of market segmentation strengthens management capabilities in meeting changing market demands.
4. Management is better able to assess competitive strengths and weaknesses. Of greatest importance, it can identify those segments where competition is thoroughly entrenched. This will save company resources by forgoing a pitched battle of locked-in competition, where there is little real hope of market gain.
5. It is possible to assess a firm's strengths and weaknesses through identifying market segments. Systematic planning for future markets is thus encouraged.
6. Segmentation leads to a more efficient allocation of marketing resources. For example, product and advertising appeals can be more easily co-ordinated. Media plans can be developed to minimise waste through excess exposure. This can result in a sharper brand image, and target consumers will recognise and distinguish products and promotional appeals directed at them.
7. Segmentation leads to a more precise setting of market objectives. Targets are defined operationally, and performance can later be evaluated against these standards. Segmentation analysis generates such critical questions as

these: Should we add another brand? Should we drop or modify existing products, or should we attempt to reposition a faded and obsolete brand image?

However, as Michael Thomas has pointed out ('Market Segmentation', *Quarterly Review of Marketing*, vol. 6, no. 1, 1980), there are at least three situations when the concept of market segmentation cannot be used, namely:

1. where the market is so small that marketing to a portion is not profitable;
2. where heavy users make up such a portion of sales that they are the only relevant target;
3. where the brand is a dominant brand in the market, there is no basis for segmenting.

But, apart from such situations which call for an undifferentiated marketing strategy, most academics and practitioners are agreed that some form of segmentation offers the best opportunity of securing a competitive advantage in the market place. This being so it will be useful to consider the various approaches to market segmentation in common use and the basis on which they have developed.

■ Bases for segmentation

According to Engel (*Marketing Segmentation*) marketing managers usually divide consumers into three classes for the purpose of marketing strategy, namely:

1. *Similarity*. All consumers are basically similar. Although differences exist among consumers (for example, age, income, and so forth), these differences are not thought to be important in affecting the purchase of their specific product class. A standard product will essentially satisfy the large majority of consumers.
2. *Unique*. All consumers are unique. The differences among consumers (for example, age, income, needs, preferences, and so forth), make a standardised product or service unacceptable. Market offerings must be tailored specifically to the needs of each individual consumer.
3. *Differences/Similarities*. Consumer differences and similarities exist and are important sources of influence in market demand. Such differences can be regarded as differences in consumer needs and wants. These differences and similarities facilitate the grouping of consumers into aggregates of *segments* according to their needs and wants and the degree to which they are present. Marketers using a segmentation approach adapt marketing programmes to match the peculiar need combinations of each of some market segment.

Geographic
Region
County Size
City (of SmSA size)
Density – urban, suburban, rural
Climate

Demographic
Age
Sex
Family size
Family life cycle
Income
Occupation
Education
Religion
Race
Nationality
Social class

Psychographic	– Producing psychological profiles or types
Life style	Straights, swingers, long-hairs
Personality	Compulsive, gregarious, ambitious, introverted, passive, authoritarian

Behaviouristic	– Effective marketing must address the needs normal consumers attempt to gratify
Purchase occasion	Should we segment people *or* their consumption occasions?
Benefits sought	Economy, convenience, prestige.
User status	Non-user, Ex-user, Potential user, First time user, Regular user.
Usage rate	Light, medium, heavy users
Loyalty status	None, medium, strong, absolute
Readiness stage	Unaware, aware, informed, interested, desirous, intending to buy
Marketing factor sensitivity	Quality, price, service, advertising, sales promotion

Figure 8.2　Major segmentation variables

Source: M. Thomas, 'Market Segmentation', *Quarterly Review of Marketing*, vol. 6, no. 1, 1980.

The obvious question is 'How do marketing managers arrive at these decisions?', to which the answer is 'By examining the variables which may be used to describe consumers and their behaviour'. According to Frank *et al.* (*Market Segmentation*, Prentice-Hall, 1972) these variables may be classified into two broad categories:

1. *General variables* where consumers are classified by broad characteristics such as demographics, personality traits or life styles.
2. *Situation-specific* variables where consumers are grouped according to consumption patterns such as frequency of usage, brand loyalty, product benefits or perceptual maps.

Thomas ('Market Segmentation') provides a useful listing of the major segmentation variables, and this is reproduced in Figure 8.2 on page 169.

Clearly, many of these variables are appropriate to individual consumers rather than to organisational buyers. That said, the preceding discussion of organisational buying behaviour should have made it clear that demographic, psychographic and behaviouristic factors will all have some influence on the way in which organisational buyers will perceive information and their reactions to it. This being so it will be both useful and relevant to examine some of the bases for consumer segmentation in more detail before moving on to the particular case of industrial and international market segmentation.

■ Geodemographic segmentation

In his editorial to a special edition of the *Journal of the Market Research Society* (vol. 31, no. 1, January 1989) on 'Geodemographics' James Rothman traces the formal use of geodemographics (the classification of small areas according to the characteristics of their inhabitants) to 1889 and the publication of Charles Booth's *The Life and Labour of the People in London*. Based upon his survey into the economic and social circumstances of all the families in London, Booth prepared a series of maps which depicted clearly and graphically the distribution and exact location of the eight categories or classes derived from his analysis.

However the real development of geodemographics dates from the 1960s and the publication of Claus Moser's *British Towns: a Statistical Study of their Social and Economic Differences* (Oliver & Boyd, 1961). Although this 'received little practical application' (Rothman, 'Geodemographics') it preceded the seminal work of Richard Webber at the Centre for Environmental Studies which was to lay the foundation for the numerous proprietary systems such as ACORN, MOSAIC, SuperProfiles and CDMS.

As Rothman points out

> Geodemographics is based on two simple principles. The first is that two people who live in the same neighbourhood, such as a Census Enumeration District are more likely to have similar characteristics than are two people chosen at random. The second is that neighbourhoods can be categorised in terms of the population which they contain, and that two neighbourhoods can be placed in the same category, i.e. can contain similar types of people, even though they are widely separated. These two principles used in combination, mean that demographic information about the neighbourhood in which a person lives can be used to provide information about the probability of their having certain characteristics.

This ability clearly offers an attractive opportunity for market segmentation and the development of targeted marketing strategies.

Several aspects of the application of geodemographics to marketing are developed in considerable detail in the special issue of the *JMRS* and should be consulted by those interested in delving deeper into this topic (e.g. store location, designing market research surveys, sampling, targeting etc.). For the purposes of an introductory text we will confine our discussion to probably the best known of the 'off the peg' systems – ACORN (A Classification of Residential Neighbourhoods).

ACORN, in common with other geodemographic systems makes use of the 1981 Census data with the Enumeration District (ED) as its basic building block. ACORN uses 40 regularly updated variables of which the most important are:

household composition;
occupation grade of each household member;
nature of occupation;
unemployment;
mode of travel to work;
number of cars owned;
household facilities;
degree of overcrowding.

Using clustering techniques CACI (the developers of the system) have defined 38 neighbourhood types which they have aggregated into 11 ACORN groups as follows:

Group	Title	*Percentage of UK* population
A	Modern family housing for manual workers	9.6
B	Modern family housing, higher incomes	7.4
C	Older housing of intermediate status	10.4
D	Very poor quality older terraced housing	9.2
E	Rural areas	5.8
F	Urban local authority housing	20.6
G	Housing with most overcrowding	2.9
H	Low income areas with immigrants	4.2
I	Student and high-status non-family areas	4.3
J	Traditional high status suburbia	19.1
K	Areas of elderly people (often seaside resorts)	6.4

To use ACORN, EDs have to be matched to post codes and it is here that most errors arise; the second main source of error being changes in housing since the last census. To help overcome these problems a number of more powerful systems have been developed.

Another well-known system developed by Richard Webber is MOSAIC which profiles consumers according to 58 life-style categories and claims to differ from competitive systems in three major respects: it analyses the country in geographical units averaging 15 households, not 150; it does not rely on 1981 Census data but uses CCN's continually updating databases to track population movements; and, finally, it incorporates information on financial behaviour at post code level by taking advantage of CCN's position as the UK's leading credit reference agency (CCN Systems Ltd is a subsidiary of Great Universal Stores PLC). In 1988 CCN launched MOSAIC Systems, a powerful PC-based product for identifying the unique characteristics of any given catchment area and designing the most effective marketing approach.

MOSAIC Systems is designed to bridge the gap between longer-term strategic decisions on matters such as product development, national advertising and pricing, and day-to-day tactical decisions on in-store promotion, distribution, coupon drops, branch location and other locally based activity. Being PC based users can test out any number of marketing tactics and have the results displayed instantly, without recourse to a bureau or to internal computing facilities. Results from the system can be either straightforward tabulation or full colour maps similar to that in Figure 8.3 which identifies areas where there are older couples in leafy suburbs within a 25-minute drive-time of central Plymouth.

On launching the system, which is supplied as an integrated software and data learning package costing up to £20 000 per annum including updates, Richard Webber claimed 'MOSAIC Systems is going to bring a hitherto unobtainable level of accuracy to local area marketing. Any one of the questions that this product addresses would have taken many hours to research. Now marketers can test out their theories in moments – quite literally at the touch of a button. It has brought the business of marketing firmly into the computer age.'

■ Preference segmentation

While demographic factors may provide a more than adequate description of a market segment and in some cases be a major influence on consumption behaviour – e.g., baby products, health care products – a marketing orientation requires that we look beyond demographics to the nature of preferences, as these will permit a much better understanding of the reasons underlying differences and similarities in actual consumption behaviour. Kotler (*Marketing Management*, 6th edn, Prentice-Hall, 1988) distinguishes three broad classes of preferences – homogeneous, diffused, and clustered – and illustrates how these may be plotted in terms of key attributes as shown in Figure 8.4 (creaminess and sweetness for ice cream).

In the case of homogeneous preference there are no apparent segments (at least in terms of the attributes selected), and one would expect all suppliers to pursue an *undifferentiated* strategy, with price and availability as key elements with advertising and promotion being used to try and develop a distinctive brand image.

Where preferences are diffused, 'A brand in the centre minimises the sum of total consumer dissatisfaction', but a more appropriate strategy might be to

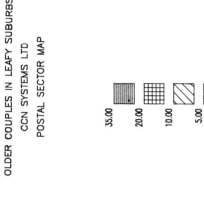

PLYMOUTH 25 MIN DRIVETIME
PERCENTAGE OF HOUSEHOLDS
IN MOSAIC GROUP L2

OLDER COUPLES IN LEAFY SUBURBS

CCN SYSTEMS LTD

POSTAL SECTOR MAP

35.00
20.00
10.00
5.00
0.00

Figure 8.3   This sample map, produced by MOSAIC Systems, identifies areas where there are older couples in leafy suburbs within a 25-minute drive-time of central Plymouth

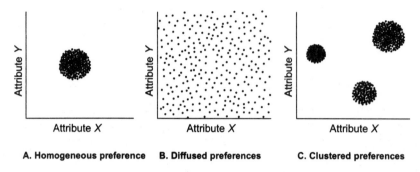

A. Homogeneous preference   B. Diffused preferences   C. Clustered preferences

Figure 8.4   **Basic market-preference patterns**

Source: P. Kotler, *Marketing Management*, 6th edn. Prentice-Hall, 1988.

concentrate on one or other dimension and seek to develop a market segment and build up brand loyalty for the distinctive, brand.

Finally, where preferences are clustered, the segments are clearly identified and the producer can either concentrate on one or else develop a series of different products targeted at each of the distinct segments – a *differentiated* marketing strategy.

Examples of identifying new market opportunities through preference segmentation are regularly reported in the 'trade' press such as *Marketing Week* and *Campaign*. At the time of writing *Marketing Week* (23 Nov. 1990) carried a report of how tissue-maker Scott was relaunching Big Value Scotties Regular 200s Tissues as a high quality facial product made from 65 per cent recycled paper in a response to Tesco, Sainsbury and Dixcel who had previously launched 100 per cent recycled paper brands to cater for those consumers concerned for the environment. In Scott's view 100 per cent recycled papers could not achieve the quality expectations associated with facial tissues and so saw an opportunity to plug a gap in the high-quality recycled sector.

Similarly, in a report 'Going Organic' Coopers and Lybrand Deloitte cite research by Mintel which indicated that roughly one in four adults would prefer processed foods to be organically grown. Although the strongest preference (best target markets) comes from those aged 25–44, the ABs and the South West, there was surprisingly little difference between sub-groups using geodemographic segmentation variables underlining that in this case it was expressed preferences which provided the best basis for segmenting the market.

■ Benefit segmentation

Another well-known approach to market segmentation is to subdivide the total market in terms of the specific benefits looked for by different consumers. This approach, pioneered by Haley, is illustrated by Table 8.1, which shows how the toothpaste market can be broken down into four distinct segments in terms of the principal benefit sought by users.

TABLE 8.1   Toothpaste market segment description

Segment name	*The sensory segment*	*The sociables*	*The worriers*	*The independent segment*
Principal benefit sought	Flavour, product appearance	Brightness of teeth	Decay prevent-ion	Price
Demographic strengths	Children	Teens, young people	Large families	Men
Special be-havioural char-acteristics	Users of spear-mint flavoured toothpaste	Smokers	Heavy users	Heavy users
Brands dis-proportionately favoured	Colgate, Stripe	Macleans, Plus White, Ultra Brite	Crest	Brands on sale
Personality characteristics	High self-in-volvement	High sociability	High hypochon-driasis	High autonomy
Life style char-acteristics	Hedonistic	Active	Conservative	Value oriented

Source: Haley, R.I., 'Benefit Segmentation', *Journal of Marketing*, vol. 32, 1968, pp. 30–5.

■ Segmentation by social character

Segmentation by social character depends heavily upon the measurement of life-style and the use of psychographics. In the article by Wells cited in Chapter 6 he provides a number of case histories to illustrate the applications of such research in profiling consumers as a basis for segmentation. The example is best illustrated by Tables 8.2 and 8.3 which comprise a demographic and psychographic profile of the heavy user of shotgun ammunition.

As Wells comments:

> In spite of this lack of focus, the data [in Table 8.3] show some interesting patterns. First, it is obvious that hunting is not an isolated phenomenon but rather is associated with other rugged outdoor endeavors. Shotgun shell buyers not only like to hunt, they also like to fish and go camping. They even like to work outdoors.

These relationships are interesting and useful because they suggest activities and settings, other than hunting scenes, that might be appropriate for shotgun ammunition advertising. They suggest products that might be especially appropriate for joint promotions or other cooperative marketing ventures, such as displaying shotgun ammunition near camping or fishing equipment in retail outlets. [Table 8.3] also shows that ammunition buyers are apt to be do-it-yourselfers, which suggests that hunters are apt to be buyers of hardware and tools.

Items in the third group [in Table 8.3] suggest some hypotheses about the psychological makeup of the shotgun ammunition buyer. Compared with the non-buyer he is definitely more attracted by violence, suggesting that detective, war, and violent Western TV programs ought to draw audiences with disproportionate numbers of shotgun users, and that action and adventure magazines ought to be considered when placing advertising associated with hunting. Relationships between product use and media exposure are always best documented by direct cross-tabulation, but when these data are not available (and they often are not) relationships suggested by life-style patterns can provide helpful direction.

The relatively high levels of agreement with the fourth section [of Table 8.3] suggest that the hunter is generally less risk-averse than is his nonhunting counter-part. To policy makers charged with keeping hunters from shooting themselves and each other, this willingness to accept risk would suggest that sober warnings about the dangers of firearms may well be ineffective. Lest this conclusion seem hopelessly naive, let it be noted that sober warnings about the dangers of firearms are exactly what some policy makers have attempted.

The relatively high levels of agreement with the fifth section suggest a combination of self-indulgence and lack of internal control that seems congruent with the attitude toward risk just noted. If the hunter is in fact self-indulgent and relatively conscienceless, it would seem unwise to rely on appeals to fair play and conservation to regulate his activities. Again, such appeals have been tried with less success than expected.

The level of agreement with 'I love to eat' and the hunter's professed willingness to spend money on himself suggest markets for premium foods designed to be taken along on hunting expeditions. These two findings also suggest the suitability of game-preparation recipes for hunting magazines, and they indicate that quantity and quality of food should get particular attention from proprietors of hunting lodges. Hunters don't mind roughing it, but they want it to be a well-fed roughness.

Finally, the relatively low level of agreement with 'I read the newspaper every day' should serve as a warning to shotgun ammunition advertisers. This is not to assert that media decisions, positive or negative, should ever be based on responses to a single survey item. Rather, it suggests that any shotgun ammunition advertiser who is spending his budget in newspapers should think twice about alternatives.

Psychographic profiles are usually developed from large-scale surveys (200–300 questions, 1000 + respondents) using self-administered questionnaires covering a wide range of attitudes, opinions, and interests and Likert scales (see Chapter 10, p. 255). Responses may be analysed by simple cross-classification techniques, but given the wealth of information it is more usual to make use of the powerful multivariate techniques available in packaged computer programs such as SPSS (Statistical Package for the Social Sciences). Using techniques such as *factor analysis* it becomes possible to reduce the mass of data into a series of principal components which distinguish major groupings within the data. The output of such an analysis is shown in Table 8.4 (again taken from Wells's article).

TABLE 8.2 Demographic profile of the heavy user of shotgun ammunition

	Per cent who spend $11 + per year on shotgun ammunition (141)*	*Per cent who do not buy (395)*
Age		
Under 25	95	
25–34	33	15
35–44	27	22
45–54	18	22
55 +	13	36
Occupation		
Professional	6	15
Managerial	23	23
Clerical/sales	9	17
Craftsman	50	35
Income		
Under $6000	26	19
$6000–$10000	39	36
$10 000–$15 000	24	27
$15 000 +	11	16
Population density		
Rural	34	12
2500–50 000	11	11
50 000–500 000	16	15
500 000–2 million	21	27
2 million +	13	19
Geographic division		
New England/Mid Atlantic	21	33
Central (N, W)	22	30
South Atlantic	23	12
E. South Central	10	3
W. South Central	10	5
Mountain	6	3
Pacific	9	13

* Number of respondents in the survey.

Source: W. D. Wells, 'Psychographics: A Critical Review', *Journal of Marketing Research*, vol. XII, May 1975.

TABLE 8.3   **Psychographic profile of the heavy user of shotgun ammunition**

Base	Per cent who spend $11+ per year on shotgun ammunition (141)*	Per cent who do not buy (395)*
I like hunting	88	7
I like fishing	68	26
I like to go camping	57	21
I love the outdoors	90	65
A cabin by a quiet lake is a great place to spend the summer	49	34
I like to work outdoors	67	40
I am good at fixing mechanical things	47	27
I often do a lot of repair work on my own car	36	12
I like war stories	50	32
I would do better than average in a fist fight	38	16
I would like to be a professional football player	28	18
I would like to be a policeman	22	8
There is too much violence on television	35	45
There should be a gun in every home	56	10
I like danger	19	8
I would like to own my own air-plane	35	13
I like to play poker	50	26
I smoke too much	39	24
I love to eat	49	34
I spend money on myself that I should spend on the family	44	26
If given a chance, most men would cheat on their wives	33	14
I read the newspaper every day	51	72

* Number of respondents in the survey.

Source: As for Table 8.2.

■ Segmentation by social grading

The use of social class as a basis for distinguishing the consumption behaviour of groups of individuals was discussed in Chapter 6. However, the validity and effectiveness of this approach has been subject to criticism in recent years and led to the establishment by the Market Research Society (in 1979) of a working party to examine the issues. An article by Francis Quinlan in the Autumn 1981 issue of the *Quarterly Review of Marketing* ('The Use of Social Grading in Marketing')

TABLE 8.4 Eight male psychographic segments

Group I 'The Quiet Family Man' (8 per cent of total males)
He is a self-sufficient man who wants to be left alone and is basically shy. Tries to be as little involved with community life as possible. His life revolves around the family, simple work and television viewing. Has a marked fantasy life. As a shopper he is practical, less drawn to consumer goods and pleasures than other men.

Group II 'The Traditionalist' (16 per cent of total males)
A man who feels secure, has self-esteem, follows conventional rules. He is proper and respectable, regards himself as altruistic and interested in the welfare of others. As a shopper he is conservative, likes popular brands and well-known manufacturers. (Low education and low or middle socio-economic status; the oldest age group.)

Group III 'The Discontented Man' (13 per cent of total males)
He is a man who is likely to be dissatisfied with his work. He feels bypassed by life, dreams of better jobs, more money and more security. He tends to be distrustful and socially aloof. As a buyer he is quite price conscious. (Lowest education and lowest socio-economic group, mostly older than average.)

Group IV 'The Ethical Highbrow' (14 per cent of total males)
This is a very concerned man, sensitive to people's needs. Basically a puritan, content with family life, friends and work. Interested in culture, religion and social reform. As a consumer he is interested in quality, which may at times justify greater expenditure. (Well-educated, middle or upper socio-economic status, mainly older.)

Group V 'The Pleasure-orientated Man' (9 per cent of total males)
He tends to emphasise his masculinity and rejects whatever appears to be soft or feminine. He views himself a leader among men. Self-centered, dislikes his work or job. Seeks immediate gratification for his needs. He is an impulsive buyer, likely to buy products with a masculine image. (Low education, lower socio-economic class, middle-aged or younger.)

Group VI 'The Achiever' (11 per cent of' total males)
This is likely to be a hardworking man, dedicated to success and all that it implies-social prestige, power and money. Is in favour of diversity, is adventurous about leisure-time pursuits. Is stylish, likes good food, music, etc. As a consumer he is status conscious, a thoughtful and discriminating buyer. (Good education, high socio-economic status, young.)

Group VII 'The He-Man' (19 per cent of total males)
He is gregarious, likes action, seeks an exciting and dramatic life. Thinks of himself as capable and dominant. Tends to be more of a bachelor than a family man, even after marriage. Products he buys and brands preferred are likely to have 'Self-expressive value', especially a 'Man of Action' dimension. (Well-educated, mainly middle socio-economic status, the youngest of the male groups.)

Group VIII 'The Sophisticated Man' (10 per cent of total males)
He is likely to be an intellectual, concerned about social issues, admires men with artistic and intellectual achievements. Socially cosmopolitan, broad interests. Wants to be dominant, and a leader. As a consumer he is attracted to the unique and fashionable. (Best educated and highest economic status of all groups, younger than average.)

Source: W. D. Wells, 'Psychographics: A Critical Review', *Journal of Marketing Research*, vol. XII, May 1975.

reflected some of its conclusions and findings. Thus he writes 'It is suggested that social-grading of almost any kind is becoming of only marginal practical interest to most marketers', and cites the fact that much consumer expenditure relates to family purchasing rather than individual purchasing, with the result that household or family income/expenditure is a much better indicator of market potential than information about the individual head of household or housewife. Similar criticism has also been levelled against life-style as a basis for market segmentation.

However, while Quinlan argues that 'teachers and textbooks of marketing should not continue to refer to social grading for segmentation purposes as if it were as simple as ABC', it has to be recognised that by combining socio-economic factors with demographic and housing characteristics even more powerful and discriminating approaches to market segmentation have been developed. The most recent and sophisticated of these approaches is the Consumer Location System, or CLS, developed by the Post Office by combining BMRB's Target Group Index and CACI Inc.'s A Classification of Residential Neighbourhoods (ACORN). The logic behind the technique is set out clearly in the PO's explanatory leaflet:

PRECISION ADVERTISING IN MASS MARKETS

The need for direct, tightly defined targeting of mass consumer markets is becoming increasingly evident. It is getting less and less feasible to write off the wastage inherent in the mass media as a marginal penalty incurred for the sake of 'cheap' media coverage – the penalties are no longer marginal.

The secret to success, however, is not simply in defining these markets more accurately, but in defining them in a way which helps maximise the advertising effort. Furthermore, by identifying the key consumer groups within a market in this way, the advertiser's options are automatically expanded to include highly targeted media such as direct mail.

Turning the theory into practice no longer presents a problem. It's now perfectly possible to:

1. Specify mass consumer markets in much tighter terms than in the past.
2. Establish a rational basis for inter-media comparisons, and consider direct mail as a consumer media option alongside TV, press, and radio – and direct mail comes out of the comparison very well in many product fields.
3. Access accurate lists of potential purchasers within the specified target market while integrating this with other media plans.

In other words, it is possible to reap the benefits of direct mail's precision and high impact in a mass market environment.

This revolutionary technique in targeting is called the Consumer Location System....

WHAT IS THE CONSUMER LOCATION SYSTEM?

CLS is a computerised system for analysing people's purchasing, reading and viewing habits, and relating these to the neighbourhoods in which they live. It will provide a refined consumer profile related to propensity to consume and will also produce media performance evaluations related to cost-effective reach of the specific target audience.

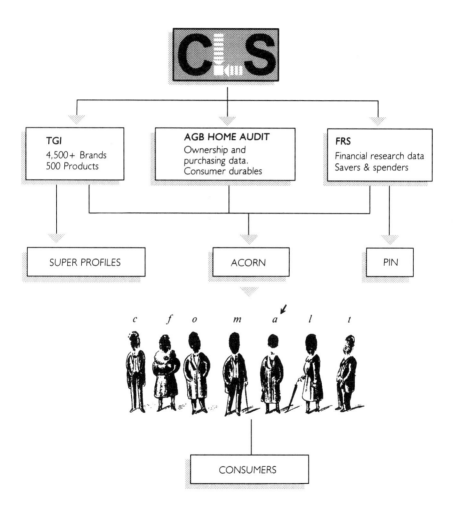

WHAT DOES IT DO?

CLS does three things. Firstly, it segments markets in a way which helps the user understand that market more fully. Secondly, it tells the user where the key consumers in that market live. It does this in a way which enables the user to reach those people through direct mail. Finally, it tells us how that market consumes different types of media – a useful gauge for those interested in the performance of different media groups in reaching their customers.

HOW DOES CLS DO IT?

It takes the data from major research sources such as Target Group Index, Financial Research Services and AGB Home Audit and it analysis markets defined by these sources using an area based classification system such as ACORN. With the use of a simple index it ranks the area types according to their level of consumption in that market. Therefore, if an area type has an index of 200 it has two times higher a level of consumption than the national average in that market – the national average always equals 100.

It also looks at the market in terms of its consumption of different media groups by taking the total level of exposure to each media group experienced by the target market, and comparing it with the expected level of exposure. For example, market 'X' may account for 10% of the total number of hours of ITV viewed in one week, but the market is only 5% of the total population. The target market is consuming twice as much ITV as one would expect (ten is twice as much as five).

HOW CAN YOU USE CLS?

You can use it as a descriptive tool which helps you to understand your market better. You can also use it to evaluate how you can reach your market most effectively with media advertising and thus reduce wastage.

The analysis will probably demonstrate that your market is heavily segmented and that a disproportionately large part of your market is situated within a small section of the population. If this is the case it may then make sense for you to exploit this fact by using the results of CLS to help you target a Direct Mail campaign.

Using the area classification and the electoral register (which is now on various computers), it is easy and inexpensive to select the names and addresses of people in your catchment areas who are the types identified by the Consumer Location System.

WHO CAN BENEFIT FROM CLS?

Anyone concerned with the task of planning the advertising of goods or services should seriously consider what the Consumer Location System has to offer. Similarly, anyone who has limited knowledge of their market's level of segmentation will find it a useful tool.

■ Industrial segmentation

While most segmentation studies are concerned with consumer markets the need is equally as great in many industrial markets, as was brought out by Richard Cardozo in his article 'Situational Segmentation of Industrial Markets' (*European Journal of Marketing*, vol. 14, no. 5/6, 1980). Cardozo identifies four dimensions which may be used separately or in combination to classify organisational buying situations which may be regarded as 'market segments', namely:

1. Familiarity with the buying task, i.e. Robinson *et al.*'s 'buyclasses'.
2. Product type. Here one may segment on the basis of product use in terms of components, materials and equipment (see Chapter 9 for a classification of industrial goods) which may be related to the 'degree of standardisation', namely.
   Custom: unique design for a particular customer.
   Modular: unique combination of standard available components or materials.
   Standard: combination of ingredients that has been offered previously.
3. Importance of purchase to the buying organisation.
4. Type of uncertainty in the purchase situation.

Clearly, Cardozo's approach seeks to add a behavioural and situational dimension to the more traditional Standard Industrial Classification (SIC) which is based on the nature of the product and encompasses very broad distinctions at the industry level (2 digit codes) as well as very narrow distinctions between firms (4 digit codes).

Another important dimension in both industrial and consumer markets is geography, particularly where this is a surrogate for national boundaries with all the implications these have for cultural, legal and political differences between markets.

■ International segmentation

Yoram Wind and Susan Douglas provided a useful schemata for segmenting international markets in an article in the *European Journal of Marketing* (vol. 5, no. 1, 1972, 'International Market Segmentation'), and this is reproduced as Table 8.5.

Based upon these characteristics the authors then propose a 2-step process for segmenting international markets. First, one defines the macro segment, which may be one or more countries with similar market characteristics and then one sub-divides the macro segment on the basis of customer characteristics with it. This may be represented by a flow diagram as shown in Figure 8.5.

TABLE 8.5   **A classification scheme of various bases for international market segmentation**

	Enduring characteristics	*Situation specific characteristics*
Country characteristics	Geographic location Demographic and population characteristics	Economic and legal constraints Market conditions
	Socio-economic Cultural patterns Political factors	Product bound Culture and life style characteristics
Customer characteristics	Demographic characteristics: age, sex, life cycle Geographic location	Consumption patterns Loyalty patterns Buying situations Attitudes (perceptions and preferences)
	Socio-economic Personality and life style characteristics	

Source: Wind and Douglas 'International Market Segmentation', *European Journal of Marketing*, vol. 5, no. 1, 1972.

■ Methods of segmentation

In the preceding section we have looked at a number of different bases for segmenting markets without addressing the question of *how* one should set about the task. As is apparent from the references already cited there is a wealth of

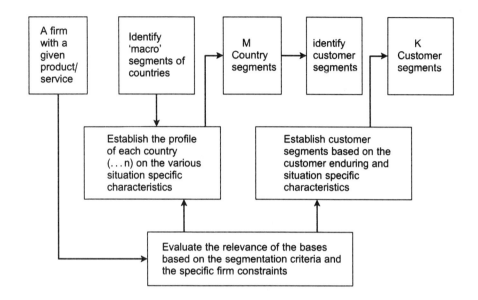

Figure 8.5 The hierarchy of segments approach to international market segmentation

Source: Wind and Douglas, 'International Market Segmentation', *European Journal of Marketing*, vol. 5, no. 1, 1972.

information on the subject and the discussion here can only scratch the surface. However, for a concise but comprehensive discussion of the topic one cannot better the article 'Issues and Advances in Segmentation Research' by Yoram Wind, which appeared in the August 1978 issue of the *Journal of Marketing Research*. The following discussion of methods draws heavily on this source.

As Wind points out, 'Four major types of models can be used in an effort to segment a market. They include the traditional *a priori* and *clustering-based* segmentation models, and the new models of flexible and componential segmentation which are based on different sets of assumptions.' He continues:

A priori segmentation models have had as the dependent variable (the basis for segmentation) either product-specific variables (e.g. product usage, loyalty) or general customer characteristics (e.g. demographic factors). The typical research design for an *a priori* segmentation model involves seven stages:

1. Selection of the (*a priori*) basis for segmentation.
2. Selection of a set of segment descriptions (including hypotheses on the possible link between these descriptors and the basis for segmentation).
3. Sample design – mostly stratified and occasionally a quota sample according to the various classes of the dependent variable.
4. Data collection.

5. Formation of the segments based on a sorting of respondents into categories.
6. Establishment of the (conditional) profile of the segments using multiple discriminant analysis, multiple regressional analysis, AID or some other appropriate analytical procedure.
7. Translation of the findings about the segments' estimated size and profile into specific marketing strategies, including the selection of target segments and the design or modification of specific marketing strategy.

Clustering-based methods are very similar to *a priori* methods with the essential difference that one does not specify in advance a dependent variable but rather looks for natural clusters occurring in a data base. Needs, benefits, attitudes, life-style and psychographic characteristics are the most commonly used factors in establishing the existence of a cluster. This approach is also known as the *post hoc* method of segmentation.

On occasion *a priori* and *post hoc* methods may be combined in a hybrid approach: e.g., one might segment first on usage and seek to determine if there are clusters or sub-groups within these segments, using benefits, needs, etc, as a basis for refining the discrimination.

As the name implies, flexible segmentation is a dynamic methodology which offers management 'the flexibility of 'building up' segments (cell or cell combination with any specific brand-switching matrix) based on the consumers' response to alternative product offerings (under various competitive and environmental conditions)' (Wind, 'Issues and Advances'). The technique depends heavily on conjoint analysis and computer simulations of choice behaviour and is particularly suited to concept and new product testing.

The fourth approach, which also depends upon sophisticated statistical analysis and extensive computing power, is componential analysis. The model, proposed by Green, differs from other segmentation models in that it seeks to predict which type of consumer will be most responsive to which product feature. The method has many similarities with flexible segmentation and is applicable to both industrial and consumer markets.

In Quinlan's opinion, flexible and componential segmentation 'has become highly academic and out of touch with real world practice', which is a view shared by Graham Hooley of the Bradford Management Centre. In an article entitled 'Multivariate Jungle – The Academic's Playground but the Manager's Minefield' (1980) he argues forcefully that the development of multivariate statistical techniques and the ready availability of massive computing power have resulted in academics presenting such methods as if they were the panacea for all ills. Such claims are regarded sceptically by practitioners and lead Hooley to propose seven commandments to govern their use, namely: 'do not be technique oriented; consider multivariate models as information for management; do not substitute multivariate methods for researcher skill and imagination; develop communication skill; avoid making statistical inferences about the parameters of multivariate models; guard against the danger of making inferences about market realities when such inferences may be due to the peculiarities of the method; exploit the complementary relationship between descriptive and predictive methods.

■ Selecting a segmentation approach

During the 1980s many marketers in the UK came to question the relevance of the traditional social class approach to market segmentation in an increasingly more egalitarian society. In order to examine the usefulness and stability of some alternative methods of measurement Granada Television commissioned the British Market Research Bureau (BMRB) to undertake research on the topic. The results of the research received the award of Best Paper at the 1988 Market Research Society Conference and were published as 'Can we at last say goodbye to social class' in the *Journal of the Market Research Society*, vol. 30, no. 3, July 1988.

In their paper the authors, Sarah O'Brien and Rosemary Ford, report the findings of a joint working party of the IPA, ISBA, ITCA and MRS whose report published in January 1981 concluded that:

1. Social grade provided satisfactory discriminatory powers.
2. No alternative standard classification variables were found to provide consistently better discriminatory powers.
3. No classification variables worked best across all product fields or data types.
4. There was no evidence to show a decline in the discriminatory power of social grade over the previous ten years (preceding 1979).

However, these findings appear at variance with reports such as those published by the Henley Centre and others on changing life-styles and the frequently observed fact that single earner AB households with children in private education frequently have less disposable income than C2D households with multiple earners occupying low cost public housing. Further, research by BARN indicated (1987) that in one year 32 per cent of their TV audience panel had changed social class. Although this was seen as exceptional the fact that between 4 and 7 per cent of the panel change social class every year clearly points to a very mobile population in terms of the factors used to define social class.

Against this background O'Brien and Ford felt it would be opportune to compare the usefulness of social class with some of the newer non-occupation based techniques for classifying consumers which had emerged in the 1970s and 1980s. Based upon a 50-minute interview with 1380 adult respondents the researchers were able to build up a very detailed picture of people's lives, motivations and possessions capable of being analysed by a range of non-standard demographic classifications. In the event three different variables were used – social class, lifestage and lifestyle. Social class was employed using the categories described in Table 6.3 but collapsing A and B into a single category. Lifestage is a classification based upon a number of variables such as age, marital and working status, and presence of children. Six groups governing 83 per cent of the adult population were defined as 'power groups' reflecting their spending power in terms of disposable income, namely:

Granny power (14 per cent) People aged 55–70, not in full-time employment and with no children or young dependent adults.
Grey power (12 per cent) People aged 45–60 with one adult working full-time and no children or young dependent adults.
Older silver power (18 per cent) Married people with older children (5–15 years) but no under fives.
Young silver power (16 per cent) People who are married with children aged 0–4 years.
Platinum power (7 per cent) Married people aged 40 or under but with no children.
Golden power (15 per cent) Single people, with no children, aged 40 or under.

The remaining 18 per cent did not fall into any of these categories.

The Lifestyle variable was derived from a factor and cluster analysis of 54 attitudinal dimensions and yielded five clusters.

The paper by O'Brien and Ford comprises an extended and rigorous analysis of the discriminatory power of the three different classificatory systems and comes to the conclusion that social class is *not* dead. In fact their conclusions are very similar to those of the Working Party reported above, namely:

- social class *does* discriminate
- no alternative classification provides *consistently* better discriminatory powers
- no *one* classification works best across all product fields.

However, the researchers also conclude that

- sometimes other classifications discriminate *more*, and frequently they are *just as powerful* as social class.

In other words, marketers should always consider other classifications when designing surveys and analysing data.

The second part of O'Brien and Ford's research looks at the stability and replicability of the three approaches and comes to the conclusion that life stage is superior to both lifestyle and social class on the following grounds:

- unlike social class it can be applied consistently at an international and cross-cultural level;
- unlike geodemographic classification it does not require a very large sample size;
- also unlike geodemographics it is not *falsely* stable (i.e. systems like ACORN are based on census data which can become out of date due to the period between censuses);
- Lifestyle data require only a minimal extension to standard demographic data and so can be collected quickly;
- in contrast to social class, lifestage data are less likely to be regarded as 'personal' which makes the interviewers' task easier.

These conclusions reinforce those relating to the discriminatory power of the different approaches (assuming the base data is valid and reliable), namely, social class may be an appropriate method for analysing markets but one should always consider alternative approaches which may be better given the particular context and the purposes to which the research is to be put.

■ Using segmentation techniques

In order to justify market segmentation most writers agree that a market segment must possess four distinct characteristics:

1. It must be *measurable.*
2. It must be sufficiently *substantial* to warrant the effort invested in it.
3. It must be *accessible* in the sense that there are channels of distribution, media, etc., which permit a focused approach to it.
4. It must respond *uniquely* to the efforts directed at it.

To these four conditions, defining a viable market segment Thomas ('Market Segmentation') adds a fifth – *stability* – by which he means that the segment's behaviour is such that its future response may be predicted.

However, authors are less agreed upon the role which segmentation has to play in marketing strategy. Some see its role as offensive, in the sense that segmentation should be used to identify opportunities and unfilled niches in the market place which can be exploited through an aggressive strategy. Conversely, other authors see market segmentation as a means of avoiding cannibalisation of one's existing products by defining distinct segments for new products and as a defensive strategy for deterring new entrants to the market.

Clearly these alternatives are not mutually exclusive for a firm with a portfolio of products, when defensive strategies will be more suited to products in the mature or decline phase of their life-cycle, while offensive strategies will be appropriate for guiding new product development and managing products in the launch phase of their life-cycle.

To conclude, however, it is well to heed the warning given by Resnik, Turney and Mason ('Marketers Turn to Counter-Segmentation', *Harvard Business Review*, Sept/Oct 1979) who state, 'Many markets today may be characterised as hypersegmented, a condition under which increasingly smaller market segments are identified and targeted.' This, fragmentation may cause consumers to become confused, retail distribution difficult to maintain, and result in major diseconomies in both production and marketing. To avoid this, Resnik *et al.* propose that marketers will have to turn to counter-segmentation', involving:

1. The elimination of market segments by dropping products.
2. The *fusion* of segments by persuading customers to accept simpler and less-differentiated products.

CHAPTER 9

Patterns of distribution

Learning Goals

The objective of this chapter is to introduce the student to the formal systems and structures which have developed over time to facilitate the physical transfer of goods from the raw material stage into ultimate consumption.

The issues to be addressed in this chapter include:

1. The role of distribution in the business system.
2. The nature of primary production, commodity markets and the channels of distribution which serve them.
3. The nature of industrial marketing.
4. Factors influencing the structure of industrial marketing channels.
5. The influence of industry concentration on channel structure.
6. The nature of retail distribution.
7. The evolution and structure of the retail trade.
8. Current trends and their impact upon competition.

On completion of this chapter you should be able to:

1. Define the nature of and role played by the distribution system.
2. Define raw materials and the distinction between finite and renewable raw materials.
3. List some salient features of extractive industries.
4. Account for the development of producer-user agreements.
5. Discuss some key aspects of agricultural production and marketing.
6. Explain the features underlying the growth of processing.
7. Describe the channels used for fresh produce and the role of Marketing Boards.
8. Identify the distinguishing characteristics of industrial marketing.
9. List the main factors which influence the structure of industrial distribution channels.
10. Describe the effect of industry concentration on industrial channels and exemplify this by reference to the distribution of steel.
11. List the main functions performed by retailing and describe their key features.
12. Describe the structure of the retail trade and the main kinds of outlets.
13. Explain the concept of the Wheel of Retailing.

14. Summarise some of the main innovations which have taken place in the past forty years.
15. Identify the advantages and disadvantages of various patterns of retail distribution.
16. Review some current trends in retailing and their implications for the industry's future.

In Chapter 1 we considered briefly some of the issues which define an economy. It will be recalled that the first of these stages was termed 'Traditional society' which is characterised by its lack of a systematic understanding of the environment and the technology and tools necessary to achieve any significant improvement in productivity. In such societies, and particularly the most primitive ones, the great majority of people's time is taken up with survival and the satisfaction of basic physiological needs. The first real step in the process of civilisation occurred when people began to establish settlements, rather than pursue a nomadic existence in which they moved from place to place seeking food and other essential materials. The point we are seeking to establish is that *place* and *location* has played a fundamental role in the evolution of exchange and the development of marketing.

Originally, the market was a physical location where people could exchange surpluses at first in kind (barter or countertrading) and subsequently through a medium of exchange such as money. The opportunity to exchange surpluses and thereby increase satisfaction encouraged task specialisation which, in turn, increased productivity and output. However, early settlements were severely limited in their production/consumption opportunities by virtue of the raw materials or factors of production available to them. Over time trade between settlements developed and further specialisation of function occurred based upon the exploitation of natural local advantages. It was observation of this pheno-menon which prompted Ricardo to formulate his *theory of comparative advantage* in which he demonstrated that through specialisation and exchange two countries could both gain even though one country had a natural advantage (i.e. was more cost-effective) in producing both the products which were to be exchanged. More recently Michael Porter in his *Competitive Advantage of Nations* (1990) has argued that the classical theory based upon the concept of factor endowment 'is at best incomplete and at worst incorrect' as an explanation of the competitive performance of nations. Porter's thesis is that while a natural endowment is important it is the way such endowments are used which is important and he points to the fact that in many cases, such as Japan, factor deficiencies have acted as a spur to innovation and superior performance. However, one does not need to develop the argument further to appreciate that the potential to innovate and specialise will only add value and increase satisfaction if the goods produced can be made available to users and consumers who have a demand for them. To achieve this requires the existence of channels of distribution and of specialists and intermediaries to facilitate the flow of goods from producers to consumers. It is this topic which forms the subject of this chapter. (Note: This chapter is concerned with the infra-structure of distribution and is largely descriptive. Its inclusion and the detail it contains are believed to be important as an understanding of existing channels of distribution and the factors which underlie or condition their structure and operation represent external factors over which the individual firm or supplier has limited control. This understanding is essential when making channel decisions and using 'place' as an element in the marketing mix. This is dealt with in more detail in Chapter 14.)

■ The distribution of raw materials

The term 'raw materials' is often used to describe the physical goods used in manufacturing without distinguishing between natural raw materials and semi-manufactured, or fabricated, materials. For example the raw materials used in the packaging industry – paper, plastics, fibre-board, etc. – are the finished goods of other manufacturers in the chemical industry. To avoid confusion the term will be used here to describe materials in their natural state such as coal, wool, wheat and rubber, which are often termed 'primary commodities'.

A broad distinction may be made between those raw materials which occur in a natural state and those which are the result of man's efforts in developing particular types of natural products through agriculture. The distinction is a logical one, for whereas man cannot alter the absolute supply of 'natural' raw materials, he can increase the supply of crops, both in absolute amount and in terms of specific varieties. Accordingly they merit separate treatment.

■ 'Natural' raw materials

This category is the one with which the so-called extractive industries are concerned and includes mineral deposits, forest and sea products. It is recognised that it is possible for man to increase the supply of both the latter, just as it may one day be possible to increase the total supply of minerals through deep excavation, or mining them on the moon. In this context, however, they will be treated as being in fixed supply for we have yet to achieve the technological breakthrough which makes such possibilities economically feasible. That this is so is evident in the conservation policies which have been widely adopted.

Another feature which is common to the supply of natural raw materials is that not only is supply fixed in an absolute sense, it is also fixed in the short term if all existing plant is operating at capacity. In other words, supply is not immediately responsive to increases in demand owing to the time-lag between such an increase becoming apparent and resources being diverted to exploit the market opportunity which such excess demand represents. Mines and sawmills cannot be opened overnight, and fishing fleets take time to construct. In the case of minerals the delay is especially protracted as most of the accessible deposits are already being exploited, so that not only do mines have to be opened but road, rail and port facilities also have to be developed. Even reopening disused mines takes time, as is evident from the efforts made in Cornwall during the 1970s and 1980s to cash in on the world shortage of tin.

Because supply cannot readily be increased in the short term, prices for raw materials react very quickly to variations in demand in the way in which economic theory predicts they will. In fact commodity markets are usually used as examples when studying supply and demand because these factors can be clearly distinguished in operation, free from the complications which advertising, sales promotion and the like introduce into consumer goods markets. Owing to the tendency for raw material prices to fluctuate widely with variations in both demand and supply, many attempts have been made to stabilise the functioning of commodity markets – usually with little success as will be seen below.

■ Salient features of the extractive industries

The extraction of raw materials is usually expensive, and involves considerable capital investment even in the case of the more common materials such as coal, iron ore, basic chemicals and mineral oil. As a result, production of these materials is usually concentrated in the hands of a limited number of firms with the necessary capital and technical resources. From the point of view of the basic industries which process and refine these raw materials, the uncertainties associated with a free market represent a considerable threat to their own security and stability, and predispose them to secure control over a substantial part of their raw material requirements. This is not always possible, however, as many countries limit, or forbid, foreign participation, particularly where they have a monopoly over available supplies. In these circumstances the firm has no option but to buy in the world's commodity markets, the operation of which is very similar to the wheat market described in detail later in this chapter. In an introductory text of this nature it is not possible to consider political interference in the operation of free markets, e.g. the Arab countries' restriction of oil supplies following the Arab-Israeli conflict in 1973 and the subsequent establishment of OPEC as a producer cartel or the sanctions imposed on Iraq following its invasion of Kuwait in 1990.

The position with regard to the less common raw materials differs in that although production tends to be concentrated for the reasons outlined above, demand is made up of a large number of consumers with limited individual requirements. To satisfy these demands, specialist markets have been developed wherein the processes of concentration, equalisation and dispersion can take place, e.g. the London Metal Exchange.

In addition to what might be termed the basic raw materials of industry such as oil, chemicals, iron ore, etc., and the rare materials such as gold, silver, tin and diamonds, there is a wide range of materials which occur regularly in nature, and are relatively easy to extract with limited capital equipment. Like many other raw materials they are usually bulky, and the cost of transportation plays a significant role in their marketing. Extraction is closely governed by the proximity of the market to the source of supply and distribution is strictly local, precluding the need for the central markets associated with less common materials. Sand and gravel are examples of such locally distributed materials.

■ Producer-user agreements

As noted earlier, the inherent instability of commodity markets has stimulated both producers and users to seek some form of agreement to minimise the impact of fluctuations in supply and demand. Under normal conditions the establishment of an agreement is beneficial to both buyer and seller, as it invariably fixes a price bracket for the commodity. Thus, producers can treat the lower limit of the bracket as a guaranteed selling price and plan their output accordingly. Similarly, the buyer can cost his own output in the knowledge that the price of the raw material content cannot exceed the upper limit set by the bracket. However, if supply and demand should get in serious imbalance such agreements are put to a test which few are capable of surviving.

The classic example of the validity of this statement must be the International Tin Council, which was long quoted as the model for such agreements. For many years the council successfully held prices within the limits agreed on by producers and users, through the maintenance of a buffer stock. As soon as the price of tin fell to the lower limit prescribed by the agreement the Council entered the market, and supported it by buying at that price until sufficient excess supply had been removed for the price to rise above the 'floor'. (These are identical to the tactics of the Bank of England in the foreign exchange market.) Similarly, at the other end of the scale, as soon as excess demand or a decline in supply resulted in the price reaching the agreed ceiling, the Council would release stocks until the price fell within the bracket. A particularly attractive feature of the scheme was that it was self-financing, as the margin between the upper and lower limits was sufficient to cover the stockholding and administrative costs involved. The Tin Council functioned perfectly on this basis until the early 1960s, when demand began to outstrip supply with the result that the market price was invariably near its upper limit. In order to keep the price within the prescribed limits the Council was increasingly called upon to release its stocks, but was never able to replenish them at the lower price. Eventually the inevitable happened and the stocks were exhausted, leaving a free market in which prices spiralled rapidly before stabilising at a more realistic level some £500 above the old limit. It is possible that the market free-for-all might have been avoided if the Council had had more funds at its disposal with which to build up stocks in time of excess supply, or had appreciated the fundamental disequilibrium earlier and raised the market price sooner. As it was, the Council's operations masked the development of imbalance between supply and demand and gave the market a false appearance of stability.

While the Council survived this crisis it collapsed in 1990 and was disbanded.

■ Agricultural products

Agricultural products may properly be regarded both as industrial raw materials and as consumer goods. In that there are significant differences in distribution, depending upon whether crops are sold direct into consumption or to manufacturers for processing it will be convenient to deal separately with these two categories. At the same time there are certain features common to both which deserve consideration prior to a discussion of the salient differences in distribution.

Probably the most striking feature of agriculture is the smallness of the average production unit. Although there has been a consistent trend towards larger unit size in nearly every industrialised country as alternative employment opportunities have become available, this is still true today. In the author's opinion there is unlikely to be a significant decline in the number of small farms and, in fact, it seems reasonable to anticipate that their numbers will increase. As the world's population continues to expand geometrically so will the demand for food increase. At present the economists' calculations are based on average income per acre, from which it is argued that farms are too small to enable the average farmer to attain an adequate standard of living. Further, it is true that increased unit size would permit more extensive use of labour-saving equipment and improve the marginal productivity of capital by comparison with investment in a small farm. These arguments neglect the fact that the small, intensively farmed unit has a significantly higher yield per acre than the large, mechanised unit – a comparison of average wheat yields as between the United States and Holland reveals that the latter are some 400–500 per cent greater than the former. In the future, as demand outstrips supply, prices will rise and thus make intensive farming not only necessary but also more profitable. If the argument is valid, it would seem that the supply of agricultural products will continue to flow from a large number of small producers albeit of a more sophisticated kind. The current 'green revolution' and the associated interest in natural or organic foods has also seen a revival in the fortunes of the small production unit.

Although agricultural products are usually thought of as being homogeneous, in fact there are considerable variations in quality, and some form of grading process is necessary before they can be offered for sale. Further, crops are perishable and need careful handling and storage to prevent deterioration. Neither of these operations can be performed economically on a small scale, nor with the limited resources at the small farmer's disposal, and a complex distributive network has been developed to facilitate the marketing of crops and foodstuffs.

■ The causes of market disequilibrium

A commonly observed feature of agricultural markets is the erratic fluctuation of price, particularly in the short term. This instability is essentially attributable to variations in supply, as the demand for most agricultural products is fairly stable and predictable in advance. Obviously, climate is a major cause of supply instability, but its effects are compounded by the behaviour of producers in the manner outlined below.

In the case of many products such as wheat, cotton, rubber and livestock, a high proportion of the total supply is accounted for by large, specialist producers. Allowing for the vagaries of climate, their output tends to be fairly constant and calculable in advance, from which it follows that the major variations in supply must be attributed to the output of the small farmers.

Most land may be used to grow a variety of crops, and the major decision facing the small producer is which crop to plant in order to gain the greatest return; a decision that must be made several months before the crop will be ready for sale. In assessing market opportunity it is natural that the farmer should be influenced by current prices, and there is a strong probability that a large number will independently decide to plant those crops which are currently fetching the best prices. The reason certain crops are fetching above average prices is clearly due to the fact that the existing supply is insufficient to satisfy the total demand, and thus the price mechanism is having the desired effect of encouraging an increase in supply. However, it would be purely fortuitous if the separate decision of thousands of producers to increase planting of a specific crop resulted in an exact balancing of supply and demand. It is nearly certain that the increased supply will depress price and fail to meet the farmer's expectations. Further, the decision to switch from, say, wheat to barley will reduce the supply of wheat and its price will go up, thus encouraging the farmer to increase his acreage under wheat and to decrease planting of barley.

It is the time-lag between the decision to sow a particular crop and its reaching fruition, the inability to go back on the decision once its is made, and the farmer's imperfect knowledge of others' sowing decisions which create fluctuations in supply that disturb market equilibrium.

■ The impact of the marginal producer

A good example of the manner in which the small farmer determines the final level of supply is afforded by the market for natural rubber.

Between the two World Wars the leading rubber-producing countries agreed to limit supply in order to ensure a fair market price for their output, e.g. the

Stephenson scheme in South-east Asia. The restriction in supply forced prices up and encouraged the peasant farmers in the Dutch East Indies to clear land, which they would otherwise have been unable to cultivate, to plant rubber trees. These trees were not given the same careful attention as is typical of the commercial plantation, and which accounts for the major production costs, they were simply left to grow for the eight to ten years necessary to achieve maturity. As soon as the trees were big enough to tap, native rubber flooded on to the market, causing prices to plummet and the producer agreements to collapse.

The native product is only slightly inferior in quality to the plantation product, and now accounts for about 30 per cent of total supply. The commercial grower's position is aggravated by the fact that although he is committed to the high fixed costs of maintaining his plantation, the native grower is not, and only taps his trees when the market price justifies the effort. Thus, whenever the market price becomes favourable from the plantation owner's point of view the marginal producers enter the market and force the price down.

Given the possible variations in supply and its diverse origins it is not surprising that man has developed elaborate marketing systems to permit concentration of output so that it may be made available to those with a demand for it. Such marketing systems possess many features in common and the discussion of the market for a single product will help to clarify these. The wheat market in the United States is particularly well documented and will be used as an example here.

■ The marketing of wheat

The first stage in the marketing of wheat is concentration at the local elevator by individual farmers. The elevator may be owned by an independent wholesaler, or by the farmers themselves as a co-operative. In either case the elevator will usually offer to purchase the grain outright at central market price, less the cost of freight to the central market and the elevator owner's commission, or, alternatively, to store the grain for a fixed charge. The farmer's decision to sell or store is based on the current price, and expectations as to its future movements, as against the cost of warehousing. (Note: there is an absolute floor to market price determined by Federal Government subsidy. This subsidy is analogous to the guaranteed farm prices offered by the British Government to ensure a minimum level of domestic production prior to entry to the EEC when the Common Agricultural Policy came into force.)

Most of the grain in local elevators is resold to manufacturers in the same area, but the balance is sold either to wholesalers in the 'terminal' markets, e.g. the 'Wheat Pit' in Chicago, or else sent to commission agents in such centres for sale at the best price available. Dealers at the central market frequently combine the functions of merchants, agents and brokers, unlike other markets where dealers tend to specialise in only one of these functions.

The merchant is usually in business for himself and buys stocks with the intention of reselling them at a higher price, so that his income is determined both by the size of the margin and by the volume of business transacted. By contrast, agents usually act on behalf of a client for a fixed commission, and so may find it more profitable to achieve a high turnover than to withhold supplies until the price rises; similarly, they lack the merchant's incentive to buy at the lowest price. Brokers occupy an intermediate position between merchants and agents as they buy and sell both for clients and on their own behalf. Unlike merchants, however, they rarely take physical delivery or hold stocks.

In order to bring buyers and sellers into physical contact and facilitate the exchange of title to goods, it is usual to find a place specifically designated for this purpose. Usually the dealers who comprise the 'exchange' or 'market' draw up rules to regulate the transaction of business, and to exclude non-members from participation in its operation. Within the market transactions fall into two main categories – spot and future trading. Spot, or cash, transactions concern existing or readily available goods, on which immediate delivery can be effected, while the futures market is concerned with contracts for sale and delivery at some future, and usually specified, time.

In fact the futures contract is not a contract to buy or sell at all, but is an option to buy at an agreed price, at a stated time. From the buyer's point of view an option ensures the future availability of supplies at a fixed, maximum price. If, when the option matures, the market price is less than that negotiated, the option is not taken up, for the commodity can be obtained for less in the open market. Conversely, if the price in the market is higher, the option will be exercised and the seller will have to bear the loss. Naturally, the dealer's success depends on his being able to predict accurately the future level of supply, and setting a price which will be attractive to the potential purchaser while exposing the dealer to the minimum of risk. To achieve this the dealer must secure a continuous supply of accurate market data as the basis for forecasting future price levels. Although some dealing in futures is purely speculative, the majority of dealers depend on it for their livelihood and so base their forecasts on facts rather than hunches. In doing so they perform a valuable service, for they reduce uncertainty concerning both demand and supply in the markets in which they operate.

■ 'Consumer' crops

Although there is a fairly clear-cut distinction between crops which comprise the raw materials of industry and those which are consumed in their natural state, it is difficult to maintain the distinction if processing is used as the delineating factor. Nowadays the distinction would seem to rest on the necessity for processing as a prerequisite of consumption, rather than the existence or absence of processing. In the case of crops which are usually classified as 'industrial', the common denominator is the fact that they must undergo some physical change before they can be consumed. This change may be relatively minor, as is the case with flour milling, or extensive – if, say, one is converting wool into a suit of clothes. By contrast 'consumer' crops may be used immediately in their natural state but in advanced economies an increasing proportion are now processed in some way or other prior to consumption.

■ Factors underlying the growth of processing

The volume of agricultural output is ultimately determined by the length of the growing season. Assuming an adequate water supply, temperature is a critical variable. Plants will not grow at or below freezing, and make very little progress until the temperature rises above 40°F. Thereafter, the rate of growth doubles approximately for every 18° increase in temperature, so that the farther one moves away from the equator the shorter the length of the growing season. Thus, from early times, man has been preoccupied with methods of preserving and storing food for out-of-season use.

The slow growth of population until recent times is at least partly attributable to lack of success in balancing excess with famine. The growth of international trade partially alleviated the problem but had to await the development of the steam ship and refrigeration to make any real impact. Similarly, a revolution in farming techniques has greatly increased our ability to increase crop yields and prolong the growing season, but the problems of preservation and storage still exist, and command ever-increasing attention.

Refrigeration is expensive in terms of capital installation, and suffers from the same basic disadvantage as canning and similar methods of preservation – the majority of the good stored is water. Although dehydration eliminates this diseconomy, traditional methods tended to so change the nature of the food that they were largely unacceptable. The development of freeze drying overcame most of the problems associated with satisfactory reconstitution, but the expense was too great to justify general commercial usage. However, research sponsored by the Ministry of Agriculture came up with a method of speeding up the process, and Accelerated Freeze Drying (AFD) was born. The improved process is less costly and has been widely adopted e.g. Batchelor's Vesta range and Surprise peas, Nestles Gold Blend instant coffee, Cadbury's Smash.

Thus we now have a situation in which the consumer is able to buy highly perishable foodstuffs at any time of the year. Not only that, as methods of preservation have improved costs have fallen, and many 'processed' foods now possess distinct advantages over 'fresh' products. Two obvious advantages are the reduction in waste and the added convenience. Canned, frozen or AFD peas are invariably of uniform quality, which is not the case with peas bought in the pod, and require the minimum of preparation.

The advantages offered by processed foods have had a marked impact on purchasing patterns, and many items traditionally associated with the fresh produce market are now sold through dry-goods outlets, i.e. supermarkets and grocery shops, as distinct from greengrocers. Retailing forms the subject matter of a later section and will not be discussed here, but a brief description of the traditional channels is called for.

■ The distribution of fresh produce

Essentially, fresh produce reaches the ultimate consumer by one of the four channels illustrated in Figure 9.1.

The functions of broker, agent and producer exchange are identical with those discussed earlier in connection with the marketing of wheat. The term wholesaler is synonymous with merchant, and is increasingly preferred to the latter designation.

The most direct channel, producer – consumer, is usually only encountered on a limited and local scale, e.g. door-to-door sales or the stall in the local market, and most growers prefer to sell through conventional retail outlets. Sales direct to retailer fall into three categories:

1. The producer acts as his own wholesaler and establishes direct contact with local outlets.
2. The producer sets up his own retail outlets or, conversely, the retailer with a chain of outlets integrates backwards into production.
3. The producer sells under contract to large retailers, e.g. the major supermarket chains, Marks & Spencer, BHS etc.

Few growers are able to dispose of their total output in this way, however, and most sales are made initially to the wholesaler, either direct or through the medium of a broker or agent. Most urban centres of any consequence have wholesalers who specialise in breaking down bulk supplies into small quantities for resale to the multiple or small retailers in their area. These wholesalers obtain supplies direct on a local basis, but also buy in the central markets from brokers and other wholesalers, e.g. Covent Garden for fruit, vegetables and flowers, Smithfield for meat, Billingsgate for fish. There can be little doubt that the degree of control exercised by some of the central markets results in diseconomies of which the producer rightly disapproves. Despite the perishability of, say, lettuce, it is difficult to account for the services which increase their value from a farm-gate price of 30p per dozen to a shop price of 40p each. Such excesses go apparently unnoticed by comparison with the criticism levelled at the promotional expenditures of the manufacturer of branded goods.

In order to ensure an adequate supply of certain basic foodstuffs the Government has seen fit to provide incentives for farmers by guaranteeing payment of a minimum price for their output. There are several methods by which this may be achieved, but the most overt and controversial method is through the establishment of a marketing board.

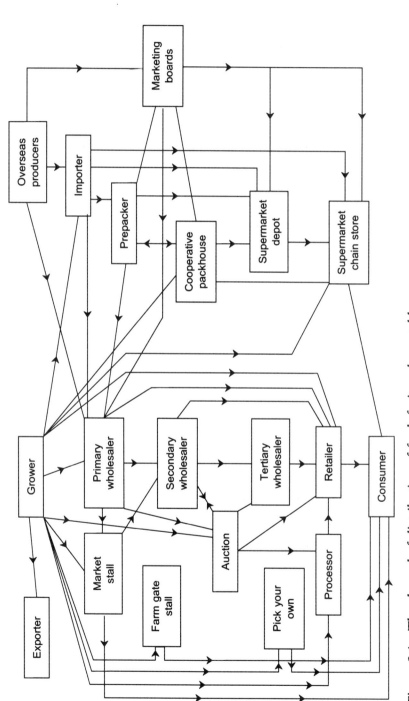

Figure 9.1 The channel of distribution of fresh fruit and vegetables

Source: Ministry of Agriculture, Fisheries and Food.

■ Agricultural marketing boards

The agricultural marketing boards operating in the United Kingdom at the present time were set up under the Agricultural Marketing Acts, 1931–58. The basic features which they have in common are:

(a) They are producer-controlled.
(b) They can only come into existence at the request of the majority of producers involved with the production of the commodity concerned, e.g. milk, hops.
(c) Their declared object is to secure the best possible return for their members.
(d) They are committed to improving quality, output, distribution and management within their own field of activity.

Space does not permit detailed consideration of the organisation and operation of the various boards, which may be obtained from their offices on request, but in view of the fact that the boards are run by producers for producers, some comment seems called for.

In essence the constitution of marketing boards results in the creation of producer-controlled monopolies and, while it is accepted that all monopolies are not necessarily harmful, they do create supply-controlled markets which are the antithesis of the marketing concept. Either the consumer must accept what the producer is prepared to offer, or he must do without. This is tolerable if there are acceptable substitutes for the monopolist's output, e.g. butter/margarine, or where the product is non-essential, but this is not the case with fresh milk, eggs, potatoes, etc.

The marketing boards pay a standard price to producers for equivalent grades of produce, irrespective of the fact that some are remote from the market and so are being subsidised by those in more economic locations. Similarly, consumers in rural areas tend to subsidise those in urban areas, particularly London, through the adoption of near-standard retail prices. It seems unlikely that maximum efficiency will be achieved so long as all farmers are treated alike and there is little incentive to concentrate on the production of those products which the consumer prefers.

At the time of writing the following agricultural marketing boards were still operating:

Milk Marketing Board (various)
Potato Marketing Board
British Wool Marketing Board

For information on these, readers should make direct contact, while for the latest information on EEC Regulations they should consult *A Report on Agricultural Marketing Schemes* (HMSO, 1978). (Students who seek a more detailed analysis of the operation of agricultural marketing boards are recommended to *Farming for Consumers*, by Graham Hallett and Gwyn James: Hobart Paper 22, Institute of Economic Affairs.)

■ The distribution of industrial goods

By contrast with the clearly defined patterns associated with the distribution of raw materials, it is difficult to generalise with regard to the channels of distribution associated with the three main categories of industrial goods – equipment, fabricated materials and supplies. Observation suggests that a number of different channels are used, and that selection is conditioned by a host of factors which are summarised in the following check-list:

■ Customer characteristics

Number of potential users.
Geographical distribution of potential users.
Frequency of purchase.
Average order size.
Distribution of users on the basis of consumption.
Relative importance of product to user, i.e. is the product an essential input from the user's point of view, or may its purchase be postponed or delayed?
Degree of user sophistication *vis-à-vis* product characteristics, i.e. does the user need technical service, if so, what type?
Credit standing.
Preferred purchasing pattern – a single preference is unlikely to emerge owing to variations in the above factors, e.g. need for after-sales service.
Degree of associated service requirements – both before and after sale.

■ Middleman characteristics

Market coverage.
Gross margin.
Proportion of salesmen's time available for selling product.
Degree of technical expertise.
Financial strength and stability.
Stock carrying capacity.
Servicing capability.
Number of substitute products carried.

■ Company characteristics

Size – both absolute, and relative to the industry/market of which it is a member.
Financial strength.
Industry position – leader or follower?
Spatial relationship between plant(s) and major users.
Degree of technical competence.
Degree of specialisation.
Breadth of product line.
Ability to provide desired services.

■ Environmental and competitive characteristics

The nature of seasonal, cyclical and secular trends in demand.
Degree of concentration in user industry(ies).
Nature and usage of existing distributive channels.
Extent and nature of legal restrictions and regulations.
The impact of taxation, e.g. on leasing.
Government procurement policy.
Consumer needs – in so far as the demand for industrial goods is derived from consumer demand shifts in the latter will have an impact on the former.

As will be seen in a later chapter, consideration of all these factors plays an important role in determining a firm's distribution policy and results in many diverse alternatives. On the other hand, it is possible to distinguish broadly similar channels operating across the whole field of industrial goods, which suggests that the most useful approach will be to identify the basic structures and illustrate them with actual examples.

■ Salient features of industrial marketing

Before proceeding to make such a review, however, it will be useful to state some of the salient features which differentiate the marketing of industrial and consumer goods implicit in the 'check-list' outlined above.

Although the basic marketing principles described in this book are felt to be equally applicable to the marketing of all types of goods and services, there are certain differences in degree that condition their relative importance. In the case of industrial goods these differences may be summarised as:

1. *Derived demand.* The demand for industrial goods, and raw materials, is derived from the demand for consumer goods in the sense that any expansion or contraction in the latter will be reflected by a corresponding shift in the former. The more distant the manufacturer is from the

production of a specific consumption good, the less direct will be the impact of a change in demand for that good.

2. *Rational buying motives dominate the industrial market.* This is frequently misinterpreted in one of two ways: (*a*) there is an absence of emotional motives in the industrial purchasing situation, or, (*b*) consumer purchasing behaviour is irrational. Neither of the above statements is correct: consumers are rational and industrial buyers are influenced by emotional factors, but there is a difference in degree, i.e. the industrial buyer will emphasise objective criteria to a greater degree than the average consumer.

3. *Concentration of buyers.* The number of potential buyers for an industrial good is generally far smaller than is the case with consumer goods. Further, industrial buyers tend to be concentrated geographically, e.g. the cotton and woollen industries. One must be careful not to overstate the importance of this distinction for, clearly, its validity depends upon the precise nature of the product. For example the market for office supplies is both large and dispersed, whereas the market for some consumer goods may be both small and concentrated, e.g. speciality goods produced on a purely local basis. It is also important to remember that although a national brand may have millions of users, the producer may concentrate his direct sales and distribution efforts upon a limited number of major buyers, e.g. wholesalers and grocery chains.

4. *The scale of industrial purchasing is greater.* In absolute money terms this is generally, but not always, true. In a proportionate sense, i.e. size of purchase, *vis-à-vis* disposable assets, the reverse may often be true.

5. *Industrial products are technically more complex.* Again this is true absolutely but not relatively. The purchaser of a car or television set is faced with a similar degree of technical complexity as the buyer of a computer – in both instances the buyer evaluates performance rather than construction, and is dependent upon the seller for both advice and service.

6. *Industrial buying is a group process.* The same might also be said of the household as a decision-making unit for consumer purchases. It is unlikely that the latter will have formalised evaluation and decision procedures, however, both of which are common in the industrial buying context.

7. *The role of service is greater.* Again this depends upon the nature of the product and the type of service. Immediate availability is a prerequisite for sale of a convenience good – this is rarely the case with even the most common of industrial goods – and consumer durables need after-sales service just as much as many industrial goods.

8. *Leasing, renting, and the extension of credit are important.* This is increasingly true of consumer goods.

From the comments made in respect of the 'distinguishing' factors it is clear that although industrial marketing may differ in degree, there are sufficient points of similarity to permit the transfer of principles and techniques from one to the other. As such, undue emphasis of differences may be harmful if it induces practitioners in either field to neglect thought and practice in the other. In particular, it will become apparent that marketing tactics are largely a function of product and market, irrespective of whether the specific product be designated 'consumer' or 'industrial', so that a given mix may be equally appropriate to products in either category.

■ Distributive channels

As noted earlier, distributive channels tend to cut across arbitrary product/ industry boundaries and attention here will be concentrated on major variations in structure.

Essentially, the same three basic alternatives are open to manufacturers of both industrial and consumer goods, namely:

1. Direct sale to user/consumer.
2. Indirect sale through the medium of a third party.
3. A combination of both direct and indirect sale.

Direct sale offers the greatest degree of control, but can be uneconomic where there is a large number of customers for the product in question. Under these circumstances some form of intermediary may be able to operate at a lower cost by combining the disparate, but complementary, outputs of several manufacturers for resale to small users of such products, e.g. building materials, office supplies. Distribution through an intermediary, or wholesaler, offers the manufacturer the opportunity to improve his overall profitability, albeit at the sacrifice of some measure of control, and so is frequently used to extend the coverage of the producer's own sales force.

Wholesalers vary considerably in terms of both the nature and extent of the services which they provide, and it is common to draw a broad distinction between 'full' and 'limited' service organisations. The full-service wholesaler usually employs his own sales force, holds stocks from which to make immediate delivery, provides information, advice and technical service, and is usually prepared to extend credit. As the name implies, limited-service wholesalers generally perform a restricted function, and often confine themselves solely to stockholding and delivery. In the latter case the manufacturer is responsible for stimulating demand and the provision of technical services.

For the most part manufacturers adopt some combination of both direct and indirect sale and, as will be seen in the chapter on channel policy, the precise mix will depend upon two basic criteria – cost and control.

■ The distribution of steel

Although the manufacturer of steel in the UK is largely concentrated in the hands of a monopoly, which limits competition between separate production facilities, it provides a good example of the need for a complex distributive structure.

Steel is frequently thought of as an essentially homogeneous product when, in reality, it is highly complex and produced in an enormous variety of shapes and to very different specifications, to meet widely disparate end-use requirements. For example mild steel sheet, used in the fabrication of consumer durables such as cars and washing machines, is very different from electrical steels used in transformers and generators, and from high carbon steels used in the machine-tool industry. To simplify matters discussion here will be confined to flat-rolled mild steel producers.

In order to meet specific end-use requirements, an order for flat-rolled mild steel may vary according to any one of the following factors:

Hot-rolled or cold-reduced
Quality/ductility
Quantity
Thickness
Sheet or coil
Width (and length in the case of sheets)
Coated or uncoated – if coated, type and thickness of coating and method of application of coating

From the user's point of view, each of these factors is highly important and will be specified precisely to meet his exact needs. From the producer's point of view, however, such variants create diseconomies as they interrupt the smooth flow of production and reduce the mill throughput. In turn, the diseconomies created by operating the mill at less than optimum efficiency to meet customer needs are reflected in the producer's price structure. However, beyond a certain point the diseconomies involved in meeting a precise specification become so great that the producer must refuse to accept less than a minimum order quantity (MOQ). The MOQ is determined by a number of complex factors which cannot be discussed here but, over the years, increasing automation has resulted in a gradual increase in the size of the minimum acceptable order. This increase has had little impact on the large-scale user, whose minimum requirements for a given specification are normally far in excess of the MOQ, but could have been a major threat to the user with a limited demand had it not been for the existence of steel wholesalers, or 'stockholders'.

Although some stockholders are subsidiaries of the steel producers, the majority are independent organisations. Given the enormous variety of steel products, all but the largest stockholders find it necessary to specialise in some category, e.g. tinplate, sheet and plate, structural steels, etc. In essence, the stockholder functions by anticipating the likely needs of small users, which he combines into an acceptable mill order, normally for a 'standard' size. In fact there are no 'standard' sizes, but certain combinations of width and length have been widely adopted as they offer the maximum benefits within the mills' price structure, and so reduce the scrap loss when cutting to the exact size required. To meet the precise size requirements specified by their customers, stockholders install shearing, slitting and shaping machines and, increasingly, are ordering in coil form, which permits them to cut to any length without loss.

In addition to breaking bulk to meet small users' requirements, the stockholder also helps to even out fluctuations in supply and demand. Steel-making is a complex, multi-stage process in which an order may be 'lost' at any stage of manufacture, necessitating a 'remake'. If an order is rejected at final inspection it can take three to four weeks to replace, assuming that it can be fitted into the mill schedule immediately. Further, production of an exact quantity is a virtual impossibility, so that most orders turn out less than, or in excess of, the specified amount. Steel buyers are familiar with the technological constraints involved in steel production and adjust their buying policies accordingly.

Where a specification is known to be difficult to produce, buyers maintain sufficient stocks to cover the possibility of late or partial deliveries. However, the maintenance of stocks ties up capital, and most buyers reduce their stock levels to the minimum consistent with normal deliveries in the knowledge that temporary shortages may be made good by buying from stockholders. From the producer's point of view the stockholder performs an equally valuable service in absorbing excess supply in the short term. In addition to buying excess production against mill orders that the customer is unprepared to accept, the stockholder provides an outlet for cancelled orders and reject materials which the mill would find it uneconomic to reclaim. Thus, through specialisation and local knowledge the stockholder performs a number of valuable functions for both producer and user, at a lower cost than would be possible if they performed these functions themselves.

Concentration ratios as a criterion (see Chapter 4 for an extended discussion of *industrial concentration*)

The factors which predispose the steel producer to adopt both a direct and indirect approach are typical of many industries with high concentration ratios. (The concentration ratio is an economic concept that is widely used in comparative industry analyses in preference to the less precise distinction between perfect and imperfect competition.) Concentration ratios take into account both the size and numbers of firms in a market, and are computed by summing the percentage of total sales accounted for by a given number of firms — thus a true monopoly would have a concentration ratio of 100 per cent, while a highly oligopolistic industry might be defined as one in which the four largest firms account for more than 50 per cent of total sales.

For the marketer faced with the decision of selling direct or through an intermediary, the concentration concept provides a useful rule of thumb when applied to purchases by users, as opposed to sales by producers. By ranking firms in terms of their consumption of the product concerned, it is relatively simple to arrive at a measure of concentration and decide whether direct sale is economically feasible and, if so, to what extent. Many analyses of this kind have revealed what has been termed the 'heavy half' phenomenon, i.e. 50 per cent of total purchases are accounted for by a small percentage of buyers.

As a generalisation, it is reasonable to state that the higher the concentration ratio the more direct sale is to be preferred, but this does not necessarily mean that the producer will attempt to make *all* sales direct. Consider, for example, the supplies of the motor-car assembly industry, where a small number of buyers account for a very high percentage of total demand. Irrespective of the producer's size, or the nature of his product, he will deal direct with Ford, Toyota, etc. Over time, however, the cars produced by these companies will require replacement parts, but it is unlikely that many components manufacturers will attempt to sell them to every garage and repair shop in the United Kingdom with an uncertain demand for such part. In consequence, the component manufacturer must decide whether to set up his own regional warehouses, to have distribution to the car manufacturer, or to use the services of motor accessory and parts wholesalers.

Similarly, the manufacturers of standardised parts such as bearings, industrial fasteners or electrical components, and the producers of general-purpose equipment such as bulldozers, fork-lift trucks or lathes will find that a high percentage of sales are accounted for by a limited number of customers. However, unless the producer has a very strong franchise with such major users and can depend upon them consistently to absorb his output, he cannot afford to ignore the multiplicity of small users that make up the balance of the market. The more numerous and geographically segregated the latter are, the less economic direct sale becomes, so that in markets with a very low degree of concentration the producer may well find it necessary to channel his total output through an intermediary. Many operating supplies produced by small, specialised producers fall into this category, e.g. stationery, hand tools, cleaning materials.

■ Manufacturers' agents

Although attention has been focused on wholesalers as a link between producer and user, many firms prefer to employ agents, either in addition to, or in place of, a sales force of their own.

From the manufacturer's viewpoint, the major advantage of employing agents is that he only pays commission on actual sales and so avoids the fixed costs associated with the maintenance of a sales force. Further, agents enter into a contractual agreement with their principal and so are subject to a greater degree of control than is usually possible when selling through an independent wholesaler.

Most agents handle a line of complementary but non-competing products, and operate within a clearly defined territory. The successful agent depends heavily upon his established contacts, and so offers the manufacturer a 'ready-made' salesman when introducing a new product or extending his geographical coverage. On the other hand, agents are not without disadvantage for, as noted when discussing the wheat market, the agent rarely has a complete identity of interest with his principal. This is particularly so when the agent is selling several different products, when he is likely to take the line of least resistance and sell what is in greatest demand, rather than devote his time to missionary selling, i.e. making cold calls to stimulate demand. Also, unlike wholesalers, the agent does not take delivery of goods, and the manufacturer must maintain and finance a larger inventory than would be necessary if he sold through a wholesaler. Hence, where there are seasonal fluctuations in demand, or the manufacturer is short of working capital, the wholesaler will usually be preferred to the agent.

From the foregoing description it is clear that there is frequently a conflict between the desire for the most economic method of distribution and management's wish to retain control over the marketing of the firm's output. This conflict will be examined in greater detail in Chapter 14, but attention now must be turned to the distribution of consumer goods, or retailing.

■ The distribution of consumer goods

As noted in the previous section, the demand for industrial goods is derived from the demand for consumer goods. Although this link may sometimes appear tenuous, it is clear that all other productive activities finally depend upon selling goods and services into ultimate consumption. Although several distributive options are open to the consumer-good manufacturer, almost all eventually involve a retail outlet of some type or other, and this section will be largely concerned with the function and operation of such outlets.

■ Retailing functions

Most dictionaries define retailing as 'the sale of goods in small quantities to ultimate consumers'. As such, the retail outlet constitutes the final link in the distributive chain, and is responsible for the performance of several important marketing functions, namely:

1. The physical movement and storage of goods.
2. The transfer of title to goods.
3. The provision of information concerning the nature and use of goods.
4. The standardisation, grading and final processing of goods.
5. The provision of ready availability.
6. The assumption of risk concerning the precise nature and extent of demand.
7. The financing of inventory and the extension of credit to consumers.

In many instances it is difficult to distinguish exactly where manufacturing ends and retailing begins, owing to the assumption of some of these functions by organisations that are not usually considered to be retailers or, conversely, by the assumption of functions by the retailer which are more often associated with manufacturers. Thus, in recent years there has been an increasing tendency for manufacturers to assume responsibility for the provision of information through extensive advertising and sales promotion campaigns, while many retailers have integrated backwards into wholesaling and even manufacturing activities. In the opinion of one authority, Professor W. G. McClelland (*Costs and Competition in Retailing*, Macmillan, London, 1966), the distinction must rest on the performance of those functions inherent in the very nature of retailing – the physical movement of goods and arrangement of transfer of title. To a lesser extent, functions (3), (4) and (5) in the above list also serve to distinguish retailing from other forms of manufacturing and distributive activity, and an examination of these five functions follows.

■ Physical movement and storage

As one would expect, there is an enormous variation in the cost of transporting and storing goods depending upon the method of transport used, the length and complexity of the journey, the amount of handling and protection required, etc. In the case of bulk cargoes for transport by sea, the cost may be as low as £0.01 per ton mile while, at the other extreme, door-to-door delivery of groceries may cost as much as £40 per ton mile. Clearly, the more homogeneous the cargo and the larger the bulk for delivery at one point, the lower the unit cost incurred. The potential savings inherent in such economies have led in recent years to the growth of larger retail units and the virtual elimination of door-to-door delivery.

Within the retail outlet, recognition of the high costs arising from counter service, both in terms of the duplication of effort in putting goods on display and then fetching them for customers on request, as well as the waste of valuable selling space, have led to widespread adoption of self-service. Competitive pressures, and the ever-growing variety of goods available for sale have also encouraged the retailer to keep the majority of his stock on display and to depend upon rapid delivery from central warehouses for replenishing his supplies. As a result there has been a strong trend towards the concentration of stocks at the wholesale level, leaving the retailer to stock only those goods for which he feels there is an immediate demand.

■ Transfer of ownership

When one considers the degree of concentration usually associated with the production of goods and the widely dispersed nature of the consumer market, it is clear that few manufacturers will be in the position to undertake direct sale. Thus the need arises for an intermediary to perform this function and effect a transfer of ownership.

In the case of shopping and specialty goods, e.g. Singer sewing machines, the customers may be prepared to make a special purchasing effort to seek out the nearest distribution point. However, in the case of many convenience goods brand loyalty tends to be low, and maximum distribution is essential to high volume sales. Like the steel stockholder, the retail outlet offers the manufacturer the opportunity to make contact with the consumer at an economic cost. By stocking a line of complementary products the retailer is able to spread the overheads involved in personal selling. Also, by catering to the separate demands of a large number of individual consumers, he is able to buy in economic quantities from the producer and still further reduce the costs of effecting a transfer of ownership.

From the consumer's point of view, retail outlets greatly facilitate the purchasing decision as they provide the opportunity to inspect and compare both the prices and quality of competing products. The location of retail outlets, and the nature of the goods in which they deal are readily ascertained, whereas the manufacturer's identity and location are not so easy to determine. Similarly, although many manufacturers publicise a recommended selling price, increased competition and the abolition of Resale Price Maintenance have resulted in a situation where the retailer is often the sole reliable source of this information on which so many buying decisions depend. Finally, the retailer often has to break bulk and the price, which represents the consideration given in exchange for ownership of the goods, cannot be determined until the consumer has specified the quantity which he wishes to purchase.

■ Ready availability

Depending upon the nature of the product, consumers are prepared to go to varying lengths to obtain goods to meet their specific needs. Given the number of competing products and outlets, both retailers and manufacturers are highly sensitive to this aspect of consumer behaviour, and adjust their stockholding policies accordingly to offer the desired level of availability.

By definition, a convenience good must be immediately available as the consumer is not prepared to wait to take delivery. From the retailer's point of view the problem is less critical than it is for the manufacturer, as he will usually stock several brands which are acceptable substitutes for one another. However, although convenience goods were defined earlier as those which the consumer buys frequently and with the minimum of effort, the ultimate distinction lies not in the product itself but in the consumer's perception of it, and what may be a convenience good for some may be a specialty good for others. Thus if the housewife is unable to find her preferred brand in one outlet she may well transfer all her custom to another where she can. In that the overall level of brand preference is reflected by the brand's share of the total market, most retailers will stock competing products in the same ratio to one another in the hope of maintaining store loyalty.

In the case of shopping goods, demand is neither so regular nor so predictable as is the case with convenience goods, and the retailer's stock policy, and ultimately his success are based on his judgement of the precise nature of consumer demand. Such decisions invariably create a conflict between the desire to offer a sufficiently wide selection to cater to variations in consumer preference, and the need to hold a sufficient stock of given products to meet the demand for them. A good example of this conflict, shared by both producer and retailer, is the demand for fashion goods in relation to the demand for more conservative styles. The demand for such fashion goods is frequently underestimated, and represents a lost profit opportunity of considerable dimensions. On the other hand, if the retailer overestimates likely demand he will incur additional inventory costs, and may have to sell at a loss to recover his working capital. Although such miscalculations ultimately have an effect on producers' sales, the majority of the risk is carried by the retailer.

■ The provision of information

Retailers supply information to both consumer and manufacturer. In the latter case, the most important information supplied by the retailer is the actual order which he places with the producer, in that it reflects future expectations concerning consumer demand by those in most direct contact with it. However, orders are subject to influence by the manufacturer's salesmen, and may represent wishful thinking rather than informed and objective opinion. Also, in the absence of information concerning stock levels, it is difficult to say whether orders are placed in anticipation of an upswing in demand, or merely to replenish stocks depleted by past demand. Even if the order does accurately reflect changing consumer preferences, it does not give the manufacturer an explanation as to the causes – to obtain such information the manufacturer will have to undertake research.

The provision of information to consumers varies considerably in terms of both amount and quality. Often the most meaningful information provided is the opportunity to examine competing products in close juxtaposition to one another. Price is a more concrete piece of information but, as the advent of the discount house has proved, it is frequently a measure of the retailer's efficiency rather than the value of the product.

Spoken information is still provided by retail sales assistants in many outlets, but consumers would seem to regard much of this information as emanating from a low credibility source, i.e. they place little reliance on its accuracy or objectivity. The adoption of this attitude is unsurprising in view of the low status and pay attached to retail selling in general, which is hardly conducive to the recruitment of highly motivated personnel. Hopefully, more retailers will follow the example of pioneers like Boots and Marks & Spencer in upgrading the quality of their employees through the provision of adequate training and incentives. As things stand at present, however, manufacturers are likely to fill the information gap by the continued use of advertising and sales promotion.

■ Processing

The increase of prepacked goods on display in retail outlets is an outward manifestation of the reduced importance of this traditional retailing function. In part this may, be attributed to consumer preference, but it is equally due to the manufacturer's desire to make his product identifiable at the point of sale.

In general, it is more economic to pack at the factory than at the point of sale, as the volume of output permits the use of the most productive machines. However, there are a number of important exceptions to this generalisation:

1. Some products may be transported more economically in a completely knocked-down state ('CKD') e.g. beds, wardrobes, bicycles.
2. Some commodities may be preserved more easily in bulk form, e.g. bacon, cheese.
3. In some cases the consumer's exact requirements can only be met by processing at the point of sale, e.g. 'three lamb chops', 'a pint of mild and bitter'.
4. Packaging can only occur after the customer is satisfied that the goods meet his requirements, e.g. clothing, fresh produce.

■ The structure of the retail trade

At a given point in time it is impossible to derive an exact measure of the size and structure of the retail trade in Britain owing to the rapid changes which are taking place. Major changes have taken place in retailing over the last two decades, and the remainder of this chapter will discuss the nature of these developments as well as outline changes in specific sectors – for example, the independent grocers and department stores.

Various social and environmental factors have affected the structure of the retail trade over the last two decades, affecting not only where goods are bought but also what is bought:

– more leisure time, longer holidays
– more working wives
– increased use of large shopping outlets
– less frequent shopping

These factors, among others, have resulted in the growth of convenience foods and frozen foods. The growth in the consumption of convenience foods has had a major impact on the structure of modern British retailing as it led to the emergence of the supermarket which has affected all forms of retailing.

Overall, the period since the Second World War has been one of increased affluence. Britain became a society with a high demand for consumer goods. By the late 1970s this pattern had begun to change, the demand for consumer durables had slowed down, and there was a small reaction against the increased use of convenience foods with a return to 'natural' foods. Competition between sectors of the retail trade became fiercer as consumers 'tightened their belts'. Some sectors of the retail trade have fared better than others under the competitive pressure. Table 9.1 and Table 9.2 compare the progress of large and small businesses, while Table 9.3 summarises the changes in the value and volume of retail sales from 1955 to 1987 and Table 9.4 summarises trade by retail sector for 1984 and 1986.

TABLE 9.1   Retail trade by type of retailer, 1984 and 1986

	Single outlet retailers 1984	1986	Small multiple retailers 1984	1986	Large multiple retailers 1984	1986	All retailers 1984	1986
Businesses number	218 700	217 050	27 399	26 331	832	904	246 931	244 285
Outlets number	218 700	217 050	70 235	66 765	60 793	60 144	349 728	343 959
Turnover (£bn)	24.9	27.9	10.4	11.9	47.5	56.5	82.8	96.4

Source: British Business, 18 March 1988.

TABLE 9.2   Percentage of retail turnover in businesses of various sizes

Businesses with:	1976	1980	1984
1 outlet	34	31	29
2–9 outlets	15	15	13
10–49	10	9	8
50–99	8	8	7
2–99	33	32	28
100–199	7	8	9
200–499	12	13	22
100–499	19	21	31
500 and over	14	17	11

Source: Retail Inquiries.

TABLE 9.3   Value and volume of retail sales (1980 = 100)(All retailers)

	Value	*Volume*
1955	12.4	61.7
1965	19.7	78.6
1975	50.8	93.5
1980	100.0	100.0
1981	108.2	100.2
1982	117.1	102.2
1983	127.6	107.1
1984	137.5	110.7
1985	149.5	115.3
1986	162.9	122.6
1987	–	129.6(est)

Source: CSO, 1987.

TABLE 9.4   Retail trade by sectors, 1984 and 1986

	Food retailers		*Drink/ confectionery and tobacco shops*		*Clothing/ footwear and leather goods shops*		*Household goods shops*		*Other non-food retailers*		*Mixed retail businesses*		*Hire and repair businesses*	
	1984	*1986*	*1984*	*1986*	*1984*	*1986*	*1984*	*1986*	*1984*	*1986*	*1984*	*1986*	*1984*	*1986*
Business number	81 680	77 301	43 226	44 379	32 000	32 711	42 916	42 785	38 617	39 395	5 644	4 853	2 848	2 861
Outlets number	105 953	100 171	56 499	56 858	58 552	58 874	60 104	60 839	50 858	51 357	11 231	10 077	6 531	5 783
Turnover (£bn)	30.9	34.8	8.5	10.0	7.6	9.2	12.1	14.7	6.9	8.2	15.6	18.2	1.1	1.3
Share of sales (%)	37.3	36.1	10.3	10.4	9.2	9.5	14.6	15.2	8.3	8.5	18.8	18.9	1.3	1.3

Source: British Business, 18 March 1988.

■ Types of retail outlet

For descriptive purposes, British retail outlets are usually grouped into three main categories:

1. Independent retailers, including small chain stores with nine or fewer branches.

2. Multiple retailers with ten or more branches, but excluding retail co-operative societies.
3. Retail co-operative societies.

The main retail outlets excluded from this classification are department stores, gas and electricity showrooms, and mail order houses.

Independent retailers have declined in recent years, both in shop numbers and in their share of retail trade. This decline is largely attributable to the aggressive price competition from supermarkets and discount houses. (See the later section on the independent grocery trade which gives a more detailed description of the decline of the independents.)

Multiple retailers have enjoyed a period of widespread expansion in the post-war period. The multiples' scale of operation enables them to employ functional specialists, to buy in bulk, and to use their extensive financial resources to acquire the best store locations. Multiple organisations may conveniently be subdivided into three groups:

(*a*) Food chain stores such as Tesco and Sainsbury.
(*b*) Variety chain stores such as British Home Stores, Littlewoods, Marks & Spencer and Woolworth.
(*c*) Speciality chain stores such as Boots, Burtons, Dolcis and Times furniture stores.

Co-operative retail societies are collectively the largest retailer in the United Kingdom but the Co-op has failed to exploit fully the economies of scale open to it and has consistently lost ground to multiple and independent alike over the past quarter of a century. Retail co-operative societies are voluntary, non-profit-making organisations which are controlled by committees elected by customers who are members of the society. In the opinion of many it is this factor more than any other which has slowed the growth of the movement by delaying the adoption of modern retailing techniques. As long ago as 1957, the Gaitskell Commission recommended that the Co-op should adopt a new management structure, in addition to the setting-up of more specialised shops and a reduction in the number of societies.

Department stores are another type of retail outlet which has been under increasing competitive pressure from supermarkets, multiples and superstores. Department stores are usually defined as establishments with 24 or more employees engaged in selling clothing, textiles and at least four other major commodity groups. Since 1980 department stores have been clasified as mixed retail businesses making it difficult to draw direct comparisons on performance before and after this date. Table 9.5 summarises the pattern of retail sales from 1980–88 by type of business. The number of department stores has stabilised at around 350, with new store openings matching closures. The large national store groups such as House of Fraser, Debenhams, John Lewis, have followed a policy of market repositioning hoping to attract a larger share of the 25 to 40 age group who tend to have the most disposable income. To pull this group away from the variety chain stores, these department stores have modernised and altered their emphasis to one of quality rather than price, improving store ambience and offering co-ordinated product ranges.

TABLE 9.5   Volume of retail sales, 1980–88. (Index numbers of sales per week (average 1985 prices) 1985 = 100)

				Non-food retailers		
			Mixed	Clothing		
Broad kind of	All	Food	retail	and	Household	Other
business	retailers	retailers	businesses*	footwear	goods	non-food
(Sales in 1985, £m)	(87 920)	(32 986)	(15 865)	(8 677)	(14 717)	(15 675)
1980	85.8	90.4	86.2	77	73	95
1981	85.9	91.0	86.5	75	74	94
1982	87.6	91.7	89.6	77	77	94
1983	92.0	94.8	93.3	85	86	95
1984	95.5	96.6	95.9	92	93	98
1985	100.0	100.0	100.0	100	100	100
1986	105.3	103.4	105.0	109	111	102
1987	111.5	107.4	111.8	119	121	107
1988	119.2	112.9	118.6	127	135	114

* Mixed retail business: Where less than 80 per cent of a business's sales, or 50 per cent in the case of food retailing, fall into the main broad kinds of business, the business is classified as a mixed retail business.

Source: Business Statistics Office, *Business Monitor* SDM28 Retail Sales (July 1989 edition, published by HMSO).

■ The 'wheel of retailing'

The 'wheel of retailing' is a major hypothesis concerning patterns of retail development. Advanced by Malcolm P. McNair, a professor at the Harvard Business School, the hypothesis holds that new types of retailers usually enter the market as low-status, low-margin, low-price operators, and gradually acquire more elaborate establishments and facilities involving increased investment and higher operating costs. Finally, they mature as high-cost, high-price outlets, vulnerable to new competitors, and the 'wheel' goes round again.

Although there are a number of exceptions which suggest that the hypothesis is not universally valid, the general pattern of British retail development conforms with it remarkably closely. As a result of wartime restrictions and controls between 1939 and 1952, the normal evolution of the retail trade was brought to a virtual standstill, but with the removal of restrictions, it would seem that it is now making every effort to make up for lost ground. In fact the scale of innovation and the changes in retail structure which have resulted are often referred to as the 'Retail Revolution'. Some of the major changes associated with this revolution are outlined below.

■ Major retailing innovations since 1950

Self-service. Although the first self-service shop in Britain was opened in 1942, the war-time restrictions referred to above delayed its development until these controls were removed: e.g., there were 10 outlets on self-service principles in 1947, less than 500 in 1950, 4000 in 1957 and nearly 9500 in 1961. There can be no doubt that self-service has been a major factor in improving the productivity of retail distribution, by increasing the utilisation of the available floor area, the carrying of stock on open shelves where it can be selected, rather than in a stockroom, and the reduction in personal service.

Self-service is particularly suited to the sale of branded convenience goods, and thus has had the greatest impact on the food sector, where it has led to the development of supermarkets. Supermarkets are defined as 'self-service shops with a minimum sales area of 2000 square feet and at least three check-outs'. Multiple traders such as Tesco and Sainsbury have been most aggressive in the development of supermarkets and have gradually expanded their product lines from foodstuffs and household requisites such as soap and cleaning materials to include hardware, paint, toiletries and cosmetics and selected soft goods. The supermarkets' scale of operation has permitted them to adopt aggressive pricing policies, and the 'battle of the high street' has forced the independent retailer and wholesaler to join forces to meet the threat through the formation of voluntary chains.

A further development in this area has been the growth of the superstore. The superstore was the natural extension of the supermarket concept. Grocery superstores are defined as stores selling a wide range of food items and other grocery products with at least 25000 square feet of selling space. In 1989 there were 578 superstores and this number can be expected to increase as superstores become more firmly established in the United Kingdom.

Voluntary chains. The growing success of the multiple outlet rests largely on the integration of both wholesaling and retailing activities. Independent wholesalers had long realised that the growing power of the multiples would place the independent retailer at a competitive disadvantage and that it was only a matter of time before this group, which comprised their chief customers, would seek to take collective action and set up their own wholesale co-operatives. To forestall such a possibility, the more astute wholesalers took the initiative and organised voluntary chains of independent retailers. Essentially, such chains are based on an agreement whereby the retailer agrees to place a minimum weekly order with the wholesaler; to submit orders by a specified time, often on specially designed forms; and to accept delivery at a prescribed time. In addition many chains, or symbol grocers as they are often called, agree to undertake co-operative advertising campaigns, to adopt a distinctive and uniform decor or 'house style', and to carry 'own brands'. In return for these promises, the wholesaler passes on economies in storage and transportation costs in the form of lower prices, organises joint promotional activities, advises on shop layout and management, and often lends capital for store modification and improvement. Spar, Mace, VG and Londis are examples of symbol voluntary groups in the grocery trade.

While voluntary chains are most active in food retailing they are also to be found in a generally less sophisticated form in other sectors: e.g., Unichem, Numark and Care serving the needs of chemists, Jen in the footwear trade, as well as a number of associations in the tobacco, confectionery and hardware trades. However, as the multiples continue to expand their share of the total retail trade one may anticipate further groupings developing among the independents.

The independent grocer. In the years 1971 to 1981 the number of independent grocery outlets almost halved, going from 86 000 to 47 000. This rate of decline was in line with that of all other outlets. However, for the multiples and co-operatives it was part of a policy of rationalisation, and for independents was the outcome of increased competitive pressure. The multiple groups have at least two advantages over the independents: first their buying power enables them to negotiate lower prices and subsequently to sell at lower prices than independents; second they have the advantage of economies of scale accruing to their large scale of operation. The independents' share of sales value and volume reflects this sector's growing difficulties. In the period 1971–81 there was a 38 per cent fall in volume, while the multiples recorded a 57 per cent increase in volume over the same period. The future does not look particularly bright for the independent grocers. In the face of continuing competition from multiples, the independents have had to move towards longer opening hours in order to survive.

Mail order. In the 1970s the mail order section of the retail trade experienced a period of rapid growth; the sales in 1979 showed an increase of 24 per cent on the previous year. Since then sales have continued to grow from £2335 million in 1980 to £3596 million in 1987 a growth of 54 per cent. However, the index of all retail sales grew by 76 per cent over the same period, indicating the sector is losing ground by comparison.

Mail-order houses fall into two basic categories – general and specialist. The latter usually concentrate on a single product group and are particularly active in the market for seeds, bulbs, plants and small horticultural items. At the other end of the scale, mail order is dominated by the general-line firms with sales well in excess of £700 million per annum, and including household names such as Littlewood's, Great Universal Stores, Grattan and Freemans. Nearly half the goods sold by mail order are clothing, and another quarter is accounted for by household goods.

Given the extensive network of retail outlets throughout the country, the growth of mail order appears at first sight to be an enigma. In fact, it reflects the marketing skills of the operators who have consistently pursued a policy of high quality, backed by a guarantee of satisfaction that is scrupulously honoured with none of the unpleasantry found in some retail establishments. Add to this the convenience of shopping in the comfort of one's home, and generous credit and repayment terms, and the combination becomes virtually irresistible.

Discount houses. The development of discount houses in Britain was delayed for some years, following their introduction in the United States, owing to the existence of Resale Price Maintenance. Since the abolition of this practice, however, they have become a growing force in the field of retailing.

In the simplest terms a discount house may be defined as a non-food supermarket, and operates on the same principle of low mark-up and rapid turnover. However, firms such as Kwiksave Discount and Asda have extended discounting principles into the food sector. In the first stage of their evolution they tend to concentrate on shopping goods and particularly on consumer durables with a high average margin, which permitted the discounter to offer savings of as much as 50 per cent on recommended retail prices – e.g. Comet, MFI. The second stage of their evolution has been marked by the turn of the 'wheel of retailing'. Discount houses have upgraded their image by improving the amenities and the range of goods and services offered. Recently there has been a move towards continental-type fresh food discount outlets which, with the renewed interest in 'natural' foods, will undoubtedly expand further.

Franchising. Franchising recently has been a growth sector of the UK economy. It is not a new type of business organisation as its origins can be traced back two hundred years to brewers' 'tied-public house' systems. The recent growth in franchising has been encouraged by the British Franchise Association formed in 1977. The Association offers guidance to prospective franchisees and has done much to stamp out malpractice in the business. In essence a franchise agreement allows an individual to set up in an established business by adopting the name and practices of its originator; e.g., Wimpy Bars have a more or less standardised layout and menu. The franchisee usually pays a lump sum to begin with and then pays a continuing royalty to the franchisor. Franchisors exercise varying degrees of control over the operation of franchisees, and provide varying levels of support which preclude generalisation. Given the attraction of running one's own business under the protective umbrella of a franchise offering specialised retailing skills and experience normally accessible only to the large organisation, it is perhaps not surprising that only a relatively small number of UK franchises fail each year. This high success rate is probably due to the great personal motivation of the franchisees and the guidance of the franchisor. Examples of franchise operations can be found in many areas of trade – British School of Motoring, Apollo Window Blinds, Dynorod, Prontaprint, Pronuptia and Youngs. The best-known franchise organisations are probably those in the catering and fast-food sectors – MacDonald's, Burgerking, Spud-U-Like, Holiday Inns, Kentucky Fried Chicken and Thorntons all come into this category.

Cash-and-carry wholesaling. Cash-and-carry wholesaling developed out of the independent wholesalers and retailers' desire to remain competitive with the multiple sector. As such it represented an alternative to the formation of voluntary chains which have already been referred to. While the setting-up of a voluntary chain resulted in formal relationship between retailer and wholesaler, cash-and-carry operations place no such restrictions on either party. As the volume of sales and the market share held by the independent grocers has fallen, cash-and-carry operators have been forced to look for new customers and for new, non-grocery lines. The catering trade has become the main cash-and-carry customer, taking over from the independent grocers.

■ Channels of distribution

In broad terms the same channels of distribution noted in respect of the manufacturer of industrial goods are also open to the consumer goods manufacturer, namely:

1. Direct to the ultimate consumer.
2. Direct to the retailer for resale to the ultimate consumer, i.e. the retail outlet is regarded as the customer.
3. Indirect sale through the medium of a wholesaler or agent.
4. A combination of any or all of these alternatives.

□ Direct sale to ultimate consumers

Direct sale to the consumer may be achieved by the manufacturer/seller of services in one of three ways:

1. Forward integration into retailing and the establishment of one's own outlets. (Usually it is the retailer who integrates backwards, however.)
2. Mail order selling.
3. Door-to-door selling.

The advantages and disadvantages of each of these alternatives may be summarised as:

1. *Own retail outlets*
Advantages:

(a) Complete control over the selling function: e.g., price setting, terms of trade, provisions of services, sales training, etc.
(b) Economies of scale in storage, transportation and administration.
(c) The ability to co-ordinate in-store promotion with advertising and other promotional activities.
(d) Closer contact with the consumers and therefore a better understanding of their needs and preferences.

Disadvantages:

(a) Limited access to the market.
(b) The assumption of all risks.

(c) The need for extensive financial resources to cover both fixed investment and working capital needs.

Examples: Boots, British Shoe Corporation, Burtons, Singer.

2. *Mail order*

Advantages:

(a) Complete control.
(b) Economies of scale.
(c) Access to the whole market, including areas with insufficient population to support conventional outlets.
(d) Consumer convenience.

Disadvantages:

(a) High delivery costs.
(b) High promotional costs.
(c) High costs of building and maintaining an up-to-date mailing list.
(d) Costs of financing credit sales.

Examples: Great Universal, John Moores, Grattan. (Note: although many of the general-line mail-order houses have their own production facilities a large part of their merchandise represents the output of other manufacturers.)

3. *Door-to-door*

Advantages:

(a) Complete control.
(b) Most effective method of selling certain goods and services where demonstration or complex explanation is necessary: e.g., vacuum cleaners, insurance policies.

Disadvantages:

(a) Unsolicited calls are viewed with suspicion.
(b) High cost – usually offset by paying low basic salary and high commission.
(c) Difficult to recruit and retain suitable salesmen owing to unattractive working conditions.

Examples: Avon Cosmetics, Kleen-Eze, Prudential Assurance, various publishing houses.

☐ Direct sale to retail outlets

In view of the high costs associated with direct sales to the consumer, most consumer-goods manufacturers prefer to sell through some form of independent retail outlet.

Given the number of retail outlets, direct sale might appear totally uneconomic at first sight. On reflection, however, it is clear that a very large percentage of sales are channelled through a very limited number of buying points and the manufacturer can gain direct access to the market through relatively few centralised purchasing agencies.

TABLE 9.6   **Concentration ratios in the UK retailing industry by broad commodity group**

	All Sales Amount (£ m)	The largest five enterprise groups accounted for:		The largest ten enterprise groups accounted for:	
		Amount (£ m)	%	Amount (£ m)	%
Food	29 080	10 070	34.6	13 805	47.5
Drink, confectionery and tobacco	14 067	2 762	19.6	4 269	30.3
Clothing, footwear and leather goods	16 568	6 080	36.7	8 101	48.9
Household goods	20 318	4 038	19.9	5 970	29.4
Other non-food goods	15 462	3 060	19.8	4 295	27.8
Hire and repair	1 681	1 094	65.1	1 164	69.2

As can be seen from Table 9.6 there is a high degree of concentration in several sectors of the UK retail trade. For example, in 1975 Nielsen estimated it was possible to gain access to 75 per cent of the grocery trade through 344 buying points. By 1980 275 buying points were estimated to control 82 per cent of all purchases but, to reach the remaining 18 per cent of the market one would have had to contact 39 000 additional buying points. The trend continues but whether such an operation is economically feasible requires consideration of the cost and control factors mentioned in the previous section and usually resolves itself into a policy decision on the relative merits of selective, versus extensive, distribution. If the latter is chosen, as it invariably is with mass consumption, widely advertised convenience goods, most manufacturers find it necessary to sell at least part of their output through an intermediary.

□ Selling through wholesalers

The advantages of selling through a wholesaler have already been examined when discussing the distribution of industrial goods, and will not be pursued further here. In general, manufacturers of consumer goods will find it appropriate to make use of the wholesaler's services under the following circumstances:

1. Where a large number of small, widely dispersed outlets account for a significant share of total sales.
2. Where the manufacturer has limited working capital and is unable to bear the costs of direct selling.
3. Where the manufacturer is new to the market and seeking to gain retail acceptance.
4. Where the manufacturer has an excess supply which could be sold under a wholesaler brand, or where he has no brand of his own.
5. Where demand is irregular and/or seasonal: e.g., fireworks!
6. Where trade custom has resulted in channel control becoming vested in the wholesaler.

■ Automated retailing systems

A recent report from ICL on *Retailing Tomorrow* opened with the following observations:

> The implications of computer-based systems in the retailing industry are enormous and far-reaching. And they are impacting on every part of the industry – retailers themselves, manufacturers, wholesalers and ultimately consumers too.
>
> In new research and statistical analysis published for the first time here in *Retailing Tomorrow* it is clear that the long-awaited technology revolution in retailing is, at last, happening. Hard evidence shows a massive upsurge in demand from UK retailers for automated systems.

In this section we will examine the benefits associated with automated retailing systems and the forces which are accelerating its take-up and use through the retail sector.

While retailers were among the first organisations to make use of large mainframe computers for central administrative functions, the use of information technology (IT) in individual stores was delayed awaiting necessary developments in both hardware and software. Among these developments may be numbered:

1. Increased standardisation of computer communications.
2. The development of British Telecom's Packet Switched System (PSS) and its X-stream networks enabling easier and more cost-effective transmission of computer signals around the country.
3. The introduction of standardised code-marking (bar coding).
4. The growth of inter-company communications enabling different computer systems to link into one another.

As a consequence of these developments the number of EPOS terminals in retail outlets has grown rapidly as can be seen from Figure 9.2 and Table 9.7.

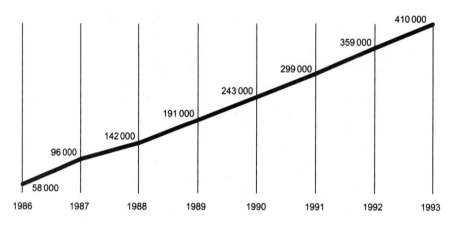

Figure 9.2   Growth in EPOS market, 1986–93 by number of units installed

Penetration of EPOS equipment in the UK retail sector as a whole will be spectacular with large and medium-sized retail organisations accounting for the bulk of this growth. Additionally, spending on equipment in the early 1990s will be supplemented by a growing level of investment in replacement systems.

Source: ICL estimates.

TABLE 9.7   Penetration of EPOS terminals by retail line of trade

	1984 (%)	1985 (%)	1986 (%)	1987 (%)	1988 (%)	1989 (%)	1990 (%)
Beer/wine/spirits	15.0	18.0	23.0	30.0	39.0	49.0	57.0
Chemists	1.0	2.0	3.0	6.0	13.0	22.0	33.0
Clothing	5.0	9.0	16.0	25.0	36.0	50.0	65.0
Department stores	47.0	50.0	57.0	65.0	75.0	83.0	88.0
DIY/Home improvement	2.5	12.0	24.0	37.0	51.0	65.0	80.0
Electrical	25.0	30.0	36.0	42.0	51.0	58.0	64.0
Speciality food	3.0	6.0	9.0	13.0	17.0	21.0	27.0
Footwear	2.0	5.0	13.0	22.0	31.0	40.0	50.0
Furniture	4.0	6.0	9.0	13.0	18.0	23.0	30.0
Supermarkets	1.7	4.5	13.0	25.0	39.0	55.0	70.0
Housewares	2.0	10.0	20.0	30.0	37.0	45.0	52.0
Jewellers	15.0	40.0	50.0	60.0	70.0	78.0	85.0
Leisure	20.0	22.0	25.0	29.0	34.0	40.0	47.0
Newsagents	1.0	2.0	5.0	11.0	19.0	27.0	36.0
Variety	10.0	13.0	16.0	20.0	26.0	34.0	46.0
Pubs and restaurants	1.0	2.5	8.0	17.0	28.0	39.0	50.0
Fast food	15.0	21.0	29.0	39.0	51.0	63.0	71.0
Petrol	2.0	6.0	12.0	19.0	29.0	40.0	50.0

Source: ICL estimates. The retail categorisations in the above statistics are based on the line of trade of major UK retail organisations and not on their respective operating philosophies.

The benefits accruing from automated retailing systems may be usefully characterised as 'hard' and 'soft'. Perhaps the most important hard benefit arises from improved stock control and management which allows for lower operating stocks with a better range on display and a greatly reduced need for mark-downs or discounting to shift slow-moving stock. ICL estimate that in the hospitality industry more accurate information can pay for an in-store system within fifteen months and quote the case of a DIY retailer which was able to cut its stock by 40 per cent without affecting the level of business. In food multiples the use of scanning equipment and EPOS terminals has resulted in greatly improved productivity with a reduction of 19 per cent in checkout labour hours for the same level of business. Checkout operators are able to handle around 25 items a minute which is a 66 per cent improvement compared with a conventional cast register/cash desk operation. Significant savings in labelling, pricing and shelf-filling have also been achieved together with savings in administrative costs due to more accurate reporting.

Another source of hard benefits has been increased cashpoint efficiency with few price identification and price ringing mistakes. Attitudes to these benefits are summarised in Table 9.8.

TABLE 9.8   Benefits of EPOS

Key	Very important			Very unimportant	
	5	4	3	2	1
Base: Benefits of introducing EPOS, where 5 = very important and 1 = very unimportant.					
Better stock control	48	28	13	6	4
Improving store level information	39	33	13	9	5
Exercising central management control	23	42	18	13	4
Better staff productivity and planning	14	26	32	20	8
Less stock shrinkage	17	28	30	14	11
Improving promotional planning	7	28	30	24	10
More effective display and store layout	2	19	33	24	22

Note: Numbers are *row* percentages, ie number in sample selecting each option.

Source: Research Solutions for ICL, UK Ltd.

On the soft benefit side the major gains arise from more and better information on which to make marketing and management decision. Automated systems also free staff time so they can give more attention to serving customers and thereby enhance perceived service levels. Customers also appreciate the benefits of fewer stock outs and the provision of more information regarding their purchases. Figure 9.3 is an example of a till receipt issued by a B & Q Supercentre which illustrates the kind of detail available.

Figure 9.3   Example till receipt

■ Teleshopping

In a paper 'Teleshopping: Just Around the Corner?' (*RSA Journal*, February 1990) Ian Miles examines the reasons underlying the optimistic expectation that teleshopping is just about to take off and its disappointing development in the UK in recent years. Miles points out that:

> Teleshopping is one of a number of new *transactional services*, such as telebanking (where money is transferred electronically) and telebooking (the ability to reserve, for example, train and theatre seats remotely). These go beyond other new services which make use of computer and telecommunications technology (these are often called *new telematics services*), such as *information services* which allow for mail, conversations, multi-user games.

However, compared with these other kinds of services teleshopping calls for a more significant change in user behaviour and possesses a number of disadvantages which are less off-putting in fields such as telematics. Table 9.9 summarises these drawbacks to teleshopping (in italics) but also suggests ways of overcoming these barriers.

Although the means of overcoming barriers to the more rapid adoption and diffusion of teleshopping may be identified it seems unlikely that they will be rapidly overcome. Given that shopping is also a social experience which provides a change from the everyday surroundings of the home it would seem reasonable

TABLE 9.9   Overcoming barriers to teleshopping

Overcoming hardware barriers
- Limited text on screen, eyestrain problems: better screens (high resolution, flat screens);
- *Lack of portability of screen and keyboard*: smaller systems, mobile communications, multiple phone sockets/data networks in homes.

Overcoming software/information barriers
- Non-user-friendly interfaces: improved interfaces, using for example 'mice', trackerballs, remote controllers;
- *Cumbersome menu systems*: simulated shopping environments, personalised 'shopping lists', natural language systems;
- *Inferior graphic quality*: photovideotex, video quality images delivered via various media: cable TV, ISDN telephony, 'downloaded' catalogues broadcast on TV and stored on videorecorders, interactive compact disc, satellite broadcasts, etc.

Overcoming social and system barriers
- Limited diffusion of hardware, software and telematics: development of wide range of consumer information technologies (home informatics);
- *Limited choice of services*: expanded range of services as critical mass of users established, and as more retailers use computerised stockholding, ordering and transactional systems, electronic funds transfer, etc.;
- *Problems with delivery schedules*: social innovations, facilitated as economies of scale in delivery possible; flexible delivery times and schedules, neighbourhood deposit centres (e.g. post offices), and household deposit centres (refrigerated post boxes, new types of doors?).

to predict that teleshopping will provide only one of many options and is unlikely to displace in-store shopping in the foreseeable future.

■ Future trends in grocery retailing

In the field of retailing, be it for groceries or financial services, it has long been recognised that convenience and accessibility have had a major influence on consumers' patronage decisions. Accordingly, past decades have seen retailers of all kinds seeking to maximise territory coverage by opening more and more outlets. While this trend is likely to continue in some of the new growth areas it seems much less likely in the field of food retailing where a stable population and static per capita food consumption point to the inevitability of saturation in this market. The consequences of such saturation were the subject of an article by Robert Duke in the *Journal of Marketing Management*, vol. 7.1, 1991 ('Post-Saturation Competition in UK Grocery Retailing').

To address the problems of saturation in grocery retailing, particularly between the 'Big Five' of Sainsbury, Tesco, Asda, Argyll and Gateway, Duke proposes the use of a strategic marketing tool called *market leakage analysis* (MLA). MLA is a technique which divides the market into two parts – the company's share of the market and the *leaked* market which the company could serve but currently does not. Figure 9.4 depicts the basis for market leakage analysis and suggests that this can arise from three main causes. In Category A the company does not have a product or service which matches precisely the needs of the consumers comprising this segment. In Category B are potential customers which the firm has been unable to reach due to deficiencies in its marketing communications or distribution strategies. Finally, Category C contains those users which the firm has tried to win and failed. Clearly, each category calls for a rather different strategy.

It seems reasonable to assume that if the market is saturated then there is no potential competitive advantage in Category B as opening still more outlets can

Figure 9.4   Market leakage analysis

Source: Ohmae (1982).

only lead to diminishing returns and reduced margins. It follows that opportunities for the future will be concentrated in Categories A and C – extending the product/service mix to match consumer needs better and intensifying one's competitive effort. While such competition has always existed it can only become more acute and focused with the elimination of new outlets as the major source of advantage.

Duke argues that few if any major retailers will wish to attempt a direct frontal assault by opening a new outlet next door to a competitor which suggests that flanking manoeuvres will be the preferred strategy. In the past geographic flanking attacks have predominated, i.e. find a location with a catchment area with little direct competition, but saturation has closed off this option leaving the 'low price flank', used by Kwik Save and Asda, and defensible differentiation as the basic alternatives. The question is, of course, what will constitute the sustainable competitive advantage which will enable a firm to pursue a differentiation strategy? As Duke points out 'innovative offers in pursuit of differential advantage (price leadership, superstores, own-label, high quality, health, green and so on) . . . are hard to keep secret and easy to copy, and so, such a *defensible* advantage has largely eluded everyone'. However, Duke goes on to suggest that as resources will not be required for massive store opening programmes so it will be possible divert some of this investment to other purposes, and proposes two general approaches. The first of these is to open new kinds of outlet in a different mould to the existing superstore and the second involves improving the offer made to customers through existing outlets.

In the latter category an opportunity clearly exists in the fifth P of marketing – people. Price competition inevitably led to a reduction in service and staffing levels and the perception of retailing as a poorly paid, low status dead-end occupation. But, as Marks & Spencer, Boots and many others have demonstrated, a well trained, motivated and rewarded workforce plays a major role in developing perceptions of quality and service in the customer's mind.

A second source of defensible competitive advantage is to be found in the adoption and use of new technology such as that available through electronic point of sale (EPOS) systems. While the technology is available to all (at a price) the competitive advantage will lie in the quality of management's interpretation of the data which such systems can generate, particularly in fine tuning the product mix and in their stocking and ordering decision. In addition, the more effective managers will see technology not just as a means of increasing operating efficiency but as an opportunity to redeploy staff into customer support activities.

In the case of new kinds of outlet the experience of the 1980s indicates that while the benefits of one-stop shopping in large, well stocked superstores with good parking facilities were appreciated there was also a need for the traditional corner-shop type of operation with long opening hours, stocks of fresh foods and other basic items needed to top-up the weekly shop, and easily accessible without making a major expedition. Convenience outlets – or C-stores are they are now known – have emerged as a major market niche. While the superstores were content to let the develop unchallenged as they concentrated on their expansion of major outlets it would be surprising, now this phase is almost finished, if they did not turn their attention to this sector in the near future. Given that about 80 per cent of a store's operating cost is the cost of goods sold it is clear that the size and scale of the Big Five will give them an almost irresistible advantage if they move into the C-store market.

Taken together Duke sees these possibilities as offering a strategic choice grid as illustrated in Figure 9.5.

Figure 9.5   Grocery multiples' strategic choice grid.

Source: Duke, *Journal of Marketing Management*, vol. 7.1, 1991.

An invaluable source of information on retailing is the Economic Intelligence Unit's publication *Retail Business*. Other recommended publications are *Retail and Distribution Management, Nielsen Researcher, Group Grocer, Business Monitor, Annual Abstract of Statistics* and the numerous Keynote and Mintel Reports. Perhaps the best source of statistics on all aspects of marketing is the *Marketing Pocket Book* and related titles published by NTC Publications Limited (22–24 Bell Street, Henley-on-Thames, Oxfordshire RG9 2BG).

Part III
THE MARKETING MIX

CHAPTER 10

Marketing research*

___ Learning Goals ___

The issues to be addressed in this chapter include:

1. The nature and scope of marketing research.
2. Organising for marketing research.
3. The planning and execution of research.
4. Forms and sources of data, their collection and use.
5. The analysis and presentation of data.
6. The role of marketing research agencies.

After reading this chapter you will be able to:

1. Define marketing research.
2. Explain the scope of marketing research.
3. Discuss the issues involved in the decision to establish a market research department and the role and function of the market research manager.
4. Clarify the distinction between primary and secondary data.
5. Summarise the nature of desk research and list some major sources of external data.
6. Describe the nature of field research and the collection of primary data.
7. Explain the survey methods available to a researcher and the differences between censuses and surveys.
8. Define the nature of sampling and review the types of sample in common use.
9. Illustrate the various methods of making contact with respondents.
10. Review some of the issues involved in the design and use of question-naires.
11. List the kinds and properties of attitude scales and their use in market-ing.
12. Set out the preferred structure and format of market research reports.
13. Describe the role of marketing research agencies and give examples of syndicated research data.

---

* Readers wishing an extended treatment of this subject are referred to *Research for Marketing* (Macmillan, 1990).

It is not without significance that this chapter is entitled 'Marketing Research' as opposed to the more familiar title 'Market Research', although some might consider it pedantic that a distinction be drawn between the two. It is reasonable to say that most of the published literature on market research is, in fact, concerned with marketing research in that it deals with the question of research in relation to marketing on a much broader front than is implied by the former description. By definition, market research is concerned with measurement and analysis of markets, whereas marketing research is concerned with all those factors which impinge upon the marketing of goods and services, and so includes the study of advertising effectiveness, distributive channels, competitive products and marketing policies and the whole field of consumer behaviour.

■ Definitions

In his *Principles of Management* (second edition), E. F. L. Brech defines market research as 'the study of all problems relating to the transfer of goods and services from producer to consumer with the aim of producing practical answers consistent with accepted theoretical principles'. At a later point the objective of undertaking research is stated as 'to reduce the areas of uncertainty surrounding business decisions'. Both these definitions indicate a function of much greater scope than is inherent in the more limited concept of the market and analysis of it.

The British Institute of Management has adopted a slightly modified version of the original definition (now superseded) of the American Marketing Association, namely: The objective gathering, recording and analysing of all facts about problems relating to the transfer and sale of goods and services from producer to consumer or user.

The last word in this definition is important for it emphasises that marketing research is equally concerned with industrial goods – a point which is frequently overlooked in definitions which refer solely to consumers, as the latter are usually interpreted as 'ultimate' consumers.

■ The scope of marketing research

Explicit in the introduction to this chapter is recognition of the fact that marketing research is concerned with the scientific investigation of *all* factors which impinge upon the marketing of goods and services. It follows, therefore, that the scope of this function is virtually limitless, and discussion here will have to be confined to those types of research most frequently undertaken in practice.

Essentially, marketing research seeks to provide answers to five basic questions: Who? What? When? Where? and How? The associated question Why? extends inquiry into the area of socio-psychology and is sometimes distinguished as a separate field known as motivation research. (Unfortunately, this title has developed certain undesirable connotations due to the dubious activities of some practitioners.) In practice, marketing research is usually concentrated on a limited number of recurrent problems, often on a continuous basis, which may be classified as follows:

Market research
The size and nature of the market in terms of the age, sex, income, occupation and social status of consumers.
The geographical location of potential consumers.
The market shares of major competitors, i.e. brand share analysis.
The structure, composition and organisation of distributive channels serving the market.
The nature of economic and other environmental trends affecting the structure of the market.

Sales research
Determination of territorial variations in sales yield.
The establishment and revision of sales territories.
Sales call planning.
Measurement of the effectiveness of salesmen.
Evaluation of sales methods and incentives.
Cost-benefit analysis of physical distribution systems.
Retail audits.

Product research
Analysis of the competitive strengths and weaknesses of existing products, i.e. both one's own and one's competitors'.
Investigation of new uses for existing products.
Product concept testing.
Product testing.
Packaging research.
Variety reduction.

Advertising research
Copy research.
Media research.
Measurement of advertising effectiveness.

Business economics
Input – Output analysis.
Short- and long-range forecasting, i.e. based on trend analysis.
Price and profit analysis.

Export marketing research
Any or all of the above where relevant.

Motivation research

This check-list is by no means comprehensive but serves as an outline of the possible scope of research activities. Although research in most of the above areas is concerned with the recording of fact, qualitative research into the nature of attitudes and opinions is also appropriate in a number of instances, e.g. product concept testing.

■ Organising for marketing research

In view of the frequent references to the increasingly competitive nature of the business environment one might expect that the majority of firms would have a marketing research department – in fact, remarkably few do. Recent data are hard to come by but a survey by the BIM in 1966 achieved only a 40 per cent response from the 265 companies contacted – presumably because the majority had no research department as such. However, it would be erroneous to assume that this implies a correspondingly low usage of research findings, as a large part of marketing research is carried out by specialist organisations. It is also true that many companies have departments which are performing a marketing research function although identified by some other title such as Economic Intelligence. The more recent BIM survey, *Marketing Organisation in British Industry* (1970), would seem to confirm this view in that it indicated that 74 per cent of the respondents undertake marketing research but only 38 per cent of the respondents have appointed somebody full time to this activity. However the most up-to-date findings, which relate to research undertaken during the 1970s and 1980s, would suggest that comparatively few firms have their own marketing research function or indeed make use of any formal marketing research. In *Marketing and Competitive Success* (Philip Allan, 1989) Baker and Hart comment as follows:

> Throughout the seventies market research was frequently associated with higher export performance (ITI Research, 1979, British Institute of Management (BIM), 1975 and Rollason, 1971). Such findings were confirmed in a recent study carried out by Baker and Abou-Zeid (1982), where 86 per cent of companies with a Queen's Award for export achievement carried out export market research. The most popular method of conducting market research was to use salesmen, while agents and government sources were less popular means of providing information. The major use to which the information was put was in selecting the foreign markets, while other uses were providing market information and identifying the required adaptation to suit the needs of these markets.
>
> Cross-national comparisons have also highlighted the importance of market research to competitive success. For example, Connell (1979) describes how innovation in Japanese firms is typically initiated by sales and marketing personnel in the light of identified customer needs. This, along with other factors which emphasise customer interaction and interdepartmental cooperation in product development, distinguished Japanese firms from British firms.
>
> Recent empirical work in the UK also lends weight to the argument that market research plays an important role in successful companies' marketing operations. Takeuchi and Quelch (1983) quote examples of successful companies who constantly monitor product quality from the buyers' point of view. The market research tactics involved include:

- conducting customer satisfaction surveys;
- tracking and recording all complaints and problems;
- having a questionnaire completed by all customers returning goods;
- carrying out extensive field tests on new products;
- analysing warranty claims;
- assessing the condition of goods received by administering a questionnaire.

Alexander (1985) shows that the use of qualitative market research by three companies (studied by her in some depth) generated information which was used to move beyond existing product concepts and to translate market requirements into innovative, successful designs. In the study by Walsh and Roy (1983), into the practices and policies of winners of the Design Council Awards, all award-winning companies paid attention to market research, and many ideas for new market opportunities, as well as design evaluation, came from market or customer research. Finally, Hooley and Lynch (1985) report that successful companies made much greater use of all types of market research than did less successful ones. Table 10.1 summarises the types of market research used by both High-fliers and Also-rans.

TABLE 10.1 Frequent use of market research techniques

	Sample	High-fliers	Also-rans	Significance
Sample size	1 504	175	1 329	'T'
Customer surveys	26.9%	33.7%	26.0%	0.05
Qualitative research	24.7%	30.9%	23.9%	0.0
Field experiments	18.5%	26.9%	17.4%	0.0
Laboratory experiments	12.4%	20.6%	11.3%	0.001

Source: Hooley and Lynch, 'Marketing lessons from UK's high-flying companies', *Journal of Marketing Management*, vol. 1, no. 1, Summer 1985.

It is logical to hypothesise, in view of the above information, that market research has a positive influence on company performance. Given the dictate of the marketing concept – that the customer is the focus of the company – it is axiomatic that market research be included in the company's operations.

However, investigation of the existence and effectiveness of market research has been called into some question. Criticism by Ames (1970), Wilson (1984) and King (1985), among others, has emphasised that counting the number of heads in marketing research departments, or estimating market research budgets, focuses on the 'trappings' of marketing, not its 'substance'. Small low-budget research teams may be as effective in gaining an understanding of customers' needs, wants and perceptions as a larger organisation.

Based upon their survey Baker and Hart found for that above-average companies made significantly greater use of market research than below-average companies as shown in Table 10.2.

TABLE 10.2   Market research in above-average and below-average companies

Research type	Above-average companies (%)	Below-average companies (%)	Variation (%)
In-house	52	31	+68
External	69	47	+47

Note: Significant at the 5 per cent level.

Some indication of the magnitude of expenditure on marketing research is provided by Table 10.3 which also contains data on users of market research and number of research agencies.

TABLE 10.3   Expenditure on market research

(i) Value of GB commissioned market research	1983 £m	1984 £m	1985 £m	1986 £m	1987 £m	1988 £m
AMSO members' turnover	96	117	136	152	177	207
Other MR companies' turnover	44	51	50	52	61	70
Total	140	168	186	204	238	277

(ii) *AMSO members' source of income by client's business*

	1981 (%)	1988 (%)
Food, soft drinks	22	16
Health & beauty aids	7	7
Alcoholic drinks	8	6
Tobacco	5	2
Other consumer products	8	6
Total consumer products	50	37
Media	5	10
Public services	2	6
Vehicles, durables	5	8
Financial services	2	6
Advertising agencies	5	6
Pharmaceutical	5	6
Retailers	3	4
Government	6	4
Industrial products/services	2	4
Tourism, travel	2	3
Other	13	6
Total services and other sectors	50	63
Total	100	100

(iii) *Nature of AMSO members' fieldwork in 1988*

	Volume	Value £207m
	Interviews (%)	(%)
Face-to-face interview	57	64
Telephone interview	25	16
Group discussion	1	11
Postal	16	9
Total	100	100

(iv) *Nature of AMSO members' research in 1988*

	Value £207m (%)
Consumer research	
quantitative	68
qualitative	6
Total consumer research	74
Other respondent groups	26
Total	100

Source: Association of Market Survey Organisations, 1989.

The decision to set up one's own marketing research department clearly depends upon an evaluation of its potential contribution to the firm's overall operation. Such an evaluation is essentially qualitative, and will vary from firm to firm, precluding the statement of hard-and-fast rules. For our purpose it will suffice if it is assumed a decision has been made to establish such a department and attention concentrated on the factors which must be taken into account. These may be summarised as:

1. The role and function of the department.
2. Its position within the organisation structure.
3. The role and function of the department manager.

■ Role and function of the department

From the check-list covering the scope of marketing research it is apparent that a very large department would be necessary to cover all the areas mentioned. If a firm is undertaking research for the first time it would be well advised to draw up a list of priorities and content itself with attempting to achieve only the more important in the first instance. This does not mean that all other research must be discouraged absolutely, as too rigid lines of demarcation can only lead to an inflexible approach and the neglect of lines of inquiry complementary to the main purpose of the research.

All too often firms make the mistake of handing over responsibility for the maintenance of routine records to the newly formed marketing research department. The transfer of such records invariably creates both friction and inefficiency – it hinders the operation of the department which depends upon such records for its routine operation, e.g. sales, and diverts the marketing research department from its main function – research. In that much routine work involved in the compilation and maintenance of records will have preceded the setting up of a specialist research department it is best if the various divisions retain this function, making the data available as and when required. In order to avoid both duplication and fragmentation of effort, each department's responsibility should be clearly stated, and only those returns essential to the marketing research department's internal research efforts should be submitted. That said, the creation of computerised information systems greatly enhances the free flow of information within an organisation and offers the market research department almost instant access to all stored data relevant to its function.

■ Organisational positioning

The positioning of the marketing research department within the organisation depends very largely on the existing structure. As a generalisation, the department should have direct access to the managing director, as it is performing a staff function and, in many instances, is providing the chief executive with the raw material upon which policy, as opposed to operating decisions, will be made. In the larger organisation, with executive directors in functional appointments, the marketing director may well be delegated responsibility for directing the efforts of the research department and deciding which reports should be submitted to the chief executive. Even so there is a strong case for a 'dotted line' relationship between the managing director and the department to ensure that reports that are critical of a particular aspect of the firm's activities are given a hearing, and to avoid straining relationships between the marketing and other functional directors. Further, the managing director is concerned with the overall effectiveness of the firm and so is in a better position to see the implications of research findings without becoming subjectively involved with the possible effect on an individual department.

Some writers recommend that the manager of the marketing research department should be of equivalent status to the managers of the major operating divisions, but it is felt that this is unrealistic in view of the discrepancy in size and responsibility that usually exists. Provided the manager has access to the board of directors his status should be directly related to the importance accorded the department within the organisation as a whole.

∎ The role and function of the marketing research manager

The job specification of the marketing research manager will vary, depending upon the size and function of the department and the degree of external control and direction. In all cases, however, the manager must be technically competent and possess personal integrity. Technical competence includes not only experience and skill in marketing and analytical techniques but also the ability to translate management problems into viable research projects capable of implementation within the constraints imposed by time, and the available budget.

Personal integrity requires that the marketing research manager interpret findings objectively in accordance with generally accepted principles of scientific inquiry. 'Lies, damned lies and statistics' can only enjoy currency so long as the unscrupulous use 'facts' to support preconceived conclusions by judicious selection, manipulation and presentation – 'massaging the data', in research jargon.

In addition to these essential requirements the manager should also possess those skills common to all managerial positions – administrative ability, an understanding of human behaviour and the ability to communicate effectively.

∎ The planning and execution of research

Marketing research activity falls into two main categories – continuous and *ad hoc*. Marketing is an on-going process in a dynamic environment, and continuous research is essential if the firm is to remain informed of changes in the demand determinants outlined in Chapter 5 and be able to modify its policies accordingly. Much data of this type is collated by specialist organisations and government departments, but is often too generalised to meet the individual firm's specific requirements and needs to be supplemented by 'in-house' research.

However, many marketing situations are unique, e.g. the introduction of a new product, and demand a specific or *ad hoc* investigation. Such research invariably follows a clearly defined sequence which includes the following stages:

1. Recognition of the need for research.
2. Analysis of the parameters which predicate this need – problem definition.
3. Exact statement of the objective of the research.
4. Formulation of an experimental or survey design based on the analysis of Stage 2.
5. Data collection.
6. Tabulation and analysis of data.
7. Interpretation of results and the formulation of conclusions and recommendations.

8. Preparation and presentation of a report containing the findings.
9. Evaluation of results of action initiated on basis of research findings, i.e. 'feedback'.

Clearly, continuous research must follow the same procedure in the first instance, but the first four stages will be omitted subsequently.

■ Primary and secondary data

The data collection phase of a research investigation draws on two main sources of information, which are distinguished as primary and secondary sources. Secondary sources consist of existing data and should always be examined first. Frequently, however, such data have been collected for purposes peripheral to the researcher's main line of inquiry and so need to be supplemented by the collection of new, or primary, data. These differences in the source of data are recognised in the distinction between Desk Research and Original, or Field, Research.

■ Desk research

Desk research into secondary data sources is a common-sense preliminary to any field research. Not only is it possible that the required information is already available, albeit in a form which requires retabulation, but also such research is essential to indicate the precise nature of the data to be obtained by survey or experimentation. Further, published sources are more accessible and offer savings in time and money if properly used.

Logically, desk research should begin with the firm's own records. It was argued earlier that the responsibility for maintaining records should be left in the hands of the individual departments, but it is the marketing research department's responsibility to ensure a sufficient degree of uniformity to permit collation of these records into a common data base for the firm as a whole. The area in which records are usually maintained from which to compile such a data base normally include:

1. Purchasing – stock levels, unit costs, usage rates, etc.
2. Production – output, material, labour, inventory, physical distribution and overhead costs, machine utilisation, etc.
3. Personnel – wage costs, turnover, efficiency levels, absenteeism, etc.
4. Marketing – promotional and administrative expenditures, market and brand data, etc.
5. Sales – by product volume, value, contribution to profit, order size
   – by type of outlet/customer
   – by area and by salesman.
6. Finance – all cost and accounting data.

In addition to these internal data, the researcher also has access to a large number of external sources, which may be conveniently grouped into five main categories:

1. Government – domestic and foreign.
2. Universities and non-profit research organisations, e.g. *Oxford Bulletin of Statistics*.
3. Trade associations, e.g. British Institute of Management.
4. Academic and professional journals, the trade press.
5. Commercial research organisations, e.g. Attwood Statistics, Economist Intelligence Unit, Gallup, Nielsen, Dun & Bradstreet, Kompass etc.

The publications of government departments are far too extensive to permit full documentation, and only a few may be detailed here. A comprehensive list is contained in the *List of Principal Statistical Series and Publications* which is number 20 in the *Studies in Official Statistics* published by HMSO. The more important Government sources are:

Annual Abstract of Statistics
British Labour Statistics Year Book
Business Monitor
Censuses of Distribution, Population, and Production
Department of Employment Gazette
Economic Trends
Family Expenditure Survey
Financial Statistics
General Household Survey
Guide to Official Statistics
Monthly Digest of Statistics
National Food Survey
Overseas Trade Statistics
Regional Trends
Report on Censuses of Production
Report on Censuses of Distribution
Social Trends
Statistical News
Trade and Industry
U.K. Balance of Payments 'Pink Book'
U.K. National Accounts 'Blue Book'

Commonly used international sources include:

Balance of Payments Year Book (I.M.F.)
E.E.C. and E.C.S.C. publications
International Financial Statistics (I.M.F.)

International Labour Review
International Travel Statistics
International Reports on Cotton, Sugar, Tea, Tin, etc.
U.N. Year Book of National Accounts Statistics
U.N. Year Book of International Trade Statistics
U.N. Demographic Year Book
U.N. Direction of International Trade
U.N. National Statistical Yearbook
U.N. Statistical Papers
Yearbook of International Trade Statistics
Yearbook of Fisheries
Yearbook of Forest Product Statistics
Yearbook of Food and Agricultural Statistics
Yearbook of Labour Statistics

An extensive listing of foreign sources is to be found in the Stationery Office publication *International Organisations and Overseas Agencies Publications.*

When using published sources it is important to ascertain the method employed in the compilation and tabulation of the data, and to avoid direct comparative analysis where this differs. Further, such data should only be used when the researcher has satisfied himself as to their validity, reliability and homogeneity.

■ Field research

When all published sources have been evaluated, the research issue may still remain unanswered, although much more clearly defined. As noted earlier, desk research is often incapable of providing answers to highly specific problems, but it will often indicate factors which have proved important in similar situations in the past. None the less, there are a number of areas in which field research is usually necessary, and these may be summarised as:

Advertising research – the effectiveness of advertisements *per se*, i.e. copy testing, and media research – usage, coverage, etc.
Consumer research – investigation of the factors underlying consumer choice and preference.
Distribution research – effectiveness of alternative channel structures, methods of handling, etc.
Packaging research – colour, design, size, shape, informational content, etc.
Product research – concept testing, acceptability of new product offerings, development of user and non-user profiles, etc.

■ The collection of primary data

Original data may be collected by one, or a combination, of three methods – observation, experimentation and sample survey. Observation is the simplest, but usually least satisfactory, alternative and consists essentially of observing the processes associated with the factor under investigation. A good example of this approach is the measurement of customer flow patterns within retail outlets, from which many principles of store layout have been derived.

Observational techniques depend heavily on the skill and objectivity of the observer, and suffer from the need for secrecy if behavioural patterns are not to be disturbed as a result of the subject's awareness that he is under scrutiny. Further, overt behaviour rarely throws much light on the subject's motivation and decision processes, and it is these that one is usually trying to determine.

Experimentation avoids the lack of control common to observational methods and is usually less expensive to undertake than a sample survey. Several examples of experimental method are contained in the section on 'Laboratory Techniques' in Chapter 16 and make it clear that the major drawback lies in the difficulty of replicating normal behaviour in the laboratory setting. In part this may be overcome by conducting such experiments in their normal context, e.g. testing pack design by putting the test item(s) on display in a shop. However, if the results of such tests are to be taken as valid it is necessary to hold constant all variables other than that which is actually under test. Difficulties in identifying both the nature and effect of other variables may be largely overcome by repeating the experiment a sufficient number of times to permit the derivation of an average or representative results, and through the use of controls. A control often consists of running an experiment identical with the test situation with the exception of the test variable, on the assumption that any differences which arise are due to this variable.

Measurement of a single variable can be both expensive and time-consuming, in view of the large number of variables which may require testing. For example in the case of a new pack one may wish to isolate the separate effect of name, colour, size, shape, information value, etc., as well as the total effect. Techniques such as Latin Square and Factorial Design have now been developed which permit multiple variable analysis of this sort, and most modern statistics texts detail their use, e.g. M. J. Moroney, *Facts from Figures* (Pelican A236, 1956). A more specific treatment is to be found in Cox and Enis's *Experimentation for Marketing Decisions* (Intext, 1973) and is the subject of chapter 3 'Experimental Designs and Models', by James Rothman in *Consumer Market Research Handbook*, 3rd revised edn, Robert Worcester and John Downham, ESOMAR (1986).

Probably the most familiar method used in the collection of primary data is the sample survey. Survey method and sampling are both subjects on which a number of specialised texts have been written, and only the briefest coverage can be attempted here.

■ Census versus sample

As will be seen, marketing researchers have access to a wide selection of survey methods and, subject to time and financial constraints, their choice will be dictated by three separate considerations:

1. Respondent selection.
2. The means of establishing contact with respondents.
3. The information required and the means of obtaining it.

Theoretically, the ideal method of collecting primary data is to undertake a census of the whole population possessing the attribute to be investigated. In practice such an exercise is near impossible and only practicable where the population, in the statistical sense of all units belonging to a clearly defined group, is both small and readily accessible. Thus, although one might successfully conduct a census of a narrowly defined population such as 'all students registered in the first year marketing course at X college', if one were to extend the population to all students in the college, or 'all students of marketing', it is almost certain that one would be unable to establish contact with some members of the population.

Even assuming one could complete a census of a large population, the cost would be enormous and the data so extensive that it would be out of date before it could be collated and analysed, e.g. the 1960 Census of Population was not published until 1964 and the 1970 Census until 1973. For these reasons most researchers content themselves with a representative sample of the population which they wish to study.

Once the marketer has precisely identified the population to be studied, e.g. 'the market for instant cake mixes', the researcher can set about the construction of a sample design which will yield the desired information within the ever-present time and budgetary constraints.

■ Sampling

Sampling is based on two fundamental principles of statistical theory which are usually termed 'The Law of Statistical Regularity', and 'The Law of Inertia of Large Numbers'. The first law holds that any group of objects taken from a larger group of such objects will tend to possess the same characteristics as the larger group. The second law holds that large groups are more stable than small groups owing to the compensating effect of deviation in opposite directions.

On the basis of these and similar principles, one can determine the size and composition of a sample which will yield a desired level of accuracy while allowing for, and eliminating, possible sources of error. In fact, a properly designed and executed sample may prove to be more accurate than a poorly conducted census.

In most instances, the researcher wants some measure of the reliability of the data he has collected, and so will select a sample design based on probability theory such that the chance that any given unit will be selected may be assigned a definite, non-zero probability. There are many types of probability-based sample design, including simple random sampling, stratified samples, cluster samples and multi-stage samples, and the interested student should consult Moser and Kalton's *Survey Methods in Social Investigation*, 2nd edn (Heinemann Educational Books, 1971) for a clear and concise exposition of their nature, usage, etc. or chapter 4 'Sampling' by Martin Collins in Worcester and Downham, *Consumer Market Research Handbook*.

Although some form of probability sample is essential if the results are to be used for predictive purposes, there is often a need for a 'quick and dirty' survey as a preliminary to such a sample, to clarify basic issues, or to provide generalised information required in a hurry. To this end three types of non-probability sample are sometimes used – the convenience sample, the judgement sample and the quota sample.

Convenience sampling consists of soliciting information from any convenient group whose views may be relevant to the subject of inquiry. Thus, one might stop passers-by on the street to ask their views on parking meters and off-street parking to get a feel for the subject, and as a basis for formulating more precise questions to be asked of a representative sample.

Judgement sampling is a slightly more refined technique in that respondents are selected on the basis of the interviewer's subjective opinion that they constitute a representative cross-section of the population to be investigated.

Quota sampling represents a distinct improvement on both these approaches in that the respondent 'type' is specified on the basis of characteristics of the population at large. Each interviewer is then assigned a quota and solicits information from people who meet the specification. Clearly, the more detailed the latter is, the more representative will be the data, e.g. if the quota calls for ten middle-class housewives between twenty and thirty-five years old, with at least one child under school age, there is a precise specification that can easily be met by visiting a residential suburb and interviewing young women pushing prams or push-chairs. In a number of cases, well-designed and well-executed quota samples have achieved results comparable to much more expensive probability samples. However, such verification can only be established in retrospect and is no basis for accurate prediction.

■ Establishing contact with respondents

Once respondents have been identified from the sampling frame, i.e. list of all members of a given population, the researcher may establish contact by one of three methods – personal interview, mail questionnaire or telephone interview.

Taking these in reverse, it is clear that the telephone possesses the major disadvantage that private subscribers represent only a proportion of all households and tend to be concentrated in the higher socio-economic groups. These factors can be overemphasised however, and researchers are becoming increasingly aware of the advantages of the telephone for quick, low-cost interviews. This is particularly true in the field of industrial market research, where the compulsion to answer the phone can often secure an otherwise unobtainable interview, or where one wishes to limit investigation to members of the higher socio-economic groupings.

To be effective telephone interviews should be both short and explicit. If they are not the interviewer runs the risks of respondent confusion and of having the interview terminated before it is complete. In the United States, where a higher proportion of households have telephones, this method is widely used to monitor reaction to radio and television programmes and to measure advertising recall.

The mail survey possesses the advantage that it enables the researcher to reach any household or business establishment in the United Kingdom at very low cost. It also avoids the problem of interviewer bias. Unfortunately, the ability to contact an individual does not ensure his co-operation, and mail questionnaires suffer from very high refusal rates – a 50 per cent response would be considered excellent. In part this may be overcome by increasing the number of potential respondents, but one cannot escape the possibility of bias which arises from respondent self-selection, i.e. it is reasonable to argue that people who do complete mail questionnaires are different from those who will not. As with the telephone interview, there is also the possibility of misinterpretation of the actual questions asked, and although this may be reduced by using short, simple questions, the value of the information obtained is correspondingly reduced.

It is because of the disadvantages associated with telephone and mail questionnaires that the personal interview remains the most popular survey technique, despite its high cost. The use of trained interviewers invariably produces a high percentage of acceptable returns with a low refusal rate. The ability of the interviewer to clarify ambiguities improves accuracy, permits the use of longer and more complex questionnaires, and greatly reduces the problem of respondent self-selection. Further, the interviewer may be able to obtain additional information from observations, e.g. type of housing, possession of durables, etc. The major disadvantages of personal interviewing are high cost, and the shortage of trained interviewers, which increase the possibility of interviewer bias, e.g. the interviewer may 'lead' the respondent, or simply record the answers inaccurately. However, many of the problems involved in data collection may be minimised through good questionnaire design. (A full treatment of the above issue is to be found in Joan McFarlane-Smith's *Interviewing in Market and Social Research* (Routledge & Kegan Paul, 1972) and in Worcester and Downham, *Consumer Market Research Handbook*, chapter 6, 'Interviewing and Field Control' by John F. Drakeford and Valerie Farbridge.)

■ Questionnaires

Most formal questionnaires are structured so that they may be administered easily to a large number of respondents, and to simplify subsequent analysis.

Conversely, unstructured questionnaires are of great value when one is seeking to get the feel of a problem, but they are difficult to interpret owing to the differences in emphasis and meaning which arise when respondents are allowed free choice of vocabulary. In either case, the questionnaire may conveniently be considered to consist of four basic elements.

First, all questionnaires must be identifiable and so must be given a title and a distinctive number. Further, where the questionnaire is to be administered by an interviewer, provision should be made for recording the date and time of the interview, the place where the interview took place, and the interviewer's number and signature.

Second, all questionnaires should make provision for the recording of basic respondent data as a basis for subsequent classification, and to permit comparative analysis with other surveys. These data may be obtained partly by questioning and partly by observations, and should include: age, sex, social class, occupation of head of household, marital status, family size and composition, level and type of education. Optional, but useful, data are: name and address, owner or tenant of property, type of property, ownership of consumer durables. Income is obviously a desirable piece of information, but many respondents consider such questions too much of an intrusion on their privacy and either refuse to answer or exaggerate. If personal questions of this type are to be asked, it is best to leave them until the end of the interview to avoid antagonising the respondent and possibly securing an incomplete interview.

Third, the questionnaire should contain control questions to check on respondent consistency and to ensure that it has been administered or completed in accordance with the instructions given. The form of such questions depends on the nature and subject matter of the survey.

Finally, the questionnaire must contain questions that will elicit the information required to provide answers to the problem under investigation.

■ Question design

Questions may be dichotomous, multiple choice or open-ended. Dichotomous questions require a straight yes or no answer and are easy to ask, understand, record and analyse. On the other hand a large number of questions will be necessary if detailed information is required, and the responses will not reveal possible shades of meaning. Thus, although they are useful for securing factual data, e.g. 'Do you have a refrigerator?', they are of limited value when seeking opinions or attitudes, when multiple choice questions are to be preferred. As the name implies, multiple choice questions offer the respondent a number of alternatives and so permit the collection of more detailed and accurate data, e.g. 'How often do you use Whizzo?'

At least once a week . . .
Once a fortnight . . .

Once a month . . .
Less than once a month . . .
Never . . .

Similarly, one can obtain a measure of the strength of opinions or attitudes, e.g. 'Old age pensions should be increased.'

Strongly agree . . .
Agree . . .
Disagree . . .
Strongly disagree . . .
No opinion . . .

Some form of pilot survey is usually necessary to ensure that an adequate list of alternatives is offered, and 'All', 'None', or 'Don't know' should be included if the alternatives are not mutually exclusive. In recent years a number of sophisticated techniques, such as multi-dimensional scaling, have been developed to improve the quality of the data obtained through the use of multiple choice questions.

Open-ended questions give the respondent complete freedom in answering and so yield the maximum information, as well as eliminating interviewer bias. They are very useful in situations where it is impossible to formulate all possible alternatives, or shades of opinion, and reveal many facets of the respondent's attitudes and behaviour beyond the scope of dichotomous or multiple choice questions. On the other hand there are several disadvantages. The answers have to be recorded verbatim, for subsequent editing and analysis, to avoid the possibility that the interviewer is only recording what he considers significant. In addition, much of the data may be irrelevant, or become so, through the need to group it into categories for purposes of analysis.

In so far as is possible, all questions should be clear and unbiased, and phrased in terms which are meaningful to the likely respondent. To meet these require-ments each question should be formulated in the light of the information which it is hoped to elicit. For example if one is investigating smoking habits there are a number of possible dimensions along which data may be secured, and it is pointless to ask a multiple-dimensional question, 'What kind of cigarettes do you smoke?', which may be answered in terms of brand, price range, whether tipped or not, etc. Similarly, the question 'Why do you smoke brand X?' may be answered in terms of quality, price or satisfaction, all of which are interrelated and so give no clear indication of the salience of such factors taken in isolation.

The sequence in which questions are asked also has an important bearing on the value of the data obtained. Most respondents are nervous or suspicious initially, and so should be asked simple questions of a non-personal nature. Conversational questions, e.g. 'Have you lived here long?', and those which seek the interviewee's preference, e.g. 'Do you like making cakes?', often help to break the ice, as well as leading naturally into more specific questions. Sequence is also important, in that each answer inclines the respondent to make use of the same ideas in answering subsequent questions, e.g. if you ask questions about price, followed by questions on reasons for brand preference, price will usually be stated as a major reason. Similarly, if you ask women questions about fashions, followed by questions on their attitude to advertising, you will get many more favourable responses than you would if you had omitted the questions on fashions.

Questionnaires should always be field tested before use to ensure that they meet this criteria outlined above.

The standard references on questionnaire design are A. N. Oppenheim, *Questionnaire Design and Attitude Measurement* (Heinemann, 1967), and S. Payne, *The Art of Asking Questions* (Princeton, 1951). An up to date discussion appears as chapter 5 'Questionnaire Design' by Jean Morton-Williams in Worcester and Downham, *Consumer Market Research Handbook.*

■ Attitude scales

While the precise nature of the link between attitudes and behaviour is subject to debate there can be no argument that attitude is one of the most important and pervasive concepts in marketing. This concept has been discussed earlier (Chapter 6) and the purpose here is to review some problems associated with the measurement of attitudes.

Many of the problems of measuring attitudes are inherent in the concept itself and in the varying interpretations of it by different theorists. However, as Gilbert A. Churchill Jr observes (*Marketing Research: Methodological Foundations*, Dryden Press, 1976, pp. 206–7) there is substantial agreement on the following:

1. Attitude represents a predisposition to respond to an object, and not the actual behaviour toward the object. Attitude thus possesses the quality of readiness.
2. Attitude is persistent over time. It can change to be sure, but the alteration of an attitude, which is strongly held, requires substantial pressures.
3. Attitude produces consistency in behaviour outcroppings. Attitude is a latent variable that produces consistency in behaviour when manifested. This consistency occurs whether the manifestations are in the form of verbalizations about the object, or approach or avoidance of the object.
4. Attitude has a directional quality. It connotes a preference regarding the outcomes involving the object, evaluation of the object, or positive-neutral-negative affectations for the object.

Of these four clusters of attributes it is the latter which poses the strongest need for measurement through the assignment of some form of number which reflects the directional nature of an attitude. This object is achieved through scaling but one must be careful to determine the nature of a scale before jumping to too hasty a conclusion of the interpretation to be placed upon it.

In brief there are four types of scale, nominal, ordinal, interval and ratio, and their properties may be summarised as:

1. *Nominal scales*. This is the weakest form of scale in which the number assigned serves only to identify the objects under consideration. Library classification schemes employ nominal scales, as does the Standard Industrial Classification (SIC) such that members of the same class will be assigned the same number but each class will have a different number. By extending the number it is possible to achieve finer and finer distinctions until a unique number is assigned to a specific object, e.g. a telephone number.

2. *Ordinal scales* seek to impose more structure on objects by rank ordering them in terms of some property which they possess such as height or weight. As with nominal scales identical objects are given the same number but the ordinal scale has the added property that it can tell us something about the *direction* or relative standing of one object to another, e.g. 1 may represent the smallest member of a group such that we can safely say that 2 is bigger than 1, 5 is bigger than 2 and 17 is bigger than 5. However, this is all we can say (other than reversing the scale) and in order to be able to draw conclusions about differences between the numbers we must know something about the interval between the numbers.

3. *Interval scales* have this property in that they are founded on the assumption of equal intervals between numbers, i.e. the space between 5 and 10 is the same as the space between 45 and 50 and in both cases this distance is five times as great as that between 1 and 2 or 11 and 12, etc. However, it must be stressed that while we may compare the magnitude of the differences between numbers we cannot make statements about them unless the scale possesses an absolute zero, in which case we would have a ratio scale.

4. *Ratio scales*. Ratio scales are the most powerful and possess all the properties of nominal, ordinal and interval scales, while in addition they permit absolute comparisons of the objects, e.g. 6 feet is twice as high as 3 feet and six times as high as 1 foot.

The above discussion is essentially descriptive – for a discussion of the mathematical properties of the various scales one should consult *Research for Marketing Decisions*, by Paul E. Green and Donald S. Tull (Prentice-Hall, 4th edn, 1978).

■ Scaling methods in marketing

Marketing researchers have borrowed a number of different scaling techniques from the behavioural sciences, among which the most important are:

Thurstone's comparative judgement technique
Likert scales
Guttman Scales

The Semantic Differential
Q-sort technique

Thurstone scales were first introduced by L. L. Thurstone in 1928 and have been very widely used ever since. In essence a Thurstone scale is an attempt to construct an interval scale by selecting a set of statements about a subject which range from very favourable to very unfavourable expressions of attitude towards the subject with each statement appearing to be equidistant from those on either side of it. Scales may contain eleven, nine or seven statements, which are chosen by a panel of judges from a pool so as to achieve the property of equal-appearing intervals, and respondents are asked to select the statement which most accurately reflects their attitude. A score is assigned to each statement and is used, often in conjunction with scores for other sets of statements, in order to provide a summary statement of attitude towards the object of inquiry.

Likert scales differ from Thurstone scales in that respondents are presented with a series of statements and asked to indicate their degree of agreement/disagreement with each. Respondents are usually offered five categories – Strongly Agree, Agree, Uncertain, Disagree, Strongly Disagree, though three or seven divisions are used by some researchers – and are asked to select the position corresponding most closely with their opinion. By scoring a series of statements on a given subject, e.g. qualities of a brand, content of an advertisement, it is possible to construct a generalised attitude towards the object with an indication of the *intensity* with which the attitude is held.

Guttmann scaling represents an attempt to ensure a highly desirable property of an attitude scale which is only partially achieved by the Thurstone and Likert methods – the property of unidimensionality, i.e. all the statements used belong to the same dimension. The construction of Guttmann scales is more complex and laborious than for Thurstone and Likert scales and is described at some length by Moser and Kalton (*Survey Methods in Social Investigation*, 2nd ed., Heinemann, 1971) – as are all the other methods referred to here. However, relatively little use is made of the method in marketing research.

In contrast the Semantic Differential technique developed by Osgood *et al.* (*Method and Theory in Experimental Psychology*, New York, Oxford University Press, 1952) is very widely used, largely because it is much simpler to construct than any of the scales discussed so far and yet yields a very high measure of agreement with these more elaborate measures. The method consists of a series of bipolar adjectives (strong-weak, good-bad, etc.) separated usually by between five to nine points. The respondent is asked to check-mark the point which best indicates their attitude. Scale positions are sometimes qualified, for example:

Extremely good. Very good. Fairly good. Neither good nor bad. Fairly bad. Very bad. Extremely bad.

However, such qualification tends to discourage selection of the extreme positions.

■ Multidimensional scaling

All the scales discussed so far use a single number to represent a person's attitude – or, as Churchill puts it, 'a linear compensatory model' (*Marketing Research: Methodological Foundations*, Holt–Saunders, 1976). Such a model rests upon the basic assumption that attitude is unidimensional such that we balance negative and positive factors in arriving at a single summary statistic.

In recent years marketing researchers have challenged this basic model and have argued that attitude is multidimensional. In turn this requires a concept of a multidimensional space rather than a unidimensional scale and considerable effort and ingenuity has been devoted to developing measures of this space.

The basic characteristic of multidimensional scaling is that respondents are asked to make judgements concerning the degree of similarity/distance between pairs of stimuli using a scale which may be either *metric* (interval or ratio scale) or *non-metric* (ordinal scale). A particularly attractive feature of non-metric multi-dimensional scaling is that it converts an ordinal input into an interval scale or metric output. Thus as long as the respondent can rank order all the stimulus pairs it is possible to convert such 'greater than', 'less than' statements into absolute statements concerning the status of all the objects.

Multidimensional scaling is based upon sophisticated mathematical techniques, a full discussion of which is to be found in Paul E. Green and Frank J. Carmone, *Multidimensional Scaling and Related Techniques in Marketing Analysis* (Allyn & Bacon, 1970), or *Theory and Methods of Scaling* by Warren Torgenson (Wiley, 1955). However, for normal use packaged computer programs such as M–D–SCAL are available which require only basic mathematical skills. 'Multivariate Analysis of Market Research Data' by C. Holmes (chapter 13 in Worcester and Downham, *Consumer Market Research Handbook*) provides a more recent source.

■ Presentation of findings

Space limitations preclude consideration of field interviewing procedures, and the techniques used in collating, tabulating and analysing the data collected. Once these steps have been completed, the findings, and recommendations based on them, must be presented in the form of a report.

Most research findings have to be presented to two distinct groups – general management and research specialists – and the different needs and orientation of these groups usually requires the preparation of two separate reports. The first of these consists of a fully documented technical report, while the second consists of a short but detailed account of the major findings, conclusions and recommendations abstracted from the first.

The Market Research Society has adopted the following standards as constituting the minimum acceptable content of a survey report:

1. The purpose of the survey.
2. For whom and by whom the survey was undertaken.
3. General description of the universe covered.
4. Size and nature of the sample, including a description of any weighting methods used.
5. The time when the field work was carried out.
6. The method of interviewing employed.
7. Adequate description of field staff and any control methods used.
8. A copy of the questionnaire.
9. The factual findings.
10. Bases of percentages.
11. Geographical distribution of the interviews.

In order to ensure that a technical report satisfies these minimum requirements and presents the material in a logical sequence, many organisations have adopted a formal layout on the following lines:

1. *Introduction.*
   Title of the report.
   Name of sponsor.
   Title of research organisation.
   Date of publication.
2. *Table of Contents.*
3. *Preface* stating terms of reference, and acknowledgements where appropriate.
4. *Statement of purpose.* This generally consists of an elaboration of the terms of reference contained in the preface. It should outline the general nature of the problem to be investigated and the specific hypotheses on which the research was based.
5. *Methodology.* This section should outline the stages through which the project passed, step by step, and include a statement of the definitions adopted, the research techniques employed, the sources of data used, details of sample size and composition, a description of the methods of analysis employed, and any explanatory observations deemed necessary by the researcher.
6. *The findings.* This section consists of an abstract of those data considered relevant to the problem under investigation.
7. *Conclusions* drawn from the findings.
8. *Recommendations* based on the conclusions.
9. *The appendices.* These should include a detailed account of the sample design and its theoretical reliability; a copy of the questionnaire and instructions to interviewers; detailed statistical tables; the bibliography and glossary of terms if appropriate; details of any tests of reliability, theoretical proofs, etc.

In reports intended for line management as opposed to other researchers it is common to find that the conclusions and recommendations follow immediately after the statement of purpose or terms of reference, and the description of the methodology is consigned to the appendixes. Reports of this nature usually also include a single-page statement of the basic purpose and findings entitled Management or Executive Summary.

■ The role of marketing research agencies

It was stated earlier that many companies utilise the services of independent marketing research agencies, either to supplement their own research effort or as a substitute for a research department of their own. To provide these services, most independent agencies are capable of undertaking all aspects of the research process' described above, and act in both an advisory and executive capacity.

In addition to undertaking *ad hoc* research on behalf of client firms, some of the bigger organisations specialise in documenting a particular area of marketing on a continuous basis. The findings from such research are usually incorporated in standardised reports which are circulated to subscribers at regular intervals. A well-known example of such a service is the Inventory Audit of Retail Sales, which is often referred to as the Nielsen Index, after its originator.

Once the manufacturer's products leave his factory there is invariably a time-lag before they are purchased and consumed. The longer this time-lag, the more difficult it becomes for the producer to exercise control over supply to meet variations in demand and modify his production to maximise profit. The Inventory Audit helps reduce these uncertainties by monitoring both sales and stock levels for three major product groups – food, drugs and pharmaceuticals. The actual audit is made in a representative sample of outlets, carefully selected from the population of all retail outlets stocking the three product groups. Each outlet enters into an agreement with Nielsen's under which all invoices are retained for inspection and auditors are permitted to take physical stock on the premises. By the simple process of adding goods invoiced to opening stock and deducting closing stock, sales of each item may be determined. These data are then circulated to subscribers, together with information covering the number of outlets stocking given brands, prices, average order sizes, merchandising schemes, etc. A fact sheet issued by Nielsen for their Food Index is reprinted as Table 10.4.

AGB Superpanel is a panel of 8500 households in which all individuals regularly record purchase data on a wide range of packaged grocery, household, fresh food, toiletry and other personally purchased products. The panel is representative of Great Britain, with regional samples sufficiently large to permit separate reporting on ten ITV regions and is run by AGB Market Information.

Data collection is via a personal data terminal (p.d.t) equipped with a light pencil, which panel members use to 'wand' the bar codes of their purchases, entering the price manually. Information on the retailer used and on unpack-

TABLE 10.4   Nielsen Food Index

The Nielsen Food Index measures the performance of product categories sold in grocers. A grocer is defined as a retail outlet with at least 20% of its total turnover in groceries and/or provisions, and a larger proportion of turnover in no other commodity unless it is one or a combination of the following: off-licence trade, bakery goods, or tobacco.

Sample size   831 grocery outlets in England, Scotland and Wales. These have been selected to allow analysis of patterns of trading by shop type and 9 regions.

Audit frequency   Audits are carried out every 2 months.

Report contents   For each brand, size, flavour etc, specified by the client and an 'all other' section.

CONSUMER SALES and Shares	Units Sterling Average sales per shop handling Weighted average sales per shop handling
RETAILER PURCHASES and shares SOURCE OF DELIVERY	Units Co-ops Multiples } direct v. other Independents
RETAILER STOCKS and Shares	Units Average stocks per shop handling Units in forward selling area
STOCK COVER PRICES DISTRIBUTION Shop, all commodity and product class turnover weighted	Days/weeks/months supply Average retail selling prices Handling Total out-of-stock Out-of-stock in selling area Purchasing Merchandising
ADVERTISING	Press, magazine and TV expenditure Group promotions

Subdivisions in the report

SHOP TYPES	NIELSEN REGIONS
All grocers	London
Co-operatives	Anglia
Multiples	Southern
Major multiples – Argyll, Asda, Fine Fare, International, Sainsbury, Tesco	Wales, West and Westward Midlands Lancashire Yorkshire Tyne Tees Scotland
Other multiples	
Total independents	
Major symbols – Mace, Spar, VG, Wavy Line	
Other independents	
Superstores – over 25 000 sq ft	

aged items without bar codes is obtained from specially created codes in a patented code book. The p.d.t is kept in a modem linked to the power supply and a telephone socket and data are polled overnight. The technique enables achievement of unprecedented levels both of data accuracy and speed of collection.

The following data are obtained about each panel home and each purchase within the audit field made by these households.

The home
1. Age of housewife
2. Size of household
3. Social class
4. With or without children
5. Claimed housewife weight of ITV viewing
6. Cat/dog ownership
7. Ownership of refrigerator
8. Washing machine ownership
9. Ownership of deep freezer
10. Ownership of colour television
11. Full-time working, part-time working or non-working status of housewife
12. Terminal age of education of housewife

The purchase
1. Brand name
2. Size
3. Flavour/variety
4. Actual price paid
5. Weight of purchase
6. Quantity bought
7. Name and address of shop
8. Type of shop

Subscribers to the Superpanel service receive standard four-weekly reports on their selected product fields, for the country as a whole and each ITV region separately. They include the following information.

1. Total consumer expenditure – for the total market, for each brand and for each size an estimate is made of consumer expenditure at actual retail prices and an estimate of volume is made.
2. Market shares – gives share of total market held by each itemised brand.
3. Product penetration – gives the percentage of households buying each brand at least once during the four-weekly period.

All data relating to each household and individual's weekly purchasing are retained by AGB and can be provided in various forms according to the particular marketing situation which needs to be analysed.

The principal types of special analysis are weekly purchasing, brand profiles, repeat purchasing brand share predictions, brand switching and source of purchase.

Other forms of analysis relating to test marketing product usage, television viewing, effectiveness of coupons, samples and special offers and cross-matching of purchasing and media data can be provided.

Further information about AGB Superpanel may be obtained from:

AGB Market Information
The Research Centre
West Gate
London
W5 3HH

Other well known sources of continuous research data are the British Market Research Bureau's Target Group Index and G & A's Home Audit. Further details of these panels are to be found in Peter M. Chisnall, *Marketing Research*, 3rd edn (McGraw-Hill, 1981).

■ Database Marketing (DBM)

One of the most valuable assets a company possesses is its knowledge of the identity and location of actual and potential customers. Such information constitutes a database. In recent years developments in computing capacity and information technology have led to the recognition that the customer database is ideally suited to the new technology and resulted in the emergence of the new field of database marketing.

In his new book *Marketing Management and Information Technology* (1990) Keith Fletcher examines the application of IT to the whole process of marketing management and its specific application to particular marketing functions and tasks. In Chapter 10 he examines the topic of sales decisions and includes a comprehensive review of DBM. While it is stated that there is no agreed definition of DBM, that offered by Stone and Shaw (1987) captures well its essential characteristics, namely:

> DBM is an interactive approach to marketing communications, which uses addressable communication media (such as mail, telephone and the sales force) to extend help to its target audience, to stimulate demand, and to stay close to them by recording and keeping an electronic database memory of customer, prospect and all communication and commercial contacts, to help improve future contacts.

The key point is that the power of electronics aided and abetted by developments in telecommunications have made it possible to increase the power of the database far beyond that which was possible when depending upon a manual system. To be fully effective, however, it must be possible for the user to interact with or relate to the database (hence *relational database*) and match any variable with any other in order to develop and exploit the potential for distinctive and focused marketing efforts. It is this use of a database for marketing planning which distinguishes DBM from *direct marketing* with which it is often confused. Specifically, direct marketing embraces 'any activity which creates and profitably exploits a direct relationship between the company and the prospect (Ogilvy and Mather, 1985) and tends to focus on the communication opportunities for this such as the new electronic media, telephone selling and direct response advertising' (Fletcher, *Marketing Management*). From this definition it is clear that direct marketing will benefit greatly from the existence of a relational database as this will increase significantly the ability to pinpoint specific targets with unique messages but much direct marketing is developed using customer databases which do not possess this property, i.e. DBM requires a more sophisticated database than is necessary for basic direct marketing.

While DBM is a suitable base for all kinds of marketing communication and effort it is particularly suited for use with the telephone. Recognising this fact British Telecom publish annually a TMS (Telephone Marketing Services) *Direct Marketing Handbook* which is available from their offices at 95 Ebury Bridge Road, London, SW1W 8RL (free of charge in 1990!) and contains excellent coverage of most aspects of direct marketing. In an article entitled 'The Emergence of Marketing Databases and their Uses' Tony Coad offers the following guidelines on what he looks for in a marketing database:

> Firstly, a Marketing Database contains the names and addresses of a company's customers, with as much individual characterisation as possible.
>
> When building consumer databases for example, each responding customer can be distinguished by their demographic and lifestyle attributes.
>
> My Company, NDL International has built over 60 consumer marketing databases for major UK companies, characterising individual customers by their individual demographic and life style qualities.
>
> Such detail – whether of individual consumers, or individual businesses – enables us to search for common characteristics among customers that relate to purchase behaviour. If we did not characterise each customer we would not be able to distinguish between them. We then could not use our database to reach people on the basis of their individuality or to help us understand the separate market segments that exist in nearly all markets.
>
> Secondly, we need to distinguish between our customers on the basis of their purchase behaviour. This is the what, when, how much, why, where of their purchase history.
>
> We now have all the data we need effectively to operate a marketing database. We can track purchase behaviour by the profile of that customer, so, in theory can:
>
>   – Find out where customers for Product X live.
>   – See how customers for the standard model differ from those of the full-feature version.
>   – Find out which types of customer pay the top price for a product or service.
>   – See which sort of people buy at different outlets then vary our point of sale accordingly.
>   – Make sure that the people who are actually buying our product are those we had in mind when promoting it.
>   – Identify prospect names and addresses, and individual lifestyles as a point of contact.

With the data, we can track purchase behaviour and profile the types of customer exhibiting that behaviour. But of course marketing databases need to present data in a form digestible to marketers, so . . .

. . .The third characteristic of a marketing database is that it should be based on relational software. This will enable any piece of data to be retrieved in any sequence and placed in any combination. Hierarchical database software does not allow this so we cannot readily identity segments and then relate those segments to names and addresses. And we should make our consumer database address-based.

Thanks to the Post Office's Postal Address File we have a means of standardising addresses – which means we can recognise duplicate entries – and can attach data from a variety of sources to the correct household with confidence.

The fourth characteristic of a marketing database is its geography. It has to be all in one place, not scattered around the company, probably on incompatible installations.

Fifthly, the output must be user friendly. Reports must be customised, friendly and rapid. Better still the output should be capable of being accepted by marketers who need not be systems analysts. PC-based output, rich in opportunities for statistical analysis, is ideal.

The sixth characteristic of a marketing database is obvious. It must belong to the marketing department and be an effective source of influence over major marketing decisions. An installation which is really part of some other function or department will never be satisfactory. The Marketing Database is now – and potentially – too important a resource to be at the wrong end of another department's priorities.

The TMS *Direct Marketing Handbook* contains a wealth of practical advice and information and is recommended for those wishing to pursue the topic in greater detail than is possible in a basic textbook.

The application of Bayesian techniques to marketing research

Traditionally, marketing research has employed a methodology based on classical statistics as exemplified by the principles stated in the section on sampling. In recent years, however, increasing attention has been given to the Bayesian, or subjective, approach to probability which incorporates the decision-maker's personal feelings regarding the likely occurrence of specified events.

The aim of marketing research is to reduce uncertainty concerning the outcome of future events or a given course of action. It is clear, however, that even the most extensive research is unlikely to result in perfect information and that even if it did, the value would not be justified by the cost. Thus, even when the results of research are available to him, the decision-maker will still be faced with some degree of uncertainty and the value of the Bayesian approach lies in its ability to quantify such uncertainties and incorporate them in an analysis of the problem. In practice, many managers make use of subjective probabilities in an informal way and always have, e.g. the sales manager forecasting next year's sales adjusts the individual salesman's estimates on the basis of his own opinion of their likely accuracy; the production manager decides to use a substitute material to meet an urgent order because he feels the chances are eight out of ten it will work.

Although the Bayesian approach is rejected by many classical statisticians, it is the author's opinion that it is a valuable technique when properly applied. While it is beyond the scope of this book, the student is recommended to consult one, or all, of the following:

1. 'Better Decisions with Preference Theory', John S. Hammond III, *Harvard Business Review* (Nov–Dec 1967) pp. 123–41. The 'best' short introduction to the use of subjective probabilities in analysing real-world problems.
2. *Analysis of Decisions Under Uncertainty*, Robert Schlaifer (McGraw-Hill, 1969). An introductory text by one of the pioneers in the field. It is difficult to follow, but involves no sophisticated mathematics. Well worth the effort of the several readings usually necessary to achieve understanding.
3. *Research for Marketing Decisions*, Paul E. Green and Donald S. Tull (Prentice-Hall, 4th edn 1978). Integrates both traditional and Bayesian approaches, as well as covering most of the new research techniques. Strongly recommended to the student who wishes to specialise in marketing research.
4. 'Making Decisions in Marketing', T. Cass, *Marketing Forum* (May–June 1968) pp. 15–24. A 'home-grown' review article based largely on Schlaifer's book.
5. Chapter 8, 'Marketing Research', in *Marketing Strategy and Management*, Michael J. Baker (Macmillan, 1985) pp. 216–27.

CHAPTER 11

Product* policy, planning and development

Learning Goals

The issues to be discussed in this chapter include:

1. The need for and nature of product policy.
2. The concept of the product life-cycle.
3. The definition of what constitutes a 'new' product and the role of new product development (NPD).
4. The NPD startegies open to the firm and the nature of the NPD process.
5. Organising for NPD.
6. The concept of the 'product portfolio'.

After reading this chapter you will be familiar with:

1. The central role of the product or service as a key element in achieving and sustaining competitive success.
2. The view that change is inevitable and that progress is achieved by the continuous substitution of new and improved solutions to consumer needs such that all products and industries follow a life-cycle from birth through growth to maturity and eventual decay.
3. The *process* of new product development through which firms identify market opportunities and develop new products to exploit them.
4. The *procedures* followed to screen ideas and translate these into successful new products.
5. Some alternative organisational structures for encouraging and managing NPD.
6. The need for a firm to develop a portfolio of products each at different stages of the life-cycle to ensure its survival and long-run success.

---

*While the emplasis here is on physical products and a separate chapter (23) deals with the special case of services, in most instances products may be regarded as synonymous with services throughout this chapter.

A cardinal principle of marketing is that firms should seek to determine the multidimensional nature of consumer demand, and then deploy their resources in the creation of products which will satisfy these demands. Acceptance of this principle recognises that the firm's ultimate success, whether measured by total profits, return on investment, market share or any other criterion, is largely dependent upon its product policy.

■ Product policy

A firm's product policy is fundamental to the whole operation of the business. Most new companies are conceived to produce a specific product or group of products, and it is this decision which dictates the industry to which they will belong, the markets they will serve, and the nature and extent of the resources, methods and techniques they will employ. These factors often tend to be overlooked, however, for most companies are long-established members of a given industry and inextricably linked with their product line. Similarly, it is often erroneously assumed that companies are irrevocably committed to their current product mix, which ignores the fact that apart from certain highly specific capital equipment, most corporate resources may be put to other uses.

The latter assumption may be attributed to the fact that companies rarely do undertake a radical change in product policy, even when environmental changes indicate that they should – a fact which prompted Theodore Levitt to write the now classic 'Marketing Myopia' (*Harvard Business Review* (July–Aug 1960)).

Levitt's thesis is that companies take too narrow a view of their market because they think in terms of their product offering, rather than in terms of the fundamental needs which these products satisfy. Thus the American railroads thought of themselves as the ultimate development in overland transportation, and failed to respond to the invention of the internal combustion engine which gave us the car, lorry and aeroplane. If the management of the railroads had thought of themselves as being in the 'transportation business', then doubtless they would have integrated these new methods of moving goods and people into their existing network. As it was, the expanding demand of a rapidly growing economy masked the impact of the new competition and lulled the railroads into the complacent belief that they could look forward to continued and uninterrupted growth. Even when the threat was appreciated the railroads chose to compete head-on, failing to realise that they could not hope to duplicate the speed and convenience offered by their rivals, with the result that until recently they have appeared to be members of a dying industry. Now, however, as the result of a belated appreciation of the marketing concept, railways in many advanced economies are enjoying a new lease of life as a result of careful analysis of their comparative strengths *vis à vis* alternative forms of transportation and a strategy of positioning based on realistic market segmentation.

The writings of Levitt and Peter Drucker, among others, have given us the concept of corporate strategy which, in essence, consists of a statement of the firm's objective, and the mix of policies to be used in the attainment of that objective. A first step in the formulation of a corporate strategy is to answer the questions 'What business are we in?' and 'What business do we want to be in?' Declining industries have invariably failed to define their business in sufficiently broad terms. Had the railroads thought of themselves as being in the 'transportation business' it is reasonable to assume that they would have been responsive to the development and introduction of new methods of transport, irrespective of whether they involved rails and locomotives.

Gulf Oil exemplifies the broad viewpoint in that it has defined its role as 'servicing the travelling public'. Although the company's past growth depended largely upon the refining and sale of petroleum products to motorists, Gulf recognised that developments in fuel cell technology and growing concern over air pollution may be sounding the death-knell of the petrol engine. The motor car represents only one stage in the evolution of personal transport, however, and it is clear that people will continue to travel even though we may not be able to predict the exact nature of the next development. While travelling, people have a need for both rest and refreshment, and to meet this continuing need Gulf developed a nation-wide network of Holiday Inns (now divested and operated as a franchise).

Hopefully, this example makes it clear that by defining the business they are in, and want to be in, Gulf did not commit themselves irrevocably to a given product mix, but will modify their product offering in the light of changes in consumer demand – this is their product policy.

■ The concept of the product life-cycle

The above examples clearly indicate that, over time, man develops new and better ways of satisfying basic needs, with the result that as new products are introduced, established products become obsolescent and eventually pass into oblivion. In time the cycle repeats itself, and the once new product suffers the fate of the product which it originally replaced. In many ways this process resembles the human life-cycle, with its phase's of birth, growth, maturity, senility and death, and has given rise to the concept of the product life-cycle.

The first stage in the product life-cycle is represented by its introduction into the market. As with human beings, this is a critical stage, for the product has little to protect it from the hostile environment into which it is introduced. (Fortunately, medical science has been more successful in protecting new-born offspring than has the marketer!) Assuming survival, new products enjoy a period of increasing demand and rapid growth, but as most innovations are merely substitutes for existing products, other' manufacturers will react strongly to the newcomer, and their own decline in market share, stemming the newcomer's growth. However, as the superiority of the new substitute becomes apparent many suppliers will switch to it to protect their market share accelerating the

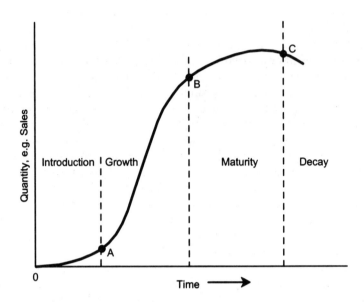

Figure 11.1   Stages in the product life-cycle

adoption of the new product and the decline of the old. The levelling out of demand for the new product represents the onset of maturity.

In time, other new products will enter the market offering advantages over the now mature product, which will experience a decline in demand as consumers switch their allegiance. This phase has been characterised as senility or decay. Classically the product life-cycle is represented as having four basic phases as represented in Figure 11.1.

If the stylised PLC shown reflects reality then clearly the change in the inflection of the curve at A heralds rapid exponential growth, at B a levelling off of demand, at C a diminution that suggests either product rejuvenation or replacement. Although the utility of the PLC concept is occasionally challenged by sceptical practitioners their criticisms tend to reflect their own failure to understand its meaning, and to the rather naive assumption that all products will exhibit perfectly symmetrical S-shaped curves.

In fact, consideration of a number of other areas reveals that some form of exponential function (represented graphically by a cumulative S-shaped curve) is typical of the manner in which objects or ideas spread or diffuse through populations of 'adopters'. Elsewhere (*Marketing New Industrial Products*, Macmillan). I have argued that the consistent and pervasive nature of the diffusion process approximates a law of nature and reflects an underlying process such that if one can initiate diffusion it will proceed to some extent automatically thereafter due to the 'bandwagon' or 'contagion' effect.

In the context of new-product marketing we find that success is usually defined in terms of achieving a predetermined sales target within a specified time period. It follows that the sooner one can achieve an initial sale the sooner diffusion will commence. In essence the logic is that proof of a sale adds conviction to the selling process, while word-of-mouth recommendation or pure visibility, e.g. a new car at the kerbside, will accelerate awareness of the new product's existence and so improve the probability of further purchases.

Put very simply then, success or failure is highly dependent upon the speed with which we can achieve initial sales and the lesson to be learned from the concept is that effort to pre-identify 'early adopters' is essential to long-run success. In the particular, however, it is impossible to be highly specific about the particular characteristics of early adopters in different contexts and situations as has been demonstrated by the lack of correlation between the findings of various research studies. Such a lack of correlation does not invalidate the utility of the concept – it merely emphasises the need for persons well versed in their own product – market interface (however we define 'product' and 'market') to apply their experience and knowledge in seeing how such a basic idea can be of use to them.

Unlike the human life-cycle, however, one cannot predict the length of any of the phases of the product life-cycle – certainly there are not the equivalent of actuarial tables for new products. Further, marketers have the option to practise euthanasia and quietly dispose of products which fail to live up to expectations, or, alternatively, to prolong the life-cycle through a rejuvenation process. The analogy is a useful one, provided that one bears in mind that it is a generalisation and says nothing specific about the duration of any given phase. However, by monitoring changes in demand, one can predict the onset of growth, maturity and senility, and vary one's marketing inputs accordingly, e.g. reduce the level of advertising expenditures during growth and emphasise production and physical distribution; step up the amount of sales promotion at the onset of maturity; retire the product when senility sets in. Table 11.1 provides a useful summary of how various characteristics such as cash flow and competition vary in accordance with the stages of the product life-cycle and their implications for managing the marketing mix.

■ What is a 'new' product?

The first stage in the product life-cycle posits the introduction of a new product – the question is, 'What constitutes a new product?' There can be no hard-and-fast answer, for newness is essentially a subjective concept that depends upon one's state of knowledge or, in the case of a firm, its current range of activity. It is possible to distinguish a spectrum of newness ranging from an invention, which Mansfield has defined as 'a prescription for a new product or process that was not obvious to one skilled in the relevant art at the time the idea was generated'

TABLE 11.1   Characteristics of life-cycle stages

Product life-cycle	Introduction	Growth	Maturity	Decline
Characteristics				
Sales	Low	Fast	Slow to decline	Declining
Profits	Negligible	Peak levels	Begin to decline	Declining to zero
Cash flow	Negative	Moderate	High	Low
Customers	Early adopters	Mass market	Mass market	Laggards
Competitors	Few	Growing	Many 'me too' rivals	Taking market
Key actions				
Strategy	Expand market	Market penetration	Defend share	Productivity
Marketing costs	High	High (declining %)	Falling	Low
Marketing emphasis	Product awareness	Brand preference	Brand loyalty	Image maintenance
Pricing	High	Maintain	Maintain/increase	Rising
Distribution	Patchy	Intensive	Intensive	Selective
Product	Basic	Improved	Broaden position / Product development / Resegment	Rationalise

Brand life ⟶

Generic life ⟶

Source: Peter Doyle. 'The realities of the Product Life Cycle', *Quarterly Review of Marketing*, Summer 1976, pp. 1–6.

(Edwin Mansfield, *The Economics of Technological Change* (W. W. Norton, New York, 1966)), to a minor change in an existing, widely known product, e.g. the addition of a new blue whitener to a detergent.

For the purpose of this book a new product will be considered anything which is perceived as such by the consumer, or with which the firm has no previous experience. The former permits the inclusion of variants in existing products, and their packaging, as well as totally new products such as satellite television, body scanners or laptop computers. The latter acknowledges that production of an existing product with which the firm has no previous experience raises the same marketing problems as does a totally new product. Further, it may also be perceived by consumers as a new product, e.g. the sale of home furnishings under the 'St Michael' brand by Marks & Spencer.

■ The role of new product development

Although it is impossible to predict the life span of a given product, there is an inevitable certainty that it will eventually be replaced by the introduction of a new substitute or even made totally obsolete as the result of technological innovation.

In Chapter 5 it was stated that branding developed in its present form as a result of the realisation that many mass markets were faced with the possibility of over-supply, such that the individual manufacturer could only protect his position by distinguishing his output from that of his competitors. Many critics of advertising would argue that the claimed differences between brands are more a figment of the copywriter's imagination than a reality, and still view products such as detergents and canned peas as homogeneous. This view is admissible if one adopts a narrow definition of a product, based solely on the function that it performs in terms of objective and quantifiable criteria. However, from the arguments advanced concerning newness, it is clear that the consumer's perception is modified by subjective considerations which are not amenable to quantification. Thus a relatively minor change in a product's composition or marketing may assume major significance in the user's eyes and result in a marked shift in demand for that product. It is argued, therefore, that branding can only succeed as a competitive strategy given the existence of perceived differences.

If this is so it follows that a competitive market will be characterised by a continual effort to develop such differences. Clearly, the producer who succeeds in distinguishing his product from that of his competitors, through the creation of a new and desirable attribute, will enjoy an advantage which will enable him to expand his sales and share of market. Such an advantage is in the nature of a monopoly, which may last for years if protected by a patent, e.g. the Polaroid camera and film, or be eroded overnight by imitative innovation, e.g. enzyme active detergents.

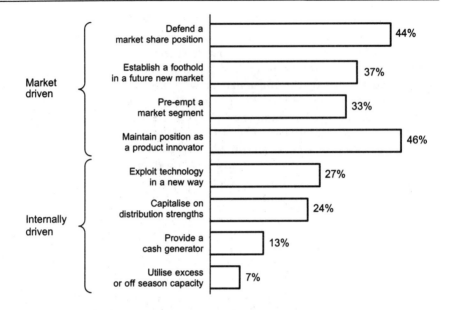

Figure 11.2   Strategic roles for sucessful new products

Source: Pierre Rodocanachi, 'The Successful Management of New Products in the 1980s', ESOMAR seminar, Athens, Nov. 1983.

The role of new product development is the creation of such competitive advantages.

Over the years the American consulting firm Booz-Allen & Hamilton has pursued the objective of seeking to understand the management approaches that result in competitive advantage with a particular emphasis upon the role of new product development. In a paper given to the Esomar seminar on New Product Development (Athens, November 1983) entitled 'The Successful Management of New Products in the 1980s', Pierre Rodocanachi presented the findings of their most recent research based upon in-depth interviews with top management of large and medium sized companies in the United States and Europe, complemented by a comprehensive mail survey of corporate executives and product managers of *Fortune 1000* companies. According to this research new products play an important and diverse role in the firm's overall strategy as can be seen from Figure 11.2.

■ The importance of new products

Any attempt to measure the contribution of new products to a firm or industry's growth and profitability is bedevilled by a lack of consensus as to what

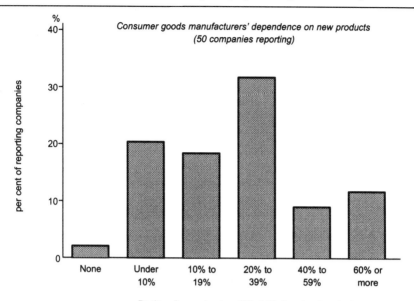

Figure 11.3 Consumer goods manufacturers' dependence on new products

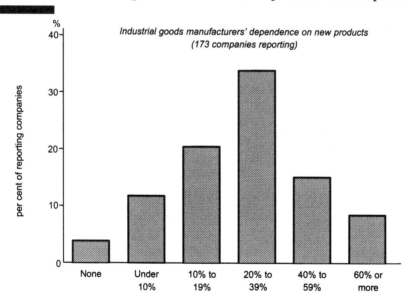

Figure 11.4 Industrial goods manufacturers' dependence on new products

(From *The Marketing Executive Looks Ahead*: 'Experiences in Marketing Management' 13, National Industrial Conference Board, 1967.)

constitutes a new product. Similar difficulties also exist when one seeks to measure the failure rate of new product introductions.

Ignoring the problems of data comparability for the present, two valid generalisations may be advanced:

1. Firms are increasingly dependent upon new products for the maintenance and expansion of sales.
2. A large proportion of new product introductions are failures in the sense that they do not achieve the expected sales level, and are withdrawn from the market.

The first generalisation is supported by Figures 11.3 and 11.4 reproduced on page 273.

More recent data are reported in Table 11.2, based on a survey of a representative cross-section of UK industry in 1974. Although more recent hard data is available the anecdotal evidence drawn from trade magazines etc. confirms this general pattern.

Estimates of new product failure rates vary enormously from the oft-quoted level of 80 per cent (Ross Federal Research Corporation, quoted in the *Wall Street Journal*, 5 April 1961), to an absolute low of 7 per cent (A. C. Nielsen Company, *How to Strengthen Your Product Plan*, 1966) if the firm makes full use of the screening and testing procedures described below.

■ Alternative new product strategies

Relatively few new products emanate from totally new companies, and attention here will be focused on the established firm with an existing product line. Such firms vary in their willingness to innovate and develop new products, and are usually categorised as 'leaders' and 'followers'.

Many industries which are highly concentrated or oligopolistic in structure are dominated by one or a small number of firms which determine the competitive character of the market along such dimensions as price, quality, distribution policy and innovation. These firms are the leaders. The remaining firms are thought of as followers in that they imitate the policies of the leaders and rarely possess a sufficient market share to affect industry practice through independent action. (Although this is not the place to enter into a discussion of the evils of monopoly/oligopoly, there is a considerable body of evidence which suggests that small firms in an industry are the most innovative, and it would be wrong to assume that it is always the industry leader who stimulates innovation.)

Whether a firm is a leader or follower, there are several distinct ways in which it can add to its product line which may be summarised as:

1. Modification of an existing product, e.g. addition of a new ingredient in a detergent, toothpaste or cake mix; increase in the cubic capacity of a car engine, adoption of disc brakes, etc.

TABLE 11.2 Inter-industry variations in dependence on new products
Where does the largest proportion of your sales come from?

Industry	Products launched within the last five years		Products launched more than five years ago		Totals	
	%	n	%	n	%	n
Building and construction	45	13	55	16	100	29
Chemicals/allied products	29	12	71	30	100	42
Clothing	67	19	33	9	100	28
Electrical machinery	38	13	62	21	100	34
Engineering/general machinery	41	71	59	102	100	173
Fabricated metal	21	8	79	30	100	38
Food, drink, tobacco	11	6	89	49	100	55
Furniture and fixtures	57	8	43	6	100	14
Iron and steel	21	6	79	22	100	28
Leather	54	7	46	6	100	13
Paper	24	5	76	16	100	21
Plastics	50	9	50	9	100	18
Printing and publishing	38	8	62	13	100	21
Textiles	50	33	50	33	100	66
Miscellaneous	64	9	36	5	100	14
Stone, glass, clay	24	5	76	16	100	21
Total	38%	232	62%	383	100%	N = 615

Source: M. J. Baker and S. T. Parkinson, 'An Analysis of the Significance of Innovation', Appendix to *S.S.R.C. Report* 1974.

2. Addition of a complementary product, e.g. a new brand of cigarette, a new flavour in a food or beverage; the development of a new model of car.
3. Entry into an existing market new to the firm, e.g. Cadbury's entry into the cake market; Rank Organisation's entry into the office-equipment market.
4. Development of a new market through the introduction of a totally new product, e.g. Polaroid camera, television, computers.

These alternatives are listed in ascending order of risk. The first strategy usually entails a low level of risk, and is frequently in response to overt public demand. Thus, offering an MG variant of its Metro and Maestro cars extended British Leyland's competitive position but required comparatively little additional investment by the firm.

The second strategy involves a greater degree of risk, as the firm has no previous direct experience of the production and marketing of the new item. However, in so far as it is a complementary product, previous experience with similar products and markets will be almost directly relevant and reduce the risk accordingly.

Entry into an existing market of which the firm has no previous experience is unlikely to be viewed favourably by the companies currently sharing that market. Thus the new entrant's inexperience is compounded by the aggressive reaction of competitors, and involves a still higher level of risk.

The fourth alternative exposes the firm to a completely unknown situation, added to which the value of fundamentally new products may take years to establish owing to the innate conservatism of the potential user. Further, it is only when a product achieves wide-scale trial that many of its limitations become apparent, which may involve the innovator in many years of adjustment and modification. At the end of this time another firm may well enter the market which the innovator has developed and deprive him of the fruits of his labours, e.g. IBM in the computer market.

The sources of new product failures identified by Cooper (1975) and Cooper and Calantone (1979) are summarised in Table 11.3.

■ New product development

Despite the risks involved, new product development is a competitive necessity and has prompted many companies to evolve formalised procedures for dealing with the complexities and uncertainties inherent in the process. In the survey undertaken by Booz-Allen & Hamilton, strong support was found for a six-stage process represented diagrammatically in Figure 11.5.

The survey also indicated a significant change of emphasis from the findings of the 1968 study. Specifically: 'Companies now conduct far more up-front analyses than in the past. Specific strategies are delineated. Ideas and concept generation are focused. Screening and evaluation are more rigorous, more attuned to strategic and performance considerations. On the whole, the up-front process receives more attention.

TABLE 11.3 Reasons for new product failure

Product characteristic	Percentage of failures
The better mousetrap no one wants (innovative, unique products rejected by the market).	28
The me-too product meeting a competitive brick wall (similar to products on the market already meeting customer needs).	24
Competitive one-upmanship (me-too products hurt by the concurrent introduction of similar competitive products).	13
Environmental ignorance (products not well-suited to customer needs).	7
The technical dog product (technically new products not performing).	15
The price crunch (products well-suited to customer needs but priced too highly).	13

Source: R.G. Cooper, 'The Dimensions of Industrial New Product Success and Failure', *Journal of Marketing*, vol. 43, Summer, 1979.

■ The location and screening of new product ideas

To be effective, any search for new product ideas should be structured, in the sense that efforts should be directed towards a specific area and pursued systematically. Most firms possess some special skill or 'distinctive competence', and it is this which they should seek to exploit in developing new products. Thus, if a firm has developed a reputation for precision engineering it should seek to build on this strength, rather than branch out into mass-produced, fabricated products. Although there are cases of firms which have achieved success following a radical departure from their original product policy, the author would argue that this is attributable to their developing a distinctive competence they previously lacked or had failed to exploit.

Figure 11.5   Six stages of product evolution

Source: Booz-Allen & Hamilton.

The adoption of search criteria is essential if the firm is to avoid wasteful exploration of the multiplicity of sources open to it. Such sources may be internal or external to the firm.

Internally, every member of the company is a potential source of new product ideas, and company suggestion schemes have thrown up many more valuable suggestions than they are generally credited with. Many companies now have their own Research and Development Department, specifically charged with developing in-house projects, in addition to which Sales, Marketing and Production usually have distinct ideas of how the current product line could be improved or extended.

Externally, the firm's distributors and customers are frequently a fruitful source of ideas, as are the product offerings of one's competitors. Another major source is the published literature of the universities and professional bodies, the technical and trade press, and the various government research departments. Much of the information to be gleaned from these sources is incapable of immediate application but is sufficient to stimulate further investigation – the AFD process described earlier in Chapter 9 is a clear exception to this generalisation.

The major source of ideas for radical innovations is undoubtedly the private inventor, whose work may be reviewed by consulting the Patent Office files or the weekly *Official Journal*. (Few inventors appreciate the commercial potential of their ideas, and those that do frequently meet with a cool reception from potential manufacturers, e.g. Xerography, the Hovercraft, but nearly all patent their ideas.)

In drawing up a short-list of product ideas for detailed investigation the search criteria mentioned earlier will also help reduce the need for subsequent screening, i.e. weeding out of marginal ideas. Such criteria usually require that:

(a) The product will meet a clearly defined consumer need.
(b) The product is consistent with the firm's production and marketing policies.
(c) The product will utilise the firm's existing skills and resources.
(d) The product will contribute to the firm's long-run profitability.

Once a short-list has been compiled, the next step is to evaluate each product's potential. To ensure consistency, many firms make use of a factor rating table similar to that reproduced in Figure 11.6, on page 280–1, which suggests the use of five ratings, ranging from Very Good to Very Poor, for seventeen different factors. By assigning a value, e.g. 10,8,6,4 and 2, to the rating, and by weighting the factors in terms of their relative importance to the firm, it is possible to compute a score for each product idea and limit further investigation to the highest scoring ideas.

Once management is satisfied that the basic idea is indeed consistent with its policies, and within its engineering and production capabilities, it should formulate a product concept, i.e. a precise statement of the need the product will fill and the form it will take. Based on this statement the marketing research department can develop a profile of the potential market and the production department can estimate unit cost at various levels of output. (The latter may necessitate the construction of a prototype(s).) Utilising these data, the marketing department can then develop its own estimate of the costs associated with varying levels of market penetration.

The emphasis upon 'front-end' analysis referred to earlier has had a dramatic effect upon the mortality of new product ideas as can be seen from Figure 11.7, on page 281, reproduced from Rodocanachi 'Successful Management' which compares the findings of the 1968 and 1981 Booz-Allen Studies.

Despite this increased emphasis upon evaluation and screening it appears that the USA still lags considerably behind Japan in the attention given to this phase, which suggests that still more effort will be applied to it in future.

■ Financial considerations

New product introductions represent an investment opportunity for the firm, and it is essential that such opportunities be evaluated in the light of all other possible uses of the firm's resources. In the normal course of events a company is faced with a disparate collection of investment opportunities, and so must develop a common denominator with which it may rank dissimilar projects in order of preference. The discounted cash flow (DCF) technique has been widely adopted for this purpose.

	Very Good	Good	Average	Poor	Very Poor
I. MARKETABILITY					
A. Relation to present distribution channels	Can reach major markets by distribution through present channels	Will have to distribute mostly by distribution through present channels, partly through new channels	Will have to distribute equally between new and present channels, in order to reach major markets	Will have to distribute mostly through new channels, in order to reach major markets	Will have to distribute mostly through new channels, in order to reach major markets
B. Relation to present product lines	Complements a present line which needs more products to fill it	Complements a present line that does not need, but can handle, another product	Can be fitted into a present line	Can be fitted into a present line but does not fit entirely	Does not fit in with any present product line
C. Quality/price relationship	Price below all competing products of similar quality	Price below most competing products of similar quality	Approximately the same price as competing products of similar quality	Price above many competing products of similar quality	Priced above all competing products of similar quality
D. Number of sizes and grades	Few staple sizes and grades	Several sizes and grades, but customers will be satisfied with few staples	Several sizes and grades, but can satisfy customer wants with small inventory of non-staples	Several sizes and grades, each of which will have to be stocked in equal amounts	Many sizes and grades which will necessitate heavy inventories
E. Merchandisability	Has product characteristics over and above those of competing products that lend themselves to the kind of promotion, advertising, and display that the given company does best	Has promotable characteristics that will compare favourably with the characteristics of competing products	Has promotable characteristics that are equal to those of other products	Has a few characteristics that are promotable, but generally does not measure up to characteristics of competing products	Has no characteristics at all that are equal to competitors' or that lend themselves to imaginative promotion
F. Effects on sales of present products	Should aid in sales of present products	May help sales of present products; definitely will not be harmful to present sales	Should have no effect on present sales	May hinder present sales some; definitely will not aid present sales	Will reduce sales of presently profitable products
II. DURABILITY					
A. Stability	Basic product which can always expect to have uses	Product which will have uses long enough to earn back initial investment plus at least ten years of additional profits	Product which will have uses long enough to earn back initial investment plus several (from five to ten) years of additional profits	Product which will have uses long enough to earn back initial investment plus one to five years of additional profits	Product which will probably be obsolete in near future
B. Breadth of market	A national market, a wide variety of consumers and a potential foreign market	A national market and a wide variety of consumers	Either a national market or a wide variety of consumers	A regional market and a restricted variety of consumers	A specialised market in a small marketing area
C. Resistance to cyclical fluctuations	Will sell readily in inflation or depression	Effects of cyclical changes will be moderate, and will be felt after changes in economic outlook	Sales will rise and fall with the economy	Effects of cyclical changes will be heavy, and will be felt before changes in economic outlook	Cyclical changes will cause extreme fluctuations in demand

D. Resistance to seasonal fluctuations	Steady sales throughout the year	Steady sales – except under unusual circumstances	Several fluctuations, but inventory and personnel problems can be absorbed	Heavy seasonal fluctuations that will cause considerable inventory and personnel problems	Severe seasonal fluctuations that will necessitate lay-offs and heavy inventories
E. Exclusiveness of design	Can be protected by a patent with no loopholes	Can be patented, but the patent might be circumvented	Cannot be patented, but has certain salient characteristics that cannot be copied very well	Cannot be patented, and can be copied by larger, more knowledgeable companies	Cannot be patented, and can be copied by anyone
III. PRODUCTIVE ABILITY				
A. Equipment necessary	Can be produced with equipment that is presently idle	Can be produced with present equipment, but production will have to be scheduled with other products	Can be produced largely with present equipment, but the company will have to purchase some additional equipment	Company will have to buy a good deal of new equipment, but some present equipment can be used	Company will have to buy all new equipment
B. Production knowledge and personnel necessary	Present knowledge and personnel will be able to produce new product	With few minor exceptions, present knowledge and personnel will be able to produce new product	With some exceptions, present knowledge and personnel will be able to produce new product	A ratio of approximately 50–50 will prevail between the needs for new knowledge and personnel and for present knowledge and personnel	Mostly new knowledge and personnel are needed to produce the new product
C. Raw materials' availability	Company can purchase raw materials from its best supplier(s) exclusively	Company can purchase major portion of raw materials from its best supplier(s), and remainder from any one of a number of companies	Company can purchase approximately half of raw materials from its best supplier(s), and other half from any one of a number of companies	Company must purchase most of raw materials from any one of a number of companies other than its best supplier(s)	Company must purchase most or all of raw materials from a certain few companies other than its best supplier(s)
IV. GROWTH POTENTIAL				
A. Place in market	New type of product that will fit a need presently not being filled	Product that will substantially improve on products presently on the market	Product that will have certain new characteristics that will appeal to a substantial segment of the market	Product that will have minor improvements over products presently on the market	Product similar to those presently on the market and which adds nothing new
B. Expected competitive situation – value added	Very high value added so as to substantially restrict number of competitors	High enough value added so that, unless product is extremely well suited to other firms, they will not want to invest in additional facilities	High enough value added so that, unless other companies are as strong in market as this firm, it will not be profitable for them to compete	Lower value added so as to allow large, medium and some smaller companies to compete	Very low value added so that all companies can profitably enter market
C. Expected availability of end users	Number of end users will increase substantially	Number of end users will increase moderately	Number of end users will increase slightly, if at all	Number of end users will decrease moderately	Number of end users will decrease substantially

Figure 11.6 Factor and subfactor ratings for a new product

Source: John T. O'Meara, Jr, 'Selecting Profitable Products', *Harvard Business Review* (Jan–Feb 1961) 83–9.

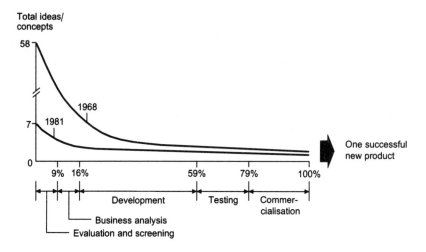

Figure 11.7   Mortality of new product ideas (by stage of evolution)

Source: Pierre Rodocanachi, op cit.

The basic principle upon which the DCF technique is based is recognition of the fact that a currently available sum of money can be invested to generate a stream of future earnings. Thus £1 invested today will be worth £1.10 a year hence if the return on investment is 10 per cent per annum. Conversely, £1 received a year hence is only worth £0.90 today if it could be invested at 10 per cent. By applying the DCF technique one can make direct comparisons of investment opportunities with very dissimilar future cash flows and select the one with the highest net present value. Naturally, the method is not infallible, as it is very dependent upon the accuracy of the predicted future cash flows. The more distant these are the less accurate they become – a factor which partially accounts for the popularity of payback and similar methods which emphasise the time in which the original investment will be recovered. Many students will be familiar with these techniques already: those that are not are recommended to refer to *An Insight into Management Accounting* by John Sizer (3rd edn, Penguin Books, 1989).

At this stage of the new product evaluation procedure it is unlikely that sufficient information exists to permit a detailed comparison of proposals, but even a rough computation will help reduce the list.

■ Testing the product concept

Given the revised short-list, the next step is a detailed feasibility study based on tests of the product concept. Such tests may have been made already, but if not, it is essential that they be undertaken prior to detailed market studies and the finalisation of prototypes. In its original form the product concept represents the marketer's perception of a product which will satisfy a specific consumer want, and may differ considerably from the consumer's own perception of what is required. As it is the latter who ultimately decides whether the product will be a success, reconciliation of any discrepancy is vital. Further, outlining the broad characteristics of a new product to a potential consumer may well stimulate the latter to suggest specific attributes previously unthought of.

In some instances the product concept is too complex to be tested verbally, and some form of mock-up or prototype must be used to communicate the idea and gain consumer reaction. For example, the concept of a cordless telephone or a pick and place robot may be difficult to convey in words but eminently simple to demonstrate.

Once the product concept has been validated, a detailed market study should be undertaken. If it is subsequently decided to market the product this study will form the basis of the marketing plan. Concurrently the engineering and production departments will develop final prototypes, and decide on the production techniques to be used if the project is adopted.

■ Product testing

In view of the high risks associated with new product introductions, field testing should logically precede firm commitment to large-scale production and marketing. Product testing consists of an objective appraisal of the product's performance, free of subjective associations created by other elements of the marketing mix, e.g. price, packaging, brand image, etc. It should not be confused with test marketing, which includes consideration of these factors.

The precise nature of a product test obviously depends upon the product itself but, essentially, all seek to determine how well it will perform in actual use. Certain product atrributes are capable of precise measurement, e.g. the efficiency of an engine, the life of an electric light bulb, whereas others depend upon consumer preference and defy exact quantification, e.g. the taste of a food or beverage. Recognised tests exist for the measurement of most items included in the product specification and subsequently incorporated in the description of the goods as offered for sale. With the passing of the Trade Descriptions Act, 1968, which came into force on 30 November of that year, the importance of ensuring the accuracy of such quantitative statements became a matter of law rather than conscience. This Act makes it an offence to use a false trade description, which is defined as covering:

(a) The composition, quality, quantity, and size of goods.
(b) Their suitability and fitness for any particular purpose.
(c) Their testing or approval by any person.
(d) The method, origin, date of manufacture, production or processing.
(e) Their history and previous ownership.

Under the provisions of the Act, the use of a false description becomes a criminal offence punishable by fine and/or imprisonment, whereas previously misrepresentation was only actionable in a civil action.

As noted, however, many product qualities are a matter of individual perception and preference, the incidence of which can only be established through actual trial. In practice a number of experimental methods have been developed, some of which will already be familiar to the reader as a result of their incorporation in television commercials.

In that the manufacturer is seeking to establish how his new offering will be perceived by the consumer, a commonly used test involves comparison with a leading competitive product. The detergent advertisement which shows two halves of a badly stained article washed in an identical manner, except for the fact that one powder is Spotto and the other Brand X, is an example of such a paired comparison. Although scientifically valid, a successful rating on a blind test in which the new product is identified solely by a code number is no guarantee of market acceptance. The purpose of such tests is to test a specific variable such as taste, texture, washing power, etc., and thus requires that all other variables be held constant. In the real world the consumer does not normally select a product along one dimension alone, even though a single factor such as washing power may predominate. Products are bundles of attributes which are viewed collectively and which create their own associations in the mind of the potential user, so that a preference for A over B based on a single variable may be reversed when all the variables are taken into account. Thus, although a successful product test is an essential preliminary to continued development, it is not conclusive evidence of market success, and many producers will only make a final decision on the product's future after large-scale market testing.

■ Test marketing

Basically, test marketing consists of launching the product on a limited scale in a representative market, thus avoiding the costs of a full-scale launch while permitting the collection of market data which may subsequently be used for predictive purposes.

In practice the term 'test marketing' tends to be used loosely, and it is important to distinguish the original concept, as outlined above, from two associated techniques commonly confused with it. The first of these is often referred to as pilot marketing, and fulfils the same function for the marketer as the pilot plant does for the production engineer, i.e. it tests the feasibility of the proposed course of action. In many instances companies become so involved with the development of a new product that by the time successful product tests have been completed they feel irrevocably committed, and any course of action other than full-scale marketing is unthinkable. However, companies of this type are usually aware of the critical importance of a well-designed and co-ordinated marketing plan, and so test its feasibility in practice prior to full-scale operations. Pilot marketing on a regional basis may also serve to give the firm valuable marketing experience while commissioning new plant to meet the anticipated demands of a national market.

The other practice often confused with test marketing is the testing of mix variables, i.e. measuring the effect of changes in the test variable, all other variables being held constant, e.g. copy testing. Such tests are often used to improve the marketing of existing products, and should not be confused with the true test market in which the collective impact of all variables is being tested simultaneously.

It is clear that if test market results are to be used to predict the likely outcome of a full-scale national launch, then the test market must constitute a representative sample of the national market. Despite the claims of various media owners it is equally clear that no such perfect microcosm exists and that test marketing is of dubious value if undertaken for predictive purposes alone. In addition to the dangers inherent in scaling up atypical test market results to derive national sales forecasts, many marketers feel that test marketing increases the risks of aggressive competitive reaction in an attempt to nip the new product in the bud. Test market validity depends heavily on the assumption that trading conditions in the market are 'normal', and it follows that any departure from such conditions will bias the results. Competitors learn quickly of test marketing operations and typically react in one of two ways. If the new product closely resembles existing brands, the manufacturers of these brands will usually step up their advertising and sales promotion in the test market to maintain existing brand loyalties and prevent the new entrant getting a foothold. These tactics also ensure the existence of 'abnormal' trading conditions during the test period. Alternatively, if the new product represents a radical departure from existing products, competitors can easily monitor its test market performance while developing their own substitutes. If the test results seem promising the imitative innovator may well enter the national market at the same time as the originator of the idea – if not before!

For these reasons many manufacturers now undertake more exhaustive tests of the mix variables and omit the test market stage altogether. This approach is strongly favoured by Jananese companies. If the new product is launched on a limited scale initially, more often than not it is in the nature of a feasibility study rather than in the hope of obtaining hard data from which to predict the outcome of a national launch.

Evidence to support this view was provided by an article in the 29 October (1984) issue of *Fortune* ('Testing Time for Test Marketing', Eleanor Johnson Tracy).

According to the author:

Revolution is coming to test marketing. Not so long ago it was heresy for a U. S. company to introduce a new product nationwide without reams of test results gleaned from 3% of the population over at least a year. But traditional test marketing is slow, expensive, and open to spying and sabotage. So some consumer goods companies now use a much smaller sample over a much shorter time to probe the market. Sometimes they bring out a new product without test marketing it at all.

Procter & Gamble, which practically wrote the primer on test marketing, is a leader in changing the rules. The Cincinnati giant tested its new encapsulated aspirin, Encaprin, for only three months in one market before rolling out nationwide in June. It put Folgers instant decaffeinated coffee on U. S. shelves without test marketing. Other companies shunning the conventional test-market route: Quaker Oats with Chewy Granola Bars and chocolate-covered Granola Dipps; Sara Lee, a division of Consolidated Foods, with frozen croissants; and Campbell Soup with its Pepperidge Farm Star Wars cookies. This year Pillsbury introduced Milk Break Bar, a cream-filled chocolate-covered wafer, without test marketing, even though it was the company's first venture into the ready-to-eat snack market.

In addition to test marketing being 'slow, expensive, and open to spying and sabotage' its demise is being hastened by the availability of alternative methods for assessing likely market response. Among these alternatives the simulated test market and, scanner-based test marketing are the most popular and widely used techniques.

In a simulated test market consumers are recruited in retail outlets, asked to read an advertisement about a new product and given a free sample of it. Subsequently, the consumer is asked to rate the product (by means of a telephone interview in the USA) and these data are used to predict market response by means of a computer programme. Apparently this method is quite successful at

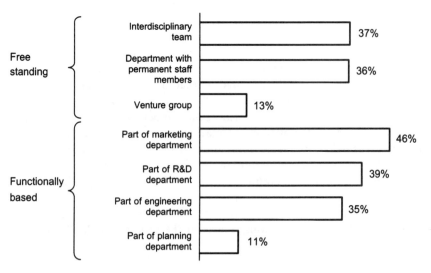

Figure 11.8　New product development structures

Source: Booz-Allen & Hamilton.

weeding out potential failures for a modest investment ($40 000) but is less good at predicting actual potential.

A more sophisticated approach is the scanner-based test in which consumers in selected markets get an identification card which is presented at the retail check-out. Using the product codes a record is made of purchase, without the consumer or competitors knowing which product(s) are being tested, which enables prediction to be made about take-up and sales potential.

■ Organising for new product development

In Chapter 19 (Organising for Marketing) passing reference is made to compromise structures suited to new product development. In the 1981 Booz-Allen survey this issue was given considerable attention and revealed the existence of two broad approaches described as free standing and functional. As can be seen from Figure 11.8, free standing approaches, which consist of an independent team, can be sub-divided into three main types while teams based in a functional department are of four main types.

According to Rodocanachi, 'Successful companies tend to use more than one organisational concept, mixing and matching not only the approach but the types of skills and leadership elements of the team.' Based on this observation three basic organisational approaches are identified as illustrated in Figure 11.9.

These approaches are described as follows:

> The first is the entrepreneurial approach, typically used for developing new-to-the-world products. The structure requires an interdisciplinary venture team and a manager with the ability to integrate diverse functional skills. This is an autonomous

Approach	Skill mix	Leadership
● Entrepreneurial	● Interdisciplinary venture team	● integrative manager
● Collegial	● New Product specialists	
	● Marketing R&D	● Functional manager
● Managerial	● Specific functions	

Figure 11.9   New product organisation

Source: Pierre Rodocanachi, op. cit.

new products 'group, usually reporting to a general manager. Success requires involvement of, and strong commitment from, top management. Typically, the process, the management structure, and the requirements for formal business planning are less rigid than other approaches. Usually, an incentive system promotes risk taking by rewarding handsomely for success.

The second is the collegial approach, typically used to enter new businesses or add substantially different products to existing lines. This approach requires strong senior-management support and participation in decision making, a commitment to risk taking, and a formal new products process to guide the effort and ensure discipline. It also requires a clear commitment to provide whatever is necessary for success and for expediting decisions.

The third is the managerial approach. This is the standard process used for existing business management. It involves strong planning and heavy emphasis on functional leadership to drive new products in manufacturing, distribution, marketing, or the like. It tends to be a rigid new products process involving many levels of management, quick promotion of successful new product managers, limited risk incentives, and rigorous application of financial criteria.

The more successful companies match all of the elements just discussed to specific new products opportunities. The organizational approach and extent of top-management support vary, based on the specific needs of each new products opportunity. As the newness of the product increases, the entrepreneurial, integrative focus of the team increases, along with the involvement and support of top management.

An analysis by *Fortune* (15 October 1984) of 'Eight Big Masters of Innovation' confirms this need for organisational flexibility when it reported:

New models of corporate organization are emerging at the innovative companies. To retain an entrepreneurial feel for their markets, most of them work hard to stay highly decentralized. 3M, for example, encourages a process analogous to cell mitosis: as they develop new products, units of the organization subdivide into new units. At Campbell Soup, $3.3 billion in sales is spread among 52 so-called strategic business units.

The ability to make use of the market information gleaned by decentralized operations seems to depend on compressing the lines of communication between the chief executive and the middle manager. Apple achieved this by flattening its organization chart: fully 15 people report to Chief Executive John Sculley, and a line manager of modest responsibility is rarely more than three reporting levels away.

All these companies believe in keeping their management ranks lean, but even those with relatively thick layers of management have developed ways of keeping top management in touch.

■ Product portfolio analysis

Thus far the discussion has tended to look at products, and especially new products, as if every firm produced only a single product. In reality most firms have a range or portfolio of products each of which may be at a different stage in its life-cycle. It is recognition of this which led the Boston Consulting Group to propose a diagnostic procedure for analysing the comparative and collective performance of different products in a firm's range which has since become famous as the 'Boston Box'. While several variants of the Boston Box have been proposed they all rest on two fundamental propositions, namely that the 'competitive value of market share depends on the structure of competition and the stage of the product life cycle' (G. S. Day, 'Diagnosing the Product Portfolio', *Journal of Marketing*, April 1977).

The importance of taking into account the stage which a product (or industry) has reached in its life-cycle is fundamental to the whole concept and practice of marketing. As we saw in Chapter 1 when reviewing the evolution of the marketing concept, survival depends upon understanding and satisfying the needs of customers and realisation and acceptance of the fact that over time these needs will change, often due to the action of marketers; hence, the product life-cycle. If, then, we accept the inevitability of the PLC it follows that even where we are concerned with a basic product such as steel with a life span of decades we would be unwise to assume that any particular formulation or, more important, method of manufacture is immune to competition and replacement. To guard against this possibility product differentiation has become a key competitive strategy and new product development an essential activity, so that even the overtly single product firm should have a range of products at different stages of development.

The emphasis upon market share as a surrogate for profitability has been extensively documented since the publication of the PIMS (Profit Impact of Market Strategy) analysis by the Marketing Science Institute based on a technique developed by General Electric. However, as Day points out, in many situations market share is a poor proxy as its use rests on the assumption that all competitors 'have the same overhead structures and experience curves, with their position on the experience curve corresponding to their market share position'. Thus market share indicates *relative* profitability between firms in direct competition (Ford *vs.* General Motors) but neglects factors which affect *absolute* profit performance when comparing dissimilar products.

Day cites a number of other pitfalls in using portfolio analysis and the issue is discussed in considerable detail in Alan Morrison and Robin Wensley, 'Boxing up or Boxed in? A Short History of the Boston Consulting Group Share/Growth Matrix' (*Journal of Marketing Management*, vol. 7.2, 1991) which the student should consult for details. However, the purpose here is to introduce a conceptual approach which has secured extensive support among practising managers for at least the three reasons cited by Day:

> They [managers] are first attracted by the intuitively appealing concept that long-run corporate performance is more than the sum of the contributions of individual profit centres or product strategies. Secondly, a product portfolio analysis suggests specific marketing strategies to achieve a balanced mix of products that will produce

the maximum long-run effects from scarce cash and managerial resources. Lastly the concept employs a simple matrix representation which is easy to communicate and comprehend.

A typical example of this matrix is reproduced as Figure 11.10 using market share and market growth (a proxy for stage in the PLC) as the relevant parameters. In this matrix no values are attached to market share or growth rate although these will usually be included when assessing the comparative performance of one's own products against those of the market leader. Hence the purpose is solely to distinguish the four basic categories of product, the desired movement of businesses over time, and the likely movement of cash between them.

Wildcat businesses (also known as problem children) represent products at the beginning of their life-cycle where hopes run high and expectations of rapid growth and profitability encourage the firm to invest heavily in its new product despite uncertainty as to its eventual success. Clearly, the hope is that by so doing the product or business will get on to the rapid growth curve when sales expand

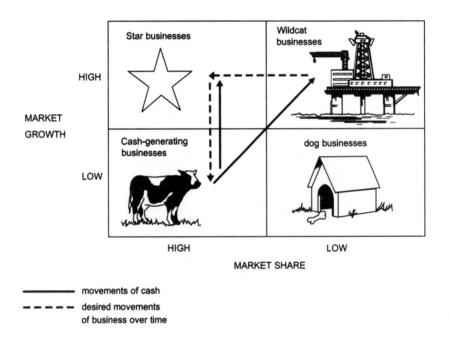

Figure 11.10   The product portfolio

Source: The Conference Board.

exponentially and costs and overheads decline rapidly as a result of economies of scale and growing experience. At this stage of market development competition is fierce as firms jockey for position to become 'stars' and seek to secure cost and price advantages which will enable them to secure the dominant share of the new market.

To achieve this all the cash generated has to be ploughed back into the business together with the profits from the products at the mature stage of their life-cycle represented as cash cows. Finally, while the transition from cash cow to dog is not a desired move the PLC concept tells us that this is inevitable as the mature phase degenerates into decay and senility with declining growth and profitability.

As noted in a 1974 report from the Conference Board, the construction of product portfolios has significant implications for the firm's corporate planning, namely:

1. Careful and continuous watch must be kept on competitors in the star businesses, lest any of them gains leadership in market share.
2. For the corporation as a whole, the overriding objective should be to maximise the net present value of the portfolio of businesses over the planning period, subject to the constraints of financial or other corporate policies.
3. It is vital to achieve a sound balance in terms of financial and managerial resources among cash cow, wild cat and star businesses.
4. The family of businesses is dynamic. In time, wild cats will become stars – or dogs. Stars will become cows – or, if inadequately nourished – dogs. Eventually, new stars or new wild cats will be needed; hence corporate management must be ever-concerned with new products, new markets and acquisitions. It should strive to postpone indefinitely corporate maturity.

While it is not possible to pursue these issues in greater detail in an introductory text, it should be clear that *Product Policy, Planning and Development* is at the very heart of the marketing process. Indeed, we can safely say that the best marketing advice we can offer is 'Build a better product at the same price as your competitor or the same product at a lower price.' While achievement of this ideal will not eliminate the need for the other elements of the marketing mix – distribution and promotion – it will go a long way to ensuring success.

Similarly, space limitations preclude discussion of the actual management of the product as it progresses through its life-cycle – particularly the variations in emphasis upon the mix elements both individually and together. However, an extended treatment of these issues is to be found in *Marketing Management and Strategy* (Macmillan, 1985).

CHAPTER 12

Packaging

Learning Goals

The issues to be discussed in this chapter include:

1. The basic functions of packaging desired by consumers and distributors and required by law.
2. The use of packaging as a variable in the marketing mix.
3. Environmental concerns and trends in packaging development.

After reading this chapter you will be familiar with:

1. The protective information and usage functions looked for in packaging by consumers and distributors.
2. The legal requirements covering disclosure of information on packaging (UK and EEC).
3. The use of packaging as a marketing mix variable and source of competitive advantage.
4. Ways in which a growing concern for environmental matters is influencing attitudes to the use of packaging materials.

Surprisingly few introductory marketing texts devote much attention to the role of packaging as an element in the marketing mix. When one considers that total packaging industry sales amounted to over £7612 million in 1988, and have risen steadily since, it is clear that packaging costs are a major marketing expenditure and deserve fuller treatment.

The present lack of attention is partially attributable to the tendency to classify packaging as a production cost, so that it is seldom isolated in the way that expenditures on advertising and promotion are. In part it is also attributable to the practical function which the pack performs, which tends to shield it from public scrutiny of the type directed at promotional expenditures whose practical virtues are less easily discernible. In reality packaging costs often exceed all other marketing costs and, in some instances, constitute the major element of total cost, e.g. cosmetics. These facts were emphasised by a cost analysis of the items in a household food basket in which it was found that while advertising only accounted for 2 per cent of the total cost packaging materials were responsible for 22 per cent or eleven times as much. In the same vein the chairman of Teacher's the whisky producers was quoted in the *Financial Times* in June 1973 as stating 'In spite of stringent control in purchasing materials at the lowest possible cost consistent with quality, the value of the packaging material in a standard case now exceeds that of the whisky.'

Although more recent data are hard to come by, it is clear that the trend for packaging to comprise an increasing proportion of the total cost of convenience goods continues. In an article in *Retail and Distribution Management* (Mar–Apr 1974) reference was made to the rapidly increasing costs of packaging raw materials, together with the observation that 'We may soon reach the situation where the plastic and cardboard wrapper around four tomatoes or half a dozen nails costs more than the goods involved.' In absolute terms it is quite clear that packaging costs have increased significantly in recent years, as can be seen from Table 12.1.

Table 12.1 Manufacturers' sales of packaging products: summary (millions)

	1983	1984	1985	1986	1987	1988
Paper and board	1267.4	1412.8	1520.4	1568.3	1682.6	1823.2
Plastic	782	883.9	975.4	1089.2	1298.5	1570.5
Metal	1141.9	1259.1	1334.5	1359.8	1412.1	1506.1
Glass	370.7	370.2	397.3	385.6	391.3	407.4
Wood	116.7	128	131.9	154.1	185.5	198
Canvas	20.1	23.3	20.6	26.7	33.4	35.5
Total	3698.8	4077.3	4380.1	4583.7	5003.4	5540.6

Source: Business Statistics Office, (1989) *Business Monitor*, London, HMSO.

■ Basic packaging functions

The basic function of any pack is to protect its contents in transit, in storage and in use. This criterion will play a major role in determining the shape, size and materials used, but in recent years there has been a tendency to subordinate such practical aspects to design and promotional considerations. In most cases there will be little or no conflict between the physical characteristics considered desirable by manufacturers and distributors and the promotional and design elements demanded by consumers. However, it will be useful to consider the requirements of these two groups separately to emphasise the varying nature of their needs.

■ Distributor requirements

As noted, the prime function of any pack is to protect the contents. From this it follows that pack design will depend very largely on the nature of the contents in terms of their value, physical composition and durability. In addition one must also take into account the length of the distribution channel, the amount of handling which the container will receive, and variations in climatic conditions which may be encountered between the point of manufacture and sale.

Most small items are bulk-packed in some type of outer container capable of withstanding the anticipated degree of rough handling. However, such containers can only reduce the shock of mishandling, so that the individual packs must also be capable of resisting such punishment. An example of the degree of protection necessary is provided by the findings of the Printing, Packaging and Allied Trades Research Association that containers which one man is just capable of handling are likely to be dropped from a height of three feet somewhere in transit. This distance corresponds to waist height, or the level of a lorry tailboard, and requires that containers should be able to withstand an equivalent shock. It was also found that heavier packages tended to receive more careful handing as two men were needed to lift them or else mechanical handling methods were used e.g. fork-lift trucks. Such methods are widely used now, and it is in the packer's interest to determine the capacity of such equipment and take it into account in establishing bulk pack size and weight. Modifications to containers to satisfy mechanical handling requirements may well increase their intrinsic cost, but such costs are invariably more than recouped through a reduction in the amount of handling required.

Breakage in transit due to rough handling is only one aspect of protection, and equal attention must be given to spoilage from other causes. Foremost among these are moisture, fungus, insects and exposure to sunlight.

Transportation and storage costs are usually computed on the basis of weight and/or volume, and it is clearly in the manufacturer's interest to use packages which make maximum use of a given space. At the retail level the space/volume factor takes on added importance, as it directly affects the number of different items which can be put on display. Sales per square foot, or per linear foot of shelf, are frequently used measures of retail productivity, and it is clear that retailers will avoid packs which occupy a disproportionate amount of space in relation to their value. However, the retailer, like the manufacturer, recognises that purely physical properties must be modified in the light of consumer preferences, and so may be prepared to subordinate these in favour of packs with greater promotional appeal.

■ Consumer requirements

Reference has already been made to the fact that the packaging of consumer goods was originally a retailing function but that competitive pressures, and the growth of branding, resulted in the manufacturer assuming responsibility for it.

Through the adoption of a distinctive pack and brand name, the manufacturer is able to differentiate his product at the point of sale and to develop advertising and promotional strategies designed to create consumer preference for his output. Further, by packaging the product himself the manufacturer is able to exercise much greater control over the condition in which the ultimate consumer will receive it, and so avoid dissatisfaction arising from poor storage and packing at the retail level.

Essentially, consumers want products, and have little direct interest in their packaging *per se*. In many instances, however, the satisfaction to be derived from a product is dependent upon its packaging, and consumers are receptive to both technical and aesthetic improvements in pack design. Many competing products are incapable of differentiation on the basis of objective criteria, and in these instances packaging and promotion often constitute the sole distinguishing features upon which the product's success or failure depends.

A clear example of this is the United Kingdom sardine market. Some years ago a number of fish packers in Britain offered a variety of brands of sardines in competition with Scandinavian and Portuguese imports. Although sardines tend to be associated with the latter countries, the domestic product was competitively priced and secured a strong following among those who could perceive no difference in product quality – real or imagined. As a group, however, sardine eaters became increasingly frustrated by the difficulties associated with opening the conventional pack, as the tag frequently broke when the key was turned, facing them with the almost impossible task of opening the tin with an ordinary tin-opener. In part the trouble was due to the fact that few people used the key correctly, but it was also due to the lock-seamed construction of the can which required that the tag be sufficiently strong to tear open a double thickness of material at the seam. The Scandinavians overcame this problem by adopting aluminium lids, while the Portuguese soldered the lid to the body, leaving a line of weakness which opened easily. Neither course was open to the British packers – aluminium is much more expensive than in Scandinavia, and high labour costs precluded following the Portuguese practice. Consumers responded enthusiastically to the new pack and the domestic share of market sagged dismally owing to the inability of the United Kingdom packers to duplicate the improved container at a competitive price. Ease of opening is clearly a significant consumer 'plus'.

Conventional demand curves indicate that as price falls the volume demanded will increase. In theory this relationship is continuous and we can establish the volume which will be demanded at any given price. In practice prices are discrete and should properly be represented by a 'stepped' demand curve. However, theory suggests that if the manufacturer can offer his product at a lower price he will be able to increase demand, and this is frequently achieved by offering the consumer a variety of different sizes. In addition to catering for variations in household size and usage rates, a range of pack sizes enables the manufacturer to reach consumers with limited purchasing power. As the retired population expands less perceptive marketers will increasingly come to appreciate that lifelong consumption patterns may well have to be modified as inflation reduces the purchasing power of fixed retirement incomes. It would be naive to expect manufacturers to offer small packs at a price proportionate to the 'standard' size in view of the high proportion of fixed costs incurred irrespective of unit size. None the less, the provision of non-standard pack sizes is not only good marketing, it is a socially desirable activity.

Many products are not consumed immediately the package is opened but are used over varying periods of time. To prevent spoilage such products must be packed in resealable containers, the most familiar of which are the screw-top bottle and jar, and the lever-lid can. Screw-top jars have long been in use for the packaging of products containing sugar, such as jam, which are susceptible to mould when exposed to the atmosphere. However, cheap metal screw caps have only recently come into their own as bottle closures as an alternative to the crown cork. The latter suffers from the disadvantage that it is difficult to remove without an opener and cannot be reused unless fitted with a plastic insert, which greatly reduces its cost advantage as a closure. Lever-lid cans are widely used for packaging hygroscopic materials such as dried milk, instant coffee, cocoa and health salts, but are losing ground to plastics for certain applications. Although ease of opening and reclosure are desirable, many mothers want a pack to be stable and 'child-proof', to prevent accidents to young children, and will show a preference for packs with the latter attributes.

Visual appeal is also an important aspect of pack design, particularly in the case of products of a luxury or semi-luxury nature where the pack itself may add to the image of product quality which the manufacturer is seeking to create. Some critics have argued that elaborate and expensive packaging is used to disguise inferior products, or to permit the seller to inflate the true worth of the product. Neither claim will sustain much examination, for poor packaging is almost always a good indicator of a poor product, and no amount of packaging can disguise a poor product for long. Similarly, few consumers are prepared to pay more for a product solely on account of its packaging unless such packaging will add to their enjoyment of the product itself – After Eight Mints are a classic example, and it is irrelevant if the added satisfaction is purely subjective to the consumer and incapable of objective measurement.

Finally, consumers demand packages which satisfy their information needs. Certain information is required by law, e.g. statement of weight and composition of product, although frequently the latter is expressed in language incomprehensible to the average consumer. In addition to this basic information, consumers favour a clearly marked price (now largely a retailer responsibility since the abolition of Resale Price Maintenance), information on how the product should or may be used, and, preferably, some view of the contents themselves.

■ Legal requirements

In addition to providing a distinctive and appealing means of identifying and protecting, the pack must also provide the user with information concerning its contents. Some of this information may be required by law. The production and design of packaging is influenced by the ever-increasing amount of information which by law must appear on it. Two examples are given of the nature of product information required:

1. *Food products* in general must be marked with:
   - a description of the contents
   - an indication of the physical form of the food
   - a list of ingredients in order of weight
   - any food which is characterised by the presence of a particular ingredient must have a declaration of the % contents of that ingredient
   - an indication of any storage conditions and its minimum durability
   - any necessary instructions for use.
2. *Cosmetics* must be marked with:
   - name and address of an EEC seller or manufacturer
   - batch number
   - description of product
   - any relevant expiry date
   - warnings or cautions necessary
   - required references to particular ingredients.

There is strong pressure for more information – America and Germany already have ingredient declarations on cosmetic products.

The rights to package designs are another legal aspect of packaging. In today's market where products are sold by the shape of the packaging as much as anything else, design registrations can be very valuable, especially in the areas of wine, spirit, toiletries and cosmetics packaging. Other means of securing the legal rights over a product package include the following:

(a) Patent Rights – for a new invention or application.
(b) Copyright – provided the existence and ownership can be proved this is a powerful weapon against imitators.
(c) Trademarks – may assist in distinguishing packaging from competitors'. Directories are available in most technical libraries. For information on existing trade names, see for example, *Trade Marks: a Guide to the Literature and Directory of Lists of Trade Names*, Brenda M. Rimmer (British Library; Science Reference Library, Occasional Publications, 1976).

To secure ownership of these legal rights you must:

1. Identify the designer. You must know who made the design, are they an employee or contracted labour? One person or several?
2. Ensure that the rights have been assigned to you. There should be a standard clause in contracts of employment concerning the ownership of

copyrights. Formal assignment documents for employees and contracted workers may be advisable.

3. Keep the original drawings. A file should be kept with the history of the development of the packaging and signed, dated original drawings.

Britain's membership of the EEC has had its effect on the legal requirements for packaging – new rules have been agreed for the labelling of packaged food and drink products, and these new labels appeared in British shops in 1983. The most important change was that all products had to list ingredients, including additives. The Food and Drinks Industry Council has anticipated the confusion that this might cause, and published an explanatory leaflet listing the purpose of every food additive. For example, butylated hydroxytoluene prevents oils on crisps and fried snacks going off, sodium nitrate gives bacon a long storage life and its pink colour, and monosodium glutamate is a flavour enhancer used in prepared meats and savoury foods.

Another effect of Britain's membership of the EEC is in the area of unit pricing. This is a system of selling products in standardised pack sizes and marking on the pack the price per unit of quantity and the actual price. This promotes easy comparison of products by consumers and thus should lead to fair competition. The current EEC status on unit prices is an optional directive concerning prescribed quantities on a wide range of products and a mandatory directive concerning unit pricing on foodstuffs. There are constant pressures to expand this to other products. Some EEC countries, e.g. Germany, enforce prescribed quantities; however, others including the UK regard this regulation with caution, preferring to operate without these regulations. Some products, however – for example, bread, jam, tea and canned products – have long had standardised pack sizes.

We have discussed here a few of the existing and future legal requirements for packaging. It is impossible to generalise any further as there is no complete summary of legal requirements in existence at present, only partial summaries as the legal requirements will vary by type of product. Specialised advice should be sought on this from any of the trade bodies and institutions included at the end of this chapter.

▌ The resolution of conflict between distributor/user requirements

Such conflict as does exist between user and distributor requirements is almost invariably resolved in favour of the user. Diseconomies in weight/volume relationships due to the use of odd-shaped containers, and losses due to breakages can often be minimised through the use of standardised outer containers. However, the manufacturer can only afford to incur such additional costs if the consumer is prepared to pay a premium for the added benefits received.

Similarly, retailers are more concerned with turnover and gross margins than with the actual number of units on display. If it can be shown that although a promotional pack may occupy twice the space of a conventional container, it will generate increased demand or help build store traffic, then the retailer will usually co-operate in the promotion, e.g. Pyrex coffee jugs filled with instant coffee.

However, manufacturers are not unresponsive to retailer demands and many new packs have been developed as a result of pressure from the big food chains, especially those employing self-service. Self-service has largely replaced counter service owing to the lower operating costs possible through the elimination of sales assistants. This in turn has stimulated manufacturers to develop new packaging materials to help the product sell itself and lead to the elimination of many traditional practices.

In the former category may be included plastic bottles, first introduced in 1964 by ICI, aluminium foil, bubble-packs, and shrink-wrapping for prepackaged meats, etc. In the latter category the one-trip bottle was developed to encourage supermarkets to carry carbonated beverages, which they had virtually dropped owing to the diseconomies associated with returning deposits and handling empty bottles. Innovation has not been confined to the development of new materials alone, and many improvements have been made in the use of traditional materials. Lightweight tinplate has reduced both the cost and weight of cans and closures, while increased strength has permitted the development of the aerosol, sales of which now amount to hundreds of millions every year. The difficulties described earlier in connection with sardine cans have now been overcome with the development of the Ziehfix can in which the lid is attached to the body by a rubber sealing ring and is easily stripped off. (It is doubtful if this innovation would have saved the sardine packer, for such cans cost more to manufacture than a conventional can. For a distinctive product such as John West's kipper fillets the added cost would appear to justify the convenience, however.) Similarly, the strip-top beer can has combined the advantages of two competing materials – aluminium and tinplate.

■ The package as a marketing variable

In recent years a number of articles have appeared describing how manufacturers have used packaging as a competitive weapon in their marketing strategy. The one-trip bottle was adopted by Schweppes in an attempt to recapture the market share lost to Beechams, who had capitalised on the supermarkets' unwillingness to handle returnable bottles by introducing the Hunt range of 'mixers' in cans. After Eight Mints' luxury image was born out of careful pack design backed up by an effective advertising campaign. Van den Bergh commissioned Rockwell glass to design a streamlined, lightweight bottle for their Tree Top line of fruit squashes to give it added appeal at the point of sale.

The contribution of packaging (reinforced by effective promotion) to the expansion of an established brand is exemplified by no. 6 in the series 'Marketing Case Studies from ITV Advertisers', which describes the campaign to reposition R. Whites Lemonade following its merger with Canada Dry in 1980. As the case study reports:

> Currently over two billion litres of colas, mixers and other carbonates worth just over £1 billion are consumed in the UK. 'Other Carbonates' account for 61 per cent of volume and 49 per cent by value.
>
> Although the Soft Drinks Market is now fairly static overall, following a period of steady volume growth in the 1970s, certain sectors are continuing to develop. Thus, whilst on-licence sales have been particularly affected by the recession, the take-home sector of the market is continuing to expand.
>
> Grocery outlets are increasing their hold on the take-home market but traditional distribution through off-licences and CTNs remains important for all forms of carbonated soft drinks.
>
> Lemonade accounts for around 80 per cent of sales of the 'other carbonates' grocery sector of the market.
>
> In line with the growth of the grocery sector has been the growing importance of own label' and a comparable increase in marketing and promotional activity by the major brands. Distribution trends have also had a major effect of packaging, particularly in terms of the development of plastic bottles able to contain carbonated drink (polythene terephalate, or PET as they are known in the trade). These bottles are not only easy to handle but, due to their lightness, facilitate larger sizes. Recently there has also been a rapid expansion in sales of the new ¼-litre can.
>
> All in all, therefore, an increasingly competitive market where the large brands are fighting it out with each other and 'own label'.

Canada Dry Rawlings Limited

R. Whites Lemonade is marketed by Canada Dry Rawlings, a company formed by the merger of Canada Dry (UK) Limited, and R. Whites & Sons Limited/H. D. Rawlings Limited, in 1980. These companies represent the soft drinks interests of Bass and Whitbread, Bass Limited owning 65 per cent and Whitbread and Company Limited 35 per cent.

Canada Dry Rawlings Limited is the third largest company in the British Soft Drinks industry. The formation of the Company means it has historic strengths in brands for each sector of the Soft Drinks market. Canada Dry Mixers, Rawlings Fruit Juices, Squashes and Cordials, R. Whites flavoured carbonates, Bass, Pilsner and Cyder Shandies, Barbican alcohol free lager, and Buxton Spring Waters. This means that Canada Dry Rawlings offers a soft drink range that is second to none for variety and quality.

R. Whites lemonade

Since 1978 R. Whites has been relatively dormant, and packaging developments within the soft drinks market has not been pursued. After the merger in 1980, the company capitalised on these trends and introduced 1½-litre PET bottles in late 1981. This pack proved to be a great success, especially in the multiple sector of the trade, and was followed in early 1982 by the introduction of the 2-litre pack. This was followed in April 1982 by the repackaging of the litre non-returnable glass bottle in a new lightweight bottle with a pre-printed wrap-around label. At the same time the R. Whites canned carbonate range was reintroduced in the new ¼-litre can.

The launch of the new packs spearheaded a massive sales and distribution drive, and at the same time the brand received overall support from television advertising in London, South and Midlands – currently the strongest sales areas for R. Whites Lemonade.

Recall of the campaign to increase awareness showed an improvement from under 20 per cent to around 60 per cent, but more important still, sales improved significantly, particularly for the ¼-litre can and 1½-litre PET bottle, under-lining the importance of using packaging as an important variable in the marketing mix.

An article in *Marketing*, 'A Nation of Importers', by Ludo Pinxt (4 October 1984), provides several powerful examples to support the author's claim that:

'Britons spend £40.85 bn on food and drink every year but British food manufactur-ers are missing out on a large chunk of this business by failing to recognise the need for new products. The result is that European companies are taking the business with more interesting products, more imaginatively packaged and displayed.' Given that true innovation in food stuffs are few and far between it is clear that processing and packaging play the critical role in a food company's marketing strategy, as Pinxt's examples clearly demonstrate.

Take coffee cream, which is a basic German supermarket line. 'The product cannot alter, but the presentation can. One maker now markets its product in a vacuum-formed container that is made in the shape of a lidded jug which works better and looks different. The result is product advantage for the manufacturer and added value for the consumer.

Pinxt also draws attention to the fact that canners of fish products like John West and Carnation have done nothing to add any excitement to standard products like tuna fish, while Saupiquet, a continental producer, offers six varieties (tuna and capers, etc.) as well as four tuna snack dishes. However, product modification is only part of the story.

With Saupiquet it was not just a product change, but a packaging change as well. Canning is seen as an outmoded concept in the UK, but this is because UK food processors have been slow to take up new packaging methods.

Saupiquet sells its new snack range in new canning packs that do away with the concept of the old hard-to-open can. The process, now well accepted in Europe, involves preprinting the entire pack design, including the top, on to a flat sheet of metal, then punching it into a can shape. This provides more scope for graphics and branding, and also makes it possible for the base to become a single ring-pull section, which does away with the need for a special opener. The new snack lines have become an instant meal purchase, competing with other forms of takeaway food.

Saupiquet produced a different product, differently packaged and displayed. The process is not unknown in Britain, but while cans of this type are seen in provincial supermarkets, the contents are invariably imported pates, salads, fish and processed meat products. When shown to a senior UK food marketing manager recently, the pack was dismissed with the claim that it could not be done. It can be done, and is being done, along with a wide variety of other technical advances in Europe, with the result that even very basic or familiar products can be re-presented with great success to consumers in the marketplace.

It is not true to say that the British won't try anything new. The concept of the wine box was taken from Australia and refined in the UK as a new marketing concept. But why not a variety of plastic containers to create product advantage and difference? All are in use on the Continent.

Multiple packaging

And why not more multiple packaging to create more choice and demand? In France and Germany, yogurt makers package up six, even twelve, different flavours in one multiple pack. The purchase appears different from endless plastic cartons, and gives consumers the opportunity to try different flavours which, individually, they might not choose.

Enlightened UK marketers show what can be achieved, with imagination. Long Clawson Dairy, a fast-growing cheese company in Leicestershire, acknowledges that its success in its first year of exporting – worth £1m – was learned from continental rivals. Marketing manager Keith Tate says: 'We have learned an awful lot, in a short space of time, from continental cheese suppliers, who pay particular attention to packaging.' And £1m on a total turnover of £11m is new business worth learning about.

In Holland, Denmark, Italy and France, the designer is always designing for markets other than the home market, pushed by marketing managers constantly looking across borders for new business. Britons tend to wait for someone else to prove a new idea, and then produce a me-too. Why wait for the Danes to import crispy fried onions such as the recent Mr Funions range?

The UK attitude of 'I don't believe it can be done' is replaced on the Continent with 'This is what we want. Find a way of getting it done.' It can be as simple as repackaging existing products – peas and carrots look tantalising in glass jars in French supermarkets even though the product is the same as the discredited canned peas and carrots in the UK.

It is a matter of approach – an approach which argues that the market is constantly looking for new products, whether new or apparently new, and that it is better to get in first, rather than come along later with a me-too. Me-too can be too late.

Many of the innovations cited in this article have now been adopted by British food manufacturers, but the advice remains sound. In a crowded market place packaging and presentation at the point of sale may be the sole means of attracting attention and purchase. The need for continuous innovation is obvious.

■ Future trends in packaging

Major changes in the areas of packaging systems and materials are few and far between because the problem is not only to develop a new idea, but that it should be of enough consequence to merit a change from the existing method of packaging. A change usually involves a good deal of capital expenditure, and this is the main factor which helps to maintain the status quo.

Today, however, there is a growing cost differential between the packaging currently being used and their possible substitutes. This can be shown by the amount of energy used in the creation of packaging materials.

Energy content:	Glass pack	6542 kJ per unit
	Metal pack	5191 kJ per unit
	Bag in box*	3046 kJ per unit

(*carton containing powdered or granulated products)

The actual costs will very approximately reflect these differences.

One recent development which is threatening the glass industry is PET (polyethylene terephthalate), a type of polyester. This is mainly produced in Britain by ICI. This material is increasingly being used in the USA, Britain and Japan, especially in the area of non-returnable soft drinks bottles. In 1982 in Britain for the first time PET took a larger share of the soft drinks packaging trade than glass; 15 per cent PET, 12 per cent glass. This growth is expected to continue, as PET is expanding into other packaging fields such as beer, wine and fruit drinks and was used in 1983 for the first time as a container for spirit miniatures by international airlines. This is because of the substantial weight reduction – PET miniatures weigh 9 gm compared with 63 gm for a glass container, and this leads to savings on fuel for the airlines.

It is predicted by V. Wolpert, a London analyst of plastics packaging materials, that glass will be forced into narrower areas such as bottles for medicines, cosmetics and pharmaceuticals. Similarly, in *Packaging Today* (October 1982), L. Fennelly declared: 'Two decades from now the glass container industry will be a small specialist area of packaging in cosmetics and decorative packs, and in quality segments of larger markets.' The glass manufacturers, however, are not simply waiting for the predicted end to come, but are employing some defensive measures to reduce production costs. The most widely publicised cost-cutting exercise has been the spread of recycling schemes and bottle banks. The Glass Manufacturers Federation represents the UK's 10 bottle manufacturers and began the bottle bank scheme in 1977. This scheme was started as a direct result of pressure from environmentalist groups. However, the industry soon began to realise that what had started as a defensive move was making good business sense. The Federation's Assistant Director, K. Stott said (*Sunday Times*, 2 May 1982): 'At that time there was a groundswell of feeling in Europe against non-returnable bottles, and it seemed that legislation was imminent.' And 'It has gone much better than we hoped, from being an act of environmental responsibility it has become a major part of the industry.' The scheme is helping to bring down energy costs by increasing the amount of waste glass in the initial melting process. Every 10 per cent of cullet (waste glass) which is added to traditional glass making materials saves 2 per cent on energy costs. Other cost saving measures are also being adopted, such as reducing the amount of glass used in making a bottle.

The 1970s saw the increasing use of electronic devices to improve the efficiency of day-to-day marketing activities. One of these innovations is the *European Article Numbering system* (EAN), used in food retailing. This system started in Britain in 1977, and originated in the USA in the early 1970s under the name of the Universal Product Code system (UPC) . This is a system of incorporating a 13-digit item identification number, both in decimal characters and bar code form, into the product packaging. See Figure 12.1 for an example of an EAN code for a coffee creamer. This code, marked on the packaging, is read by an optical scanner at the supermarket checkout desk, which retrieves the price and product description and displays this to the shopper whilst printing out this information onto the receipt (see Chapter 9).

The EAN system is in use in food retailing in Europe, Australia, Japan and South Africa. America and Canada are the only countries operating the UPC system which has a 12-digit code. This 12-digit UPC code did not have sufficient capacity for use as a world-wide system, hence the adoption of the 13-digit code. However, both the American system and the EAN system are very nearly compatible and the majority of scanning devices being used can scan 12- or 13-digit codes.

The system has benefits in inventory control, checkout productivity and it eliminates the need for marking the price on every item in the shop. Prices are displayed near the item on the shelf. The retailer can analyse the performance of new items, advertising and the comparative performance of similar items in different supermarkets. A list of possible benefits are set out in Table 12.2.

5 000114 201213

Figure 12.1　An example of a European article numbering code

TABLE 12.2   Potential benefits to food retailers from adoption of
UPC-orientated systems

Front-end benefits	*Merchandising benefits*
Improved throughput	Point of sale movement data
Checker productivity	Advertising analysis
Reduced misrings	Vendor analysis
Tender reconciliation	New item performance analysis
Cash reporting	Location analysis (for within and between
Store funds control	stores)
Check authorisation	Price management
Store operation benefits	*Inventory management benefits*
Eliminates price marking and re-marking	Shelf space allocations marking
Permits routine ordering	Reduced out-of-stock
Reduces shrinkage	Reduced backroom inventory

Warehouse and Transportation workload balancing

Source: IBM Corporation, 1975.

■ Environmental concerns

In its August 1990 issue *Which* magazine examined a number of issues related to
packaging including the incidence of misleading and excessive packaging,
problems with opening packaging and environmental concerns.

In terms of environmental concerns *Which* claim that packaging makes up
around a third of the rubbish by weight which we put in our dustbins. Of course,
packaging plays an important role in the protection. distribution and marketing
of products, as discussed earlier in the chapter, but it also impacts on the
environment in a number of ways. First, packaging consumes scarce natural
resources some of which are non-renewable. Second, the manufacture of
packaging materials consumes energy (itself a natural resource) which generates
carbon dioxide emissions which contribute to the 'greenhouse' effect. Third, it
results in waste, which has to be disposed of, and, litter which has to be cleaned
up.

In total the UK consumes about six million tonnes of packaging a year which is
equivalent to about six billion glass containers, 14 billion cans and 700 000 tonnes
of plastic. Paper and cardboard make up the balance. In theory all these materials
can be recycled but in practice only a fraction is. In the case of glass the UK
recycles about 20 per cent, 10 per cent of cans, 30 per cent of paper and cardboard
and less than 1 per cent of plastic. Many European countries have better records

than this, e.g. Germany recycles 40 per cent of its glass bottles and the Netherlands 60 per cent, and the UK government has set a target for 50 per cent of recyclable household waste to be recycled by the year 2000. Given that the *Which* survey indicated that 59 per cent of the respondents said they would be more likely to buy a particular brand of a product it the packaging was less likely to damage the environment, against 20 per cent who said they would not, the Government's target would seem achievable and with obvious implications for marketers.

We have briefly covered some of the current and future trends in the packaging materials industry, concentrating on the area of consumer goods packaging. For further information on this and other areas of packaging, see some or all of the trade journals listed below:

Packaging News
Packaging Review
Packaging Technology
Packaging Today

Some sources of information

Institute of Packaging
Fysonby Lodge
Nottingham Road
Melton Mowbray
Leicestershire LE13 0NU
0664-500 055

Packaging Industry Research Association (PIRA)
Randalls Road
Leatherhead
Surrey KT22 7RU
0372-376-161

Food Manufacturers' Industry Group
6 Katherine Street
London WC2B 5JJ
071-836-2460

Institute of Purchasing & Supply
Easton Hall
Easton on the Hill
Stamford
Lincolnshire
PE9 3NZ
0780-56777

Article Numbering Association
6 Katherine Street
London EC2B 5JJ
071-836-2460

British Standards Institution
101 Pentonville Road
London N1 9ND
071-62909000

Industry Council for Packaging and
the Environment
Premier House
10 Greycoat Place
London SW1P 1SB
071-222-8866

CHAPTER 13

Pricing and price policy

Learning Goals

The issues to be addressed in this chapter include:

1. The role of price in competitive strategy and the marketing mix.
2. The importance of price in competitive strategy and the marketing mix.
3. The nature of internal and external factors influencing the pricing decision.
4. The establishment of pricing objectives.
5. Methods of pricing.
6. The selection of a pricing strategy.
7. Perception and pricing.
8. An alternative model of pricing behaviour.

After reading this chapter you will be able to:

1. Explain why pricing has often been relegated to a secondary role in competitive strategy and the marketing mix.
2. Identify some reasons why pricing may receive more attention in the 1990s.
3. Describe and analyse the influence and impact of both internal and external factors on price determination.
4. Discuss pricing objectives.
5. Understand price 'formulas' or methods and give their advantages and disadvantages.
6. Explain the two main pricing alternatives, and suggest where each would be used.
7. List pricing strategies used in practice and give some reasons for their use.
8. Identify the influence of perception on the pricing decisions of both buyers and sellers.
9. Consider and evaluate a dynamic model of pricing behaviour.

■ Introduction

As we saw in Chapter 5 when discussing Demand and Supply, price is the mechanism which ensures that the two forces are in equilibrium. In other words, if demand exceeds supply then the price will rise to the point where the volume demanded by those willing and able to pay that price is equivalent to the volume available. Conversely, if supply exceeds demand then prices will fall until sufficient new buyers have entered the market to ensure the consumption of the available supply. Thus it is the price mechanism which determines whether firms will wish to enter or leave a given market because of the returns which may be earned on a given investment of resources. It follows that if all markets were perfect and infinitely flexible then the return on investment would be the same in them all.

Of course these conditions do not prevail and the aim of the investor/ entrepreneur is to get out of industries where returns are falling and into those where they are rising – usually because demand exceeds supply. But what will happen if the overall capacity to supply exceeds the overall capacity to consume? The answer is obvious – in the short run, factors of production will be surplus to requirements and become idle, as happened during the recession in Britain in the 1980s where over 2 million people are unemployed at the time of writing. During a recession and in the short-to-medium term at the microeconomic or firm level the emphasis is more than ever on survival and the need to ensure that revenues, which depend upon the volume sold and the price earned, exceed the costs of producing, distributing and selling that volume. Clearly, costs and prices must be primary considerations in the development of a marketing strategy.

The present propensity to produce more than we can consume is not entirely new, for as we saw in the opening chapter, it was the threat of such a situation at the beginning of this century which led to the 'rediscovery' of the marketing concept. It also led to the emergence of product differentiation supported by promotional effort as the preferred competitive strategy. Foremost among the reasons for this change of emphasis from a concern with producing the largest volume at the lowest cost, was recognition of the fact that if products are perceived as homogeneous then consumers will prefer the lower-priced offering and that economies of scale will invariably mean that the firm with the largest output will have the lowest costs and so be able to undercut its rivals. More correctly it is the firm with the largest market share which will enjoy the maximum benefits of the scale and experience effects and it will use its cost advantage to maximise its returns and/or dominate its immediate competitors. In such a situation the firm with a lesser market share either has to accept the going market price or it can seek to position its product in such a way that it will be perceived as different by a sufficient number of customers so that in effect it will have its own little monopoly and can charge a differentiated price (hence, *monopolistic competition*). It is for these reasons that while price occupies a central role in economic theory, in marketing it tends to be relegated to a secondary role and much more attention is given to other elements of competitive strategy and the marketing mix. This is born out by the findings of numerous surveys. For example, during 1990 Cath Byrne of Strathclyde University undertook a survey in several European Countries on behalf of Honeywell Ltd in which she asked respondents to identify their key purchasing criteria. The results were as follows:

Key factors:	Technical ability, quality.
Very important:	Flexibility, reliability, delivery scheduling, ordering convenience.
Important:	Price, personal contact, service.
Quite important:	Reputation, innovations, after sales service, previous contact.
Not at all important:	Image, location, payment terms, salesmen.

Similarly Ughanwa and Baker (*The Role of Design in International Competitiveness*, Routledge, 1989) found price ranked third out of 16 critical success factors behind 'Performance in operation' and 'Reliability' (see p. 84). Results such as these may be accounted for by one or more of the following reasons:

1. Perfect competition prevails. Under these circumstances the firm cannot have a 'price policy', it must accept the market price.
2. Under conditions of imperfect competition there is a tendency towards 'rigid prices', and for competition to be concentrated on non-price elements such as product differentiation, advertising, service, etc. Thus competitors prefer to avoid direct price competition, which could lead to a price war, and adopt the price level of the industry leader.
3. The construction of a demand schedule is considered impossible owing to the enormous number of interacting variables which condition consumer preference. Even if it were possible to quantify demand at various price levels the value of the information would not justify its cost, thus a trial and error approach, or acceptance of the 'going rate', is to be preferred.
4. Marketers lack an adequate understanding of the theoretical concepts and so avoid the complexities involved in developing a 'scientific' price policy.

In every field of marketing activity the suppliers emphasis upon new product development and differentiation confirms their reluctance to compete on price alone. That said it is clear that no seller can ignore the price dimension, albeit that, as the composite model of buyer behaviour proposed in Chapter 6 indicates, consumers will place more emphasis upon fitness for purpose in short-listing products for possible purchase. The more similar the products the more important price will be in determining the final choice, and only if both product and price are very similar indeed will the subjective association created by promotion have a significant influence on that decision.

TABLE 13.1 The relative importance of marketing activities in all types of products[a]

| | Rank | | | Resultant | |
	1,2	3,4	5,6	Rank	n
Pricing[*]	63%	27%	10%	1	357(100%)
Customer service	51%	34%	15%	2	306(100%)
Product research and development	41%	31%	28%	3	274(100%)
Product services	40%	38%	21%	4	207(100%)
Sales management	28%	38%	34%	5	264(100%)
Physical distribution	23%	36%	41%	6	173(100%)
Advertising and sales promotion	20%	30%	50%	7	173(100%)
Marketing research	25%	24%	51%	8	140(100%)
Marketing cost, budgeting and control	19%	24%	48%	9	123(100%)
Distribution channels control	21%	32%	47%	10	81(100%)
Extending customer credit	15%	38%	47%	11	81(100%)
Public relations	13%	33%	54%	12	66(100%)

[a] Based on 244 industrial goods, 55 durable goods and 108 non-durable goods.
[*] To be read: 63 per cent of 357 producers of industrial, durable and non-durable goods ranked pricing as the most important policy area.
n = number of mentions.

Source: Hanna A. Said, 'The Relevance of Price Theory to Price Practice', unpublished Ph.D. Dissertation, University of Strathclyde, 1981.

TABLE 13.2 Importance of factors in gaining business related to product category

Factor place 1, 2 or 3 in importance	All companies	Product category				
		Consumer durables	FMCG	Repeat industrial	Capital industrial	Services
Product performance	74.7%	63.9% (86)	77.9% (104)	84.0% (112)	91.9% (123)	61.7% (87)
Product design	43.1%	57.4% (133)	42.2% (98)	38.4% (89)	59.4% (136)	34.9% (81)
Consumer research	10.6%	11.1% (105)	14.4% (136)	5.4% (51)	4.8% (45)	13.4% (126)
Sales force management	32.2%	28.6% (89)	31.5% (98)	34.5% (107)	33.5% (104)	32.1% (100)
Advertising and promotion	28.9%	41.2% (143)	48.1% (166)	15.7% (54)	9.5% (33)	27.6% (96)
After sales service	26.3%	20.9% (79)	10.7% (41)	29.6% (113)	39.6% (151)	31.4% (119)
Pricing	53.3%	61.2% (115)	58.6% (110)	63.3% (119)	46.0% (86)	43.3% (81)
Distribution	25.0%	32.4% (130)	36.0% (144)	37.9% (152)	14.8% (59)	10.7% (43)
Finance and credit	8.3%	8.3% (100)	9.0% (108)	10.2% (123)	10.1% (122)	6.0% (72)
Transport and storage	5.7%	5.1% (89)	7.3% (128)	9.4% (165)	3.4% (60)	3.5% (61)
Public relations	10.7%	6.1% (57)	7.8% (73)	6.3% (59)	5.2% (49)	19.0% (178)

Source: G. J. Hooley, C. J. West and J. E. Lynch, *Marketing in the UK: A Survey of Current Practice and Performance*, Institute of Marketing, 1983.

The paradox is, therefore, that while price may not be the most important element in competitive strategy, and receives comparatively little attention in the marketing literature, it can never be far from the strategists' thoughts. In other words, a competitive price is a necessary but not sufficient condition for marketing success. Further, in the short term, price may be the most effective tactical weapon, as we shall see later in this chapter and also when considering the role of sales promotion particularly in a recessionary environment.

Indeed the results of a survey of 'The Relevance of Price Theory to Price Practice' by Hanna Said (unpublished Ph.D dissertation, University of Strathclyde, 1981) undertaken at the depth of a recession provided results which are at variance with those of nearly all other recent studies as can be seen from Table 13.1.

In Said's view, 'These differences may be accounted for by today's inflation which may lead firms to perceive price as the most important element of strategy. It can also be explained by the fact that this study is mainly concerned with pricing and our respondents probably are those who think that pricing is of more importance so they 'perceived it to be the most important area.' Certainly, the survey by Hooley *et al.* (G. J. Hooley, C. J. West and J. E. Lynch, *Marketing in the UK: A survey of current practice and performance*, Institute of Marketing, 1983) supports the general view as can be seen from Table 13.2. However, Simon's 1986 survey would seem to support Said as can be seen from Table 13.3 and he suggests a number of reasons why the significance of price has increased in recent years which may be summarised as follows:

Table 13.3   'Pressure' in various marketing areas as perceived by managers

	Europe 0% — 100%	USA 0% — 100%
Pricing	78.0	80.6
Product quality	73.6	63.3
New products	68.2	78.5
Internal staffing and training	67.6	67.1
Selling costs	67.2	70.4
New competition	64.2	55.0
Government regulation	63.0	50.1
Product differentiation	62.6	62.6
Distribution	60.4	64.6
After sales service	53.8	66.4
Advertising	47.8	56.4

Source: USA, *Marketing News*, 11 June 1986, p. 1; Europe, Author's study 1986.

1. High inflation rates have led to higher price consciousness.
2. Stagnating or declining real incomes have induced consumers to switch to cheaper products.
3. Increased competitive pressure (and the difficulty of sustaining an advantage through differentiation) has enhanced the role of price particularly in industrial markets.
4. Aggressive pricing is a major competitive weapon in buyers' markets as suppliers seek to maintain market share.
5. New competitors use aggressive pricing strategies to break into markets and secure a foothold, e.g. Japan, Korea.
6. Consumerism and legislation on competition (see Chapters 4 and 24) have resulted in greater market and price transparency and encouraged buyers to compare price and quality more systematically.

In developing a price policy it is clear that one has to consider both the external environment in which one has to compete and also the internal factors which condition and control the courses of action open to the firm. A brief review of these follows.

■ External price determinants

A major determinant of price policy is the structure of the market in which the firm is selling its output. Many authors tend to confuse industry structure with market structure, and limit their attention to the size and number of firms engaged in creating perfect substitutes. Thus it is common to find references to monopolistic and oligopolistic industries when the total output of a given product is concentrated in the hands of one, or a few, firms. Although it is acknowledged that the true monopolist is a price-maker, and that oligopolistic industries frequently exhibit price rigidity owing to the price leadership of a dominant firm, it is felt that the industry view oversimplifies the true situation.

Conventionally, the industry approach would distinguish the manufacture of aluminium, steel, glass, paper and plastics on the basis that their output possesses different physical properties and is the result of distinctive production processes. Each would be classified as a separate industry, yet all compete with one another for the packaging market. This suggests that one must take into account not only the prices of perfect substitutes but also the prices of all goods which compete for the same market and can be used to satisfy the same basic wants. Certainly no self-respecting buyer is going to confine his attention to a single material when several acceptable alternatives are available, and the technique of value analysis has been developed largely to permit comparative cost analysis of competing substitutes.

If the above arguments are accepted, then it follows that the firm must look beyond the narrowly defined industry of which it considers itself a member, and should evaluate the price structure of its end market and the policies of all firms/ industries operating in that market. (In the language of the economist, one must analyse the cross-elasticity of demand.)

The second major external price determinant is best summarised by the economist's concept of elasticity. Essentially elasticity measures the responsiveness of demand to changes in price, i.e. it is a measure of price sensitivity. Thus if a 1 per cent change in price results in a change in the amount demanded of more than 1 per cent demand is said to be elastic, if less than 1 per cent then demand is inelastic, and a directly proportionate change indicates unitary elasticity. Elasticity of demand is conditioned by the importance of the product in the consumer's scale of preferences, by the disposable income of existing and potential consumers, by the existence of substitutes and a number of other, lesser factors. As a summary measure it is of great value in determining the firm's basic attitude to price – if demand is elastic pricing will be a major policy area, if inelastic it will be of secondary consequence.

Thirdly, the firm's pricing policy will be influenced by government policy as expressed in the extant and proposed legislation in such areas as price maintenance, monopolistic practices, minimum performance standards for products, etc., e.g. the introduction of cut-price detergents by Procter & Gamble and Lever Brothers following the Monopolies Commission recommendation to this effect.

■ Internal price determinants

The major factor conditioning the firm's price policy is its own definition of the business it is in, for this will determine the products it will produce and the nature of the markets it will seek to exploit. The product mix identifies the firm with an industry, while its market specifies the firms, industries and products with which it will compete, and the dimensions along which it will compete.

Traditionally, the firm's success has been measured by its profitability, which is simply a measure of the amount by which income exceeds expenditure. If, as implied earlier, the majority of firms accept the going market price, it is evident that profits will depend very largely on the firm's ability to minimise expenditures or costs. To this end considerable effort has been devoted to the development of sophisticated cost measurement and control systems, and management is often happier to immerse itself in the tangible realities of such systems that grapple with the complexities of price determination. Further, both shareholders and the Government require the firm to account for the way in which it spends its income, and so emphasise the need for detailed cost analyses and statements. As will be seen below, such data are widely used in the formulation of prices.

The third internal constraint on the firm's price policy is the nature and extent of its corporate resources, which are discussed in Chapter 19 and will not be reiterated here.

It follows from the brief outline above that the price-setter's discretion is circumscribed by a number of factors, admirably summarised by Joel Dean as:

1. The number, relative sizes and product lines of competitors who sell products to do the same job.
2. The likelihood of potential competition.
3. The stage of consumer acceptance of the product.
4. The degree of potential market segmentation and price discrimination.
5. The degree of physical difference between the seller's product and those of other companies.
6. The opportunities for variation in the product-service bundle.
7. The richness of the mixture of service and reputation in the product bundle.

(Joel Dean, *Managerial Economics* (Prentice-Hall, New York, 1951) p. 402.)

■ Pricing objectives

In an article entitled 'How to Price for Maximum Profits' (*Management Methods*, November 1956), Jules E. Anderson quotes a survey by the National Industrial Conference Board which revealed that only 4 out of 155 leading US manufacturers used a clear-cut, written procedure in setting prices. Although dated, these findings tend to confirm a widely held belief that most firms lack clearly defined, explicit pricing objectives and formalised pricing procedures. It is the author's opinion that this belief is erroneous, and based upon faulty data derived from poorly designed surveys. This opinion tends to be supported by the findings of more sophisticated researchers, in particular those of Robert Lanzillotti ('Pricing Objectives in Large Companies', *American Economic Review*, XLVIII (Dec. 1956) pp. 921–40) and W. Warren Haynes (*Pricing Decisions in Small Business*: University of Kentucky Press, Lexington, 1962) both of whom have undertaken extensive field research into the firm's pricing objectives.

Lanzillotti's findings were: 'The most typical pricing objectives cited were: (1) pricing to achieve a target return on investment; (2) stabilisation of price and margin; (3) pricing to realise a target market share; and (4) pricing to meet or prevent competition.' The main conclusions drawn from this study are considered sufficiently significant to be quoted verbatim, namely:

The general hypothesis which emerges is that (a) the large company has a fairly well-defined pricing goal that is related to a long-range profit horizon; (b) its management seeks – especially in multiproduct multimarket operations – a simultaneous decision with respect to price, cost, and product characteristics; and (c) its pricing formulas are handy devices for checking the internal consistency of the separate decisions as against the general company objective. Under this hypothesis no single theory of the firm – and certainly no single motivational hypothesis such as profit maximisation – is likely to impose an unambiguous course of action for the firm for any given situation; nor will it provide a satisfactory basis for valid and useful predictions of price behaviour (pp. 938–9).

It seems reasonable to conclude that the pricing policies are in almost every case equivalent to a company policy that represents an order of priorities and choice among competing objectives rather than policies tested by any simple concept of profit maximisation (p. 939).

Another relevant aspect of the data for theoretical analysis is the conception of the market held by managements of large corporations. Individual products, markets, and pricing are not considered in isolation; the unit of decision-making is the enterprise, and pricing and marketing strategies are viewed in this global context. Because of the tremendously complex joint-cost problems and lack of knowledge of actual relationships between cost and output or sales, on the one hand, and the joint-revenue aspects of multiproduct companies, on the other, pricing is frequently done for product groups with an eye to the over-all profit position of the company. This means that costing of products ends up as a result of price policy rather than the reverse. In view of the various external pressures on the company and the nature of the strategy of the enterprise, it is doubtful if price would have any closer relationship to actual costs were detailed cost data available to management. The incentive to realise target rates of profit for the long haul better suits the objectives of management-controlled companies than any desire to profiteer or seek windfall profits (p. 940).

From these conclusions it is clear that firms do establish pricing objectives, even though they may not be stated explicitly. Frequently such objectives are implicit in the company's overall objective, in other cases they may take the form of a generalised statement such as:

'All prices must cover fully allocated costs.'
'Prices will not exceed those asked by immediate competitors.'
'Prices will be set which will discourage the entry of new firms into the market.'
'All prices must yield a return of investment not less than X per cent.'

In the analysis by Said, referred to earlier, the findings did not support conventional price theory which assumes that profit is the sole and principal motivation of business firms. Indeed her evidence suggests strongly that firms are motivated by many objectives simultaneously related to profitability, security and sales. As can be seen from Figure 13.1, survival is seen as the most important goal, followed by short-term profits, liquidity, medium-term profits, market share, sales revenue, with long-run profits seen as of relatively little importance. Not evident from the figure but of considerable interest is the fact that divisional managers and accountants placed much more stress on short-term survival/liquidity/profit goals than did managing directors and marketing managers who took a longer-term perspective and emphasised market share and long-run profitability.

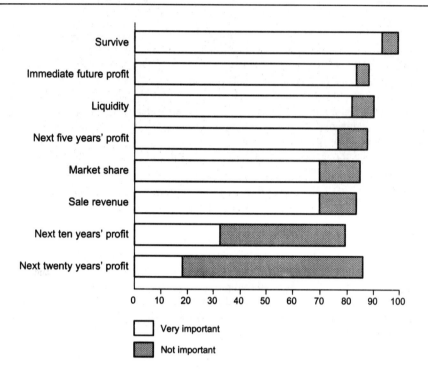

Figure 13.1   Values of importance quoted to pricing objectives

Source: Hanna A. Said, op. cit.

■ Pricing 'formulas'

Even though the firm may not have committed itself to a formal statement of price policy, in practice its pricing behaviour is usually sufficiently consistent to permit identification and classification. Observation indicates that there are a limited number of pricing formulas, or methods, in general use, and these may be classified as:

Full-cost or cost-plus pricing. In simple terms, all this involves is the addition of a predetermined margin to the full unit cost of production and distribution, without reference to prevailing demand conditions. In practice, it is doubtful if the firm can establish its true unit cost in advance, owing to uncertainty as to the volume it can make/sell. Broadly speaking, all costs may be classified as fixed or variable. Fixed costs are incurred irrespective of the volume of output and are the result of management policy, e.g. the depreciation of fixed assets, the level of selling, general and administrative overheads, while variable costs fluctuate more or less directly with the volume of output, e.g. raw material and labour costs. In that unit cost is computed by dividing total cost by output in units, it is clear that this can only be established when the two quantities are known. The price-setter may forecast sales volume and compute unit cost on the basis of this estimate, adding the predetermined margin in order to arrive at a price. It would be purely fortuitous if demand at this price were to coincide exactly with the available supply, with the result that the seller will either be left with unsold units or else will sell his total output at a lesser profit than could have been obtained. Further, as Lanzillotti implies, the allocation of fixed costs to given products tends to be arbitrary, so that the unit cost used as the basis for a price may bear no relation to true cost at all.

Although cost plus a fixed margin may be a valid method to adopt when deciding whether to enter a new market, most sellers would be prepared to vary this price in the light of potential consumer reaction to it, implicit in current market prices. If this is so, then the price-setter's decision rule is rather different from that generally associated with full-cost pricing – cost plus a predetermined margin is not the price, it is a minimum acceptable price and the actual price adopted may be any amount greater than this. This being so, it is erroneous to contend that prices based on cost take no account of consumer demand. However, cost-plus pricing has a number of drawbacks admirably summarised by John Winkler in Table 13.4.

Table 13.4 Drawbacks of cost-plus pricing

- Difficult, in advance, to determine such costs as construction, material price changes, and similar costs.
- Difficult to allocate joint costs to specific products.
- Not based on realistic profit goal or market share objective.
- Ignores elasticity of demand.
- Generally disregards competition.
- Buyers are more concerned about the cost and value of product to them than about production and selling costs to supplier.
- Does not distinguish between out-of-pocket and 'sunk' costs.[*]
- Difficult to determine 'fair' return.
- Ignores capital requirements and return on investment.
- Many costs vary with volume, and volume depends on price charged.

---

[*]Those which are spent, regardless of production level.

Source: Chapter 16 'Pricing' by John Winkler in *The Marketing Book*, 2nd edn, Michael J. Baker (Heinemann, 1991).

Figure 13.2   Break-even chart

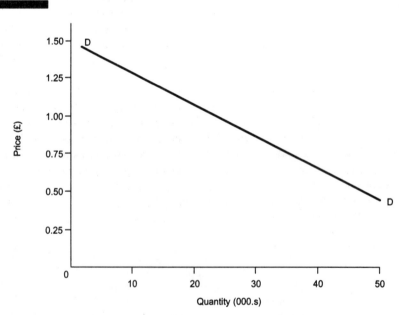

Figure 13.3   Hypothetical demand curve

Break-even analysis. Break-even analysis utilises the concepts of fixed and variable costs, and enables the price-setter to investigate the implications of any number of price-volume alternatives.

The first step in a break-even analysis is to compute the firm's total cost curve by adding the variable costs incurred at different levels of output to the fixed costs, e.g. if fixed costs (FC) = £10 000, and unit variable cost (VC) = £0.25, then total cost (TC) = £10 000 + £0.25x where x = the number of units produced. The next step is to compute total revenue (TR) curves for the range of prices under consideration and plot these graphically as shown in Figure 13.2.

Clearly the 'break-even' point for a given price lies at the intersection of the total revenue curve for that price and the total cost curve, e.g. with a price of £0.75 the firm will break even at a sales volume of 40 000 units. On its own, this information is of little value to the price-setter, unless he has some feeling for the likely volume of demand over the range of prices for which he has calculated break-even points. In reality, the price-setter will usually have at least a preliminary analysis of the potential market for the product, from which he may derive a hypothetical demand curve as shown in Figure 13.3.

By reference to the demand curve it can be seen that at a price of £0.75, 36 250 units will be demanded and the firm would incur a loss. Closer inspection would seem to indicate that the best price is £1.00, at which 20 000 units will be sold.

Marginal costing/contribution analysis. Break-even analysis allocates fixed costs to a product at a predetermined rate in such a way that, collectively, the firm's products will absorb the firm's total fixed costs. Many price theorists contend that this conventional accounting approach can lead to incorrect decisions, and advocate the adoption of techniques based on marginal analysis as developed by economists.

In essence the marginal approach states that one should ignore fixed costs and concentrate on the relationship between variable cost and revenue, usually termed the 'contribution'. For example, if the variable cost of producing a unit is £0.25 and this unit may be sold for £0.50, then the contribution is + £0.25. It is understood that contribution means 'contribution to fixed costs, variable marketing costs, and profits', and the firm's objective in setting price should be to maximise the total contribution. If average unit cost is used as a criterion, then it is likely that the firm will reject any price less than average cost, and so forego the contribution which sale at such a price would generate. A simplified example will help clarify this point.

During the day many trains in the London area carry only a few passengers, and it seems clear that the revenues earned must be less than the average cost of running a train. Ignoring the social responsibilities of a public transportation authority, such a practice seems economically suicidal. However, marginal analysis reveals that elimination of these services would lead to lower profits (bigger losses!), in that the incremental cost incurred in running a train is negligible. The fixed investment necessary to cope with rush-hour traffic flows has already been made and is a 'sunk' cost; maintenance and engineering crews have to be paid to keep the rolling stock and track in good repair, as do railwaymen to operate the signals, drive the trains, etc. While it is true that some of the latter may work a split shift, the majority do not, and two shifts must be employed as a minimum. Thus, running off-peak trains adds little to the fixed costs to which the transportation authority is committed if it is to provide reasonably adequate commuter services – the cost of the power used and a slight increase in maintenance and operating cost. Provided that sufficient passengers use the off-peak services to cover the cost of these variables, then a contribution will be earned towards fixed costs.

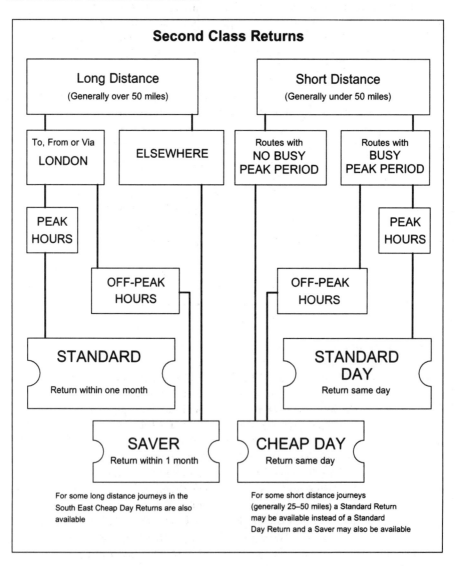

Figure 13.4 Pricing – an example of decision criteria

Source: Railnews, October 1984.

An article in *Railnews* (October 1964) illustrates how British Rail used these principles in seeking to maximise its revenue through a carefully thought-out pricing strategy:

> A new range of rail fares is to be introduced next May to make ticket categories more understandable, and bring prices more into line with our markets.
>
> By introducing the changes, the passenger business aims to increase revenue, encourage off-peak travel and compete more effectively in the travel market.
>
> Earnings are expected to increase by £10 million – £15 million a year, mostly on Inter-City travel. Passenger-miles are also expected to rise about 500 million miles a year.

Figure 13.4 illustrates the factors taken into account in arriving at the decision to offer four basic fares – Standard, Standard Day, Saver, and Cheap Day – and provides a clear example of how a once-declining industry is using marketing principles to restore its fortunes. (While British Rail now use a different fare structure it follows similar principles in seeking to optimise revenue from a combination of peak and off-peak pricing.)

Many managers find it difficult to ignore fixed costs and so make incorrect decisions. The argument that a firm has spent £x million in developing a product, and so must continue with its production and sale in the face of unfavourable use reactions, is a classic example. The best advice in such a situation might well be 'Don't throw good money after bad.'

Contribution analysis does not simplify the problems inherent in forecasting demand and costs, but it does ensure that management does not reject projects which would improve the firm's overall profitability solely because they are not self-supporting on an average cost basis.

Other techniques. The pricing formulas described above are the best known, and most extensively used, techniques at the present time. As a basis for 'scientific' decision-making, they are beset with faults and difficulties, and a number of new techniques have been evolved in recent years in an attempt to remedy these defects. It is impossible to do justice to these in an introductory text and the student should refer to the following sources for detailed coverage: Robert D. Buzzell, *Mathematical Models and Marketing Management* (Graduate School of Business Administration, Harvard University, Boston, 1964) ; Ronald E. Frank, Alfred E. Kuehn and William F. Massey, *Quantitative Techniques in Marketing Analysis* (Irwin, Hornewood, Ill., 1962): Paul E. Green, 'Bayesian Decision Theory in Pricing Strategy, *Journal of Marketing*, xxvii i (Jan. 1963) pp. 5–14; Alfred Oxenfeldt, David Miller, Abraham Schuchman and Charles Winick, *Insights into Pricing* (Wadsworth, Belmont, California, 1961).

Some insight into current practice was provided by project MACS (Baker and Hart, *Marketing and Competitive Success*, Philip Allan, 1989) as indicated by Figure 13.5.

Figure 13.5 **Pricing in successful and less successful companies**

More up-to-date information on pricing methods and the use of cost in pricing setting is to be found in Said's thesis 'Relevance of Price Theory' and is reproduced in Tables 13.5 and 13.6. From these tables the following conclusions may be drawn:

(1) Considerable attention is given to cost even when prices are not finally based on cost.
(2) Full cost methods are used much more extensively than marginal cost methods.
(3) Firms are flexible in their approach to pricing with the great majority varying their profit margin to reflect market conditions.

■ Pricing strategies

In *Price Management* (1989) Henry Simon confirms that while it is the product which provides value, benefit or utility it is price which enables one to make comparative assessments between different products and it is this alone which 'determines the amount a customer must sacrifice to acquire a product'. However, in addition to its importance in establishing the price value relation Simon cites six reasons why price is an important element in the marketing mix.

TABLE 13.5 Pricing methods

	Extent of using the method						(a) X	Total response n	N
	Very great extent	Great extent	Moderate	Little extent	Very little	Not applic-able			
(1) Domestic market									
Adding a percentage to cost (cost plus).	*87(29%)	30(10%)	52(18%)	33(11%)	52(18.0%)	42(14%)	3.199	296(100%)	356
Fixing required gross profit margin on selling prices.	84(29%)	50(17%)	53(19%)	22(8%)	49(17.0%)	28(10%)	2.951	286(100%)	356
Prices to realise a specified level of profit on sales.	62(23%)	57(21%)	54(20%)	33(12%)	37(13.5%)	31(11%)	3.069	274(100%)	356
Following market leader.	28(10%)	27(10%)	43(16%)	45(17%)	62(23.0%)	66(24%)	4.048	271(100%)	356
Charging what the market will bear.	161(50%)	73(22%)	43(13%)	13(4%)	24(7.4%)	12(4%)	2.086	326(100%)	356
(2) Export									
Adding a percentage to cost (cost plus).	72(34%)	22(10%)	29(14%)	18(9%)	27(13.0%)	41(20%)	3.139	209(100%)	275
Fixing required gross profit margin on selling prices.	49(25%)	25(13%)	42(21%)	20(10%)	32(16.0%)	30(15%)	3.258	198(100%)	275
Prices to realise a specified level of profit on sales.	37(20%)	33(17%)	33(17%)	19(10%)	31(17.0%)	35(19%)	3.420	188(100%)	275
Following market leader.	11(6%)	16(9%)	21(12%)	22(12%)	42(23.0%)	68(38%)	4.511	180(100%)	275
Charging what the market will bear.	126(55%)	31(14%)	25(11%)	11(5%)	17(7.0%)	18(8%)	2.193	228(100%)	275

* To be read 87(29%) out of 296 companies use cost plus in the home market to a very great extent.

(a) The greater the mean, the less the extent of using the method.

X = the arithmetic mean.

n = number of valid observations.

N = number of cases included in the sample for export = number of firms' exports.

Source: Hanna A. Said, 'The Relevance of Price Theory to Price Practice', unpublished Ph.D. dissertation, University of Strathclyde, 1981.

TABLE 13.6 Type of cost used for different pricing methods

	Full cost	Marginal cost	Do not use cost	n	N
Domestic market					
Adding a percentage to cost (cost plus)	69% (175) *	28% (70)	3% (9)	100% (254)	356
Fixing required gross profit margin on selling price	75% (192)	22% (57)	3% (9)	100% (258)	356
Target pricing	73% (178)	24% (57)	3% (8)	100% (243)	356
Following market leader	75% (153)	21% (43)	4% (9)	100% (205)	356
Charging what the market will bear	71% (224)	25% (78)	12% (9)	100% (311)	356
Export					
Adding a percentage to cost (cost plus)	59% (99)	39% (65)	2% (4)	100% (168)	275
Fixing required gross profit margin on selling price	65% (99)	31% (53)	4% (6)	100% (168)	275
Target pricing	64% (97)	33% (51)	3% (5)	100% (153)	275
Following market leader	55% (73)	30% (34)	4% (5)	100% (112)	275
Charging what the market will bear	64% (133)	33% (70)	3% (7)	100% (210)	275

* To be read 69 per cent (175) of 254 firms which use cost plus refer to full cost in deciding their selling prices.

n = number of valid observations.

N = number of cases included in the sample.

Source: Hanna A. Said, op. cit.

1. Price elasticity is twenty times greater than advertising elasticity, i.e. a 1 per cent change has a sales effect twenty times as big as a 1 per cent change in advertising expenditure.
2. The sales effect of a price change is often immediate, and so measurable, while changes in other mix variables are usually lagged and difficult to quantify.
3. Price changes are easy to effect compared with varying other mix variables.
4. Competitors react more quickly to price changes.
5. Price does not require an initially negative cash flow as do other marketing expenditures such as advertising which have a lagged effect.
6. Price and the product are the only two mix elements which feature significantly in strategic planning concepts.

So far, attention has been focused on quantitative aspects of price determination and little consideration given to the qualitative factors which shape the final pricing decision. Given the difficulties involved in constructing a demand schedule, pricing formulas can only give a broad indication of the range within which the desired sales volume might be achieved. Hence, the final price decision must depend upon a judgmental assessment of the impact of a given price strategy. In broad terms there are two alternatives open to the marketer – a high price approach aimed at 'skimming the cream' off the market, and a low price strategy aimed at preempting a significant share of the total market.

High price strategies are appropriate to mature or saturated markets, which show a degree of segmentation on the basis of quality, design features, etc., or to the introduction of a product which differs significantly from anything currently available. In the case of existing markets, consumers in the higher income groups are often prepared to pay a premium for products which are differentiated from those appealing to the mass market, e.g. a Rolls-Royce or Toyota Lexus compared with a Renault or a Ford Escort. Owing to the limited demand at the higher prices, a small, high-quality producer can maintain a profitable level of sales without building up a sufficiently large market share to attract the competition of firms catering to the mass market. This does not mean that the latter type of firm will not diversify into the high price segment to make fuller use of its resources, but the established reputation of the quality producer will provide a high degree of protection against such competition.

Skimming the market is also attractive to the firm with a new and unique product. As noted earlier, new product development invariably represents a considerable investment on the part of the innovator, and a high initial price offers the opportunity to limit the costs of launching the product into the market while earning monopoly profits. A good example of such a strategy is the launching of the Polaroid Land camera, which was originally put on the market at a price of around £100, with very limited distribution and promotion. The novelty of a camera which could produce a finished print within a matter of seconds attracted a lot of free publicity, as well as being something of a status symbol because of its price. As demand at the initial high price was exhausted,

Polaroid lowered prices and 'slid down the demand curve', with the result that a basic camera is now available at around £10. It is interesting to note that in the United States, where the camera was developed and first put on sale, a rather different strategy was adopted and the camera offered originally at a relatively low price. The reasoning in this instance was that the purchase of a camera tends to be once and for all, whereas there is a continuing market for film, thus the more cameras that were sold the greater would be the demand for film. As the film was unique, and protected by patents, competition from other manufacturers such as Eastman–Kodak was precluded and offered greater long-run profitability, provided sufficient cameras could be sold.

When adopting a skimming strategy, with the intention of subsequently reducing price to appeal to a wider market, it is important not to create ill will by reducing price too quickly. This danger may be reduced by differentiating the appearance of the product and offering it as a 'stripped-down', or economy model. The use of this strategy is to be seen in the marketing of PCs and electronic calculators and may be anticipated very shortly in the market for cam corders.

A low price policy recommends itself in a number of circumstances pre-eminent among which is entering a market with a high price-elasticity of demand. The newcomer will have to achieve a certain level of sales in order to break even, and in the short run may only be able to wrest sales from existing products through the medium of an attractive discount on current prices. Penetration pricing, as this strategy is sometimes termed, usually involves the firm in accepting a loss initially, while achieving sampling of the product and the development of brand loyalty. As suggested earlier, however, few firms are willing to buy market share openly for fear of setting off a price war, and a penetration policy is usually disguised as some form of sales promotion, e.g. price-off labels, coupons, etc. Where the firm possesses a cost advantage it has little to fear from a low price strategy, but it is rare that a new entrant into a market can undercut the existing brand leaders owing to the economies of scale open to them. In fact, contrary to popular belief, oligopolists often practise a low price policy to discourage the entry of new competitors into the market.

In 1954 E. R. Hawkins elaborated on these two basic strategies when he listed the pricing policies described by 'marketing specialists' (Edward R. Hawkins, 'Price Policies and Theories', *Journal of Marketing*, XVIII (Jan. 1954) pp. 233–40). These policies may be summarised as:

1. *Odd pricing* – i.e. the adoption of prices ending in odd numbers. This policy is notably prevalent in food retailing, and is also used extensively on low ticket items in general. The adoption of such prices implies the existence of a stepped or discontinuous demand curve, i.e. avoidance of intermediate prices ending in round numbers suggests that the price-setter believes that demand is totally inelastic at that price, e.g. reducing an item from 25p to 24p would not increase demand so price is reduced to 23p.

2. *Psychological pricing.* This differs from odd pricing in that the price need not be an odd number but merely one that has an apparent psychological significance for the buyer, e.g. 95p instead of £1.

3. *Customary prices.* Such prices are fixed by custom, e.g. the old 6d bar of chocolate. Like the first two strategies the adoption of such prices assumes a kink in the demand curve. (The abolition of resale price maintenance and inflation seem to have seen the demise of customary prices for products like shoes and confectionery where they were formerly commonplace. However, 'psychological' prices still prevail, and 99p seems to have assumed a particular significance in this context. However, with the disappearance of 1p and 1 cent coins in many countries this will have to change!)

4. *Pricing at the market/meeting the competition.* This strategy presumes a marked inelasticity of demand below the current market price, such that a price reduction would not be justified by increased sales revenues. This approach is frequently adopted to avoid price wars.

5. *Prestige pricing.* This strategy implies a skimming approach in which the seller gives prestige to his product by asking a price well in excess of those asked for near perfect substitutes, e.g. Estee Lauder cosmetics, After Eight Mints.

6. *Price lining.* This policy of adopting specific prices for certain types of merchandise is common among retailers and is closely related to both psychological and customary prices, e.g. women's dresses, nylon stockings.

7. *Geographic pricing.* This policy is sometimes used where the marketer serves a number of distinct regional markets and can adopt different prices in each without creating consumer or distributor ill will. Petrol is priced in this way, depending on the distance of the garage from the nearest bulk terminal.

8. *Dual pricing strategy.* The marketer sells the same product at two or more different prices. Within the same market it is necessary to use different brands, but in distinct regional markets it may be possible to justify price differentials on the grounds of varying distribution costs, cf. petrol.

The arguments for skimming and penetrating strategies are admirably summarised by Simon (1989) in Table 13.7.

In the Introduction to this chapter it was noted that pricing tends to be relegated to a secondary role in the formulation of competitive strategies. To a large degree this is due to the fact that price is highly visible and readily understood by consumers and competitors alike, whereas other elements of the marketing mix are less capable of direct and objective assessment.

However, as was noted in the Introduction to this chapter, an increasingly competitive climate has resulted in much more attention being given to the use of price as both a tactical and strategic weapon. An extended discussion of the topic is to be found in A. F. Millman's 'Price Wars' published in the January 1983 issue of the *Quarterly Review of Marketing*, in which he cites several markets where

TABLE 13.7   Arguments for skimming and penetration strategies

Skimming strategy	*Penetration strategy*
• high short-run profits little affected by discounting. • quick pay-back for real innovation during the period of monopolistic market position, reduces long-run competitive risk, quick amortisation of R&D expenses. • high profit in early life-cycle phases, reduces the risk of obsolescence. • allows for price reduction over time. • avoids the necessity of price increases. • high price implies positive prestige and quality. • requires fewer financial resources. • requires lower capacity.	• high total contribution through fast sales growth in spite of low unit contribution margins. • takes advantage of positive intrapersonal (consumer goods) or interpersonal (durable goods) carryover effects, builds up a strong market position (with the potential of higher prices and/or higher sales in the future. • takes advantage of short-run cost reductions through (static) economies of scale. • allows for fast increase of the cumulative quality by accelerating the experience curve effect. Achieves a large cost advantage that competitors will find difficult to match. • reduces the risk of failure; low introductory price gives some assurance of low probability of failure. • deters potential competitors from market entry, or delays their entry.

Source: H. Simon, *Price Management*, Elsevier Science Publishers, BV, Amsterdam (1989).

price has been used extensively as a competitive weapon – retailing, airline seats, petrol, motor cars, cross channel ferries, etc. In some cases, such as Tesco's *checkout* campaign, the results have been spectacular and beneficial; in others, such as Freddie Laker's *Skytrain*, they have been spectacular and fatal.

In his analysis Millman covers a number of issues not discussed here including the attitudes to risk of marketing executives and the legal implications of the Resale Prices Act of 1976. He also makes a useful distinction between price wars and price attrition and argues that the latter 'are characterised by long periods during which the total price *package* is gradually worn down' interspersed with short bursts of high activity. By contrast a price war is 'typically the result of a battle for market share which can easily get out of hand if there is no pressure group or check mechanism with sufficient mobility and authority to restore order'.

It was Fellner who described price as 'the blunt instrument of competition'. Under the right conditions its use may bring quick and beneficial results but you are more likely to remain in good health if you can avoid being the victim of price warfare.

■ Perception and pricing

In Chapter 6 we proposed a composite model of buying behaviour which placed considerable emphasis upon the mediating influence of selective perception in determining not only what cues or stimuli are given conscious attention but also on the interpretation given to the information. It is the phenomenon of selective perception which modifies the strictly economic explanation of the manner in which demand will react to supply at different prices and so may be seen to contradict the concept of 'economic rationality'. Accordingly to the latter concept buyers will always select the supplier offering the lowest price but, in reality, the market for many goods and services will contain a variety of different prices for superficially similar offerings. The explanation is, of course, that even if the offerings are objectively perfect substitutes one for another buyers may perceive them subjectively as being different. Much of the effort of competing suppliers is directed specifically at achieving such perceived differences through the creation of reputation, brand loyalty and the augmentation of the core product.

Simon (*Price Management*, Amsterdam, Elsevier, 1989) devotes a chapter to the subject of 'Price Management and Psychology' and provides a comprehensive summary of the variables which influence price perception and evaluation which is reproduced as Table 13.8.

From Table 13.8 it is clear that a multiplicity of factors bear upon the buyers' (both consumer and industrial) perception of price. In addition, their relative influence may well vary from one buying decision to the next as a consequence of changes in the buyers' status and/or the circumstances or context in which the decision has to be made. Thus, while there has been much research which suggests that buyers (particularly individual consumers) have poor price recall it would be wrong to assume that this reflects price insensitivity of lack of consideration for price in making a buying decision. Indeed, there is also a considerable body of research which indicates that at the time when a buyer makes a purchase decision they have a good feel for what is available in the market place so that the decision is 'rational' in terms of what the buyer is seeking to optimise at that precise time and in that specific context.

Of particular interest in terms of the psychology of pricing is the case where the price itself becomes of major importance in influencing the prospective buyer's perception of the quality of the offering. Simon provides an excellent overview of the evidence that price is used as an indicator of quality and cites Zeithman's (1988) finding that much of this is contradictory. That said, and despite the lack

TABLE 13.8   Variables which influence price perception and evaluation

Motivational variables	Cognitive variables	Situation variables

• personal involvement
 	
• striving for
  – social recognition
  – quality
  – cognitive consistency
  – shopping convenience
  – saving
	• ability to compare quality
	
	• ability to remember and compare prices
	
	• experience
	
	• trust in the supplier
	
	• self-confidence
	
	• application of simplified decision rules (brand loyalty, etc.)
		• way of exhibiting price (form and quality, etc.)
		
		• mode of payment
		
		• time pressure
		
		• competitive products and prices
		
		• complexity of purchasing task
		
		• variability of prices
		
		• price labelling
		
		• product use
		
		• financial situations of buyers
		
		• price image of the store

Source: H. Simon, *Price Management*, Elsevier Science Publishers, BV, Amsterdam (1989).

of much empirical support, Simon proposes 16 conditions or contexts where 'we expect the phenomenon . . .' to occur, namely:

Conditions under which quality will be inferred from the price.

1. Brand and manufacturer names do not play an important role, e.g. rugs, furniture.
2. Consumers have little or no experience,
   – because the product is new. Note that the quality indication is effective only if the new product is not a genuine innovation which is beyond the existing reference system.
   – because the purchase interval is long; that is, for frequently purchased 'low involvement' products.
   – because it is not usual for people to share their experience with the product.

3. Objective quality is difficult to evaluate,
   - because of the technical complexity,
   - because of the particular importance of such attributes as durability, reliability, etc.
4. Considerable quality differences are perceived.
5. Price itself is an important product attribute.
   - prestige products (Snob, Veblen effect),
   - use or display of the product are associated with social risk (wine, liquor, cosmetics, fashion products, clothing, gifts, etc.).
6. Absolute price is not too high. For very expensive products, the search for objective quality information can be rewarding. In other words, the reliance on price alone can be costly.

With respect to situational conditions, the role of price as quality indicator is the greater,

7. the greater the time pressure is during the purchase,
8. the more complex the purchase task is,
9. the lower the price transparency is (e.g. with respect to the variation of prices for the same product),
10. the more the buyer trusts the supplier of the price information.

With respect to personal characteristics, price-dependent quality evaluation should be the most important,

11. the less self-confident the buyer is,
12. the less frugal the buyer is,
13. the stronger the desire is to purchase quickly and conveniently,
14. the stronger the desire is to avoid cognitive dissonance,
15. the better the economic situation of the household is,
16. the less product-related information the buyer has.

Source: H. Simon, *Price Management*, Elsevier Science Publishers, BV, Amsterdam (1989).

The important point to be made here is that if these are widely held expectations (and we believe they are) then they will have an important bearing upon the way in which suppliers set their prices.

In other words, if these 'hypotheses' reflect the pricing decision maker's perception of the situation then it is this which will govern his pricing decision. Similarly, under the conditions proposed by Simon, it would seem to make a lot of sense for the buyer to use price as an indicator of quality where the opportunity cost of getting better information is very high together with the perceived risk of making the wrong decision. Hence, while IBM equipment is often 25 per cent more expensive than comparable competitive products there is considerable support for the view that 'Nobody ever got fired for buying IBM'.

■ A strategic pricing framework

In the *Journal of Consumer Marketing* Hugh Cannon and Frank Morgan present 'A strategic Pricing Framework' which conceptualises pricing outcomes or objectives as a function of pricing strategies constrained by environmental factors. The essence of their framework is reproduced in Figure 13.6 and provides a very useful summary of the key issues to consider in pricing decision making.

The model comprises three central elements:

- a series of Rules (R)
- a selection of pricing methods (P)
- a set of possible pricing objectives (O)

Readers should consult the original source for the precise definitions used by the authors but in broad terms P1 and P2 (target profit and cost-plus pricing) are both variants of cost-based methods. P3 and P4 (perceived value and going-rate pricing) are based upon what the market will bear, while P5 (sealed bid pricing) and P6 (negotiated pricing) are self-explanatory. Similarly, the rules and objectives are fairly clear, the point about the first rule being that if the customer is small then it is unlikely the seller would entertain sealed bid or negotiated prices (P5 and P6) so these are eliminated from the feasible set. Otherwise one proceeds through the decision tree using the rules and objectives to help one select a preferred pricing method.

■ An alternative model of pricing behaviour

Based on her extensive analysis of pricing behaviour, Said offers us an alternative model in Figure 13.7, on page 336, which she describes as follows:

> As a first step, there is the decision about objectives which business firms seek to achieve through their pricing policy.
>
> The process of price determination comprises both the firms' approach to pricing and the techniques used, which includes the following:
>
> - Decisions concerning the methods of pricing either cost or not cost related.
> - Decisions concerning methods of costing for pricing purposes.
> - Decisions concerning profit policy, the techniques used in calculating profit margins and their flexibility between products.
> - Decisions concerning price changes in response to demand and cost fluctuations.
> - Decisions concerning price review.
> - Decisions concerning pricing systems to be used.
> - Decisions concerning discount structures to be operated.

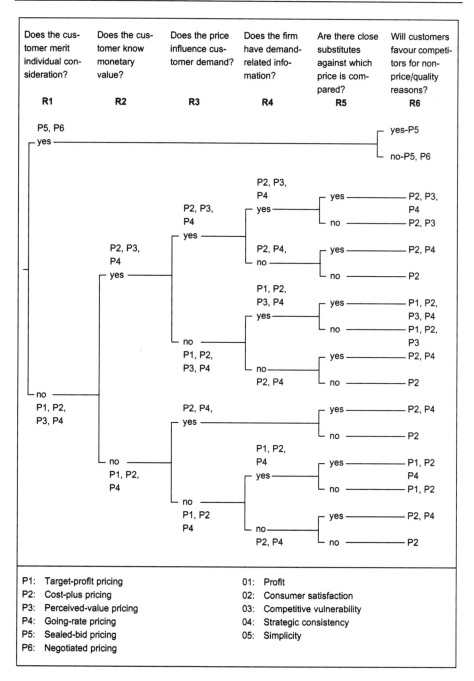

P1: Target-profit pricing
P2: Cost-plus pricing
P3: Perceived-value pricing
P4: Going-rate pricing
P5: Sealed-bid pricing
P6: Negotiated pricing

01: Profit
02: Consumer satisfaction
03: Competitive vulnerability
04: Strategic consistency
05: Simplicity

Figure 13.6 A strategic pricing decision model

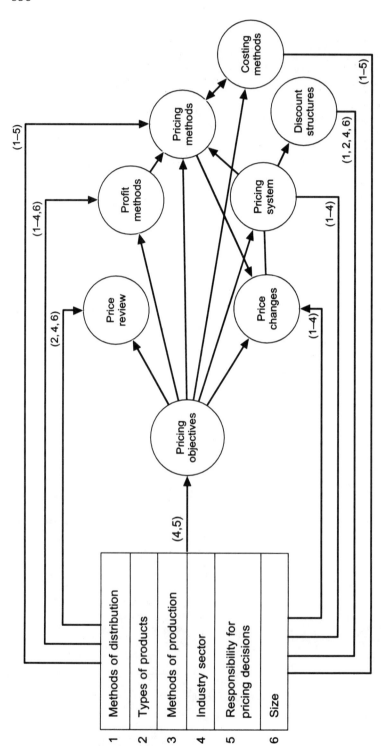

Figure 13.7 A model of pricing behaviour

Source: Hanna A. Said, op cit.

As suggested in the model, pricing behaviour is a function of a complex of objective and subjective variables. The objective variables indicated in the model are the type of product, methods of production, methods of distribution, industry sector and size. The subjective variables are the choices made by executives responsible for pricing and the type of respondent manager.

To begin with pricing objectives, the model shows a link between pricing objectives and industry sector, type of manager responsible for pricing decisions and type of respondent manager.

Firms' approach to pricing and techniques used are functions of all these objective and subjective variables combined with pricing objectives. More specifically:

- There is an association between the pricing methods used in business firms and their pricing objectives, the type of product they produce, the methods of production and distribution they use, the industry sector they fall in, and the type of manager responsible for setting prices.
- There is an association between the costing methods used in business firms and their pricing objectives, pricing methods, the type of product, methods of production and distribution, industry sector and the type of manager responsible for pricing.
- There is an association between profit policy employed by a business firm and its pricing objectives, pricing methods, type of product, methods of production and distribution, industry sector and size.
- There is an association between price changes and pricing objectives, pricing methods, type of product, methods of production and distribution, industry sector and pricing systems.
- There is an association between firm's policy in reviewing prices and pricing objectives, pricing methods, type of product, industry sector and size.
- There is an association between pricing systems employed by firms and their pricing objectives, the type of product, methods of production and distribution and industry sector.
- There is an association between discount structures operated by business firms and their pricing systems, type of product, methods of distribution, industry sector and size.

As shown in the model, the relationship between the different aspects of pricing behaviour is cross-sectional or one way, which indicates the case in a static analysis. However, over time these associations will show a two way relationship, indicating a dynamic state and the adjustment of policy and practice in the light of experience. For example, a price review can result in a change in the firm's pricing objectives, which in turn will cause a change in its profit policy, pricing methods, pricing systems, price changes and so on. A change in profit policy can cause a change in pricing objectives, pricing methods, costing methods, etc. Also a change in costing methods can cause a change in pricing methods, which in turn influence profit policy, pricing objectives and consequently all the process of pricing.

This model might fill an existing gap in the pricing literature on two counts:

First, it suggests a link between pricing behaviour and certain variables which play an important role in pricing, but which have received little attention previously.

Second, while recognising the interdependence and interrelationship of the various aspects of the pricing process, it considers them to be influenced significantly by the firms' overall pricing objectives, of which there may be several, and so conditioned by them.

These two points suggest the complexity of pricing decisions, which is emphasised by Livesey, Oxenfeldt, Tucker, Hague, and many others, that pricing decisions constitute a complex web, and that successful pricing requires an awareness of the many interrelationships among pricing decisions.

CHAPTER 14

Distribution policy and the selection of marketing channels

Learning Goals

The issues to be addressed in this chapter include:

1. The functions of the distributive channel.
2. The determinants of channel policy.
3. The selection of a distributive channel.

After reading this chapter you will be able to:

1. List the five essential functions performed by a distribution channel.
2. Review the advantages and disadvantages of the three basic alternatives available when selecting a distribution policy
   - direct sale
   - sale through an intermediary
   - a dual policy.
3. Explain the channel policy decision in terms of the resolution of conflict between cost and control.
4. Summarise the factors to be considered when selecting a distribution channel.

In that Chapter 9 dealt extensively with 'Patterns of Distribution', this chapter may well appear superfluous at first sight. However, the earlier chapter was essentially descriptive, and it now remains to investigate *how* the marketer selects the most appropriate distribution channel.

■ Distribution: a neglected subject

It is generally agreed that the subject of marketing owes its origin to economists' inquiries into the nature of the distributive process at the end of the last century.

However, despite this early interest, it is only in recent years that the firm has turned its attention to the role which distribution has to play as an element of competitive strategy.

In a review of the status of distribution in the 1960s, Donald Bowersox advanced two reasons which he felt accounted for the delay in the development of this area of marketing: (*a*) the lack of computers and applied analytical tools sufficient to deal with the complexities of the problem; (*b*) the absence of adequate motivation (Donald J. Bowersox, 'Physical Distribution Development, Current Status and Potential', *Journal of Marketing*, XXXIII (Jan. 1969) pp. 63–70). Of these it was felt that the latter was the more important, and two main factors may be distinguished which were to provide the necessary motivation – technological innovation and increased competition.

Writing in the April 1962 issue of *Fortune*, Peter Drucker characterised distribution as the 'Economy's Dark Continent' and noted that whereas the cost of physical distribution accounted for as much as half of the total cost of finished goods, it had received relatively little attention by comparison with managements' cost reduction efforts in other directions. Since the publication of this article there has been an enormous expansion in the literature of physical distribution, but it is significant that little of the research represented by this literature has been concerned with the strategic implications of channel policy. As Bowersox notes, extant concepts assume vertical integration or, alternatively, take the viewpoint that physical distribution operations and responsibilities cease where a transfer of ownership occurs. The latter ignores the fact that many manufacturers sell at least part of their output through intermediaries, and implies that they take no further interest in the sales process once their output has passed into the wholesaler's inventory. Similarly, vertical integration is atypical of present distributive structures.

Given the competitive pressures attributable to escalating costs, increased industrial concentration as the result of acquisition and mergers, and the threat of product obsolescence inherent in accelerating technological innovation, it is clear that distribution policy has become a question of acute importance to the marketer.

■ The function of the distributive channel

Although the functions performed by distributive channels have already been described in respect of various types of goods, it will be useful at this point to synthesise common features into a series of empirically valid generalisations. In order to avoid misunderstanding, a channel of distribution is here defined as: 'The structure of intra-company organisation units and extra-company agents and dealers, wholesale and retail, through which a commodity, product or service is marketed. This definition was designed to be broad enough to include: (*a*) both a firm's internal marketing organisation units and the outside business units it uses in its marketing work and (*b*) both the channel structure of the individual firm and the entire complex available to all firms (*Marketing Definitions*: American Marketing Association, 1962). The Macmillan *Dictionary of Marketing and Advertising* (2nd edn, 1990) explains further 'a channel consists of all those steps through which a product must pass between its point of production and consumption'.

As economies develop there is an increasing emphasis on specialisation and the division of labour, as a result of which a 'gap' develops between producer and user. The primary purpose of a distributive channel is to bridge this gap by resolving spatial and temporal discrepancies in supply and demand. Irrespective of the extent of these discrepancies, certain essential functions need to be performed which may be summarised as:

1. Transfer of title to the goods involved.
2. Physical movement from the point of production to the point of consumption.
3. Storage functions.
4. Communication of information concerning the availability, characteristics and price of the goods.
5. The financing of goods in transit, inventory and on purchase.

The importance of these functions varies, depending upon the nature of the goods themselves. Physical movement and storage tend to predominate in the case of bulky raw or part-processed materials such as basic chemicals, petroleum products and steel, where price and specification are standardised and the market is comprised of a limited number of buyers and sellers. As the complexity of the product increases the provision of information and product service becomes predominant. In the case of consumer goods, advertising and sales promotion constitute the major communication channel, but industrial goods depend more on personal selling owing to the more heterogeneous nature of the goods involved and the possibility of modifying them to meet end-user requirements. Some indication of the possible complexity of the distribution channel for a common-place product like the broiler chicken is shown in Figure 14.1.

In essence, then, the functions are common to all distributive channels, but in the particular it is necessary to consider the precise nature of the product, and seller-buyer relationships, to determine their relative importance.

As noted previously, the manufacturer is faced with three basic alternatives when deciding upon a distribution policy:

(*a*)   Direct sale.
(*b*)   Sale through an intermediary.
(*c*)   A 'dual' policy combining direct sale with the use of an intermediary.

The advantages and disadvantages commonly associated with these alternatives may be summarised as:

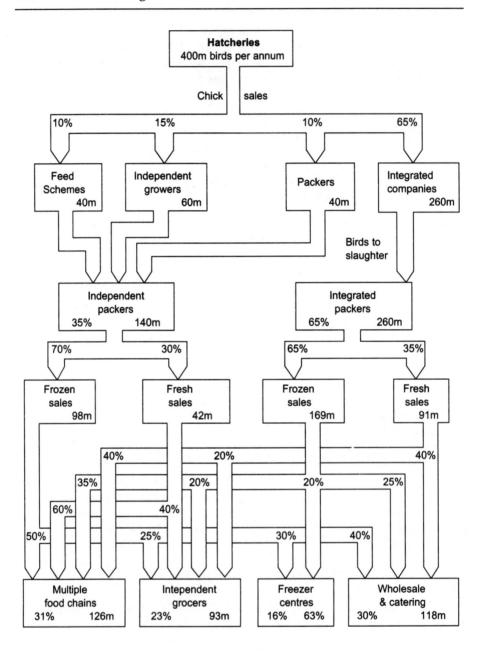

The flow chart is prepared only as an example, the information contained therein is not an accurate analysis of the broiler industry (Prepared by Produce Studies Limited, Newbury, England.)

Figure 14.1   British broiler production, flow plan

■ Direct sale

The major advantage associated with direct sale is that it permits the seller to retain full control over the total marketing process. Its usage is favoured by the existence of:

A limited number of potential buyers.
A high degree of geographical concentration of potential buyers.
A high degree of technical complexity requiring extensive service.
A high level of technological innovation.
Stable demand conditions, i.e. the absence of seasonal and cyclical trends which necessitate stockholding.

Any of these factors in itself may be sufficient to predicate adoption of a policy of direct selling; in combination they are virtually irresistible. Conversely, a conflict between, say, the number of buyers and their geographic dispersion may make direct selling a totally uneconomic proposition – the major disadvantage linked with this approach.

■ Sale through an intermediary

When cost considerations militate against the adoption of direct selling, manufacturers frequently make use of an intermediary who, by acting on behalf of a number of buyers and sellers, is able to perform the necessary functions more economically, i.e. the gross margin demanded by the intermediary is less than the on-cost which would be incurred through providing the same services oneself. The advantages and disadvantages of using an intermediary may be summarised as:

Advantages:
1. Cost advantages: use of an intermediary
   • Minimises the cost of a field sales organisation.
   • Eliminates warehousing costs.
   • Minimises inventory financing charges.
   • Minimises sales costs – invoicing, financing of accounts, etc.
   • Minimises the risk of loss through inventory obsolescence.
   • Minimises loss through bad debts and reduces the cost of credit control.
   • Eliminates local delivery costs.
   • Reduces the costs of processing to meet non-standard orders.
2. Coverage. The use of intermediaries allows the producer to reach all potential users without having to incur the fixed costs which would arise if direct selling were used.
3. Provision of service. Intermediaries can provide immediate availability and necessary pre- and after-sales service on a local basis more effectively than many producers.

Disadvantages:

The major disadvantage associated with the use of an intermediary is the loss of direct control over any, or all, of the following:

Selling effort – Customer selection
　　　　　　 – Call frequency
　　　　　　 – Product emphasis
　　　　　　 – Promotion and missionary selling effort.
Pricing.
Delivery.
Service – Standard and availability.

Clearly, the importance attached to retaining control over these functions will vary from product to product and manufacturer to manufacturer.

■ Dual distribution

In order to try and reconcile the conflict between the desirability of direct contact and the economies offered by selling through an intermediary, many manufacturers have adopted a compromise solution, usually referred to as 'dual' distribution. Under this alternative the manufacturer sells part of his output direct but entrusts the balance of his sales effort to an intermediary. As noted elsewhere, this policy is favoured by the existence of the 'heavy half' phenomenon, where a limited number of users constitute the major demand with the balance fragmented among a large number of small or irregular users.

The major disadvantage associated with dual distribution is the difficulty intrinsic in determining a fair division of the market between producer and intermediary.

■ Major determinants of channel policy

Fundamentally, the channel decision requires resolution of the often conflicting forces of cost and control.

Cost is readily understood even if it is sometimes difficult to quantify, and several aspects of control have already been stated. However, the concept of control must be broadened to recognise the fact that a firm's ability to exercise control is a function of its competitive strength *vis-à-vis* other channel members. Thus it is usual to find that one member of the distributive channel dominates its practices and is regarded as the 'locus of channel control' (see Louis P. Bucklin, 'The Locus of Channel Control', *Proceedings of the Fall, 1968, Conference of the American Marketing Association*, pp. 142–7). In general the dominant members are either producers or users/consumers, but there are situations where a channel intermediary may be dominant and so condition the structure and operation of the channel. The latter situation is most likely to occur where both producers and users are small and the market is geographically dispersed, and is equally true of retailer/wholesalers in the consumer goods market as it is of the industrial goods wholesaler. Overall, dominance or control is determined by a number of factors which may be summarised as:

Buyer/seller concentration ratios in terms of production/consumption, and spatial relationships.

Technical complexity. In the case of technically complex products, dominance will be conditioned by the relative sophistication of the producer *vis-à-vis* the intermediary and/or user. Thus a small firm may exercise considerable influence over much larger users or intermediaries.

Service requirements – the more complex these are the more likely it is that the producer will exercise control.

In the final analysis, however, the determining factor is economic advantage, i.e. which channel member can perform the necessary channel functions at the lowest cost consistent with the required degree of efficiency. At a given point in time the structure of a trade channel serves as a rough and ready guide as to the relative efficiency of its members, but it is clear that over time environmental changes may predicate the adoption of an alternative structure to better meet the needs of users/consumers. Similarly, lack of control may persuade a channel member to modify his policies in order to protect his position – a tendency which is implicit in Galbraith's concept of 'countervailing power'.

Examples of competitive reaction within the distributive channel are well documented in the field of consumer goods but less so in the industrial sphere. The growth of dominant retailing institutions was noted in Chapter 9, together with the response of the independent wholesaler whose livelihood was threatened, and similar trends are to be observed in industrial markets.

Among the latter may be noted the adoption of contract purchasing, also known as systems contracting, stockless purchasing, automatic ordering or 'Just in time' (JIT) purchasing. Under this system, buyers negotiate contracts for the continued supply of standard requirements from a single source at a fixed price. Effectively, this reduces the actual stock of parts, supplies or components to the absolute minimum consistent with day-to-day operations, and transfers the inventory costs and risk of obsolescence to the supplier. Such contracts are invariably based upon a total cost analysis rather than on a basis of minimum price. Associated with contract purchasing there is a growing trend in the United States towards computerised ordering systems in which standardised and routine orders are placed direct with the supplier (producer or wholesaler) through the medium of electronic data processing equipment, e.g. Data Phone, WATS-line and Flexowriter. In that these practices not only result in operating economies but also free the purchasing agent to devote more time to non-routine buying decisions, they are resulting in a fuller and more sophisticated evaluation of competitive offerings. In the UK Kwik-fit operates such a system for all its outlets.

To counteract the growing sophistication of buyers, many sellers have switched to systems selling, in which they offer a complete 'package' of related products and services which would formerly have been purchased from a variety of different sources. Similarly, the appointment of market managers, as opposed to product managers, recognises the need to adapt marketing practice to the specific needs of different end-use markets.

■ The channel decision

Whether one accepts profit maximisation as the basic corporate objective or not, it seems reasonable to affirm that uncertainty about the future business environment and the competitive activity of other firms will predispose the firm to reduce costs to the minimum level consistent with achievement of its own stated objective. If this is so, then the channel decision may be viewed as a three-stage process. The first stage consists of a qualitative assessment of the environmental opportunity which the firm is best suited to exploit, conditioned by less tangible objectives such as 'To build the best product'. 'To provide the best after-sales service'.

Once the broad strategy has been determined, management must decide which mix of policies offers the optimum probability of attaining the desired result. Such decisions cannot be made in isolation, for the success of a strategy demands that the separate marketing policies in respect of price, distribution, promotion, etc., be synthesised into a consistent and cohesive whole. Usually, however, one variable will take preeminence over the others by virtue of the basic strategy decided upon – the 'strategic variable'. For example, if the basic strategy is to sell mass consumption convenience goods, extensive or mass distribution may well be considered the key or strategic variable, and will condition policies adopted in respect of other mix elements. Similarly, if the basic strategy is to build a reputation for high product quality the product itself will become the strategic variable, and probably result in a high price, selective distribution policy.

In order to decide which distribution channel or combination of channels is to be preferred the marketer should then quantify the costs associated with the available alternatives. This analysis should be based initially on a check-list similar to that in Chapter 9, followed by a detailed cost breakdown for direct sale to the number of accounts thought to be necessary to achieve the desired sales volume. Such a breakdown would normally include consideration of the following:

Number and geographical distribution of accounts.
Number of calls per account adjusted to allow for potential order size.
Average sales per call.
Average time per call.
Number of salesmen necessary to achieve the optimal call pattern.
Salaries and commission payable.

Travelling and administrative costs incurred.
Costs of holding inventory.
Costs of financing receivables.
Costs of extending credit.
Costs arising out of bad debts.
Costs of providing necessary services.
Costs of invoicing, order processing, expediting, etc.
Transportation costs.

On the basis of such a cost analysis one may then compute the average selling, general and administrative costs per unit sold, and compare this with the gross margin asked by intermediaries for providing the same services and market coverage. Obviously, if the margin asked is greater than the average unit cost, direct sale will appear more attractive, and vice versa. The outcome of such an analysis is rarely clear-cut, however, and even when it does appear so it does not necessarily represent the optimal strategy. The latter may only be determined effectively on a marginal or contribution basis, which in turn will usually require the use of a computer to cope with the enormous number of possible combinations and permutations.

As inferred earlier, the selection of a strategy is basically a judgmental process. Only under certain limited circumstances will the decision-maker be without prior information, and in most cases his evaluation will be based upon a consideration of alternatives related to current practice. Although he will still be faced with considerable uncertainty, the existence of prior information suggests that the channel decision should be amenable to analysis using a Bayesian approach.

The application of Bayesian methodology to the channel selection decision is discussed in *Planning and Problem Solving in Marketing* by Wroe Alderson and Paul E. Green (Richard D. Irwin, Homewood, Illinois, 1964) pp. 311–17. The example used is highly simplified, and ignores the difficulties associated with quantifying the cash flows attributable to different courses of action and the complexities inherent in different channel combinations. None the less, it does demonstrate that if the decision-maker can quantify his expectation as to the probability of the occurrence of basic events, he will be better able to select the policy which will maximise profits or other preferred criterion.

Once the optimum distribution policy has been quantified, the final step in the analysis should be to review the original qualitative assessment in the light of the quantitative data and to eliminate any inconsistencies, e.g. the quantitative analysis may suggest that the original decision would not optimise the opportunities open to the firm.

Readers should consult Chapter 12 of *Marketing Strategy and Management* (1985) for a more detailed analysis of the issues involved in selecting a distribution policy.

CHAPTER 15

Marketing communications

Learning Goals

The issues to be discussed in this chapter include:

1. The definition of communication and basic models of the communication process.
2. The way in which advertising works.
3. The role of communication in the marketing mix.
4. Marketing communications as information processing.

After reading this chapter you will be familiar with:

1. The concept of a channel of communication linking communicators with an intended audience.
2. The view that effective communication is the consequence of a process similar to that described in the hierarchy of effects models, i.e. moving an audience from unawareness to awareness, interest and action.
3. The distinction between personal and non-personal influence and their combination in the theory of the two-step flow of communication.
4. The paradigm of the innovation-decision process comprising the four stages of *knowledge*, *persuasion*, *decisions* and *confirmation* and its use in planning and communication strategy.
5. The nature of opinion leadership and the characteristics of opinion leaders.
6. The influence of source effect.
7. The concepts of consonance and dissonance.
8. The relationship between message and medium.
9. The role of communications as a marketing mix variable.
10. The view of marketing communications as a form of information processing in which consumers play an active role.

■ Introduction

In the view of some authors (e.g. M. Wayne DeLozier, *The Marketing Communications Process*, McGraw-Hill, 1976) all the marketing-mix variables and indeed all company activities may be regarded as marketing communication variables. Conversely, E. J. McCarthy and William D. Perreault Jr. (*Basic Marketing*, 8th edn, Irwin, 1984) take a more narrow approach and regard marketing communications as the *promotional* activities of personal selling, mass selling, which they see as comprising advertising and publicity, and sales promotion. Our own discussion will incline towards the latter, narrower, functional treatment as it is felt to be more appropriate to an introductory text. However, an attempt will be made in this chapter to put this basically factual and descriptive treatment into a theoretical perspective by reviewing some of the major concepts and ideas which have found their way into the marketing literature in recent years.

To this end the chapter begins with a definition of communication and proceeds to examine some of the basic models of the communication process in current circulation. References will be made to the role of attention and perception as prerequisites of action by the receiver – usually in the form of some attitudinal or behavioural change, or both – as well as to the relevance of learning theory to the propagation and understanding of marketing communication. Both these topics were introduced in Chapter 6 ('Consumer Behaviour').

The chapter then looks more closely at some of the major components of any marketing communication – the source, the message and the medium – and concludes with a discussion of the role of communication in the marketing mix. Finally, we examine a suggestion by Crosier (1983) that we should abandon traditional models of the kind discussed in this chapter in favour of an alternative explanation based upon information processing theory.

■ Communication defined

Wilbur Schramm defined communication as 'the process of establishing a commonness or oneness of thought between a sender and a receiver' (*The Process and Effects of Mass Communications*, University of Illinois Press, 1955, p. 3). Central to this definition is the concept that for communication to occur there must be a transfer of information from one party – the sender – which is received and understood by the other party – the receiver. In other words both receiver and sender play an active role in establishing communication – a fact which is given particular point when one considers that the average consumer is estimated to be exposed to approximately 3000 promotional messages a day but only receives nine of these messages. My colleague Keith Crosier has drawn to my attention the fact that while I assert that 'both receiver and sender play an active role' this is not clear from Schramm's model nor the pictorial representation of it in Figures 15.1 and 15.2. I agree – in fact the arrows in the figures tend to convey unidirectionality and cast the destination in a passive 'receiver' role. I do not believe Schramm intended this, and I certainly do not, in that my composite model of consumer behaviour described in Chapter 6 stresses strongly the point just alluded to – it is the receiver who decides whether or not to 'switch on' and thus plays an active role in the process. This point is of particular importance as much of the criticism of advertising rests on the assumption that promotional activity is something done to or exercised on passive consumers with no opportunity to control or influence the process.

Pictorially the simplest model of the communications process is shown in Figure 15.1. However, this simple model ignores the fact that it is necessary to convert ideas into a symbolic medium to enable them to be transmitted via a communication channel. To allow for this we must introduce two more elements into the model – encoding and decoding – as shown in Figure 15.2.

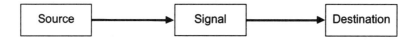

Figure 15.1   Simplified communication model

Figure 15.2   Communication channel model

As Schramm points out, this model can accommodate all types of communication so that in the case of electronic communication the encoder becomes a transmitting device – microphone, teletype, etc – and the decoder a receiver – radio or television set, telephone, etc. In the case of direct personal (face-to-face) communication then one person is both source and encoder while the other is decoder and destination and the signal is language. It follows that if an exchange of meaning is to take place, then both source and destination must be tuned in to each other and share the same language. Put another way, there must be an overlap in the field of experience of source and destination – which Schramm illustrates as follows:

We must also recognise that all communication is intended to have an effect and introduce the notion of *feedback* into our model of communication, for it is through feedback that the source learns how its signals are being interpreted. In personal communication feedback is often instantaneous through verbal acknowledgement or gesture but in impersonal communication through the mass media it may have to be inferred from other indicators, e.g. audience size, circulation, readership, or monitored by sampling opinion.

The final element in Schramm's model, which is not immediately apparent from the figures other than in the existence of arrows linking the other elements, is the *channel* or, more correctly channels, for messages are rarely transmitted through a single channel. Thus in personal communications it is not merely the words which convey the message but the intonation of our voice and the gestures which accompany them although some might regard these as coding rather than channels. In the field of marketing communication then the channel tends to have the specific connotation of the *media classes* which are the subject of more extended treatment in the next chapter.

The marketer's version of Schramm's model employs slightly different terminology, but contains all of the following elements (see C. Shannon and W. Weaver, *The Mathematical Theory of Communication*, University of Illinois Press, 1962):

Who . . .	*says what* . . .	*how* . . .	*to whom* . . .
Communicator	*Message*	*Channels*	*Audience*

with what effect

Feedback

Kotler defines these basic elements as follows:

Communicator: the sender or sources of the message

Message: the set of meanings being sent and/or received by the audience

Channels: the ways in which the message can be carried or delivered to the audience

Audience: the receiver or destination of the message

From his model Schramm derives four basic 'conditions of success in communication . . . which must be fulfilled if the message is to arouse its intended response'. These are:

1. The message must be so designed and delivered as to gain the attention of the intended destination.
2. The message must employ signs which refer to experience common to source and destination, so as to 'get the meaning across'.
3. The message must arouse personality needs in the destination and suggest some ways to meet those needs.

4. The message must suggest a way to meet those needs which is appropriate to the group situation in which the destination finds himself at the time when he is moved to make the desired response.

Consideration of these four requirements should strike a receptive chord in the memory of the reader who is methodically working his way through the book, for they echo closely points discussed in Chapter 6 concerning hierarchy-of-effects models in consumer behaviour. In fact Schramm's four conditions are very similar to Strong's basic AIDA model – Attention, Interest, Desire and Action. It will be useful, therefore, to recapitulate on this earlier discussion but specifically in the context of marketing communications. In doing so we will first provide a broad overview and then pick out certain key concepts for a fuller discussion, namely diffusion theories, opinion leadership and the two-step flow of communication, source credibility and cognitive consonance and dissonance.

■ How advertising works

One of the earliest explanations of how advertising works is based upon the stimulus – response theory of learning in which advertising is perceived as a stimulus and purchasing behaviour the intended and desired response. However, it is clear that advertising, even when very intense does not lead automatically to purchase and it was postulated that the act of purchase is the culmination of a whole sequence of events. If this is so then it is argued that advertising's role is to move people up the steps from a state of unawareness to purchase and a number of models of varying levels of sophistication have been put forward including Strong's AIDA model (Attention, Interest, Desire, Action), Lavidge and Steiner's 'Hierarchy of Effects' Model (Awareness, Knowledge, Liking, Preference, Conviction, Purchase) , and Roger's 'Innovation Adoption' Model (Awareness, Interest, Evaluation, Trial, Adoption). (See p. 125.)

The models referred to above are all old (the most recent is 1961) and relate specifically to personal communication rather than the broader field of marketing communication which is our concern here. Keith Crosier addresses this issue directly in Chapter 6 of the companion volume *Marketing: Theory and Practice* (ed. M. J. Baker, 2nd edn, Macmillan, 1983) and the reader is strongly advised to consult this for a much extended discussion of marketing communications in general and the role of hierarchical models in the particular. However, all these models suggest a sequence of events which observation and experience often contradict, particularly' in the case of low involvement and/or impulse purchases and Crosier underlines the trenchant criticisms of, *inter alia*, Copland, Palda, Krugman, Ehrenberg and Ray. Indeed this conflict of opinion is but another manifestation of the conundrum as to whether attitude change leads to behavioural change or vice versa, there being substantial evidence for both schools of thought. However, notwithstanding this conflict of opinion, it is clear that most advertisers find the learning model intuitively appealing and often set objectives in terms of moving potential customers up the various steps from unawareness to purchase.

Two basic problems may be identified immediately: first, audiences are comprised of persons who differ from each other in many demographic and psycho-social respects; second, there is likely to be considerable variation in the levels of knowledge and awareness of different members of the audience at any given point in time. As a consequence individuals will vary in their response to the advertisers' message and the channels through which it is communicated. It follows that insight into the understanding of how such variance occurs is of vital importance in designing marketing communications.

Many communication experts subscribe to McLuhan's thesis that 'the medium is the message' (*Understanding Media: The Extension of Man*, McGraw-Hill, 1965) and so would argue that once a target audience has been identified the primary decision is selection of the medium or channel to be used. Conversely others point out that media planning is a complex activity only because there are so many similar media that choice between them is difficult. This being so, then it is the message which must be selected first and this will help identify the most appropriate medium to reach the target audience. In reality, however, it seems that both approaches are used and that preference is situation-specific. But on balance the channel seems to exercise the greater influence and will be dealt with first.

In general channels may be divided into two major categories: *personal* and *non-personal*. As the name implies personal channels embrace all those situations in which a direct, face-to-face communication takes place, while non-personal channels comprise all media through which messages are transmitted *without* face-to-face communication, e.g. press, television, exhibitions, etc. The available evidence suggests that both types of channel have a role to play and it is usually held that non-personal media are most effective in establishing awareness and interest, while personal influence is necessary to move the members of an audience up the hierarchy through desire to action. Further, it has been found that personal influence is most effective in high-risk purchase situations, i.e. where the consumer is expending relatively large amounts and purchases infrequently (shopping goods) or where the product/service has social connotations which link brands with social groups (speciality goods). (The obverse of this is that mass communication is most appropriate for convenience goods.)

As indicated, however, it is usual to find a combination of both personal and non-personal channels used in a given campaign. Research by Lazarsfeld (*The People's Choice*, Sloan & Pearce, 1944) showed that impersonal channels are often mediated in their effect by personal channels – the so-called 'Two-step flow of communication'. According to this model certain members of the population act as filters and amplifiers for messages and these persons have been designated *opinion leaders*. It follows that if the two-step model applies then the communicator should identify the *opinion leaders* and transmit his messages through them. Often opinion leaders are best reached via impersonal channels and themselves become a personal channel performing the role of unpaid salesmen.

Clearly, the achievement of direct face-to-face communication could be expensive and impersonal channels help reduce the cost of conveying messages to consumers. However, many messages transmitted through the mass media compete for our attention and most of these are screened out by the psychological defence mechanisms of selective *perception, distortion* and *retention*. As a result the power of mass communication as a persuasive influence is largely discounted nowadays and the mass media are seen primarily as leading to learning and reinforcement over time. Further, different media act in different ways and the skill of the media planner lies in selection of the medium or combination of media best suited to the audience he is seeking to reach

Reference has been made to the message on several occasions and its importance is obvious, for, as Kotler says, it is the means 'by which the communicator attempts to make the product meaningful and desirable to the buyer'. Perhaps the most important point about the message is that it should be designed so that it is meaningful to the recipient after the distortion which will inevitably occur on transmission through the chosen channel or channels and its selective screening by the audience. It follows that the message is an infinitely variable element in the communication process, as it must be tailored to the differing needs and levels of knowledge/experience of a constantly changing audience. However, two broad schools of thought exist concerning message structure and content, one favouring *consonance* (i.e. conforming with held beliefs, aspirations, etc. – 'pleasant' messages) , the other dissonance (i.e. contrary to held beliefs and so creating discomfort or dissonance). We return to these concepts later in the chapter.

The final element is the communicator himself. His influence is both direct – identification of audience, selection of channel, choice of message – and indirect – the way he is perceived by the audience as the source of the message (the 'source effect'). Again, it is important to stress that the source is not necessarily the communicator himself but rather the origin of the message as perceived by the audience (cf. the testimonial advertisement). In turn the audience's perception of the message will be governed by its interpretation of the *source credibility* – a concept developed by Kelman and Hovland and seen as comprising two elements – expertness and trustworthiness. Fundamentally the precept is 'the higher the source credibility the greater the effectiveness of the communication'. However, source effect decays over time and must be reinforced through repetition. Further discussion of source effect is to be found on pp. 360–1.

■ Diffusion theories

In discussing hierarchy-of-effects models in Chapter 6 reference was made to Everett Rogers's five-step adoption model – awareness, interest, evaluation, trial, adoption – which has been used extensively in many studies of new product marketing and marketing communications. However, Rogers' basic model has been subject to a number of criticisms. Specifically, it suggests that adoption is a consequence of the process when in fact the decision might be to reject the innovation, or even to 'wait and see', i.e. deferred rejection/adoption. Second, the five stages need not occur in the sequence proposed (cf. impulse purchasing) and it seems likely that evaluation is not a discrete phase but takes place throughout the process. Further, in many instances the trial phase may be omitted. Finally, some critics have pointed out that adoption (purchase of a product) is not the final stage in the process, as post-adoption activity will occur leading to feedback which will influence subsequent behaviour.

To meet these criticisms Rogers joined forces with Floyd Shoemaker and proposed a revised 'paradigm of the innovation – decision process' containing four stages (see *Communications of Innovations*, 2nd edn, Free Press, 1971):

1. *Knowledge.* The individual is aware of the innovation and has acquired some information about it.
2. *Persuasion.* The individual forms an attitude, pro or con, towards the innovation.
3. *Decisions.* The individual performs activities which lead to an adopt-reject decision about the innovation.
4. *Confirmation.* The individual looks for reinforcement regarding his decision and may change his earlier decision if exposed to counter-reinforcing messages.

Clearly this model is more flexible and less mechanistic than the original and permits the accommodation of the criticisms outlined earlier. Diagrammatically the model appears as shown in Figure 15.3. The reader will be familiar with the antecedent variables, for these were reviewed in Chapter 6, so attention will be focused on the process itself. However, before doing so it will be useful to introduce the concepts of *adopter categories* and *diffusion*.

Under another name (the concept of the product life-cycle, PLC – see pp. 267 ff.) the diffusion process is one of the most familiar and fundamental of marketing ideas. In essence the PLC and cumulative adoption curves are the same and show that after a slow initial start sales grow rapidly and then begin to level off until saturation is achieved. If these sales are plotted against elapsed time from introduction of an innovation, then a normal distribution results and this has lead to attempts to analyse and classify the adoption/buying behaviour of individuals in terms of the properties of the normal distribution. Figure 15.4 illustrates this.

It follows that if we are able to identify beforehand certain individuals as being more receptive to a given innovation, then we should be able to accelerate adoption by focusing our initial marketing efforts upon them. In turn, because the diffusion process is probabilistic, this will accelerate the whole diffusion process and result in enhanced profitability.

Returning to the process of adoption it has been determined that certain communication mixes are more appropriate than others at different stages and this knowledge is of great value in planning a communications strategy.

356

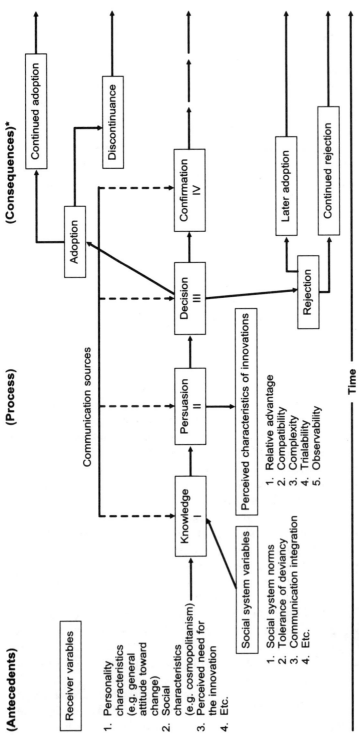

Figure 15.3 Paradigm of the innovation decision process
(Note: A modified version of this figure is to be found in Everett M. Rogers, *Diffusion of Innovation*, 3rd edn, New York, Free Press, 1983, p. 165.)

Source: Everett M. Rogers with Floyd Shoemaker, *Communication of Innovations*, 2nd edn, New York, Free Press, 1971.

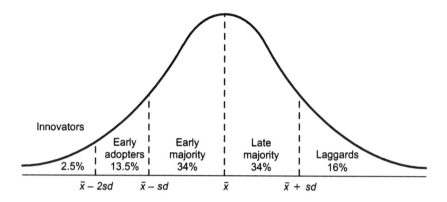

Figure 15.4   Adopter categorisation on the basis of innovativeness

(The innovativeness dimension, as measured by the time at which an individual adopts an innovation or innovations, is continuous. However, this variable may be partitioned into five adopter categories by laying off standard deviations from the average time of adoption.)

The *knowledge* stage is one of awareness and preliminary information-seeking in which impersonal sources tend to dominate. Other things being equal one could conceive of a situation in which all potential buyers of a new product were exposed to information about it simultaneously but because of selective perception and distortion relatively few would react to the information. Early adopters are those who do react quickly and they have been found to possess a number of characteristics which distinguish them from later adopters. Specifically, they make it their business to be well-informed and so make greater use of mass media and personal sources of information – both social and professional (i.e. sales personnel or 'change agents') – and they also tend to be better-educated, extrovert and more cosmopolitan than later adopters.

The second stage in the process is that of *persuasion*, in which the potential user moves from a state of neutral awareness to the development of an attitude towards the new object. In my model (pp. 142 ff.) this change is initiated by 'precipitating circumstances' and leads to formal evaluation of possible solutions to the felt need. In the Rogers and Shoemaker model this evaluation is based upon the perceived characteristics of the innovation – relative advantage, compatibility, complexity, trialability and observability. At this stage prospective users will seek to extend their information base and make greater use of personal sources. It is at this juncture that opinion leadership assumes great importance as the potential user will seek the advice of those he sees as knowledgeable about the item under consideration.

Relative advantage is defined as 'the degree to which an innovation is perceived as better' than an existing idea or object and it is stated that the higher the relative advantage the greater the likelihood of adoption. Compatibility and complexity are self-explanatory and tend to vary inversely with one another, i.e. the more compatible an object is with one's field of experience, attitudes and value structure, etc., the less complex it is likely to seem and vice versa. Trialability, or the extent to which an individual can try out an innovation before coming to a decision, is an important factor in reducing perceived risk and an aid to speeding up decision-making (it works both ways!). Finally, observability refers to the visible effectiveness of the innovation.

While these perceived characteristics enjoy wide currency I am not overly fond of them myself. For example, relative advantage is really a catch-all for all the other characteristics and it is tautologous to state that the greater the perceived advantage the faster the adoption – even the clinically insane act in the manner which maximise their own perceived self-interest however misguided some people may regard it. Accordingly the reader is warned that while the concept is appealing one must beware that it is not meaningless due to circularity of definitions, e.g. the greater the relative advantage the faster adoption but the faster the adoption the greater the perceived advantage. Certainly it is difficult to operationalise the concept, for the perception of characteristics tends to be individual-specific.

Following his evaluation the potential user will make a decision to adopt or reject which, as the model shows, is open to subsequent modification, i.e. an adopter may continue in use or reject and vice versa for a rejector. Once made the decision is subject to *confirmation*, in which the person seeks to validate the rightness of his decision and therefore alleviate any post-decision cognitive dissonance (discussed below). This being the case it might be more accurate to show confirmation following the actual decision: 'Adoption' or 'Rejection'.

Like many marketing concepts Rogers' diffusion model is most valuable for the insights which it gives rather than in providing direct practical applications. Thus it provides a framework for organising one's thinking about the decision process and the stages which the individual goes through which can be related to the specific features which distinguish a particular marketing problem.

▌ Opinion leadership and the two-step flow of communication

Early models of communication regarded both impersonal sources (the mass media) and personal sources as establishing direct contact with an audience – the so-called 'hypodermic effect'. Belief in this model leads to speculation concerning the influence of the mass media upon voting behaviour – thus the undertaking of one of the most celebrated pieces of communication research, reported in Paul F. Lazarsfeld *et al.*, *The People's Choice* (Sloan & Pearce, 1944).

Lazarsfeld and his colleagues set out to study the influence of the mass media on individual voting behaviour in the 1940 presidential election in the United States. Contrary to expectations it was found that influence did not flow directly from a medium (press, radio, etc.) to an audience but was channelled through an intermediary who was designated the 'opinion leader'. It was this finding which gave rise to the two-step model which has had a significant influence on communication research and practice ever Since. However, it must be emphasised that the two-step hypothesis does not exclude the possibility of a direct flow (one step) and its main contribution is in introducing the mediating effect of personal influence on impersonal communications. Thus nowadays the mass media are regarded primarily as *information* sources and considerable attention is focused upon the nature and behaviour of opinion leaders – how to identify them and how to communicate effectively with them. Engel *et al.* (1986) emphasise that contemporary models of social influence are built on a multi-stage interaction model in which the mass media can prompt seekers of information to approach opinion leaders and vice versa. But while opinion leaders do not *mediate* the flow of information their potential influence as personal sources remains significant.

In simple terms an opinion leader is one to whom others turn for information and advice. However, it must be emphasised that in the usual marketing context opinion leaders are not a distinct and easily classified group in the sense in which Cabinet Ministers or Managing Directors of major companies are. More often than not opinion leaders are people just like you and me, for if they are to be effective at a personal-influence level they must be accessible, which implies that they are members of reference groups with which people have contact. In fact most reference groups develop around shared interests and some members will be seen as more influential than. others in the context of that interest. But we belong to many reference groups, leader and follower roles may be reversed, e.g. the captain of the football team may well seek the first reserve's opinion on the merits of hi-fi systems. It is this tendency which makes identification of opinion leaders difficult but, despite this, a number of studies have been completed which permit some generalisations to be made. Writing in 1971 Thomas S. Robertson (*Innovative Behavior and Communications*, Holt, Rinehart & Winston) offered those shown in Table 15.1.

Research in the past two decades has done nothing to modify significantly these generalisations and Elihu Katz's summary (cited by Robertson, *Innovative Behavior*, p. 180), made in 1957, would still seem to be valid:

> influence is related to (1) *personification of certain values* (who one is), (2) *competence* (what one knows), and (3) *strategic social location* (whom one knows). To the extent that an individual represents or personifies group values, he stands a better chance of leadership. Thus if the group emphasises an 'in' manner of dress, the person who dressed most accordingly may well be influential. Again, to the extent that an individual is highly knowledgeable, he stands a better chance of leadership. Finally, to the extent that an individual is available and active in the everyday interpersonal communication process, the better his chance of leadership.

TABLE 15.1   Summary profile of opinion-leader traits

Characteristics	Findings
Age	Varies by product category
Social status	Generally same as advisee
Gregariousness	High
Cosmopolitanism	Limited evidence that higher than advisee's
Knowledge	Generally greater for area of influence
Personality	No major distinguishing traits
Innovativeness	Higher than advisee's

Source: T. S. Robertson, *Innovative Behavior and Communications* (Holt, Rinehart & Winston, 1971) p. 179.

Engel *et al.* (*Consumer Behavior*, 1982) conclude from their survey of the available evidence that opinion leaders gain satisfaction from one or more of five basic motivations – product involvement, self-involvement, concern for others, message involvement, and dissonance reduction. Conversely people accept opinion leadership where there is limited alternative information available, where their own knowledge is inadequate, where there is a high degree of perceived risk and, of course, because there is little or no cost to such information.

From the above summary it follows that marketers must identify the opinion leaders for their own product/service category. Certain of the generalised traits outlined above will assist in this identification, as will the trait of innovativeness. It is also clear that opinion leaders maintain their status, which gives them satisfaction, from being well-informed and so are likely to make greater use of both personal and non-personal sources of information.

■ Source effect

As the basic model of communication makes clear, all communication originates from a source and this source has a marked bearing upon the subsequent interpretation of the message. In a marketing context it is important to distinguish between the true source – the organisation which is responsible for the generation of the message and pays for its communication in promotional channels – and the perceived source, which is the consumer perception of its origin. This distinction is important because we (consumers) often identify messages with the communicator (sales agent, personality in the television commercial) or the channel (*Good Housekeeping, Reader's Digest*, Radio Clyde) rather than the company 'behind' the message.

A great deal of attention has been given to source effect and extended discussions are to be found in several of the texts cited. Typical of these is DeLozier (*Marketing Communications Process*) who provides the following summary:

1. In general, a source is more persuasive when his audience perceives him as high, rather than low, in credibility.
2. A source's credibility, and thus his persuasiveness, is reduced when his audience perceives that the source has something to gain from his persuasive attempts (intention to manipulate).
3. Over time the opinion change attributed to a high-credibility source decreases, whereas the opinion change induced by a low-credibility source increases, resulting in about the same level of retained opinion change for both low- and high-credibility sources.
4. Reinstatement of a high-credibility source some time after his initial message presentation results in higher opinion change retention than if no reinstatement occurs; whereas reinstatement of a low-credibility source some time after his message presentation results in lower opinion change retention than if no reinstatement occurs.
5. The low-credibility source can increase his influence by arguing for a position which is against his own self-interest.
6. A communicator increases his influence if at first he expresses some views already held by his audience, followed by his intended persuasive communication.
7. A communicator increases his persuasiveness if at the beginning of his message he states that his position on the topic is the same as that of his audience, even though he may argue against that position.
8. The more similar members of an audience perceive the source to be themselves, the more persuasive the communicator will be.
9. What people think of a communicator's message affects what they think of him (his image).
10. A source is more persuasive when he holds a positive, rather than a negative, attitude towards himself, his message and his receiver.
11. The more powerful and attractive a source is perceived to be, the more influence he has on a receiver's behaviour.

As Keith Crosier has pointed out to me, one must treat such apparently authoritative statements with considerable circumspection for much of the evidence on which they are based is derived from situations far different from those encountered in the market place (e.g. students' reactions to views communicated by their professors). For an extensive and up-to-date interpretation of marketing communications as such, then students are strongly recommended to supplement this chapter with Chapter 6 of *Marketing: Theory and Practice*.

■ Consonance and dissonance

At various places in the text reference has been made to dissonance and it will be useful to indicate the role this concept has to play in marketing communications.

In the discussion of perception (pp. 115–18) it was indicated that we seek to organise perceived stimuli (cognitions) into coherent and consistent patterns which are in accord with our knowledge, beliefs and attitudes – in other words we are seeking a state of *consonance*. If two cognitions are not consonant, they may be either irrelevant, i.e. they have no relationship to one another, or dissonant, i.e. in conflict with each other. Clearly dissonant cognitions create a state of psychological tension which the individual will seek to avoid, reduce or eliminate. It is also clear that in any choice situation there is a potential for dissonance, as the recognition of choice implies alternative solutions to a perceived need. In many consumer purchasing situations these alternatives are very similar and the propensity for dissonance is correspondingly greater.

Attention was first focused upon this phenomenon by the publication of Leon A. Festinger's *A Theory of Cognitive Dissonance* (Row & Peterson, 1957) and has been the subject of much interest ever since. It is generally agreed that dissonance can arise from one of three basic causes – logical inconsistency, a conflict between attitude and behaviour or two behaviours, and when a strongly held belief is contravened or negated. Faced with a state of dissonance we tend to use a number of approaches to remove the state, and all these contain elements of selectivity. *Avoidance* is a clear example in which we screen out stimuli which conflict with our preferred interpretation (this can occur both before a decision and after and may be subconscious), while in the case of *rationalisation* we interpret the stimuli to suit our preferred belief (cf. the example of the American football match on p. 117). Alternatively we can *seek additional information* which supports our choice – again on a selective basis or *forget* or *suppress* the inconsistent information we have. It follows that dissonance can occur at any stage of the purchase decision, though most interest has been shown in the post-purchase phase when commitment has been made to a particular choice, and is likely to be most acute in the case of major purchase decisions.

In a paper given at the 1970 Market Research Society Annual Conference ('The Complementary Benefit Principle of How Advertising Works in Relation to the Product') Peter Hutchinson suggested that the existence of cognitive dissonance has two basic lessons for practitioners:

1. Perfect in manufacture those product benefits which are readily available.
2. Advertise those attributes which are not immediately observable or easily learned.

The first recommendation underlines the importance of ensuring that those dimensions on which direct comparisons can be made are highly developed in one's product, while the second emphasises the need to provide the potential user with additional reasons for preferring your alternative to all the others.

■ The message and the medium

Earlier in the chapter reference was made to Schramm's four basic conditions for successful communication, all of which involved the basic element of communication – the message. The message is the subject of a separate chapter in DeLozier (*The Marketing Communications Process*) and this source should be consulted for a full discussion of the topic. Only a brief overview can be presented here.

There are three dimensions of messages which demand particular attention – structure, appeal or content, and the symbolic code (words, music, gesture, etc.) in which the message is couched.

The structure of a message embraces three main considerations – whether it should be a one-sided or two-sided presentation, the sequence in which information should be presented, and whether a conclusion should be offered. In fact there is no single preferred structure, for this will vary according to the audience. For example, one-sided messages are most effective with people who agree with the source, are poorly educated and unlikely to be exposed to any counter-arguments, while a two-sided message is better suited to convert persons inclining to an opposite opinion, better educated and likely to be exposed to counter-arguments Similarly, in the case of sequence some messages are more effective when they build up to a climax (high audience interest), others to an anti-climax (low audience interest), while in the case of two-sided arguments controversial material is most effective when presented first (the *primacy* effect) and bland or uninteresting information is favoured by *recency*, i.e. the material presented last is more effective. Finally, while messages are in general more effective if a conclusion is presented, this applies more to persons of low intelligence than persons of high intelligence and is less so in all cases where the source is seen as having a vested interest in the conclusion. Much of the same applies where drawing a conclusion would insult the audience's intelligence.

In the case of message appeal DeLozier cites six alternative approaches – fear, distraction, participation, emotion *versus* rational, aggression arousal, and humour. Of these the most controversial are the use of fear appeals and distraction methods. Much criticism has been levelled against advertisements for consumer products which suggest that non-possession will lead to loss of status or social unacceptability (e.g. deodorants), while the use of fear is widely supported in health and safety advertising. Distraction is also criticised on the grounds that it diminishes/influences critical judgement concerning the prime subject of the communication, e.g. the expense-account lunch or the use association in consumer advertisements. Overall the evidence regarding the efficiency of different message appeals confirms that it is situation-specific and must be varied in light of the circumstances they are expected to encounter.

Some mention has already been made of the symbolic code in which a message is couched. Here the evidence is more clear cut and indicates that while choice of words can have an important bearing upon the interpretation of a message, non-verbal communications are often more important in conveying ideas and meaning than words alone. The validity of this is readily apparent in television commercials when sound and movement can be combined to enhance the impact of the purely verbal message to be put across.

At this juncture no reference will be made to the advertising media through which a message is conveyed to an audience, as this is discussed at some length in the next chapter.

■ The role of communication in the marketing mix

As a process marketing is firmly founded on the assumption of effective two-way communication – of consumers telling firms what they want and firms informing consumers what they have to sell. In this sense communication is central to everything the firm does and pervades all its activities. However, when we speak of marketing communications we do so in the more restricted sense of those functional activities which are collectively known as 'promotion' – advertising, personal selling, public relations and sales promotion. Each of these topics is treated at some length in the chapters which follow but before turning to these it will be useful to summarise the basic objectives of promotional strategy.

Martin Bell (*Marketing: Concepts and Strategy*, 2nd edn, Houghton Mifflin, 1972) rightly observes that each item on an exhaustive list of promotional objectives would need a chapter to itself and contents himself by selecting seven for specific mention:

1. Increase sales.
2. Maintain or improve market share.
3. Create or improve brand recognition, acceptance or insistence.
4. Create a favourable climate for future sales.
5. Inform and educate the market.
6. Create a competitive difference.
7. Improve promotional efficiency.

Clearly there is considerable overlap between these seven objectives but the distinction between them is important because emphasis upon any one will tend to lead to a different *promotional mix* being required. For example, creating a favourable climate for future sales is most appropriate for industrial products and consumer durables where there is a long repurchase cycle. Thus customers need to have the wisdom of their previous purchase confirmed in order to reduce post-purchase cognitive dissonance and will also respond favourably to advice on how to get the best out of their purchase. Conversely if one is seeking to win customers from other manufacturers, then one may be seeking to engender cognitive dissonance by suggesting the currently preferred brand is inferior to your own. To achieve these objectives it will often be necessary to use different messages and different channels – a requirement which will only be apparent if one has carefully defined the objective in advance.

Bell also cites five key conditions which favour the use of promotion in the marketing mix:

1. A favourable trend in demand.
2. Strong product differentiation.
3. Product qualities are hidden.
4. Emotional buying motives exist.
5. Adequate funds are available.

While a favourable trend in demand will usually result in a greater apparent return on one's promotional investment, it should not be overlooked that maintaining sales under conditions of stagnant or declining demand is equally and sometimes more important. Similarly, while the existence of strong product differentiation will allow clear distinctions to be drawn with competing products, it must also be remembered that the greater the departure from known and trusted concepts, the greater the intrinsic resistance to change. For these reasons it often happens that the most effective promotions are those which communicate hidden product qualities (purity, taste, durability, etc.) which can only be recognised in use, coupled with promotions which appeal to emotional buying motives. (As noted in my model of buying behaviour in Chapter 6, faced with a need to discriminate between two objectively similar competitive brands, the subjective/emotional factors may be trivial but determinant.) Finally, it is a truism to extol the need for adequate funds but it is a factor which is often overlooked, as will be noted when discussing advertising appropriations in the next chapter.

Marketing communications as information processing

In earlier editions reference was made to the eclectic nature of the foregoing review of marketing communications which was supported by a recommendation that the reader consult the named sources for a fuller treatment. At several places reference has been made to Keith Crosier who has made many helpful and cogent criticisms which I have attempted to accommodate in this revision. However, his most radical suggestion – that I completely restructure the chapter – I have chosen largely to ignore, on the grounds that he is concerned with the latest state of the art in marketing communication theory whereas my perception of an introductory text book is that it must record and analyse the received wisdom and practices which enjoy *common* currency. That said it is also important that the reader should be exposed to the latest thinking and this section examines Crosier's argument, referred to in the introduction to the chapter, that we abandon traditional theories in favour of one based on information processing.

Clues to Crosier's thinking are to be found in chapter 6 of the Second Edition of *Marketing: Theory & Practice*, but even this recent contribution lacks the integrative framework which becomes possible by using information processing theory. Thus his proposals are to be found in an article entitled 'Towards a Praxiology of Advertising' (*International Journal of Advertising*, vol. 2, no. 3, July–September 1983) the abstract of which states:

> This article argues for the need to abandon traditional models of advertising effect, if a theory is to be developed which is capable of fitting the observable reality that people use advertisements deliberately rather than being used by them. Using information processing theory as the best available organising principle, it proposes a number of candidate elements of a future, fully grounded theory of advertising.

In the opening paragraph we are told that 'Praxiology is the study of human action. The term is used here to express the crucial idea that people voluntarily and deliberately consume and use advertisements, in contrast to the commonly implied alternative that advertising manipulates people.' Crosier then goes on to argue that:

> Where advertising is concerned the prevailing grand theory is operant conditioning, expressed in the form of various hierarchical models of advertising effect all implicitly conforming to the stimulus-response – or at best stimulus-organism-response – paradigm of human behaviour. In the half century since Pavlov died at the age of 87, the social and cultural influences upon response to stimuli such as advertisements have of course changed considerably.

Thus we need to reconsider the relevance and applicability of this model by observing how people actually behave when reacting to modern advertising.

As we have inferred earlier, 'The conversation and publications of advertising practitioners, social critics of advertising, consumerists and politicians very often hinge upon an important implicit hypothesis: that advertising is something powerful firms do to powerless (though sometime stubborn) consumers.' But this is an assumption rejected by our earlier composite model of buying behaviour and by Crosier's conceptualisation of Advertisement Processing Behaviour reproduced as Figure 15.5.

In support of his model Crosier cites Sternthal and Craig's proposal that 'purchase and consumption decisions are viewed in terms of how individuals acquire, organise and use information' (B. Sternthal and C. S. Craig, *Consumer Behavior: An Information Processing Perspective*, Englewood Cliffs, N.J., Prentice-Hall, 1982). According to this view, consumers are active seekers and users of information although they may indulge in such behaviour for purposes other than specific product purchase decisions. (Crosier proposes six other uses in addition to 'hard' information – entertainment, added value, implied warrant, reassurance, involvement, vicarious experience.) Thus without departing entirely from the classical operant conditioning or stimulus-response process implicit in the hierarchical models, the information processing model assigns much greater important to consumers as participants rather than passive objects and so is more in keeping with the view of behaviour advanced in Chapter 6.

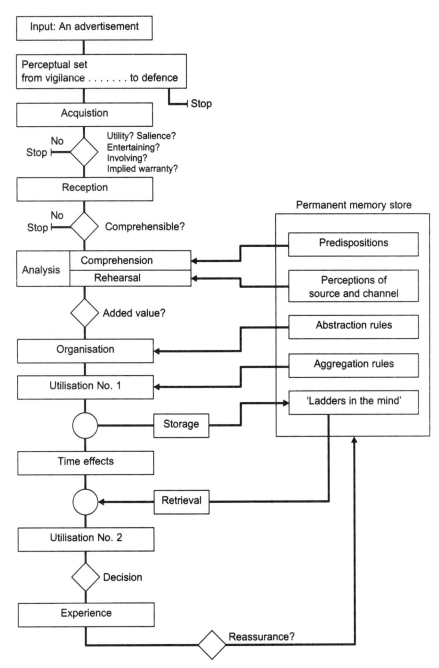

Figure 15.5   A model of advertisement-processing behaviour

Source: Keith Crosier, 'Towards a praxiology of advertising', *International Journal of Advertising*, vol. 2, no. 3, July–Sept. 1983.

CHAPTER 16

Advertising*

Learning Goals

The issues to be addressed in this chapter include:

1. The nature and objectives of advertising.
2. The evolution of advertising.
3. The structure of advertising in the marketing mix.
4. The role of advertising in the marketing mix.
5. The organisation of advertising in terms of both advertisers and agencies.
6. Agency selection and remuneration.
7. The characteristics of the major advertising media.
8. Campaign planning and setting the advertising appropriation.
9. The measurement of advertising effectiveness.
10. The economic and ethical aspects of advertising.

After reading this chapter you will be able to:

1. Define advertising.
2. List specific objectives which advertising may be used to achieve.
3. Describe the historical development and evolution of advertising.
4. Cite some vital statistics to help describe the size and nature of the advertising industry.
5. Outline the structure of the advertising industry and distinguish the roles of the three main parties involved in the advertising process – advertisers, agents and media owners.
6. Discuss the role of advertising in the marketing mix.
7. Suggest how a firm might organise for advertising.
8. Review the role and function of advertising agencies.
9. Explain the basis of agency remuneration.
10. Give advice on agency selection.
11. Indicate how to evaluate different advertising media.
12. Summarise some of the key features of the national press, regional press, Sunday newspapers, magazines, television, commercial radio, outdoor advertising, the cinema and direct mail.

*I am grateful to Jennifer Skene for her assistance in updating the factual content of this chapter.

13. Outline the procedure to follow when planning an advertising campaign.
14. Review alternative methods for setting advertising appropriations.
15. Describe methods for answering advertising effectiveness.
16. Indicate some of the economic and ethical issues associated with advertising.

■ Definitions

Essentially advertising is a means of spreading information. This is too broad a description, however, to be useful as a definition, or to distinguish it from other forms of communication. The American Marketing Association has adopted the following as a definition: Any paid form of non-personal presentation and promotion of ideas, goods or services by an identified sponsor. This is certainly a very succinct statement and merits some elaboration. Firstly, advertising is paid for, it is a commercial transaction, and it is this which distinguishes it from publicity. It is non-personal in the sense that advertising messages, visual, spoken or written, are directed at a mass audience, and not directly at the individual as is the case in personal selling. Direct mail is, of course, targeted at individuals but is still regarded as an impersonal source in the terms of this definition. Finally, advertisements are identifiable with their sponsor or originator, which is not always the case with publicity or propaganda.

The nature and role of sales promotion are dealt with in the next chapter, but it will be useful at this point to give the AMA's definition to avoid confusion with advertising *per se* in the meantime. Sales promotion: those marketing activities, other than personal selling, advertising and publicity, that stimulate consumer purchasing and dealer effectiveness, such as displays, shows and exhibitions, demonstrations, and various non-recurrent selling efforts not in the ordinary routine.

■ Objectives

The ultimate purpose underlying all advertising is increased awareness. Many authors would also ally this with some form of statement concerning an increase in profit, but this is anticipating an end result applicable only to trading organisations, which is also attributable to a host of other factors (clearly, advertisements sponsored by government departments concerning road safety, or the health hazards of smoking, are not designed to increase profits).

Despite the problems inherent in measuring the effectiveness of advertising, which are the subject of a subsequent section of this chapter, it is only realistic to state that firms invest in advertising expenditures in the expectation of an improvement in profitability. If one examines the specific objectives which may motivate a particular advertising campaign, it is clear that an improvement in profit varies from a primary, to a very subsidiary, motive. An examination of the specific objectives listed by Matthews, Buzzell, Levitt and Frank (*Marketing: An Introductory Analysis*, McGraw-Hill, 1964) makes this clear.

1. To build primary demand.
2. To introduce a price deal.
3. To inform about a product's availability.
4. To build brand recognition or brand preference or brand insistence.
5. To inform about a new product's availability or features or price.
6. To help salesmen by building an awareness of a product among retailers.
7. To create a reputation for service, reliability or research strength.
8. To increase market share.
9. To modify existing product appeals and buying motives.
10. To increase frequency of use of a product.
11. To inform about new uses of a product.
12. To increase the number or quality of retail outlets.
13. To build the overall company image.
14. To effect immediate buying action.
15. To reach new areas or new segments of population within existing areas.
16. To develop overseas markets.

The above list is by no means exhaustive, but it does indicate that the aim underlying a campaign may be directed at a short-term increase in sales volume (price deals and other promotional offers), the development of a new market, an increased share of an existing market, or the building of a favourable attitude to the company as a whole (corporate advertising). The latter, like an increase in retail distribution, is a long-term objective for which it would be difficult to assess the actual return on the advertising investment.

Whatever the specific objective or purpose, it is generally agreed that its statement in explicit terms is an essential prerequisite of a successful campaign. Similarly, it is also agreed that certain conditions are more favourable to successful advertising than others, for example an expanding market, or possession of a feature which differentiates the product from its competitors. This point will be returned to when discussing advertising strategy.

■ The evolution of advertising

It is often erroneously assumed that the advertising function is of recent origin, a point commented on by Henry Sampson in his *History of Advertising*, published in 1874: 'It is generally assumed – though the assumption has no ground for existence beyond that so common among us, that nothing exists of which we are ignorant – that advertisements are of comparatively modern origin.'

There is some evidence to suggest that the Romans practised advertising, but the earliest indication of its use in this country dates from the Middle Ages with the adoption of surnames indicative of a man's occupation, as opposed to some other distinguishing designation (Harrison = Harry's son). The producer's name is of equal importance today as a means of identifying the source of goods and services.

Signs represented the next stage in the evolution of advertising, acting as a visual expression of the tradesman's function as well as a means of locating the source of goods at a time when the numbering of houses was unknown. One can still see vestiges of the practice in the barber's pole, or the symbolic boot or glove.

The craft guilds of the Middle Ages disapproved of competition among their members, but were not averse to competition with one another in the adoption of distinctive liveries, or the sponsoring of mystery plays – an early form of institutional advertising! At the same time many guilds adopted trade marks as a means of identifying the producer, and as a guarantee of quality – the adoption of corporate symbols, as a more immediate means of recognising the firm's identity than the written word, is an interesting reversion to this practice.

Although Caxton had invented the hand press by the end of the fifteenth century, the use of the written word in advertising was limited by the low level of literacy, so confining written advertisements to the clergy. By Shakespeare's time posters had made their appearance, and the few remaining examples make it clear that advertising had assumed the function of fostering demand for new products as well as increasing demand for existing products.

Another important development at this time was the emergence of the pamphlet as an advertising medium, early examples of which disclose their sponsorship by companies bent on generating goodwill for their activities. (Later examples are more veiled as to their origin and, properly, should be considered as propaganda.) However, the seventeenth century was a period of unrest in England, resulting in government censorship which was to hinder the development of regular publications. From 1620 onwards a number of Mercuries, Gazettes, etc., made their appearance, but were mainly short-lived, and carried few advertisements.

The high cost of posters and handbills encouraged a number of publishers to experiment with the issue of free papers comprised solely of advertisements. Their success was limited, however, and posters and handbills continued as the main media until the early eighteenth century. An examination of the periodicals of the early 1700s, such as the *Tatler* and *Spectator*, reveals an increasing number of advertisements, but this growth was abruptly curtailed in 1712 by the imposition of a tax on both papers and advertisements. The first Stamp Act levied a tax of ½d per copy on publications and 12d per advertisement, supposedly to raise revenue but in fact intended to curtail a libellous and seditious press.

The effect of the tax was virtually immediate – the majority of unsubsidised papers ceased publication, and the legitimate businessman severely curtailed his use of advertising. On the other hand, the quacks and charlatans, with their enormous profit margins to fall back on, continued to advertise, and it is worth noting that the generally unsavoury nature of the advertising of this time was a direct consequence of government censorship and heavy taxation. Under the circumstances neither government control nor taxation would appear to be as effective as modern critics of advertising would have one believe.

The tax on advertisements was abolished in 1853, at a time ripe for the development of mass advertising as we know it today. Mass production was a reality, and channels of distribution were being developed to cope with the physical movement of goods, creating a need for mass communication to inform consumers of the choice available to them. This need was soon recognised by the forerunner of today's advertising agent – the space salesman. Initially space salesmen located customers for the media owners, receiving commission on the space they sold. Gradually the position changed, and the agent became a space-broker, or middleman, buying space wholesale from the media owner and reselling it retail, often at a profit of 25 per cent. The profits to be earned attracted competition and the agents found it necessary to offer incentives to advertisers to purchase space from them, in preference to their competitors. Thus the practice evolved of giving the advertiser free assistance in preparing his copy and later, as the number of publications increased, of selecting the media which would prove most effective in reaching the advertiser's potential customers. In essence this is the system which still obtains today, with the agent looking upon the advertiser as his client, while deriving most of his income from commissions paid by the media owner. (Many advertising agents now charge a service fee on smaller accounts, or where additional work is undertaken on-behalf of the advertiser.)

Towards the end of the last century increased competition between advertising agencies led to the practice of 'commission rebates' in both Britain and the USA whereby the agencies offered the client a discount or rebate from the commission received by him from the media owner. The practice was frowned upon by the more professional agencies, on the grounds that it could only lead to lower standards of service, but after a few years the issue ceased to be contentious, presumably because the practice was limited. Recently, however, competitive pressures have seen a revival of rebating in the UK with strong attacks on the system headed by Allen Brady and Marsh who argue that a 15 per cent commission only yields 2 per cent net profit after tax for the typical full service agency. ABM stated publicly that they would refuse to work for a client seeking a rebate, and in 1983 resigned the £3.5 million B & Q account on just those grounds. While a negotiated fee system would seem to be the safest way of ensuring that both client and agency receive what they expect, there is no indication that the commission system will be changed in the foreseeable future.

Reference to ABM's campaign to discourage rebating underlines an important facet of the practice of advertising: namely, that while it is subject to a certain amount of statutory regulation it has been particularly successful in retaining responsibility for its own *self-regulation*. Thus while the Television Acts and the 1973 Sound Broadcasting Act which superseded them imposed a duty to establish an obligatory pre-clearance of commercials, press advertising is subject to the

Advertising Standards Authority Code of Advertising Practice which is a logical evolution of earlier codes of practice devised by the profession in response to criticism of certain kinds of advertisement. Full details of the ASA's code and *modus operandi* are contained in leaflets published by them and additional information may be obtained from both the Advertising Association (AA) and the Institute of Practitioners in Advertising (IPA).

■ Industry statistics

Before looking at the present-day practice of advertising and the salient characteristics of the major media it will be helpful to review some of the industry's vital statistics.

In 1989 total advertising expenditure by UK advertisers amounted to £7555 million while the Institute of Sales Promotion estimates total expenditure for 1989 at £5500 million. The breakdown of this expenditure and some comparisons with other budget headings are contained in Tables 16.1 to 16.9 inclusive. While accurate at the time of writing the sources cited should be consulted regularly for up-to-date statistics.

TABLE 16.1   Total UK advertising and sales promotion expenditure per capita, 1989

	Advertising (£)	Sales Promotions (£)
Per man, woman and child*	137	100
Per member of working population†	343	250
Per household‡	343	250

* 55m (*Marketing Pocket Book*, 55 643 000).

† 22m (1990 National A/cs, 22 236 000).

‡ 22m (Eurostat, from *Euro Marketing Pocket Book*, 22 042 000).

TABLE 16.2   Comparison with selected items of annual national expenditure, 1989

	£m
Social Security	57 255
Health	25 332
Defence	20 979
Housing and community amenities	7 654
Transport and communications	7 161
(Advertising	7 555)*
(Sales promotion	5 500)

* Advertising Association

Source: CSO, 1990.

TABLE 16.3   Comparison with selected items of annual household expenditure, 1989

	£m
Alcohol	19 818
Tobacco	8 196
Post	610
Buses and coaches	2 320
Television and video hire charge, licence fee and repairs	3 144
(Advertising	7 555)*
(Sales promotion	5 550)

* Advertising Association

Source: CSO, 1990.

TABLE 16.4   Advertising expenditure by media category, 1980–89

	Advertising expenditure (inc. direct mail) at constant prices £m('85)									
	1980	*1981*	*1982*	*1983*	*1984*	*1985*	*1986*	*1987*	*1988*	*1989*
National newspapers	603	590	600	650	719	747	816	890	973	1 003
Regional newspapers	905	865	858	910	977	1 003	1 064	1 188	1 366	1 401
Consumer magazines	272	253	243	249	265	267	289	317	373	370
Business & professional	303	281	288	307	330	344	361	378	450	491
Directories	116	123	144	171	193	209	258	288	323	360
Press production costs	184	185	179	202	229	245	268	283	316	319
Total press	2 382	2 296	2 312	2 490	2 713	2 815	3 057	3 344	3 800	3 946
Television	979	1 023	1 080	1 235	1 324	1 376	1 620	1 739	1 882	1 877
Direct mail	368	378	397	333	344	444	458	448	469	622
Poster and transport	151	145	144	153	159	164	186	200	216	222
Radio	76	76	81	90	91	82	88	103	123	130
Cinema	25	23	21	18	17	18	18	20	24	29
Total	3 982	3 941	4 036	4 318	4 648	4 899	5 428	5 855	6 514	6 825

Total advertising expenditure (inc. direct mail) percentage of total

	1980	*1981*	*1982*	*1983*	*1984*	*1985*	*1986*	*1987*	*1988*	*1989*
National newspapers	15.1	15.0	14.9	15.1	15.5	15.2	15.0	15.2	14.9	14.7
Regional newspapers	22.7	21.9	21.3	21.1	21.0	20.5	19.6	20.3	21.0	20.5
Consumer magazines	6.8	6.4	6.0	5.8	5.7	5.5	5.3	5.4	5.7	5.4
Business & professional	7.6	7.1	7.1	7.1	7.1	7.0	6.6	6.5	6.9	7.2
Directories	2.9	3.1	3.6	4.0	4.2	4.3	4.8	4.9	5.0	5.3
Press production costs	4.6	4.7	4.4	4.7	4.9	5.0	4.9	4.8	4.9	4.7
Total press	59.8	58.3	57.3	57.7	58.4	57.5	56.3	57.1	58.3	57.8
Television	24.6	26.0	26.8	28.6	28.5	28.1	29.8	29.7	28.9	27.5
Direct mail	9.2	9.6	9.8	7.7	7.4	9.1	8.4	7.7	7.2	9.1
Poster and transport	3.8	3.7	3.6	3.5	3.4	3.3	3.4	3.4	3.3	3.2
Radio	1.9	1.9	2.0	2.1	2.0	1.7	1.6	1.8	1.9	1.9
Cinema	0.6	0.6	0.5	0.4	0.4	0.4	0.3	0.3	0.4	0.4
Total	100.0	100.0	100.0	100.0	100.0	100.0	100.0	100.0	100.0	100.0

Source: Advertising Association, *Advertising Statistics Yearbook, 1990*.

TABLE 16.5   Trends in UK advertising expenditure

	Advertising expenditure (£m)	GDP at market prices		Consumers' expenditure	
		£m	Adv as %	£m	Adv as %
1970	554	51 770	1.07	32 114	1.73
1971	591	57 735	1.02	36 010	1.64
1972	708	64 631	1.10	40 750	1.74
1973	874	74 188	1.18	46 428	1.88
1974	900	83 757	1.07	53 491	1.68
1975	967	105 718	0.91	65 854	1.47
1976	1 188	124 982	0.95	76 560	1.55
1977	1 499	145 699	1.03	87 530	1.71
1978	1 834	168 123	1.09	100 847	1.82
1979	2 137	197 831	1.08	119 516	1.79
1980	2 555	231 272	1.10	139 016	1.84
1981	2 818	254 294	1.11	154 701	1.82
1982	3 126	278 408	1.12	169 816	1.84
1983	3 579	303 634	1.18	185 895	1.93
1984	4 059	324 443	1.25	198 895	2.04
1985	4 455	355 317	1.25	217 023	2.05
1986	5 138	390 928	1.35	239 535	2.15
1987	5 823	418 610	1.39	264 120	2.20
1988	6 831	465 895	1.47	296 165	2.31
1989	7 555	508 859	1.48	324 348	2.33

Source: Advertising Association, *Advertising Statistics Yearbook, 1990*

TABLE 16.6   Annual expenditure by product category, 1989

	£m
Government	503.6
Food	379.8
Automotive	322.4
Toiletries and cosmetics	168.9
Leisure equipment	159.8
Household appliances	99.7
Tobacco	44.0

Source: Advertising Association, 1990.

TABLE 16.7   The top 10 holding companies' advertising expenditure in 1989

Rank 1989	1988	Holding company	Total press and TV expenditure (£000)
1	1	Unilever	133 060
2	3	HM Government	119 970
3	2	Procter & Gamble	76 510
4	5	Nestlé Holdings (UK)	72 320
5	4	Mars (UK)	67 810
6	8	The Electricity Council	50 340
7	6	Kingfisher plc	49 550
8	7	British Telecom	47 550
9	7	Kelloggs (UK)	45 180
10	—	Ford Motors Company Ltd	42 680

Source: *Marketing Week Magazine*, 23 March 1990.

TABLE 16.8   The top 25 advertisers in 1989

Rank 1989	1988	Advertiser	Total Adspend (£000)	TV share (TV%)
1	1	Procter & Gamble	53 943	98.8
2	2	British Telecom	47 499	71.9
3	3	Kellogg	45 138	92.9
4	11	Lever Brothers	40 883	93.5
5	12	Ford	40 837	37.1
6	4	Nestlé	37 882	69.5
7	–	Water Authority Association	36 877	65.6
8	9	The Rover Group	36 794	55.2
9	7	The Electricity Council	35 709	63.2
10	6	Mars Confectionery	32 721	95.9
11	14	Kraft General Foods	32 277	87.0
12	5	Pedigree Petfoods	28 985	93.8
13	29	VAG (UK)	28 636	49.2
14	8	Vauxhall Motors	28 176	34.0
15	20	HJ Heinz	27 033	79.6
16	40	Dixons Stores	26 830	3.8
17	13	Gallaher Tobacco	26 490	5.2
18	23	British Gas	25 726	43.1
19	15	Elida Gibbs	25 430	83.4
20	22	National Westminster Bank	25 054	46.6
21	18	Bass	24 673	95.4

Rank 1989	1988	Advertiser	Total Adspend (£000)	(continued) TV share (TV%)
22	19	Renault	24 575	40.5
23	41	Halifax Building Society	23 561	43.7
24	33	Midland Bank	23 358	54.7
25	10	Brooke Bond Foods	23 065	87.6

Source: *Marketing Week Magazine*, 23 March 1990.

TABLE 16.9   The top 15 UK advertising agency groups in 1989

Rank 1989	Group		Billings in £m
1	WPP Group	: Worldwide capitalised	9 970
		: UK capitalised	1 855
2	Saatchi & Saatchi	: Worldwide capitalised	9 831
		: UK capitalised	1 050
3	Omnicom UK		452
4	The Lowe Group		416
5 }	Young and Rubicam Holdings (UK)		360
5 }	Grey Communications		360
7	Lopex		337
8	WCRS		318
9	Interpublic		302
10	D'Arcy Masius Benton and Bowles		280
11	Collett Dickenson Pearce		194
12	Abbott Mead Vickers		193
13	Austin Knight Advertising		133
14	Yellowhammer		96
15	The Brunning Group		89

Source: *Campaign* (23 February 1990).

■ The structure of advertising

The above description outlining the evolution of advertising makes it clear that at least three separate parties are involved in the advertising process:
- The advertiser
- The advertising agent
- The media owner.

In market terms, advertisers constitute buyers and media owners sellers, and consequently they take considerable direct interest in each other's activities. In many instances advertiser and media owner will negotiate direct with one another, but beyond a certain point the intervention of a third party becomes desirable, which accounts for the existence of advertising agents.

From the advertiser's point of view the agency constitutes a reservoir of skills which it would be difficult to duplicate in even the largest company at an economic cost – for the smaller company it would be impossible. Further, the discount on the purchase of time and/or space in the various media is usually restricted to established and recognised advertising agencies, which enables the agency to offer its services free of charge to the advertiser under normal circumstances. From the media owner's point of view, agencies act as wholesalers, bulking together a host of orders from a variety of sources, thus reducing the area of contact between buyer and seller to manageable proportions. In addition the agent is familiar with the media owner's language and method of operation, and, in a sense, acts as an interpreter between the parties. Both these factors create economies which the media owner considers justification for the payment of commission.

In addition to these three major participants at least two others have emerged in recent years – the *creative* specialist and the *media* specialist. Advertising agencies of the kind referred to above had traditionally handled all aspects of their clients advertising business and so were known as *full service* agencies. However, their ability to provide the depth and quality of service across the board was questioned by some and led to the establishment of 'boutiques' or 'hot shops' specialising solely in the creative aspects of campaign planning. Not being eligible for commission on media buying, creative specialists work on a fee basis. By contrast media specialists are eligible for media commission and, because they have lower overheads, often rebate part of this as an inducement to advertisers.

Before examining the interaction of the parties in the development of an advertising campaign it will be useful to look at the role of the three major parties – advertiser, agents, and media owners – in somewhat greater detail.

▌The role of advertising in the marketing mix – the advertiser's viewpoint

As was noted earlier, the justification for advertising from the advertiser's point of view is that it increases profitability, even though it is difficult to quantify precisely to what extent. (Mail order is the only case where a sale can be directly credited to the publication of an advertisement.) Advertising is but one variable in the marketing mix, albeit an important one, and it is difficult to separate its contribution from that of the other mix elements. As was implied in the list of advertising goals in the section on 'Objectives', there are a number of ways in which advertising may increase the profitability of the firm (R. H. Colley lists 52 specific goals in *Defining Advertising Goals*, Association of National Advertisers, New York, 1961) and these are stated more explicitly below:

1. To increase demand to the point where economies of scale are achieved. The larger the fixed costs of production, the greater the unit contribution once the break-even point has been reached – 'leverage'. The advertiser may wish initially to build primary demand for the product group as a whole, anticipating that he will benefit proportionally from the overall growth of the market. Once product acceptance has been achieved, advertisers usually concentrate on building brand recognition and loyalty. Colour television is a good example of this in that early advertisements for sets tended to emphasise the benefits of colour as compared with black and white, i.e. selling colour rather than brand A, B or C. As the market becomes more competitive, advertisers concentrate on extolling the features of their product which differentiate it from that of other producers.

2. The building of a 'brand image' in a competitive, mature market has other benefits in addition to maintaining or improving the firm's competitive position. Brand recognition and brand loyalty relieve the producer of his dependence on the distributive channels. This is particularly true of convenience goods, but is also applicable to shopping goods where the manufacturer can place little reliance on either the ability or interest of the retailer to sell his specific product. Only where a retailer is a sole distributor can the producer rely on an equal and corresponding interest in the sale of his product.

3. Information gathering invariably precedes the purchase of a product to some degree and, clearly, the ready availability of such information in the form of advertisements reduces the prospective purchaser's dependence on personal selling. Personal selling is a cost to the producer, both directly, in the payment of his sales force, and indirectly, through the margin he has to offer middlemen to perform the service on his behalf. The physical separation of producer and prospective buyer, coupled with competition, make advertising a more economic means of communication than personal

contact in both the industrial and consumer selling field. Further, a good advertisement can go a long way to achieve the first two stages of the sales process – the creation of awareness and interest.

4. Most firms are subject to a fluctuating demand for their output, be it seasonal, cyclical or secular, and advertising can do much to minimise such fluctuations though its impact is greatest in the case of seasonal variations. Ice cream and soup are classic examples of building year-round demand for products formerly consumed during a particular season, through informing consumers of alternative uses by means of advertising.

5. Finally, it is maintained that advertising improves profitability in a less tangible way by creating goodwill for the firm as a whole and by improving the morale of its employees; everyone likes to work for a well-known firm.

■ Organisation for advertising within the firm

Recognising the enormous disparity in the size and nature of firms, it is clear that the formulation of generalisations about the nature of the advertising function within the firm is fraught with danger. At the same time, some description of the mythical average' firm is useful in that it provides a starting-point for an examination of actual practice in a company with which one is familiar by association, or through reading the practitioners' journals. This caveat should be continually borne in mind, however, in reading this section.

Whatever the specific objective behind the mounting of an advertising campaign, the maximum return on expenditure will only be achieved if the right information is conveyed to the right people in the right way. This is unlikely to be the case unless those responsible for the firm's advertising have a thorough understanding of:

(a) The nature of the market.
(b) The nature of the product.
(c) The nature of the channels of distribution.
(d) The nature of the channels of communication – the media available, and their characteristics.

From the discussion of the structure of advertising earlier it is clear that advertisers have four options open to them. First, they can do it for themselves 'in-house'; second, they can hand over the responsibility entirely to a full service agency; third, they can buy in creative services but handle the remainder themselves; and, fourth, they can develop their own campaigns but devolve media buying to a specialist. In fact any combination of options could be used and this so-called 'A la carte' approach is proving increasingly popular, so that working relationships in the advertising business can be represented as in Figure 16.1.

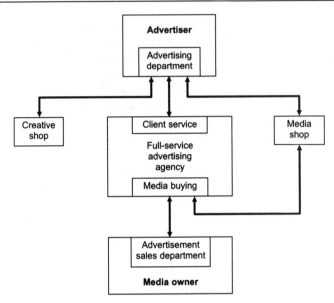

Figure 16.1   Working relationships in the advertising business

Source: K. C. Crosier, Starthclyde University, MBA Marketing, Distance Learning Module.

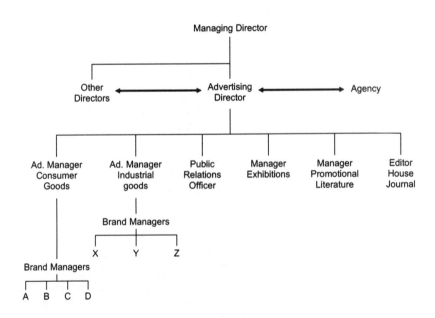

Figure 16.2   Organisation chart for the advertising department of a large, diversified company

In so far as the services of the full service agency and media specialist are 'free' it makes sense for the advertiser to use those wherever possible and avoid duplication within the firm. The critical factor is ability to communicate to the agency what the firm wishes to achieve, and what it has to offer the consumer which differentiates it from its competitors. Essentially, therefore, the advertising manager's role is one of liaison and interpretation (i.e. explaining management's objective to the agency and vice versa).

In the large firm the percentage of revenue allocated to advertising may constitute a very large sum in absolute terms and necessitate the employment of a number of persons to manage it effectively. The organisation chart in Figure 16.2 indicates the appointments that might typically be found in such a company – the actual number of staff employed in each section depending on the importance of advertising and promotion to the firm's marketing effort, and the financial resources allocated to it.

■ The advertising agency

The modern advertising agency of today has advanced a long way from the space salesman of a century ago, to the extent that some feel it would be more appropriate to call it a marketing agency.

With increasing competition, advertising agents have extended the range of services available to clients, the scope of which is indicated in the organisation chart for a large agency in Figure 16.3. Figure 16.4 indicates more clearly the functions and relationships within a full-service agency. Despite the apparent extent of the agency's expertise implied, it would be incorrect to assume that the agency could substitute for the firm's own marketing department. As was suggested in the preceding section, the advertiser might regard the agency as an extension of his own business, in that it would be uneconomical to duplicate its skills in terms of the creative aspects of advertising, but, at the same time, it would be foolish to delegate the whole marketing function to a third party specialising in only one aspect of it. It is a rule of agencies not to hold competing accounts, and for this reason alone it is unlikely that one could secure the services of an agency with the necessary experience to handle the total marketing of a specific product. It is also true that accounts change hands, so that one might be able to engage an agency with experience in the relevant product field, but this experience will invariably be limited to the advertising problems involved.

If one accepts that the agency is expert in the advertising function, it follows that it will only be able to perform effectively if it is given the full support and confidence of the advertiser. Much of the conflict which arises between advertiser and agent is the direct result of the former only giving the latter part of the information necessary to devise a successful campaign; it is the advertiser's responsibility to feed in the marketing inputs and data around which to build the

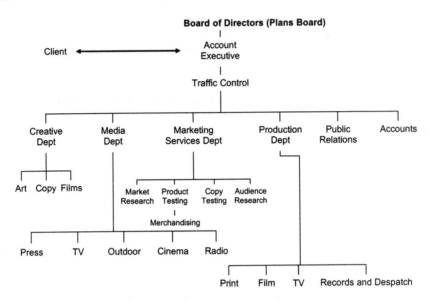

Figure 16.3   Organisation chart for a large advertising agency

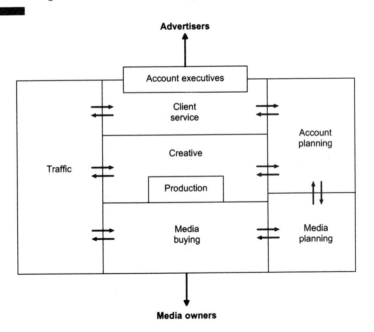

Figure 16.4   Functions and relationships in a conventional full-service advertising agency

Source: K. C. Crosier, Strathclyde University, MBA Marketing Distance Learning Module campaign. While on the subject of the advertiser/agency relationship, it is appropriate to comment that there seems little evidence to suggest, that agencies 'wear out', in the sense of losing their creative touch, a belief which prompts some advertisers regularly to change agencies to avoid such an occurrence. Most of the firms which are well known for the quality of their advertising have enjoyed a long and unbroken association with their agency, which suggests that mutual confidence improves over time, as does the expertise of the agent in advertising a particular product.

■ Agency remuneration

Passing reference has already been made to the fact that most, if not all, of the full-service agency's income is derived from commission paid by media owners, but a fuller explanation of this practice will be helpful here.

First, media commission is payable only to *recognised agencies* which have been approved by a consortium of trade associations acting on behalf of the media owners. Two criteria are of particular importance – competence and liquidity – and evidence of both must be provided.

Second, while the arithmetic of commission payments is simple enough it is widely misunderstood, as Crosier makes clear (Strathclyde University, MBA D.L. materials):

> Suppose that the total *rate-card cost* of media bookings, as published in the media owners' rate cards and in British Rate and Data ('BRAD'), is £234 567. A recognised agency is actually charged 15 per cent less than that figure by the media owners concerned. This figure has been the norm since Volney B. Palmer invented the system in 1841, though it took some time to standardise in Britain thereafter. Having said that, it is important to note that smaller-circulation newspapers and magazines give only 12½ or 10 per cent, and that only the five major media (press, television, posters, radio, cinema) offer commission at all; in the business, they are therefore sometimes designated 'above the line', all other vehicles being 'below the line'.

> Assuming a straightforward fifteen per cent transaction in this case:

Rate card cost	£234 567
Less 15%	£35 185
Charge to agency	£199 382

The agency invoices its client £234 567, the full cost which the latter can readily check in BRAD, and thereby earns £35 185 on the transaction – from the media owners not from the client who has ostensibly 'employed' them.

However, it is widely accepted that 15 per cent media commission is insufficient to cover all the costs involved in a major advertising campaign and it has become accepted that all 'production charges' and some creative costs will be charged direct to the advertiser by the agency. In addition, if the agency buys in services such as market research or sales promotion materials for its client it will add 17.65 per cent to the price, as this will be equivalent to a commission of 15 per cent on the new 'total' price. (Consult the section on Marketing Arithmetic on p. 503 if you're still not clear!)

The commission system was declared a restrictive trade practice by the OFT in 1978 but the ruling has had little apparent effect so far. However, it seems likely that EEC rulings will require a change to either negotiated commissions with the media owners or a service fee between agency and advertiser.

■ Agency selection

From the above comments it is clear that the selection of an advertising agent is not to be undertaken lightly, and the following is suggested as a structured approach to the problem. (This is based on the method adopted by Gateway when selecting an agency.)

1. Prepare a short-list of agencies that you think might be suitable. Details of agencies and their existing accounts can be obtained from the Advertiser's Annual. There is nothing to prevent you approaching an agency currently handling a competitor's account, but if they are prepared to drop the existing account to bid for yours, it is unlikely that you will achieve lasting success in this direction. Subjective information on agencies may be obtained from business acquaintances, or by asking media owners to identify the agency responsible for advertisements which you admire.
2. Construct a check-list of the factors on which you intend to base your decision and assign each a weight commensurate with the importance which you attach to each, e.g.:
   Creativity (i.e. ability to develop a distinctive/novel approach) – 10
   Previous experience in the product field – 8
   Ability to undertake *ad hoc* research – 6, etc., etc.
3. Draw up a questionnaire to:

   (*a*) Elicit the agency's grasp of the problems inherent in marketing your product, and its approach for dealing with them.
   (*b*) Provide a basis around which to build a 'Presentation' – i.e. an outline for a campaign.

4. Approach the agencies on the short-list and ask them if they are interested in competing for the account. (Some indication should be given of the

annual appropriation to be allocated to advertising.) Once the news gets around that you are looking for an agency it is quite likely that several agencies not on the short-list will ask if they may make a presentation. One should resist the temptation to expand the field, if the initial selection was undertaken thoroughly, as it will only serve to confuse the issue, unless there is some very valid reason, e.g. an agency thought to be unavailable having severed its connection with a competitor.

5. Rate the completed questionnaires in line with the previously determined weights.

6. Convene a selection board from the company's executives, e.g. Managing Director, Marketing Director, Advertising Manager, and rate the presentations made as for the questionnaires. (To avoid difficulty in resolving the final outcome it is recommended that both the weights and rating scale be given a large spread, i.e. instead of rating from 1 to 5 use an interval of 5; Worst 5 . . . Best 25.)

In a survey conducted for *Marketing* (15 November 1990) with marketers in 120 companies to find out what clients really think of their agencies the most important factors in choosing an agency were reported as:

Understanding of client needs	8.9*
Creativity	8.6
Media buying	8.0
Brand strategy and planning	7.8
Accessibility of senior management	7.4
Willingness to negotiate on fees	7.0

* Mean score based on clients scoring
   different aspects of agency performance
   on a scale of one to ten.

A survey undertaken almost simultaneously by *Marketing Week* provided slightly different results as can be seen from Table 16.10, on page 388.

Even if one follows a methodical selection procedure such as the one advocated above there is ample evidence that the result may not be satisfactory and a change of agency will be called for. Ken Gofton examined the agency – client relationship in an article in *Marketing* (27 September 1984) entitled 'What moves the client', and points to J. Walter Thompson's loss of the Guinness account as a classic example of the break-up of an apparently perfect partnership. To throw light on the question, *Marketing* undertook a survey of 100 companies that had changed agencies recently, and concluded that 'The ability of an agency to understand the client's marketing problem and to get the staff of both organisations pulling in the same direction emerged as one of the crucial issues.' The findings of the survey are reproduced on the following pages as Tables 16.11 and 16.12.

TABLE 16.10   Criteria ranked in order of importance for overall assessment of agency performance

Rank 1989	Rank 1990		On 10 point scale Percentage rating 9 or 10 'very important'	Change in % rating very important 1989 to 1990	Average rating
1	1	Creativity	61%	−3%	8.7
2	2	Value for money in results achieved	55%	+9%	8.3
3	3	Media buying and placement	42%	−9%	7.7
5	4	Attentiveness and adaptability to client companies	32%	+4%	8.0
4	5	Quality of account managers	31%	−5%	8.0
6	6	Marketing strategy and analysis	23%	−4%	7.1
7	7	Coverage of major markets outside the UK	3%	−2%	3.3

Source: Marketing Week, 16 November 1990.

TABLE 16.11   Why clients sack their agencies (% mentioning)

In a rut – needed new ideas	41%
The results fell short of our expectations	36%
They didn't understand our problems	32%
Couldn't develop the right chemistry with the staff	30%
We weren't getting value for money	25%
Needed to rationalise the agencies used	20%
Product launch or relaunch coming up	14%
Changes of personnel in the agency	11%
Not sufficiently competitive on media buying	11%
Conflict of interests between accounts	9%
Not sufficiently international	9%
Expected more marketing support	7%
We weren't big enough for them	7%
Competitors activities meant we needed to take a fresh look	5%
Needed to spread our work between more agencies	5%
Offices too distant for easy communication	5%
We'd outgrown the agency	5%
Agency wouldn't negotiate on fees/commission	2%
Security	—

Source: K. Gofton, 'What moves the client', Marketing, 27 Sept. 1984.

TABLE 16.12   What clients look for when choosing an agency (% mentioning)

Creative record	77%
Evidence that the agency understands my marketing problem	64%
Good personal chemistry with staff	61%
Good media buying record	34%
Marketing skills to supplement those of in-house departments	20%
The agency made the best pitch	16%
A range of services other than marketing	7%
Specialised knowledge of my industry	7%
Appropriate size – our wish to be big fish in the agency pool	5%
A recommendation from people I trust	2%
Location	—
Security	—
Willingness to negotiate on commission fees	—

Respondents were asked to choose three factors from the list.
100 companies were polled, of which 44 replied. Of these, 13 were in food and drink, ten in other FMCG areas, eight in consumer durables, five in services, five in business-to-business or industrial marketing and three in retail.

Source: K. Gofton. 'What moves the client', *Marketing*, 27 Sept. 1984.

Of course the success of an agency in meeting its clients' objectives will depend very heavily upon the quality of the briefing it receives. As to what constitutes an ideal brief, Crosier suggests 'First, there should be *general* broad guidelines on creative and media strategies . . . Thereafter, the following *specific* ingredients should preferably be included:

1. Unequivocal, measurable objectives
2. Product profile – technical specifications *and* satisfactions deliverable
3. Company image/style/atmosphere
4. Market analysis
5. Production capacity
6. Price structure
7. Distribution
8. Media and creative allocations
9. Criteria for evaluation of effectiveness.

Clearly, given such a brief the potential for misunderstanding is greatly reduced and the likelihood of a harmonious working relationship much improved.

■ The media

The third party to the advertising process is the media owners, and the aim of the following section is to review briefly the salient characteristics of the media available. Before proceeding to this review it will be helpful to outline a check-list as a basis for assessing the value of the various media. In common with most other similar lists appearing elsewhere, the outline given below is based on Hobson's *Selection of Advertising Media*, published by Business Publications on behalf of the IPA.

An evaluation of an advertising medium requires consideration of four major factors:

1. The character of the medium.
2. The atmosphere of the medium.
3. The coverage of the medium.
4. The cost of the medium.

Two further factors which should be taken into account are the size and position of the advertisement.

Character. The character of a medium may be largely determined on an objective and factual basis through consideration of the following:

(*a*)   The geographical coverage of the medium, e.g. national, regional, local.
(*b*)   The socio-economic composition of the audience.
(*c*)   Composition of the audience by age and sex groupings.
(*d*)   The medium's physical characteristics – visual, oral, standard of reproduction, availability of colour, possibility of movement, etc.
(*e*)   Frequency of publication. Allied to this is the duration of interest in the medium – most daily papers are thrown away the same day, while magazines may be kept for several weeks and read by a number of people. The frequency of publication also has a direct effect on the booking of time or space, i.e. the timing of the appearance of an advertisement.
(*f*)   The power to reach special groups – this is closely related to (*b*) and (*c*) above, e.g. *Punch* or the *Financial Times, Vogue*, etc., preselect a particular type of audience and so are especially suited to selling to this segment of the population. Further, the association of a product with a medium may give that product favourable connotations by transferring confidence in the publication to items advertised therein, e.g. *Good Housekeeping*.

Atmosphere. The atmosphere of a medium is difficult to define in that it is based on a subjective evaluation of its content, presentation, etc. A broad distinction may be drawn between acceptable and intrusive media, in that the latter create impact through intrusion and irrelevance to context, e.g. television commercials, whereas many magazines are purchased as much for their advertisements as their other content. The concept will become clearer when related to individual media.

Coverage. The essential criterion on which coverage is judged is the actual number of persons exposed to the medium, in the sense of being made aware of its content. For example, the number of people who actually see a poster is considerably less than the number that have the opportunity to see it; on the other hand, the readership of a magazine may well exceed ten times its actual circulation.

Cost. For purposes of comparison the cost of publishing an advertisement is usually expressed in terms of 'cost per thousand', which is arrived at by dividing the cost of publication by the audience in thousands. The difficulty in ensuring comparability in the measurement of audience size in terms of coverage, as defined above, makes this a rough measure at best, and media planners are actively seeking more sophisticated measures of cost effectiveness.

Advertising expenditure by media for the years 1980 to 1989 is indicated in Table 16.4.

Size. The effect of increased size or duration of an advertisement is to increase effective coverage, but on a progressively diminishing scale. Larger advertisements enable the advertiser to make more selling points, or to create greater impact when properly used. It is also contended that 'bigness', of itself, creates confidence and prestige.

Position. Detailed studies of the positioning of advertisements within a medium have shown that certain 'slots' consistently achieve greater coverage than other positions. Further, certain positions can be very useful in isolating a particular segment of the general audience. (Timing has the same effect for broadcast messages on radio and television.)

In the following pages are given synopses of the various media available to the advertiser. While correct at the time of writing this type of information is subject to constant change and very quickly becomes dated. For detailed and up-to-date information the reader should consult *British Rate and Data* (BRAD). Contact with The Advertising Association (Abford House, 15 Wilton Road, London SW1V 1NJ, Telephone: 071-828-2771, Fax: 071-931-0376) is also strongly recommended as they publish an excellent range of material including a set of 'Student Briefs' covering various aspects of advertising. Chapter 19 in *The Marketing Book* (2nd edn, Michael J. Baker, Heinemann, 1991) also contains an excellent survey of media characteristics by Keith Crosier.

■ The national press

Since the publication of the previous edition there have been radical changes in the national press. Writing in 1985 the erosion of advertising revenues due to competition with commercial television was seen as a major threat to several of the national dailies following the collapse of the *News Chronicle*. In a report from the Economist Intelligence Unit it was argued that publishers needed to charge economic selling prices which are estimated to be twice the then cover cost. A conservative attitude to change on the editorial side and the absence of marketing were also cited as threats to the national dailies existence. In the period since then not only have we seen significant changes in ownership and editorial attitudes, the introduction of a successful new 'quality' paper (*The Independent*) and the widespread adoption of modern marketing techniques but we have also witnessed a radical change in working practices and the conversion to modern information technology in place of the antiquated methods of yesteryear.

Following Hobson's 'check-list', the salient characteristics of the national press may be summarised as:

Character. Newspapers are bought largely for their news value and so are singularly appropriate for announcing new products and new developments of existing products. Because of their frequency of publication they are also well suited to 'opportunity' markets, e.g. advertising anti-freeze during a sudden cold spell, such- and-such a race was won on X tyres, Y petrol, Z oil, etc., etc. Despite their short life, newspapers have a high attention value and it is estimated that an 11 × 3 advertisement (i.e. 11 inches long by 3 columns wide) is seen by one-third of the readers. Further, the advertisements in the national press are more likely to be seen by the retailer (also true of T.V. commercials) than are those appearing in magazines, and so have an indirect effect on the distributive channels.

In addition to their news content newspapers are also bought for the regular features they carry, and certain days have been developed to cater to specific reader interests, e.g. Thursday and Friday for grocery products, as the majority of grocery purchases are made on Friday and Saturday; mail order advertisements on Saturday and Sunday, to coincide with the weekend letter-writing peak, etc.

As their name implies, the national papers have national coverage. Their regional strength varies, however, and up-to-date data should be sought from *BRAD* or JICNARS (Joint Industry Committee for National Readership Surveys).

Atmosphere. In general terms this may be summarised as a sense of urgency and importance coupled, to a varying degree, with a certain authority. Most people read a newspaper which confirms their own view of the world and so is regarded as a high credibility source (i.e. the content is accepted at face value). To a certain extent, the authority of the factual content is transferred to the advertisements and may be regarded as 'assistance to selling' under the heading of 'Character'.

TABLE 16.13 Press – national newspapers

	Tabloid/ Broadsheet	Circulation (1) 000	Adult readership (2) 000	Adult readership (2) %	Sex Men %	Sex Women %	Age 15/34 %	Age 35/54 %	Age 55+ %	Class ABC1 %	Class C2DE %	Rates(3) scc £	Rates(3) Mono £	Rates(3) Page 4 Colour £
Population profile					48	52	37	31	32	41	58			
National dailies														
The Sun	T	3 949	10 791	24	53	47	45	30	25	24	77	110	26 000	32 800
Daily Mirror	T	3 087	8 845	20	55	45	37	31	32	26	73	109	28 300	35 000
Daily Mail	T	1 676	4 349	10	49	51	30	34	35	57	44	82	20 664	45 000
Daily Express	T	1 555	3 900	9	52	48	28	32	39	52	48	85	20 825	36 000
The Daily Telegraph	B	1 095	2 493	6	54	46	21	35	44	82	18	66	29 500	25 000
The Star	T	907	2 665	6	61	39	51	29	20	18	82	38.50	9 432	
Daily Record (Scotland)	T	774	2 163	5	53	47	42	31	27	26	73	33	8 640	9 225
Today	T	575	1 774	4	62	38	50	32	18	43	58	24	6 200	6 750
The Guardian	B	433	1 279	3	64	36	39	41	20	79	21	35	15 500	17 000
The Times	B	433	1 097	3	57	43	35	43	22	87	14	32	14 000	26 000
The Independent	B	415	1 156	3	62	38	45	39	16	79	21	29	12 500	17 000
Financial Times	B	199	702	2	71	29	35	51	15	84	17	50	22 400	35 000
National Sunday														
News of the World	T	5 056	13 043	29	51	49	46	30	24	27	72	118	28 000	34 500
Sunday Mirror	T	2 880	9 249	21	52	48	40	31	29	30	71	100	25 900	27 300
The People	T	2 617	7 522	17	51	49	34	30	35	28	73	77	20 550	
The Mail on Sunday	T	1 871	5 457	12	50	50	42	34	23	61	40	94	25 000	
Sunday Express	B	1 762	5 169	11	49	51	26	32	42	60	39	105	47 040	14 245
Sunday Post (Scotland)	T	1 274	3 534	8	47	53	29	28	43	30	69	31.70	7 200	
The Sunday Times	B	1 214	3 638	8	54	46	39	41	19	79	20	80	36 000	55 000
Sunday Mail (Scotland)	T	880	2 348	5	51	49	41	32	37	29	70	27.25	7 135	10 100
Sunday Telegraph	B	598	1 964	4	54	46	19	34	37	78	22	48	21 850	25 500
The Observer	B	589	2 208	5	60	40	37	37	25	76	24	47	22 000	26 000
Sunday Sport	T	475	1 813	4	71	29	74	21	5	27	73	55	12 302	14 245
Sunday Correspondent	B											24	10 500	13 200
The Independent on Sunday	B											28	12 000	16 500
Weekend colour magazines														
Sunday		5 056	12 376	27	50	50	47	29	23	27	73		25 000	28 500
Sunday Mirror Magazine		2 880	8 854	20	51	49	40	31	29	31	70		17 250	23 000
You Magazine (The Mail on Sunday)		1 871	5 409	12	49	51	43	34	23	61	40		13 700	16 700
Sunday Express Magazine		1 702	5 119	11	48	52	27	32	41	61	38		22 400	22 400
The Sunday Times Magazine		1 214	3 690	8	52	48	40	41	20	78	21		9 500	15 000
Telegraph Weekend Magazine		1 095	2 708	6	50	50	24	35	42	81	18		10 200	12 750
The Observer Magazine		589	2 214	5	58	42	38	38	25	76	25		6 500	9 600
Independent			2 214	5	57	43	46	39	15	80	19		5 750	5 750
Sunday Correspondent Magazine			1 325	3									3 750	4 500

Sources: (1) ABC data Nov. 1989–April 1990; ABC Data July–Dec. 1989 (2) JICNARS Jan.–Dec. 1989 (3) BRAD July 1990 min. rates. From Marketing Pocket Book 1990, NTC Publications Ltd: 0491–574671.

Quantity/Coverage. Table 16.13 gives recent circulation figures for the best-known national newspapers. Clearly, an evaluation based solely on the number of copies bought would be an inadequate guide to the suitability of a particular paper for a particular advertisement, and these 'raw' data must be related to the demographic composition of the audience *vis-à-vis* the consumer profile of the product or service in question. (This is a useful rule-of-thumb guide to media selection – i.e. define the demographic characteristics of the target consumers, and then select the medium which offers the closest match to this profile.) Table 16.14 shows national newspaper circulation trends for 1977–88.

TABLE 16.14   National newspaper circulation trends, 1977–88

	1977 (000)	1984 (000)	1985 (000)	1986 (000)	1987 (000)	1988 (000)	+ or − 1977/1988
National dailies							
Daily Express	2 339	2 002	1 902	1 729	1 690	1 637	
Daily Mail	1 900	1 864	1 815	1 732	1 810	1 759	
Daily Mirror	3 905	3 494	3 033	3 339	3 128	3 157	
The Star	—	1 633	1 455	1 278	1 137	967	
The Sun	3 883	4 084	4 125	4 050	4 045	4 219	
Today	—	—	—	307	340	548	
Popular dailies	12 027	13 077	12 331	12 235	12 150	12 287	+ 2.2%
The Daily Telegraph	1 326	1 235	1 202	1 132	1 169	1 127	
Financial Times	178†	218	234	254	307	278	
The Guardian	267	472	487	507	460	438	
The Independent	—	—	—	303*	361	387	
The Times	291	457	478	467	447	436	
Quality dailies	2 062	2 382	2 401	2 662	2 744	2 666	+ 29.3%
National Sundays							
The Mail on Sunday	—	1 607	1 631	1 601	1 854	1 919	
News of the World	4 978	4 698	5 103	4 954	5 096	5 360	
Sunday Express	3 187	2 542	2 449	2 181	2 228	2 033	
Sunday Mirror	3 949	3 489	3 009 †	3 046	2 894	2 953	
Sunday Sport	—	—	—	—	—	551	
The People	3 973	3 253	2 962 †	2 983	2 856	2 743	
Popular Sundays	16 087	15 589	15 155	14 765	14 928	15 559	− 3.3%
The Observer	678	744	736	769	764	722	
Sunday Telegraph	821	713	686	686	739	693	
The Sunday Times	1 348	1 260	1 251	1 147	1 250	1 315	
Quality Sundays	2 847	2 717	2 673	2 603	2 753	2 730	− 4.1%
All national newspapers	33 023	33 766	32 560	32 496	32 575	33 242	+ 0.7%

Source: * A.B.C data Oct.–Dec. only. † 5 month A.B.C. data only (excl. Aug). From *Marketing Pocket Book 1990*, NTC Publications Ltd: 0491–574671.

Cost. Most newspaper advertising rates are based on a charge per standard column centimetre (SCC) – i.e. one column wide by one centimetre deep. The actual column width varies, as does the cost, from paper to paper. In general, the cost per thousand tends to be roughly equivalent, but once again reference should be made to *BRAD* for exact and up-to-date information. Table 16.13 lists 1990 rates. Charges also vary within each paper depending on the actual position of the advertisement – see 'Position' below.

Size. As a general rule, readership does not increase with the size of the advertisement in a directly proportional manner. Despite diminishing returns, the consensus of opinion favours larger advertisements because of the greater impact which they achieve and because readers 'select' advertisements to a certain extent, i.e. there is a tendency to notice those of direct interest to the reader. This means that a series of small advertisements, costing the same as a single large advertisement, may be seen many times by the same people, but pass unnoticed by those with a latent demand – it is unlikely that a full-page advertisement will pass unnoted by these potential customers in the same way.

Position. The location of advertisements within the medium is at the discretion of the advertising manager, who, naturally, attempts to satisfy as many clients as possible. Owing to the demand for certain positions, however, it has been found both simpler and more lucrative to charge special rates for these favoured positions. It is clear that certain pages preselect a particular segment of the readership owing to the nature of the features on that page, e.g. the women's and sports pages. It follows that if one is advertising a product which has a particular appeal to a segment of the readership, there is a greater probability of it coming to their attention if it is located on a page that caters to that interest.

The actual position within the printed media may be defined by one of the following, largely self-explanatory, terms:

Top, centre, bottom.
Inside, i.e. towards the fold, or outside.
Next matter, i.e. next to editorial content.
Under matter, next and under matter.
Island position, i.e. matter on at least three sides.
Solus, on its own, no other advertisements appearing on the same page.
Semi-solus, only one other advertisement on the same page.

Research evidence on the value of such positions is inconclusive, but media planners contend that better results are obtained from some positions than others. For example it is contended that as the eye is accustomed to starting at the top of a piece of printed matter there is a greater possibility of catching the reader's attention if the advertisement is on the upper half of the page. Intuitively one is inclined to agree with observations of this type until adequate research either confirms, or confirms the hypothesis.

■ The regional press

At the time of writing there were 1,660 regional newspapers published on a regional basis in the United Kingdom. In many respects the characteristics of the regional press are similar to those of the national dailies already described, and this summary will be confined to noting certain differences, and the major advantages and disadvantages of local papers as an advertising medium.

First, local papers have the advantage that they achieve concentrated coverage of a limited area, and so are likely to achieve a greater density of readership than a national paper. Because of the 'local' content they also tend to receive closer scrutiny, but against this must be set the greater authority of the national paper.

Second, regional papers are ideally suited to developing regional markets based on local preferences – an examination of consumption patterns on a regional basis soon indicates that the British population is far from homogeneous in this respect.

Third, the limited circulation of the regional and local papers makes them a good medium for copy testing (i.e. running different versions of an advertisement in order to measure their relative effectiveness as a basis for final selection). The lower circulations of these papers also makes them more economical, although the CPT rate may be comparable to, or even greater than, those of the nationals.

Fourth, and this also applies to the national papers to a lesser degree, the frequency of publication permits the development of a theme by instalments, or early repetition if desired to 'stiffen up' a campaign.

Finally, evening and weekly papers have the advantage over morning daily papers that they are taken *into* the home, and so are likely to be seen by more members of the household at greater leisure.

The major disadvantages associated with both regional and national papers are:

(a) The poor quality newsprint does not permit a very high standard of reproduction – this may be improved by colour printing 'inserts' on a glazed paper that will accept a smaller screen size than ordinary newsprint, e.g. *Daily Express*.

(b) News dates rapidly, so most papers are scanned rapidly on the day of issue and discarded, i.e. a newspaper advertisement is virtually a 'one-shot' attempt at attracting the public's attention and so will usually require a number of repetitions if it is to be seen by the majority of the paper's readers.

■ Sunday newspapers

J. D. Hughes of Hobson, Bates and Partners wrote of this group: 'The British Sunday press is a unique phenomenon. No other country possesses anything remotely like it. It is, moreover, a phenomenon rooted deeply in the habits and behaviour of the people it serves' (*Advertiser's Weekly*, 21 Oct 1966). When one considers that the *News of the World* alone has a readership of 29 per cent of the United Kingdom *adult population*, one begins to appreciate how deeply ingrained is the Sunday newspaper habit.

Unlike daily papers, which tend to be scanned, the Sunday paper is perused at leisure and so achieves greater attention value. The readership figures are given in Table 16.13; however, the actual composition of the readership varies from paper to paper, and the serious student should consult the JICNARS for a detailed breakdown on both a national and regional basis.

A second feature of the 'quality' Sunday papers (*Sunday Times, Sunday Telegraph* and *Observer*) which used to differentiate them from most of the dailies is the colour magazine, which largely overcomes the criticism of low standards of reproduction associated with newspapers in general (the 'popular' press has now entered the Sunday newspaper magazine market, e.g. the *News of the World* and the *Sunday Express*).

■ Magazines

The major factor which differentiates a magazine from a newspaper is that the former preselects its readership through the nature of its content. A second distinguishing feature is that it is read at leisure.

Magazines, as a group, may be further subdivided into categories, and media planners have adopted the following classification:

1. General magazines – so designated because of their general appeal, as contrasted with:
2. Specialist magazines, which cater for the readership with clearly defined and specific interest – e.g. doctors, philatelists.
3. The retail trade press. This subdivision is justified because of the medium's importance in 'selling-in' a product prior to the start of a campaign aimed at the consumer.

General magazines. This category may be further subdivided into those which have a predominantly male or female readership, as compared with those which appeal to both sexes. For example *Woman* has a predominantly female readership, *Autocar* male, *Radio Times* male and female. Overall, the characteristics of the general magazine are so diverse that one should properly attempt to rate each separately by reference to the check-list. At the same time there are a number of points which justify generalisation, namely:

Character
Read at leisure.
Preselect their audience by the content, e.g. *Popular Gardening, Homemaker, Punch.*
Better standards of reproduction than newspapers.

Longer duration of interest – e.g. of the ultimate readership of a woman's weekly, 60 per cent see it within two weeks of publication, 30 per cent in the next two weeks, and the remaining 10 per cent over a period of six months or longer.

Readership may be ten to fifteen times circulation.

The lower frequency of publication necessitates booking of space well in advance, i.e. magazines are less flexible in this respect than newspapers.

Atmosphere

More stable than that of the newspaper, which is affected by the news it carries.

Higher standards of reproduction convey a greater sense of luxury than is possible with a newspaper, particularly where colour is used.

Coverage/Cost

Difficult to estimate on a comparative basis owing to the variation in page size, on which rates are based, and of readership. Overall, the C.P.T. is higher than that for the national or regional press, and ranges from about £0.70 – in the mass circulation broadcasting publications, to around £1.50 – in the glossy fashion magazines. This higher cost is offset by the greater intrinsic worth of the advertisements to the reader, which ensures a higher 'page traffic', i.e. number of readers per page expressed as a proportion of the total readership.

Specialist magazines. Detailed information on specialist magazines is more limited than in the case of the general magazine, largely because so few of them are included in the National Readership Survey. In addition to the above generalised comments, one may add that the magazines in this category are even more selective in their readership appeal. Further, the advertising content is often of equal interest to the editorial content, e.g. collectors' magazines listing objects for sale, technical magazines detailing new products and product improvements. With the exception of direct mail, the specialist magazine offers the greatest opportunity of reaching a highly specific audience.

Retail trade magazines. The need to ensure adequate distribution and availability of a product prior to the opening of a campaign directed at the ultimate consumer is advanced as the main reason for using this medium. Some media planners are sceptical as to its value, owing to the generally low level of readership – around 25 per cent – which is compounded by the sheer volume of advertisements, thus making the actual possibility of any particular advertisement being seen correspondingly small. It is also argued that the smaller retailer, at whom much of the effort is directed in the anticipation that it will reduce the amount of direct selling required, is an ordinary mortal who reads newspapers, watches TV, etc., and that advertisements in these media are more likely to be seen and carry regular authority. In the light of these arguments it is clear that each case should be considered on its merits, and that particular attention should be given to position within the medium.

A review of print media would not be complete without some reference to controlled circulation papers and annuals and directories.

There has been a considerable growth in controlled circulation papers in recent years, particularly in the trade, technical and professional fields. Papers or magazines with a controlled circulation are not sold but are distributed free of charge to persons with a known interest in the magazine's editorial content. As with all other media, space is sold on the basis of the medium's ability to reach an audience which in this instance is closely defined. Many of these publications claim virtually total coverage of the predefined audience. This assertion should be treated with circumspection, but it is indisputable that some achieve spectacular results.

Annuals and directories may be subdivided into four categories:

1. Annual special numbers – these are published by the parent publication, usually a magazine or newspaper, as a completely separate entity, i.e. they are not a 'special issue'. Example: *Country Life Annual*.
2. Annual consumer reference books. Examples: *Whitakers Almanack, Daily Mail Year Book, Pears Cyclopaedia*.
3. Trade, technical and professional diaries, buyer's guides, year books. These usually contain a mass of information which the practitioner may require at a moment's notice. Example: *Electrical Trade Directory*.
4. Annual street directories and shopper's guides. (Telephone directories might be considered to come within this category, especially the classified directories or 'Yellow Pages'.)

Obviously the greatest disadvantage associated with this medium is the low flexibility that is a concomitant of annual publication. Against this may be set low cost – *AdWeekly* published a 'case history' of Automat some years ago which demonstrated how this company had concentrated its limited advertising appropriation in trade directories and, through careful positioning and repetition, achieved excellent results (25 Aug 1967).

■ Television

Television advertising is the most recent development in the field of advertising media and, as inferred when reviewing the national press, its impact has been enormous. In terms of expenditures, TV is second only to the press as a whole, and its growth in recent years has consistently exceeded that of all other media. The importance of the medium is reflected in the publication of books devoted solely to the subject of commercial television, and the serious student should refer to these sources for a detailed description. Limitations of time and space dictate that the barest outline can be developed in this context.

Character. Above all commercial television is a mass medium: it can be received in over 99 per cent of all British homes. On an average evening over 50 per cent of these homes will be tuned in to a commercial television station and, in the course of a day, an average of 2.9 hours of commercial transmissions will be received by the households capable of tuning in. Although, in theory, it would be possible to reach all these households simultaneously with a single advertisement, few advertisers would in fact attempt this as coverage is subdivided among fourteen contractors, who cover thirteen geographical regions, namely:

Thames TV ⎱	
London Weekend Television ⎰	London
Central Ind. TV	Midlands
Granada TV	North West
Yorkshire TV (Link)	Yorkshire
Scottish TV Central	Scotland
HTV	Wales and West
TVS	South and S. East
Tyne Tees TV (Link)	North East
Anglia TV	East
TSW	South West
Ulster TV	N. Ireland
Border TV	Border
Grampian TV	N. Scotland

Thus, while national coverage is possible, most advertisers tend to advertise selectively on a regional basis. This trend is encouraged by the contractors, who on the one hand stress the purchasing behaviour which differentiates the consumers within their area from those in other areas, thus making a case for regional marketing, while on the other hand they publish statistics that demonstrate that their audience is an accurate reflection of the national audience and so suitable for a national campaign. If a note of scepticism is detected, the reader should consult some of the commercial television contractors' own publicity material to see how it is possible to substantiate essentially opposing claims from the same basic data. (This tendency is most marked in the case of those companies offering test marketing facilities, where a representative sample is a desirable prerequisite – it is difficult to accept that the inhabitants of central Scotland are identical with those of Kent and Sussex, or vice versa!)

With such a large potential audience, it follows that commercial television reaches all socioeconomic groups. As might be expected, there is a slight bias towards the lower social groups, to larger families and to housewives, but as these constitute the mass market for consumer goods, this has clear advantages for the marketers of such products.

The great advantage of television over all other media, with the exception of the cinema, is its ability to combine sound, vision and movement. This combination permits the use of advertisements that demonstrate the product and its advantages, which, most would agree, is far more effective than a written or static visual representation.

Commercial television channels operate seven days a week, mainly between the hours of noon and midnight, with the result that the composition of the audience varies according to the time segment selected: e.g. programmes for housewives in the afternoon, children's programmes from 4 to 6 p.m., 'family programmes' 6–9 p.m., adult programmes from 9 p.m. onwards. The composition of the audience also varies from day to day, and once again the student is referred to *BRAD* or the publications of the Joint Industry Committee for Television Advertising Research (JICTAR) for a detailed breakdown.

Television commercials themselves vary from 7-second 'spots' through multiples of 15 seconds to a normal maximum of 2 minutes. In practice, few advertisements exceed 60 seconds and most are in the 15-, 30- and 60-second bracket. A readily observed feature of television commercials which is infrequently commented on is the fact that the advertisements are concentrated into a series of 'natural breaks'. To the author's knowledge research has yet to be undertaken on the effect that this has on the viewer. Some media planners have commented adversely, however, to the effect that viewers must find it difficult to assimilate a fairly large number of advertisements within a short space of time. (An examination of peak loadings, in terms of water and electricity consumption, might lead one to believe that in fact the majority of viewers avoid the problem by attending to their toilet and making cups of tea during such breaks!)

Atmosphere. It is often claimed that a major advantage of television is that it is viewed in the home, in a relaxed atmosphere, when the audience is more receptive than is normally the case when exposed to advertising messages. Against this one must set the disadvantage that the injection of advertising into a programme is both intrusive and irrelevant. While attention may be concentrated on the programme itself, the popularity of the first and last 'spots' in the break would seem to indicate that media planners recognise that attention may wander once it is realised that a break has started, and only returns in anticipation of the commencement of the programme. With the introduction of infra-red remote controls a new phenomenon known as 'zapping' has emerged. Simply put zapping consists of switching channels during commercial breaks just to see what is going on on other channels and so reduces exposure to the advertisements being screened. No satisfactory data to quantify the possible effect of this behaviour was available in 1990.

The more successful television advertisers, judged on the basis of their sales results, appear to have recognised both the intrusive and irrelevant aspects of commercials, and to have made a virtue out of necessity by issuing advertisements that superficially appear to have both these characteristics. Judging by the adverse comments directed at a margarine that gave one delusions of grandeur, one should be surprised to learn that at a time when margarine sales were in a decline the only brand showing an absolute increase in sales happened to be the one with the 'stupid' commercial.

Coverage/cost. With fourteen contractors, each with its own rate structure that varies both in terms of the time of day and the day of the week, little of general use can be said.

Position in terms of television commercials refers both to the time segment and the position within the segment.

Size is measured in terms of the duration of the commercial.

At the time of publishing the previous edition considerable interest had been generated by the establishment of the Cable Authority in 1984 with the task of overseeing the establishment of a hi-tech cable network in the UK. The Authority (which is due to be absorbed into the new Independent Television Commission in 1991) was also made responsible for awarding franchises and overseeing programme standards. It was believed this initiative would lead to a major expansion in cable TV which previously had been confined to areas with difficult reception. In the event, by July 1989 only 1.3 per cent of homes were connected to a cable system which was just under 20 per cent of homes passed by a cable and it seems unlikely there will be any significant increase in penetration with the introduction of Direct Broadcasting by Satellite (DBS) in February 1989 when SKY TV first came on the air (DBS covers television transmissions via satellites which can be received on dishes less than 1 metre in diameter). SKY TV uses the Astra satellite which carries 16 channels eight of which are in English including Sky one, Sky Movies, Sky News and Eurosport. Early in 1990 a second company, BSB, entered the UK market using its own Marcopolo satellite carrying five channels and capable of being received on much smaller dishes only 35 cm in diameter. Take up of the services was disappointing and by the middle of 1990 the two companies merged in an effort to reduce the wasteful competition between them. Whether such a merger will be acceptable (e.g. to the OFT) remains to be seen as does the success of the new medium.

■ Commercial radio

Until the autumn of 1973 the only commercial radio transmissions which could be received in this country were those of Radio Luxemburg. However in October 1973 Capital Radio came on the air as the first of approximately sixty local commercial radio stations authorised for the country as a whole. A second London station, London Broadcasting, came on the air shortly afterwards, while the third, Radio Clyde, started transmissions on New Year's Day 1974. There are at the present 45 local radio stations and the whole ILR network has an average weekly reach of 49 per cent of the total adult population. Stations are allowed to include up to nine minutes of advertising in each hour of broadcasting. Time is sold on a 'spot' basis (like TV) but peak periods are different being highest in the morning and evening rush-hours (especially in-car reception).

■ Outdoor advertising

(The 'check-list' approach will not be used for the remaining media – the student may like to formulate his/her own.) Outdoor advertising is often thought of as consisting solely of the poster medium. This ignores transportation advertising, illuminated signs and several lesser media which properly fall into this category.

As with the press and the cinema, the advent of commercial television resulted in outdoor advertising having to reappraise its role as an advertising medium. It was realised that television had become the prime medium for the advertising of a wide range of mass consumption goods which had formerly depended far more on press, poster and cinema. There are still instances in which outdoor advertising may be used as the prime medium, but in the majority of cases outdoor advertising is sold as a complement to a television campaign on the grounds that it serves as a reminder at, or near, the actual point of sale. This fact is supplemented by a gradual increase in audience size due to increased personal mobility.

The main outdoor medium is the poster, which suffers from three main disadvantages. First, to ensure that its message is conveyed quickly and concisely it can only accommodate a short copy story. Second, posters are not seen in the context of other matter of editorial or entertainment value. Finally, production costs are relatively high, as are maintenance costs. Offsetting this are a number of advantages.

It has been estimated that over 90 per cent of the population goes out of doors in the course of a week and thus has an 'opportunity to see' a poster. Actual poster sighting will obviously be considerably less than this but, unlike most other media, an accurate predictive model has been developed which enables the prospective advertiser to determine in advance the type of campaign he will have to mount to reach an audience of a given size. (See Mills and Rockley's Studies and the IPA Audience Measurement Study, 1964.) Current information on the poster audience can be obtained from OSCAR (Outside Site Classification and Audience Research) which is controlled by JICPAR and funded by the poster contractors. Second, poster advertising offers greater geographic flexibility than virtually any other medium; one may use a single site in a specific locality, cover all or part of a town, or all or part of the country. Third, the cost of poster advertising is relatively low, so that an advertiser with a limited appropriation can mount both an extensive and prolonged campaign for an amount that would make little impact on television when ranged against the large budgets of the major television advertisers. (This is not to say that posters will have more impact than a television commercial as such, but rather that impact is relative such that a limited television campaign would tend to be completely dominated by that of a major advertiser on the medium.) Fourth, posters can make full use of colour and achieve high standards of reproduction. Posters are increasingly being used with great dramatic effect and more thought is going into the use of the medium. The advertisements for 'Araldite' adhesive are a good example of this. In this poster campaign an actual motor car was attached to the poster seemingly by Araldite to show the great adhesive qualities of the glue.

Poster sites come in a range of sizes: 4-sheet, 60″ × 40″; 12-sheet, 60″ × 60″; 16-sheet, 120″ × 60″; 48-sheet, 120″ × 240″; supersite, 10 feet high by a range of widths from 27 feet upwards. The cost of a poster site depends on its location, and it is therefore difficult to generalise. The poster industry offers advertisers various ways of mounting a poster campaign. From 'line by line' where the contractor offers individual sites to build up a specific display to suit particular marketing objectives, and 'key plans' which are specially built displays offered by Independent Poster Sales Ltd. Details are given in Table 16.15 and further information can be obtained from *BRAD*.

TABLE 16.15   Posters

Campaign

Adshel Limited
4 sheet posters on bus shelters (20 000 sites available)

	14 days	28 days
National 2000	£80 000	£152 000
Adshel 1000	£45 000	£50 000

National Solus Sites

	No. of Panels	Price/m
12 sheet display National	500	£80 000
16 sheet display National	1000	£65 000
32 sheet display National	650	£117 000
48 sheet display National	400	£128 000

(Price and number of sites available dependent on site location. Sites are throughout England, Wales and Scotland, Regional or National/TV regions.)

More O'Ferrall Ltd

	No. of panels	Cost/m
270 campaign: 2 campaigns covering (27ft × 10ft – 64)	500	£285 000
	(250 panels each campaign rotated after 15 days)	
National 96: (40ft × 10ft – 96)	2 campaigns covering 300 (150 panels each campaign rotated after 15 days)	£225 000
London 96 (40ft x 10ft – 96)	50	£100 000

Source: BRAD 1990 (March).

Transportation advertising (see Table 16.16) is a familiar aspect of our everyday lives which should not be overlooked when considering media selection. The general points made with regard to posters apply equally to transportation advertising, so that further description will be confined to a review of the sites available and the approximate costs associated with them.

TABLE 16.16   Transportation advertising

		Rate £/m
Bus sides		
LTA	T sides	115–175
British Transport Adv	T sides	155
Primesight	T sides	75–140.00
C.A.N.	T sides	90–125
London Underground sites		
Stations	4 sheets	50–55
	12 sheets	80–95
	16 sheets	120–150
	48 sheets	465–670
	Lifts and escalator panels	18–25
Trains	Tube-car panels	3–4.70
British Rail Station sites		
London terminal	4 sheets	£100
Intercity stations	4 sheets	£80
Other stations	4 sheets	£60
Contractor: British Transport Advertising		

Taxicabs	Rate: £/space	
	Interior	*Exterior*
Barker Taxi Media North	£.60–.80/wk	£4.85/wk
Cabvertising	16.25–33.75/m	£19.15–23.05/m
Louis Barnett & Sons Ltd	£4.50–5/m	£19–20/m
National Outdoor Adv (Taxi Division)	£4–8/m	£21–30/m

Source: BRAD 1990 (March).

■ The cinema

The impact of television on the cinema is readily apparent in any major town where former sites have been converted into bingo halls, warehouses or simply pulled down to make way for redevelopment. Although many may regret the passing of the local cinema and retain nostalgic memories of a 9d seat in the stalls, there can be no doubt that the competition of television has forced the cinema industry to undertake a massive face-lift. Cinema operators have realised that if they are to persuade customers to leave the comfort of their own fireside, and the hypnotic attraction of the 'box', they must make cinema-going an event. Despite the closure of many cinemas, many of which were themselves a mute reminder of the days of music-hall, there can be no doubt that the improvement and rebuilding programmes have greatly improved the standards of comfort offered to patrons. At the same time the film producers have concentrated on the competitive advantages which they possess, and which cannot be duplicated on the small screen – size and colour. The box office success of the James Bond films, and films like *Star Wars* and *Indiana Jones and the Temple of Doom* testify that the formula is a good one.

An examination of the composition of the cinema audience provides an interesting insight for the media planner.

Clearly, the Screen Advertisers Association's claim that it is the medium for reaching 'young adults' is justified by these statistics. This audience is of particular interest to the manufacturers of both semi-luxury goods, such as cosmetics, and consumer durables, appealing to single persons with high discretionary spending power, engaged couples and young marrieds.

Television can still offer a lower cost per thousand for the same audience but lacks the high attention value of a captive audience, viewing under ideal conditions over which the advertiser, not the viewer, has control, e.g. sound volume, quality of picture.

An indication of the cost of using the cinema for an advertising campaign may be judged from Table 16.17.

TABLE 16.17   Cinema advertising and audience composition

(i) Costs

ISBA Area	No. of screens	Weekly 30 secs	cost all screens 60 secs
		£	£
London	316	17 318	34 636
Southern	125	4 814	9 628
East of England	77	2 563	5 126
Midlands	197	7 586	15 172
Yorkshire	121	4 168	8 336

North East	61	2 112	4 224
Lancashire	163	4 865	9 730
Wales & West	122	3 376	6 752
Border	20	367	734
Central Scotland	94	4 239	8 478
Northern Scotland	26	705	1 410
Northern Ireland	33	992	1 984
Total	1 401	54 272	108 544

Source: BRAD, July 1989; CAA 1989.

(ii) Audience Delivery Plan

Cost per thousand admissions (30 seconds)

London/Southern	£29.30	All other areas	£21.50

Network average admissions 1.6 million per week

Source: Cinema Advertising Association September 1989.

(iii) Adult Audience Composition

	Average audience profile	UK population profile		Average audience profile	UK population profile
	%	%		%	%
Men	51	48	Class AB	26	18
Women	49	52	Class C1	30	23
Age 15–24	62	19	Class C2	26	28
Age 15–34	81	37	Class DE	18	31
Age 35 +	19	63			

Source: CAA/JICNARS, January–December 1988.

(iv) Coverage and Frequency (using all screens)

	8 weeks duration		16 weeks duration	
Target audience	% Cover	Av. OTS	% Cover	Av. OTS
Adults 15–24	33.7	2.1	46.6	3.1
Men 15–24	34.2	2.2	47.3	3.2
Adults 15–34	24.8	2.0	35.6	2.8
ABC1 15–34	32.6	2.0	45.7	2.8
Men 15–34	25.5	2.0	36.7	2.8
All adults 15–64	15.3	1.8	22.6	2.5

Source: CAA/JICNARS, January–December 1988. From *Marketing Pocket Book 1990*, NTC Publications: 0491–574671.

Advertisements are normally of 15, 30, 60 and 120 seconds in length. Actual rates vary by cinema and may be obtained from the Screen Advertising Association's master list of cinemas.

Although the cost per 1000 of using the cinemas is greater than for television the Screen Advertisers Association justifies this on the grounds that the cinema possesses undeniable qualitative advantages, particularly the combined impact of colour, sound, and the big-screen presentation upon a captive audience.

■ Direct mail

The great advantage of direct mail, by comparison with all other media, is its selectivity. Postal delivery is possible in every part of the country – a potential which enables the advertiser to reach a small, closely identified audience with a precision that could not possibly be duplicated by any other medium.

In the author's opinion direct mail is grossly underrated as an advertising medium, probably because of the dangers inherent in generalising from the particular. The common belief that the recipients of a direct mailing 'shot' immediately consign it to the waste-paper basket without a glance is not borne out by a recent American survey, which showed that approximately two-thirds do read the advertisement, and that more than 30 per cent subsequently make a purchase of the item advertised. Similar findings are reported by the British Market Research Bureau in its *Direct Mail Summary of Research*.

Direct mailing lists may be compiled by the advertiser himself from customer records, or from the same basic sources used by the direct mail house – classified telephone directories, trade directories, etc. Where it is intended to mount a campaign designed to increase one's market or to enter a new market, the cost would be disproportionate by comparison with the cost of 'buying' a list from a specialist direct mail house. (Lists are rarely sold as such – the rate quoted is for a mailing using the direct mail company's list.) The price of a direct mail shot depends upon the production costs of the items to be mailed and the size, volume, folding, inserting and labelling requirements of the mailing. In addition to the production charges, the postage must be paid and the Post Office offers discounts and incentives for direct mailers. Some statistics on direct mail advertising are given in Table 16.18 and a guide to planning a direct mail campaign suggested by the Royal Mail is given in Figure 16.5 (The Royal Mail is an excellent source of advice on the whole topic.)

As with other aspects of advertising, the employment of an agency is to be recommended owing to the specialisation which they can bring to bear on the advertiser's problem. Those direct mail shots which do finish up in the waste bin most frequently do so because of either incorrect identification of a 'prospect' or poor copy and layout. A good agency will not be guilty of either of these faults.

TABLE 16.18   Direct mail advertising – volume and expenditure

	1983	1984	1985	1986	1987	1988
Volume (millions of items)	1 084	1 262	1 303	1 401	1 626	1 766
Expenditure (£million)						
Production	187	203	301	325	300	326
Postage	112	121	144	149	183	204
Total	299	324	445	474	483	530
Total advertising expenditure all media excl. direct mail (£million)	3 579	4 059	4 441	5 117	5 781	6 731
Direct mail share of expenditure % of all media incl. direct mail	7.7	7.4	9.1	8.5	7.7	7.3

Source: Post Office.

On average a direct mailing will cost £250–£300 per thousand, which, when it is considered that three mailings is considered a desirable target to aim at, makes a campaign of any size an expensive undertaking. Against this must be set the precision with which potential customers may be reached by comparison with the lower costs of the 'buck shot' approach of the other media. A further advantage of direct mail is that its effectiveness can be measured directly, which, as a later section will show, is not the easiest of things to achieve. A summary of key areas to look for is provided by the Royal Mail's 'Planning a Direct Mail Campaign' as shown in Figure 16.5, on page 410.

An off-shoot of direct mail is door-to-door distribution of advertising material. Several companies offer this service for the distribution of samples, coupons and leaflets, utilising the services of part-time employees under the control and supervision of a full-time area supervisor, e.g. Vernon's Distributors. Rates vary, depending upon the nature of the material to be distributed, and the frequency, i.e. every house, every tenth house, etc. The Post Office will also deliver unaddressed mail to all 21 million UK homes.

■ Some other advertising media

The following list, on page 412, gives examples of other types of advertising media, and typical rates at November 1990.

Planning a Direct Mail campaign is a logical step-by-step process. Whether you are using a direct mail agency or mailing house, or doing it yourself, it is important to make sure you have built these steps into your plans . . .

Define your objectives.
What do you want your campaign to achieve?

Establish your budget.

Identify your target market.
What sort of people do you want to reach?

Select a mailing list or lists which match your target market.

Design the mailing package.
What should its components be? (Typically: envelope, letter, illustrated leaflet, reply device.)

Write the mailing package.
Speak directly to the addressee; make sure the tone of voice is appropriate to your target market.

Print/production.
Check that your creative designs can be produced within budget and on time.

Mailing.
The collation of all the components, addressing and posting. Check that you are using the most appropriate and cost-effective Royal Mail service for your needs.

Response and fulfilment.
Ensure you have laid on resources for handling response and fulfilling orders.

Analysis.
Check campaign results against your objectives. Any lessons to learn for future campaigns?

Analysis of results can be more or less sophisticated, depending on your resources and the complexity of your campaign. The important thing is to use your defined objectives as the benchmark for measuring your success.

Key areas to look at are as follows . . . .

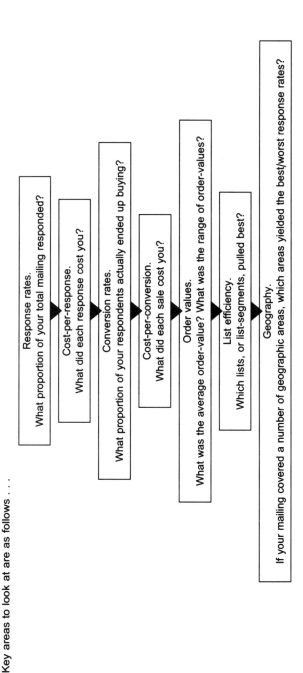

Collate all this information and you will have not only an accurate analysis of the success of your campaign but also a set of valuable planning data to apply to your next campaign.

Figure 16.5 How to plan a direct mail campaign

Some other advertising media

Media	Typical rates
Aerial advertising (aircraft-towed banners)	£250–£400 per hour
Book marks	£47 per 10 000
Local authority advertising	£15–30 per 1 000 with rate demand etc.
Matchboxes	From £54 per 1 000
Playing cards	£220 per 100 packs with single colour printed
Parking meter advertising	£140–£350 per 100 displays
Teleguide (telephone recordings)	Recruitment ads: £200–£400 per week
	Product ads: £190 per week
Travel wallets	£23 995 for 1m wallet advertisements
Hot air balloons (8 man)	£750 per day
Electronic outdoor advertising display	From £200 per 10 sec transmission per week
Lorry-side posters	£75 per side per month
Ships advertising	£44 per site per month (summer rates, Sealink I.o.W. service, double crown size)
Litter bins	£25 per panel per month (minimum 4 panels)
Advertee golf signs	£1 per week per tee (minimum of 6 tees)
Video tape publications	£1 852–£21 000 per minute
Video in Post Offices	£10 950 for 30 sec spot every 15 min over 5 weeks
Taxi cabs	Tip up seats from £3.50 per month, exteriors from £25 per month

Note: Other advertising media listed in *BRAD* include calendars, year planners, business cards, car blinds, milk bottles, sporting events, town maps, exhibition centres, airships, airports.

Source: Advertising Association.

■ Campaign planning

An excellent treatment of this subject used to be available in Olaf Ellefsen's *Campaign Planning* published by Business Publications on behalf of the IPA but, sadly, this is now out of print. No suitable substitute has been identified and the following notes will have to suffice until a fuller treatment becomes available.

Earlier in the chapter a number of advertising objectives were stated, and it was noted that the determination of such an objective was an essential prerequisite to the formulation of a campaign plan. Assuming that management has given its advertising agency a clear statement of what it wishes to achieve, it then becomes the agency's responsibility to devise a campaign that will maximise the return on the appropriation allocated. As was inferred when discussing the agency/client relationship, the preparation of a campaign plan will require close co-operation between the parties. This will become clear if one considers the stages leading up to the introduction of a new product.

The first stage in the process is the recognition of a business opportunity. Once this has been identified, the marketer will undertake marketing research as a basis for quantifying the nature and extent of this opportunity. As a result of such research a consumer profile will be drawn up stating the demographic characteristics of the potential consumer, the geographical location of the market, the frequency and method of purchase, etc.

Armed with this 'blueprint' of the intended consumer, the next stage in the process is the development of a product to satisfy the demand represented by recognition of the original opportunity. Once developed, the product will be tested. It is at this stage that the agency should be brought in. Given the consumer profile, the nature of the product and a statement of the features which differentiate it from competitors' offerings, the proposed channels of distribution and intended price bracket, the agency will be in a position to suggest an appropriate name and package. The continued growth of self-service retailing, described in Chapter 9, demands that very careful attention be paid to the latter two factors (name and package), as recognition at the point of sale is a vital stimulus to purchase. For these reasons alone the advertiser will want to feature both the brand name and pack in his advertising. If concept and product testing have been carried out the comments of the respondents should also be made available to the agency, as they invariably provide leads as to the copy platform to be adopted. A good example of this was Johnson's Wax in the United States. When housewives were asked to list the most important properties of a floor polish, the majority gave considerable weight to the polish's ability to resist scuffing. Although 'scuffing' was not a word in common currency, the panel housewives had independently selected it as the most descriptive. When Johnson introduced their new brand it was advertised as the 'non-scuff' polish and achieved immediate success – it was just what housewives were looking for!

A further reason for bringing in the agency at this time is to discuss the method of launching the product – test market, regional or national launch – and the timing, from selling in to the channels of distribution to the product's appearance in the retail outlet. On the basis of all this information, the agency will draw up a plan for submission to the advertiser comprising two major elements – the copy platform and the media schedule.

The copy platform is the theme around which the campaign is based, e.g. 'It's the real thing. Coke', while the media schedule lists the media in which the advertisements are to be published with details of size, timing, frequency and cost. The advertising literature is full of advice on the selection of USPs (unique selling points), EBTs (emotional buying triggers) and the like, but for an insight into the preparation and execution of advertising campaigns the student is strongly recommended to read one, or all, of the following books: David Ogilvy, *Confessions of an Advertising Man*: a highly readable and somewhat unconventional description of how Ogilvy became one of America's top advertising men, packed with information and advice for the aspiring advertising agent; and his more recent book *Ogilvy on Advertising*; Rosser Reeves, *Reality in Advertising*: a short but highly concentrated coverage of do's and don't's in advertising, full of actual examples of advertising campaigns; Martin Mayer, *Madison Avenue*: a colourful and interesting description of what goes on at the heart of the US agency business, a little dated now but still worth reading.

■ Setting the advertising appropriation

The decision of how much to spend on advertising and other promotional activities is one of the more difficult budgeting problems that management is called upon to make. As will become clear in the next part of this chapter, the measurement of advertising effectiveness is, to say the least, difficult. In the absence of a directly measurable relationship between the volume of advertising and the overall profitability of the firm, the majority of managements have adopted one, or a combination, of the following 'rule-of-thumb' approaches.

Fixed percentage of sales. Under this method management allocates a percentage of either past or anticipated sales to advertising. A BIM *Survey of Manufacturers' Marketing Costs* (Information Summary No. 111) published in 1964 indicated that there is a considerable variation in the percentage allocated to advertising, even within an industry, which, in turn, is a reflection of the different competitive strategies adopted by marketers. Although dated, this observation is equally true in 1991 as it was in 1964. In this context it is noteworthy that total expenditures on advertising have remained a virtually constant percentage of the GNP in most advanced economies during this century.

Adoption of this policy may be justified on the grounds that it is rational to allocate a fixed proportion of sales revenue to advertising in the absence of a model which permits a prediction of variation in sales volume in response to variations in the volume of advertising. On the other hand, it ignores the fact that a decline in sales volume will result in a contraction of the advertising appropriation at the very time when increased advertising may be the stimulus necessary to halt the decline or reverse the trend.

In the case of companies operating in markets with an inelastic demand, the policy helps stabilise the competitive situation, always providing that it is a commonly accepted practice. Certain oligopolistic industries appear to exhibit this characteristic – the knowledge that increased advertising will not result in an increase in primary demand dissuades individual firms from attempting to improve their market share through increased advertising owing to the strong competitive response which it is bound to provoke. (This tendency was also noted with regard to the use of price reductions as a competitive weapon, unless the instigator had a clear cost advantage over his competitors.)

The 'me-too' approach. The adoption of this 'policy' was implied above, and constitutes the adoption of a level of advertising which corresponds to that of one's competitors. This is a purely defensive and negative reaction. Clearly, the firm is interested in what its competitors are doing as a guide to the policies it should adopt, but it also follows that if the firm is to improve its competitive position it must pursue policies that will enable the consumer to distinguish it from the competition and perceive it as superior.

TABLE 16.19 Method used to set advertising budgets' frequency

Method used	Regularly (%)	Tried it (%)	Heard of but not used (%)	Never heard of or no reply (%)
1. Percentage of expected sales	38.4	15.7	21.2	24.8
2. Match competition	8.3	15.5	39.8	36.4
3. What we can afford	48.5	16.6	10.8	24.2
4. Desired share of voice	11.4	12.0	27.8	48.7
5. Objective and task	39.8	13.4	15.0	31.9
6. Accept agency proposal	4.2	19.9	35.4	40.5
7. Experimentation and testing	13.6	20.9	28.5	37.1

Source: G. J. Hooley, C. J. West and J. E. Lynch, *Marketing in the UK: A Survey of Current Practice and Performance*, Institute of Marketing, 1983.

What we can afford. This method tends to relegate expenditures on advertising to the bottom rung of the corporate budget ladder. It implies that whatever remains after-meeting operating costs, dividend payments, etc., will be spent on advertising. As with the fixed percentage of sales method, the most likely outcome is that as sales fall the unit contribution will decline to the point where no advertising can be afforded at all. Conversely, as sales rise an increasing amount will become available and the possibility of wasteful expenditures will become a reality.

The 'task' approach. In the absence of a normative model of the relationship between various levels of advertising and profitability, this method is to be preferred to any of the above practices. The first step in this method is the definition of a clear objective. Given the objective, one can prepare a campaign plan that would achieve this goal. An examination of the costs of mounting such a campaign may indicate that it is beyond the company's available resources. Within this constraint, the plan may be modified by closely evaluating each of its component parts and dispensing with the least essential. Obviously the end result will be a lesser objective than originally laid down, but it will be a realistic statement of what the firm can hope to accomplish related to current resources.

The BIM *Survey of Marketing Organisation in British Industry* (Information Summary 148) indicated that the respondents used the following basis for determining their advertising appropriations.

	%
Proportion of expected future sales	39
Analysis of needs or objectives	19
Proportion of past sales	11
Proportion of profit	7
Historical expenditure	2
As much as can be afforded	1

Table 16.19 reports the findings of the survey undertaken by Hooley, West and Lynch on behalf of the Institute of Marketing (1983) into methods of setting the advertising appropriation. More recently (*The Marketing Book*, 1991) Crosier has reported that analysis of a number of surveys in the UK and USA between 1970 and 1985 indicates that on average 44 per cent of companies based their spend on actual or projected sales, 21 per cent used judgement ('all you can afford', 'notional sum', 'arbitrary method', 'affordable approach' etc.), 18 per cent used a task approach with all other methods accounting for the remaining 17 per cent.

■ The measurement of advertising effectiveness

When discussing media selection, frequent reference was made to *BRAD* and the IPA Readership Surveys as a source of information on audience composition. Head counting is a long-established practice that yields sound demographic data. A measure of audience size is of interest to the advertiser but, ultimately, he is much more concerned with the effectiveness of his advertising, i.e. he wants a measure of the results of exposure to advertising. Five basic methods have been evolved to measure advertising effectiveness and these are reviewed below.

The measurement of awareness. Awareness is defined as 'knowledge about a company or its product without reference to the source of knowledge'. As, by definition, awareness tests do not relate knowledge to source they provide only a rough and ready guide to advertising effectiveness, and are usually undertaken as a preliminary to further tests. In the case of a new product it may be possible to isolate the source of awareness, but this is virtually impossible in the case of an established brand.

Actual measurement is obtained by asking respondents:

(a) Straight dichotomous questions, e.g. Have you ever heard of the XYZ company?'

Yes . . . No . . .

(*b*) An open-ended question, e.g. 'Do you know of any companies that make a detergent with a blue whitener?'

(*c*) Check-list questions with rating scales, e.g. 'How familiar are you with the XYZ company?'

> Very familiar . . .
> Know something about . . .
> Know very little about them . . .
> Never heard of . . .

Low cost and speed are cited as the major advantages of this method.

The measurement of recall. Recall – what people can remember about advertising messages – is the most frequently used measure of advertising effectiveness, on the basis that if. the message has left a memorable impression it has fulfilled its communicative function. If the advertising objective is to communicate information then the method is appropriate, but in many instances the objective is to promote action, e.g. mail-order advertisements. Recall is also a useful measure when copy testing.

Recall studies are capable of measuring several dimensions of advertising effectiveness. At the lowest level they consist of the respondent's describing the basic theme of an advertisement, and progress through association of the correct theme with the product advertised, measures of comprehension, credibility and conviction, to significance.

Essentially, the method employed is to ask the respondent to reconstruct what he or she can remember having seen or heard advertised, either unaided – unaided recall – or with a varying degree of assistance to direct the respondent's thinking along particular lines – aided recall. Aided recall is generally preferred, as few people will spontaneously recall past events without some stimulus, in which case the researcher must guard against bias arising from too much assistance, or false answers resulting from guessing. Gallup and Robinson conduct regular surveys of recall, and attempt to minimise bias by first establishing that the respondent has read the issue being tested by showing him the cover, and then asking him to establish knowledge of its content. Once the respondent has demonstrated familiarity with the test issue, he is then asked to reconstruct his memory of the advertisements without opening the magazine. The final stage is to show the respondent brand names, advertisement logotypes, etc., and after telling him that some did not appear in the issue in question, ask him to identify those he remembers. A sample of 400 is used, the interviews are recorded verbatim and, after editing, are compiled into an index of recall – the 'proved name registration'. A PNR is calculated for the medium as a whole, for the product group and for the specific brand. Although it is difficult to assign an absolute value to a PNR, it provides a useful guide to the advertiser in that he can measure his advertisement's performance against that of all other advertisers in the magazine and that of his immediate competitors. Further, over a period of time he can determine whether the impact of his advertising is increasing, declining or static.

A hybrid test which incorporates both aided and unaided recall is 'working along the time line'. For example you ask a respondent to describe what he did yesterday evening, anticipating that he will recall an event which involved consumption of a product in which you are interested. If the product group is mentioned, e.g. 'I washed, cleaned my teeth and went to bed,' you might ask the name of the brand of soap or toothpaste and lead into further questions related to these products. If the product group is not mentioned then the interviewer will ask directly 'Did you clean your teeth?', etc.

Three problems are inherent in all recall studies:

1. Respondent confusion, due to either confusing the advertisement and its sponsor – Kellogg's Puffed Wheat – or identifying advertisements correctly from recollections of previous campaigns.
2. Recall of advertising messages in the interview situation is not the same as recall at the point of sale (a strong argument for both poster advertising and POS display), nor does it indicate an intention to buy.
3. The ever-present danger of misinterpretation of the results.

For the two latter reasons recall investigations are often combined with:

Attitude surveys. A favourable attitude towards a company or its product nearly always precedes a decision to buy, even if this favourable predisposition is at the preconscious level, i.e. a consumer picks up a product on impulse without consciously identifying the motivation to purchase.

Attitude measurement may consist of a general assessment or be restricted to various dimensions of a specific brand – acceptance, preference or insistence – of either one's own or one's competitor's product. Unfortunately, it is difficult to construct a true measure of a person's attitudes, and several techniques are frequently used in combination to permit cross-checking. The more common methods are:

(a) Direct questions of the 'Do you like X?' type, followed by a request to explain why you do, or do not, like X. Direct questions suffer from their inability to distinguish between varying degrees of intensity of feeling. Rating scales provide a partial solution and are amenable to rapid analysis, but suffer from the disadvantage that the choice of phrases which are precise, yet universally understood, is extremely difficult; that, however large, the scale may still not permit a truly accurate expression of intensity of feeling; that intermediate positions are capable of varying interpretation, e.g. 'What is your attitude to Widgets?'

Favourable . . .
Mixed . . .
Indifferent . . .
Unfavourable . . .

Alternatively, one might use the scale: Excellent, 4,3,2, Poor, or even a seven-or ten-point scale.

(b) A second method is to ask the respondent to complete a checklist by indicating the most appropriate answer/description of those assigned to each question. By undertaking a preliminary survey it is usually possible to design questions that will cover the attributes which consumers, as opposed to advertisers, think important.

(c) A semantic differential test, in which a respondent indicates where a brand or company stands on a scale of paired opposites, either descriptive adjectives or phrases, e.g. reliable–unreliable.

(d) Partially structured interviews, in which the interviewer memorises the points to be covered and 'discusses' the subject with the respondent, rather than posing formal questions from a questionnaire. The lack of trained interviewers, the length of the interview and difficulties of interpretation severely limit the use of this method.

Attitude related to usage is usually considered a more significant measure of advertising effectiveness than attitude on its own, and it is usual to obtain a measure of usage as a basis for a comparison of attitudes.

Psychological measurement. The three techniques described above are designed to measure a respondent's reaction to advertising at the conscious or preconscious level. Psychological techniques are designed to probe deeper and reach to the subconscious mind. At this level the respondent is unaware of the reasons which result in certain expressed patterns of behaviour, although if asked, he will usually advance an acceptable and rational reason. As most advertising messages are directed at large audiences, the peculiarities of the individual are of little or no consequence unless they are common to a large number of individuals. It is to determine basic motivation that advertising researchers, among others, use psychological methods where direct questioning might lead to rationalisation or evasion.

Psychological techniques have limitations which require great care in their execution and interpretation, and it must be recognised that the results will be qualitative not quantitative. As noted above in regard to partially structured depth interviews, the lack of suitably qualified interviewers usually restricts the use of these techniques to small samples from which it is difficult to make acceptable projections of consumer behaviour.

The most frequently used method is the unstructured depth interview of from one to three hours, in which interviewer and respondent talk about a specific subject in the belief that if the respondent is kept talking about the same thing long enough some of his unconscious attitudes will begin to emerge.

A popular variation of the depth interview is the focused or directed group interview, in which a skilled interviewer leads a group of six to twelve people in an unstructured discussion that relates to the product and/or its advertising.

Other projective techniques used include thematic apperception tests, picture probes, narrative probes, sentence completion tests and word association tests.

Sort and count. Many advertisements contain an invitation to interested parties to write in to the advertiser for further information, free samples, etc. By sorting and counting the requests generated by such advertisements the advertiser can obtain much useful information at low cost.

Despite the potential bias due to respondent self-selection, this method does give valuable information in relative terms of the pulling power of different media, of different copy platforms and advertisement make-up, and of different sizes and positions within the media. The advertisements are usually keyed, i.e. given a coding, to assist identification, either by including the code in the address, e.g. Dept DM7 for an edition of the *Daily Mail*, or by requiring the respondent to clip the coupon on which the information is similarly recorded.

As mentioned by Ogilvy (in *Confessions of an Advertising Man*), direct mail advertisers have a continuous feedback of the pulling power of their advertisements, which supports his suggestion that those selling though more conventional channels might do well to adopt some of the former's advertising practices, e.g. use of long copy.

Others. Under this heading are a number of techniques which attempt to measure a causal relationship between advertising and measurable indicators of the firm's performance such as increased distribution (on the premise that if retailers are asked for goods not in stock they will seek supplies) or sales volume. The 'dealer playback' technique also deserves mention, and has been used by Black & Decker in a competition designed to increase sales push at the retail level. (Company representatives visit stores selling the goods in question, express an interest in them, and note the number of selling points suggested in their recent advertising that the salesman advances as a reason for purchase.)

In May 1990 AGB announced a new development in measuring advertising effectiveness and claims that it can demonstrate not only whether a particular TV campaign has worked, but which viewers bought more products as a result of the advertising and how the budget should be deployed to bring the best sales results (*Marketing Week* 1 June 1990). AGB's claim is based on the use of a technique called *data fusion* which involves the integration of two existing data sources. Ideally the answer to many research questions is to use single source data in which a representative sample of consumers can be surveyed in terms of their purchasing behaviour related to their reading, viewing and listening habits. However, attempts by Central Adlab and Neilsen and HTV's Statscan to set up sufficiently large panels to provide such data proved to be prohibitively expensive and had to be abandoned.

To overcome this problem BMRB launched its Target Group Ratings service in April 1990 which is based on the fusion of TGI which measures product usage, and BARB which measures viewing. The aim of Target Group Ratings is to enable advertising agencies to plan campaigns more accurately by selecting programmes watched by the users of their products rather than more broadly defined demographic groups. However, the AGB service differs in that its primary purpose is to aid campaign evaluation by quantifying the effect of advertising on sales. The AGB method also uses BARB data but fuses it with information from its own TCA panel which measures product purchases in 6500 homes. *Marketing Week* reported:

> By developing a computer model of TV viewing behaviour, based on the individual viewing patterns of housewives on the BARB panel, AGB can now predict when an individual housewife on the TCA panel is likely to be watching ITV or Channel 4. From this it can work out the number of times she is likely to have seen a particular commercial.
> The model depends on certain key demographic characteristics and viewing claims, such as the fact that non-working women are much more likely to watch TV during the day than those who are out at work.

In a test on a new fmcg the fusion model showed that among heavy viewers who saw a commercial an average of 8.6 times their purchases increased by 44 per cent compared with an increase of only 29 per cent by light viewers who saw the commercial on average 2.7 times during the campaign. The analysis also showed that advertising primarily increased trial of the brand and sales to occasional buyers rather than increasing the purchase rate of regular buyers demonstrating that the ads were much more effective with some demographic groups than others.

Clearly such results are very promising but, as *Marketing Week* cautions, they also depend heavily on the judgement and integrity of the researcher. Only when sufficient case histories are available will we be able to assess fully the potential of data fusion as a means of both campaign planning and measuring advertising effectiveness by merging existing databases.

Laboratory techniques for pre-testing advertisements

A number of techniques have been developed to try and obtain an objective measure of people's response to advertisements, which interviewing methods are unable to elicit owing to an inability to verbalise or a tendency to rationalise. The use of the instruments listed below is based on the knowledge that emotional arousal in a human being results in various responses which are under the control of the autonomic nervous system and thus largely independent of conscious control. These responses include increases in pulse and respiration rates, erection of hair follicles, changes in pupil size and electrical brain pulses, perspiration rates, etc. As each person reacts to different stimuli to a varying degree, ideally one should measure all responses simultaneously, but this is clearly impossible under normal conditions. As such it is necessary to select the method(s) which provide the most reliable results in monitoring reactions to the specific variable under test with the minimum disturbance to the subject. The most frequently used are:

(a) *The psycho-galvanometer.* This instrument measures changes in the activity of the sweat glands via electrodes attached by suction to the subject's hands. Prior to exposing the subject to the test advertisements the basal level must be established for control purposes and care taken to maintain a constant temperature throughout the test. The highest reading recorded indicates maximum arousal.

(b) *The eye observation camera* is used to measure pupil dilation. As light also affects the pupil, care must be taken to ensure that both control and test material are of the same luminosity. The material to be tested is back-projected into a closed box while the camera records the pupil dilation over a period of time. The greatest change occurs with the highest level of arousal. The camera may also be used to measure the subject's blink rate – the higher the rate the greater the arousal. Blinking is partly under conscious control, and is also affected by humidity, irritation and fatigue, all of which must be controlled if an accurate measure is to be obtained.

(c) *The tachistoscope* is an instrument used for exposing material for controlled periods of time ranging from $\frac{1}{100}$ of a second to several seconds. Its main use is in measuring the impact of an advertisement by determining either the point at which its features are registered (noting and legibility studies) or its visual impact (what is communicated) when exposed for only a brief period. As individual 'thresholds' vary, a norm must first be established for each subject.

(d) *The eye-movement camera* tracks the movement of the eye over an advertisement by filming a point of light projected on to the eyeball. The track indicates the order and degree of attention given to the features of the advertisement.

All the above methods are subject to criticism on the grounds that they are unrealistic as a result of the laboratory situation; that only a limited number of respondents may be tested (owing to the high cost of the test and data processing equipment required), and these may not be representative; that no indication of the direction of the response is given, so that respondents have to be questioned as to their feelings, which reintroduces subjectivity into the test, i.e. a marked reaction may be due to either repulsion or attraction.

In mitigation, any test is better than no test if it helps in establishing whether or not advertisements are communicating their basic point to the subject. Further, it is only through experimentation that satisfactory techniques for measuring advertising effectiveness will be evolved.

■ Advertising case histories

An excellent series of case histories of different advertising campaigns is available from ITCA, 56 Mortimer Street, London W1, and two of these are reproduced below with their kind permission. (*Campaign, Ad Weekly and Marketing* also publish such case histories on a regular basis.)

An increasing number of retail advertisers are now putting greater emphasis on the strategic use of television advertising to achieve corporate long-term objectives compared to those using the medium to communicate short-term tactical price promotions. Argos successfully combined the two as this case study demonstrates.

■ Argos

Argos is a wholly owned subsidiary of BAT Industries and is managed by the BAT Stores division which also takes in International Supermarkets and Jewellers Guild. BAT acquired Argos, which was part of the Green Shield operation, in 1979. At that time the chain comprised just 17 showrooms; today and expanding at an annual rate of 15–20 units, there are over 140, with an annual turnover in excess of £300 million at retail selling prices (rsp). The Argos concept of catalogue/showroom retailing is unique in the UK and originates from North America where it has operated successfully for many years. It comprises catalogue browsing in the showroom and/or home, merchandise display in the high street, filling in a purchase selection form and then payment/collection in the showroom.

■ The market

The total value of retail sales in the 25 plus markets in which Argos currently operates is worth around £1000 million rsp (source: AGB). These markets include electricals excluding white goods (Argos has significant penetration of kitchen, domestic and personal electrical appliances) ; also toys where Argos with around 5 per cent of the market shares leadership with Woolworths; garden equipment and furniture; and jewellery where, in a fragmented market, Argos has 3 per cent penetration and is thought to be one of the most important named retailers. Penetration by Argos varies, according to AGB between 1 per cent and 13 per cent sterling in the 25 markets covered with around 2 per cent in total of all the markets in which it competes; the showrooms stock around 2800 individual lines in all.

Competing with a wide diversity of other retailers due to the broad range of products stocked, Argos offers a distinctive means of shopping and a very competitive price proposition. Bulk buying in branded goods and efficient modern systems of retailing produce resources that give prices comparable with if not lower than the specialist chains as well as the department and superstores. The Argos system means minimum shop assistants, optimum merchandise display and computerised stock control, the economics of which are passed back to the consumer in the form of lower prices. The prime vehicle for communicating the broad choice of products available is the catalogue backed up by showroom displays.

■ Developing a long-term strategy

In just over 10 years Argos grew from virtually nothing to a massive multiple chain and an enormous amount of research has gone into evaluating and improving the showrooms, the catalogue, the shop locations (via Acorn data in particular) and in communication. The chain has become mass market but in consumer perception is perceived to be more down market and discount than is in fact the case. Consumer research confirmed that this was an inhibiting factor in what otherwise would have given Argos even greater market penetration and in the longer term, with continuing competitive improvements, was a problem which needed to be resolved to ensure long term prosperity.

At the same time the company needed to, each year, re-launch the catalogue to ensure that it reached the maximum number of potential customers and also to ensure maximum awareness and current use. In this form of retailing, catalogue awareness and usage are the keys to offtake; passing traffic and window shopping following Argos research confirmed that 80 per cent of Argos purchases were decided before the consumer entered the showroom but that only just under half of the people in possession of a catalogue were actually persuaded to buy.

Over the last five years, the company's activity has tended to be promotional rather than strategic, comprising press advertising of the catalogue linked with price promotion and accurately targeted catalogue door to door distribution involving around 21 million households. Whilst tactically delivering short term results, this promotion was not providing any longer term benefits in terms of attitude shifts; furthermore the mechanics of printing and distributing the extra millions of catalogues were becoming cumbersome to the degree that it was seriously inhibiting marketing, pricing, product buying and stock control since the time pressure and lead times were considerable. The increasing size of the chain compounded the problem.

The company decided that it simply needed to improve attitudes as fast as it possibly could to take advantage of the rapidly growing markets in which it operated and also to combat an increasingly competitive number of high street retailers which were also beginning to diversify and specialise. To do this it needed to increase familiarity of the Argos shopping concept through advertising and first hand experience. The key was to increase awareness and usage of the catalogue but at the same time to promote more positively the concept of catalogue shopping. The decision was made in 1983 to use television in a big way to achieve both a tactical and immediate offtake of catalogues as well as a strategic change of attitudes.

■ Why television

Television was chosen by Argos and their agency Chetwynd Haddons because creatively it provided the opportunity to humanise through gentle humour the rather clinical and unusual nature of the store, but at the same time had a proven track record in delivering immediate sales offtake (in this case the object was catalogue uptake). The other reasons for choosing television were as follows:

- the facility to test and to weight the advertising according to areas of sales strength;
- the opportunity to, in effect, place the catalogue in the actual home of the potential customer;
- the greater prestige that using television imparts, which was important to Argos in combatting the second division high street retailer image that they had among many people;
- and last but not least television could counter criticism of inertia selling often levelled at door to door distribution.

■ Advertising objectives

1. To maximise offtake of the new Argos catalogue.
2. To improve attitudes and imagery towards the Argos system of high street shopping.
3. To penetrate the wide non-user and aware visitor to Argos.

■ The commercials

Four 20-second commercials were developed by Chetwynd Haddons and as a result of pre-testing three were finally chosen to run. Announcing the catalogue in a humorous,' slightly anti-establishment way, the commercials succeeded also in communicating the two key customer benefits of convenience and economy. Through situations in a courtroom, a government department and a hospital outpatients, the commercials invited people to get their catalogue from Argos showrooms; the whole campaign was summed up in the line: 'You can't put a good book down'.

The campaign was tested in Central and Anglia from August 15 to September 11 1983; in Central the campaign achieved 81 per cent housewife coverage and 5.9 opportunities to see (OTS) ; in Anglia the comparable figures were 86 per cent and 7.5 OTS. In Spring 1984 the test was extended to London, all three areas accounting for around 50 per cent of Argos sales. The ratecard spend in Spring 1984 was over £250 000.

■ Campaign results

● In strictly controlled measurement conditions, there was a 33 per cent increase in catalogue up-take in the areas carrying television advertising compared to those not receiving TV. This success was achieved in Autumn 1983 and repeated in Spring 1984.
● £ sales in the television areas were up between 20 to 30 per cent on the previous year compared to a 10–15 per cent increase in the areas without television support.
● Well after the television advertising had finished, the plateau of sales was significantly up on the preceding year and higher than in those areas without television advertising. These extra sales were achieved profitably since no additional price promotion was used in the TV areas.
● Pre- and post-awareness and attitude research showed a sharp increase in awareness and a significant increase in the numbers of catalogue-aware potential customers intending to purchase.

■ The future

In the light of these results, Argos have extended the campaign to all areas in Autumn 1984 with a ratecard spend in excess of £1 million. According to Stuart Colley, marketing manager, Argos 'Television has provided a better opportunity in return on investment than alternative promotional activity and as a result we are looking to expand our investment in the medium into 1985. We are particularly pleased with the strategic possibilities of the medium which the campaign has proved can be achieved at the same time as meeting immediate tactical objectives. Its intrusiveness and ability to convert inertia into energy has been aptly demonstrated for us at Argos!' The success of this strategy is confirmed by its continuing use into the 1990s.

■ Swatch Quartz

Characterised by falling unit prices, the UK watch market remained almost static in volume during the late 1970s and early 1980s, declining in real value by between 20 and 30 per cent. During this period Japanese brands dominated the market. It is all the more remarkable, therefore, that a unique concept of a watch from Switzerland has achieved sales in excess of £12 million at retail selling prices (rsp) in just 18 months. Branded 'Swatch', the product was launched solely on ITV and Channel 4 opening up, as this case study demonstrates, an entirely new sector of the market.

■ Louis Newmark

Louis Newmark Limited was founded in the 1880s as an importer of quality Swiss watches and clocks, and soon established a strong position in the UK market. It has always enjoyed a strong working relationship with the Swiss watch industry and, in 1981, it acquired the rights to the Avia name, a brand which it had marketed since the 1920s. The decision to appoint Louis Newmark to market Swatch was therefore to be expected.

Today, Louis Newmark has diversified into a wide range of technological fields, encompassing the Aircraft division, which manufactures the flight control systems for the Sea King Helicopters and Hawk fighter aircraft; and the subsidiary company McMurdo which manufactures the safety lights used by all the world's major airlines. The combined turnover of the company is now 30 million per annum.

■ The UK watch market

According to Louis Newmark, around 11 million watches were sold in the UK in 1983, worth in excess of £200 million rsp. This excludes very cheap watches selling below £5 which are estimated to account for a further 2 or 3 million units. (This market is notoriously difficult to quantify because of variations in trade mark-ups; all figures are therefore approximate.) Unit growth has been healthy but due to dramatic falls in the average price following the introduction of new technology, the value of the market has remained almost static. By price, the market segments as follows: £5–25 (65 per cent); £25–60 (30 per cent) ; and over £60 (5 per cent) – source: Louis Newmark.

Traditional buying patterns have been upset by both the frequency of product innovation, although in recent years the market has returned to the traditional analogue style pioneered by the Swiss, and changes in the nature of distribution.

Worldwide, the Swiss watch industry has witnessed a decline in volume, with its retention of the traditional movement in the face of intense Japanese competition; only in the premium sector did the traditional qualities of the Swiss industry ensure a dominant hold on the world market.

The watch market has also undergone a dramatic change in the nature of retail distribution. The strength of the long-established traditional jeweller has been progressively eroded by the opening up of non-traditional stockists, including departmental stores, W H Smith, Boots, Underwoods, Dixons and others which have taken a substantial slice of the market, particularly at the cheaper end. This has been paralleled by the growth of the mail order business and outlets such as Argos and the other discount operators, who have similarly established large shares at the cheaper end of the market.

■ Swatch – creating a new market sector

Swatch is the direct result of intense research and development carried out by ETA, the Swiss watch industry group and represents a major product breakthrough. Although retailing at less than £20, it provides the consumer with similar technology found in the very expensive Swatch 'Delerium' which sells at over £3000.

In essence, Swatch is based on a solid case into which the movement is built and sealed with the dial and glass, providing the consumer with a totally shock- and water-resistant product. The combination of high technology, durability and fashionable appearance at a low unit cost positions Swatch uniquely in the watch market.

Louis Newmark and their agency Shackle Hanmer commissioned a series of research studies to establish the most effective UK launch strategy in terms of positioning, targeting and communication. Initially available only in a man's version, the product benefits highlighted by research indicated a major opportunity for Swatch amongst the younger (aged under 35) watch purchasers, both male and female who pursued an active lifestyle, or at least believed that they did.

In this respect, one important feature emerged. It was not essential for the target group to actually have participated in any of the activities featured, but rather that they 'felt' they participated. The term vicarious participation might be most properly applied because many potential consumers felt they were actually involved in a sport by virtue of following it on television or elsewhere.

The product was seen as being particularly appropriate for sporting and other outdoor pursuits, yet was equally suited for wearing on fashionable occasions. Research also indicated that Swatch would have a particular appeal during the summer months, which was significant, since some 60 per cent of watch sales occur in the last week before Christmas.

■ Television – an essential element of the launch

Television was seen as essential to the successful launch of Swatch for the following reasons:

- Research amongst both 'traditional' and 'new' watch retailers showed that the trade felt television was essential to generate the immediacy of awareness and high speed offtake that they required from a watch priced at under £20;
- the trade referred to the success of Japanese watches launched on television as well as many consumer durables with which they were familiar;
- television provided the benefit of colour – vital to a product range which was differentiated essentially in terms of colour and features;
- and, most important of all, television provided the facility for movement, vital to ensure the effective demonstration of the key product benefits.

The decision was made to test market in one area and then progressively roll out across the country. No other advertising medium was used.

■ Advertising objective

To create awareness of Swatch amongst the prime target audience of all adults aged 25 or over as a unique form of watch combining fashion and durability.

■ The commercial

The 30-second launch commercial utilised a quick-cut still treatment to demonstrate the watch being used in a series of energetic sporting situations by young people with whom consumers could identify. Although shot on location in the USA, the treatment proved very economical as well as effective, the high beat music track helping to pull the fast-changing frames together into one communication.

This unusual execution compared to other advertising in the watch market aided recall and impact. A 10-second version supplemented the initial 30-second launch commercial; in year two the treatment was extended to include women (for the launch of the ladies version of Swatch) which demanded a greater emphasis on fashion, and to suggest a change of season. Again the music, lifestyle and situations featured were chosen only after a considerable amount of qualitative research.

■ Summer campaign

The launch campaign in the Summer of 1983 commenced on Central TV in June and rolled out to include Granada and London (LWT and Thames) during the latter part of the month, and July. The agency took full advantage of the available discounts to purchase an effective £723 000 rate card expenditure.

The initial campaign on four ITV stations achieved 241 adult ratings producing 79 per cent coverage and 5.3 opportunities to see (OTS) ; Channel 4 was used to help build coverage and frequency of the under 35s in particular.

The campaign was extended pre-Christmas, using the same commercials in 30- and 10-second time lengths, and with the addition of STV, Tyne Tees and additional spots on TV am. In 1984 advertising for Swatch was totally national running throughout June and July and planned for pre-Christmas.

■ Campaign results

● In 18 months Swatch achieved sales of £12 million rsp, exceeding all sales targets by a considerable margin. Thus in 1983 150 000 units were sold against a target of 50 000; in 1984 the target is 500 000 units and already Swatch looks set to exceed this. In 1983 sales in areas with television were 300 per cent up on those without.

● Distribution targets have been vastly exceeded and the brand is generally recognised to have received unparalleled trade support in such a short period of time. Every major multiple jeweller, the majority of independents, most department stores, W H Smiths, Dixons, Underwoods, Duty Free shops, even some airlines, are currently stocking Swatch.

● These results have been achieved profitably and without recourse to price cutting. Furthermore, sales have maintained their high volume long after television advertising was halted, each new burst of TV moving the sales growth even higher.

■ The future

Ted Day, managing director of Louis Newmark Limited Watch Division, states 'Swatch is the most significant development in the UK watch industry for 5 years and we confidently predict the brand will sell three quarters of a million units worth £15 million rsp next year. Television has been the major factor in this success and 90 per cent of an increased budget will be deployed in the medium in 1985'. In 1991 Swatch is firmly established as a major and distinctive brand in the watch market.

■ Economic and ethical aspects of advertising

The above review of advertising has concentrated on the practical aspects of the subject in so far as they affect the marketer. At the same time one must be aware that advertising is frequently the subject of criticism, and the aim of this section is to summarise the arguments both for and against. In view of the author's interest in marketing it follows that he has a favourable attitude towards advertising, and the reader is warned that this treatment is bound to be somewhat subjective.

The economic argument. Essentially the question is 'Is advertising productive in the economic sense, i.e. does it maximise satisfaction through the utilisation of scarce resources?' The cliché 'It pays to advertise' is tacit recognition of the fact that advertising improves the profitability of the advertiser, but this is not to say that it necessarily makes any real contribution to the welfare of the community as a whole.

From the economist's point of view, the acid test of any economic activity is the utility of the output of that activity, which is measured by the extent to which it satisfies wants. For the economist the difficulty of accepting that advertising creates utility in this sense is both semantic and conceptual. The economist would argue that rather than satisfy existing wants the advertiser seeks to create wants for something that is already available. Advertisers would probably argue that you cannot create wants – you can only create better ways of satisfying existing wants, and that consumers derive satisfaction from advertised goods is undeniable. Similarly, to argue that advertising persuades people to consume things they do not want is to deny one of the basic assumptions of the economist – that, by and large, people are rational in their purchasing behaviour.

Many economists draw a distinction between 'informative' and 'combative' advertising, following the definition of Alfred Marshall in his book *Industry and Trade*, published in 1919. The distinction was further elaborated in the March 1928 issue of the *Economic Journal* (Braithwaite), where it was claimed that advertising which contains information may be regarded as a true selling expense, whereas advertising designed to stimulate demand is non-essential and largely unproductive. In the April 1962 issue of the same journal, Samuel Courtauld was to assert 'most competitive advertising is a costly national extravagance'.

It would seem, therefore, that the critics concede the value of informative advertising as a means of making the consumer aware of the existence of goods and services and their basic properties, but that they consider combative or persuasive advertising to be a wasteful use of resources. It is difficult to see how the distinction can be maintained, since an advertisement for a new product may be justified as informative in that it makes consumers aware of the existence and characteristics of this product, but combative in that it seeks to persuade consumers to buy the new product in preference to a previously available substitute.

All advertisements contain some information, and it is a fruitless exercise to try and evaluate their individual utility in any precise manner as the informative/persuasive distinction will depend entirely on the existing state of knowledge of each individual member of the audience.

Partial recognition of this fact has diverted many economists, and other critics of advertising, to accept that 'persuasive' advertising can be beneficial, providing that it results in lower prices. Unfortunately, this distinction ignores that price stability is the same as a price reduction under conditions of inflation, and that a consistent improvement in quality may represent the equivalent of a price reduction in that it increases consumer satisfaction for the same nominal money outlay.

To summarise, the case against advertising may be stated as:

1. Advertising leads to higher prices by conditioning demand and so leads to distortion of the productive machine, e.g. maize may cost only £0.01 per pound, but when converted into branded cornflakes it retails at about £0.80 per pound.
2. Advertising leads to non-price competition, e.g. the use of promotions. This creates diseconomies due to difficulties associated with the accurate measurement of demand, and results in a high proportion of product failures.
3. It is an unreliable guide as to value and satisfaction.
4. It leads to oligopoly and monopoly.
5. It is a waste of national resources.

Proponents of advertising would argue that:

1. Advertised goods are cheaper because:

    (a) Advertising brings about economies in 'true' selling costs, e.g. by reducing the need for direct selling, encouraging the development of self-service, etc.
    (b) It raises the scale of production, helps to stabilise output and promotes standardisation.
    (c) Competition ensures that the benefits of these economies will be passed on to the consumer.

2. Advertised goods are better goods because:

    (a) The identification of the product with the manufacturer through branding constitutes a guarantee of quality which must be maintained if the manufacturer is to secure repeat purchases from users.
    (b) To maintain market share manufacturers must constantly strive to improve their product to meet, or exceed, the claims of competing products.

3. Branded and advertised goods create a freedom of consumer choice that was unknown when the same articles were sold from bulk.
4. Advertising improves the standard of living by making new developments quickly available to the public and, by stimulating demand, creates investment, production and employment opportunities.

The ethical argument. Advertising is indicted on ethical grounds on the basis that it encourages the development of materialism. F. P. Bishop, in his book *The Ethics of Advertising*, defines materialism as ' . . . an acquisitive ideology in which the satisfaction of material desires is held up as the sole or principal end for the individual or group'.

In the creation of a materialistic society advertising is charged with deliberately concentrating on those motives that are least desirable in man and of the least value to society. One can be shown innumerable advertisements that appeal to one or more of the 'seven deadly sins', or that play on the emotion most easily stimulated in the human animal – fear. Fear of being left out, of being socially unacceptable, or of being considered socially inferior in some way or other, e.g. dull, lifeless hair; B.O.; halitosis; X washes whiter – and it shows.

Advertising is further indicted in that it sets out to eliminate nonconformity and discourage originality in thought, word and deed. Admass leaves no room for reason, and cultivates the herd instinct.

Finally, in the words of A. S. J. Baster in *Advertising Reconsidered* (1935), 'The major part of informative advertising is and always has been a campaign of exaggeration, half-truths, intended ambiguities, direct lies, and general deception' (quoted by Bishop).

Most marketers would readily agree that the acquisition of material things is a means to an end and not an end in itself, but would also argue that man has free will and therefore the right to decide for himself what level of material consumption he will seek to attain. Religion and philosophy offer us a wide range of alternatives from which to choose a set of principles that will constitute a 'good life'. Whereas mere possessions are unlikely to result in satisfaction in the total sense, it is also true that a certain level of material goods is essential to the maintenance of life. Over and above these essentials, the desired level of material possessions will depend on the society of which we are a member, our education and income.

It is also appropriate to point out that it is only in this century that the possibility of a reasonable standard of living for all members of society has been achieved, and this, as yet, only in advanced economies. Earlier civilisations were largely based on the sweated labour of the masses and only the aristocracy could afford the luxury of philosophising about the 'good life' – only in the next world was it conceivable that all might share in the material comforts enjoyed by the few. (It is an interesting reflection on middle-class morality that the demand for labour-saving kitchen equipment only really got off the ground in this country with the passing of personal servants following the creation of alternative opportunities for female employment in the Second World War.)

Present-day 'welfare economics', designed to remove 'poverty in the midst of plenty', have grown out of the belief that we are now capable of producing sufficient to permit an adequate standard of living for all, and that the major problem is a more equitable distribution of output. At the same time, experience of a full employment policy in the post-war period has taught us that in the absence of adequate demand, production is frustrated and both human and physical resources lie idle. Many would argue that restriction of demand in recent years has mainly resulted from government policies designed to curb inflation, rather than from the inability of the productive machine to create goods in demand. It is my opinion that the inflationary trend is largely the result of a lack of demand.

In the case of the average consumer, the material possessions which constitute the good life are limited to a relatively small number of goods and services. There is a latent demand for many other goods and services, but their utility is less than the effort necessary to earn sufficient to pay for them owing to the disincentive of increasingly punitive levels of taxation. Consequently there is no incentive to work more effectively and improve productivity, an attitude which is compounded by the Government's provision of a range of social services that caters for virtually all of life's emergencies.

Even after ten years of Thatcherism both government and management have been singularly ineffective in explaining the real benefits that will accrue from increased productivity, and the working man resists measures to achieve this in the belief that he may be making himself redundant. The possibility of redeploying labour into new industries creating new products to satisfy existing wants is overlooked. On the other hand if the consumer could be made to want dishwashing machines, VCRs, DSB, electric toothbrushes or any other similar but 'non-essential' item, this might provide sufficient incentive to call forth the increase in productivity that is so urgently required.

In a sense, therefore, materialism and an acquisitive society are necessary if we are to maintain and improve the quality of life for both ourselves and those less fortunate in the developing economies. The more wealth we create domestically, the greater will be our ability to help others.

The other argument for the retention of advertising is that it helps preserve freedom of speech and freedom of choice. Modern media are dependent upon advertising revenues for their continued existence. On their existence largely rests the continued freedom of speech for, as noted when discussing the evolution of advertising, one of the first acts of a dictatorship is to secure control of the means of mass communication. (See Crosier, *The Marketing Book* for an extended discussion of these issues.)

CHAPTER 17

Sales Promotion

Learning Goals

The issues to be addressed in this chapter include:

1. The nature and objectives of sales promotion.
2. Determining the sales promotion appropriation.
3. The types of promotion in current usage.
4. The selection and use of a given promotion.

After reading this chapter you will be able to:

1. Distinguish between 'above and below the line' promotional activities.
2. Set out the objectives which may be achieved through the use of sales promotion.
3. Explain how to determine the size of the appropriation for expenditure on sales promotion.
4. List and describe the major types of sales promotion in current use – sampling, off-price labels, banded offers, premium offers, competitions and personality promotions.
5. Review the issues to be considered in deciding whether to run a promotion.
6. Evaluate the factors to be taken into account when choosing a particular type of promotion.
7. Describe the legislation related to the use of sales promotion.
8. Relate in detail the use of sampling as a major promotional activity.
9. Summarise typical sales promotion problems and their solutions.

Introduction

The previous chapter was concerned solely with media, or 'above the line', advertising. The balance of promotional expenditure 'below the line' is accounted for by a wide variety of sales promotion activities which, collectively, now account for around 60 per cent of the total promotional spend. However, despite the magnitude and importance of sales promotion, comparatively little attention is given to it in most textbooks and journals, a fact which no doubt prompted the title of an article in the 1 November 1984 issue of *Marketing* by Christian Petersen – 'Cinderella in the Limelight'.

Petersen points out that it was not until 1977 that sales promotion expenditure exceeded advertising expenditure but, as noted, it now accounts for 60 per cent of the average UK marketing budget, which is approximately equal to the proportion in the USA and other European markets. For 1988 the Institute of Sales Promotion estimates expenditure at £5.5 billion of which approximately £3 billion will be on price-related promotions.

In a book of this type it is impossible to do justice to all aspects of marketing and this is very much the case with a subject like sales promotion. However, *Marketing Week* magazine runs regular features and special reports on the subject and is a mine of up- to-date information, while Ogilvy, Benson & Mather have published an excellent handbook on the subject. Ogilvy, Benson & Mather have kindly consented to the reproduction of extracts from this handbook (*A Guide to Consumer Promotions*, A. Morgan, 2nd edn, 1976) which, although somewhat dated now, provides an excellent overview of when and how to use sales promotion.

In addition to the above sources several of the major market research agencies publish reports on the subject and the current revision has benefited greatly from reference to Key Note Publications Ltd 1989 analysis *Sales Promotion*.

■ Definition and objectives

The Institute of Sales Promotion (ISP) defines sales promotion as follows:

> Sales promotion is a facet of marketing which is adding value, usually of a temporary nature, to a product or service in order to persuade the end user to purchase that particular brand.

Much advertising also satisfies this definition which accounts for the difficulties of distinguishing the precise division between above and below the line expenditure, a problem which is further compounded by the distinction between consumer and trade promotions. Thus the ISP's estimate of total spend, which remains at around £5.5 bn per annum, is reckoned to include 60% on trade promotions leaving between £2 bn and £2.5 bn for promotions targeted directly at the end user. This expenditure is claimed to be increasing by about 20 per cent per annum but data published by MS Surveys and Promotional Services suggests that the *number* of promotions declined steadily from 16 964 in 1980 to 12 886 in 1988 – a fall of 24 per cent. Clearly, readers need to consult the sources listed for up-to-date information.

The basic objective underlying all promotions is an increase in sales. This aim may be further subdivided, in terms of the time dimension, by devising strategies designed at achieving either short- or long-term gains. Hopefully, both aims will be achieved, but the immediate objective will condition the strategy and the promotional tools employed.

Although display advertising can be very effective in making consumers aware of the existence of a product, inertia frequently prevents consumer sampling and some additional incentive is required to persuade non-users to try it. Promotions are designed fo provide this incentive. Consumers invariably view trial of a new product as containing a risk element – perceived risk – yet without trial there is no possibility of repeat purchases. A product may be totally new, in the sense that it has never previously been offered for sale, or new in the sense that the individual has no previous experience of it. A different strategy will apply to each of these situations.

In the case of a totally new product the initial campaign will seek to obtain the widest possible trial and will employ a combination of methods, e.g. coupons, free samples, in-store trial, banded offers, etc. Where the brand is already established and has a known brand share, the promoter will adopt a more selective approach and concentrate on those segments of the market with the lowest usage rates. A totally new offering will also merit a more prolonged campaign to encourage repurchase; this would not be justified for an established brand because of the cost of 'subsidising' users who would have bought the product without a promotion. Against this element of subsidy must be set the fact that a 'bonus' helps maintain brand loyalty in the face of one's competitors' promotions.

In highly competitive markets, where product differentiation is difficult, if not impossible, such as detergents, breakfast cereals, petrol, etc., promotions are frequently employed to secure short-term increases in sales in the knowledge that once the promotion is finished the new buyers will revert to their former brand, or a competitive brand which is running a promotion. Clearly, promotions of this type are subject to criticism on the grounds that they are combative and do nothing to increase primary demand, and it is argued that the consumer would be better served by a permanent price reduction. From an industry viewpoint there is some truth in the argument, but from the position of the individual firm there is little incentive in adopting such a policy. Faced with an inelastic demand all firms would follow suit and reduce price, but would still be faced with the need to continue promotional activity to protect their individual brand shares. If it is assumed that the manufacturer would protect his profit margin, one is drawn to the inescapable conclusion that such a price reduction would eventually lead to an overall decline in product quality.

In the case of a product like petrol, which has to conform with a technical specification, a reduction in quality of this kind is not permissible. It follows that unless a price cut or promotion can be offset against lower raw material prices then the only justification for either tactic must be the hope that the resulting increase in market share will offset the costs involved. But as the upsurge of promotional activity by the major British petrol companies in recent years has showed, petrol is essentially a commodity with convenience and price the major choice determinant. The result is that gains in market share tend to be short-

TABLE 17.1   Consumer attitudes to sales promotion

	Agree a lot (%)	Disagree a lot (%)	Percentage variation
Promotions save you money	15	13	+2
Promotions make shopping fun	9	30	−27
Promotions encourage you to try new products and brands	10	21	−11
Competitions are fixed	18	21	−3
I prefer no frills	47	4	+43
I welcome the return of trading stamps	13	33	−20
Manufacturers try to put one over on ordinary people	28	7	+21
Saving packet tops is not worth it	39	11	+28

Source: Marketing Week/Harris International/Key Note 1989.

lived as the suppliers to an oligopolistic market react in the way theory predicts they will. None the less, the 1964 promotional wars sparked off by Shell's revival of its Make Money campaign, after ten years of almost no promotional activity and an emphasis on price cutting, did demonstrate the benefits of modifying the marketing mix and making a significant short-term gain. Thus for an outlay of around £2 million Shell picked up 2 per cent market share in a virtually stagnant market. (See *Marketing Week*, 11 May 1984, for a full analysis.)

To sum up, sales promotion can be used to achieve a number of marketing objectives which were summarised in the *Quarterly Review of Marketing* (C. D. Moss, P. Thorne and P. Fasey, 'The Distribution of Coupons', January 1963) as follows:

1. to gain customers and convert them to regular users – particularly for new or improved products;
2. to widen the distribution of a product;
3. to influence stock levels which may be too high or too low;
4. to reduce sales peaks and troughs and maintain economic production levels;
5. to cushion the effect of a price increase;
6. to create new interest in an established product and improve results from in-store displays.

■ Determination of the appropriation

A distinct advantage of promotions as compared with display advertising is that the former is capable of reasonably accurate costing in terms of a desired result whereas the latter is speculative.

In setting the appropriation a two-stage approach is possible. The first stage requires the quantification of only two variables, which are reasonably accessible to the company – sampling cost and the additional contribution arising from the sale of a marginal unit. The second stage requires the determination of three further, and less accessible, facts – the conversion rate from sampling to regular usage, frequency of purchase among regular users, number of purchases by those sampled who do not adopt the product and become regular users.

The sampling cost can usually be calculated in advance and comprises two elements – the distribution cost and the value of the sample or coupon. Where the promotion consists of a coupon redeemable on purchase of the item being promoted, the value of the unit discount must be adjusted in line with the anticipated redemption rate to arrive at a total cost – previous experience usually provides a reliable estimate of this rate.

The growth of the promotions business has resulted in the setting up of firms which specialise in all its aspects, several of which are wholly owned subsidiaries of agencies like Young & Rubicam, J. Walter Thompson and LPE. These companies are well qualified to advise on all aspects of promotions, and will provide estimates of redemption rates with a reasonable degree of accuracy.

Once the sampling area has been defined and the nature of the offer decided, it is a relatively simple matter to calculate the redemption rate/sales volume which will ensure break-even in the short term. In order to allow for the long-term potential of a promotion an estimate must be made of the three second-stage variables referred to above. Conversion rates, like redemption rates, may be estimated with reasonable accuracy on the basis of past experience. The same is true of the percentage of those who will 'make subsequent purchases without becoming 'brand adopters'. (Many large companies undertake continuous market research which enables them to predict at an early stage in the life of a promotion exactly how repurchase patterns will develop.) Product usage is also quite well documented, both by independent firms like Nielsen and by the larger agencies and manufacturers. Armed with this data it is possible, with a little educated guesswork to formulate an acceptable forecast of the long-term benefits.

In the article by Moss *et al.* on 'The Distribution of Coupons' referred to earlier there is a very useful example of the methods of distribution available, the comparative costs and the likely redemption rates. For example, in 1961, 73 per cent of all coupons (7614 million) were distributed through the national press and accounted for 16 per cent of the 324 million redemptions at an average media and distribution cost of 12.4p per redemption (of which 6p was the coupon value). This is equivalent to a redemption rate of 0.93 per cent of coupons distributed while other methods showed the following returns:

Method	Redemption rate
In/on pack	37.70%
Door to door	5.25%
Magazine	2.16%

Table 17.2 provides the most recent data available in 1990. More up-to-date information is, of course, available directly from Nielsen.

TABLE 17.2   Coupons – volume and expenditure

	1983	1984	1985	1986	1987	1988
Number of coupons distributed (millions)	2994	3045	2907	4592	4695	3934
Number of coupons redeemed (millions)	243	274	263	343	411	290
Total value of coupons redeemed (£m)	23.3	31.0	34.2	47.3	60.4	51.9
Coupon's average face value	9.6	11.3	13.0	13.8	14.7	17.9
Manufacturers' average handling allowance to retailers (pence per 100 coupons)	93.4	99.1	108.0	138.0	148.0	169.0
Distribution medium of coupons redeemed (%) (excl. retailer tailor-made promotions)						
Newspaper	8	5	5	8	6	5
Magazine	5	4	5	6	6	7
Door-to-door	30	24	37	34	38	34
In/on pack	42	49	39	38	34	32
In store	..	..	..	..	5	10
Others	17	18	14	14	11	12
Average redemption rates by media (%) (excl. retailer tailor-made promotions)						
Newspaper	..	2.0	..	1.9	2.0	..
Magazine	..	2.5	..	2.6	2.4	..
Door-to-door	..	8.5	..	9.8	9.3	..
In/on pack	..	24.8	..	23.6	24.2	..

Source: Nielsen Clearing House.

■ Promotions in current usage

As every consumer is aware there is a bewildering array of promotional offers available. A short review of these is given below.

Free samples. Of all the promotions this method offers the greatest chance of getting a consumer to actually try the product. At the same time it is the most expensive, and its usage is invariably restricted to brands with potential annual sales of several million pounds. A number of companies seek to reduce sampling cost by co-operating in a joint promotion of non-competing products on similar lines to the gift pack given to mothers of first babies.

Off-price labels. In terms of consumer acceptability the label featuring X*p* off the regular price is the most popular promotion. It is also popular with retailers as it involves none of the diseconomies associated with coupon redemption and also provides the opportunity to feature a price reduction in their local advertising.

The actual extent of the price reduction is an important determinant of the level of sampling, and careful thought, and preferably testing, must be given to the selection of a discount. As discussed in the chapter on pricing, some prices have the apparent effect of being perceived as less than they really are, and it is these which have the greatest impact on impulse purchases. Obviously, if sales volume can be increased sufficiently the firm may be able to both even out seasonal fluctuations and make a profit.

A price reduction is a short-term strategy, however, and the simplest for one's competitors to duplicate. For these reasons it is avoided by companies that are sensitive to a price war wherever possible, which probably accounts for the revival of promotions by the major petrol companies in 1984.

Banded offers. This type of promotion takes two forms:

(*a*) The use of an existing and well-known brand to 'carry' a free sample of another non-competing product. Both products may be produced by the same firm, e.g. soap and toothpaste, which has the dual advantage of increasing sales of the carrying brand while securing trial of the carried brand, or complementary products of different producers, e.g. instant coffee and sugar.

(*b*) Two-for-the-price-of-one.

Premium offers. There are three main varieties of premium offer:

1. *The free gift.* This may be contained in the package – plastic animals in breakfast cereals – attached to it – a plastic rose, tea-towels, etc. – given out at the checkout to those purchasing the item carrying the offer – bowls, china, waste-paper baskets, etc. In some instances the offer will be the pack itself, as is the case with instant coffee packed in storage jars. A common feature of these promotions is that they encourage a collecting habit and so achieve extended trial as the consumer builds up the collection.

2. *The free, sendaway premium.* This type of promotion offers a free gift in exchange for proof of purchase of the product. This approach has greater appeal to the retailer than those promotions which require him to stock 'giveaways', especially as the promotion usually involves point of sale material that builds store traffic and stimulates impulse purchases. From

the promoter's angle an added advantage is that many people buy the product intending to send off for the premium but in fact never do.

3. *Self-liquidating premiums.* These differ from the other type of premium in that the consumer has to send both money and proof of purchase to obtain the offer. The advantage to the consumer is that he secures merchandise, often carrying a leading brand name, at a significant discount on its normal retail price. The promoter benefits in that, as the name suggests, the offer pays for itself. If combined with a collecting habit, offers of this kind may run for years ensuring long-term usage, e.g. Kellogg's silverware offer.

Competitions. Like all other promotions these are no newcomers to the marketing scene (Lever Brothers were spending £1 million a year on promotions at the turn of the century), but they have attracted more than their usual share of attention of late as a result of tangling with the betting and gaming laws. Interest in competitions is considerable owing to the attraction of a very large prize, together with a sufficient number ot consolation prizes on an area basis to encourage people to continue to try their luck. National newspapers frequently offer prizes of £1 million in their bingo games and even *The Times* entered the fray with its Portfolio game.

Personality promotions. As with the door-to-door distribution of samples, this type of promotion is limited to the big brands with large advertising appropriations. The method employed is to offer a prize if the housewife has the advertised product in her home when the personality (Egg-chick, Ajax Superman, etc.) calls, provided that she can answer a simple question. Including in-store displays, leaflet distribution, etc., but excluding display advertising, this type of promotion can cost in excess of £400 000.

TABLE 17.3   Types of promotion (percentage share of total promotions), 1884–88

	1984	1985	1986	1987	1988
Premium	41	42	44	44	44.5
Special offer	23	21	17	9	7
Multi-pack	16	13	14	17	19
Coupon	11	11	11	11	11
Reduced price offer	9	9	10	14	14
Other	–	4	4	5	3.5
Total	100	100	100	100	100

Source: MS Surveys & Promotional Services Ltd.

From the above description of the major types of promotions, it is clear that there is a wide choice of alternatives. Ogilvy, Benson & Mather offer both general and specific advice on how to evaluate these, and the following sections are reprinted from their handbook. It should be stressed that the section on sampling has been chosen for illustrative purposes only and all the other major alternatives are given the same detailed treatment. Table 17.3 summarises the share of different types of promotions for the period 1984 to 1988.

How to decide whether to run a promotion and which promotion to choose*

■ Introduction

Consumer promotions are not a panacea. They have, unfortunately, become fashionable. A belief has developed that they are *the* modern marketing technique. This is nonsense. Consumer promotions are just one part of the marketing mix, not a substitute for it. If a promotion is run it will normally work better as a part of the whole, fitting in with the advertising, product development, packaging, trade incentives and salesmen's incentives as a logical development of the marketing strategy.

In particular, it must be made clear that 'promotions' and 'advertising' are complementary techniques, not substitutes for each other. There is a growing body of evidence that companies who switch their marketing expenditure exclusively 'below-the-line' make temporary gains in volume at the expense of permanently undermining their brand-image and the loyalty of their most regular buyers.

A well-designed promotion can help solve certain specific marketing problems, and together with the rest of the marketing mix help to achieve a marketing objective. Therefore, before discussing whether to mount a promotion at all, and certainly before selecting the type of promotion, the *marketing objectives* of the brand must have been agreed, specific *marketing targets* set, and the problems to be overcome identified.

This assumes that the following information is available:

(*a*) Who is the target market for the brand.
(*b*) Why they use the product and how.
(*c*) How frequently it is bought and where.
(*d*) Who are its main competitors.
(*e*) How the consumer rates the brand compared with its competitors.

If these facts are not known then what is needed is not a promotion but basic research into the brand to determine its problems and marketing positioning.

*The extract quoted (pp. 443–53) is reproduced by kind permission of Messrs Ogilvy, Benson & Mather. As noted it is now dated on points of detail but the issues and approaches discussed are still valid.

■ How to decide whether to run a promotion

(a) Determine, in order of priority, the problems facing the brand.

(b) Determine the money available to solve the problems.

(c) List and cost all the possible alternative solutions to the problems: e.g. more advertising, consumer promotions, pricing strategy, product change, etc.

(d) Estimate (or guesstimate) the effectiveness of each solution.

(e) If the answers to (c) and (d) suggest that a promotion is the most efficient answer to the brand's problem and if the answer to (b) shows there is enough money for a successful promotion then a promotion is indicated.

(f) It does not make sense to run a promotion simply because a competitor is running one unless this has caused problems for your brand which a promotion would solve. If the problems confronting your brand, at that time, would not be solved by a promotion, then it would be a costly mistake to allow your competitor's action to stampede you into panic action. His problems or his perception of his problems may be quite different from those confronting your brand.

■ Which promotion to choose?

(a) The one most likely to solve the brand's problem successfully, within the available budget.

(b) You can help to decide this by looking up your problems in the chart (in the next section).

(c) Then for each promotion listed as likely to help, look up the separate section on that type of promotion.

(d) Look initially at the sub-sections on

    (i)   Advantages
    (ii)   Disadvantages
    (iii)   Essentials for success
    (iv)   Points to look out for
    (v)   How much will it cost?

(e) Does the promotion offer an incentive to the market target, from their point of view?

(f) Consider the impact of the promotion on the image of the product. An expensive, high-quality product, should have an expensive, high-quality promotion.

(g) Consider whether the consumer has any problems which the promotion could solve: e.g. if a product is messy to use, it may be worth considering a free spreader or spatula.

(h) Promotions are tactical tools. There is no formula for picking the correct one. They will usually be better if they are designed in the context of the individual brand's consumers, its market and its trade practices.

(*i*) Because of this need for bespoke designing it is usually better not to copy other companies' promotions but to think ideas out from scratch.

▌ Problems and an indication of the consumer promotions most likely to help in solving them

These are suggestions, not hard and fast rules. Altering the design of a promotion may make it a suitable solution for other problems. The nature of the product, the company and the trade will also affect the best solution to any problem.

	Promotions which may help
(*a*) To get consumer trial of new or existing product	Free with-, in- or on-pack premium Money-off voucher Money-off offer Sampling Proprietary promotions
(*b*) To obtain repeat purchasing	Any premium offer of a collectable item (free or 'self-liquidating promotion') Competition Free mail-in Free continuous mail-in (coupons) 'Money-off voucher promotion' 'Self-liquidating promotion'
(*c*) To obtain long-term consumer loyalty	Continuous 'self-liquidating promotion' (coupons) Trading stamps
(*d*) To increase frequency or quantity of consumer purchase in the short run	Competition Free on-, with-pack premium Free mail-in Household stock reward scheme (personality promotion) In-store self-liquidator Money-off offer (including banded packs) Shop-floor promotions Tailor-made promotions
(*e*) To move high stocks out of stores	Competition Free with-pack Free mail-in

                                    Shop-floor promotions
                                    Tailor-made promotions

(f) To get consumers to visit your   Free gifts
     premises   Money-off voucher
                                    Shop-floor promotions
                                    Tailor-made promotions
                                    Trading stamps
                                    Proprietary promotions

(g) *To get increased distribution.* This will call for trade and salesmen's incentives primarily although a consumer promotion may be necessary to 'pull the product through'. However the choice of consumer promotion will really depend on other problems facing the brand at the time.

(h) *To obtain increased stock levels/stocking in depth.* As with the increased distribution this calls for trade and salesmen's incentives. The choice of a consumer promotion to 'pull the product through' will depend on other problems facing the brand at the time.

(i) *To obtain information on consumer product usage.* This is a research, not a promotional problem.

Points which may arise in connection with any promotion

■ Legal clearance

The number of UK Statutes with which marketing activity has to comply has proliferated in the last decade. Key Acts are quoted throughout this document.

The EEC is developing a body of Directives towards harmonisation of the laws of member countries, which include 'misleading advertising', 'premium offers' and 'informative labelling' among other market topics. These could affect planning for the long-term, or a continuing promotion.

In addition there are several voluntary codes of practice. Most important is the British Code of Sales Promotion Practice (CAP Committee 1977). Compliance with this code reduces but does not eliminate the risk of illegality.

For multinational operations, also consult the series of Codes by the International Chamber of Commerce.

It is important to check for copyright. Similarity to a previous promotion by another company might give rise to a claim of 'passing off' or breach of copyright (apart from causing confusion among consumers and retailers!). If an outside agency is involved it should be made quite clear whether or not any work done by the agency is their copyright.

■ Claimed value of premium items or gifts or prizes

These must comply with the provisions of the Trade Descriptions Act 1966. It is also wise to check whether a prize or premium is on public sale and at what price. It is advisable to be aware of the practices deemed acceptable and unacceptable by the Office of Fair Trading in their Consultative Document on 'Bargain Offer Claims' (1975). While no legislation is in prospect, it offers guidelines for any promotion in which the price of the product is modified temporarily or where some other product is offered in connection with it.

The EEC is developing legislation on 'unit pricing' whereby both the price of the pack and of the relevant unit (pound, kilogram, litre, etc) must be quoted. This will also apply to price modifications.

■ The printing of any promotional offer on the pack

The following problems arise:

- (a) Ensuring adequate supplies have reached direct and indirect outlets by the time advertising breaks (IPA regulations).
- (b) The Advertising Standards Authority requires that details of the closing date and of any limitations on an offer (e.g. 'while stocks last') must appear on the outside of the pack or label.
- (c) While the special pack is on offer, the retailer may put away 'Normal' merchandise which may have deteriorated when it is returned to the shelves.

The sending of items or literature by post:

- (a) There are restrictions of overall size, weight and nature of items that can be sent by post.
- (b) The GPO will not pay compensation for the loss of items with a monetary value, unless sent by registered mail. (Postal regulations concerning paper money introduced 3/10/66.)
- (c) Substantial discounts are available for bulk postage if some regional pre-sorting is done.
- (d) Care should be taken that goods sent by mail to adults should not fall into the hands of children.

■ Promotions advertised on TV

There are ITCA rulings:

- (a) That such promotions must be available to all consumers whether viewers or not.

(*b*)   That if a promotion is limited to certain sizes or packs, this must be made clear in the advertisement.

■ Promotions aimed at offering prizes to children

Promoters should take extra care that the promotion accords with the letter and spirit of the laws and guidelines. There are specific and stringent ITCA rulings related to:

(*a*)   Exaggerated claims and trade puffery, such as the use of the word 'free' or 'free with'.

(*b*)   Promotions on a product whose brand choice cannot normally be considered to be a child's prerogative, e.g. floor polish, soap.

(*c*)   Promotions where the premium, gift or reward is dependent upon collecting a number of items.

(*d*)   In the case of children under 16, entry forms should require the consent of a parent or guardian (particularly where a prize or gift is a holiday, a pet, or goods to the value of £50 or more).

■ Company administration

Check that there is provision in salesmen's order forms, accounting procedure, etc, for special packs sold alongside normal packs.

Check that any liabilities incurred by the promotion are adequately covered by your insurance or that of the promotion company concerned.

Check that all advertising and promotional material include closure dates and adequate descriptions of the rules of the promotion.

Check that all liabilities to *tax* are included when budgeting the costs of a promotion. Even when an item is given away 'free', the promoter may be liable to VAT on its value. Consult the VAT General Guide, or the Customs and Excise.

■ Sampling

■ Definition

The consumer is either:

(*a*)   given some of the product free; or

(*b*)   allowed to use the product freely during a given period.

The size of the product give-away may vary from a taste or spray to a full-sized pack.

The samples can be distributed in a number of ways:

(*a*) Given by a demonstrator in a store. These are usually used instantly, e.g. a tasting of food or drink, a spray of perfume, a cigarette to smoke.

(*b*) Given away with another product.

(*c*) Distributed in some medium, e.g. a shampoo sachet in a magazine.

(*d*) Delivered door-to-door.

(*e*) Sent on application from the consumer.

(*f*) Given to visitors to some specific location, e.g. hotels, exhibitions, showrooms, race tracks, etc.

(*g*) Where the consumer is invited to use the product freely, e.g. a car or television set, then the 'sample' is delivered, by arrangement, to the home or place of business.

■ Advantages

The advantage to the consumer is immediate and obvious (this does not apply if the consumer has to apply for the sample).

The consumer has to make no effort, is involved in no expense (again except in the case where he has to apply for it).

Mass sampling is by far the quickest way of obtaining widespread consumer trial.

Demonstrates to the consumer the product's qualities, and the manufacturer's faith in his product.

Creates excitement.

■ Disadvantages

This is very expensive.

Considerable administration is involved in distributing the samples.

The special costs of trial-sized packs can be as expensive as a normal pack.

The product needs to have an advantage, or difference, that the consumer can perceive.

It will not increase usage by existing consumers.

■ Essentials for success

A good product.

Efficient distribution, especially in:

(*a*) getting the samples to the potential market

(*b*) preventing samples going astray.

Where the sample is left with the consumer, it should be of sufficient size for the consumer both to appreciate the product's qualities and to form the habit of using the product. Consumers show disproportionately more gratitude for a 'full-size' sample.

Trade co-operation. This is very important. If the nature of the product makes a large sample necessary it may be necessary to persuade the trade that you are not depriving them of the profit they could have made selling the product.

A product that regular users are likely to buy frequently.

Advertising support.

Good distribution for the product so that consumers who are persuaded by the sample have the maximum opportunity to buy.

That consumers are informed where they can obtain further supplies of the product.

While not essential the conversion rate to product usage will be increased, if the consumer is given a money incentive to make the first purchase. Thus if the sample is distributed in a store the consumer's attention can be drawn to a money-off offer. If the sample is distributed away from the store or shop the sample should be accompanied by a money-off coupon or voucher.

■ Decisions that have to be taken

What size sample to distribute? This will depend on:

(a) The nature and value of the product.
(b) Consumer usage, e.g. do not give consumers a year's supply, preferably sample the size you most want them to buy.
(c) How apparent is the difference or advantage, e.g. can it be discerned on the first try or bite of the product?
(d) The method of distribution to be used, e.g. you cannot put a pound pack inside a magazine; retailers prefer in-store samples to be small.
(e) The cost of special sample packaging.
(f) The promotional budget.

How to distribute the sample. This will depend on:

(a) The size of the sample.
(b) The nature of the product, e.g. is it breakable?
(c) The market target. If it's not a mass market product there is no point in distributing door-to-door.
(d) The possibilities for sample misuse.
(e) The promotional budget.
(f) The promotional objects.

■ How research can help

It could help to determine the most efficient sample size, e.g. how little of the product is needed to convert the consumer to the product (but see also (third para.) under Disadvantages). There could, however, be a security problem here with a new product.

Subsequently, in measuring conversion rate to the product and in planning further operations.

■ Points to watch/problems which may arise

In connection with any form of sampling operation. That there is adequate check on samples at all stages of distribution.

That the packaging of the sample will stand up to its method of distribution. It is advisable to check this in action. The standard pack may encounter much rougher treatment in a distributor's sack than in a standard outer moved by a forklift truck.

That any quotation received for distribution has been made with knowledge of both the weight and dimensions of the sample.

That there is no chance of the sample tainting other products or of being tainted by them.

See also. 'Points which may arise in connection with any promotion'.

Sampling in stores and shops. That all details are fully discussed and agreed with the store in advance, e.g.

(a) Dates.
(b) Amount of space.
(c) Location of space.
(d) Hours the demonstrator will work. It can cause conflict if these are markedly different from store staff.
(e) Any necessary equipment, e.g. electrical socket.

That demonstrators are subject to adequate supervision and spot checks.

That adequate provisions are made for demonstrators to have clean overalls, etc. under all circumstances.

That if food is being sampled to eat, all food hygiene rules are strictly observed.

Samples given away with another product. That the market target for the two products is similar.

That the products are non-competitive.

Samples distributed in a Press medium. That there are no disputes between media owners and their distributors that will interfere with sample distribution.

Samples distributed door-to-door. Medicinal samples may not be distributed door-to-door.

Both the Board of Trade and CAP require manufacturers to exercise care in putting samples through letter boxes. Complaints have been made of products dangerous to children or dogs and where there is any danger of this CAP recommend personal handing over of the sample instead of distribution through the letter box.

TABLE 17.4   Typical problems and possible promotional solutions

Problem	Solution
1. To increase consumer awareness:	In-store raffle/display; phone-ins; sweepstakes; free draws; competitions.
2. To increase penetration of new or existing products:	Free offers (with in or on-pack) ; money off coupons or offers; sampling; refund offers; multibrand schemes; banded packs, reduced price offers.
3. To improve repeat purchase:	Competitions; free offers; on-pack money-off coupons; reduced price offers; refund/buy-back offers; giveaways; self-liquidating premiums; re-usable container premiums.
4. To increase consumer loyalty:	Premium offers; money-off offers; personality promotions; coupons; buy one, get one free offers; twin packs; refund offers; re-usable container premiums.
5. To increase purchase frequency or amount bought:	Competitions; share-outs/giveaways; free offers; personality promotions; tailor-made promotions; multibrand schemes; in-store promotions; banded packs; reduced price offers.
6. To move high stocks out of stores:	In-store raffles/competitions; free offers; tailor-made promotions; in-store merchandising.
7. To attract consumers to premises:	Free gifts/trials; tailor-made promotions; money-off coupons.
8. Trading up to larger sizes:	Consumer choice coupons; refund offers; multibrand schemes.
9. To increase distribution:	Tailor-made promotions; multibrand schemes; trade competitions; salesman's incentives; sample distribution.
10. To encourage display:	On-pack premiums; banded packs; premium offers; heavy price cuts.

Source: John Williams, 'Picking the winners', *Marketing*, 26 April 1984.

That a sample intended to go through a letter box can go through the average letter box and that instructions cover premises with no letter boxes.

That a household sample is sufficient for a household. If it is something desired and there is not enough to go round you may cause ill-will and the market target may never even see the sample.

■ How much will it cost?

The following list includes some of the main costs likely to be incurred:

(*a*) Cost of sample contents.
(*b*) Sample packaging.
(*c*) Distribution.
(*d*) Advertising.
(*e*) Display material.
(*f*) Merchandising force.
(g) Supporting trade and salesmen incentives.

■ Picking a promotion

The foregoing extract from OBM's Handbook relates specifically to sampling, which is but one of many methods available. While the others are discussed in similar detail it will be helpful here to provide a summary of typical sales

TABLE 17.5 The promotional brief

Brand(s) or service(s)	Other comments/constraints in particular,
Pack size(s) involved	space available for on-pack promotions
Area(s) involved	Legal
Outlets involved (if appropriate)	Cautionary information to be included
Timing	Printing restrictions – number of colours
Budget	permitted, print area, use of drawings/
Target group	photographs, etc.
Promotional objectives	Other support activity planned
Restrictions as to type of promotion	Other relevant information – e.g. logo
(if applicable)	references, pack dimensions
Promotion communications e.g. if	Confidentiality
on-pack the number of packs	Standard of response required – concepts,
involved, leaflet circulation, etc	roughs, presentation layouts
Proofs of purchase required	Response from consultancy

Source: John Williams, 'Picking the winners', *Marketing,* 26 April 1984.

promotion problems and possible solutions. Table 17.4 is taken from 'Picking the Winners' by John Williams (who is the author of *The Manual of Sales Promotion*) and appeared in the 26 April 1984 issue of *Marketing*.

John Williams also offers a very useful outline of the factors to be included in a promotional brief, and this is reproduced as Table 17.5, together with a check list of criteria for effective promotions – Table 17.6.

TABLE 17.6   Criteria for efficient and effective promotions

1. The promotional objectives, budget and success criteria have been specified.
2. It does not attempt to do what other items in the mix can do better.
3. It is the best promotion for achieving the objectives.
4. It has maximum effect for the least cost.
5. It is consistent with the behaviour pattern of those to whom it is addressed.
6. It is consistent with brand image.
7. It gets attention and has urgency and action built into it.
8. It does not use complicated or confusing copy and is simple, clear and easy to act on and understand.
9. It uses emotional as well as rational appeals to self-interest.
10. It is legal and decent and evidently honest.
11. It sufficiently rewards all on whom its success depends.

Source: John Williams, 'Picking the winners', *Marketing*, 26 April 1984.

In selecting a promotion the OBM Handbook emphasises the need to conform with both statutory requirements and the various codes of practice. Of the latter the most important is the British Code of Sales Promotion Practice, the fifth edition of which was launched in July 1990. The 13 principles are reproduced in Table 17.7.

TABLE 17.7   Promotions: legal, decent, honest, truthful

BASIC PRINCIPLES

All promotions should be legal, decent, honest and truthful

The following basic principles apply to all sales promotions. Guidance should therefore be sought on this section when, in particular circumstances, the rules leave any room for doubt. These principles will be taken by both ASA and CAP as the basis on which to determine good practice in any question for which no precedent exists.

1 Legality
All sales promotions should be legal. The Code is designed to complement legal controls, not to usurp or replace them. Promoters are reminded of their responsibility to comply with the law and to take legal advice where necessary before implementing any promotion. This applies especially to prize promotions.

2 Spirit of the Code
The Code is to be applied in the spirit as well as in the letter with the aim of eliminating practices which might lead sales promotion into disrepute.

3 Fair competition
All sales promotions should adhere to the principles of fair competition as generally accepted in business.

4 Consumer interest
All sales promotions should deal fairly and honourably with consumers and should be seen to do so. No promoter, or other person engaged in the conduct of a sales promotion, should abuse the trust of consumers or exploit their lack of experience or knowledge to their detriment.

5 Consumer satisfaction
Sales promotions should be so designed and conducted as not to cause avoidable disappointment.

6 Fairness
The terms and conduct of promotions should be equitable to all concerned.

7 The public interest
Neither the design nor the conduct of a promotion should be such as to conflict with the public interest. In particular, promotions should contain nothing which is likely to provoke, or may appear to condone, violent or anti-social behaviour, the causing of nuisance or injury to any member of the public, or damage to property.

8 Truthful presentation
The presentation of a promotion should be clear and honest and should not be likely to mislead those who are addressed, or those to whose attention such material is likely to come.

9 Substantiation
When called upon by the Advertising Standards Authority or the Committee of Advertising Practice, promoters should be ready to present such evidence or argument as may be necessary to establish the compliance of their promotion with this Code and of any advertising material with the British Code of Advertising Practice.

10 Limitations
Any factor likely to affect a consumer's decision to participate in a promotion should be made clear *before* the consumer is committed to any purchase upon which participation depends.

11 Suitability of promotion to those reached by it
Promoters should take all reasonable steps to ensure that neither advertising nor promotional material reaches those for whom the promotion concerned may be inappropriate.

12   Administration

Promotions should be conducted promptly and efficiently so as to provide no justifiable grounds for complaints from consumers.

13   Responsibility

The prime responsibility for all aspects of a promotion *always* rests with the promoter. Agents and intermediaries share responsibility to the extent of their involvement.

CHAPTER 18

Personal selling and merchandising

___ Learning Goals ___

The issues to be discussed in this chapter include:

1. The role of personal selling.
2. The economics of personal selling.
3. The deployment of the sales force.
4. The employment, training and compensation of salesmen.
5. The nature and role of merchandising.

After reading this chapter you will be familiar with:

1. The complementary nature of personal selling and impersonal methods employing advertising and promotion.
2. The various roles performed by salesmen and the distinction between 'order-takers' and 'order-makers'.
3. The costs and benefits associated with personal selling.
4. Factors governing the deployment of the field sales force.
5. Newton's four-way classification of selling styles – trade selling, missionary selling, technical selling, new-business or missionary selling.
6. Factors which influence the selection and training of salesmen.
7. Methods of salesmen's compensation together with their various advantages and disadvantages.
8. Criteria for evaluating salesman performance.
9. Factors underlying the increased importance of merchandising and its influence on in-store behaviour.
10. Merchandising services available from TV contractors.

Despite the importance of advertising and sales promotion in disseminating information and stimulating interest in products and services, there are many circumstances where personal contact is necessary to effect a sale. Of necessity most advertising is generalised, and so cannot answer all the consumer's information needs; it cannot elaborate upon specific points perceived as significant by the individual, nor can it resolve doubts as to suitability in a particular context. Further, there can be no guarantee that the potential user's media habits will expose him to advertisements for a given product, or that if he does see the advertisement he will perceive it as relevant.

The function of personal selling is to provide the specific inputs which advertising, or non-personal selling, cannot offer at the individual level. It should be remembered that advertising and personal selling are complementary activities, and that their relative importance will vary depending upon the nature of the product and the buying behaviour associated with it.

TABLE 18.1   The relative importance of elements of marketing communications

Type of marketing activity	Industrial goods	Consumer durables	Consumer non-durables
Sales management and personal selling	Very high	High	High
Media advertising	Very low	Moderate	High
Special promotions	Low	Moderate	Moderate
Pack, brand, other	Low	Low	Moderate

5-point scale: Very low, low, moderate, high, very high.

Source: Bill Donaldson, *Sales Management* (Macmillan, 1990).

Many theorists stress the nature of the product as a determinant of the appropriate promotional mix and are collectively identified as the 'Characteristics of Goods School'. Members of this school would argue that advertising will be dominant in the case of small, simple and frequently purchased items of low unit value, while personal selling is appropriate to high-priced, technically complex products which are bought infrequently.

According to this view the appropriate promotional mix might be represented diagrammatically as in Figure 18.1, while the relative importance is suggested in Table 18.1.

Although useful, this approach is oversimplified, for the user's perception of any given product defies classification into convenient categories, such that a 'convenience' good may be perceived as a 'shopping' good and vice versa, depending upon the individual's frame of reference. The importance of allowing for the behavioural dimensions of perception is implicit in the different promotional strategies adopted by firms selling near-perfect substitutes in the economic sense, e.g. Avon sells cosmetics door-to-door, Estée Lauder products are available

Figure 18.1 Selecting the promotional mix

Source: Based on *Selling in a Modern Perspective*, R. J. Robinson and Bent Stidsen (Boston, Allyn & Bacon, 1967)

in less than 150 outlets, Yardley and Coty are available in some 7000 department stores and chemists' shops, while Miner's brands are sold through variety chains and supermarkets. There are no hard-and-fast rules which dictate the adoption of a given promotional strategy for a product.

■ The evolution of the salesman

Although our stereotype of a salesman probably owes more to the music-hall comedian than to reality, there can be no doubt that selling has long occupied a relatively low position in our social and economic hierarchy. Fortunately, there are signs that this state of affairs is slowly changing and that selling is increasingly regarded as a profession rather than a trade. Several factors may be distinguished as contributing to this change and the resultant increase in the flow of better qualified recruits, namely:

1. 'Salesman' applies equally to all persons engaged at all levels of selling, from the retail sales clerk to the negotiator of multi-million-pound contracts. In that the former greatly outnumber the latter, selling tends to be identified with the functions performed by retailers rather than with manufacturer's salesman. However, increased labour costs have led to wide-scale reduction in personal selling at the retail level and have thus brought more sophisticated sales functions into sharper focus, i.e. an emphasis on creative selling as opposed to mere order-taking.
2. Growing awareness of the need for personal selling in the service sector e.g., banks, insurance and other professional services – has resulted in a

significant improvement in both the visibility and credibility of the function.

3. The concentration of retail buying power has resulted in a clear distinction between the negotiating skills demanded in organisational buying situations and the merchandising effort called for at the point of sale with a consequent increase in the salesman's status and importance.

4. The pressures of international competition have made it clear that the manufacturer can no longer leave his product to 'speak for itself' – effective selling and promotion are essential.

5. Increased product complexity, and more sophisticated buyers demand high-calibre salesmen. The scarcity of such personnel has boosted salary levels above those offered in many other occupations, improving selling's economic status and attracting in better-qualified recruits.

Collectively, these factors have made a career in sales more respectable, and resulted in a better understanding of the sales function.

■ The salesman's role

In view of the possible variations in product and market characteristics it is virtually impossible to formulate a single definition of the saleman's role.

Where a user/consumer has previous experience of a product the salesman is often a passive 'order-taker' whose function is to price the product specified, take payment and effect delivery, e.g. 2 lb of potatoes, a packet of Whizzo, 50 tons of cold-reduced mild steel sheet. Such a situation is very different from the case where the potential buyer has no previous experience of the product and is actively seeking information, and different again from the situation where the consumer has only an ill-defined or latent demand for a product to fill a given need. In the latter situations the salesman becomes an 'order-maker' and plays an active role in the purchasing decision.

Although there is more than an element of truth in the generalisation that retailers are order-takers, whereas manufacturers' salesmen are order-makers, no such clear-cut distinction exists in reality. Many manufacturers have become sensitive to the important influence which the retail sales assistant can have on the purchasing decision, and have installed their own employees in leased departments or provided training for their customers' staff. Similarly, the high cost of personal selling has persuaded many manufacturers to adopt standardised reorder procedures and to eliminate unnecessary or uneconomic sales calls. Alternatively, less experienced personnel are assigned to perform routine functions, leaving the salesman free to devote more time to missionary and developmental selling.

Although emotional factors undoubtedly influence both industrial and consumer purchasing decisions at all levels it is felt that there is a tendency to overemphasise these and, consequently, to overstress the salesman's role as a 'persuader'. In everyday speech, 'persuasion' is often used to suggest that a person has been, or can be, induced to act against his better judgement – this is certainly the context in which Vance Packard views 'The Hidden Persuaders' of advertising. In reality it is doubted if consumers are persuaded by spurious arguments as frequently as Packard suggests, and the salesman's role might be more usefully viewed as a problem-solving activity in which facts and arguments are used to justify the selection of a given product to satisfy a specific want. The salesman's skill lies in his ability to perceive the attributes which the 'prospect' considers important, and to structure his presentation so that his product's suitability along those dimensions is adequately conveyed to the potential customer. Thus, the car salesman will emphasise performance to his male customers, and finish and trim to his female customers – if he is a good car salesman he will also realise that the middle-aged bank clerk's concept of performance is rather different from that of the junior account executive and so on. (There is more than a grain of truth in the old adage 'Let the customer tell you what he wants and then sell it to him', i.e. given the wealth of detail which you could give the customer, concentrate on the points in which he expresses interest.)

■ The economics of personal selling

A recurring theme of this book is that the well-managed firm will seek to develop strategies that will enable it to achieve certain predetermined objectives. Fundamental to the firm's ability to achieve its stated aims is the need to earn profits, so that the adoption of policies, and the strategies by which they will be implemented, will revolve largely around cost/revenue considerations. This point has already been stressed at some length elsewhere but it is particularly relevant in the context of personal selling.

In absolute terms personal selling is the most expensive method whereby the producer can establish contact with the potential consumer. A guide to the cost of employing a salesman in 4 industry sectors is provided in Table 18.2. Relatively, however, it is often the least expensive method owing to the higher conversion factor achieved by direct selling *vis-à-vis* the use of middlemen or other promotional efforts. Whether the manufacturer should employ his own sales force, how big it should be, and how he should deploy it to maximum effect are questions which may only be resolved through a full evaluation of the alternatives. Although it is possible to quantify many of the parameters, no single prescriptive formula is available, but a number of steps can be offered as the basis for structuring such an evaluation.

1. The company should state its sales target for the coming year and for the next five years or so.
2. The promotional budget should be reviewed in the light of the sales target to ascertain whether the proposed expenditures will be sufficient to generate the desired sales volume – see 'The "task" approach' in Chapter 16.

TABLE 18.2   Guide to the cost of employing a salesman

	Overall annual cost	Daily cost based on 200 working days	Total no. of selling calls per day	Cost per call
Manufacturer's salesman selling to retail trade	£27 000	£135	10–12	£13.50–11.25
Pharmaceuticals salesman selling to doctors and hospitals	£38 000	£190	6–8	£31.66–£23.75
Industrial salesman selling to OEMs	£38 000	£190	4–6	£47.50–£31.66
Capital goods salesman selling to end users	£45 000	£225	3–5	£75–£45

Source: John Lidstone, 'Putting Force Back into Sales', *Marketing*, 22 September 1983.

3. Personal and non-personal selling are complementary activities and should not be segregated when determining the size of the promotional budget, i.e. management should decide how much it is willing to spend on all promotion, before attempting to allocate it to specific promotional efforts.
4. The optimum mix of personal and non-personal promotional efforts will vary by product, firm, industry and market, and is subject to change over time, therefore the total budget should be allocated roughly in accordance with the relative importance attached to each.
5. The adequacy of the sales budget may be evaluated by reference to past sales data or, if the firm has no previous experience of direct selling, by reference to the industry/product data published by trade associations, the BIM, the trade press, etc. A rough and ready guide is to substitute such data into the formula:

$$\text{Sales} = \frac{\text{Sales budget}}{\text{Average cost per call}} \times \text{Average sales per call}$$

In the absence of hard data, the firm would have to rely upon its own subjective estimates of likely events, and could easily test a large number of alternatives by running a simulation on a computer.

Once a field sales force is in existence, a continual process of adjustment is necessary to maximise its productivity. Ideally, salesmen should be used to the point where the marginal cost of making a sales call is equivalent to the marginal revenue which it generates. In practice, adoption of this principle is rarely feasible because of the high fixed costs associated with the addition of an 'incremental' salesman, unless payment is on a straight commission basis.

■ Deploying the field sales force

Optimum deployment of the sales force is an ever-present problem for the sales manager. Essentially this problem has three dimensions:

(a) The geographical dispersion of potential customers.
(b) The nature of the company's product mix.
(c) The buying needs of customers.

The geographical dispersion of customers imposes a major constraint on sales force productivity in that time spent travelling between customers is largely wasted. The amount of travelling time will vary considerably depending upon a number of factors but, on average, it is estimated that salesmen only spend 40 per cent of their time actually in contact with customers. Clearly a major objective must be to minimise the spatial distribution of accounts, which suggests that the sales force should be organised on a territorial basis.

However, such an organisational structure may conflict with the essential requirement that a salesman know his product. For the single product company, or the company with a limited range of closely related products, this may not create any problems, but as product line diversity and/or complexity increase, so product specialisation becomes progressively more essential. In the steel industry it would be impossible for any individual to be completely familiar with all products, and specialists are required for the sale of tinplate, mild steel sheet and plate, electrical steels, billets and bars, etc.

In turn, product knowledge must be backed by an understanding of the buying needs and practices of different customer groupings. Thus the detergent manufacturer's salesman will find it necessary to adopt a very different approach when selling to a major grocery chain as opposed the small independent outlet. Similarly, it will be necessary to use a very different strategy when selling to industrial users.

There is no simple rule which dictates that the manufacturer should organise his sales force on a territory, product or market basis and, in fact, many companies have adopted a composite structure. Many of the arguments examined when discussing product and market management in Chapter 19 are equally applicable in this context, but it is important to recognise that the internal organisation of the marketing department on either product or market lines does not automatically require that the sales force be organised in the same way. For obvious reasons of economy most sales forces are organised on a territorial basis, but within these boundaries salesmen may specialise on either a product or customer needs basis. The role of the product or market manager is to supply the salesman with detailed information of the most appropriate marketing inputs, such that several product managers may brief a single salesman on the 'best' tactics to be used in respect of each of their different products. Similarly, the market manager will lay down the nature of the selling approach most suited to the particular customer grouping for which he is responsible.

At the territory level a number of techniques have been evolved in recent years to improve sales efficiency. The sales call pattern is in the nature of a 'transportation problem' in the language of operations research, and is capable of at least partial solution through the use of linear programming techniques. In order to permit analysis it is necessary to adopt a number of simplifying assumptions, e.g. the relationship between time spent with buyer and size of order, the value of new account development or 'prospecting', etc., and it is clear that no true optimum solution is possible. None the less, the discipline of developing empirically valid generalisations is in itself worth while as it can lead to valuable insights into the more effective deployment of the field sales force.

■ Selling situations classified

One of the central themes of this chapter is that selling situations vary across a number of dimensions and that one must be careful to distinguish between them. At the same time there are sufficient similarities to permit the identification of a number of situations in which a particular kind or type of selling will be appropriate. It will be useful, therefore, to outline the basis characteristics of each as a first step towards identifying the sales situation facing the company and the necessary sales inputs to cope with it effectively.

In an investigation into sales management practice undertaken by Dr Derek Newton of the Harvard Business School, a preliminary report of which was published in the *Harvard Business Review* ('Get the Most Out of Your Field Sales Force' (Sept–Oct 1969) pp. 130–43) a secondary finding was that . . . one can effectively isolate four basic styles of selling that cut across industry boundaries to a large degree . . . '. These four styles are characterised as:

1. Trade selling.
2. Missionary selling.
3. Technical selling.
4. New business selling.

Although there is nothing new in identifying selling styles and attaching labels to them, this classification is preferred by the author in that it offers the broadest level of categorisation consistent with utility. In summary the characteristics of the four styles are:

Trade selling
   (a)   Major aim to build sales volume by providing customers with promo-
           tional assistance, i.e. selling *through*, e.g. food, textiles and wholesaling.
   (b)   Personal selling subsidiary to non-personal activities.
   (c)   Low-pressure selling, with an emphasis on continuity and a thorough
           understanding of customer practice.

Missionary selling
- (a) Primary aim is to build sales volume by providing direct customers with personal selling assistance, i.e. to persuade ultimate users/consumers to buy from the company's immediate customers.
- (b) Most typical of firms selling to distributors for resale.
- (c) Low pressure but requires energetic, articulate men capable of making a large number of calls in order to cover all the potential users, e.g. medical representatives.

Technical selling
- (a) Primary responsibility is to increase sales to present customers through the provision of technical advice and assistance.
- (b) Requires an ability to identify, analyse and solve customer problems, and so places a premium on technical and product knowledge.
- (c) Continuity is an important factor in building up buyer confidence and goodwill.

New business selling
- (a) Primary aim is to secure new customers.
- (b) The high level of rejection of new product propositions favours the employment of mature, experienced salesmen who can take an objective view of 'failure' and have a wider range of techniques to deal with buying objections.

The recruitment, selection and training of salesmen

■ Attributes of the successful salesman

Given the possible variations in the role which salesmen are called upon to play in different selling situations, it would be surprising to find that potentially successful salesmen may be identified by the presence, or absence, of a stereotyped set of personality variables. On the other hand, the high costs of selection and training make it essential that wastage through salesmen turnover be minimised, and have prompted the construction of innumerable check-lists which purport to identify the attributes of a successful salesman. The majority of such lists emphasise factors such as 'intelligent, extrovert, energetic, self-confident', etc., and a number of selection tests have been devised to measure such characteristics.

Collectively these lists, and the associated tests, presume the existence of a stereotype the validity of which is doubted by the author. This doubt would appear to be supported by the findings of Samuel N. Stevens, who has summarised '. . . the major conclusions which social scientists have reached in regard to social and psychological characteristics of salesmen . . .' as follows:

1. There is no significant relationship between intelligence test scores and sales success.
2. No significant relationship has been found between independent measures of personality traits and sales success.
3. No correlation exists between age and sales success.
4. There is no correlation between measurable character traits and sales success.
5. There is no significant correlation between level of education and sales success.
6. No significant correlation exists between level of sales activity and sales success among individual salesmen.
7. Each of the above factors has significance when studied in relation to all of the others in individual salesmen.
8. Such a study as that indicated in point 7 above can provide a useful tool for selection and development.
9. Salesmen are more likely to succeed when chosen with regard to the kinds of customers they will deal with than in terms of the types of products sold.
10. Salesmen differ from non-salesmen in four important ways

    • Salesmen are persuasive rather than critical.
    • Salesmen are intuitive rather than analytical.
    • Salesmen have higher average energy levels (expressed in activity).
    • Salesmen are more strongly motivated by the desire for prestige, power, and material gain than by a service ideal or the need for security.

11. Salesmen's interests cluster around a dominantly persuasive common core.

('The Application of Social Science Findings to Selling and the Salesman', *Aspects of Modern Marketing* (AMA Management Report no. 15, American Management Association, New York, 1958) pp. 85–94.)

■ Recruitment

As noted in point 7, factors 1–6 have no individual significance and their collective importance will vary depending upon the selling task to be performed – point 9. If this is so, then it follows that firms should develop their own selection procedures based on a job specification appropriate to their own sales policies and objectives. Such a job specification is vital to efficient recruitment and selection.

Most sales positions are advertised in the classified columns of the major newspapers and trade journals, and media representatives frequently quote the number of applications received by advertisers as an indication of their publication's 'pulling power'. Such statements would seem to confuse volume with quality, and usually indicate that the advertisement has failed in' its function as a screening device. On occasion a loosely worded advertisement is a useful guide to the calibre of people who are actively seeking new jobs – as a means of securing applicants for a specific post it is both a wasteful and 'sloppy' approach. (A leading firm of management consultants once informed the author that they had received over 800 applications for a sales manager's post requiring previous experience with a highly specialised product. As there could not have been more than fifty people with such experience, either the consultant was 'fishing' for applicants to fill other vacancies, or he didn't know his job. In either case he was wasting his client's time and money.)

Most job advertisements require applicants to submit details of their previous experience and other evidence to indicate their potential suitability for the post. Where the job specification is fairly loose or the employer intends to give recruits extensive training, standardised application forms greatly assist the preparation of a short-list as they ensure that all applicants supply information considered important by the prospective employer.

■ Selection

Once a short-list has been prepared, the final selection of candidates usually involves some combination of tests and interviews. If a job specification has been prepared the purpose of the selection procedure will be to identify the applicant who most closely matches the job profile. In the absence of a job specification selection is likely to be overly subjective.

Although many factors will be common to all sales positions, and permit the use of structured interviews, the relative importance of these factors will vary depending upon the precise nature of the selling job to be performed. To deal with this problem and permit the development of standardised selection procedures, it is recommended that some form of factor rating be employed, similar to that described in connection with the screening of new product ideas.

In recent years an increasing number of firms have adopted some form of psychological testing in addition to the traditional personal interview. Such tests are seen as a cross-check on both interviewer bias and respondent consistency, and fall into four main categories:

Aptitude
Interest
Mental ability
Personality

Tests of this kind conform more with the American than with the British ethic and are most frequently used in companies with strong links with the United States, e.g. Esso, Procter & Gamble, Mars.

Criticism of psychological tests is not based solely on cultural differences, however, and a number of American marketers are equally as sceptical as their more conservative British counterparts. For example, David Mayer and Herbert Greenberg ('What Makes a Good Salesman?', *Harvard Business Review*, XLII

(July–Aug 1964) pp. 119–25) discern four reasons which appear to account for the failure of aptitude tests:

1. Tests confuse interest with ability.
2. It is possible to fake answers and give the response the interviewer is looking for.
3. Tests favour conformity not individual creativity.
4. Tests concentrate on personality traits in isolation and fail to measure the person as a whole.

In the companion volume *Sales Management: Theory and Practice* (Macmillan, 1990) Bill Donaldson reports that an increasing number of firms are now using assessment centres which employ a variety of techniques and may appraise six to eight candidates over one to three days using a team of selection specialists.

However, psychological testing techniques are becoming increasingly sophisticated and it is anticipated that they will come into wider use in the future.

■ Training

The function of the selection procedures described above is to recruit candidates who are potentially suited to the company's selling tasks. Often the firm will use previous experience as a selection criterion, although a BIM survey indicated that only forty of the seventy-five respondents stipulated that this was essential. (This survey, *Methods of Selecting and Training Salesmen* (Information Summary 87, 1966) provides useful background data but is based on too small a sample to permit valid generalisation.) Even where the new recruit has previous experience it is unlikely that this is directly relevant to the products, markets and administrative procedures particular to his new employer, and some training will be necessary.

The objective of training is to make the salesman more effective *as judged by the firm's criteria*. As is evident from the distinction drawn earlier between trade, missionary, technical and new-business selling, sales volume is only one criterion, and may be totally inappropriate in some circumstances. Although the need for training is clearly greatest in the case of new, inexperienced recruits it should be looked upon as a continuing process. Over time products, channels and markets change, and the well-managed firm will adjust its policies accordingly – continuation training is fundamental to the effective implementation of such changes in policy.

The length, content and cost of the sales training programme varies enormously between companies, but all seek to cover two main areas – knowledge and skills. knowledge is concerned with the acquisition of facts and will normally include coverage of:

The company – its history, structure, policies and procedures.
The product(s) – composition, manufacture, performance and usage.
The market – size, structure, composition, buying behaviour, etc.

Skills may be subdivided into two categories – technical and behavioural. Technical skills cover training in techniques appropriate to various stages of the buying process such as securing interviews, opening the interview, overcoming objections and the 'close'. If the product can be demonstrated this would also be considered a technical skill.

Behavioural skills are concerned with the development of empathy between buyer and seller. They are difficult both to define and to acquire, and are usually described in texts on salesmanship under titles such as 'How to be a good listener', 'How to excite curiosity', etc.

According to John Lidstone ('Putting Force Back into Sales', *Marketing*, 22 September 1983) the modern salesman must develop his knowledge and skill in three key areas:

> First, he must have a fluent confidence in the financial facts upon which buying and selling are based, and in the impact of his product on his buyer's business and on his own company's costs, profits and cash flow. In a world of constantly changing costs and prices, the salesman must be capable of ensuring not only that an order is obtained, but also that it is a profitable one.
>
> Second, he must know how to prepare, in far more detail than before, strategies for each major customer. He must know how to ensure that all the company's resources are harnessed to achieve both short- and longer-term customer satisfaction, at a profit. Such strategies, skilfully and imaginatively implemented, will do much to eliminate the pyrrhic sale' produced by a salesman under pressure from management, which too often has resulted in short-term gains but the long-term loss of an account.
>
> Third, he must know how to negotiate a mutually satisfactory order and long-term business, rather than just using persuasive techniques to conjure up the 'your turn next' type of order. Many of the larger buyers have no option but to purchase from the major suppliers. But the key to success is the terms on which the contract to trade is agreed.
>
> Negotiation skills of the highest order must be developed to deal on equal terms with these major customers, many of whom have been trained to buy. So far, little more than lip service has been paid to this fact. Indeed, an uncomfortably large number of sales managers, let alone salesmen, still think that negotiation is just a smart word for selling. It is nothing of the sort.

■ Salesman compensation

Selling is a function which lends itself to some kind of payment by results in the majority of cases. If it is borne in mind that every incentive has a corresponding disincentive, then it follows that one must determine which incentive is most appropriate to a given selling situation.

Surveys into the remuneration of salesmen by the TACK organisation and the BIM indicate that about 18 per cent of salesmen are paid a straight salary, with no bonus or incentive, while the remaining 82 per cent all receive some form of financial incentive. Every method has its advantages and disadvantages and these may be summarised as:

Salary only
  (a) The salesman's income is based on his overall performance and not subject to fluctuations beyond his control, e.g. the impact of a credit squeeze or marked seasonality of demand.
  (b) The method is fairest where the salesman is engaged in missionary selling or required to spend much of his time providing technical services.
  (c) Where there are variations in territory potential it prevents friction between salesmen, and gives flexibility in sales and journey planning.
  (d) It simplifies payment and avoids complications in the salary structure of the company as a whole.

As suggested, each of these advantages has a built-in disincentive:

  (a) Sales effort will not be maximised when most needed.
  (b) The quality of the services rendered will affect sales volume and so should be measured in just the same way.
  (c) Territories should be designed so that they have the same potential to encourage salesmen to compete with one another.
  (d) If incentives are properly designed they will ensure that all members of the company receive a reward proportionate to their contribution.

Salary and commission
This is the most frequently used method on the grounds that:

  (a) The salary provides a basic income while the commission provides the incentive to extra effort to achieve a better standard of living.
  (b) Variable commissions on different products ensure that salesmen give them the degree of attention desired.

Commission only
In practice this method is found very infrequently – TACK reports 5.5 per cent, BIM nil – as it has little attraction to any but the most confident of salesmen. From the employer's point of view it has the great attraction that payment is directly related to the results achieved, but it can also create considerable friction among other employees owing to the very high earnings which can be achieved by a good salesman.

Bonus schemes
Bonuses may be paid in addition to commission, either as an individual or group incentive, as a reward for sustained effort or the achievement of a predesignated target, or where a purely quantitative assessment would not adequately reflect performance, e.g. reduced sales on a falling market when such sales still represent an increase in market share.

A survey by a postgraduate student at Strathclyde University (C. K. Manolis), reported by Donaldson (*Sales Management*, Macmillan, 1990), revealed that 30 per cent of UK salespeople were on straight salary, 35 per cent on salary + commission, 17 per cent on salary + commission + bonus and 5 per cent on commission only.

■ Evaluation of salesmen

In the preceding section little reference was made to the methods used in evaluating salesmen's performance, on which most remuneration schemes are based. Once again it is necessary to reiterate that the relevant criteria will depend upon the company's own sales policies and objectives but, in general, performance will be measured in both quantitative and qualitative terms. Quantitative criteria include:

Sales volume.
Number of orders secured.
Number of sales calls made.
Number of service calls made.
Expenses incurred.
Territory contribution to profit.

Among the qualitative criteria in common use are:

Degree of product knowledge.
Quality of sales presentation.
Rating on personality traits such as initiative, judgement, etc.
Self-organisation, i.e. use of time, handling of correspondence, reports, etc.
Customer relationships.

Once the relevant criteria have been selected, some basis for evaluation must be chosen. Methods based on past performance, or involving a comparison of salesmen, suffer from the disadvantage that present conditions may differ markedly from those obtaining in the past, and that sales territories, and hence salesmen, are rarely, if every directly comparable. To overcome these difficulties many companies prefer to measure performance against prescribed standards, e.g. actual sales versus forecast, number of new accounts secured versus target, expenses incurred versus budgeted expense, etc.

■ Merchandising

In the chapter on patterns of distribution reference was made to the transference of some of the 'traditional' retailing functions to the manufacturer intent upon securing greater control over the marketing of his output. Subsequently, the role of packaging, advertising and sales promotion were examined in the context of generating demand for particular goods and services. It now remains to consider merchandising as an extension of the selling process whereby the manufacturer seeks to ensure that the retailer sells his products as quickly and as profitably as possible.

From the manufacturer's point of view the retail outlet provides the ready availability and convenience which are so expensive to achieve by direct selling methods. Once the retailer has taken delivery of goods from the manufacturer they become his property until he can effect their resale to ultimate consumers, and it follows that until he is able to achieve this he will have neither space nor capital with which to purchase further supplies from the producer. Clearly any assistance which the manufacturer can give the retailer to stimulate demand and encourage purchase will be to their mutual advantage – this is the role of merchandising.

To maximise sales volume the sales force must ensure that its products are in the right place at the right time, in order to translate potential demand for them into effective demand. The right place means not only the outlets with the highest turnover or largest clientele but also the right place within the outlet to achieve the maximum impact on the prospective purchaser. Given the cost of a salesman's time, plus the cost of point-of-sale display material, it is obvious that merchandising efforts must be concentrated on the larger outlets which promise the greatest potential return. Within outlets, research has shown that certain locations are to be preferred. Thus in self-service outlets the best positions have been found to be:

1. At the end of gondolas facing the main traffic flow. (A gondola is a shelving unit on the main floor area which subdivides this area into a series of aisles.)
2. At eye level on the shelves around the sides of the shop. Impact can be further improved by siting the product immediately prior to the area normally set aside for display of the product group.
3. In dump displays in the main traffic aisles as these tend to cause congestion and focus attention on them.
4. Immediately next to the checkout – here again congestion creates a 'captive' audience.

In shops which still retain counter service the preferred positions are:

1. On the counter itself. If this is extensive, then next to the till or scales.
2. At eye level behind the counter.
3. In a dispenser placed in front of the counter.
4. Next to a complementary product, e.g. cream next to tins of fruit.

Timing is also an important factor underlying successful merchandising. Research indicates that the majority of purchases are made at the weekend and so emphasises the need to ensure adequate display at this time. Similarly, seasonal products such as mincemeat, Easter eggs and the like must be put on display in plenty of time, as must goods which are to be the subject of heavy promotion.

The major pitfall to be avoided by the salesman is that of becoming a merchandiser first and a salesman second. The salesman's role is to instruct retailers in the use of proven techniques to stimulate demand at the point of sale, and it is undesirable that he should become involved in routine activities associated with stocking shelves and putting goods on display. The salesman's job is to ensure that his products are given sound merchandising and a fair share of the favoured sites, and the normal call frequency precludes his devoting much time to in-store promotion.

In view of the heavy demands on the salesman's time, many firms now employ personnel whose sole function is to assist the retailer with the creation of effective store displays. Much merchandising is purely mechanical and so can be performed by part-time or less highly paid employees than is the case when salesman are required to do their own merchandising. In view of the desirability of achieving maximum impact simultaneously over a wide area at the commencement of an advertising campaign, several independent television companies now offer additional sales and merchandising support to supplement the advertiser's own efforts.

Tyne Tees, Border, Granada and HTV all have their own retail sales force. The remainder less LWT and Ulster offer this service through a contracted company. London and South & S. East England are the exceptions with Thames TV and TVS not offering this service. Some indicative costs using the Television South West retail force are set out in Table 18.3.

TABLE 18.3   Costs of TSW's contract sales force

Cost per salesperson day inclusive of fee and expenses		
(TSW – £59)		£65.00
Briefing per operative, inclusive of fee and expences		
(TSW – £65)		£70.00
Supervision and administration (covering production of		
all documentation plus reporting)	2 weeks	£500.00
	3 weeks	£600.00
Agency representative travel to attend briefing in Plymouth		£150.00
Sales bonus – allowance per person		
	2 weeks	£30.00
	3 weeks	£50.00
Total costs		
2 weeks (800 call) Grocery/CTN campaign		
(TSW – £3845)		£4145
3 weeks (1200 call) Grocery/CTN campaign		
(TSW – £5420)		£5970
2 weeks (500 call) Licensed grocer campaign		
(TSW – £3255)		£3495

The foregoing discussion of merchandising has tended to emphasise the manufacturer's involvement. It is important to stress, therefore, that increasingly retailers are adopting much more sophisticated approaches to extract the fullest possible return from their space and so are likely to have strong views on in-store promotions and point of sale material. Some clues to their attitudes are to be found in two articles published in successive weeks in *Marketing* – 'Centres of Attraction' by Brian Seymour (6 September 1984) and 'Supermarket Scientists' by Maureen Johnson (13 September 1984). In the first article Seymour points to the growing difficulty experienced by FMCG manufacturers in getting in-store display space to influence customers near the point of purchase and advocates that such manufacturers should follow the US pattern and seek to get display in shopping centres.

Johnson's article provides a number of insights and findings based on studies by Research Bureau which illuminate the dynamics of point of sale activity. For example, 20 per cent of purchases are decided in-store (worth £1 billion plus). For 2 per cent of purchases the brand is undecided before the shopper enters the outlet, and 9 per cent of purchases involve switching from intended purchase on entering the store, while 9 per cent are impulse or reminder buys. Clearly, the ability to influence such decisions with effective p-o-s display and in-store promotion is considerable.

■ Telemarketing

The 22 June issue of *Marketing Week* in 1990 contained a review of telemarketing in which it reported the findings of the British Direct Marketing Association that half of companies already use the phone to win business and currently spend about £5 billion on telemarketing. Currently, the main use is to fix sales appointments or to take enquiries for brochures but with the radical changes in technology which have occurred in recent years *Marketing Week* predicts that increasingly the telephone will come to be seen as a strategic sales medium.

A recent Key Note Report shows that use of the telephone as a major marketing technique grew 126 per cent between 1987 and 1990 as compared with a 63 per cent growth in the use of direct mail over the same period. Currently 87 per cent of all households own a telephone which approaches levels in the USA and the day is not far off when access to both households and organisational customers will be almost 100 per cent. Perhaps equally important to the growth of telemarketing is the change in attitude to the telephone as an information and communication medium greatly encouraged by the break-up of the old Post Office monopoly and the introduction of competition between British Telecom and other suppliers such as Mercury, i.e. the telephone companies are marketing their services too.

In addition to establishing initial contact with potential new customers (cold calling) e.g. double glazing, time shares, financial services etc., the telephone is seen as providing an increasingly important role in improving service levels and maintaining customer loyalty. *Marketing Week* cites the general Electric Answer Center in Louisville, Kentucky as a prime example of how to use the telephone to add value. GE products promote a toll-free number for consumers to call if they have any questions or problems. Staff have access to 750 000 items of information about GE products to help callers when washing machines go wrong, recommend a type of refrigerator, and so on. GE found that such a service encouraged consumers to buy more from the company, and then to recommend it to others. Similarly, research by the Technical Assistance Research Program for Coca-Cola established that complaints and queries could be answered more effectively by telephone than by letter. Given that Nielsen studies show that only one out of 50 unhappy customers complain – the rest simply switch brands – any service which can keep customers in contact with suppliers must add value and help retain customer loyalty.

Increasingly sophisticated technology such as automated call distributed (ACD) systems and predictive dialling will undoubtedly accelerate the growth of telemarketing. In the case of ACD, calls are routed to available operators automatically with full details of the caller being displayed on a computer terminal while, with predictive dialling, the computer will estimate pick-up rates and average call length to determine how many calls can be handled at any one time. However, the UK has banned the use of equipment which dials an endless list of telephone numbers linked to a computer which then makes the sales call.

Part IV

MARKETING IN PRACTICE

CHAPTER 19

The company: organising for marketing

Learning Goals

The issues to be addressed in this chapter include:

1. Basic organisational structures.
2. The organisation of the marketing department.
3. The nature of product and market management.
4. The impact of marketing on organisational structure.
5. The nature of corporate resources.

After reading this chapter you will be able to:

1. Recognise different forms of organisational structure.
2. Explain the need for both *differentiation* and *integration* in the effective organisation.
3. List and describe seven basic methods of organising a marketing department.
4. Describe the origin, evolution and application of the product manager concept.
5. Describe the market manager concept and compare and contrast it with the product manager concept.
6. Discuss the relationship between the marketing concept, marketing orientation and organisational structure.
7. List some of the influences on the structure of an organisation and particularly the various corporate resources it may have at its disposal.

The change from a seller's to a buyer's market in the 1950s precipitated a rash of literature promising managerial salvation through adoption of the marketing concept. With the desperation of a drowning man corporations in every field of activity seized the straw, and marketing staff appointments proliferated. As anticipated profits failed to materialise, disillusionment set in and marketing became the scapegoat. Supporters of marketing responded by pointing out that adoption of the marketing concept requires a complete reorientation of the firm's activities which renaming the sales function was unlikely to bring about.

Superficial as this description is, it serves to underline that the firm's organisational structure is critical to marketing success. In the era of excess demand, top management attention was rightly focused on increasing output, and a production orientation was both necessary and understandable. However, a firm is more than a collection of individuals, it is a social system with its own norms, status structure and system of rewards and punishments. It is unrealistic to assume that these can be changed overnight, yet many firms which have rejected the marketing concept have done to because they failed to appreciate the inherent organisational implications, or else instituted extensive changes without full consideration of the possible ramifications. Fortunately, the unhappy experiences of the disillusioned have served to concentrate attention on the organisational implications associated with a marketing orientation.

■ Basic organisational structures

Given the possible variations in the extent of corporate resources, the products they manufacture and the markets they serve, it is clear that there can be no single organisational structure of universal applicability. Despite the infinite variations in degree, the fundamental organisational choice revolves around grouping activities by product or function. This dilemma was the subject of an article by two well-known authorities on organisation behaviour, Arthur H. Walker and Jay W. Lorsch ('Organizational choice: product *vs.* function', *Harvard Business Review*, XLIV, vi, Nov–Dec 1968, pp. 129–38), on which the following discussion draws heavily.

Traditionally, organisational theorists have suggested that the appropriate structure should be decided on the basis of three criteria:

1. Which approach permits the maximum use of special technical knowledge?
2. Which provides the most efficient utilisation of machinery and equipment?
3. Which provides the best hope of obtaining the required control and co-ordination?

Walker and Lorsch feel that these traditional criteria ignore the trade-off between functional specialisation and difficulties of co-ordination, and product specialisation which promotes collaboration between specialists but tends to lose identification with functional goals. To make good this omission the authors propose that three findings from the behavioural sciences should also be taken into account, namely:

1. Functional specialists tend to develop patterns of behaviour and thought that are in tune with the demands of their jobs and their prior training, and as a result these specialists (e.g. industrial engineers and production supervisors) have different ideas and orientation about what is important in getting the job

done. This is called *differentiation* and is necessary for functional specialists to perform their jobs effectively.

2. Differentiation is closely related to achievement of co-ordination, or what behavioural scientists call *integration*. This means collaboration between specialised units or individuals. Recent studies have demonstrated that there is an inverse relationship between differentiation and integration: the more two functional specialists (or their units) differ in their patterns of behaviour and thought, the more difficult it is to bring about integration between them.

3. While achievement of both differentiation and integration is possible, it can only occur when well-developed means of communication among specialists exist in the organisation and when the specialists are effective in resolving the inevitable cross-functional conflicts.

It is suggested that these findings raise three basic questions which must be answered when choosing between a product, or functional basis of organisation.

(*a*) Does it permit sufficient differentiation for the effective performance of specialist tasks?
(*b*) Is the degree of differentiation consistent with the desired level of integration?
(*c*) How will the structure affect intra-firm channels of communication?

Although the appropriate structure will depend upon external factors, Walker and Lorsch suggest two useful generalisations:

1. The functional type of structure is appropriate where the firm is faced with a routine and repetitive task. Under these circumstances integration can be achieved through plans, and conflict resolved by the hierarchy.
2. Where the task involves problem-solving, i.e. dealing with new situations, then the product organisation is more appropriate.

However, as the authors note, most firms are faced with a combination of both routine tasks and problem-solving, e.g. the marketing of established products and new product development. As a result most firms find it necessary to adopt some form of compromise as is evident from current organisation charts. The question of the most appropriate structure for the firm as a whole will be returned to following a consideration of the organisation of the marketing department *per se*.

■ Organisation of the marketing department

In practice organisation suggests that the marketing department may be organised in one of seven basic ways:

1. Functionally oriented.
2. Product oriented.
3. Market/customer oriented.
4. Regionally oriented.

5. Functional/product orientation.
6. Functional/market orientation.
7. Functional/regional orientation.

A marketing department organised on functional lines is illustrated in Figure 19.1 below. Under this structure, personnel are grouped by functional specialisation and their activities are co-ordinated by the marketing director or manager. Such a system enjoys the advantages of simplicity and clearly designated areas of responsibility. On the other hand such advantages are often negated by the restricted outlook which such compartmentalisation inevitably breeds. There is a tendency for each department to plough its own furrow, and efforts to co-ordinate the diverse interests of specialists imbued in a specific functional practice can be exceedingly wasteful of managerial time and effort. The larger the company the worse the problem becomes.

Firms with broadly differentiated product lines frequently organise their marketing functions of a product or product group basis. This form of structure, depicted in Figure 19.2, is only viable where each product/product group generates sufficient sales volume to justify the inevitable duplication of effort. Consequently, this form of structure is usually found in large, decentralised companies, where each division is concerned with the manufacture of a specialised product and may be regarded as a strategic business unit or SBU.

As an alternative to a product orientation, the hypothetical firm illustrated in Figure 19.2 might prefer to organise on a market or customer basis, when its organisation chart would appear as shown in Figure 19.3

A regional marketing organisation is most frequently found in the case of a large, decentralised company with extensive markets capable of subdivision into distinct geographical units. It is particularly appropriate to multi-national firms but, in common with the product and market structure, it suffers from duplication of effort, and problems of communication and co-ordination.

Figure 19.1   Marketing department organised on a functional basis

Figure 19.2 Product-oriented organisation

Figure 19.3 Market-oriented organisation

In an attempt to overcome these defects, many firms have adopted a line and staff structure which seeks to combine the benefits of functional specialisation with the varying demands of different products and markets. Currently there is considerable debate about the relative merits of organising on a product or market basis and some discussion is appropriate here.

■ The product manager concept

It is often implied that the product manager concept is of recent origin but there is evidence to suggest that General Electric had adopted such a title in the United

States as early as 1894, while Libby, McNeil & Libby claim to have appointed product managers in 1919. Generally, however, the introduction of the concept is credited to its leading exponent, Procter & Gamble, who appointed a brand manager for Lava soap in 1928. (Product manager and brand manager are interchangeable terms for the same basic function.)

Essentially, the product manager's function is to co-ordinate all activities associated with the marketing of a given product – a function which became critical with the adoption of a product differentiation as a major dimension of competitive strategy. Opinions differ as to the precise responsibilities and authority of the product manager but, in general, it is possible to discern four major activities:

1. *Planning.* At the tactical level the product manager is usually responsible for the preparation of detailed plans for the marketing of his product, e.g. the preparation of budgets and determination of the precise mix of marketing inputs. At the strategic level he is responsible for anticipating change and the preparation of plans to deal effectively with this change, e.g. new product development.
2. *Information seeking and evaluation.* In order to anticipate change it is necessary continually to scan the environment and monitor the strength and direction of relevant trends. Specifically, this involves keeping track of competitors' activities in the widest sense, i.e. one must not only keep informed about directly competing substitutes but also attempt to identify the less immediate threat implicit in new products and processes. Equally, one must be sensitive to marketing innovations such as the development of automatic vending machines, systems selling, etc.
3. *Co-ordination.* As the product 'expert', it is the product manager's responsibility to co-ordinate all those company functions which impinge upon the successful marketing of that product. Of all the functions, this presents the greatest challenge to the product manager as it inevitably requires him to be all things to all men. On the other hand these are the same skills required of top managers, and the product manager position can prove a valuable training and proving ground for senior appointments.
4. *Control.* This function not only incorporates the familiar price/cost and budgetary dimensions but also includes the introduction of new products and the phasing out of old products.

No valid generalisation can be offered as to the relative importance attached to these four activities in practice as, of necessity, this will vary from firm to firm.

In an article in the *Quarterly Review of Marketing* ('Product Management versus Market Management', Summer 1982, pp. 22–5) Michael J. Thomas looked at the role of the product manager and commented:

A long-time complaint of most product managers is that they are given responsibility without commensurate authority. But companies who have been filling product manager positions with younger, less experienced people have had to question how much responsibility should be delegated to their product managers. Responsibility often has been assigned for achievement of sales volume, market share, and sometimes profit goals but the product manager has no line authority over the functional departments that execute his plans.

Yet, we know that product management works to the satisfaction of many companies. The key to understanding why is found in the expertise of the product manager. He knows more about his product and the marketing plan that supports it than anyone else, and this expert power is the source of his being able to enlist the support of others. Thus the product manager is 'a recommender, a co-ordinator, and a watchdog who keeps an eye on his product and market place and sounds the alert when danger or opportunity arises' (Richard M. Clewett and Stanley F. Stasch, 'Shifting Role of the Product Manager', *Harvard Business Review*, Jan–Feb 1975).

■ Market managers

As with any organisational innovation, the product manager system has not enjoyed unqualified success and many firms that adopted such a system during the first flush of enthusiasm in the late 1950s have since discarded it. In those instances where the product manager system has 'failed', examination usually reveals that the company was fundamentally unsuited to such an organisational structure. In a company like Procter & Gamble which is producing a group of nearly identical products from the same manufacturing facility, all of which are to be sold through the same distributive outlets, the product manager system ensures that each brand is given the individual attention it needs. On the other hand, where a company is selling the same product into a number of different end-use markets, emphasis on the product will be inappropriate. As noted earlier, the concept of market segmentation rests on the proposition that there are differences in the needs, and buying behaviour, of sub-groups which collectively comprise the aggregate demand for a product. From this it follows that a different marketing strategy will be appropriate to each segment, which, in turn, predicates the appointment of market managers.

In the author's opinion the appointment of a market manager represents the purest implementation of the marketing concept, for it is implicit that consumer requirements will take precedence over all other activities. It is an overt recognition that different market segments represent distinct, and often dissimilar, needs, not only in terms of precise product specification but also in terms of service requirements and buying behaviour. Further, in the case of industrial goods, it recognises that many buyers have a need for a series of related products which may usefully be combined into a 'system', e.g. National Cash Register do not just sell business machines, they sell accounting 'systems' tailor-made to the end-user's specific requirements. Emphasis on the product may well result in the employment of salesmen specialising in given products and thus miss out on such opportunities.

As a broad generalisation it would seem that where customer buying habits are conditioned by the nature of the product and are similar across industry or user categories, then the responsibility for marketing should be vested in a product manager. Conversely, if it is possible to distinguish marked differences in the needs or buying behaviour of separate customer groups, then these should be regarded as different markets and market managers appointed.

However, as Michael Thomas points out in the article cited earlier, it would be a mistake to assume that the product-manager and market-manager approaches are mutually exclusive options. Thus:

> When companies have a variety of products channelling to a variety of markets, neither the product manager approach not the market manager approach alone is appropriate. This is a situation when a dual management approach could be utilised. If the product manager is used alone, it is very unlikely that he will be able to collect data and utilise market information for the entire market. On the other hand, if the market manager is used, he well most likely be concerned with the welfare of his own market and not care about anyone else's. He may want all the products and attention for his own market which can have a damaging effect on other markets and, in turn, on the overall effectiveness of the company.

Clearly, running product managers and market managers in tandem is a potential source of conflict, but Thomas and others regard this as a positive force which can be beneficial if managed correctly. Thomas cites B. Charles Ames ('Dilemma of Product/Market Management', *Harvard Business Review*, March–April 1971, pp. 66–74) who offers six rules for achieving this:

1. Determine the need for dual management.
2. Define each manager's role.
3. Change the information and planning systems.
4. Select the right candidates.
5. Explain the concept to key functional managers.
6. Monitor the activities of both product and market managers.

Provided one can achieve and control the kind of matrix organisation which is required for such a dual management system, then 'The benefits of increased market opportunities, stronger competitive position, and, in the long run, greater profits far outweigh the added costs and conflict that will arise with its use' (Thomas, 'Product Management'). Table 19.1 taken from Nigel Piercy's book *Marketing Organisation* (George Allen & Unwin, 1985) summarises well the advantages and disadvantages of various kinds of marketing structures.

TABLE 19.1   Comparison of marketing structures

Form	Advantages	Disadvantages	Situational indicators
Functional	Specialisation in task activities to develop skills. Marketing tasks and responsibilities clearly defined.	Excess levels of hierarchy may reduce unity control. Direct lines of communication may be ignored. Conflicts may emerge. Integration problem for CME.	Simple marketing operations. Single primary product/ market.
Product/ brand	Specialisation in products/ brands. More management attention to marketing requirements of different products/ brands. Fast reaction to product-related change.	Dual reporting. Too much product emphasis. More management levels and cost. Conflict.	Wide product lines sold to homogeneous groups of customers, but sharing production/ marketing systems – i.e. proliferation of brands and diversified products requiring different skills/activities.
Market/ customer/ geographical	Specialisation in a market entity– focus on customer needs. Fast reaction to market-related changes.	Duplication of functions. Co-ordination problems. More management levels.	Limited, standardised homogeneous product line sold to customers in different industries – i.e. proliferation of markets each meriting separate efforts.
Product/ market overlay	Advantages of func-tional product and market specialisation and integration.	Allocation of respons-ibilities is difficult. Duplication inefficiences.	Multiple products and multiple markets.

 # The impact of marketing on organisational structure

In the organisational context, marketing may be viewed as both a function and a philosophy. All firms have marketing function, even if it only involves selecting an intermediary to sell their output, but few firms have a marketing philosophy as embodied in the marketing concept and described in Chapter 1. Unfortunately, the distinction between the function and the philosophy is rarely stated explicitly, and has resulted in considerable misunderstanding and even acrimony.

As a function, marketing is no more, nor less, important than finance, legal, personnel, production, purchasing, research and development, or any other conceivable area of specialisation. In a given context it is only natural that more emphasis will be accorded to a specific function, which will tend to predominate over the others, but there is nothing to predicate that it will, or should, be marketing. The widely held misconception that marketers are seeking to take over other functional areas is a myth, albeit one fostered by the profession, which largely owes its existence to the high 'visibility' of marketing in the consumer goods field. Even so, firms manufacturing private brands will probably place far greater emphasis on production economies and quality control than on marketing. In the industrial goods field this tendency will be even more pronounced.

As a business philosophy, marketing requires the firm to do what it has always set out to do – combine the resources at its disposal in the manner which will best enable it to achieve its long-run profit goals. What distinguishes it from other business philosophies is that marketing perceives consumption as a democratic process in which consumers have the right to select preferred candidates and elect them by casting their money votes. As the political critics of marketing, and advertising in particular, should appreciate, you may delude the electorate once with spurious campaign promises but you had better not seek re-election. Further, unless you propose policies of which they approve you will have to give way to the candidate who does.

In the democratic environment of a free enterprise economy, success comes to the firm which sets out to discover the nature of human wants and develops products to satisfy such wants in highly specific ways. Satisfying customers can only be achieved through the concerted efforts of all members of the organisation recognising this as a common goal and working towards it. Thus, the production manager who insists on maximising productivity, in the conventional sense of maximum volume at lowest cost, by excluding non-standard items from his production schedule lacks a marketing orientation. He fails to see that the non-standard item might develop into a market leader, or that the fact that his salesman cannot offer it will predispose the firm's largest customer to switch to the company that can. Conversely, the production manager who balances the conventional criteria against such considerations is marketing oriented, despite his function and job title.

Acceptance of the marketing concept by individuals is insufficient in itself to make the firm marketing oriented – it must also develop an organisational structure that will permit it to translate thought into action. In today's increasingly competitive environment this demands that the firm be more creative and flexible than in the past; specifically, it requires:

(a) That the firm continually scan the business environment, i.e. the firm must develop its own early warning system so that it is in a position not only to meet change but also to initiate it.

(b) That the firm utilise incoming data to formulate creative plans stating not only what it wishes to achieve, but also how and in what sequence.

(c) That these plans be communicated effectively to those charged with the responsibility for their implementation, and that such responsibility be backed with the necessary resources and authority.

(d) That the firm make full use of new managerial techniques developed to assist the decision-maker in arriving at an informed decision, e.g. operations research and Bayesian decision theory.

At a given point in time, however, the firm's immediate success depends on its existing product line. If previous planning has been effective the production and sale of these products should be routine and demand a functional organisation. As noted, however, planning and new product development are problem-solving activities for which a functional structure is unsuited and some form of compromise structure is called for.

One solution is the setting up of project teams comprised of representatives from each of the functional departments (sometimes referred to as a 'matrix' organisation). Such a team may be formed on an *ad hoc* basis to suggest solutions to a particular problem, or to review suggestions from functional departments. Alternatively, the team may be established on a permanent basis and function as a separate department, e.g. many companies have set up Long-range Planning Departments.

Another solution is evident in the trend to what has been termed 'recentralised decentralisation'. During the 1950s concepts such as the 'span of control' predisposed the management of large, diversified companies to decentralise

TABLE 19.2   How is your marketing organised?

	Total sample (1298)	Better performers (160)	Others (1138)	Better performer variation from others
All products under one manager	40.7%	30.0%	42.2%	-21%
Separate product managers	15.9%	17.5%	15.7%	+ 11%
Separate market managers	12.6%	16.9%	12.0%	+ 41%
A combination of the above	30.8%	35.6%	30.1%	+ 18%

Source: G. J. Hooley, C. J. West and J. E. Lynch, *Marketing in the UK: A Survey of Current Practices and Performance*, The Institute of Marketing, 1984.

authority on a divisional basis. Under this system each division operates virtually as a separate company, and sets up its own production and marketing organisations. In many instances, however, the benefits of specialisation were negated by diseconomies arising from duplication of effort and poor co-ordination, and prompted top management to recentralise certain functions at corporate headquarters. Foremost among these are purchasing and marketing. Centralised purchasing offers clear benefits due to the economies of bulk buying, while centralised marketing services permit greater specialisation and the development of a consistent marketing approach across the whole field of the firm's activities.

Some indication of the preferred from of marketing organisation is to be found in the findings of a survey undertaken by Hooley *et al.* as shown in Table 19.2, on the previous page.

Clearly many companies use a combination of methods, the trend being most marked among larger and consumer goods companies.

The extent to which a firm can improve its competitive standing through organisational change is, in the final analysis, conditioned by the resources at its disposal and some reference to this dimension is called for.

■ Corporate resources

The resources which a company has at its disposal are of two main types – human and physical. Such resources may be internal to the organisation, or they may be external to it in the sense that the firm can gain or exercise control over them, e.g. the distributive channel.

Within the firm, resources, both human and physical, tend to be specific, and so limit the possible range of production/marketing activities which the firm can undertake. In the long run, however, the firm can change its 'resource mix', and the aim of planning is to determine:

(*a*)   What activities will maximise the productivity of existing resources?
(*b*)   What markets offer the greatest potential in future?
(*c*)   What changes need to be made in the present resource mix to enable the firm to exploit these future opportunities?

Clearly, the answers to these questions must be based on an analysis of existing resources, which will be facilitated by the use of a check-list on the following lines:

1. *Physical resources*
    Land   – as a source of raw materials.
           – as a location for manufacturing and distributive activities.

Buildings – general purpose or specific, i.e. designed for light engineering, assembly, storage, etc., or for heavy manufacturing requiring special foundations, services, etc.

Availability of and access to – power supplies, drainage and waste disposal
– transportation: road, rail, canal, port facilities, etc.

Plant equipment – general purpose, e.g. lathe, press
– specific, e.g. steel rolling mill, foundry, etc.

2. *Technical resources.* Essentially these reside in the technical expertise of the firm's employees, together with the possession of patents, licences or highly specialised equipment.
3. *Financial resources.* These are comprised of the liquid assets in the firm's balance sheet, the ability to secure loans against fixed assets and the ability to raise capital in the market on the basis of past and anticipated future performance. They also comprise the skill of the firm's financial management.
4. *Purchasing resources.* Managerial expertise backed by any special advantage enjoyed by the firm by virtue of its size or connection e.g. reciprocal trading agreements.
5. *Labour resources.* The skills, experience and adaptability of the work force.
6. *Marketing resources.* The degree of consumer/user acceptance or 'franchise' developed through past performance. Access to and degree of control over distribution; the specialised skills and experiences of its personnel.

The above list is by no means exhaustive but serves to indicate the factors the firm must take into account when appraising its own ability to undertake a given course of action. Clearly, the importance attached to any particular factor will depend upon the unique nature of the problem under consideration.

■ Summary

In this chapter it has only been possible to look at the organisation of the marketing function in a superficial way when, as many readers will know, the topics of organisation design and development are the subject of books and courses in their own right. Before leaving the issue, however, it is vital to stress that while organisational forms and structures may have an important part to play in determining a firm's efficiency and performance as we saw in Chapter 3 it is the corporate culture which most often determines whether a firm will succeed or fail in the market place.

Although the concepts of climate and corporate culture have been around for several decades (indeed I used them myself in the 1960s and 1970s when researching innovativeness (see *Marketing New Industrial Products*, Macmillan, 1975) it is only in the 1980s that they have moved to centre stage with the recognition that it is the 'people factor' which ultimately determines the quality of a firm's performance. Given the accelerating pace of technological change and the growth in telecommunications it is now estimated that even radical innovations will be diffused world-wide within 18 months of their first appearance. Maintaining a differential advantage in terms of the actual product or service has become increasingly difficult even in multinational corporations firmly committed to a policy of continuous new product development. Indeed, it is this very commitment which results in the rapid erosion of tangible product advantages and leads to shorter and shorter life-cycles. Under these circumstances it is the relationship between a supplier and user which is critical to user patronage and loyalty. In turn the maintenance of the relationship depends upon the commitment and quality of the implementation by the supplier.

The validity of this claim has been borne out by the findings of numerous management books published in the 1980s based upon both anecdotal and rigourous survey based research (see, for example Peters and Waterman's *In Search of Excellence*, McBurnie and Clutterbuck's *The Marketing Edge*, and Baker and Hart's *Marketing and Competitive Success*). It is also the central theme in Stephen King's article 'Brand Building in the 1990s' (*Journal of Marketing Management*, vol. 7.1, 1991) in which he argues that the absence of objective differences will make consumers increasingly dependent upon the company 'brand'. He argues:

> It's arguable that in a competitive situation getting the company brand right is the most important job for the management. Equally, it's clear that not many companies have organised their management structures with that in mind.
>
> The companies behind the classic brands are not by any means a good model (indeed they may be increasingly wrong for their own purposes). They tend to rely too much on the traditional 'family tree' type hierarchy. That means they are too split by function to lead naturally to the innovation and imagination that any brand constantly needs. Decisions tend to be made too tactically, too low down in the organisation, with too little guidance from the top.
>
> The right organisation for a company brand implies that brand management should reside right at the top. And since inventive organisations tend to be based on small, flexible, interactive, multidisciplinary working groups, I think that our model (at a symbolic, rather than organisation chart, level) should be something like the figure on the following page:
>
> The skills needed for this management working group would be those of *production* (the organisation and efficient running of the company's products/ services); *personnel* (recruitment/training/inspiring of the people who make up the corporate brand); *communications* (all aspects of communications, marketing and consumer/customer research); and possibly as a separate skill that of *brand designer* a new type of animal, concerned with design in its broadest sense (Lorenz, 1986), from R & D to adding services to products and vice versa, with a passion for the totality of the brand). The whole group to be led by the *CEO* – he's the real brand *manager*.
>
> However, such a model is translated into reality, it seems to me that many companies need to take a new look at their organisation charts, with brand-building

in mind. Most authorities (e.g. Pascale and Athos, 1981; Doyle, Saunders and Wong, 1990) seem to agree what there will have to be a more flexible and less hierarchical approach, with more informal networking, in order to get the rapid response and to attract the rare skills that a successful company brand needs.

It clearly goes a lot further than organisation. What the best company brands represent is a common culture – common aims, standards, language, approaches and style. A common personality, rather than a book of rules. This may sound a little abstract and qualitative, but it is what consumers value in company brands (IBM, ICI or Marks & Spencer, for instance). That puts an enormous premium on sheer leadership from the top (Hamel and Prahalad, 1989). A company brand cannot succeed if the individuals doing the detailed work are zombies who aren't allowed to take any initiatives. Equally, it will not be a brand at all if there are no common links or if they don't know how they're expected to behave.

Implicit in all of this is the belief that it is the truly marketing oriented company which is most likely to have the kind of corporate culture which will ensure that its objectives match precisely those of its intended customers.

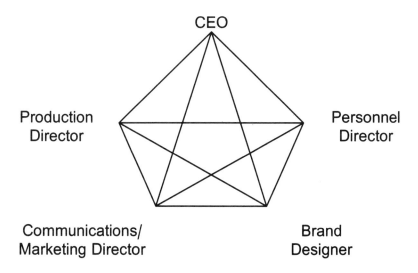

THE NEW BRAND MANAGEMENT

CEO

Production Director

Personnel Director

Communications/ Marketing Director

Brand Designer

Source: S. King, 'Brand Building in the 1990s', *Journal of Marketing Management*, vol 7.1, 1991.

CHAPTER 20
Planning for marketing

__ Learning Goals __

The issues to be discussed in this chapter include:

1. The concept of corporate strategy.
2. The nature of the marketing audit.
3. The preparation of marketing plans.
4. Financial measures for marketing analysis and control.

After reading this chapter you will be familiar with:

1. The nature of corporate strategy and the key phases in the strategic process – appreciation, plan and implementation.
2. The design and execution of marketing audits.
3. The design, layout and content of a formal marketing plan.
4. The calculation of mark-ups, discounts and stock turn.
5. The application of standard costing and budgetary control to marketing planning.
6. Ratio analysis and its use in competitive analysis.

Planning is a pervasive human activity by which we seek to exercise some degree of control over the future. As a process it will vary enormously depending upon a number of variables, foremost among which will be the complexity of the activity and the degree of uncertainty concerning the future situation in which the activity will take place. Fundamentally, however, all planning seeks to arrive at a present decision concerning future action – the more complex the activity and the more uncertain the future, the greater the need for formal, systematic planning procedures. The purpose of this chapter is to provide a brief synthesis of the separate treatment given the marketing environment and the various mix elements, and to indicate how the marketer can integrate all these considerations into a marketing plan. It must be stressed that this is the briefest of introductions to a large and complex subject, which is dealt with at length in *Marketing Strategy and Management* (Macmillan, 1985) which was written specifically for those students who have completed an introductory course of the kind provided for by this text. Marketing planning does not figure in such introductory courses and the brief discussion provided here is intended solely to emphasise the point that the various marketing functions described earlier need to be seen as part of a coherent and integrated action plan if they are to be used effectively.

■ The concept of corporate strategy

Some reference has already been made to the concept of corporate strategy, as, for example, when discussing new product development, but some elaboration is necessary here. Like comparative marketing, corporate strategy is an old concept in a new and revitalised form. Probably the most important distinction between strategy as practised by earlier generations of entrepreneurs and today's professional managers is that the latter consciously and explicitly state their aims and objectives and develop plans designed to achieve them.

In his book *Strategy and Structure* (Massachusetts Institute of Technology Press, 1962), Alfred D. Chandler defines corporate strategy as 'The determination of the basic long-term goals and objectives of an enterprise, and the adoption of courses of action and the allocation of resources necessary for carrying out these goals'.

This definition suggests three distinct phases in the strategic process:

Appreciation
Plan
Implementation.

Each of these stages is capable of further subdivision, and Kotler (in *Marketing Management*) offers the following progression:

Diagnosis: where is the company now, and why?
Prognosis: where is the company headed?
Objectives: where should the company be headed?
Strategy: what is the best way to get there?
Tactics: what specific actions should be undertaken, by whom, and when?
Control: what measures should be watched to indicate whether the company is succeeding?

Similarly, the Marketing Science Institute (see Patrick J. Robinson and David J. Luck, *Promotional Decision Making Practice and Theory*, Marketing Science Institute series, McGraw-Hill, 1964) has developed a model called APACS (Adaptive Planning and Control Sequence) which recognises the following stages which were first discussed in Chapter 7, namely:

Step 1. Define problem and set objectives.
Step 2. Appraise overall situation.
Step 3. Determine the tasks to be accomplished and identify the means to achieving these aims.
Step 4. Identify alternative plans and mixes.

Step 5. Estimate the expected results arising from implementation of the alternative plans.

Step 6. Managerial review and decision.

Step 7. Feedback of results and post audit.

Step 6. Adapt programme if required.

In turn, each of these models is capable of further subdivision, but the basic three-stage model will serve our purposes here.

■ Appreciation: the marketing audit[*]

In 1959 the American Marketing Association published an extensive management report entitled 'Analysing and Improving Marketing Performance: Marketing Audits in Theory & Practice'. While much has been written since, this still remains the most comprehensive treatment of the subject and provides the framework for this section.

According to Edward B. Reynolds, 'The term "audit" is generally understood in business usage to mean a review or appraisal of some business function or activity. As a management tool, it is traditionally used to determine the accuracy and adequacy of accounting and financial operations . . . In the field of marketing, however, the application of the audit technique as a device for evaluating not only the operational aspects of marketing but also the philosophy and policies upon which marketing operations are based is still a far from common practice.' This is certainly not the case today in marketing where auditing is also used as a device for evaluating possible future courses of action in addition to its traditional role as a means of assessing past performance. Thus, while audits first came into use as a diagnostic device for sick and ailing companies they are now used by many organisations for a regular 'check-up'.

In his Introduction, Reynolds discerns a wide range of views on the nature and practice of the audit but identifies general agreement on four basic points:

1. A planned review is an essential requirement not only for the company in difficulty but also for the company enjoying an apparently sound marketing operation.
2. The evaluation of the marketing operation must be all inclusive, involving not only every marketing activity and every marketing practice but also the underlying marketing philosophy and policies upon which these activities and practices are based.
3. The most significant requirement for successful appraisal is the establishment of valid and realistic standards of performance.
4. The evaluation process must not confine itself to the marketing operation as it exists today but must range into the future to explore untapped marketing possibilities.

---

[*] This section builds on the ideas first introduced in Chapter 3.

Subsequently, Abe Shuchman argues that it is important to distinguish the marketing audit from the continuous evaluations which executives make of the various marketing mix functions, on the grounds that such appraisals are far too limited in scope and are not undertaken in a planned and coherent fashion. 'They do not, within a specified interval, examine each and every facet of the *total* operation. There is no integrated, co-ordinated, comprehensive appraisal encompassing all marketing activities and executed systematically in accord with a planned program and schedule.' Thus he defines a marketing audit as:

a systematic, critical, and impartial review and appraisal of the total marketing operation: of the basic objectives and policies of the operation and the assumptions which underlie them as well as of the methods, procedures, personnel, and organisation employed to implement the policies and achieve the objectives.

Shuchman also emphasises that the marketing audit is a prognostic as well as a diagnostic tool:

The audit is, in addition, concerned with identifying the particular strengths of the marketing operation. It is a search for opportunities, existing and potential...

Continued success requires continual adaptation to a constantly changing environment. It requires, therefore, continual scrutiny of the environment and of the firm's relationship to the environment, with the aim of spotting the ones which indicate both a need for modifying the firm's marketing program and the direction such modification should take. It requires an unremitting search for emerging opportunities that can and must be exploited if the marketing operation is to remain highly successful.

The need to implement a formal programme of market auditing is that otherwise marginal adjustments to facets of the mix may well result, collectively, in the operation getting out of synchronisation with its environment, i.e. there is a difference between 'fine tuning' and 'tinkering'. Similarly, auditing needs to be continuous: 'in marketing as in home maintenance the time to fix the roof is when the sun is shining'.

Shuchman identifies several problems associated with auditing:

1. Defining appropriate criteria or measures for assessing the effectiveness of the mix elements and marketing activity.
2. Selection of auditors.
3. Scheduling the audit.
4. The impact of the audit.

Alfred R. Oxenfeldt ('The Marketing Audit as a Total Evaluation Program') argues that in the absence of a formal plan of evaluation some aspects will be appraised frequently and possibly at excessive costs while some phases of the business go unappraised for very long periods – often until the company is experiencing serious difficulties. Accordingly, a marketing audit must comprise the review of objectives, policies, organisation, methods, procedures and personnel in a total evaluation programme. He then proposes 5 broad approaches:

1. Audits classified by major marketing functions.
2. Audits classified by managerial aspects.
3. Audits classified by standards of appraisal.
4. Audits classified by frequency of evaluation.
5. Audits classified by sources of evaluation.

In auditing the marketing mix it is essential to do this in an integrated way so that the contribution of the individual elements may be related to each other and not just looked at in isolation. In the latter case it is quite likely that optimising on one dimension will lead to sub-optimisation on others and it is the maximum overall effect which is being looked for. In other words, one is seeking to achieve the optimum 'balance' between the various mix elements while, at the same time, one is monitoring them for incipient problems.

Auditing in terms of the major managerial aspects of the marketing function(s) is complementary to the auditing of the actual functions themselves and should be executed in terms of the six dimensions (objectives etc.) identified previously.

When auditing the objectives of a given activity one should ask the manager responsible to give you an explicit statement. Frequently such statements reveal important differences in emphasis and approach and it is essential to ensure that such differences do not render specific objectives incompatible with each other or with the overall purpose of the organisation. In a recent consultancy assignment for a national non-profit organisation, it was found that Headquarter's concern with the level of subsidy required by its operational units which had led to exhortations to these units to increase their revenue generation activities, was diametrically opposed to the objective that the units give priority access to designated users at nominal charges – i.e. the direct opposite of normal commercial practice whereby priority is given to those able and willing to pay the highest price and surplus capacity is sold off at marginal rates. Clearly, until one resolves such a contradiction of scrambled objectives, operating managers will be unable to determine the appropriate policies and tactics for the management of the function or operation for which they are responsible.

As Oxenfeldt notes, it is sometimes difficult to distinguish sharply between objectives and policies in practice, but in principle the difference is clear. 'Objectives represent goals and targets; policies represent broad principles which indicate how management believes these goals can best be achieved, and therefore are guides for decision and action.' Such a distinction underlines the desirability of seeking to specify objectives and policies with the greatest possible clarity in order to avoid confusion between ends and the means of achieving them.

Once the objectives and means of achieving them are clear the auditor must seek to determine whether the remaining four elements of organisation, methods, procedures and personnel are appropriate to each sub-function, such as advertising and sales, as well as to the marketing function overall.

The third approach to classifying marketing audits suggested by Oxenfeldt is in terms of the standards of appraisal used. By definition auditing is a process of making comparisons, usually between current and past achievement, so that one can assess the rate and direction of change in the parameters being evaluated. In turn such an analysis is an essential prerequisite to the formulation of future objectives against which performance can be evaluated.

In making a comparative analysis one may use both quantitative and qualitative methods and there is a fairly vigorous debate about which is most appropriate in what circumstances. The nature of the argument is well exemplified by the comparisons which many academics and managers make between leading business schools, such that Harvard is seen as being concerned with a qualitative emphasis upon judgemental decision-making while Chicago stresses precise measurement and quantitative analysis. In turn this leads commentators to classify Harvard as a school for general (line) managers and Chicago as a school for specialist (staff) managers. Of course, what the example points out is that you can make comparisons by emphasising differences while, at the same time or for other purposes, one could easily have stressed similarities and argued that Harvard and Chicago are identical in that they are first-rate business schools. As in most things the truth lies somewhere in between and an effective marketing audit will call for a judicious blend of both quantitative measurement and qualitative judgements. That said, there is much to be said for seeking to quantify subjective and judgemental appraisals through the use of Bayesian analysis as described in Chapter 10.

A further factor which has to be taken into account when devising marketing audits is the frequency of evaluation. The basic guide here must surely be the cost effectiveness of the auditing procedure, and one must beware of dissipating managerial time upon the collection of data for its own sake. Similarly one must not gravitate to the other extreme of assuming that managers are paid to make judgements and so need not dwell upon facts.

Finally, Oxenfeldt addresses the question of who should carry out the auditing function (source of evaluation). Five basic alternatives suggest themselves.

First, auditing may be considered the responsibility of the person in overall charge of an activity – 'auditing from above'. Second, one may invite a person from another functional area but at the same level in the organisation. Third, one can commission a 'task force' of individuals from various other areas in the organisation. Fourth, one can adopt a scheme of self-appraisal. And finally, one can bring in outside consultants to carry out the task. Each of these alternatives has its merits and demerits but as a general principle an audit is only likely to enjoy the confidence of a management group if it is actually involved in the auditing process itself to some degree. That said, most authors prefer a task force approach where this is feasible (usually restricted to large companies) followed by the use of external consultants. Where a company is attempting a marketing audit for the first time and needs to establish both a base line (where we are today) and a procedure for implementing auditing on a continuous basis, then it is unlikely to possess the necessary expertise from within its own ranks and so will prefer to commission an experienced consultant to perform the task.

In the same manner that an overall management audit is an essential prerequisite of corporate planning, so the marketing audit is an essential prerequisite of marketing planning. In making this implied distinction, that corporate and marketing planning are different, one must be sensitive to the issue raised in Chapter 1 concerning the difference between the marketing concept and the marketing function. Following this distinction, all marketers and the great majority of successful managers would argue that in setting its corporate objectives the organisation should give priority to the needs of the market – in other words the corporate plan should be marketing orientated. However, this does not make it a marketing plan for, to be strictly accurate, such a plan is concerned with the management of the marketing function *per se* and its interface with the other functional areas of the business. These other functional areas will have management plans of their own (R & D; Purchasing, Production, Finance), each of which will be designed to implement the overall corporate plan. By the same token a corporate management audit will involve an evaluation of all the functional areas and go far beyond the scope of a marketing audit internally. Externally, however, the position is very different and it is this which sometimes leads people to perceive corporate and marketing audits and plans as being the same thing.

Because it is through the market that the organisation seeks to realise its objectives, much of its external evaluation of threats and opportunities is highly consonant with the primary concerns of the marketing function. Such distinction as one would make would tend to emphasise the corporate analysis of its environment as being conducted at a macro level while the external marketing audit is largely concerned with micro aspects. However, to conduct a micro analysis of, say, brand shares it is necessary to have some feeling of the status of the market itself and whether it is expanding, contracting or stationary *vis-à-vis* other competitive markets – namely, the macro position. For these reasons corporate and marketing audits of the external environment will possess a high degree of overlap although their emphasis will differ substantially. In the next chapter (The Written Analysis of Cases) we return to some of the specific factors which might be looked at in both an internal and external audit.

■ Planning

At this stage in the process it is important to distinguish clearly between the environmental constraints within which the firm must operate and those activities over which it can exercise control It is also important to recognise that in the long run all fixed constraints are variable in some degree – thus in the short term management must accept the existing distributive network, in the long term it can modify it through its own action, just as it can develop new markets and shape the nature of competition. However, in time the environment will change too owing to technological innovation and competitive activity, and the firm must seek to develop objectives which are sufficiently well defined to require commitment, yet flexible enough to permit a change in emphasis and direction as the situation evolves. 'Servicing the travelling public' is a good example of an overall long-term objective which meets these criteria. In the short term, the skill lies in developing strategies which make the best use of available resources in moving the firm from where it is to where it wants to be.

■ Implementation

In essence a strategy is a broad statement of the means to be employed in achieving a given objective, while the actual methods used constitute the tactics. Thus, a firm's strategy might be based on skimming the cream off the market, which suggests that the appropriate tactics would be:

High product quality
Distinctive design and packaging
High price
Selective distribution
Direct sale
Extensive after-sales service
Low pressure advertising, etc.

At the risk of overstating the obvious, the success of a given strategy depends upon the co-ordination of the tactics into an integrated, complementary and cohesive whole. There is a finite number of alternative strategies open to the firm and, in a given market, it is usual to find several competing firms pursuing the same basic strategy simultaneously. If this is so, then observed variations in performance must arise out of the quality of the plan, or statement of tactics, and its execution. Factors such as motivation and morale have an important bearing on the execution of a plan, but also tend to be a function of the plan's quality and credibility.

■ The preparation of a marketing plan

If the author has segmented the textbook market correctly, many readers will be preparing for examinations, such as those set by the Chartered Institute of Marketing, which require the student to analyse a case study and prepare a written marketing plan. Hopefully, the following outline will help the student in preparing such an analysis:

Analysis of the situation; appreciation. There is little point in restating the descriptive content of a case as the objective of an appreciation is to define the central issue. This is probably best achieved by a systematic analysis of the available material in terms of:

(a) What business is the company in and what are the salient features of this business?

(b) What is the firm's goal, explicit or implied?

(c) What resources has the company – Productive
                                   – Technical
                                   – Financial
                                   – Marketing?

(d) What policies, explicit or otherwise, has it adopted in respect of these resources?

(e) Is there a single strategic variable which dominates all others – if so, what is it?

(f) Has the firm any special skill or distinctive competence?

In analysing the case (or problem, in real life), one should seek to isolate those areas which bear directly upon both the immediate problem and the more general problem of which it is symptomatic. Once these areas have been defined they should be ranked in some rough order of importance and analysed in detail. For example, if a major issue is the nature of the product itself, one should list all the advantages and disadvantages which one can think of to permit an overall conclusion to be drawn. Similarly with all other issues. The conclusions drawn from the separate analysis of the relevant issues should then be summarized and stated as the basis upon which the plan has been based. This statement should also make explicit any assumptions which have been made, together with the reasons which support their adoption.

The marketing plan. This must be realistic in the light of the analysis described in the appreciation, and should commence by stating the overall objective or aim. If the student feels that the company's stated aims are incapable of attainment he must be able to present a very convincing argument as to why, and how, they should be changed. Thus the statement of the long-term aim must be supported by an exposition of all those factors which will affect the company's ability to achieve its objective, paying particular attention to environmental changes and changing consumer needs.

Following the statement of the long-term aim, the plan should state the short-term objective and the specific policies to be adopted to achieve it. In the interests of both clarity and coverage of all salient factors, some form of outline should be used similar to that given below.

1. Short-term, aim, e.g. to increase market share by 5 per cent.
2. Forecast of market conditions for the period of the plan.

3. Statement of further marketing research to be undertaken to provide feedback on performance and to be used in the preparation of future marketing plans.
4. Statement of product policy.
5. Statement of pricing policy.
6. Statement of packaging policy.
7. Statement of distribution policy.
8. Statement of advertising and sales promotion policy.
9. Statement of sales policy.
10. Budget statement with explanation of how it is to be used for control purposes.
11. Outline of how plan is to be financed.
12. Timing for implementation of various policies.

Clearly, the amount of detail will vary considerably depending upon the central issue identified in the appreciation, and the data available. It should be remembered, however, that the overall marketing plan cannot be expected to go into the same detail as would be expected of, say, the media plan, but it should provide the skeleton around which such plans can be prepared by the various functional specialists. In an examination context, the main intention is to discover whether the candidate has acquired a sufficient understanding of theoretical principles, and these should always be outlined, even though case data is not available for purposes of exemplification. For example, if the case concerns a convenience good the student may consider sales promotion relevant, even though it is not specifically referred to, and so might suggest the use of a banded offer designed to increase consumer sampling, achieve increased consumer and retail inventories, etc.

Finally, the impact of a marketing plan will be lost if it lacks clarity of expression, no matter how logical the sequence or how sophisticated the analysis. To this end, the student must practise expressing himself clearly and concisely in order to convey the maximum information in the least number of words.

■ Marketing arithmetic

On first acquaintance one of the more confusing aspects of marketing is the basic financial data associated with selling – mark-up, discounts, and stock-turn – and that necessary to monitor the financial health of the marketing function – standard costing, budgetary control and ratio analysis. While these factors, and the latter particularly, are more properly the province of a financial text a brief overview is essential to underline their relevance to marketing and encourage more detailed study. (It is appreciated that many students will be pursuing a broadly based course which includes a study of accounting and finance. Such students should regard the next few pages as basic revision material.) Each of the topics identified is the subject of separate treatment in the following pages.

■ Mark-up

This is the amount which a firm adds to its cost of goods in order to arrive at its selling price, i.e.

$$SP = C + M$$

Where SP = selling price, C = cost of goods, and M = mark-up or margin.

The mark-up, or margin as it is sometimes termed, is intended to cover *selling, general* and *administrative* expenses ('SGA' in some accounting texts and case studies) as well as a percentage for profit. The convention which frequently causes confusion is that mark-up is usually expressed as a percentage of selling price rather than cost, probably due to sellers working backwards from a going market price, as would be essential under conditions of perfect competition. That is, one accepts the market price, deducts the desired profit, assesses the SGA associated with the anticipated volume of sales and deducts this, and is left with the amount for which the product will have to be made. If this amount is less than actual cost, one will have to accept a lower profit, or even a loss, or decide not to produce, while if it is greater an above-average profit becomes possible.

Four basic calculations are frequently called for in connection with margins/mark-ups and these are as follows:

1. Determination of selling price when costs and percentage mark-ups are given. Since the selling price always equals 100 per cent we can substitute the data given into a simple formula to arrive at the retail price, i.e.

$$C + M = SP$$

Thus if cost = £100 and the mark-up = 25 per cent then

$$£100 = SP - 25\%$$
$$= 100\% - 25\%$$
$$= 75\%$$

$$\therefore £SP = \frac{£C}{100\% - M}$$

$$= \frac{£100}{75\%}$$

$$= £133.33$$

2. To find the margin given cost and selling price, using the same figures as above, we have:

$$C + M = SP$$
$$M = SP - C$$
$$M = £133.33 - £100$$
$$M = £33.33$$

This may be expressed as a percentage of the selling price:

$$M = \frac{£33.3}{£100}$$

$$= 33.3\%$$

3. To convert a margin based on selling price to one based on cost. Here the formula is

$$\% \text{ margin on cost} = \frac{\% \text{ margin on selling price}}{100\% - \% \text{ margin on selling price}}$$

$$= \frac{33.3}{100 - 33.3}$$

$$= 50\%$$

4. To convert a margin based on cost to one based on selling price:

$$\% \text{ margin on selling price}$$

$$= \frac{\% \text{ margin on cost}}{100\% + \% \text{ margin on cost}}$$

$$= \frac{50}{100 + 50}$$

$$= 33.3\%$$

Discounts
The calculation of discounts is a constant source of confusion due to the fact that a discount is always expressed as a percentage of the *reduced* price and not the original retail selling price. For example, a 25 per cent discount on £100 is in fact £20 and not £25, i.e.

$$\text{discount} = \frac{\text{amount of discount}}{\text{original price} - \text{discount}}$$

$$= \frac{20}{80} \text{ (i.e. } 100 - 20)$$

$$= 25\%$$

(*Note*: in American texts/case studies, discounts are often termed 'mark-downs'.)

■ Stock-turn

As the term suggests, the stock-turn is the number of times the stock 'turns over' during a given period and gives a useful indicator of how a particular type of outlet is performing. Clearly the rate of stock-turn will vary enormously according to the nature of the goods sold, being fastest in fresh foods and slowest in durables such as furniture or luxuries such as jewellery, cameras, etc. There is usually a direct relationship between the margins which manufacturers anticipate in recommending a retail selling price and the stock-turn of the average outlet. It follows that more efficient outlets (i.e. those with lower operating costs) will earn higher net profits if they maintain margins and achieve average stock-turn. However, in recent years many retailers have pursued a more aggressive strategy designed to increase market share, and thereby long-term profitability, by offering discounts and increasing stock-turn.

To compute stock-turn one must divide net sales for the period by the average inventory (at selling price) for the same period. Average inventory is simply:

$$\frac{\text{opening stock} + \text{closing stock}}{2}$$

while net sales is total sales less any returns or allowances.

■ Standard costing and budgetary control

Traditionally the accounting function concerned itself solely with recording the historical performance of an organization. It is for this reason that many people seek to differentiate between the major business functions by characterizing accounting as an orientation to the past. By the same token production is seen as being preoccupied with the present – a 'present orientation' – and marketing is conceived of as a 'future orientation', with an emphasis upon the planning and control of future activities. Nowadays such a simplistic distinction would be very far from the truth, for all business functions are conscious of the need for forward planning and the need to control operations so as to achieve the desired outcome. Standard costing and budgetary control have been developed for just this purpose.

In his excellent introduction to the subject, *Costing: A Management Approach* (Pan Management Series, 1974), A. H. Taylor expresses the view that defining standard costs as predetermined costs or yardsticks fails adequately to 'convey the fundamental change in viewpoint of costing which occurs when a standard costing system is instituted in place of an historical costing system'. Taylor goes on to say:

> The standard cost is what the cost of an operation or service ought to be under given conditions and subject to given conventions of costing. It is thus a notional amount

which depends entirely on the conditions predicted. It is this notional amount which is treated as the value of the stock and the cost of the goods sold.

The conditions associated with a standard cost are essentially a standard of efficiency and a level of activity. Using material as an example, the standard material cost of a product implies the purchase of the required quantity of material at an economic price and in economic lots. This in turn implies the existence of a production plan and a storing policy. All the standards inherent in the elements of cost which comprise a product cost or the cost of an operation are interdependent. To carry the argument to the extreme, it could be said that the standard costs derive from the corporate plan.

Put another way, using standard costs is very similar in principle to the economist's use of *ceteris paribus*: it enables one to predict outcomes due to the interaction between factors under consideration given no change in all the other factors which might influence that interaction. In this sense standard costs do act as yardsticks, for they enable management to ascertain whether the business is performing as planned according to the predetermined conditions necessary for that achievement – conditions which it is management's responsibility to create. Any departure or variance from the standard will immediately warn management of a difference between planned and actual which will enable it to analyze the nature of the variance and the possibility of rectifying it. Of course, all variances are not negative, though this is most often the case in periods of inflation when costs are often rising in an unpredictable manner which cannot be accommodated when setting the standard cost. However, when positive variances do occur it is equally important that management be aware of the fact so that they may capitalize on an opportunity if such exists, e.g. a seasonal fall in raw material prices.

It must also be emphasised that conformity with the standard should not be accepted at face value, for it may well conceal countervailing trends – for example, a fall in cost due to greater machine efficiency counterbalanced by increased labour or material costs. Thus to use a standard costing system as one of management by exception could be dangerous. Its major benefits lie in its requirement that one should plan future operations i.e. prepare a budget, identify the conditions necessary for the successful execution of the plan, the creation of such conditions and the comparison of actual and planned performance as the basis for controlling activities (hence 'budgetary control').

To cite Taylor again:

The merits of a standard costing system may be summarized as follows:
1. Information is provided for managerial control through the comparison of actual expenditure against standard expenditure.
2. The analysis of variances between actual expenditure and standard expenditure saves managerial time, because the managers need only give their attention to those operations where substantial variances occur.
3. Stable and presumably, sound figures of cost are provided to assist price determination.

4. Stable values are assigned to stock and work in progress, thus eliminating
    . . . anomalies . . . and assisting in the production of a true and fair view of
    profit and a reliable trend of profitability.

For a discussion of the anomalies mentioned, of costing principles and their
managerial use the reader is referred to the original source.

■ Ratio analysis

In most countries trading organizations are required to publish an annual
statement of their financial affairs – most usually a balance-sheet, which
summarizes the financial position, and a profit-and-loss account, which is a
statement of income and expenditure. The manner in which companies choose to
publish these financial statements varies enormously, from the elaborate and
extensive documents put out by large public companies to the minimum required
by law characteristic of most private firms. However, even this minimal
information can provide an analyst with a great deal of insight into the strengths
and weaknesses of an organization and the purpose of this section is to indicate a
small number of ratios which can enable such an evaluation to be made. (Such
analysis is particularly important for students preparing for formal examinations
using the 'case method' (see Chapter 21), as most cases contain financial
statements. Only if you are able to interpret these can you decide whether or
not they are relevant to the marketing problem you have been asked to solve.)

In *The Meaning of Company Accounts* (Gower Press, 1971) Walter Reid and
D. R. Myddelton group the more common ratios under three headings:

Investment measures

(*a*) Return on equity $= \dfrac{\text{Profit after tax}}{\text{Shareholders' funds}}$

(*b*) Earnings per share $= \dfrac{\text{Profit after tax}}{\text{Number of shares issued}}$

(*c*) Price/earnings ratio $= \dfrac{\text{Market price per share}}{\text{Earnings per share}}$

(*d*) Dividend yield $= \dfrac{\text{Dividend per share}}{\text{Market price per share}}$

(*e*) Dividend cover $= \dfrac{\text{Earnings per share}}{\text{Dividend per share}}$

Measures of performance

(f) Return on net assets $= \dfrac{\text{Earnings before interest and tax}}{\text{Net assets}}$

(g) Profit margin $= \dfrac{\text{Earnings before interest and tax}}{\text{Sales}}$

(h) Asset turnover $= \dfrac{\text{Sales}}{\text{Net assets}}$

Measures of financial status solvency

(i) Debt ratio $= \dfrac{\text{Long-term debt}}{\text{Capital employed}}$

(j) Interest cover $= \dfrac{\text{Earnings before interest and tax}}{\text{Interest}}$

Liquidity

(k) Current ratio $= \dfrac{\text{Current assets}}{\text{Current liabilities}}$

(l) Acid test $= \dfrac{\text{Liquid assets}}{\text{Current liabilities}}$

The purpose of all the foregoing ratios is to enable an analyst to conduct a spot check on the financial health of an organisation in much the same way that a doctor takes one's pulse, temperature, blood pressure, etc. Diagnostically ratios are used in combination so that a satisfactory outcome for one test is not sufficient to guarantee that all the others will yield the same result. Accordingly it is necessary to work systematically through a series of tests before a clean bill of health can be issued. Which series of tests is most appropriate will vary according to one's viewpoint, but in general all analysts will wish to consider *liquidity*, *solvency* and *performance*, with less importance attached to investment measures *per se*. (For a discussion of how to interpret ratios one should consult Reid and Myddelton, *The Meaning of Company Accounts*, or B. K. R. Watts, *Business and Financial Management*, 3rd edn (M and E Handbooks, 1978) ch. 10.) Another excellent source is chapter 6, 'Profitability – Measurement and Analysis', in John Sizer's *An Insight into Management Accounting*, 3rd edn (Penguin Books, 1989).

CHAPTER 21

The written analysis of cases

Learning Goals

The issue to be discussed in this chapter is the preparation of a formal, written analysis of a marketing problem particularly of the kind used in examination case studies.

After reading this chapter you will be familiar with:

1. The purpose of using case studies as a basis for classroom discussion and formal examination.
2. Approaches to defining problems and developing a formalised approach to problem solving.
3. The objectives of problem analysis.
4. The conduct of internal and external audits (see also Chapters 3 and 20).
5. Problems associated with the quantity and quality of information.
6. The structure and presentation of formal reports.

While case studies are usually employed as the focus for a classroom discussion, they are being used increasingly as the basis for a written assignment. This is particularly so where the case method of instruction is followed in a formal course of study when the written analysis of a case is frequently adopted as the appropriate means of examination. Similarly, case studies often provide excellent material for examining students who have-pursued a more conventional programme of instruction by means of lectures and tutorials. For these reasons it will be useful to consider the objectives of a written analysis and suggest some approaches to the execution of such an exercise. (It goes without saying that the following observations apply equally to case analysis, where a formal, written analysis is not required.)

■ Objectives

Despite the fact that most European teachers tend to spend more time upon the discussion of an individual case study than their North American counterparts, it is still rare for such an extended consideration to cover all the issues contained in a given situation. Certainly, if the case study is used as a catalyst for encouraging an exchange of ideas between students, it is unlikely that spontaneous contributions will occur in the logical or ordered manner one would expect in a formal lecture. Indeed, one suspects that if the case leader succeeds in eliciting a structured analysis, then it can only be at the expense of ruthlessly discouraging digressions and diversions, some of which inevitably would prove both stimulating and illuminating. Clearly the latter approach would eliminate much of the interest and involvement engendered by a lively debate in open forum, which is one of the strengths of the case method.

However, it is generally recognised that while case discussion has a vital role to play in management education, it possesses deficiencies which can best be remedied by alternative teaching methods. As implied above, case discussions frequently lack the cogency and impact which can be achieved by marshalling one's thoughts in a logical sequence, as well as neglecting issues of possible relevance and importance. Further, at the individual level discussion can result in a superficial treatment as students soon learn that their fellows have often not undertaken a rigorous analysis, and so will not challenge apparently complex analyses of data, while the case leader may not have opportunity. A similar danger exists in that the student can struggle through by 'debating' the points made by others, or simply by preparing a detailed analysis of one issue which is regarded as his 'contribution'.

The basic objective of the written analysis is to eliminate these deficiencies while developing skills in:

(*a*)   problem definition
(*b*)   analysis
(*c*)   presentation

We consider each of these in turn.

■ Problem definition

There is wide support for the view that problem definition is the most critical and most difficult step in problem-solving. This view is generally predicated on the grounds that while problem definition is invariably cited as the first stage in problem analysis, in fact it only becomes possible after an extensive consideration of a wide range of other issues. Consider two popular statements of the normative approach to problem-solving.

First, there is the Adaptive Planning and Control Sequence (APACS) proposed by Robinson and Luck which we introduced in the previous chapter and which comprises eight steps:

Step 1   Define problem and set objectives
Step 2   Appraise overall situation
Step 3   Determine the tasks to be accomplished and identify the means to achieve these aims
Step 4   Identify alternative plans and mixes
Step 5   Estimate the expected results arising from implementation of the alternative plans
Step 6   Managerial review and decision
Step 7   Feedback of results and post audit
Step 8   Adapt programme if required

Second, there is the operational approach to research suggested by Ferber and Verdoorn (*Research Methods in Economics and Business*, Collier-Macmillan, 1962) with six stages:

1. Formulating the problem
2. Development of working hypotheses
3. Planning the study
4. Collecting and processing the data
5. Analysis and interpretation
6. Presentation of results

While the second model may appear rather different from the first, in fact they both cover the same basic elements. Similarly, both convey the impression of an orderly sequence stemming from the identification and statement of a problem, though steps 7 and 8 in the APACS model suggest that feedback and revision of the initial problem definition are omitted by the second model.

In reality we feel that feedback and adjustment of the original problem statement will be a major feature of the whole problem-solving process. This is not to suggest that no problem is ever solved, but rather than the depth analysis of one issue will inevitably raise questions concerning related but previously unconsidered issues. Given the dynamic nature of the business environment it would be surprising if this were not the case. However, we make this point solely to reinforce the fact that the steps in the problem-analysis model are neither discrete nor necessarily sequential and, having given-this warning, we will immediately find it simpler to treat them as if they were both.

In simple terms we can distinguish two alternative scenarios for the case analyst:

(a) he is given a case study and a problem statement, or
(b) he is given a case study with no indication of the specific problem to be addressed.

The first alternative is typical of the examination situation and also encompasses certain cases in which the opening or closing paragraphs contain a statement of the problem as perceived by the case writer or a character in the case itself. Such a situation corresponds well with the circumstance where an organisation has identified the existence of a problem and wishes to brief a consultant (internal or external) to analyse and solve it. The second alternative is much more open-ended and usually adopted by teachers where they wish their students to decide whether in fact a problem exists at all. A real-world parallel of this approach might be the study of an industry, market or company by a financial analyst. Fundamentally the case analyst is well advised to treat both situations in the same way.

If given a brief, then it is necessary to establish that it does reflect the real issue to be investigated rather than a symptom or effect of the real problem. Similarly, it is essential to eliminate any possible ambiguities in the problem statement or brief and to define any terms capable of differing interpretations. Equally it is of vital importance to establish the precise parameters of the topic how long is 'the short term', 'the long term', 'the future', what firms are to be taken as comprising 'the textile industry', what is understood by 'competition' – immediate and direct competition from firms producing similar products or services, or is it intended to include competition from substitute products? Clearly exactly the same points need to be taken into account when preparing a brief of one's own.

Naturally the above is a counsel of perfection. If, for example, one knew that declining sales were directly and solely attributable to a specific cause, then, as claimed earlier, the problem is largely resolved, for one can focus all one's efforts upon eliminating or avoiding that cause. While pedants will argue that such elimination or avoidance is itself a problem requiring resolution, it is believed that it will usually be a relatively trivial one. If, for example, one is certain that declining sales are the result of product inferiority due to the absence of an ingredient or feature present in a competing product, it would seem that all that needs to be decided is

(*a*) Do we wish to increase our sales to their former level?

(*b*) If yes, can we improve our product at a cost which will enable us to sell them at a price and volume which will earn us a satisfactory profit (including issues of complementarity, goodwill, etc.) ?

(*c*) If the answer to (*b*) is 'no', then clearly we must revise our original position.

On the other hand, if the problem has been incorrectly identified and the decline in demand has resulted from other causes, then treating the wrong symptoms (product composition) is unlikely to have much effect. Of course, if one could survive long enough it might permit problem-solving by elimination!

Essentially we are arguing that it would probably be more accurate to define the first stage in problem analysis as 'setting up a working problem definition' in much the same way as the scientist sets up a null hypothesis. In this way we acknowledge that problems exist because of imperfect information and uncertainty – it would be surprising if the acquisition of more information did not help to reduce uncertainty and so permit more exact problem formulation. How, then, should we set about acquiring more and better information?

■ Analysis

Armed with a working problem definition and a declared objective the analyst is well placed to commence formal investigation. At this juncture it is well to accept that while one may be embarking upon a voyage of discovery many other explorers have done the same and much can be learned from their experience. In other words there is a body of knowledge and experience concerning problem-solving which is relevant to the solution of any particular problem. While several different approaches have been proposed (and we will only discuss our own preferred method) all are agreed on the fundamental point that a structured procedure is to be preferred. This claim does not deny the utility of unstructured methods such as brainstorming, lateral thinking or the like but would suggest that these are techniques to be used in particular circumstances and especially where a structured analysis has revealed deficiencies which cannot be remedied by more formal methods. Further, the more complex the problem, the more necessary is a detailed and structured approach to its solution. Thus where the nature of the problem is very well understood, as, for example, launching a space probe or landing an aircraft, it is usual to develop a check-list of all the steps to be taken in the sequence in which they are to be taken, and to follow this unswervingly unless there are indications to the contrary. Even in the latter case, for example a pilot observes an obstruction on the runway just prior to touchdown, alternative procedures are also likely to be highly specific.

Of course, business problems are far less amenable to the highly structured analytic method characteristic of the sciences, and appropriate to science-based activities, e.g. flying and aerodynamics, largely because business is an activity arising from the interaction of people who are far less predictable in their behavioural patterns than are materials. However, experience would seem to suggest that human behaviour patterns are perhaps more open to observation and prediction than has generally been appreciated. If this is so, then an ability to predict how a person or organisation would react under a specified set of circumstances must help reduce the uncertainty faced by decision-makers and so reduce the need to exercise judgement. Unfortunately it often appears that many decision-makers confuse the amount of judgement they exercise with the quality of the decisions made. While it is true that the true exercise of judgement is the function and responsibility of the decision-maker, none but a fool would seek to substitute uncertain judgement for fact or known risk where the alternatives can be completely specified and probabilities attached to their occurrence (as in life insurance). None the less it seems that this is just the error to which so many would-be decision-makers fall prey they cannot be bothered with the labour, much of it boring, repetitive and trivial, necessary for a rigorous analysis and so flee into the exercise of 'judgment'.

From the above comments it is clear that I am proposing at least two steps to formal analysis, namely:

1. The identification and measurement of all facts which impinge upon the problems.
2. The application of judgement to the uncertain areas which are the residual remaining following the factual analysis.

The first step is frequently described as a 'management audit' and is usually sub-divided into two parts – internal and external.

■ The internal audit

The purpose of the internal audit is to develop a comprehensive list of the organisation's resources, together with an assessment of their relative importance *vis-à-vis* each other. As suggested in Chapter 19 this audit should encompass all of the following:

1. *Physical resources*
   Land – as a source of raw materials
        – as a location for manufacturing and distributive activities.
   Buildings – general purpose or specific, i.e. designed for light engineering, assembly, storage, etc., or for heavy manufacturing requiring special foundations, services, etc.
   Availability of and access to – power supplies, drainage and waste disposal
                                 – transportation: road, rail, canal,
                                         port facilities, etc.
   Plant and equipment – general purpose, e.g. lathe, press
                       – specific, e.g. steel rolling mill, foundry, etc.

2. *Technical resources.* Essentially those which reside in the technical expertise of the firm's employees, together with the possession of patents, licences or highly specialised equipment.

3. *Financial resources.* These comprise the liquid assets in the firm's balance-sheet, the-ability to secure loans against fixed assets and the ability to raise capital in the market on the basis of past and anticipated future performance. They also comprise the skill of the firm's financial management.

4. *Purchasing resources.* Managerial expertise backed by any special advantage enjoyed by the firm by virtue of its size or connections, e.g. reciprocal trading agreements.

5. *Labour resources.* The skills, experience and adaptability of the work-force.

6. *Marketing resources.* The degree of consumer/user acceptance or 'franchise' developed through past performance. Access to and degree of control over distribution; the specialised skills and experiences of personnel.

While such an audit should provide a good summary of the nature and extent of the company's assets, together with an indication of the relative importance of the major business functions, its value can only be realised by comparison with similar data for companies with which it is competing. To obtain this one must carry out an external unit.

■ The external audit

An assessment of the environment in which the company has to operate should be carried out at two levels. First, one should appraise the overall economic climate and seek to establish whether it is growing, static or declining and for what apparent reasons. Second, within this broad framework one should evaluate the industry/market in which the company is competing. Our own preferred approach to this stage of the analysis is to use the framework developed by the well-known management consultants McKinsey & Co. and built on by Michael Porter in his 'value chain analysis'.

The basis of the McKinsey approach is to sub-divide the business system into a series of sub-systems, as indicated in Fig. 21.1. Starting with raw material extraction the analysis proceeds by examining each major sub-system in turn in order to establish the interrelationship and interdependence between them in terms of:

(a) The degree of *competition* within and between each sub-system, e.g. raw material extraction might be in the hands of only one or a few producers so that conditions are oligopolistic while retail distribution could be characterised by thousands of small sellers none of whom could influence the market. Clearly the latter circumstances describe perfect competition, and both sets of conditions apply in the oil industry. Thus in establishing the nature of competition one should measure:
    (i)   the number of competitors;
    (ii) their profitability;
    (iii) their degree of integration;
    (iv) their cost structure;
    (v)   the existence and nature of any barriers to entry, e.g. technological, size of investment in production and/or marketing.
(b) Where, in the total system, *value* is *added* by the activities of members of the production, distribution, or servicing sub-systems. For example, a significant proportion of turnover in many consumer-durable industries is accounted for by after-sales servicing and the efficiency of this sector may have a radical influence upon the market shares of individual suppliers, as well as on industry profitability.

Figure 21.1   The business system

(c)   The location of *economic leverage* in the system. Does this arise from being a fully integrated producer, or can one exercise leverage by avoiding the extensive fixed investment implicit in vertical integration and concentrating on only one sub-system?

(d)   Where is the system's *marketing leverage*? Usually this is associated with control of a scarce resource which might be an essential raw material, a patent on a process, control of a distribution channel, a brand name ('Hoover', 'Elastoplast') or some other type of consumer franchise.

Once the analyst has established the major characteristics of the production, distribution and servicing sub-systems his next task must be a thorough documentation of the consumer or user. Such documentation requires one to supply answers to the five basic questions which underlie all market research – who, what, where, when and how.

1.   *Who* buys in terms of demographic and socio-economic criteria such as age, sex, income, education, occupation, marital status, etc. (for consumers), or status, authority, functional specialisation, etc. (for users)? Who *consumes*? (Compare consumption and purchase of breakfast cereals; of hand tools in a factory; etc.)

2.   *What* do people buy in terms of variety, design, quality, performance and price characteristics?

3.   *Where* do people buy? In specialist outlets, in general purpose outlets, by mail or telephone from a catalogue, in the home or on their premises, i.e. how important is direct selling through representatives versus indirect selling via the media?

4.   *When* do people buy? Are purchases seasonal, regular, irregular, associated with another activity, etc?

5.   *How* do people buy? Impulsively, after considerable deliberation, in large quantities, small quantities, from multiple sources or a single source, etc?

A sixth and equally important question is 'Why?' Unlike our other five questions one cannot usually supply a definitive and factual answer. However, when one considers that consumers (or users) do not buy products, as such, but rather the satisfactions yielded by the product, then even a partial understanding of the satisfactions looked for will go a long way towards explaining actual behaviour in the market-place.

Where in the system are company's measurable strengths and weaknesses?

(How company compares with competition – today and future)

| Raw materials | → | Production | → | Wholesale distribution | → | Retail distribution | → | Consumer or user | → | After-sales service |

How does company compare in raw materials?
- Do they have advantages in supply?
- Degree of integration?

How does company compare in technology?
- What is their rate of product, process improvement?
- How good is process efficiency?
- Advantages in location of facilities?

How does company compare in cost and profit?
- Raw material costs?
- Processing costs?
- Profit?
- Return on investment?
- Access to capital?

How does company compare in channels?
- In which channels are company's sales concentrated?
- Do products reach point of sale faster or more efficiently?

How does company compare in distributors?
- Have they more, larger, or more effective distributors?
- Share of channel's sales?

How does company compare in economics?
- Compensation of distributors?
- Distribution costs?
- Service costs?

How does company compare in products?
- Have they greater variety, better design or quality, lower price, superior performance?
- Share of market?

How does company compare in customers?
- Who are core buyers; core customers?
- Do these customers buy more frequently in larger quantities or more consistently?
- How is company's product used?
- Who are core competitors?

How does company compare in service?
- Does company have a service advantage – type, quality or quantity?

How does company compare in pricing?
- Do they have price advantage (price/ quality relationship)?
- Are they price leader?

How does company compare in economics?
- Service costs?
- Cost of consumer marketing?

Figure 21.2 Company's measurable strengths and weaknesses

At this juncture one should have developed a good understanding of both the company and the environment in which it is operating. It now remains to combine the two threads of the analysis in order to isolate the company's particular strengths and weaknesses in terms of the environmental threats and opportunities. An indication of the sort of questions appropriate to such a comparison is given in Fig. 21.2, which is taken from McKinsey's model.

Thus far we have proceeded as if information were freely available and also as if it were of a known value. Rarely will these conditions be satisfied; in fact the most frequently voiced complaint of case students is 'lack of information'. Accordingly we turn now to consider this.

■ The quantity and quality of information

It is tautologous to point out that certainty exists where there is perfect information, from which it is a simple step to deduce that problems exist because of the absence of perfect information.

It is for this reason that we have stressed the methodical collection of as much information as possible as an essential prerequisite to problem-solving. However, in this task we are faced with three major difficulties – data are frequently incomplete, second much information is presented in the form of opinion, or, third, may only be inferred from the apparent relationship between facts or events. It follows that a major job of the analyst is to screen all the available evidence for accuracy, validity and reliability as a preliminary to determining whether any relationships exist between acceptable facts that are suggestive of a solution to the problem in hand. There are many textbooks which deal with these issues at length and only a brief review is merited here.

While complete accuracy constitutes truth it would be erroneous to infer that less than complete accuracy is untruth and thereby unacceptable. In a business context it is rare that one requires the degree of precision necessary in the scientific laboratory, or even the engineering workshop, and a reasonable estimate will often suffice. What is reasonable depends upon the circumstances and may vary by several percentage points around the true value, e.g. an estimate of market size. Essentially the need for accuracy depends upon how sensitive the final outcome of one's analysis is to changes in the value of constitutent elements – if the end-result appears to be largely insensitive, then approximation will suffice; if highly sensitive, then the more accurate the point estimate the better.

A good example of this is provided by a feasibility study of the suitability of a Scottish mountain for development as a ski-slope. While access to the slope, nature of the uplift facilities and back-up facilities (car parks, toilets, cafes, etc.), price to be charged, growth trends in total demand, etc., all have a bearing upon the decision, estimates of all these parameters are relatively unimportant compared with the value of the critical or limiting factor – the prevailing weather conditions. In the event analysis revealed that when one deducted the number of days when it would not be possible to ski due to high winds or poor visibility from the total days on which snow could be guaranteed, the residue was so small as to make it quite obvious that a commercial venture was impractical almost regardless of the values one attached to any of the other parameters.

The mark of a good analyst is an ability to isolate the critical factors and then focus all available resources in eliciting the most accurate information available concerning them. When using data from published sources one must distinguish between the credibility to be attached to government statistics gathered by census and estimates extrapolated from samples by trade associations, consultants and those with a vested interest in the interpretation of the data they convey. One must be conscious of recency and assess how delay in publishing data may affect its current validity. One must also be sensitive to changes in the collection and recording of data over time and satisfy oneself as to the comparability of such data.

Such strictures are all very well when dealing with information from published sources, but how does one deal with opinion and hearsay? Much information in case studies falls into the latter category and is often conflicting in its indication of the true state of affairs. A classic example of this is to be found in the Barnstaple case study, in which three executive managers responsible for the finance, production and sales functions each attribute the company's declining fortunes to a different cause. However, by carefully adducing factual data in the case, or inferences which may be drawn from *these data* with a very high degree of confidence, it can be clearly demonstrated that only one manager's opinion is acceptable. Herein lies a key skill of the analyst – an ability to pick out relevant pieces of information, while discarding those which only serve to confuse an issue, and link them together to demonstrate a functional relationship.

It is possible to distinguish three different levels of analysis in this sorting and synthesising process – deduction, inference and the formulation of assumptions. A deduction is made when one derives a logically necessary conclusion about a specific case from perfect information concerning the general case – for example, all retailers of cars operate on a 20 per cent gross margin; the XYZ company is a retailer of cars: *deduction* – the XYZ company operates on a 20 per cent gross margin.

The status of an inference is less clear cut than is that of a deduction. An inference may be defined as the interpretation placed upon evidence by an observer, from which it follows that the quality of an inference may range from excellent, i.e. a very high probability that it reflects reality, to very poor. Assuming, however, that the correct inference is drawn, then the distinction rests in the fact that there is always an element of uncertainty associated with an inference while there is none with a deduction. However, by linking logical deductions with reasonable inferences one can proceed a long way towards the solution of a problem.

The need for assumptions only arises where there is an absence of evidence necessary to link other information which seems to bear upon the problem. Assumptions may be of two kinds – working assumptions and critical assumptions. Working assumptions are those necessary to move an argument along and provide links in the chain of reasoning, but unlike critical assumptions they are not vital to the final decision. In every case an assumption should only be made as a last resort when it is obvious that other information is not available. When setting out an assumption, and especially a critical assumption, it is important to state clearly the evidence considered in deriving one's assumption, the reasons for selecting and rejecting particular points, and the precise form of the final assumption made. Only by careful attention to these factors will the analyst be able to communicate the thought processes leading to his conclusion; without them his argument will be open to criticism and lack conviction.

From the foregoing it is obvious that *both* the drawing of inferences *and* the formulation of assumptions demand the exercise of judgement, and this is the proper role for its application. In all other cases a strictly formal and factual approach should be followed.

■ Presentation

Skill in problem definition and analysis is of little consequence if the analyst is unable to communicate his findings to others. There are several good books on report writing including:

Gallagher, William J., *Report Writing for Management* (Addison-Wesley, 1969)
Mitchell, John, *How to Write Reports* (Fontana, 1974).

and the student should consult these for detailed guidance on how to set about writing a report. However, in doing so it will become apparent that even the textbook writers are not in complete agreement and Gallagher and Mitchell suggest different formats for writing management reports. My own preference is for the Gallagher sequence, namely:

Summary
    Purpose
    Scope
    Conclusion(s)
    Recommendations
Introduction
Body
Appendix

However, for a Written Analysis of Cases (WAC) the Mitchell approach may be more appropriate:

Statement of the problem
Factors causing the problem
The effects of the problem
Examinations of possible solutions and their implications
Conclusions

Recommendations
Appendices

Whichever method is preferred two final words of warning seem appropriate. First, the student can assume that the examiner is familiar with the case and so should avoid the regurgitation of descriptive material unless it is introduced for a specific purpose. Second, facts seldom, if ever, speak for themselves.

For students seeking an extended discussion of the issues raised in this chapter, Geoff Easton's *Learning from Case Studies* (Prentice-Hall, 1982) is essential reading. Based upon a seven step approach,

Understanding the situation
Diagnosing problem areas
Generating alternative solutions
Predicting outcomes
Evaluating alternatives
Rounding out the analysis
Communicating the results

Easton uses a series of short cases to exemplify and reinforce the key stages in a rigorous and logical analytical approach which adds greatly to the abbreviated treatment here.

CHAPTER 22

Marketing in foreign environments

Learning Goals

The issues to be discussed in this chapter include:

1. The stages of development through which economies pass in order to become advanced industrialised economies with a strong marketing function.
2. The contribution of marketing to economic growth.
3. The nature of comparative advantage and theories of international trade.
4. The identification of market opportunities.
5. Globalisation versus differentiation as international marketing strategies.
6. Marketing in a foreign environment.
7. The impact of the single common market (1992) on the UK's competitive performance.

After reading this chapter you will be familiar with:

1. Rostow's concept of the stages of economic growth and development.
2. The reasons why the marketing function adds value and improves productivity even in countries with endemic supply deficiencies.
3. Ricardo's Theory of Comparative Advantage and benefits which flow from specialisation and international trade.
4. The factors which encourage firms to enter foreign markets.
5. Sources of information and methods for establishing the existence of foreign market opportunities.
6. The differences between a globalised or undifferentiated marketing strategy compared with the use of a segmentation (differentiated or concentrated) approach.
7. The alternative approaches to marketing in foreign environments.
8. The implications of the single common market post-1992 for UK marketing strategy.

As with the previous edition this chapter seeks to provide a synoptic and greatly simplified introduction to three questions.

1. To what extent are the principles and practices discussed in this book relevant to other countries at different stages of economic development?
2. For what reasons might countries wish to engage in international trade?
3. What alternatives are open to firms wishing to sell in another country?

Thus the intention of this chapter is to provide the reader with an introduction to some of the issues associated with marketing in foreign environments. It cannot and does not pretend to be an exposition of the important subfield of marketing known as International Marketing which is the subject of text books and courses in its own right.

■ Stages of economic development

Perhaps the best known, and some would argue most important, discussion of the stages in economic development is to be found in W. W. Rostow's *The Process of Economic Growth* (W. W. Norton & Company Inc., 2nd edn, 1962). In his preface to the second edition, Rostow states 'The objective here is to provide a framework of theoretical concepts within which the variety of growth experiences can be systematically arranged, similarities and differences systematically isolated. ' The outcome is summarised in the penultimate chapter 'The Stages of Economic Growth', in which he distinguishes the following:

1. The traditional society.
2. The preconditions for take-off.
3. The take-off.
4. The drive to maturity.
5. The age of high mass consumption.
6. Beyond the age of high mass consumption (subsequently Rostow designated this stage 'The search for quality').

The arguments underlying Rostow's thesis are not amenable to the kind of simplification which is necessary when addressing a sub-issue in an introductory text book and merit consideration in full. However, his 'stages' have proved to be a very robust concept and provide a useful framework for distinguishing between economies at different stages of development and, thereby, for discussing the relevance and application of various marketing principles and practices. It will be useful, therefore, to identify the salient characteristics of each stage.

Traditional societies are characterised by a lack of systematic understanding of their physical environment and 'the technology and tools necessary to achieve any significant improvement in productivity. In such societies 75 per cent or more of all activity is focused on the food production necessary to sustain the society and any surplus tends to be controlled by rich land owners who dissipate it rather than invest in new technology.

The initial *preconditions for take-off* were created in Western Europe out of two characteristics of the post-medieval world which interacted and reinforced each other: the gradual evolution of modern science and the modern scientific attitude; and the lateral innovation that came with the discovery of new lands and the rediscovery of old, converging with the impulse to create new technology at certain strategic points. *The widening of the market* – both within Europe and overseas – brought not only trade but increased specialisation of production, increased inter-regional and international dependence, enlarged institutions of finance, and *increased market incentives* to create new production functions (Rostow, *Process of Economic Growth*, my emphasis).

The *take-off* consists, in essence, of the achievement of rapid growth in a limited group of sectors, where modern industrial techniques are applied. Technically, take-off is distinguished as occurring when society is able to sustain an annual rate of net investment. of around 10 per cent, and 'usually witnesses a definitive social, political and cultural victory of those who would modernise the economy over those who would either cling to the traditional society or seek other goals'. To achieve this, 'the corps of entrepreneurs and technicians must be enlarged, and sources of capital must be institutionalised' so that it can be deployed into the most promising growth opportunities.

The *drive to maturity* is defined by Rostow as 'the period when a society has effectively applied the range of [then] modern technology to the bulk of its resources', and he offers the following symbolic dates:

Great Britain	1850
United States	1900
Germany	1910
France	1910
Sweden	1930
Japan	1940
Russia	1950
Canada	1950

Of maturity, Rostow makes the following trenchant observation:

At maturity, however, the professional managers become more important – the nameless, comfortable, cautious committee men who inherit and manage large sectors of the economy, while the society begins to seek objectives which include but transcend the application of modern technology to resources.

The *age of high mass consumption* is only one of three such objectives which Rostow distinguishes – the other two being increased security, welfare, and, perhaps, leisure to the working force; and enlarged power for the mature nation on the world scene. As he notes, 'A good deal of the history of the first half of the twentieth century can be told in terms of the pattern and succession of choices made by various mature societies as among those three alternatives.'

While commentators like Galbraith (*The Post Industrial Society*) would seem to agree that there is another stage *beyond high mass consumption* but the nature of this has yet to be determined, and, like the highest stage in Maslow's need hierarchy 'self actualisation', may even consist of a recycling to the values of the traditional society, in *The Marketing Book* (2nd edn, 1991) I suggested in the final chapter that Rostow's 'search for quality' has become the dominant theme in the advanced industrialised economies and seems likely to remain so for the foreseeable future.

The evolutionary and sequential nature of Rostow's 'stages' demonstrates close parallels with our now familiar concept of the product life-cycle, albeit that it is not clear whether stage 5 represents a decline into decadence and senility and stage 6 a new PLC or a rejuvenation of the existing life-cycle/progression. None the less, the concept does possess the advantages which have led us to advocate the PLC – it describes a process and it distinguishes a number of discrete phases which can be used both as a basis for classification and for prognosis. Thus as our discussion of 'The Evolution of an Economic Theory of Consumption' in Chapter 1 shows we can both diagnose the stage of development which an economy has reached and propose strategies and policies for reaping the maximum advantage from its existing status as well as suggesting how it might best move to a more advanced stage if this is desired and possible.

The question as to whether economic growth and development are desirable objectives may seem a naive one, but it is important to recognise that much of the criticism levelled against marketing arises from its close association with the stage of high mass consumption. Indeed marketing is often seen as both the agent and engine of mass high consumption which is criticised for its emphasis on excessive materialism (Galbraith), its wasteful use of resources (q.v. *The Waste Makers* by Vance Packard, or *Limits to Growth*, Meadows *et al.*) and its destruction of our environment. If these things are bad, and most would agree that they are, then it is all too easy to see marketing as guilty by association. At least two points deserve to be made in this context.

First, while marketing as we know it *appears* to be a consequence of an ability to create an excess supply of particular goods and services, which only exists to a significant degree in mature, high consumption economies, this is not the same as proving that its concept and practice are only relevant to this phase of economic development. Second, the most vocal adversaries of economic growth are those who directly and indirectly are enjoying its benefits to the full and so have both the leisure and the means to proselytize their views. Things doubtless look different to a subsistence farmer with an annual income measured in hundreds rather than thousands of dollars.

In a book called *In Defence of Economic Growth* (Cape, 1974), Wilfred Beckerman sums up the basic issue succinctly when he observes that 'The growth problem is a problem of how resources should be allocated over time. Economists, and we hope politicians too, are concerned primarily with maximising welfare, which may be seen as comprising two elements – the level of consumption and the equality of its distribution. In addressing the problem of how to maximise welfare it is of the utmost importance that we consider the time dimension, for it is apparent that future consumption is highly dependent upon present *consumption*, in the sense that investment in new plant and equipment, in research and development, in education, etc. requires us to accept a lower level of current consumption in order to reap greater benefits (or welfare) in the future. It follows, as Beckerman pointed out, that 'the essential point is that it is *consumption* over some relevant time period which should be maximised, not the growth rate'.

To be correct we should recognise that what we are seeking is *optimum* growth, which we can define as the growth rate at which the sacrifice of present consumption necessary to promote future growth is just balanced by the extra future consumption this will generate.

In assessing what is an optimum growth rate we are again faced with the intractable problem identified earlier – namely, that 'optimum' is a subjective concept and will be perceived differently by different pressure groups. Thus influential critics like Galbraith have suggested that mankind keeps on raising the definition of optimum instead of being satisfied with what it has got. If we regard the United States as the pacemaker, in that its citizens enjoy the highest standard of living in the world, we can see immediately that standards there have increased significantly in the past decade – for the rest of us trying to catch up we are faced with an ever-receding frontier. And so we come to the crux of the controversy, for it is marketing which is cast in the role of villain in the piece. In *The Affluent Society* (Penguin, 1974) Galbraith comments:

> As a society becomes increasingly affluent, wants are increasingly created by the process by which they are satisfied. This may operate passively. Increases in consumption, the counterpart of increases in production, act by suggestion or emulation to create wants. Or producers may proceed actively to create wants through advertising and salesmanship. Wants then come to depend on output.

In the same vein Professor Harry Johnson of Chicago made the following observation in his *Money, Trade and Economic Growth*, 2nd edn (Allen & Unwin, 1961): 'The fact that wants are created and not original with the individual, raises a fundamental philosophical problem, Whether the satisfaction of wants created by those who satisfy them can be regarded as social gain. ' It would appear, then, that while growth is essential to ensure an improved standard of living, for most of us the marketing function is in some way responsible for exaggerating consumption needs to the point where the level of growth necessary to sustain such consumption is beyond the optimum and becomes wasteful.

■ Marketing and economic growth

From the foregoing discussion it seems reasonable to conclude that while one may have some reservations about both the nature and extent of consumption in affluent and mature economies, the achievement of such a state is desirable and one to be pursued by economies at lower levels of development. That said it seems reasonable to inquire into the relevance which marketing has both in advanced economies, where it has been accused of creating conspicuous consumption, and in developing countries, which by definition are foreign environments when compared with the UK and where many point to the scarcity of basic commodities as evidence that it is production not marketing which is needed.

Let me deal first with the advanced economies. While marketing is often identified with materialism it is important to recognise that this is not the same as proving that marketing is a materialistic business philosophy. It is probably nearer the truth to assert that, as a business philosophy, marketing is neutral and that overtones of materialism merely mirror society's preoccupation with improving the standard of living. In turn, this laudable objective became embroiled with a perceived need to maintain a high level of employment; and employment results in increased production of goods. Obviously, if such increased supplies are not consumed, the process becomes sterile so we get into a vicious circle of stimulating consumption to increase demand and maintain employment opportunities. If we are not careful we lose sight of our real objective of improving human welfare and begin to confuse the means (growth) with the end (a better standard of living). The standard of living is concerned primarily with the quality of life and, while an increase in the quantity of goods and services may be an essential part of that quality, the two are not synonymous. In fact in advanced countries it would seem that beyond a certain point the consumption of physical goods is subject to diminishing returns and may reduce the quality of life due to environmental pollution, creation of stress, loss of leisure and recreational opportunities, etc.

It seems to me both ironical and paradoxical, assuming that marketing is so powerful in persuading people to consume more against their own interests, that no one suggests that these same skills and techniques cannot be used in the interest of conservation and moderation. In fact they can, and I predict that this will increasingly be the case. Thus in post-industrial society marketing will have a crucial role to play in identifying the satisfactions which people are seeking, for, as we have seen, the central economic problem is that of maximising satisfaction from the consumption of scarce resources. Where marketers tend to differ from economists is in the emphasis they give to measuring individual consumer preferences as the basis for resource allocation – in other words they give greater attention to the subjective and qualitative dimensions of demand than is common with economists.

As has been pointed out to me on numerous occasions on visits to developing economies, their problem is seen very differently. Supply deficiency or scarcity is seen as the fundamental problem and marketing is regarded as superfluous when there is such an obvious imbalance between supply and demand. Such a viewpoint is perfectly valid if you think marketing is a sort of sophisticated selling and concerned solely with demand stimulation by means of advertising, promotion and packaging.

To recapitulate, economies are concerned with maximising the satisfaction gained from the consumption of scarce resources. It is the satisfaction of individual consumers we are concerned with, and it would be paternalistic, not to say presumptuous, to assume that any single person is able to specify just what gives people the greatest satisfaction without asking them. To point to the fact that the available supply is consumed is not to prove that we are maximising satisfaction – it only goes to prove that something is better than nothing. My need for shoes is stronger than my need for brown shoes. If you only produce black shoes which I do not particularly like, they are still preferable to no shoes at all, but you are not maximising my satisfaction. Certainly you are not going to motivate me to work harder to own two pairs of shoes I do not like. (In passing it should be mentioned that one of the reasons why marketing is now practised in Soviet countries is that they had an awful lot of black shoes no one would buy!)

In a thoughtful analysis of the relevance of marketing to developing countries Fred Austen ('The Relevance of Marketing to Developing Countries', Paper presented to the Marketing Education Group of the United Kingdom, North Region Workshop, 1978) discusses the following ten areas which he considers to be characteristic features of developing countries:

1. *Segmented.* In Western countries considerable skill and ingenuity is displayed in dividing homogeneous groups by social purchasing-power grouping, consumer attitudes, etc. In developing countries no such ingenuity is necessary. Peasants and townsmen, rich and poor, are clearly separated. Even a medium-sized country like Nigeria has not merely three main religious groups but 200 different tribes, each with its own tradition and language.

2. *Fast-changing.* The cries of woe from the beggars for foreign aid disguise the fact that growth in national income is commonly as fast as in England during the heyday of the industrial revolution and the change in balance between town and country is taking place at a staggering rate. Places like Kathmandu, Dar-es-Salaam and Jakarta are not only now enormous by any standard but are growing at an alarming rate.

3. *Badly administered.* Fast growth, plus major, often frequent, political changes, combined with little administrative tradition and ambitious concepts of state control, have almost universally overstretched the administration. The prevailing tribal and family loyalties are a further important cause which lead administrators and executives to have priorities out of line with good practice or optimum effectiveness.

4. *Low general purchasing power.* Not only are the countries poor, with general money incomes usually well under £250 p.a. per head, and in many countries well under £100 p.a. per head, but much of the work is absorbed in subsistence farming, or food purchase. The well-off, who have purchasing power high even by our standards, contribute comparatively little to the move towards Western or

Soviet styles of market economy. The rich in developing countries, like Adam Smith's feudal barons, spend a disparately high proportion of income on servants, imported luxuries or purpose-made articles, none of which are generators of low-cost, mass-market structures.

5. *High military expenditure.* A reflection of insecurity – and the influence of military leaders – is shown by the staggering expenditure on defence. George Dalton, in *Economic Systems and Society* (Penguin, 1974), looked at developing countries, defined somewhat more broadly than we have, and quotes 1970 figures of 200 billion dollars, compared with 168 billion dollars for education and half that for public health, with rates of growth (1961–70) of 8 per cent, nearly four times the growth rate in developed countries, and often well over 10 per cent of GNP. Looked at slightly differently, according to figures quoted by Dalton, developing countries spent twenty times on armaments of what they received in aid.

6. *State dominated.* Almost regardless of political complexion the state plays a greater role in the economy than in developed nations. Partly this is due to balance-of-payments problems, partly due to ideology, partly to the absence of an existing management and commercial infrastructure. Normally the economy is geared to a five-year plan, handsomely printed but indifferently executed. Restriction of imports is particularly common. Foreign capital aid normally operates through state channels.

7. *Monopolistic.* In most products monopoly or oligopoly is the rule and competition the exception. This largely follows from the common import restrictions, small fragmented markets and the associated problem complex.

8. *Poor infrastructure.* Both social items, such as roads, hospitals, schools, sewers, postal and telephone services, and also private networks in the transport, finance and media fields are deficient, causing a completely different pattern of requirements and opportunities.

9. *Vulnerable exports.* In general developing countries are dependent on a few products. Characteristically one primary product will be 55–85 per cent of total exports (see *Industrialisation of Developing Countries*, Moscow, Progress Publishers, 1973) and apart from the recent rises in commodity prices (petrol, cocoa, coffee, tea especially) the long-range terms of trade appear to be moving against developing nations (see *Terms of Trade Policy for Primary Commodities,* Commonwealth Secretariat, 1975). This can largely be attributed to the fact that the goods produced by developing countries stayed the same, while the markets changed and the more sophisticated countries changed products and product mixes in line with market valuations. It also reflects the fact that the sharpest discrimination was by developing countries against other developing states. Tyagunenko quotes revealing figures which show that from 1955 to 1971 trade

with the developed Western countries and Soviet bloc countries rose by 2–3 per cent for each bloc (as a percentage of the total), which was balanced by a 5 per cent drop in the already small trade (about a quarter of the trade) with other developing countries. Incidentally the same figures show how insignificant the proportion of trade with the Eastern bloc is when compared with the massive (about three-quarters) proportion of commerce with capitalist countries. If anything this situation is worsening in the 1990s rather than improving.

10. *Inadequately documented*. British marketers envy the information commonly available in the United States, while industrial marketers similarly respect the published consumer data, but differences between our fields are as nothing when compared with most developing countries. Even where there is a superficial veneer of sophistication in the presentation of figures, they are nearly always out of date, generally ineffectively collected and frequently deliberately tailored. It must be appreciated that with the differences in culture it is often almost impossible to get urban, numerate patriates who can still communicate with the predominantly rural peasant population. Beyond this, in a subsistence economy with a population which is largely illiterate, worried about tax implications and with no general traditions as to the integrity of information and the importance of figures, one cannot expect good primary statistics, or find gathering secondary statistics easy.

To overcome the barriers to economic growth implicit in these features of developing countries, Austen argues that 'It is clearly vital, therefore, that the management process at organisation level, as opposed to governmental planning level, which optimises and predicts the relationship of inputs to outputs over time, i.e. "Marketing", should play an increasingly significant role' an assertion which echoes the sentiments of such well-known authors as Galbraith, Drucker and McCarthy.

Consider what Drucker had to say as far back as 1958 ('Marketing and Economic Development', *Journal of Marketing*, Jan 1958, pp. 252–9) :

> My thesis is very briefly as follows, Marketing occupies a critical role in respect to the development of such 'growth' [i.e. underdeveloped] areas. Indeed, marketing is the most important 'multiplier' of such development. It is in itself in every one of these areas the least developed, the most backward part of the economic system. Its development, above all others, makes possible economic integration and the fullest utilisation of whatever assets and productive capacity an economy already possesses. It mobilises latent economic energy.

In the first instance most would agree with Kindleberger (*Economic Development*, McGraw-Hill, 1958) that whether markets stimulate development or vice versa, distribution systems tend to be neglected and are the source of considerable inefficiency. It follows that improvements in physical distribution are likely to have a high pay-off and help break the vicious circle so typical of the developing economy, where surpluses are small or non-existent, leaving little or nothing for investment to provide the necessary stimulus to growth. Allied with developments in physical distribution it is also clear that efficient retail practice has a significant contribution to make in optimising the satisfaction derived from the available supply. Austen cites a study by Slater which showed that ten years after supermarkets were introduced into Puerto Rico they accounted for 40 per cent of all food sales in San Juan and offered lower prices than traditional small outlets. In a similar vein several studies in Latin America have claimed that mass retailing methods used by Sears, Roebuck have been an important contributor to economic growth.

However, marketing can perhaps make the greatest impact by ensuring that scarce resources are channelled into those products which offer the greatest consumer satisfaction. Unfortunately in economies where scarcity is endemic it is often difficult to persuade managers that an ability to sell everything they can make is not necessarily the same as maximising satisfaction. A simple case history will help make the point.

In Nigeria soft drinks such as coke, lemonade and orangeade are extremely popular and often difficult to obtain. A survey of marketing students at the University of Nigeria in Enugu showed that although the major bottling company was able to sell all its output, customers were not entirely satisfied with the product mix, which emphasised coke and contained relatively small proportions of orange and lemon flavours. It appeared that consumers had a very strong preference for orange and deliveries were consumed immediately; lemon ranked second, but it was only after both orange and lemon were sold out that coke became acceptable as third best, but still preferable to no soft drink at all. Because demand exceeded supply the manager assumed that all was well and paid little attention to new firms being set up concentrating mainly on orange and lemon flavours. In ignoring this potential competition he clearly had forgotten that some years previously coke had built up its sales in preference to beer, which had now lost its dominant place in the beverage market.

The moral is as clear in developing economies as it is in developed ones – an understanding of consumer needs is fundamental to long-run business success, and therefore to optimising the allocation of scarce resources. In turn it is clear that the scarcer resources are, the greater the need to optimise the return from them, so that even where growth is restrained voluntarily marketing practices and techniques have a major role to play in ensuring the greatest possible return in terms of consumer satisfaction.

By improving the efficiency of the marketing function we improve profitability, and increased profitability means a larger surplus to invest in expanding production facilities. In other words marketing productivity is an essential contributor to reducing and solving the scarcity problem.

To conclude, it seems to me that the marketing concept is universal to all stages of economic development and to ignore it is to slow down the optimum rate of growth as I have defined it – put another way, neglect of the marketing concept wastes scarce resources. When it comes to application of the concept then it is clear that different marketing functions are more relevant in some situations than in others. In developing countries one needs market research as an essential input to planning future development; one needs greatly improved distribution to ensure that the limited goods available are put into consumption in the most efficient manner possible; one needs greater control over distribution to eliminate distortion of the price mechanism through diversion into a black-market operation. One has proportionately a much lesser need for promotional and selling activities than is the case in advanced economies, where supply and demand are much closer to equilibrium. However, these differences do not deny the relevance of marketing, merely a better understanding of its application.

It follows, therefore, that in principle the concepts and practices discussed in this book are of relevance to all countries whatever their stage of economic development. However, in seeking to apply the ideas in this book one should be mindful of Robert Bartel's conclusions when addressing the question 'Are Domestic and International Marketing Dissimilar?' (*Journal of Marketing*, July 1968), namely:

(a) Marketing is a process of twofold character: technical and social.

(b) Marketing technology, i.e.' . . . the application of principles, rules, or knowledge relating to the non-human elements of marketing', has universal validity and potentially universal applicability.

(c) 'The applicability of marketing technology is dependent upon circumstances of the environments in which it is applied', i.e. cultural and societal factors condition the technical factors.

(d) There are wide differences in cultural and societal factors between countries and, therefore, in marketing practice. Despite these differences the *relationships* between marketing practice and environment are susceptible to generalisations in analysis termed 'comparative marketing'. Thus, although the marketer may expect both differences and similarities between foreign and domestic markets, 'both are embraced within a consistent body of marketing theory'.

So much for marketing within countries at different stages of economic development. What about trade between them?

■ International trade

While trade between nations is of almost equal antiquity as exchange between individuals the theoretical explanation for it had to await the statement of David Ricardo's 'Theory of Comparative Advantage' in the early nineteenth century. To demonstrate the application of his theory and the benefits which would flow from specialisation by nations Ricardo used the following example (see *Dictionary of Modern Economics*, ed. David W. Pearce, Macmillan, 1981).

	Labour Hours required to produce	
	1 gallon wine	1 yard cloth
Portugal	80	90
England	120	100

Portugal has an absolute advantage in the production of both commodities since the input requirements are less than those for England. Portugal's comparative cost advantage for wine is 80:120 which is less than the rate of 90:100 for cloth. If Portugal specialises in accordance with her comparative cost advantage then for every yard of cloth she ceases to produce she can have $1\frac{1}{8}$ gallons of wine, for each embodies 90 labour hours. If, as Ricardo postulates, the exchange rate after trade between cloth and wine is 1:1, then Portugal can exchange her $1\frac{1}{8}$ gallon of wine to obtain $1\frac{1}{8}$ yards of cloth. In other words, Portugal can obtain $1\frac{1}{8}$ yards of cloth for the 90 labour hours which would only have yielded 1 yard of cloth produced domestically. However, England gains too, for despite her absolute inferiority she can translate the 120 hours required to produce a gallon of wine into the production of $1\frac{1}{5}$ yards of cloth which by international exchange can be converted into $1\frac{1}{5}$ gallons of wine.

Nowadays, modern theory has established that the only necessary condition for the possibility of gains from trade is that price ratios should differ between countries but the essential concept remains the same – that by specialisation and through trade countries improve their overall standard of living. Recently the strict application of this doctrine has been challenged by Bruce Scott in an article in the *Harvard Business Review* ('National Strategy for Stronger US Competitiveness', Mar–April 1984).

According to Scott one must reject the static theory of comparative advantage in favour of a dynamic approach founded on a national strategy towards long-run competitiveness. Thus:

> Japan's remarkable post-war economic growth is based, in considerable measure, on the Japanese government's rejection of static, conventional economic theories. Japanese leaders recognised that Japan could create competitive advantages by mobilising technology, capital, and skilled labour to attack problems or identify opportunities in selected sectors. They created a strategy of dynamic comparative advantage at the national level that parallels the strategy of a diversified company as it shifts resources from less to more promising areas. As a high level MITI official explained in a 1970 OECD publication:

> 'Should Japan have entrusted its future, according to the theory of comparative advantage, to these industries characterised by intensive use of labour? [With a population of 100 million] had [Japan] chosen to specialise in this kind of industry, it would almost permanently have been unable to break away from the Asian pattern of stagnation and poverty . . .'

The Ministry of International Trade and Industry decided to establish industries which require intensive employment of capital and technology, such as steel, oil refining, petrochemicals, automobiles, aircraft, industrial machinery of all sorts, and later electronics, including electronic computers. From a short-run, static viewpoint, encouragement of such industries would seem to conflict with economic rationalism. But, from a long-range point of view, these are precisely the industries where income elasticity of demand is high, technological progress is rapid, and labour productivity rises fast. It was clear that without these industries it would be difficult to raise [our] standard of living to that of Europe and America; whether right or wrong, Japan had to have these heavy and chemical industries.

As Scott points out, Portugal should have chosen to specialise in the growth industry of the day (cloth) and forsaken the production of port wine! (In *The Comparative Advantages of Nations* (Macmillan, 1990) Michael Porter dismisses Ricardo's theory as inadequate and incomplete and proposes that the only lasting, sustainable advantage is a country's people, This book is essential reading for those seeking the most modern and detailed analysis.)

However, Japan's success in penetrating world markets with its modern products confirms the necessity for international trade, for without imports it would be impossible to produce these and exports are essential to pay for them.

Of necessity, Britain has long been involved in foreign trade in order to make good her limited endowment of land and raw materials. During the middle of the last century we had a virtual monopoly of international trade, but since that time our share has declined continuously. In large degree this decline has been due to the enormous expansion in international trade, for in absolute terms our total trade today is many times greater than it was during the last century. Several factors may be distinguished as having contributed to this growth, including:

(a) Nationalistic policies, emphasising self-sufficiency, have yielded to the logic of the theory of comparative advantage, i.e. that countries will maximise their growth by specialising in those activities with the greatest marginal product, and exchanging excess supplies for the surplus output of other specialised economies. The creation of international trading communities is an implicit recognition of this, e.g. EEC, EFTA, LAFTA (Latin America Free Trade Association), etc.

(b) Politically, it has been realised that the removal of trade barriers will not only stimulate the growth of economies but will also lead to cultural exchange and the easing of international tension.

(c) The 'population explosion' has created new mass markets and expanded the demand for all types of goods and services.

(d) Developments in communications and transportation have opened up hitherto inaccessible markets.

(e) The removal of trade barriers has intensified competition in formerly protected markets, and encouraged domestic manufacturers to develop new products and to look farther afield for markets in which to sell them.

▌ Factors which predispose the firm to enter international markets

Fundamentally, entry into any new market, domestic or foreign, is undertaken to increase overall profitability. In turn, the decision to enter the international market may arise from any combination of a number of factors, among which may be distinguished:

1. Loss of domestic market share due to increased competition. Whereas a price reduction in the home market might be suicidal, the firm using a contribution approach may be able to increase total profits by selling at a lower price in foreign markets. (This strategy is often precluded by the existence of anti-dumping agreements.)
2. Loss of domestic market share due to product obsolescence. In many cases products made obsolete by the introduction of more sophisticated substitutes are still appropriate to less advanced countries, e.g. oil lamps.
3. Saturation of the domestic markets precluding the attainment of scale economies. Unlike the previous points, which presume the existence of excess capacity, this situation suggests that an increase in market size will permit the firm to expand its production and reduce average cost. In turn, this will permit the firm to expand its domestic market, as well as compete more effectively overseas.
4. The provision of incentives. Incentives to enter international markets are of both the 'push' and 'pull' variety, and invariably originate at government level. International agreements such as GATT (General Agreement on Tariffs and Trade) frequently exclude the provision of direct subsidies to exporters, but there are a number of ways in which a government can provide indirect support.

In addition to the information and promotional support represented by these expenditures, the exporter can also call upon other departments such as those of the DTI for specialised help, can insure against loss through the Export Credits Guarantee Department, and receive preferential tax treatment for expenses incurred.

'Pull' incentives are those offered by foreign governments to encourage entry into their national market. Originally, such incentives included import licences and tax relief on profits, but these are less common now. Most developing economies wish to develop domestic industry, in order to create employment opportunities, as well as wishing to conserve foreign exchange. Consequently, pull incentives are now largely designed to attract foreign firms to establish subsidiaries, rather than to attract the importation of finished goods. Probably the strongest incentive of all, however, is the existence of potential demand backed by purchasing power. Essentially, such market opportunities are of three types:

Type 1. One can offer an equivalent product at a lower price.
Type 2. One can offer a better product at a competitive price.
Type 3. One can offer a product which is not available in the foreign market.

In view of the high labour costs/low productivity of many of our industries, few type 1 markets are open to British exporters and attention is largely concentrated on type 2 and type 3 situations.

Over the years many traditional British exports have built up a reputation for quality, soundly based on product superiority, e.g. woollens, speciality cotton textiles, china, machine tools, etc. Unfortunately, complacency and poor marketing have allowed competitors to pre-empt many type 2 markets, although personal experience of the American consumer goods markets suggests that these markets are not irretrievably lost, as many British products of unrivalled quality could be sold at twice their domestic price and still undercut the Japanese imports which predominate.

Type 3 markets offer the greatest profit opportunity of all, but are the least common. Further, the small size of the domestic market, and insular thinking, frequently delay the development of technological innovations, allowing other countries to overtake us, e.g. the Hovercraft. Hopefully, membership of the EC and the pact of 1992 (see end of chapter) will encourage the adoption of more aggressive, and less risk-averse, R and D and marketing policies which will fully exploit our inventive genius.

■ The location of market opportunity

In general, the identification of foreign market opportunities will result from systematic marketing research of the type described in Chapter 10. In the particular, however, it is usually necessary to modify this approach for a number of reasons:

(a) Most companies are seeking a market for an existing product with which they have had considerable domestic experience, i.e. one is seeking to match needs with a product, rather than develop a product to satisfy identified but unfilled needs.

(b) Few companies or executives have any 'feel' for foreign markets, which tend to be totally unknown quantities in a way which the home market can never be. Some might argue that this is an advantage in that it demands a fuller and more scientific analysis, with less dependence on subjective, judgemental opinions.

(c) Few countries possess the wealth of published data available for use in domestic desk research, making precise quantification difficult.

(d) Field research using survey methods is frequently precluded because of language difficulties, the non-availability of trained personnel, cost, etc.

(e)   There are literally dozens of countries which might represent a potential market, and some form of screening procedure is essential to reduce the list to manageable proportions.

In the latter context the development of comparative marketing as an area of study offers considerable hope in that it is concerned with 'The identification and analysis of common factors and differences in marketing concepts, systems and techniques among various societies, including nations' (David Carson, 'Comparative Marketing – A New–Old Aid', *Harvard Business Review*, May–June 1967). As the title of Carson's article suggests, comparative analysis is a long-established technique, but it is only in the 1970s that it became the subject of formal study in the marketing context. As a result of these studies a number of formal classificatory systems have been, or are in the course of being, developed which take into account economic, geographic and human factors. Although none of these systems has yet been accepted as definitive, reference to any or all of them should permit early elimination of countries which are clearly unsuited as potential markets for a given product or service. Similarly, a study of the differences and common factors between countries should sensitise the marketer to their relative importance when formulating a marketing strategy.

■ Sources of information

In the nature of things, the classificatory systems being developed by comparative marketing theorists are based largely on generalisations, and should be regarded as a screening device. Once a short-list of potential markets has been decided upon, the researcher must seek out more detailed data. A number of sources are available to assist him in this task, some of which have already been quoted in Chapter 10. These may be supplemented by reference to:

The Department of Trade and Industry
Chambers of Commerce
Commercial Officers of the Diplomatic Service
Export Councils
Federation of British Industries
Institute of Directors
Chartered Institute of Marketing
National Association of British Manufacturers
Trade Associations
The Foreign Departments of the major banks, etc., etc.

(The DTI publishes a wide selection of free publications which are available on request and contain full details of sources of information, export services available, etc.)

Many of the sources quoted can provide first-hand information on specific opportunities, as well as advising on the procedure to be followed, and the pitfalls to be avoided, when entering specific markets.

■ Field research

Although it is generally true that few countries have market research organisations capable of undertaking field research, this certainly does not apply to the advanced, affluent economies which represent the best potential markets for British goods. On the other hand few companies are prepared to make a large-scale entry into a foreign market, and so baulk at the expenditure that an extensive survey would involve. Consequently, many would-be exporters confine their field research to a 'fact-finding' tour in which they solicit the opinions of informed sources, the quality of which varies enormously. Owing to the uncertainties associated with entry into a foreign market, as opposed to risks which are quantifiable, many marketers prefer to enlist the support of a third party in the country concerned, i.e. an indirect approach, which is usually regarded as a substitute for field research.

■ Globalisation versus segmentation

Since the publication of 'Marketing Myopia' in 1960 Ted Levitt has been recognised as one of the foremost marketing thinkers of our time with the added advantage that he can and does communicate his ideas clearly and vigorously. This is certainly the case with his article which appeared in the May–June 1983 issue of the *Harvard Business Review* – 'The Globalisation of Markets' – which opens with the following sentences:

> A powerful force now drives the world toward a single converging commonality, and that force is technology. It has proletarianised communication, transport, and travel, making them easily and cheaply accessible to the world's most isolated places and impoverished multitudes. Suddenly no place and nobody is insulated from the alluring attractions of modernity. Almost everybody everywhere wants all the things they have heard about, seen or experienced via the new technological facilitators that drive their wants and wishes. And it drives these increasingly into global commonality, thus homogenising markets everywhere.
>
> The result is a new commercial reality – the explosive emergence of global markets for globally standardised products, gigantic world scale markets of previously unimagined magnitudes.

The article, which is reprinted in his book *The Marketing Imagination* (Free Press, 1983), develops this theme at some length, and argues that countries (Japan) and firms (Coca Cola) which have appreciated this trend enjoy enormous economies of scale in production, distribution and marketing, and by using price as a competitive weapon are able to devastate the competition. This trend is accelerated by the newly industrialising countries' (NICs) desire for modernity, as a result of which they have run up enormous external debts, and made the old patterns of international trade obsolete. As a consequence the multinational corporations which have dominated the scene for so long are giving way to the global corporation, and:

> The multinational and the global corporation are not the same. The multinational corporation operates in a number of countries, where in each case it adjusts with accommodating care and therefore high relative costs to the presumptive special conditions of the particular country. In contrast, the global corporation operates with resolute constancy and therefore at low relative costs as if the entire world (or major regions of it) were a single, largely identical entity; it does and sells the same things in the same single way everywhere.

My own view is that 25 years from now this thesis will be seen as being as overstated as 'Marketing Myopia' was. The weakness in Levitt's argument is that he is overlooking a basic concept of marketing, which is that one can pursue three quite different strategies, distinguishable as undifferentiated, differentiated, and concentrated. Global corporations pursue an undifferentiated strategy, while multinationals follow a differentiated and sometimes concentrated approach, i.e. they adjust the product/service to what they perceive as the particular needs of different groups of customers or 'market segments'. Of course Levitt has to recognise the existence of such segments which, if nothing else, will continue to exist because of the unequal distribution of income, and has to admit that the global corporation will appeal only to those who don't mind an undifferentiated product.

Now, under certain circumstances an undifferentiated product will be preferable to no product at all, as we saw in the example of coke in Nigeria cited earlier, but, as I have pointed out elsewhere ('Maxims for Marketing in the Eighties', *Advertising*, no. 66, Winter 1980/81), one of the marketing's maxims is that 'The act of consumption changes the consumer. ' In other words, the Model T at $500 was much preferable to no car at all, but once you had come to appreciate its basic benefits you also became aware of its basic faults, including that 'you can have any colour you like so long as it's black', and so come to want a product which is differentiated in some way or other. General Motors recognised this fact when Ford would not accept it and displaced him as market leader – permanently.

Experience suggests that while one can pursue an undifferentiated (global?) strategy successfully for some of the time, ultimately you will have to change it – at least to a different undifferentiated strategy, but probably to a differentiated or concentrated strategy. As such this argument is inconsistent and contradictory – a fact which is emphasised with some irony by chapter 4 in the same book, *Marketing Imagination*.

This view would certainly seem to be shared by Alvin Toffler in his book *Previews and Promises* (Pan, 1984) when he observes:

Take mass production. Nothing was more characteristic of the industrial era. Yet we're already moving from a mass production, mass consumption economy to what I've called a 'de-massified' economy.

In traditional mass manufacturing, factories pour out a stream of identical objects, by the million. In the Third Wave sector, mass production is replaced by its opposite: de-massified production – short runs, even customized, one-by-one production, based on computers and numerical controls. Even where we turn out millions of identical components, they are frequently configured into more and more customized end products.

The significance of this can't be overestimated. It's not simply that products are now more varied. The processes of production are themselves transformed. The smokestack – that symbol of the industrial, assembly-line society – is becoming a relic.

We still think of ourselves as a mass production society, yet in the advanced sectors of the economy, mass production is already an outmoded technique. And the idea that we can keep our old mass manufacturing industries competitive indefinitely is based on ignorance of what is actually happening on the factory floor.

The new technologies make diversity as cheap as uniformity. In fact, in many industries, it's customize or die. This is exactly the opposite of what was required in the Second Wave economy.

In fact, it is almost a dialectical return to pre-industrial, one-of-a-kind production, but now on a high technology basis.

And exactly the same trends are visible in the distribution system, too, where we see more and more market segmentation, direct mail targeting, specialty stores, and even individualized delivery systems based on home computers and teleshopping. People are increasingly diverse, and, as a result, the mass market is breaking into small, continually changing sectors.

Perhaps the most telling indictment against the globalisation argument is that it is production-orientated in the sense that it seeks to 'drive' the wants and wishes of potential users toward commonality rather than modify the supply to match a varying demand. As we shall see in the next sections, which look at different approaches to marketing in foreign environments, such an approach is reasonable when one is entering foreign markets for the first time or has only a limited interest in selling to such markets and wishes to minimise the risk. Otherwise, given the diversity of behaviour discussed in Chapters 6, 7 and 8 (Consumer Behaviour, Organisational Buyer Behaviour and Market Segmentation), it would be surprising, to say the least, if extending the geographical scope of one's marketing did not increase this diversity.

■ Approaches to marketing in foreign environments

As we have seen, there are numerous threats and opportunities which might predispose the firm to consider selling in foreign markets – the question is 'How does one set about it?' In ascending order of commitment the alternatives available may be summarised as:

Exporting
Licensing
Contract manufacturing
Management contracting
Joint Venture
Establishment of subsidiaries

Direct exporting is essentially direct selling in a foreign market, and thus requires the firm to take full responsibility for establishing contact with potential customers. Indirect exporting occurs when the exporter employs the services of middlemen to look after the distribution, and often the complete marketing, of the product.

Channel policy is a technical aspect of marketing, and the general principles discussed in Chapter 4 and elsewhere are equally applicable to foreign and domestic markets. Thus, the same considerations of cost versus control should be evaluated in the context of direct versus indirect exporting. The decision to export direct will almost always necessitate the establishment of sales offices and the appointment of full-time employees to staff them, although other functions, such as physical distribution and advertising, may be delegated to agents. Supporters of the direct approach argue that the setting up of branch offices and the employment of salesmen are reassuring to potential buyers as they represent a definite commitment to the market, as well as giving the marketer direct control over elements such as price, credit policy, after-sales service, etc.

In the case of technically complex industrial goods, with a small, clearly defined potential market, the direct approach is probably to be preferred. However, where the product is simple, largely undifferentiated and aimed at a mass market, most manufacturers prefer to use middlemen and test the market before committing themselves to an extensive sales and distribution network. As in the home market, middlemen fall into two main categories – merchants or wholesalers who purchase goods outright for resale, and agents who act on the manufacturer's behalf in return for a fee or commission on sales. The same problems of control discussed earlier have to be discounted against the economics of using middlemen, although it is probably true to say that the middleman's contacts in a foreign country are more valuable to the manufacturer than they are in a domestic market.

In a recent survey ('Strategy and Performance in British Exporters', *Quarterly Review of Marketing*, Spring 1990) Rick Brown and David Cook provide an excellent overview of current practice. Some key tables are reproduced below (Tables 22.1–22.6).

TABLE 22.1   Reasons for exporting

	% 1–3	Respondents 4–6	Ranking 2–6
Gain more sales	73.4	3.7	77.1
Long-term survival	52.9	16.7	69.6
Achieve market leadership	36.5	24.3	60.8
Lack of UK opportunities	32.7	27.6	60.3
Exporting more profitable	21.4	28.5	49.9
Absorb overheads	12.6	34.5	47.1
			(H = 214)

TABLE 22.2   Methods of overseas market research

Rank	Number of companies using	Weighted mean
Exploratory trips by management	173	5.96
Distributors/agents	143	5.64
Salesmen	134	5.82
Government agencies	111	4.44
Banks/Chambers of Commerce	65	3.34
Consultancies	58	4.55
In-House researcher	54	5.31

TABLE 22.3   Export product policy

	Number	%
Standard UK product	31	15
Standard UK product with limited customisation	80	40
Substantially different from UK product	20	10
Custom designed for each customer	71	35
Total	202	100

TABLE 22.4   Export pricing

	Number	%
Different for each market related to local circumstances	98	47
Based on assessment of customer value	33	16
Based on UK price list	39	19
Based on total costs	30	15
Based on marginal costs	8	3
Total	208	100

TABLE 22.5   Success factors

	Number of companies ranking	Weighted mean
Quality	173	3.88
Effective selling	122	2.80
Delivery	114	2.75
Design specification	112	3.50
Agents/distributors excellence	97	2.95
Service	95	2.43
Ability to tailor products	86	2.60
Low price	59	3.03
Market research	48	3.08
Agent/distributor relationship	48	2.85
Advertising/promotion	36	2.19

	By number of companies ranking	*By weighted means*
Top three	– quality – effective selling – delivery	– quality – design specification – market research
Bottom three	– market research – agency/distributor excellence – advertising/promotion	– ability tailor products – service – advertising/promotion

TABLE 22.6   Failure factors

	Number of companies ranking	Weighted mean
Price	114	4.43
Specification problems	68	3.16
Delivery	58	3.21
Finance	58	3.24
Quality	49	3.76
Adaptation problems	35	2.63
Company image/reputation	31	2.65
UK image/reputation	24	2.89
After sales requirements	22	2.32

The top and bottom 3 factors are:

	By number of companies ranking	*By weighted means*
Top three	– price – specification problems – delivery/finance	– price – quality – finance
Bottom three	– company image/reputation – UK image/reputation – after sales requirements	– UK image/reputation – adaptation problems – after sales requirements

Source: Rick Brown and David Cook, 'Strategy and Performance in British Exporters', *Quarterly Review of Marketing*, vol. 15, No. 3, April 1990.

■ Other alternatives

Broadly speaking, three other alternatives are open to the firm which wishes to operate on an international scale:

1. It can license a foreign company to manufacture to its specification, e.g. Pilkington has licensed Corning Glass to manufacture float glass in the United States.
2. It can undertake a joint venture with another company, e.g. Gerber's alliance with Corn Products.
3. It can set up a subsidiary company.

Licensing has several factors to recommend it:

(a)   It avoids the risk of expropriation of assets by the 'host' country, already familiar to many British companies with subsidiaries overseas.

(b)   It avoids direct competition with the licensee on his home ground. (Obviously, the licensee must have the same skills and resources as the licensor or there would be no point in taking up the licence.)

(c)   It allows the capital resources that would be tied up in increased capacity, at home or abroad, to be deployed in other profitable opportunities. In the absence of the necessary capital resources, it permits the earning of increased profits which would otherwise be unattainable.

(d)   It enables the product to be produced at a competitive price, which might not be possible if it were to be exported as a finished good, e.g. float glass is both bulky and fragile and transportation costs would probably price it out of every foreign market where it is currently produced under licence.

(e)   Licensing avoids import tariffs and restrictions, and minimises the possibility of loss due to a change in trade policy.

(f)   It avoids the risks of product failure.

The major disadvantage to licensing is that the royalties are invariably less than the normal profits which would be earned if the product were manufactured and sold by the licensor.

Joint ventures require a greater commitment by the firm than is necessary in the case of licensing, but if successful, offer greater rewards for the risks assumed. An alliance with a well-established foreign distributor or manufacturer smoothes the exporter's entry into the market, but can lead to bitter conflict over policy and practice (e.g. Concorde).

The establishment of a foreign subsidiary exposes one to all the risks which licensing minimises. Tax incentives are often offset by requirements that nationals of the foreign country hold a majority of the shares in the subsidiary, in which case it becomes a joint venture. It is also probably true to say that such incentives are directly proportionate to the risks.

In politically stable countries, however, the wholly owned subsidiary frequently offers the greatest potential – a factor which tends to be overlooked by restrictions on overseas investment. Economies of local production can be reinforced by the parent's technical, financial and marketing expertise and resources. Past experience would seem to suggest that the parent should avoid keeping too tight a rein on its subsidiary, and should be prepared to appoint foreign managers and delegate authority for all but major policy decisions to them. Long established European companies active in international markets would appear to have accepted this principle, but American firms have only lately begun to come round to this point of view, after some fairly costly attempts to retain full control at 'head office'.

Space limitations preclude fuller analysis of international marketing, for which the reader must refer to specialised texts on the subject. It is worth reiterating, however, that such texts rest on the same marketing principles as have been discussed in this book, so that their major contribution lies in the descriptive content rather than in their treatment of marketing technology.

■ The marketing challenge of 1992

Quelch *et al.* (John A. Quelch, Robert D. Buzzell and Eric R. Salama, *The Marketing Challenge of 1992*, Addison-Wesley, 1990) consider that while effective marketing will be especially critical to competitive success in Europe post-1992 the economic studies prepared for the Commission largely ignore or take for granted the marketing processes by which many of the benefits must be achieved. More specifically they identify new product development for a 'Euromarket', the rationalisation of distribution systems and the development of new advertising and promotion programmes as calling for particular attention.

The need for an initiative which would release the latent potential of the EEC as an economic grouping able to compete effectively with the United States and Japan is readily apparent from an analysis of the EC's performance from its inception in 1957 to the publication of the White Paper in 1985. Over this period Europe steadily lost ground against the other members of the Triad. However, as Quelch *et al.* point out, what was particularly worrying was that following the recession triggered by the oil crisis of 1979 Europe recovered more slowly than either Japan or the USA despite an effective reduction in exchange rates of 35 per cent which should have significantly improved it competitiveness. Worse still, Europe was losing share in the technology based industries of the future while recording gains in sunset industries such as leather and footwear goods, wood and furniture, and textiles and clothing. Thus 'Europe's performance was best in those areas where research and development was relatively unimportant and where economies of scale could often be realised (at least in production terms) at the national market level (for example, food, drink, tobacco, textiles, clothing, and building materials).'

Recognition of the threat to Europe's competitiveness was not new and had been the subject of constant comment and criticism since the 1960s (e.g. J.J. Servan-Schreiber's *The American Challenge*, 1967). What was different in the early 1980s was the identification of non-tariff barriers to trade and the fragmentation of European markets as a major contributory factor underlying a lacklustre competitive performance. The detailed analysis of academics, which documented specific cases of diseconomies due to conflicting national standards and to wasted R & D due to unnecessary duplication, were reinforced by industry's calls for European wide standards and the elimination of discrimination between national governments within the community. Clearly the community was failing to achieve the vision of its architects as spelled out in the original 1958 Treaty of Rome which, *inter alia*, called for:

- the removal of customs duties and quotas and any other regulatory measures which would impede the free flow of imports and exports.

- the establishment of a common commercial policy and customs tariff toward non-member countries.
- a common competition policy to prevent distortions between members.
- common transport policies and the free movement of people, services and capital between member states.
- the coordination of member states' economic policies and procedures to achieve equilibrium in international competition.

This failure to realise the potential of a united Europe was even more depressing when one considers the basic advantages which an effective coalition could build upon. As James Dudley points out (*1992 Strategies for the Single Market*, Kogan Page, 1990):

> Half the world's trade is conducted in the European Community, The combined gross domestic product (GDP) of all its members make it the second largest economic bloc in the world, behind North America. The EC has an approximate population of 323 million people, making it the second largest populated market in the free world behind India.
>
> It has 228 of the top 1000 companies in the world – behind Japan with 310 and the US with 345. Europe has 115 companies with profits exceeding $200 million compared with Japan with 58 and the US with 205. Even so the EC has a technology deficit of $10.6 billion with its competitors mainly Japan and North America.

However, and despite the successive failures of the Fouchet plan (Foreign Policy), the Werner plan (economic and monetary union) and Tindeman's proposals for a European Union, which foundered on the protectionist policies of nationalistic governments, in 1985 the European heads of state agreed to a programme of legislation which would lead to a single unified market by 1992. The benefits which such unification would confer were summarised in the Cecchini Report to the European Commission and are set out in Tables 22.7 and 22.8.

What was different about the 1985 Single European Act was that while its primary objective was as in 1958 to create 'an area without internal frontiers in which the free movement of goods, persons, services and capital is ensured' this time 300 separate pieces of enabling legislation were spelled out and the Act provided for decisions to be made by a majority of 54 votes of a possible 76. Prior to this decisions required the unanimous agreement of all members with the inevitable result that progress was at best slow and often non-existent.

Quelch *et al.*, Dudley and others provide extended discussion of the particular provisions for the programme of legislation to be completed by 1992 and these will not be repeated here. What is often overlooked as Quelch *et al.* point out is that while the legislation changes the rules of the game they will not by themselves confer gains or losses on individual companies. As in any other competitive situation such changes represent both threats and opportunities and it will be the response of competing firms which will determine whether they benefit or lose out as the result of a changed environment.

TABLE 22.7 Potential gains in economic welfare for the EC resulting from completion of the internal market

	Billions Ecu	Per cent of GDP
Step 1		
Gains from removal of barriers affecting trade	8–9	0.2–0.3
Step 2		
Gains from removal of barriers affecting overall production	57–71	2.0–2.4
Gains from removing barriers (sub-total)	65–80	2.2–2.7
Step 3		
Gains from exploiting economies of scale more fully	61	2.1
Step 4		
Gains from intensified competition reducing business inefficiencies and monopoly profits	46	1.6
Gains from market integration (sub-total)	62*–107	2.1*–3.7
Total		
– for 7 Member States at 1985 prices	127–187	4.3–6.4
– for 12 Member States at 1988 prices	174–258	4.3–6.4
– mid-point of above	216	5.3

* This alternative estimate for the sum of steps 3 and 4 cannot be broken down between the two steps.

Source: Commission of EC, study of Directorate-General for Economic and Financial Affairs.

In general there is a wide measure of agreement that the creation of a unified single market will be beneficial to firms, to industries and member nations. That said, it is also clear that many of these perceptions are founded on the belief that such firms, industries and nations will be winners rather than possible losers (see, for example, Chapter 2 in Quelch *et al.*). Given the necessarily limited scope of an introductory textbook we shall confine ourselves here to the implications for UK firms and industries.

The Chartered Institute of Marketing has developed an action check-list for business in collaboration with the Department of Trade and Industry in which they summarised the marketing realities of 1992. Some of the key points of this paper were as follows:

TABLE 22.8   Macroeconomic consequences of EC market integration for the Community in the medium term

	Customs formal ities	Public procure ment	Financial services	Supply side effects	Average value	Total Spread
Relative changes (%)						
GDP	0.4	0.5	1.5	2.1	4.5	(3.2–5.7)
Consumer prices	−1.0	−1.4	−1.4	−2.3	−6.1	(−4.5– −7.7)
Absolute changes						
Employment (millions)	200	350	400	850	1800	(1300–2300)
Budgetary balance (percentage of GDP)	0.2	0.3	1.1	0.6	2.2	(1.5–3.0)
External balance (percentage of GDP)	0.2	0.1	0.3	0.4	1.0	(0.7–1.3)

Source: HERMES (EC Commission and national teams) and INTERLINK (OECD) economic models.

The stated objective for 1992 is to have goods, services, capital and people moving freely between the twelve member states of the European Community.

By then, 'The Internal Market' will be an area without internal frontiers.

To achieve this will require the elimination of physical, technical and fiscal barriers, and the action to this end is already well under way.

If the goal is achieved as planned (and there are some reservations that it will be in full by 1992), new business opportunities will arise, and ways of doing business in Europe will change significantly.

What it does not mean is that there will be a huge, single, uniform European market of 320 million people. There will still be twelve different national markets an many sub-markets within each, and most small and medium sized companies will only be able to trade in a few of them.

Languages, cultures, lifestyles, industrial, retailing and commercial operations will still vary considerably from country to country, region to region. There will also continue to be separate national banks, individual currencies, education and legal systems and other fundamental differences.

What 1992 also does not mean is that non-Community international markets should be ignored, in North America, the Middle East and the Far Eastern Pacific basin.

The achievement of a Single European Market is intended to provide not only internal market opportunities, but to give Community companies the stronger base they need to compete more effectively in wider global markets.

So, although cross-border movement within the Community should be barrier-free by 1991 and will therefore make actual exporting much easier and cheaper (once you have the order), the actual winning of the order will become much more difficult.

What were formerly national markets with varying degrees of protection, will be opened up to greatly increased aggressive competition, not only from other Community countries, but from countries outside who will see European markets with free movement, as even more attractive than they presently are.

The Marketing Implication of 1992
In essence, the changing Europe is simply a major new facet of the international marketing scene, but by its nature, it will be complex, competitive and potentially very rewarding.

To exploit the opportunities and to counter the threats, will call for the same effective marketing skills and disciplines that international marketing has always required; but with the added complexities of Europe '92, they will have to be honed to a very sharp competitive edge.

Clearly, each company will have to examine its individual situation and determine what opportunities exist for its particular product or service, and how they can be exploited. Each company will also have to consider the threats it is likely to face from new competitors with more attractive offerings.

However, in such a market environment, a number of common denominators still apply.

The Common Denominators for the Single Market
The basic questions which need positive answers, are;

1.   Is the chief executive and senior management of the company orientated and committed to the international market-place and international competition, and more specifically to the reality of Europe '92?
    Without that orientation and commitment, the future is likely to be bleak.

2.   Has the company thought through and defined its objectives and the strategic marketing focus required to achieve them?
    With many markets in Europe, most companies will have to be very selective and avoid going for a non-existent 'European' market.

3.   Does the company have a real understanding, as opposed to simply a knowledge of, the influences on the European environment and the markets in which it operates, or is planning to operate? Is it monitoring what is a constantly changing scene?

4.   Has it assessed honestly its positive and negative assets, and how they stand against the requirements of the Europe '92 situation? Is it aware that in a constantly changing market environment, strengths can become weaknesses and vice versa?
    How does its cost structure, prices, product quality, packaging, technology, distribution and marketing capabilities match up to the European market environment and competitors?

5. Has it identified the particular segments or niches where real opportunities exist for the company, as opposed to being all things to all people?

Will these market segments involve existing or new products and services? Does a development facility exist or need to be established?

6. Does it know the direct and indirect competition it faces, what makes it tick, its strengths and weaknesses, and how it is likely to act and react?

7. Having defined where it is going to compete, has the company established how it is going to compete? What is its competitive edge and is it really meaningful to the chosen market segment customers?

Creating a real competitive edge requires a deep understanding of both customers and competitors.

8. How creative is the company in its interpretation of market influences, customer needs, development, packaging, presentation and promotion of products or services, and in the facilities and organisation to support them?

9. Does it have the people and the organisation to compete effectively in its chosen European markets? Do they have the necessary language and logistical skills? Do they understand the culture and the thinking of European customers? Are they properly trained and motivated to promote and sell in Europe?

Have responsibilities for European development been clearly defined?

Will the operation be direct, through branches, subsidiaries, links with local firms, agents, partnerships or acquisitions?

10. Is there total commitment to being successful in Europe? Has the European marketing plan been developed and communicated effectively throughout the organisation?

CHAPTER 23

The marketing of services*

Learning Goals

The issues to be addressed in this chapter include;

1. The nature of factors which underlie the growth of services in the economy.
2. The types of services available.
3. The characteristics which distinguish services from physical products.
4. Specific issues involved in the marketing of services.

After reading this chapter you will be able to:

1. Identify and describe three basic factors which account for the growth of the service sector.
2. List the basic types of services available.
3. Specify and describe the four characteristics – intangibility, inseparability, heterogeneity and perishability and fluctuating demand – which are used to distinguish services from physical products.
4. Compare and contrast the view that service marketing is the same as the marketing of goods with the opposing view that it is significantly different and calls for a distinctive approach.
5. Define and describe the seven Ps of the service marketing mix – product, process, price, place, promotion, physical evidence and people.

■ Introduction

One of the most striking features of the last two decades has been the enormous growth in the service sector within the world's advanced industrial economies. In part this growth has been due to the relentless acceleration in the pace of technological change which has resulted in significant improvements in productivity. In part it is due to the fact that the slowing down of population growth in these countries has reduced the expansion of demand for physical goods. Taken

* I am indebted to my former research assistant Marie-Clare Cameron for her assistance in developing this chapter.

together these trends have seen a marked shift in employment from the secondary or manufacturing sector to the tertiary, services sector accompanied by a similar shift in expenditure patterns from goods to services. In this chapter we will first review the nature and extent of this growth in services before examining the factors or characteristics which are seen as differentiating services from physical products – intangibility, inseparability, heterogeneity, and perishability and fluctuating demand.

Examination of these distinguishing characteristics leads naturally into a discussion of whether the marketing of services is similar to or different from the marketing of physical goods. As one might expect two schools of thought exist – those who claim they are the same and those who claim they are different! Our analysis will suggest a compromise and argue that, while the basic principles are equally applicable to both, the distinctive nature of services calls for an extended marketing mix comprising seven elements with process, physical evidence and people being added to McCarthy's familiar four Ps of product, place, price and promotion. Each of these is explored in some detail and points to the potential for applying marketing principles and ideas to the whole range of economic activity, including the service sector.

TABLE 23.1   Some typical differences between manufacturing industry and service industry

Manufacturing	Service
The product is generally concrete	The service is immaterial
Ownership is transferred when a purchase is made	Ownership is not generally transferred
The product can be resold	The product cannot be resold
The product can be demonstrated before purchase	The product cannot usually be effectively demonstrated (it does not exist before purchase)
The product can be stored by sellers and buyers	The product cannot be stored
Consumption is preceded by production	Production and consumption generally coincide
Production, selling and consumption are locally differentiated	Production, consumption and often even selling are spatially united
The product can be transported	The product cannot be transported (though 'producers' often can)
The seller produces	The buyer/client takes part directly in the production
Indirect contact is possible between company and client	In most cases direct contact is necessary
Can be exported	The service cannot normally be exported, but the service delivery system can

However, in the same manner that it is necessary to adjust the nature of the marketing mix to suit the nature of the product and the market which it serves so it is with services. In the case of services this need is emphasised because as Shostack (1982) has observed:

> the difference between products and services is more than semantic. Products are tangible objects that exist in both time and space; services consist solely of acts or process(es), and exist in time only.

She believes that:

> the basic distinction between 'things' and 'processes' is the starting point for a focused investigation of services. Services are rendered; products are possessed. Services cannot be possessed; they can only be experienced, created or participated in.

Table 23.1 summarises some typical differences between manufacturing and service industries.

■ Growth of services

The growth in service can be seen by the increase in employment in the service sector and the growth of services' contribution to GDP. In 1980, services accounted for 62 per cent of GDP whilst in 1982, the share of employment in the service sector was 63 per cent. The reasons for the growth in services can be attributed to the following:

1. *Impact of technology* – The major technological breakthroughs achieved in recent years have been one reason for the growth in services. Technology has had a significant impact on the volume and quality of products now available, and it has been suggested by Markin (1982) that more goods or products often lead indirectly to an increased demand for services (the 'knock on' or 'multiplier' effect).

2. *Deregulation and increased competition* – In certain industries there have been changes governing the market entry requirements for firms which has resulted in greater opportunities for service companies to offer more services to customers more easily. For example, this has been a prominent feature of the financial sector in the UK, where building societies can now offer cheque accounts, and created a competitive advantage over the bank by offering interest on these accounts which the banks have had to match. Likewise, banks now offer mortgages to customers and estate agents can now provide complete legal services as part of a house sale and purchase for clients.

3. *Customer sophistication* – As society becomes wealthier and people have more time available compared with 30 to 40 years ago, the basic needs in life such

as housing and food are more easily satisfied, and society begins to place their income towards wants, rather than needs. In this respect, they do not need more cars, refrigerators or clothing, but increasingly use their income to follow other, more leisure-based activities, such as holidays, eating out or taking up new hobbies.

■ Types of services

Services can be mainly professional or consumer oriented. Professional service firms may serve in the business-to-business market, serve the private individual or may serve in both market segments. Professional services are often characterised by the following: advisory and problem solving; provided by a qualified professional known for their speciality; include an assignment requested by the client; provided by a professional who is independent and not connected with other suppliers; supervised by professional associations which attempt to define the nature of the profession, to lay down requirements of competence, to control the practice of the profession and to enforce a code of ethics (Gardner, 1986). These would include services like financial advice, advertising, business and management consultancy, engineering, architectural and interior design, legal, and medical (Gardner, 1986) to which may be added other agencies and brokers, such as estate agents, stock and insurance brokers and market research agencies (Yorke, 1990). Those firms which tend to be non-professional again may either be in the business-to-business market, or be consumer oriented. Those services which may be included in the former category can include office catering services, cleaning services or offer cash transference services such as Securicor. Those service firms which may be in the latter category are the ones which the consumer is more acquainted with, such as holiday tour companies (e.g. Thomsons, Lunn Poly), fast food outlets (e.g. Burger King, MacDonald's) or entertainment companies (e.g. Mecca, Canon).

■ The nature and characteristics of services

The characteristics of services have been classified into four main headings, namely intangibility, inseparability, heterogeneity, perishability and fluctuating demand. (Stanton, 1981)

■ Intangibility

Intangibility is probably the single most important factor in distinguishing services from goods. While it is possible to describe the nature and performance of physical products using objective criteria, this is only possible to a limited extent in the case of services. Intangibility has two dimensions (Bateson, 1977) –

the physical inability to touch an item and the mental difficulty in accepting an idea. Whilst it may be possible to elicit opinions or attitudes from friends or colleagues about a service before purchase is made, these characteristics have important implications for marketing planning. The evaluation of competitive services are more difficult *vis-à-vis* goods purchasing since the customer can touch most products to evaluate them, whereas the customer has to search for tangible clues of the service in order to evaluate it.

Another important aspect of the intangibility factor is the ease with which services can be imitated and the lack of formal patent protection – which leaves the service organisation the problem of distinguishing themselves from their competitors. Shostack (1982) states that 'while "that which is marketed" may still be a simple product or unadorned service, it is often a more complex combination of products and services.' She illustrates her point in Figure 23.1, on the following page.

However, some marketers regard the physical nature of a product as secondary in the sense that buyers are primarily concerned with the 'bundle of satisfactions' which flow from the product, rather than the product itself – for example the technical specification of a television set is rarely considered by the user, who will probably judge it on the basis of picture and sound quality as they appear to him. Further, as it has been pointed out (Wickham *et al.*, 1975), for many products tangibility does not permit physical evaluation in any meaningful way, so that such products tend to be selected on the basis of reputation, advice and experience rather than on the basis of physical examination. If this is the case, a consideration of ascertaining the *benefits* that consumers want or expect would be a more powerful means of developing effective marketing strategies.

■ Inseparability

The second differentiating factor of services is inseparability – that is to say, there is no distinction between *delivery* and *use* due to many services being produced and consumed simultaneously. Unlike manufacturing firms, the sale of the service must be made before production and consumption occurs and the customer receives the 'product' they are buying at the same time as it is being supplied. For example, you must be physically present at the dentist to receive dental treatment or at the hairdressers to have you hair cut. In this way therefore, a retail outlet may encounter problems with unobliging staff, a restaurant may have a poor chef; or a businessman may be unhappy with the bank teller's attitude on a Monday morning. Alternatively, the service company also must realise the significance of customer participation in the process. For example, customers may not have the ideal knowledge of filling out an application form for a mortgage or bank loan, or know how a self-service petrol pump works. This then breaks down the production/consumption interface because the customer is behaving in a difficult way for the firm. Therefore, service firms need to control the production side of the service as much as possible through the use of internal

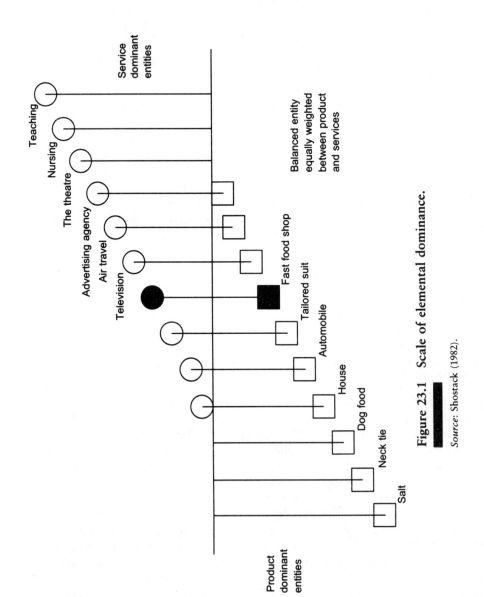

Figure 23.1 Scale of elemental dominance.

Source: Shostack (1982).

marketing as customers' perceptions of the service can be badly affected by the quality of the input as well as making the service easier to use for customers. The company must remember that some customers may not complain to the service firm directly about the poor quality service they received, but would rather show their dissatisfaction by taking their custom elsewhere or spreading the news around their friends or colleagues about the poor treatment they received.

■ Heterogeneity

The third characteristic which distinguishes services from goods is the ability to be uniform or standard. Services are heterogeneous, that is, variable, while goods are usually uniform. One would usually know what to expect when one buys a car, but it is difficult to predict whether a rock band will give the same quality of performance at a concert on the opening night of their tour versus the final night performance, or for that matter, whether the same performance would be appropriate for their fans anyway. This problem of expecting people to perform in an identical way each time is hampered due to the high level of contact between 'producer' and consumer – for example, how would you feel if a customer is aggressive towards you or if a sales assistant is too impatient to answer your queries? Therefore it is difficult to forecast and ensure provision of the same quality of a service over time when the quality itself can be affected by both the performance of the provider of the service, at the time at which it is provided, as well as the behaviour of the consumer. Due to this inseparability it therefore is difficult, if not impossible for the service organisation to standardise output and gain economies of scale in much the same way as a manufacturing organisation.

■ Perishability and fluctuating demand

The fourth major dimension which distinguishes between services and goods is that services cannot be stored or inventoried in the same way as physical goods. This inability to store services means that unused service capacity and revenue is lost forever. For example, empty seats in theatres, unsold air tickets, and unbooked rooms in hotels illustrate the risk inherent in service perishability. This problem is overcome usually, in certain service industries such as tourism and communications where service firms encourage the ordinary consumer to take a weekend break at a quiet time of year or to use the telephone at off-peak times in order to encourage people to use these services and thereby ensuring the service organisation will not suffer from too great a fluctuation in demand. Demand management in services is far more subtle than it is for products and it would be much more constructive to think in terms of capacity availability that is, one can only consume what is available, and yet this point is frequently ignored in developing marketing strategies for services.

■ Managing services marketing – the seven Ps

Many marketing scholars have been preoccupied with discussing whether the marketing of services is similar to or different from the marketing of physical goods. There are two different schools of thought with regard to the applicability of product marketing concepts and techniques to services marketing – that is product-based versus service-based approaches. One school of thought believes that services are not different from physical goods, and that therefore the same concepts and techniques used in goods marketing can be directly translated to services marketing. Most of the arguments suggested by the adopters of this view centre round the following two points:

1. The claimed differences between goods and services are exaggerated and provide little insight to understanding either of them. In addition the preoccupation with such a simple service-product classification is myopic and likely to be unsuitable. Instead more multi-dimensional classifications are needed in which the marketing strategy of the firm is a function of offer characteristics, market characteristics and characteristics of the exchange process (Wickham *et al.*, 1975; Goodfellow, 1983).
2. The most important criterion to be considered when marketing any product (including physical goods, services, ideas etc.) is the buyer's expectations. Many commentators argue that consumers are not buying goods or services, but the value satisfaction of the offering. So it is suggested that the process of marketing strategy formulation should start with a product concept which recognises the bundle of benefits, often including both tangible and intangible aspects as it is perceived by the potential buyer (Levitt, 1974; Donnelly and George, 1981).

Dissatisfaction with this approach leads many authors to take their thinking to the other extreme and call for a theory for marketing services. According to the service-based approach, it is argued that services possess certain distinguishing features which make them fundamentally different from physical goods. Therefore the suggestion advanced is that service marketers must develop a unique process of marketing strategy formulation for services which differs from the traditional one.

The development of a service marketing theory of a frame of reference which guides the marketer's thinking deals with either the service area (that is, its organisational aspects (Blois, 1982), consumer behaviour (Blois, 1982), marketing mix activities (Shostack, 1984; Donnelly, 1976) or a specific aspect of it, for example, professional services (Gummesson, 1979)).

According to this approach, it is argued that the marketing of services is much more complex than the marketing of goods due to fundamental difference in the end products and the simultaneous production and consumption processes. As such it is suggested that service marketers need new tools, strategies and organisation structures to carry out the process of marketing services effectively.

Drawing on the similar concept of McCarthy's four P's for product marketing, the services marketing mix has been extended to seven P's (Cowell, 1984, adapted from Booms and Bitner, 1982). These have been described as product, process, price, place, promotion, physical evidence and people.

■ Product

From Chapter 11 it can be clearly seen that the marketer of physical goods has a variety of strategic options open to him when determining his product range. In the same way, the service marketer is faced with similar decisions in developing his product mix. The product mix should take into account that services are made up of two parts – the 'core service' and the 'auxiliary service' (Gronroos, 1980). The core service is similar to what Kotler (1988) termed the 'core product', i.e. it is the basic service which is offered, for example, dry cleaning. The 'auxiliary' service is similar to Kotler's (1988) 'augmented product', that is to say, the added benefits which differentiate the service from competitors. In the case of dry cleaning, this could be same day delivery service to your home or office so that you do not have the hassle of picking the garment up at the end of the evening. The quality of the service can be divided into two types – technical quality, i.e. the actual cleaning of the garment, and the functional quality, i.e. how the service is actually presented or delivered (Gronroos, 1982). This aspect of the service is important with respect to 'physical evidence', as the customer will evaluate anything which is tangible about the service, such as the care with which the garment is packed or the uniform of the delivery boy, so it is therefore necessary to ensure all aspect of the product, be it core or auxiliary are of a high standard.

■ Process

The process element of the service marketing mix is concerned with the way in which the service is delivered to the customer. This has two points of interest to the service marketer. First, the inseparability characteristic of services has an important implication for how the service company's personnel deliver the service to the customer and how the customer participates in the service delivery process. Secondly, the 'auxiliary' aspect of the service, i.e. the added value of the service becomes an important competitive weapon in differentiating the service from competitors when the service is experienced by customers. One example of how process can be used to competitive advantage is through the marketing of financial services. The basic need for a bank is to store money in a safe place until we need access to it. This access has been improved considerably over the last few years by banks when they introduced services such as ATMs (Automated Teller Machines), charge cards, and through a variety of cheque book accounts on offer. However, when ATMs were first introduced, although advances in technology did increase the availability of the service, customers did not know how to use them, and they were then left to work it out for themselves. Therefore, the overall effectiveness of the service process fundamentally depends on how the customers use the service. Lowe (1988) reinforces this point that services have been defined as 'acts rather than things' and this casts some light on the concept of 'process'. Many benefits from services occur not so much as a result of what is offered, as in the way in which it is offered.

■ Price

Pricing a service is generally believed to be more difficult than the pricing of manufactured goods as discussed in Chapter 13. Cowell (1984) has produced a useful table highlighting the variety of prices for selected services.

TABLE 23.2   Price terminology for selected services

Terminology	Typical service
Admission	Theatre entry
Charge	Hairdressing
Commission	Stockbroking service
Dues	Union membership
Fare	Transport
Fee	Legal service
Honorarium	Guest speaker
Interest	Use of money
Premium	Insurance
Rate	Municipal services
Rent	Property usage
Retainer	Consultant's services
Salary	Employee services
Subscription	Membership
Tariff	Utilities
Toll	Road use
Tuition	Education
Wage	Employee services

Source: D. Cowell, *The Marketing of Services* (Oxford: Heinemann, 1984).

From Table 23.2, it is clear that services range from those supplied by the private company, to public utilities and professional service groups. It is also fair to assume that there are many different factors which influence price, one of which can be the service's role in society. For example, the pricing for public transport such as buses or trains will to a large extent be determined by public regulation in order to make the service attractive, and within reach to the majority of people. Pricing in professional services such as solicitors' and stockbrokers' fees are largely governed by professional bodies, whereas services such as hairdressing or car hire charges are largely governed by market demand. This classification by Rathmell (1974) has proved useful in clarifying how prices in the service sector can be set, but it leaves a great deal to be desired when setting price at the tactical level and using price as a marketing weapon. Wilson (1972) believes 'Outside the areas of fixed, standard or customary prices, the use of pricing in the marketing mix remains primitive and awaits only intelligent application for substantial rewards to be reaped'. This is echoed by Cowell (1984) who believes 'pricing has not yet received the attention it deserves' with regards to service marketing, and that 'As with other marketing mix elements, the price of a service should be related to the achievement of marketing and organisational goals and should be appropriate for the service organisation's marketing programme'. The difficulty, it is said, lies in the diverse nature and characteristics of services which leads to sweeping generalisations.

Cowell (1984) discusses how the characteristics of services can influence the service price, although he emphasises that these should be considered *in addition to* the traditional forces which influence price, these being costs, competition and demand. There are five categories which he considers:

1. Service perishability – since services cannot be inventoried like manufactured goods, service companies have to be prepared for fluctuations in demand at certain times of the year. Cowell (1984) cites the example of the holiday tour market, where price discounts can be made at the last minute, in order to sell unused holidays. However, he warns against increasing 'customer sophistication' where buyers almost expect these bargains to be made available at certain times of the year, and therefore hold back until the cheaper holidays are advertised, since they know the tour operator will be more keen to sell at a cheaper price then to have unsold holidays. However, in order to offset this trend and encourage potential customers, some companies have offered discounts of up to £100 off summer holidays to those customers who book early.

2. Competition between service companies increases in certain industries when customers can afford the luxury of postponing the use of the service and be able to 'shop around' for the best deal by telling the interested parties how little other companies have offered, e.g. van removals.

3. Intangibility – since the possibility of customers using the service for the first time may not know how to evaluate what they are receiving for their money exactly, they may evaluate the service on the basis of the tangible features of the service that they receive. Taking you back to Shostack's (1977) tangibility/intangibility continuum, (Figure 23.1) most goods have a degree of the service element attached to them, and likewise, most services have a degree of tangibility as well. 'The higher the material content, the

more will prices set tend to be based on costs and the greater the tendency towards more standard prices. The smaller the material content the more customer orientated and the less standard will prices be' (Cowell, 1984).

Service companies can use this to their advantage when, if a customer negotiates a lower price for the use of the service, the company has at its disposal the ability to vary the quality of the service according to what it perceives the customer is getting for their money.

4. When services are more or less standardised with regards to their use (e.g. laundrettes), prices are usually very competitive. Alternatively, companies may be subject to regulations regarding the minimum price they may charge, or they may have the freedom to sell at whatever price the market will bear.

5. Inseparability – The degree of price competition in the market will to a large extent be influenced by the number of competing firms within that area. Customers may be limited to a small geographic area in order to experience the service or only be able to use the service at particular times, which will influence the price service companies can charge.

The price of services is influenced by a number of factors, namely: the planned market position for the service product; the stage of the life-cycle of the service product; elasticity of demand; the competitive situation; and the strategic role of price (Christopher *et al.*, 1980). Gabor (1980) identified two methods for pricing services:

1. *Cost-based pricing* – either a profit oriented method, where price setting is done by professional associations, or government controlled.

2. *Market-oriented pricing* – the company is either setting prices for competitive reasons or because the firm is customer oriented.

Cowell (1984) feels that 'many of the tactical price techniques used to sell tangibles can be used to sell intangibles', citing such tactics (as identified by McDonald and Stromberger, 1969) as differential or flexible pricing; discrete pricing; discount pricing; diversionary pricing; guarantee pricing; high price maintenance pricing; loss leader pricing; offset pricing; and price lining which can be suitable for setting prices in services. He also outlines three additional aspects of service pricing which are inherent to services:

1. *Price negotiation* – many services' prices can be negotiated before the client receives the service, such as interest payments on loans or advertising agency fees.

2. *Competitive bidding* – this is more prominent in organisational markets and it is when the client can shop around for the best deal.

3. *Price awareness* – similar to the pricing of goods, this is when the service company can set its pricing strategy according to how the market perceives the nature of the pricing in that particular service industry. When the customer is relatively unsure of the price, the service company can use this

to its advantage, as they tend to perceive price as an indicator of quality, due to the lack of evidence available (Eiglier and Langeard, 1977).

However, in summary, Cowell (1984) believes that the pricing of services 'still remains largely a combination of good management, experience, trial and error, intuition and good luck'.

■ Place

This is the environment in which the service is assembled and where the firm and customer interact, and any tangible commodities which facilitate performance or communication of the service.

Place has a number of aspects of concern to the service marketer – the actual location of the premises, the look of the premises, and the channels of distribution used. All of these aspects vary in importance of course, depending on the service offered, and the preferred channel(s) of distribution of the service marketer.

First, the inseparability characteristic of services means that the distribution channels are far shorter than for a goods manufacturer – the customer almost always has to visit the 'manufacturer' in order to receive the service. Therefore the location of the premises is an important factor. The location of a dentist will vary according to whether he would like to be based in a local community where the customers' main requirements would be to visit somewhere nearby for treatment, or whether he should set his surgery in the middle of a large town, where it would be convenient for commuters to visit him during the day without too much disruption to their working day, and thereby saving them the inconvenience of taking a day off work to visit the dentist. This means that in order to expand, service firms have to either build more outlets (unlike goods manufacturers who expand production facilities or make them more efficient). This has an important drawback in that it is a very capital intensive process. Alternatives to service firms may be to franchise the operation or to use agents to promote the service. However, although this may solve the expansion problem, the service company is faced with losing control over the quality of the service since it will not be their own staff they are training and who will be providing the service.

As far as the look of the premises is concerned, the client will be searching for physical clues in assessing the success of the company. For example, the client would not have a great deal of confidence in a solicitor if the solicitor's office was poorly furnished. This would imply that the solicitor either did not care about his job, and therefore the client's problems, or that they were not successful enough even to afford to pay a few hundred pounds to have the office decorated, in which case, there may be something wrong with the solicitor's services or reputation.

The channels of distribution available to a number of service marketers have improved considerably over recent years due to improvements in telecommunications. This is especially the case in banking, where transactions can be made using either the telephone, television or at the ATMs.

■ Promotion

From Chapters 16 and 17 the uses and benefits of promotional techniques such as advertising, sales promotion, and public relations became clear for physical products, but how appropriate are these same techniques for the promotion of services?

Service firms are very rarely national or international in size and scope, but they tend to be local firms servicing the local community. There are of course exceptions to this, especially with regards to franchise operations such as the Body Shop and Tie Rack and the international professional service firms, such as advertising agencies, management consultancies and accountancy firms. However, by and large, most service firms are based locally. By implication, therefore, this would mean that most service firms undertake promotion only at the local level. However, the effectiveness of promotional campaigns has been disputed regarding the advertising of services. Rathmell (1974) has stated that the intangibility feature of services means that the service cannot be viewed physically, and it therefore cannot be advertised or shown in the same way as physical goods, but needs to be presented as an idea. The difficulty is made even more acute in trying to use sales promotion techniques such as demonstrations, money off coupons, and posting samples of the service around the areas you would like to target because of the intangibility feature. Unwin (1975) echoed this difficulty in saying:

> service advertising is difficult. It offers no tangible rewards, no immediate sensations. The service advertiser has to deal in abstractions like prudence, safety and peace of mind. He is often left with describing the invisible, articulating the imaginary and defining the indistinct. It is difficult to know what to highlight and where to draw the line. And how many service customers really know what they want, or even if they want it?

In order to minimise the problems associated with advertising a service, Shostack (1977) recommended neutralising the intangibility of the service by associating some form of tangible evidence to the service in the promotional material. Berry (1980) also feels that this would make the service more 'palpable' (i.e. understandable) for the consumer. Other strategies could be through seeking professional endorsements by trade associations or using popular personalities in order to create or improve customer confidence. Lowe (1988) has found that word-of-mouth promotion is perhaps the best for service companies.

> The intangible nature of services means that people find it difficult to make a judgement on relatively objective grounds, so they rely on the experience of those

who actually used the service to a greater degree than might be the case if a tangible product were involved.

■ Physical evidence

Since a service is inherently intangible, it is important for the client to search for tangible or physical clues which enable him to evaluate the service. 'Service firms must be aware that every aspect of the company with which the consumer comes into contact will be used as a measure of the level of service that he can expect from the organisation' (Lowe, 1988). Physical evidence are those tangible clues which the consumer may receive during the process of receiving the service, which 'verify either the existence or the completion of a service' (Shostack, 1982). She further classifies physical evidence into two categories – peripheral evidence and essential evidence.

Peripheral evidence – is usually 'possessed as part of the purchase of a service, but it has little or no independent value'. She cites the example of a cheque book which is not of any use without the funds transfer and storage service that it represents.

Essential evidence – is 'unlike peripheral evidence . . . [as it] cannot be possessed by the consumer'. However, Shostack believes that essential evidence may be 'so dominant in its impact on service purchase and use that it must be considered virtually an element in its own right'. She cites the example of a consumer who purchases transportation in the form of an airline ticket (peripheral evidence) who will probably have been influenced by the type of aircraft that 'facilitates' the service since it will have a strong impact on service perceptions and even purchase.

However, one important point should be made about the management of physical evidence. Research should be conducted in order to assess the expectations of the target market's perceptions of the service environment – what may represent the standard of physical evidence expected from a particular service organisation, may seem like an expensive luxury which will be passed on to the client in the form of higher prices or fees. An example of this would be having a doorman in splendid livery outside a restaurant.

■ People

Of all the controllable variables the marketing executive has at his disposal, the people factor in the services marketing mix is perhaps the least he can rely on in getting his marketing mix 'right' and the most important one he *has* to get right. The problem lies in inseparability of the production/consumption interface, and therefore, the satisfaction of not only the recipient of the service, i.e. the customer, but also the providers of the service, i.e. the company's own personnel become extremely important.

Service personnel are present at two levels within the organisation – contact personnel and support personnel. Contact personnel are those individuals whom the customers see – such as waiters or receptionists – and whom the customers judge the service upon when they search for tangible clues as to the quality of the service. The value they attribute to the service relies a great deal on the conduct of the contact personnel. It is very rare for customers to meet the chefs who prepare the meals or the cleaning staff who prepare guests' bedrooms. Imagine being served by a waiter who has an unkempt appearance when you are visiting a restaurant or being told by a member of the cabin crew that the only difference between paying for a first class air ticket and club class is that you have spent £200 more than the other passengers. This type of behaviour is hardly conducive to developing customer loyalty in the medium-to-long term, and yet both are real examples of the behaviour of service personnel. Had the individuals been happy with their jobs, this type of ill-mannered and off-putting behaviour could have been avoided and customer satisfaction maintained. How can a company ensure that its personnel at both levels will provide a quality service leaving a favourable impression on customers? The answer lies in 'internal marketing' (Gronroos, 1982), the purpose of which is to have 'motivated and customer-conscious employees'. Employees are seen as internal customers, and jobs as internal products, who work in an organisation that should 'create an internal environment which supports customer consciousness and sales-mindedness among their personnel' (Gronroos, 1982). Employees need to become 'ambassadors for the organisation' (Lewis, 1989) as the 'quality of the service and the quality of the service providers are inseparable' (Chase, 1978). The more competent the customer contact personnel, the better the service- business-client relationship will be, which will culminate in the service organisation receiving a positive reference. This relationship has been termed 'positive circles' (Normann, 1985).

So how should the service company attract and maintain the type of desirable personnel who will leave a positive impression on customers? Lowe (1988) attributes the use of good communications within the organisation since 'customer contact personnel cannot be expected to perform well if they are not fully informed about what the company is doing, and why'. In addition, it has been recommended (Berry, 1980) that a service employer apply traditional marketing tools such as market research and market segmentation in order that '(1) the best possible people can be employed and retained and, (2) they will do the best possible work' by identifying and satisfying employees needs, wants and aspirations.

Considerations an employer needs to make regarding the company guidelines and practices would be working conditions, shift work, flexible working hours, day-to-day benefits, either financial or in-kind (e.g. tips, taxi fares home or free meals at the end of the shift), holiday entitlement, training, career development opportunities, promotion prospects, career evaluations, pensions and life assurance. By identifying what he is able to afford to give personnel, and the minimum standard of benefits personnel are prepared to take, he is partially on the way to satisfying the personnel he would like to hire. The marketing executive can also apply market segmentation techniques when it comes to identifying the ideal personnel to hire. 'Market segmentation is relevant as people are as different as employees as they are as consumers' (Lewis, 1989). The aim of internal marketing is to 'increase job satisfaction, increase productivity and decrease absenteeism . . . and to train personnel to enhance their skills and to encourage a customer orientation; and to supervise and evaluate their performance' (Lewis, 1989).

However, internal marketing has been viewed as insufficient, and it is believed that internal marketing should be viewed as a managerial philosophy that has strategic as well as tactical implications throughout the company and its various business functions. In other words, it should permeate the whole of the service company.

> If service organisations care about both employees and customers, the pay-off will be in terms of increased motivations and satisfaction; a high level of service quality as compared to the quality expected by customers, and therefore customer satisfaction; and in turn, hopefully, customer loyalty and increased level of business activity (Lewis, 1989).

In the same manner, two other functions to be performed in a service firm have been suggested (Gronroos, 1989), namely the interactive marketing function in order to manage all the resources involved in the buyer-seller interface (that is, the physical/technical environment, the contact personnel, and the customers), and the internal marketing function which is concerned with satisfying the employees as the first market of the service firm.

The proposition of a 'relationship definition of marketing' which states 'marketing is to establish, maintain, enhance and commercialise customer relationships (often, but not necessarily long-term relationships) so that the objectives of the parties involved are met. This is done by a mutual exchange and fulfilment of promises' (Gronroos, 1989). The relationship and the transaction definitions of marketing would be enhanced by developing a service culture amongst most if not all employees, and treating each customer as an individual, rather than a one-off single financial transaction. Relationship building skills have been classified into such categories as joint problem definition, and to 'listen, be patient and modest' (Kubr, 1976), but these have been taken further (McGivern, 1983) with the need for high levels of interaction between parties, the need for trust, and the contingency of the methods used being advocated.

However, this basic marketing mix has been criticised (Gronroos, 1989) with the emphasis being put on continuously adapting the supplier's operations to meet customer's needs and more particularly to match customers' expected and perceived needs. This continuous adaptation (Yorke, 1990) will involve many people at different levels within the organisation, but the overall objective would still be to protect the existing customer base resulting in continuing exchanges and lower marketing costs per customer.

It is concluded (Yorke, 1990) that at least in professional service firms, organisations should adopt a more client-centred or market-oriented approach to their planned growth. The organisation should not focus entirely on production efficiency, current service offerings or sales, but on meeting the needs of particular clients, recognising, in addition, that client needs are rarely static but continue to evolve as the nature of *their* business changes.

This would suggest that this 'strategy demands new thinking on the part of professional organisations, not only in continually appraising client needs, but also in developing a flexibility of operation involving changes in organisation structure and the continuing education of partners and employees in dealing with client problems'.

■ Conclusion

The importance of services to the British economy has been growing both in terms of employment and in relation to GDP. This growth can be attributed to the impact of technology, deregulation and increased competition and increasing customer sophistication. Services may be professional or consumer oriented, and there is a great deal of cross-over between the two categories. Services also have characteristics which differentiate them from goods and which make marketing planning more difficult – namely, intangibility, inseparability, heterogeneity, and perishability and fluctuating demand. The service marketing mix has since been extended to seven Ps, which may be product, price, process, promotion, place, physical evidence and people, although some opinions are now stating that the emphasis should be placed on continuously adapting the supplier's operations to meet customers' expected and perceived needs.

■ References

Bateson (1977) 'Do we need service marketing?', in Eiglier, P. (ed), *Marketing Consumer Services*, Boston, Mass.: Marketing Science Institute.

Berry, L. L. (1980) 'Services Marketing is Different', *Business*, May–June, pp. 24–9.

Berry, L. L. (1981) 'The Employee as Customer', *Journal of Retail Banking*, March.

Berry, L. L. (1983) 'Relationship Marketing', in Berry, L. L., Shostack, G. Lyn and Upati, G. D. (eds), *Emerging Perspectives on Services Marketing*, Chicago: American Marketing Association.

Berry, L. L., Zeithamil, V. A. and Parasuraman, P. (1985) 'Quality Counts in Services Too', *Business Horizons*, May–June, pp. 44–52.

Blois, K. (1982) 'Organisational Structure and Marketing Policies in Service Firms', Paper presented at the 11th Annual Conference of the European Academy for Advanced Research in Marketing, April.

Booms, B. H. and Bitner, M. J. (1982) 'Marketing Strategies and Organisation Structures for Service Firms', in *Marketing of Services*, Chicago: American Marketing Association, pp. 47–51.

Chase, R. B. (1978) 'Where Does the Consumer Fit in a Service Operation?', *Harvard Business Review*, vol. 56, November–December, pp. 137–42.

Christopher, M.G., Kennedy, S. H., McDonald, M. M. and Wills, G. S. C. (1980) *Effective Marketing Management*, Aldershot: Gower.

Cowell, D. (1984) *The Marketing of Services*, Oxford: Heinemann.

Donnelly, J. H. Jr (1976) 'Marketing Intermediaries in Channels of Distribution of Services', *Journal of Marketing*, vol. 40(1), January, pp. 55–7.

Donnelly, J. H. Jr and George, W.R. (eds) (1981) *Marketing of Services*, Chicago: American Marketing Association.

Eiglier, P. and Langeard, E. (1977) 'A New Approach to Service Marketing', in *Marketing Consumer Services: New Insights Report*, Boston: Marketing Science Institute, pp. 77–115.

Enis, B. and Roering, K. (1981) 'Services Marketing: Different Product, Similar Strategy', in Donnelly, J. Jr and George, W.R. (eds), *The Marketing of Services*, Chicago: American Marketing Association.

Gabor, A. (1980) *Pricing Principles and Practice*, London: Heinemann, Ch. 10, pp. 168–76.

Gardner, C. A. (1986) *Dissertation proposal*, Washington DC: George Washington University.

Goodfellow, J. H. (1983) 'The Marketing of Goods and Services as a Multidimensional Concept', *The Quarterly Review of Marketing*, Spring, pp. 19–27.

Gronroos, C. (1980) 'Designing a Long Range Marketing Strategy for Services', *Long Range Planning*, vol. 13(2), pp. 36–42.

Gronroos, C. (1981) 'Internal Marketing – an Integral Part of Marketing Theory', in Donnelly, J. H. Jr and George, W.R. (Eds), *Marketing of Services*, Chicago: American Marketing Association, pp. 236–8

Gronroos, C. (1982) *Strategic Management and Marketing in the Service Sector*, Helsinki: Swedish School of Economics and Business Administration.

Gronroos, C. (1984) 'A Service Quality Model', *European Journal of Marketing*, vol. 18(4).

Gronroos, C. (1989) 'A Relationship Approach to Marketing of Services: some Implications', *Proceedings from the 18th Annual Conference of the European Marketing Academy*, Greece: Athens School of Economics and Business Science.

Gummesson, E. (1979) 'The Marketing of Professional Services: an Organisational Dilemma', *European Journal of Marketing*, vol. 13(5), pp. 308–18.

Hakansson, H. (ed.) (1982) *International Marketing and Purchasing of Industrial Goods*, New York: John Wiley.

Kotler, P. (1988) *Marketing Management: Analysis, Planning, Implementation and Control*, 6th edn, Englewood Cliffs, NJ: Prentice-Hall.

Kotler, P. and Bloom, P. N. (1984) *Marketing Professional Services*, Englewood Cliffs, NJ: Prentice-Hall.

Kubr, M. (ed.) (1976) *Management Consulting: a Guide to the Profession*, Geneva: ILO.

Lewis, B. R. (1989) 'Customer Care in service Organisations', *Marketing Intelligence and Planning*, vol. 7(5/6), pp. 18–22.

Levitt, T. (1974) *Marketing for Business Growth*, New York: McGraw-Hill.

Lowe, A. (1988) 'The Marketing of Services', Unit 19, University of Strathclyde MCom in Marketing for Industrialising Countries by Distance Learning, Glasgow: Strathclyde University.

McDonald, E. H. and Stromberger, T. L. (1969) 'Cost Control for the Professional Service Firm', *Harvard Business Review*, January–February pp. 109–21.

McGivern, C. (1983) 'Some Facets of the Relationship Between Consultants and Clients in Organisations', *Journal of Management Studies*, vol. 20(3), pp. 367–86.

Markin, R. (1982) *Marketing Strategy and Management*, New York: John Wiley.

Normann, R. (1985) *Service Management: Strategy and Leadership in Service Businesses*, London: John Wiley.

Rathmell, J. M. (1974) *Marketing in the Service Sector*, London: Winthrop.

Sasser, W. E. (1976) 'Matching Supply and Demand in Service Industries', *Harvard Business Review*, November/December, pp. 133–40.

Shostack, G. L. (1977) 'Breaking Free from Product Marketing', *Journal of Marketing*, vol. 41(2), pp. 73–80.

Shostack, G. L. (1982) 'How to Design a Service', *European Journal of Marketing*, vol. 16(1), pp. 49–63.

Shostack, G. L. (1984) 'Designing Services that Deliver', *Harvard Business Review*, January–February, pp. 133–9.

Stanton, N. J. (1981) *Fundamentals of Marketing*, New York: McGraw-Hill.

Tarver, J. L. (1987) 'In Search of a Competitive Edge in Banking: a Personnel Approach', *International Bank Marketing*, vol. 5(1), pp. 61–8.

Thomas, M. (1981) 'Customer Care: the Ultimate Marketing Tool', in Wensley, R. (ed.), *Reviewing Effective Research and Good Practice in Marketing*, Warwick: Marketing Education Group, pp. 283–94.

Unwin, S. (1975) 'Customised Communications: a concept for Service Advertising', *Advertising Quarterly*, vol. 44, Summer, pp. 18–30.

Wickham, R. G. *et al.* (1975) 'Marketing of Services: an Evaluation of the Theory', *European Journal of Marketing*, vol. 9(1), pp. 59–67.

Wilson, A. (1972) *The Marketing of Professional Services*, London: McGraw-Hill.

Yorke, D. A. (1990) 'Interactive Perceptions of Suppliers and Corporate Clients in the Marketing of Professional Services: a Comparison of Accounting and Legal Services in the UK, Canada and Sweden', *Journal of Marketing Management*, vol. 5(3), pp. 307–23.

CHAPTER 24

Current issues and trends

Learning Goals

The issues to be addressed in this chapter include:

1. An evaluation of marketing as a new philosophy of management.
2. Consumerism.
3. Marketing as a social process.
4. The implications of change for marketing practice in the 1990s.

After reading this chapter you will be able to:

1. Explain how and why environmental change has resulted in the need for a revised approach to exchange relationships and the 'rediscovery' of marketing.
2. Suggest why marketing and a marketing orientation appear to offer the best chance for corporate success in an increasingly competitive environment.
3. Describe the origins of consumerism and indicate why marketing should be regarded as a response to these concerns rather than the cause of them.
4. Propose why consumer concern should be regarded as a marketing opportunity.
5. Review the arguments which suggest that marketing is a pervasive activity or social process which is relevant to all kinds of exchanges, both for profit and not-for-profit.
6. Discuss the view that consumer choice will increasingly be determined by subjective perceptions as the objective differences between goods and services are increasingly eroded by competitive imitation.

■ Introduction

As in previous editions the purpose of this chapter is to identify and evaluate significant trends in the development of marketing thinking and practice and to speculate on where they might be taking us.

In retrospect it is gratifying to find that the major trends identified in earlier editions are still of both relevance and importance, although it is surprising that progress has been slower than anticipated in some areas concerned with the application of technology, and particularly information technology. In the earlier editions considerable importance was attached to the development of consumerism and to the evolution of marketing from a commercial practice to a social process. Both trends are still with us and reflect the continuing transition from an era of mass consumption into a post-industrial society. Accordingly they will figure prominently in this chapter and, to a considerable degree, subsume our 1979 prognostication that in the 1980s perhaps the most important developments will occur in four main areas:

1. The interface between marketing and public policy, with the choice between self-regulation from within and imposed regulation from without becoming more acute.
2. The growing importance of services in advanced economies and the transfer of product marketing techniques and practices into the service sector accompanied by 'demarketing' of physical consumption goods.
3. An increased emphasis upon the transferability of the marketing concept and marketing practice into the not-for-profit sector.
4. A growing recognition of the benefits of marketing in centrally planned and developing economies.

■ Marketing – a new philosophy of management?[*]

In recent years it has become increasingly fashionable to talk of accelerating technological change, increased international competition and environmental turbulence. Taken together these trends are seen as calling for a radically different approach to business and management than that which has prevailed for the better part of this century. In response to this call for a radical change in business attitudes and practices 'marketing' has emerged as both a philosophy of business and a business discipline best suited to survival and success as we move into the twenty-first century. To assess the validity of this claim it seems to me that we must first establish the nature and implications of the changes in our environment. Next, we must attempt to define just what marketing is, or is claimed to be. And, finally, we must examine whether marketing, as defined, does seem to offer the best prospects for increased consumer satisfaction in the years ahead and, if so, what is needed to promote its full acceptance.

[*]This paper was given as the 1988 'BOWDEN ADDRESS' at the Worshipful Company of Marketers Dinner on 20th October 1988, London.

■ Environmental turbulence

It has become increasingly fashionable in recent years to speak of environmental turbulence as if it were a new phenomenon discovered by later twentieth-century man. Given that the origins of the word are to be found in the Latin *turba* meaning 'confusion or uproar', from which 'disturb' is also derived, this is a typical case of modern arrogance. That said, the increased incidence of flying has made many of us aware of the uncomfortable unease engendered by physical turbulence in our environment and endowed the term with an immediacy and impact which it may previously have lacked.

Fortunately most turbulence is predictable in that it originates with a discontinuity such as those between pressure systems in the atmosphere or when approaching the sound 'barrier'. Normally we can measure and plot these discontinuities and, while we are occasionally taken by surprise by clear air turbulence, in the majority of cases we can take actions to minimise or avoid interruptions to a smooth progression from where we are to where we want to be. It follows that environmental forecasting is as important to the corporate strategist and marketer as meteorological forecasting is to the airline pilot. Unfortunately, and to pursue the analogy, the further in advance that we try to predict specific events the less accurate our specific predictions become and the less willing many people become to make the effort. A major consequence of this managerial myopia has been the emphasis upon short-term financial milking and paper entrepreneurialism which dulled the competitive edge of the UK and USA and allowed the Japanese, West Germans and others with a long-term vision of the future to penetrate our domestic markets and steal our foreign markets.

Despite the fact that the history – and progress – of man is one of continuous change people prefer to act and behave as if the future will be like the present and so ignore, avoid or resist change. But, not only is change continuous – it is accelerating. It follows that if management is to fulfil its primary roles of analysis, anticipation, planning and control then it must give particular attention to the nature and direction of change. In doing so, it is clear that, as Martel has argued, change as a process exhibits distinct regularities or patterns 'with dimensions of direction, magnitude, pace and duration that can be seen and measured'.

Martel argues that failure to recognise and use change leads to three common errors:

1. Believing yesterday's solutions will solve today's problems.
2. Assuming present trends will continue.
3. Neglecting the opportunities of future change.

He cites the American automobile industry as an example of Error 1 in that it is still pursuing Alfred Sloan's manufacturing and marketing strategy enunciated in the early 1920s. Basically this strategy is founded on the concept of trading-up or 'upsizing' and is facilitated by trade-ins and instalment buying. The economies of scale for a full line of cars exist in using many of the sub-assemblies and components of cheaper models in the more expensive models enabling, in

Sloan's words, 'the mass production of automobiles to be reconciled with variety of product'. But, the strategy does not work in reverse so that when the market wants small, high quality, low cost cars 'downsizing' is not a feasible route to continued profitability. As a result foreign competitors, who had anticipated the change, were able to penetrate the US market and establish a foothold from which it has proved extremely difficult to dislodge them.

Martel points to 'a variant of this error' in the so-called 'sailing ship' phenomenon' whereby the introduction of steam ships stimulated conventional shipbuilders to build better sailing ships rather than switch to the new technology. Numerous example of the phenomenon are to be found, not only in product development but also in systems and procedures, especially as a result of recent advances in IT.

Error 2 assumes present trends will continue – an assumption of linearity totally belied by the cyclical behaviour of most phenomena. Thus, while one may be able to project a theoretical trend or smooth past oscillations to represent past change as a continuous process, the reality is that attempts at achieving equilibrium invariably result in over-correction around the central trend and give rise to bursts of acceleration and deceleration, of stop and go clearly apparent in the business and related economic cycles.

The energy crisis of the 1970s provides clear evidence of the impracticality of the inevitable logic of extrapolation *if one assumes no reaction to restore equilibrium*. If one assumes that consumption of any finite resource will continue to grow in accordance with past trends then, inevitably, the finite resource will become exhausted. But, such projections precipitate actions which themselves initiate counter-reactions.

Thus projections of future oil scarcity encourage supply restriction and price rises; but price rises encourage the exploitation of previously marginal resources (which increases supply) conservation and energy saving practices (which decreases demand) and innovation to find alternative energy sources (which may make the previously scarce resource obsolete). As Martel points out, oil demand declined by over 15 per cent between 1979 and 1984, prices plummeted and the oil producers, both countries and companies, have moved from growth to recession.

Error 3 is the neglect of the opportunities offered by change and is usually illustrated by reference to the small number of radical innovations which have subsequently revolutionised an industry/market. In reality such examples are the exception rather than the rule and, while they will always enjoy the attention given to exceptions, the managerial requirement to plan and control require than innovation and change should be managed in such a way as to try and dampen the violent oscillations which discontinuous or radical change can precipitate. Clearly, the need is to recognise that change is inevitable and so welcome it as an opportunity rather than regarding it as a threat to the comfortable familiarity of the status quo.

Once we accept that change is inevitable then clearly we will be more prepared to meet and even modify it. It is for this reason that in successful companies so much effort has been devoted to environmental analysis in an attempt to define broad underlying trends and assess their implications in terms of future scenarios. Thus a survey of top European CEOs in the early 1980s identified eight factors which characterise the environment facing top management, namely:

1. A demand for quality and advice.
2. A move towards a service culture.
3. An emphasis upon the specialist.
4. Shortening strategic time horizons.
5. Scenario planning is replacing forecasting.
6. A reduction in head office functions.
7. A wider international outlook.
8. Tighter legislation.

These trends correspond closely to those identified by Naisbitt in his best-selling book *Megatrends*. According to Naisbitt we are changing from an industrial to an information society, from a national to a world economy in which decentralisation and diversity are replacing centralisation and homogeneity and in which participation and self-help are replacing representative democracy and institutional help. This shift from an industrial society founded on high mass consumption to a post-industrial information era reflects a change in emphasis from quantity to quality, from standardisation to customisation, from centralisation to decentralisation, from dependence to self-help, from autocracy to participation, from hierarchy to network, from transportation to communication and from information scarcity to information overload.

Clearly these are massive changes and call for equally massive changes in the way we think about and do business. In fact the conditions which precipitated what I have always referred to as the *rediscovery* of the marketing concept.

■ The rediscovery of marketing

As we all know there are almost as many definitions of marketing as there are persons willing to formulate one. Despite this variety most contain the common elements that start with and concentrate upon the consumer as the catalyst for an exchange relationship which give satisfaction to both buyer and seller. In recent times, and in my own opinion, there has been a tendency to overemphasise the interests of the consumer and my own preferred definition of marketing is that it is concerned with *mutually* satisfying exchange relationships. If this is the case then it is ironic that marketing as both a philosophy of business and business function should be perceived as new. In reality marketing came into existence with the first exchange of goods and services and has been the catalyst for economic growth through its encouragement of task specialisation and the division of labour which, in turn, have led to the emphasis upon the pursuit of comparative advantage and involvement in international trade.

Given the existence of unsatisfied basic needs it is unsurprising that society perceives its main priority as increasing the volume of output of such basic goods. The pursuit of efficiency in the application of technology to production results in it becoming concentrated and requires the creation of channels of distribution to enable mass production to be converted into mass consumption. The consequence of this, of course, is that the producer loses direct contact with his customer and tends to perceive demand as the homogeneous entity beloved of economists rather than representing the differentiated needs of a heterogeneous collection of individuals who comprise the 'market'.

It is unsurprising, therefore, that as our ability to increase supply accelerates and the natural growth of markets decelerates through a slowing down of population growth there begins to develop a mismatch between the producer's perception of consumer needs and the reality. One consequence of this misperception which became apparent in the 1950s and early 1960s was the rise of consumerism and environmentalism. Many marketing scholars claim that consumerism is the shame of marketing. My own view is that it is exactly the opposite – consumerism is in fact a protest against the absence of marketing.

The origins of the consumerist movement were prompted by the scholarly writings of persons like John Kenneth Galbraith, who pointed to the excesses of materialism, and the populist works of people like Vance Packard in books such as *The Waste Makers* and the *Hidden Persuaders*. In turn, particular focus was given by Ralph Nader's indictment of the quality of American motor cars in his 'Unsafe at any Speed'. Sued unsuccessfully by General Motors, Nader became the giantkiller and numerous others sprang to his cause. While this groundswell of complaint against the lack of perceived quality and value for money in many goods and services was undoubtedly justified one must remember that this was and is a relative perception that requires a high level of material wellbeing before it is likely to find expression. Beggars can't be choosers and, as Maslow's well-known hierarchy reminds us, we progress upwards from satisfying basic physiological needs through higher order needs for safety, love and esteem before we arrive at the point where we have a sufficient level of material satisfaction that we can become concerned with the more abstract and spiritual 'better' things of life. Elsewhere I have suggested that Maslow's esteem stage corresponds to Walt Rostow's age of high mass consumption in his model of economic growth. In Rostow's model the final stage of economic development was originally but unoriginally labelled the 'age beyond high mass consumption'. In a revised version which reflected the changes in American society during the 1950s and 1960s Rostow relabelled the ultimate stage of economic development as 'the search for quality'. Clearly, a search for quality implies that the individual will want to define quality more precisely in terms of their own particular needs and wants. It follows that if producers are to succeed then they, too, must spend more time and energy in defining individual needs and aggregating them into worthwhile market segments.

In essence, then, marketing is a very simple philosophy which requires producers to start with the identification and specification of consumer needs and then mobilise their companies' assets and resources to achieve a mutually satisfying exchange relationship from which both parties derive the benefits they are seeking. While this is a simple and appealing proposition there is no doubt that producers have been very slow to change. Levitt articulated the need in 1960 in his seminal article entitled 'Marketing Myopia' but despite his emphasis upon the inevitability of change in the ways in which basic human needs like transportation and entertainment may be satisfied comparatively few managers and companies fully appreciated the implications. As is so often the case it took a crisis to precipitate a change but in the process there were many casualties. Thus, the energy crises of 1974 and 1978 and the recessions which followed in their wake have resulted in a widescale reappraisal by producers as to the changes in organisation and activity which are called for by the new environment in which they find themselves.

■ What now?

The past decade has witnessed a flood of managerial bestsellers purporting to contain the secrets of competitive success. Few would argue that something called a marketing orientation has a major part to play in achieving this goal. The problem rests in converting managers to a true belief in consumer sovereignty, which constitutes the substance of marketing, rather than allowing them to drift into the acquisition of the trappings of a marketing function. Such a change will require a fundamental shift in attitude of a kind which may only be accomplished by effective education and communication.

Given that human beings exercise control over the other factors of production, it seems reasonable to claim that output or performance is a function of the interaction between the knowledge, skills and attitudes of those people. The reason why people speak of knowledge, skills and attitude in that sequence is because it reflects the sequence of personal development. Knowledge is distilled experience of the way things are and the way in which they work. Equipped with knowledge we can attempt particular tasks and acquire skills in the practice and application of that knowledge. In the process we will develop attitudes which will tend to reinforce the importance of the knowledge and skills acquired. It is unsurprising, therefore, that people will resist change which challenges their knowledge base or seeks to make obsolete the skills they have acquired. To accomplish change one must first change attitudes for only if this is accomplished will people be willing to acquire new knowledge and skills.

As I have indicated the changes in the balance between demand and supply have been apparent for decades and, with the benefit of hindsight, it is not difficult to understand the social and economic turbulence which exist at the interface between a society concerned with increasing quantity to one which is able to pursue an enhanced quality of like.

I believe that attitudes have changed, that quality will now take precedence over quantity and that, ultimately, this depends upon the quality of management and implementation. Thus, as we move towards the millenium, we have rediscovered the importance of defining quality from the consumer's point of view and have recognised that its achievement depends upon the supplier's understanding of that need and his skill in matching it. This, in my view, it the very essence of marketing. But, if marketing starts and ends with the consumer, why is it that significant numbers of well-educated consumers have found it necessary to band together in order to challenge the complacency of an establishment which at best seems unaware or indifferent to this precept? To answer this question it is necessary to review the origins and evolution of consumerism.

■ References

Naisbitt, John, *Megatrends*, Futura Publications, 1984.

Galbraith, John Kenneth, *American Capitalism: The Concept of Countervailing Power*, Houghton Mifflin, 1956: *The Affluent Society*, Houghton Mifflin, 1958.

Packard, Vance, *Hidden Persuaders*, Pelican, 1957: *The Waste Makers*, McKay (NY), 1960.

Levitt, Theodore, 'Marketing Myopia', *Harvard Business Review*, July–Aug 1960, pp. 45–60.

Maslow, Abraham, *Motivation and Personality*, Harper & Row, 1954.

Nader, Ralph, *Unsafe at Any Speed*, Pocket Books, 1966.

Rostow, W. W., *The Stages of Economic Growth*, Cambridge University Press, 1962.

■ Consumerism

In the first chapter of this book we examined the nature of the marketing concept and suggested that a somewhat simple statement of it might be:

'If economies are comprised of people, and we are endeavouring to allocate scarce resources in order to maximise satisfaction, then it is the satisfaction of people which we are aiming at. This being so it is essential that we determine first what people want and then allocate our resources accordingly.' In other words, we must determine the nature and strength of demand and create supplies of goods and services to satisfy these demands.'

Further, we suggested that free market economies largely permit the evolution of consumer sovereignty by allowing consumers to express their preferences as between goods and services through the daily casting of their money 'votes'.

It would be naive to suggest that any such system is or ever could be perfect. None the less, market economies and the marketing philosophy rest upon the same fundamental proposition that consumer preferences will determine the allocation of available inputs to the creation of the most desired outputs.

So much for marketing. What is consumerism?

The term 'consumerism' first came into currency in the 1970s when it was applied to a number of issues which had first attracted serious concern in the 1950s. Vance Packard was one of the first to use the expression in relation to these concerns foremost among which were planned obsolescence (see *The Waste Makers*), declining quality and the absence of satisfactory after-sales service, particularly in saturated mass consumption markets for convenience goods. This connotation was gradually extended as the 1960s progressed. In 1962 Rachel Carson's *Silent Spring* drew attention to the impact which pollution of the environment was having upon plant and animal life. In 1962 President Kennedy addressed his first consumer message to Congress in which he stated four basic consumer rights:

1. *The Right to Safety* – to be protected against the marketing of goods which are hazardous to health or life.
2. *The Right to be Informed* – to be protected against fraudulent, deceitful or grossly misleading information, advertising, labeling or other practices, and to be given the facts needed to make an informed choice.
3. *The Right to Choose* – to be assured, wherever possible, access to a variety of products and services at competitive prices and in those industries in which Government regulations are substituted, an assurance of satisfactory quality and service at fair prices.
4. *The Right to be Heard* – to be assured that consumer interests will receive full and sympathetic consideration in the formulation of Government policy and fair expeditious treatment in its administrative tribunals.

(Quoted by Senator Warren G. Magnuson, 'Consumerism and the Emerging Goals of a New Society', in Gaedeke, Ralph M., and Etcheson, Warren W. (eds), *Consumerism* (Canfield Press, San Francisco, 1972).)

Still later in the decade (1966) Ralph Nader was to publish *Unsafe at Any Speed*, a book which might well have gone unremarked had it not been for General Motors' attempts to discredit Nader which resulted in their losing a lawsuit brought by him. The publicity attendant upon the trial focused intense attention upon the standard of car manufacture and resulted in Nader himself being cast in the role of consumer champion.

It was from these grass roots that the consumerist movement developed to the proportions it has now achieved when scarcely a day goes by without the publication of some book or article on the subject, or statement by some or other government department. In fact we now have a Minister of Consumer Affairs and an extensive body of new legislation whose existence is directly attributable to the impetus generated by the movement. It is not anticipated that there will be any lessening in this interest which, in the longer term, will concentrate upon two basic areas: (*a*) the more equitable treatment of consumers through the provision of choice and information, reinforced by legislation where necessary, and (*b*) protection of the physical environment or conservation.

■ The consumerism–marketing interface

Oversimplified as they may be, the foregoing statements on the nature of marketing and consumerism reflect a fundamental paradox for while they are invariably seen as being in conflict both activities possess the same basic objective – consumer satisfaction. A still more fundamental paradox is that while everybody is in favour of consumer protection there is still a need for it.

At various points in the text reference has been made to particular issues where consumerists and marketers appear to be at cross-purposes with each other. Among those which the reader may wish to explore in greater depth are the following.

1. *Product Policy*	– Issues of Quality/Brand proliferation Planned obsolescence After-sales service
2. *Pricing Practices*	– Recommended prices and Price-off promotions Unit pricing
3. *'Truth in Advertising'*	– By category of product – By media
4. *Pollution*	– By product, e.g. motor-cars, enzyme detergents – By packaging – non-returnable containers; non bio-degradable materials
5. *'Truth in Lending'*	– Statement of true costs of borrowing

In considering these and similar salient issues it would be unreasonable to follow the practice favoured in certain quarters of ascribing all the blame to private industry. We must accept that existing institutions have succeeded very well in terms of their aims and objectives as originally stated. Because society now questions the desirability of continued and rapid economic growth due to excesses derived from its past pursuit, society is not entitled to belabour those organisations which previously enacted its collective will. A more constructive attitude recognises that the emergence of the marketing concept reflects an awareness of the side-effects of mass production and mass consumption, and that enlightened self-interest will predispose business to vary its response to consumer needs as these change. In a far from perfect world we cannot expect all firms to be equally responsive to these changed needs, and so will have to resort to legislation to ensure compliance with certain minimum standards. In the long run, however, we see no reason to believe that the greatest success will not continue to accrue to the firms most sensitive to their markets' needs.

■ Consumerism – threat or opportunity?

Because of the manner in which many consumer concerns have been expressed, many firms have tended to react defensively. In consequence of this defensive reaction there is a growing tendency in certain quarters to regard the consumerist movement as a threat to business. It would be more constructive to regard it as an opportunity.

One particularly salient feature of consumerism is that it is both overt and vocal, which is a marked contrast with most market situations where considerable time, effort and money has to be expended upon eliciting consumer attitudes and opinions. In other words, expressions of consumer concern clearly indicate the wishes of at least a sizeable segment of particular markets and reduce the need for research activity. More astute companies have already perceived this opportunity. Consider the following examples.

Increased concern over pollution and the quality of the environment has enabled many firms to cash in on devices for monitoring, reducing, alleviating, or avoiding pollution. Thus firms have developed instruments to measure the nature and extent of pollutants discharged into the air and water and clearly this market will grow as states seek to enforce laws against pollution and firms try to ensure that they comply with such laws. Having detected the existence of pollutants then a need arises to remove or mitigate their effect resulting in a demand for sewage and effluent treatment, water purification, air filtration plants and so on. Similarly, alternative solutions are required as in the case of the internal combustion engine, or fossil fuel sources of energy.

At a lesser level, firms can cash in on explicit anxieties such as the need for more informative labelling by providing it, of non-returnable containers by making them returnable, of packaging waste by making it capable of re-use through recycling. Similarly the express demand for after-sales service represents considerable scope for creative marketing – if leasing television sets is possible why not other household consumer durables?

The foregoing examples are very limited but, hopefully, they indicate the scope for constructive and positive responses rather than defensive and negative ones. The same comment applies equally to the extension and application of marketing ideas and methods into the non-business sector another basic theme of this chapter.

◼ Marketing as a social process

Probably the first influential statement of a need to re-examine the scope of marketing was contained in a seminal article by Philip Kotler and Sidney Levy ('Broadening the Concept of Marketing', *Journal of Marketing,* vol. 33, Jan 1969). In the opening paragraphs the authors review briefly the traditional emphasis on the marketing of products in a business context and go on to assert: 'It is the authors' contention that marketing is a pervasive societal activity that goes considerably beyond the selling of toothpaste, soap and steel. '

In essence the argument that marketing is a pervasive societal activity is predicated on the observation that as man's productive capability has grown so he has been able to devote more of his energies to social activities and that in order to do so he has had to develop organisations other than business firms. In reality, many non-business organisations have a longer history than the now dominant business firms, e.g. the Church, universities, government departments, hospitals, etc. However, the very forces which were to lead to an emphasis on marketing, namely the ability to create supplies in excess of basic consumption needs (see Chapter 1), were also necessary to permit such non-business organisations to realise their potential. Thus, only when we can release human and physical resources from the treadmill of satisfying the basic needs of food and shelter can we turn our attention to the satisfaction of higher needs such as education, the Arts, health, and social welfare. Further we require new forms of social organisation to cope with enfranchisement of the whole population, i.e. political societies, the need for organised labour to be able to express its view, i.e. the trade unions, and so on.

As Kotler and Levy point out, all these social organisations perform the classic business functions. Finance is necessary to pay for the organisation's operations and a personnel function is necessary to ensure that people are available to discharge such operations. A production function is necessary to organise the most economic use of inputs to achieve the desired level of outputs. Purchasing is necessary to acquire these inputs and presumably marketing is required to dispose of them. If the marketing function has not been particularly conspicuous, however, we should not be surprised for, as we have seen in earlier chapters, the need for such a function has only just become apparent in the case of physical goods.

But, given the exponential acceleration which has characterised all spheres of human endeavour throughout history we may anticipate a rapid diffusion of the marketing concept through non-business organisations within the next few years. To determine *how* the marketing concept may be applied we must first identify those ideas which have appeared generally useful in marketing other goods and services. We have already argued when discussing the marketing of industrial goods (Chapter 9) that in our opinion there is no fundamental difference in principle as compared with the marketing of consumer goods. This I believe is equally true of the marketing of services whether they emanate from profit or non-profit organisations.

In the same spirit Kotler and Levy suggest that a useful basic approach is to think in terms of three fundamental constructs or ideas – products, consumers, and tools.

First, products. All organisations produce a product although in the interests of definitional clarity we frequently prefer to differentiate as between categories of products. Thus in Chapter 5 we offered specific definitions for categories of consumer and industrial goods. To these may be added services which are intangible, such as insurance and banking, although they may confer a tangible benefit such as health and welfare services. Such services may be offered by private or public organisations which may or may not have a profit motive. Evidence of the marketing of such services is most marked in the case of those private firms such as banks which are profit-orientated and least evident in the case of public sector welfare services. To these easily recognised categories Kotler and Levy add persons, organisations and ideas, while in a more elaborate statement ('Beyond Marketing: The Furthering Concept', *California Management Review*, Winter 1969, vol. XII, no. 2) they add 'places'. In the case of these latter categories a limited marketing activity may be noted In the past but it has largely concentrated on public relations type activity supported by a limited amount of paid promotion. Clearly, there is considerable scope for the use of other elements of the marketing mix, especially in the field of marketing research, to better define consumer needs. This observation leads naturally to consideration of the second basic construct.

In a limited sense consumers are viewed solely as those persons or organisations which consume the output of another organisation. In the wider concept 'consumers' includes at least three other groups with a *direct* interest in any given organisation. First, there are persons responsible for the control of the organisation. These may be shareholders in a company or those nominated by them (directors), they may be the trustees of a private foundation, or the elected ministers who control our government departments and so on. The second category is comprised of persons/organisation which take a direct interest, and the third of those with a passive or *indirect* interest. Examples of the former are, say, consumer organisations or government departments in the case of business firms, former students and local and central government in the case of a university; while the latter category conveniently encompasses all those who might be influenced by or wish to influence the organisation at some future time.

The third construct is that of the tools of marketing. Among these we may distinguish the four 'p's of product, price, place (distribution) and promotional policy, each of which has an important role in marketing the output of any type of organisation. We have already stressed that change is symptomatic of the world in which we live – accordingly all organisations must continually reappraise and update their 'product' in order to best satisfy changing needs. Pricing has an important role to play although it frequently seems to be ignored in the provision of many public services. It is difficult for the individual citizen to decide whether the collective taxes we pay are being allocated to the ends we most desire except in a very gross way. Certainly it is impossible in the particular to determine whether we are getting value for money and the suppliers often seem insensitive to the concept of cost-benefit. Indications of changing attitudes in the latter area are to be seen in the concept of contract research in which the researcher is required to produce results in line with a prearranged budget and the suggestion that individuals be given 'tickets' which they can exchange for, say, education. In the present social climate it seems unlikely that the latter idea will gain support but its currency does imply that the consumers of such services would like a more effective way of demonstrating their wishes other than at general elections. Equally some of the dangers of monopoly power which we monitor so closely in the private sector merit more attention for they appear to exist in the pricing and quality decisions of many public services.

In the case of distribution and promotion there is also scope for the application of marketing techniques, although perhaps somewhat less than in the product and price areas. Distribution still merits attention, however, in that in many cases it appears to be dictated by the convenience of the supplier rather than the consumer. Similarly, some of the promotional techniques already in use would no doubt benefit from comparison with the sophistication typical of the promotion of consumer goods.

Essentially, therefore, we are arguing that the philosophy and techniques which have apparently worked so much to the advantage of private profit-oriented organisations are equally relevant and meaningful to all other forms of organisation. Three things must be appreciated, however. First, one must not strain the analogy between business and non-business organisations too far and so try to force the latter to fit patterns which have proved successful in the former context but which may be wholly inappropriate to non-business organisations. Second, success in marketing depends upon commitment – mere lip-service to the concept and changing the sales function's title is insufficient. (See, for example, B. Charles Ames, 'Trappings vs. Substance in Industrial Marketing', *Harvard Business Review,* July–Aug 1970.) Finally, success depends upon matching skills with opportunities (see Chapter 20).

Collectively, these three caveats indicate that the greatest benefit is likely to accrue where one attempts a transfer of basic ideas from the traditional content of marketing physical products rather than promote the wholesale adoption of particular marketing techniques. An example will help make our meaning clear.

To conclude, however, perhaps we should enquire what marketing is likely to mean in the 1990s for the archetypal fmcg companies in which it was first 'rediscovered' over 100 years ago.

■ The company as a brand

In 'Brand Building in the 1990s' (*Journal of Marketing Management,* vol. 7.1, 1991) Stephen King identifies six areas of change which are exerting pressure on companies and which are likely to intensify over the next few years, namely:

More confident consumers.
New concepts of quality.
Shortage of skills.
Tightening of the competitive screw.
The side-effects of new technology.
Restructuring.

In respect of consumers King points out that they have become more confident, readier to experiment and trust their own judgement, have more disposable income and are more worldly wise. They have a greater understanding of 'marketing' in all its activities and this understanding will help ensure customers in business-to-business marketing become more demanding too. Consumers have strong views on what gives them satisfaction and are less tolerant of goods and services that do not live up to their expectations. Finally, and probably as a consequence of the preceding changes, they have become more independent and closer to the highest level of Maslow's need hierarchy – self-actualisation. The World may be a global market but its tribes and their members still have a need to distinguish themselves from one another to express their growing individualism. Nowhere is this more the case than in consumers' increasing demand for quality and a quality founded on real values which go together to make up 'the good life' such as green products rather than products which consume non-replaceable resources, pollute the atmosphere or cause pain or suffering to other species.

Satisfying the needs of these 'new' consumers will call for radical changes on the supply side but here skills shortages, due to declining birth rates, and insufficient education and training pose a threat to our ability to make these changes. However, international competition looks certain to intensify and will become even more acute as the leading players seek to secure the necessary labour inputs.

While it has become a cliché to talk of accelerating technological change the trend persists. As King observes 'Constant innovation will be a necessary part of normal commercial life, but few companies will be able to rely on having any *demonstrable* product or service advantage for more than a few months'. In the absence of objective criteria to guide the choice decisions then the *relationship* between seller and buyer will assume even greater importance. In consumer markets King believes this will reinforce the retailer's position as the consumer's friend at the expense of the manufacturer.

Faced with changes of the kind discussed above, producers will continue to restructure in an effort to secure economies of scale in manufacturing and marketing. In many cases this will involve mergers and takeovers, in others the striking of strategic alliances. Inevitably it will result in still greater concentration of market power in the hands of a small number of global players in the majority of industries.

In order to survive King, amongst others, is of the opinion that success will depend critically on *brand-building* which he defines as

> using all the company's particular assets to create unique entities that certain consumers really want; entities which have a lasting personality, based on a special combination of physical, functional and psychological values; and which have competitive advantage in at least one area of marketing (raw materials/sourcing, product/design/patents, production systems, supply/sales/service networks, depth of understanding of consumers, style/fashion, and so on).

Only through brand building will it be possible to

- build stable, long-term demand,
- add values looked for by customers,
- develop a sound base for future growth and expansion,
- resist the growing power of intermediaries,
- become recognised as a company with a reputation and going places that people will want to work with and for.

However, King believes that brand building in the 1990s will be quite different from that of the past which led to the emergence and dominance of classic single-line brands like Coke, Pepsi, Marlboro, Persil, Oxo, Kit-Kat and Andrex. As King points out, in 1969 19 of the 25 top spending brands in the UK were repeat purchase packaged goods; in 1989 it was just one. Now the trend is to the *company brand* in which it is the subjective, difficult-to-define aspects of service and reputation associated with a company which will position it in the consumer's mind and the market place.

> In essence, brand-building in the 1990s will involve designing and controlling all aspects of a company, leading people and activities will beyond the traditional skill of the marketing department and the agencies that it employs. It will be a lot closer to the marketing of services (such as airlines, hotels, retailers, building societies) than to the brand-building of the classic brands. (King, 1991)

But such brand-building will have to be very different from most managers' current perception of 'brands' as fmcg or possibly the company's logo and corporate identity programme. In future the company 'brand' will have to encapsulate and communicate what an organisation is and what it stands for – its mission, culture and aspirations. In doing so it will be as important for the internal marketing of the firm as it is for its efforts to win a distinguished and distinctive place in the perception of its actual and prospective customers. To achieve this will require organisations to be market orientated and customer driven in a manner which embraces all members and functions of the organisation.

■ Epilogue

In the introduction to this chapter we recalled the prediction that in the 1980s the most important developments would occur in four main areas. The marketing of services was the subject of Chapter 23; and the broadening of the marketing concept was discussed earlier, while a third – the benefits of marketing to centrally planned and developing economies – was touched on in Chapter 22, Marketing in Foreign Environments. What then of the fourth development, the interface between marketing and public policy? Well, as predicted, the choice between self-regulation from within, and imposed regulation from without has become more acute, particularly as the pressures increase to harmonise consumer legislation within the EEC with the introduction of the 'single market' in 1992.

In the Appendix we provide a synopsis of some of the more important UK legislation, while in Table 24.1 we reproduce a very useful summary table of Codes of Practice developed in consultation with the OFT. The table is taken from an article in the Summer 1984 *Quarterly Review of Marketing* by C. P. Moss and W. Richardson, 'Consumerist Self-regulation – An assessment of the Office of Fair Trading Codes of Practice', which provides a concise review of the problems of ensuring the effectiveness of self-regulation.

TABLE 24.1   Codes developed in consultation with OFT

Association	Good/Services Covered	% of Industry Turnover Covered
1. Association of Manufacturers of Domestic Electrical Appliances 2. Radio Electrical and Television Retailers Association 3. England and Wales Electricity Boards 4. Scottish Electricity Boards	Electrical Repairs and Servicing	80%
5. Association of British Travel Agents – Tour Operators 6. Association of British Travel Agents – Travel Agents	Travel Trade	90%
7. Footwear Distributors Federation	Footwear	60%
8. National Association of Shoe Repair Factories and St. Crispin's Boot Trade Association Ltd (and Others)	Shoe Repairers	60%
9. Motor Agents Association and the Society of Motor Manufacturers and Traders Limited	Motor industry	85%
10. Vehicle Builder and Repairer Association 11. Scottish Motor Trade Association (Defunct)	Vehicle Body Repairs Used Cars	70%
12. Furniture Associations (Five) Branded Furniture Society; British Furniture Manufacturers Federated Associations; National Association of Retail Furnishers; National Bedding Federation Limited; Scottish House Furnishers Association	Furniture Industry	80%
13. Photography Associations (Seven) British Photographic Association; British Photographic Importer's Association; Photographic Dealers Association; National Pharmaceutical Association; Association of Photographic Laboratories; Institute of Photographic Apparatus Repair Technicians; Institute of Incorporated Photographers	Camera Films and Photography Sales & Servicing	80%
14. National Association of Funeral Directors	Funerals	80%
15. Association of British Launderers and Cleaners Limited	Launderers and Dry Cleaners	90% Launderers 70–75% Dry Cleaners
16. Mail Order Publishers' Association 17. Direct Sales and Services Association 18. Mail Order Traders' Association	Direct Selling	85%
19. Post Office	Postal Services	90%
20. Telecommunications Services	Telecommunications	90%
21. Glass & Glazing Federation	Home Improvements	80%

Source: Quarterly Review of Marketing, Summer 1984.

As an example of regulation imposed from without we need look no further than the Data Protection Act, 1984, designed to implement the Council of Europe Convention on Data Protection. An excellent summary of the major provisions and implication of this Act are to be found in 'Up to Date on Data' by Tony Painter (*Marketing*, 11 October 1984). In essence the Act is designed to ensure that data are accurate and socially acceptable and, in the opinion of a member of the Lindop Commission on whose report the Act is largely based, 'requires no more than prudent and good business practice'. Of course, if all firms were prudent and good the Act would not be necessary, and the fact that it is reflects the need to respect the privacy of the individual as the new computer-based technologies make it possible to build up detailed files and use this information for marketing purposes.

Finally, it seems safe to forecast that as the marketing concept diffuses and spreads, its practice will be characterised by evolution rather than revolution and ensure that the broad principles discussed in this book remain current for many years to come.

■ Appendix

■ Consumer Legislation

As noted in the chapter there has been a spate of legislation in recent years designed to protect the consumer. 'A very useful summary of this legislation and other provisions such as Codes of Practice is to be found in *Fair Deal* published by HMSO on behalf of the Office of Fair Trading. However, this field of legislation is subject to constant change and some parts do not apply to Scotland. As such the content of this appendix should be regarded as indicative rather than definitive and the latest sources consulted to determine the up-to-date position.

Here are three typical shopping problems:

1. You've just bought a pair of shoes. After a week, the seams come apart and the heel on one shoe wobbles. You haven't treated them badly nor used them for rock climbing for which they clearly were not intended.
Can you insist on a pair to replace them?

2. You want a food processor. You choose one and ask the manager if it is powerful enough to knead bread dough. He assures you it is. But when you start to make your first loaf, the processor can't cope. The shop doesn't have another model of any use to you and offers a credit note. You, however, want your money back so you can buy elsewhere.
Have you the right to demand cash back?

3.   You send for a blue blanket from a mail order company. It turns out to be pink even though the box is labelled 'blue'. You don't want the pink one (it doesn't match your colour scheme) nor do you want to pay for the return postage. *Can you claim for the postage at the same time as you ask for the correct blanket?*

'What are my rights?'

■ Sale of Goods Act 1979

The answers are in the *Sale of Goods Act 1979* which covers all goods (including food) bought from a trader, whether from shops, street markets, doorstep salesmen, in sales, at parties in private homes, or by mail order. It does not make any difference whether the goods are paid for in cash or by credit. Once the seller has accepted your offer to buy, a legally enforceable contract has been made which gives both of you rights and obligations. It does not matter if nothing is written down. When you say or indicate 'I'd like to buy this, please' and he says 'certainly' or goes to wrap it up for you or simply takes your money, the contract is made.

The seller has three main duties to ensure:

1. That the goods are of 'merchantable quality'
'Merchantable quality' means that goods must be reasonably fit for their normal purpose, bearing in mind the price paid, the nature of the goods and how they were described. The new shoes in example 1 should not fall apart after only a week's normal wear; and a new cassette recorder should not tear up a brand new tape. If goods are very cheap, secondhand, labelled as 'seconds', or 'sale' items, you probably cannot expect top quality – but they must still be merchantable.

2. That the goods are 'fit for any particular purpose' made known to him
If you ask for goods (like the food processor in example 2) to perform in a particular way, and the seller assures you that they will, he has broken his contract with you if they do not.

3. That the goods are 'as described'
Goods must be 'as described' – for example on the package, display sign or by the seller. The blanket in example 3 did not meet the description applied to it.

■ Getting your money back

If any of these obligations have not been met the seller has broken his contract with you and you may be entitled to your money back or compensation.

You should always complain to the seller, not to the manufacturer, since in law it is the seller who is responsible for the goods.

You are not entitled to anything if you:

- examined the item when you bought it and should have seen the faults then;
- were told about any fault (e.g. the goods were described as 'fire damaged');
- ignored the seller's skill or judgement as to the suitability of goods for any particular purpose you described to him (e.g. he told you that the food processor you were buying would not knead bread dough – as you wished).
- ignored the seller's claim that he was not expert enough to advise you correctly about your purchase (e.g. he told you he did not know whether the glue you were buying would stick metal to plastic);
- simply changed your mind about wanting the article. Some shops do refund money or give credit notes in these circumstances, but they do so for commercial goodwill and not because they have to. Such traders may insist on seeing a receipt. And they will not usually take back something you have damaged;
- received the goods as a present (the *buyer* must make any claim).

■ Price display

With a few exceptions (see below) a trader does not have to display prices for his goods.

Unless anything is said to the contrary, it is assumed that when you contract to buy goods, you are agreeing to pay the currently display price including Value Added Tax (VAT) if applicable. Traders may, if they wish, display a notice saying 'All prices are exclusive of VAT'. Prices for food and drink consumed on the premises must, however, be VAT-inclusive.

Under the *Prices Act 1974* shops must display the prices of all items of food and drink. Where they are sold by weight, as are meat and most (though not all) fruit and vegetables, the unit price (e.g. the price per lb) must be shown.

With food and drink consumed on the premises, the price must be displayed where consumers can make their choice. Pubs, cafés and restaurants myst display a selection of prices for meals and drinks. Garages must display the price of petrol on the pump.

Although a trader does not have to sell you goods, he commits an offence under the *Trade Descriptions Act 1968* if he deliberately displays a lower price on something than the price he actually charges for it.

■ Misleading prices

'Special offers', 'fantastic bargains', 'prices slashed'

These are a few of the many slogans traders use to entice you into their shops, particularly at sales time. But are the goods they offer really such bargains? The law has a good deal to say about the way prices are displayed. The *Consumer Protection Act 1987* will make it a criminal offence for a trader to display misleading price indications about goods or services. There will also be an official code of practice to guide sellers on how to avoid misleading price indications. As a general principle, prices and price comparisons must be genuine. Shops will have to take particular care with marked-down prices and comparisons with 'recommended' prices. A trader will also commit an offence if he claims that his price is lower than some other 'price' which does not exist.

if you think that a price is misleading in any way, contact your local Trading Standards Department as soon as possible.

■ Descriptions of goods and services

The *Trade Descriptions Act 1968* makes it a criminal offence for a trader to say or write something that is not true about the goods or services he is selling. This applies to many different kinds of description – what the goods are, who made them, how they work, and so on. If a car has 20,000 miles on the clock or a trader tells you 'This pan has a non-stick coating', these statements must be true. Similarly, if a photograph on the label of a packet of prawn curry shows lots of juicy prawns, the contents must live up to the description. In the case of textile products, special regulations ensure that the fibre content is marked on them. The Trade Descriptions Act also affects services but does not apply to property (e.g. an estate agent's description of a house for sale).

The local Trading Standards Officer enforces the Trade Descriptions Acts, which also give him power to enter premises, inspect and seize goods. If you suspect the law is being broken you should let him know. He may decide to prosecute. If convicted, a trader can be fined or imprisoned. In England, Wales and Scotland the courts can award you compensation if you have suffered as a result of the offence. You may, of course, sue the trader yourself.

■ Misleading advertisements

If an advertisement seriously misleads (e.g. by wrongly describing an item or service, or leaving out important facts) then it, too, is covered by the Trade Descriptions Act. If you see an advert like this, you should contact your local Trading Standards Officer.

But apart from these statutory provisions, there are standards of taste and truthfulness which advertisments should meet. These are laid down in the British Code of Advertising Practice which is administered by the Advertising Standards Authority. You should contact the ASA if you see an advert that you think objectionable or misleading in a paper or magazine. Enclose a copy of the advert if you can, or say where and when it appeared. If the ASA upholds your complaint, it can ask the advertiser to modify or withdraw the offending advert.

If you want to complain about an advertisement on TV or local radio, contact the Independent Broadcasting Authority (IBA).

Under the *Control of Misleading Advertisements Regulations 1988*, the Director General of Fair Trading has 'long-stop' powers to step in following a complaint but *only* if the public interest requires that a misleading advert complained of should be stopped by a court injunction. His role is to support and reinforce existing controls – *not* to replace them. And, in any event, he has no powers over TV/radio or cable advertisements, or many of those dealing with investments (which are a matter for the Securities and Investments Board).

Most complaints remain a matter for your local Trading Standards Officer or the Advertising Standards Authority to look into.

■ Food

The law gives you valuable protection when you buy food. The *Food Act 1984* makes it a criminal offence to sell unfit food, or to describe food falsely, or to mislead people about its nature, substance, or quality, including the nutritional value. Regulations cover food hygiene wherever food is sold, manufactured, packed, processed or stored for sale. Under the *Food and Drugs (Control of Food Premises) Act 1976*, when someone has been convicted under the food hygiene regulations, the courts can close down his premises if they find that they are insanitary and a danger to health. (There are equivalent provisions for Scotland and Northern Ireland.)

■ Food labelling

Regulations under the Food Act also state that food must be labelled clearly so you know what you are buying. Labels must include the name of the contents, a list of ingredients, in descending order of weight, the address of the labeller or packer, and any food additives used. The *Food Labelling Regulations 1984* of the European Community Labelling Directive, state that water used as an ingredient in food must be shown on the label in its place in the list of ingredients.

Labels must usually show the date by which food should be eaten. Most foods must have a 'Best before' date, or in the case of food lasting less than six weeks a 'Sell by' date. The label should also tell you how the food should be stored. (Foods not dated include fresh fruit and vegetables, bread, flour, sugar, deep frozen food and long life foods.) Local authorities (in Northern Ireland, District Councils) are responsible for enforcing these regulations. Scotland is covered by the *Food and Drugs (Scotland) Act 1956* and Northern Ireland by the *Food and Drugs Act (Northern Ireland) 1958*.

Under the *Weights and Measures Act 1985* the quantity of the contents (by weight, volume, or in a few cases, number) must be marked on the container of most packaged grocery items and many other goods. Items such as meat, fish, cheese and sausages (frequently sold as pre-packs in self-service shops) must either have their weight marked on the package, or the weight must be made known before purchase. Not all pre-packed goods must be marked, however: e.g.

everyone recognises a one-pint milk bottle. There are also exceptions in the case of small packets. The Acts also make it an offence to give short weight or inadequate quantity, and to mark goods with a wrong indication of their amount.

Most pre-packed goods (such as sugar, butter, tea, flour) must be sold in prescribed metric quantities – e.g. flour can be sold only in quantities of 125, 250, 500 and 1000 g (or in multiples of 500 g).

Since 1979 the 'average system' of quantity control for certain packaged goods has been in operation. Under this system responsibility for the contents of these packages has largely switched from the retailer to the packer, who must make them up so that the quantity on the container is within certain tolerances laid down in the legislation. Enforcement generally takes place on the packing line.

Packers, importers and traders who do not conform to the weights and measures laws can be prosecuted and fined.

Trading Standards Officers are responsible for enforcing the law and ensuring that weights, measures and scales are accurate. (In Northern Ireland, the Trading Standards Branch of the Department of Commerce is the enforcement authority.)

■ Safety

The law recognises that what you buy should be safe. Under the *Consumer Protection Act 1987*, which extended and updated earlier consumer safety laws, it is a criminal offence for a trader to sell unsafe goods. Products must meet the general safety requirement. This means that the goods must be reasonably safe taking into account all the circumstances, including the way in which the goods are marketed, any instructions or warnings given with them, any existing safety standards and any reasonable means of making them safer if possible. Some goods have to comply wiht specific safety regulations.

Breach of the safety laws is a criminal offence.

There are a number of symbols which show that goods meet certain safety standards.

■ Product liability

The Consumer Protection Act also makes manufacturers and importers liable for injury and damage caused wholly or partly by a defective product *made after 1 March 1988*. In the case of injury or death, anybody can claim – not just the purchaser. Anyone whose property is damaged by a defective product can also claim under this Act – but only if the damage exceeds £275. But seek advice if you have been harmed by a product. You will have to show that the product did have the defect that caused the damage, but you will not have to show negligence or fault on anyone's part. The manufacturer or the importer (or the supplier if neither can be identified) might well contest the case. They might, e.g. try to show that you misused the product – but the burden of proof is on them.

A 'defective product' is one that does not provide the standard of safety you are entitled to expect, bearing in mind its use and age. But a manufacturer cannot be held responsible for something he could not have known about at the time the product was made, such as dangers revealed only by later research or experience.

These provisions add to your existing rights relating to defective goods – e.g. your rights to claim a refund or damages from a retailer. In Northern Ireland, there are similar provisions under the *Consumer Protection (Northern Ireland) Order 1987*.

■ Supply of Goods and Services Act 1982

The *Sale of Goods Act 1979* is concerned with the sale of *goods*. In the main the 1982 Act protects you when you make a contract for a *'pure' service* (e.g. the dry cleaning of a suit) or a contract for both work and materials. When contractors – builders, car mechanics and electricians – supply some parts or materials in the course of their work, your contract with them is for 'work and materials'. The materials must be 'as described', 'of merchantable quality' and 'fit for their purpose'. You have the same rights as you would had you bought the materials yourself.

The Act also sets out the standard you should expect to receive from someone who does work or supplies a service whether with or without supplying materials.

Unless you and the supplier have agreed otherwise, any service must be carried out:
- *with reasonable care and skill*
  so complain if your newly-cleaned suite is damaged or your new home extension lets in the rain;
- *within a reasonable time* (unless you agree on a set time)
  so complain if a shop takes three months to repair your TV.

■ Trade Descriptions Act 1968

Descriptions of services, just like descriptions of goods, must be accurate. If a sign promises '24-hour dry cleaning' or 'while-you-wait repairs' or a tour operator's brochure claims that a hotel is 'only half a mile from the beach' then the service should match the description.

The Act, as it refers to goods, is described on p. 593. The same provisions apply to services, except that a trader commits an offence only if he knows the description of the service he is providing is wrong, or if he does not care whether it is true or not.

■ Unfair Contract Terms Act 1977

Some firms try to escape their responsibility by using 'exclusion clauses' or 'disclaimers' on their premises, tickets, contracts or booking forms – for example, 'Articles left at owner's risk', 'We take no responsibility for ...', 'Departure times subject to variation without notice'. These statements try to limit the firm's responsibility for any loss you may suffer or for any damage to you or your property which occurs because of their negligence or failure to carry out their side of the contract properly. But they are not valid unless the firm can prove, in court, that the terms are fair and reasonable in the circumstances. And the notices cannot limit the firm's responsibility if personal injury or death is caused through the firm's negligence.

Review questions and problems

Many of the following questions are taken from papers set for the Certificate and Diploma examinations of the Chartered Institute of Marketing (coded I.M.) and are reproduced by permission. Questions coded U.S. are taken from papers set for the Degree of B.A. in Marketing – at the University of Strathclyde. Questions have been taken from papers set for the Certificate and Diploma examinations of the C.A.M. Education Foundation Ltd and are marked C.A.M. Questions coded S.B.E.C. are taken from papers set for the S.H.N.C. and S.H.N.D. by the Scottish Business Education Council (now SCOTVEC).

Chapter 1
1. Why is there no single, generally accepted definition of marketing? Should there be such a definition? If so, what developments are necessary to permit its statement?
2. What is the 'marketing concept'? Is it solely applicable to firms selling goods and services, or is it a 'philosophy' which can be usefully adopted by all formal organisations?
3. Why is it that marketing has only recently become an issue of central concern to producers/sellers of goods and services?
4. What do you understand by the phrase 'accelerating change'? What factors underlie this phenomenon? Will they continue to apply in the future?
5. What is the 'marketing mix'? How useful is the concept to practitioners? In what respects?
6. Marketing: art or science? Discuss.
7. 'The marketing concept is applicable to all business organisations irrespective of their size or the nature of the goods or services marketed.' Give reasons for agreeing, or disagreeing, with this view. (I.M.)
8. How would you counter the view that marketing exists only as a loose collection of techniques practised by specialists? (I.M.)
9. What contribution can comparative data on world markets, marketing structures and behaviour, make to the generation of theory in marketing? (U.S.)

599

10. Industry in general, and marketing practice in particular, would reap great benefits from the availability of fully developed and reliable marketing theories. Discuss. (U.S.)
11. Since we cannot observe demand curves, there is little need for the marketing manager to be acquainted with economic concepts. Critically appraise this statement. (I.M.)
12. Henry Ford is often quoted as having said 'You can have any colour you like so long as it is black.' Contrast this approach with a modern marketing approach and include in your answer an explanation of the limitations to adopting a total freedom of choice. (C.A.M.)
13. Many companies are still confused about the distinction between marketing and selling. As a newly appointed marketing manager how would you explain to your managing director the differences between the two. (I.M.)

Chapter 2
1. 'In each country commerce constitutes a sub-system within the general structure of society' (Beaujeu-Garnier). What factors control the development of this sub-system?
2. Do most firms have a choice between adapting to or controlling their environment?
3. Using an industry of your choice as an example, explain the role of an environmental analysis, and how it might help a firm within the industry.
4. What is the significance of separating the 'task environment' from the 'wider environment' in an environmental appraisal of the firm? Give practical examples to illustrate your main points.
5. Given the present Soviet interest in restructuring its economy, do you consider that it is possible for a centrally planned economy to establish a free market place? Discuss with examples drawn from the Soviet bloc or the People's Republic of China.
8. Since the mid-1980s the industrial, political, legal and social environment under which firms and consumers operate has undergone fundamental changes. Identify some of these major changes, and explain how they have affected a marketeer's response to the market place.
7. Describe the means at your disposal to evaluate the possible effects of changes in uncontrollable variables on the consumer market-place.
8. The commercial structure of any country develops, some argue, in stages, and is related to the stages of economic development. Describe these stages, and any action that governments can take to influence the progress of development.
9. How does 'going international' affect the environmental perspective of a firm?
10. Examine the importance of environmental scanning in the development of an international marketing strategy. In your answer, clearly identify the key components of the environment of concern to the international marketer, and their marketing implications.

11. How might the study of macromarketing influence the thinking of an industrialist in developing a marketing strategy and a government minister in considering competition policy?

Chapter 3

1. 'The product life cycle (PLC) concept is seriously deficient as a management tool, but continues to receive a great deal of management attention.' Why do you think this is, and how far do you consider that the PLC can play a useful part in shaping companies' new product development and launch strategies?
2. Critically evaluate the use of the Boston Consulting Group Matrix and the Ansoff Matrix in portfolio analysis.
3. What are the major headings that you would include in a situation analysis; what are their relevance to future decisions on strategy?
4. Discuss the ways in which Portfolio Planning Matrices can be of value to multi-product multi-market firms in formulating marketing strategy.
5. Assess the implications of the product life cycle (PLC) concept for strategic marketing planning.
6. Explain how knowledge of either: (a) the Boston Consulting Group Matrix or (b) the product life cycle concept might influence a firm's choice of marketing strategy.
7. 'Constraints and responsibilities severely limit the freedom of strategic action' (Ansoff, 1965). Discuss this statement in terms of the selection of marketing options open to a company seeking to grow.
8. In *Marketing Strategy and Management* it is suggested that a major implication of the product life cycle is that a firm should seek to develop more than one product so that as some lines mature and decline others are being developed to replace them. It is also suggested that as soon as a company has more than one product it becomes necessary to allocate resources between them, and an important tool for achieving this is provided in the Growth Share Matrix developed by the Boston Consulting Group. Explain, giving some typical examples, how both these concepts are important in the process of developing a firm's marketing strategy.
9. Explain the nature and importance of situation analysis as a first stage in marketing strategy.
10. The 'bottom line' of an internal appraisal of a firm's marketing system is to identify strengths and weaknesses; the environmental appraisal yields opportunities and threats.
    (a) How are strengths and weaknesses related to opportunities and threats in devising the marketing strategy for a firm?
    (b) How could you systematically search for strengths and weaknesses in a marketing strategy?
11. Discuss the ways in which a marketing manager might assess the position of a product in its life cycle.

Chapter 4

1. It is said that oligopolies could not be created except by means of heavy consumer advertising. The advertisers maintain that the security created by this relatively stable situation gives protection and time to embark on product development and improvement. Discuss this statement in relation to the detergent market. (U.S.)
2. What are the advantages and disadvantages of industries which are dominated by a few large-scale companies manufacturing similar, but differentiated products? (I.M.)
3. What does the Government mean when it refers to its 'industrial strategy? Say whether you think the strategy is viable and describe, using examples, the effect it has had on the structure of UK industry. (I.M.)
4. What relationship is there between oligopoly and the concept of product differentiation? (I.M.)
5. To what extent do you accept the statement that much so-called planned obsolescence is actually the working out of competitive and technological factors, both signifying a dynamic economy? (U.S.)
6. Under what circumstances might a fall in the price of a commodity lead to a decrease in the quantity demanded? (I.M.)
7. Define and distinguish between price elasticity of demand and income elasticity of demand. (I.M.)
8. In an oligopolistic market, why do prices tend to respond slowly to changes in market conditions? (I.M.)

Chapter 5

1. Complete the following 'shopping list' of needs and wants:

Need	*Want*
Bread	. . .
. . .	P.G. Tips
Meat	. . .
. . .	Radion
Cooking fat	. . .
. . .	Blue Band
Floor cleaner	. . .
. . .	Birds Eye Frozen Peas
Heat	. . .

2. What factors would you consider *most* important in forecasting the demand for:

    Automatic washing machines
    Classical records
    Colour television
    Enzyme detergents

Fluoride toothpaste
Frozen dinners
Package tours?

3. Which 'personality theory' do you subscribe to? Why?
4. What utility has reference group theory for the practising marketer?
5. How is Maslow's 'hierarchy of needs' reflected in the nature of consumer demand?
6. One of the most difficult decisions any marketing executive has to take concerns the determination of those consumer characteristics which can be used to segment a market in the best possible way. What are the particular difficulties he has to face? (I.M.)
7. The IPA socio-economic grading of the population should be of fundamental importance to the practitioners of marketing. To what extent is it so, and how accurate are the results obtained from its use? (I.M.)
8. Why has product differentiation superseded price as the major dimension of competitive activity in consumer goods markets?
9. Discuss the advantages/disadvantages of:

(*a*) Individual brands,
(*b*) Family brands.

10. Account for the widespread development of private branding in recent years.
11. How useful is the classification of goods described in the text? Suggest an alternative classificatory system.
12. How, and on what grounds, would you classify the following products:

(*a*) Branded pain remedies, butter, detergents, frozen peas, matches, petrol, shirts, stockings?
(*b*) Cement, lathes, lubricants, sulphuric acid, transistors, wood pulp?

13. Describe the problems confronting the marketing executive when he sets out to discover what the consumer wants. (I.M.)
14. Clearly explain what you understand by the term 'demand'. In what sense can a knowledge of this economic concept have practical application? (I.M.)
15. Demand is made up of two elements, the ability to buy and the willingness to buy. Discuss the advantages to be gained from studying the effects of both elements separately. (U.S.)
16. Explain what is meant by family and individual branding, and under what circumstances it would be advantageous to use either of these methods of branding. (U.S.)
17. Identify some of the effects that the current recession and high levels of unemployment will have on spending patterns, decision patterns and family roles. (U.S.)

Chapter 6

1. Attitudes have a central role in the development of behavioural patterns. Consider the use of attitude studies as a guide to the marketing practitioner. (U.S.)
2. Consider the value of the life-style concept as an approach to market segmentation. (U.S.)
3. The main alternative to problem-solving behaviour is habitual behaviour. Discuss the application of these patterns of behaviour to the market-place. (U.S.)
4. Measures of social class have been both valuable and misleading as an aid to market segmentation. Discuss the use of social class, and the possibilities offered by the addition of complementary psychographic techniques. (U.S.)
5. Should the marketer assume that organisational buying decisions are always based upon rational/economic considerations? (U.S.)
6. What do you understand by the term 'learning'? Briefly outline any one learning theory and discuss its relevance to an understanding of consumer behaviour. (I.M.)
7. Maslow's theory of motivation postulates five general types of needs. Define these needs and explain with examples how their economic importance can be exploited by advertising. (I.M.)
8. Culture has a pervasive influence on consumption patterns. Discuss the implications of cultural factors in new product diffusion. (U.S.)
9. Why do groups have such a considerable influence on individual consumer behaviour? What are the implications of this for product promotion and advertising? (I.M.)
10. Explain how an understanding of how consumers make decisions might aid the marketer in developing his strategy. (U.S.)
11. Discuss the relationship between social class membership and consumption patterns. (U.S.)
12. Examine the view that psychological explanations of consumer behaviour may be useful theories but they are of little practical value to the marketer. (U.S.)
13. What are attitudes? Can they be changed? What is the relevance of attitudes to communications, advertising and marketing? (C.A.M.)
14. 'The consumer is not the completely rational animal dreamed up by the classical economists and fondly termed Economic Man' (Shanks). To what extent do you agree, and give reasons for your viewpoint. (C.A.M.)
15. In what way can a knowledge of the Behavioural Sciences (Sociology, Psychology) help the marketing/advertising executive to have a better understanding of consumer choices and purchasing behaviour? (C.A.M.)
16. Homogeneous products are for homogenous consumers. Discuss. (U.S.)

Chapter 7

1. 'The importance of conceptual knowledge (models) of buying behaviour in understanding and predicting the possible response of the relevant market

segments is widely accepted when the buyers are individuals and households: it is largely ignored, unfortunately, when the buying unit is an organisation.' (Webster and Wind, 1972). What factors do you think may have contributed to the apparent neglect of organisational buying behaviour suggested by this quotation, and what factors explain the current higher level of interest in the subject? (U.S.)

2. Why is the post purchase stage included in some models of the buying process? (U.S.)

3. Describe, preferably with the aid of a diagram, Sheth's or any other recognised model of industrial buyer behaviour. (I.M.)

4. Discuss the main behavioural influences affecting organisational buying behaviour. (I.M.)

5. Discuss the relevance of product classification schemes (Hill and Hillier 1977) to the analysis of industrial buying decisions. (U.S.)

Chapter 8

1. 'Whenever a market for a product consists of two or more buyers then it is capable of division into meaningful buyer groups.' Discuss the validity of this statement. (U.S.)

2. 'Without market segmentation there can be no marketing strategy.' Briefly define these terms and discuss the extent to which the statement is true. (C.A.M.)

3. Discuss the concept of reference groups as a basis for market segmentation. (S.B.E.C.)

4. The same market can sometimes be segmented by a number of variables. What are some of the problems that might be encountered in segmenting a market under such conditions? (U.S.)

5. Market segmentation is a recognition of the classification of products by consumers. Discuss. (U.S.)

6. Explain the problems associated with market segmentation and whether it is desirable or feasible in all situations. (U.S.)

7. Recommend the ways most likely to improve your marketing efforts by using a segmentation approach in each of the following markets:

   (*a*)   women's magazines
   (*b*)   toilet soaps
   (*c*)   computers

   Give reasons for your decision. (C.A.M.)

Chapter 9

1. Discuss the efforts of producer/users of primary commodities to stabilise markets by agreeing upon quotas, price, etc. What are the advantages/ disadvantages of such agreements?

2. How valid is the argument that farm size will remain small in order to attain the yields sufficient to satisfy the demands of a rapidly expanding population?

3. What factors account for the erratic short-term price fluctuations in market for agricultural products?

4. What are the essential features of:

   (a) Spot transactions?
   (b) Future contracts?

5. Distinguish between agents, brokers and merchants.

6. What advantages/disadvantages have processed foodstuffs over fresh produce, and how has this affected consumer purchasing patterns?

7. Discuss the pros and cons of agricultural marketing boards in the United Kingdom.

8. There are no fundamental differences between the marketing of industrial and consumer goods. Comment.

9. What basic distributive alternatives are open to the manufacturers of industrial goods? Which do you consider most appropriate to the sale of:

   Basic chemicals
   Computers
   Electronic components
   Machine tools
   Office supplies
   Plastic pipe?

   Why?

10. Describe the economist's concept of concentration ratios. How useful is this concept to the marketer – industrial or consumer? In what way?

11. What functions add value to the product, or merely add to its final cost without adding to its value?

12. It is frequently contended that industrial buying is an essentially rational process whereas consumer purchasing is not. State your reasons for agreeing/ disagreeing with this statement.

13. Does the industrial market merit special consideration or is it merely a particular application of general marketing principles? (U.S.)

14. Do we understand enough about how buyers and sellers interact in industrial markets to be able to predict industrial buying (or selling) behaviour? If yes, discuss; if no, why not? (U.S.)

15. In industrial marketing there is normally a much closer link between the information-gathering and promotional sides of marketing than is found in consumer goods marketing. Discuss. (I.M.)

16. Evaluate the usefulness of models of the industrial buying process (like Robinson and Faris's buygrid framework) in industrial marketing decisions. (U.S.)

17. Describe the major features which distinguish industrial marketing from consumer markets, and illustrate their implications for marketing management in consumer and industrial companies. (U.S.)

18. There is considerable variation in the retail mark-up on a bar of soap, a household electrical appliance, a suite of furniture and a diamond ring. As all retailers perform the same basic functions why should this be so?

19. In what ways do retailers provide consumers with product information?

20. How well does McNair's concept of the 'wheel of retailing' fit post-war changes in retail distribution in the United Kingdom?

21. What is a 'voluntary chain'? To what do they owe their existence, and what role do you expect them to play in future?

22. What basic distribution alternatives are open to the manufacturers of consumer goods, and what are the major advantages/disadvantages associated with each?

23. Evaluate the factors for and against the establishment of out-of-town shopping centres.

24. The last decade has witnessed an ever-increasing concentration of power into the hands of a reducing number of multiple retailers. Discuss the main ways in which manufacturers have attempted to meet this challenge, indicating what degrees of success have been achieved. (U.S.)

25. Account for the predominance of direct manufacturer-to-user channels in the marketing of capital goods in comparison to the almost pervasive use of some type of middleman in the marketing of consumer goods. What factors determine the choice of channel in each sector? (U.S.)

26. Outline the principles involved in the development of the hypermarket, and show how the conditions in Europe favoured their application in the 1960s. (U.S.)

27. Mail-order marketing has been particularly successful during recent years. How has advertising helped this growth? Your answer should outline the various methods of mail-order operation and use of media. (I.M.)

28. Examine the factors which, since 1945, have principally affected the development of retailing. (U.S.)

29. What methods have been used to measure and compare efficiency between different retail organisational types? Comment on the usefulness of the methods. (U.S.)

30. Describe some of the important trends in the retailing sector, and how this might affect marketing. (U.S.)

31. Discuss the possible reasons which might be applicable in the decisions of retailers to develop 'own labels', and manufacturers who refuse to supply 'own labels'. (U.S.)

32. Compare and discuss the relative advantages/disadvantages for a manufacturer of a consumer durable for the distribution of his goods through three of the four methods below:

    (*a*) own retail outlet

    (*b*) selective distribution

    (*c*) using wholesalers

    (*d*) franchising. (C.A.M.)

33. Why are large manufacturers with their own brand willing to supply retailers with a 'retailer' brand? What are some of the consequences of doing so? (U.S.)

34. The ANA reported recently that nearly 50 per cent of goods carried bar codes. What significance does this statement have for manufacturer and retailer? (U.S.)

Chapter 10

1. What factors, and what sources, would you take into account in preparing a forecast of the potential market for:

    (*a*) A new 'snack' food?

    (*b*) Frozen T. V. dinners?

    (*c*) A combined refrigerator/freezer unit with a capacity of 14 cubic feet?

    (*d*) Computer time sharing services?

    (*e*) Industrial catering equipment?

Make whatever assumptions you like about the 'product', but state them clearly.

2. Under what circumstances would you consider a non-probability sample a useful and valid market research technique? What disadvantages do you associate with such samples?

3. Compile a short questionnaire:

    (*a*) For sampling the opinion of industrial users on the benefits of containerisation.

    (*b*) To elicit the opinions of housewives about freeze-dried coffee. You should stipulate how the questionnaires are to be administered and to whom.

4. What is market segmentation? What variables would you use in segmenting the market for:

    (*a*) Detergents?

    (*b*) Fractional horse power electric motors?

    (*c*) Motor cars?

    (*d*) Vacuum cleaners?

5. Provide an explanation of the following methods of structuring samples for market research surveys:

    (*a*) systematic sampling,

    (*b*) cluster sampling,

(*c*) area sampling, and

(*d*) quota sampling.

In each case, give an example of a marketing situation in which the particular method could be most effectively employed. (I.M.)

6. Formulate the main rules to be kept in mind when designing a questionnaire. How important is question order in securing a satisfactory response? (I.M.)

7. Describe the main guidelines to be followed when framing market research questionnaires to be administered by interviewers to a large sample of respondents. (I.M.)

8. Qualitative research is often criticised as producing results subject to the bias of the investigator. How far do you think this is dangerous, and what compensating advantages do you see in the qualitative approach? (U.S.)

9. Give a definition of an 'attitude', and discuss the difficulties of providing such a definition. Why do marketing researchers concern themselves with attitude measurements? (U.S.)

10. Users of a motorway service area on leaving are to be interviewed to find out, among other things, whether their decision to shop at that particular service area was dependent on their immediate need for petrol or refreshment, the distance or time since their last stop (and where that was), or on other factors. Draft a section of a face-to-face questionnaire designed to establish which of these was or were most influential, and which facilities the respondent in person has used in the current visit. Do not show any coding data or any introductory section. (U.S.)

11. (*a*) Describe the nature and source of the statistical information provided in the United Kingdom Department of Employment Gazette. (10 marks)

    (*b*) Describe two sources, other than government departments of any country, from which you would expect to obtain statistical information and indicate the nature of the information available. (10 marks) (I.M.)

12. It has been said that the art of management consists of 'taking account simultaneously of the inner workings of the firm and its interaction with external forces'. Describe the contribution of marketing research to the understanding of these external forces. (U.S.)

13. What are the similarities and differences between market research for a fast-moving food product and market research for major capital plant? How would you account for the differences? (I.M.)

14. What are the essential stages in developing a proposal for market research? What differences would you expect to see in a proposal for industrial market research compared with a proposal for consumer market research? (U.S.)

15. What useful information could you hope to obtain through market research when planning to enter the market with a totally new product, based on a recent invention, about which the marketplace has no knowledge? (I.M.)

16. Distinguish between primary and secondary marketing research data. What are the main sources of data in each case? (I.M.)
17. It has been said that the initial research showed that there was no market for a dry copying machine. However, Rank Xerox ignored the findings and proceeded to establish a successful international company based on the dry copying concept. How would you explain this contradiction and does it invalidate the use of marketing research data as a planning tool? (I.M.)

Chapter 11

1. Why is the firm's product policy of such central importance to its continued growth and development? Describe a declining firm or industry, and suggest how it might improve its fortunes by adopting a macro view of its markets.
2. Describe how the product life-cycle concept might be of operational use to the marketer.
3. Suggest a system for classifying 'new' products. What are the parameters on which your classification rests, and how were they selected?
4. What advantages do you perceive in being (a) a leader, (b) a follower, in terms of product innovations?
5. Design a rating table for evaluating new product ideas, specifying the industry in which the table is to be used.
6. How would you product test:

   (a) An instant soup mix?
   (b) A new plastic resin?
   (c) A new model car?

7. Summarise the advantages/disadvantages of test marketing.
8. Is the fact that intuition and judgement are important factors in the development of new products a valid argument against the use of formal sequential procedures in this area? (U.S.)
9. Distinguish between product and market testing. Explain the contributions and limitations of each in both the consumer and the industrial goods field. (U.S.)
10. Is it possible to reconcile grocery manufacturing companies' continuous introduction of new products with a supermarket policy of variety reduction? (I.M.)
11. Define 'product policy'. What is the role in product strategy of the product life-cycle? Under what circumstances would it be advisable to try to arrest a declining sales curve? Discuss the alternatives to attempting to arrest such a decline. (I.M.)
12. Explain the significance and implications of the timing of a new product launch. (I.M.)

13. What scope is there, in your view, for the successful introduction of strict management control and evaluation procedures in the area of product planning and new product development? (U.S.)
14. Outline the major 'steps' in the new product evolutionary cycle, and assess the extent to which these are amenable to systematic organisation, management and control. (U.S.)
15. Comment on the value of a systematic approach to new product development. Can such development be planned? (U.S.)
16. Discuss the benefits that accrue to a company in setting up a system of regular, detailed product marketing plans. (U.S.)
17. Examine the limitations of test marketing exercises as a guide to full-scale product launch. (U.S.)
18. The rate at which new products are introduced into the marketplace has increased greatly in the last decade. This has been attributed to: (*a*) evidence of economic progress, OR (*b*) an increase in planned obsolescence. Develop an argument supporting ONE of these stands. (S.B.E.C.)
19. New product development may be just as important for non profit organisations as it is for business organisations. Discuss. (S.B.E.C.)
20. How can diffusion theory be used to improve the chances of a successful new product launch? (U.S.)
21. Identify and evaluate the strategies a company could adopt to extend the life cycle of a product. (S.B.E.C.)
22. Critically appraise the usefulness of the product life cycle concept to marketing management. (I.M.)

Chapter 12
1. What considerations would you take into account in selecting the basic packaging material, e.g. tinplate, glass, etc., for the following items (stipulate the material to be used and the reasons for your choice in rank order of importance, i.e. cost, strength, etc.) :

Breakfast cereal
Jam
Hand cream – (*a*) standard quality
            – (*b*) de luxe quality
Frozen vegetables
Chocolates
Panty-hose
Men's shirts
Instant coffee
Salt
Shampoo.

2. A well-known book on packaging is entitled *The Silent Salesman*. Discuss.

3. Summarise: the consumer's requirements of a satisfactory pack; the retailer's requirements.
4. Select any three well-known consumer products and analyse packaging's contribution to their marketing.
5. What contribution can motivation research make to the packaging decision? Quote specific examples to illustrate your answer.
6. Account for the increased importance of packaging as an element in the marketing mix of a typical fast-moving consumer good in recent years. (U.S.)
7. Packaging plays a major part in the promotion of branded products. Discuss this contribution in the light of growing dissatisfaction from conservationists and consumerist interests throughout the world. (I.M.)
8. Write an essay on the social psychology of colour in packaging and sales promotion. (I.M.)

Chapter 13
1. How valid do you consider the reasons offered to explain the relatively low rating of the importance of price policy in the Udell study? Why? What alternative explanations can you think of?
2. Summarise the major factors that should be taken into account in developing a price policy.
3. Discuss the advantages/disadvantages of each of the price 'formulas' discussed in the text.
4. Under what circumstances would you recommend (*a*) a 'skimming' approach, (*b*) a 'penetration' policy? Identify a current example of each and document the reasons which you believe prompted its selection.
5. Discuss the importance of price as an 'indicator of quality'.
6. What relevance have the concepts of the product life cycle and market segmentation for pricing policy?
7. Describe three ways in which product pricing policy can be used as a means of creative marketing. (I.M.)
8. Explain the statement that optimal pricing policies should be based upon a combination of contribution analysis techniques and a marketing-oriented view of customers. (U.S.)
9. Describe the uses of break-even analysis as a tool of effective marketing management. (I.M.)
10. Explain and comment on the view that optimal price is that price which best serves the central aims of the business. (U.S.)
11. What have recent studies revealed about the effect of price differentials on consumers perceptions of product quality? (I.M.)
12. Under the existing Price Code, what freedom does the marketer retain to manipulate prices to optimise long-term net profit? (I.M.)
13. In *How British Industry Prices*, the authors found that 63 per cent of the firms investigated used the absorption (full) costing approach to establish the cost and selling prices of their products.

(*a*) What are the problems which can arise when this method is used to calculate the selling price?

(*b*) Discuss the use of marginal (direct) costing and indicate how this method can be particularly important during a period of depressed economic conditions.

Illustrate your answer with simple numerical examples. (U.S.)

14. Consider the differences of emphasis placed upon 'price' by economists and marketers. Does the decision of Tesco to drop trading stamps and to use price cuts as an alternative marketing tool indicate that the economist's views are correct? (U.S.)

15. A surprisingly large number of companies relegate price policy to a secondary role in the planning of their marketing strategy. What factors might cause a company to act in this way? (U.S.)

16. How do contribution analysis and break-even analysis relate to each other? What use is made of them in marketing? (I.M.)

17. Tooth-i-Pegs Ltd make and sell 100 000 toothbrushes per month at 40p each. The total unit cost is 38p and fixed costs amount to 10 000 per month. Market research has revealed that there would be an increase in sales to 125 000 brushes per month if the price was reduced to 38p per brush. Assuming that there is excess manufacturing capacity available, should Tooth-i-Pegs Ltd reduce its selling price? Prepare an advertising and marketing plan. (C.A.M.)

18. Write notes on FOUR of the following: (i) mark-up pricing, (ii) target pricing, (iii) price discrimination, (iv) loss-leaders, (v) prestige pricing. (I.M.)

Chapter 14

1. Rank the 'essential distributive functions' cited in the text in order of importance for each of the following:

(*a*) Steel stockholder
(*b*) Primary commodity wholesaler – (i) perishable goods.
  – (ii) non-perishable goods.
(*c*) Packaged-food wholesaler.
(*d*) 'Main' car dealer.

2. Which distribution policy do you consider most appropriate to the sale of the following products:

  Car accessories
  Car tyres
  Ethical pharmaceuticals
  Household cleaning materials
  Luxury cosmetics
  Transfer presses?

Stipulate the assumptions underlying your selection of a given policy and cite actual examples wherever possible.

3. Discuss the impact of vertical integration on the structure of traditional distribution channels.

4. Selection of a distribution policy invariably demands a compromise between cost and control. Discuss.

5. Evaluate the possible effect of mail order, automatic vending and door-to-door selling on retail distribution in the coming decade.

6. How can a manufacturer evaluate the following choices in the construction of a marketing/distribution system:

   (a) Own retail sales force and direct delivery with own transport system.
   (b) Own retail sales force and commercial warehousing/delivery service.
   (c) Wholesale salesmen and own transport system delivering to wholesalers only.
   (d) Any other combination. (U.S.)

7. Describe the variables which affect the design of distribution channels and comment on their relative importance. (U.S.)

8. What are the possible sources of innovation in distribution, describing some you are familiar with, and comment on the process of adoption or of rejection. (U.S.)

9. Describe the variables which affect the choice of distribution channels by a manufacturing firm. (U.S.)

10. Fundamentally the (marketing) channel decision requires resolution of the often conflicting forces of cost and control. Discuss. (U.S.)

11. Argue the case for managing the physical distribution of a company's products as an aspect of its marketing strategy. (I.M.)

12. What problems are inherent in producing a definition of the term 'channel of distribution'? (U.S.)

13. What do you understand by the total distribution cost concept? Outline the scope of the constituent centres involved and relate the importance of an understanding of the concept to the marketing manager. (I.M.)

14. Discuss the major considerations in designing a channel system. (S.B.E.C.)

15. Why is the decision about the type of channel system to be used by a manufacturer often critical to marketing success? (S.B.E.C.)

16. By what criteria would you judge the efficiency of a particular channel of distribution? (I.M.)

17. Identify and discuss some of the factors that should increase the trend towards vertical marketing systems. (S.B.E.C.)

Chapter 15

1. It has been suggested that the major thrust of consumer protection activities should be concentrated on the provision of information. Can this be justified? (U.S.)

2. Sandage and Fryburger's 'model' of how advertising is thought to work is based on four stages: exposure/perception/integration/action. Describe what takes place at the *integration* stage. (U.S.)

3. How might the characteristics of the 'message' itself affect the success or failure of an advertisement? Discuss with specific examples. (U.S.)

4. With regard to the source of a communication, what factors can provoke attitude change in the recipient? What alternatives to attitude change are open to the recipient? (I.M.)

5. Do we really know how advertising works? What theories have been advanced that might help you to explain matters to a person who asks such a question? (I.M.)

6. Identify the main elements in a marketing communication system and say what factors are likely to limit the effectiveness of the communication. (I.M.)

7. Discuss the contribution of models of the hierarchy of effects to the development of advertising theory. (I.M.)

8. Distinguish between personal and non-personal communications and outline the marketing communications functions that each can perform. (I.M.)

Chapter 16

1. Your company is considering changing its advertising agency. How would you undertake the selection of a replacement?

2. Analyse the following publications, using the 'check-list' described in the text: *Punch, T.V. Times, Vogue, Financial Times, Woman.*

3. Discuss the merits of the cinema as an advertising medium.

4. Develop an outline campaign plan for either frozen concentrated orange juice or off-peak travel on British Rail, assuming an annual budget of £500 000.

5. What are the economic arguments for and against advertising? Which do you find more convincing? Why?

6. How would you determine the advertising budget for a new household detergent with an expected sales volume of 5 million, a recommended retail price of 0.50, and a gross margin of 25 per cent? Distinguish between above- and below-the-line expenditures.

7. What problems do you associate with the derivation of a measure of advertising effectiveness?

8. What are the objectives of sales promotion? What type of promotion would you use:

    (a) When launching a new consumer product?
    (b) During the growth phase?
    (c) When the product has reached maturity?

9. Evaluate each of the following statements:

   (*a*) Advertising costs the consumer millions of pounds every year. If advertising were eliminated, prices could be reduced and everybody would benefit.

   (*b*) Most advertising is a social waste because it merely diverts demand from one firm to another.

   (*c*) Advertising is of no value to the consumer because it consists of doubtful claims of small differences between similar products. (U.S.)

10. 'We believe in advertising; it is an essential factor in the economics of modern industry.' Discuss. (I.M.)

11. State your views on the purpose and value of sales promotion and merchandising schemes, ranging from contests to premium offers, as additions or alternatives to conventional advertising. What effect are they likely to have on brand loyalty? (I.M.)

12. 'People in advertising are parasites. They contribute nothing to the real wealth of the community.' These sentences occur in a letter in your local newspaper. Write a reply, putting the case for advertising and advertising agencies. (I.M.)

13. Summarise and evaluate any five different methods by which a national advertiser can determine the annual advertising appropriation. (I.M.)

14. 'It is not possible to make a realistic test of the effectiveness of a (television) commercial in a laboratory situation in advance of real-life exposure' (Alan Hedges). Explain. (U.S.)

15. What are the main print media? What are the main electronic media? List each. Take one media group from each category and describe its advantages and limitations. (U.S.)

16. Repetition is the key to advertising success. Evaluate the values and limitations of a repetitive campaign. (U.S.)

17. The Stimulus-Response Theory, as applied to advertising, stresses the importance of frequency and recency of exposure to advertisements by target audiences. Explain why this theory cannot by itself offer a satisfactory explanation of the influence of advertising on consumer buying behaviour. (I.M.)

18. What social benefits, if any, do the community derive from creative/display advertising? Explain your opinion with examples. (U.S.)

19. 'Personal influence is seven times more effective than magazine or newspaper advertising in the persuasion of women to switch brands of household products' (Katz and Lazarsfeld). How can this factor be employed in media planning? (U.S.)

20. Explain the advantages and disadvantages of exhibitions and trade fairs for the industrial advertiser. (U.S.)

21. Write a headline and 50–60 words of copy for a quarter page ad for a teenage magazine selling a two-week desert tour of Morocco by minibus. Describe or draw the illustration if you want to use one. (U.S.)

22. The economist Alfred Marshall (1922) drew a distinction between 'constructive' advertising and 'combative' advertising. Can such a distinction usefully be made? Discuss with examples. (U.S.)

23. Describe the main functions of a full-service advertising agency. Explain how advertising agencies are remunerated. Discuss the viability of alternatives to the advertising agency system. (U.S.)

24. Discuss three methods used in setting an advertising budget for a particular product, discussing their advantages and disadvantages. (U.S.)

25. Summarise the arguments for and against the proposition that advertising has a beneficial economic effect. (I.M.)

26. 'Advertising tends to encourage gross materialism and dissatisfaction.' (Labour Party Green Paper 1972.) Discuss. (U.S.)

27. Recently the Direct Mail Sales Bureau has been set up to promote the medium to both advertising agencies and advertisers. Explain what you know about the Direct Mail medium and consider situations where Direct Mail could become an integral part of the total media plan. (C.A.M.)

28. Explain the importance of campaign planning and indicate the elements which you would expect to be included in a campaign plan for the launch of a new toothpaste. (C.A.M.)

29. It is likely that before long the availability of cable and satellite TV will give a television viewer as many as 50 channels from which to select, thus offering to the advertiser a range of specialised audiences. What are the implications for the marketer of this fragmentation of TV audiences? (I.M.)

30. Following on from the VCR revolution in terms of viewing, what are your opinions on the future of cable television within the UK? What are the likely problems and/or solutions in the following areas: (1) measuring the growth of cable homes, (2) research measurement of audiences, (3) mechanics of wiring up homes, (4) the interface of satellite and cable viewing. (C.A.M.)

31. 'In the end a client gets the advertising he deserves, from an advertising agency.' What does this mean, and do you agree? (C.A.M.)

Chapter 17

1. 'Unlike Advertising, there are no accurate national expenditure figures available for Sales Promotion, because many companies are undertaking such promotion without realising that they are doing so.' Explain this statement and outline some of the major uses of Sales Promotion. (U.S.)

2. From some situation in your experience, illustrate the role of 'below-the-line' sales promotion as part of the overall promotional campaign. Show how the 'below-the-line' component integrated with and contributed to the success of the total. (I.M.)

3. Define 'selling-out' and 'selling-in'. Show how a well-designed promotional campaign keeps the two elements in balance. (I.M.)

4. It is often suggested that the main role of 'below-the-line' expenditures for sales promotion is to encourage the marketer's and dealer's sales people.

Give examples of such promotional activities, some of which would tend to support and others to refute this view. (I.M.)

5. In deciding on the promotional mix for a particular range of products, what circumstances would tend to favour special emphasis on:

    (a) dealer incentives
    (b) sales force activity
    (c) sampling. (I.M.)

6. There are a wide variety of types of sales promotions – coupons, competitions, price-off etc. – from which a brand manager may choose in writing his annual product promotional plans. What factors does he consider in his selection/rejection process? (U.S.)

7. Define sales promotion and give FOUR examples of the kind of marketing objective that can be achieved by the use of sales promotion. Say which techniques you would use to achieve the objective in each case. (I.M.)

8. Name the four major components of the promotional mix. What function does each perform and how does the marketing manager determine the amount of money to be allocated to each element in order to achieve a given communication objective? (I.M.)

9. Account for the boom in sports sponsorship in the last ten years. (I.M.)

Chapter 18

1. Direct selling is the most expensive method of establishing contact with the potential customer. Under what circumstances is this expense justified?

2. Distinguish the essential differences between trade, missionary, technical and new-business selling. What 'type' of salesman do you consider to be best suited to each?

3. Compare and contrast the various methods of salesman compensation discussed in the text. Which would you select in each of the following situations? Why?

    (a) Sale of capital equipment.
    (b) Sale of industrial lubricants.
    (c) Door-to-door selling of cosmetics, encyclopedias, etc.
    (d) Sale of packaged goods to independent retail outlets.

4. Account for the recent emphasis given to merchandising.

5. What is systems selling? What advantages does it have over the traditional product specialisation approach?

6. Critically examine the alternative methods of compensating salesmen. (U.S.)

7. 'There is something of the salesman in every good buyer. However, very few salesmen would ever make good buyers.' Discuss this view. (U.S.)

8. How should a sales manager determine the size of his sales force? (I.M.)

9. What do you think is the ideal way in which to recruit and select salesmen? (I.M.)

10. Show how a knowledge of interaction and influence processes in personal selling can contribute to an enhancement of sales-force productivity. (U.S.)
11. To what extent are psychological tests of value in the selection of salesmen? (I.M.)
12. What are the main factors which sales managers should bear in mind when evaluating the performance of their sales forces? Give your views on the extent to which remuneration of salesmen should be related to their performance. (I.M.)
13. Outline the value of a retail audit operation in helping to control the efficiency of a sales force. (U.S.)
14. What are the most important things a salesman can do to improve his sales performance? How can management help him to do these things? (I.M.)
15. How would you decide to divide available resources between direct sales representatives and other promotional activities? (I.M.)
16. What factors should be taken into account when designing sales territories? (I.M.)
17. Write a job description for a salesman in a company manufacturing electronic components. (I.M.)

Chapter 19

1. Distinguish the salient differences between the functional and product forms of organisational structure. Under what circumstances is each to be preferred?
2. What is the 'product manager concept'? Name five firms which have adopted this concept. (See the classified ads for clues!)
3. How does the concept of market management differ from product management? When is the former organisational structure to be preferred?
4. What distinguishes the marketing oriented firm from those which have not adopted the marketing concept?
5. Using published data, e.g. annual reports, articles in the trade press, etc., and/or personal knowledge/experience, summarise the corporate resources of a major manufacturing company. Based on your summary, what recommendations would you make to the firm's top management concerning its future strategy, i.e. on what markets/products should it concentrate its efforts?
6. Discuss the proposition that the position of the marketing department in the total organisation is particularly difficult because of the types of conflicts which tend to occur between the logic of customer satisfaction and the cost minimisation logic pursued by other departments. (U.S.)
7. The system of organising marketing divisions around the job of the brand manager, or product manager, has recently been widely criticised. What criticisms of this system would you expect to be valid in practice, and what opportunities does this system offer for more effective marketing management? (I.M.)

8. The marketing function is so central to the company's continued success that it requires to be carefully controlled by those in charge of the company. Outline a comprehensive system of such controls on marketing to ensure top management retain the responsibility with which they are charged. (U.S.)

9. Indicate the types of conflict which might arise in a firm employing sales, marketing and product managers and the ways in which these might be organisationally resolved. (I.M.)

10. Write a job description for a product manager in either:

    (*a*) a typical company making products for industry
    (*b*) a typical consumer goods company. (I.M.)

11. In what ways would the Marketing Manager of a large company be able to do a more effective job, if he were appointed to the Board as Marketing Director? How would his responsibilities change? (I.M.)

12. It should be possible to assess the extent of a company's commitment to marketing by looking at its organisation chart. Discuss. (I.M.)

13. Companies differ greatly in the organisation of their marketing functions. Discuss these differences and explain the reasons for them. (U.S.)

14. How does a production/sales based business organisation differ from a marketing-based one? (I.M.)

15. Discuss the organisational implications of a company progressing from being sales oriented to being marketing oriented. (I.M.)

Chapter 20

1. 'Management's sensitivity to strategy should be proportionate to the instability of the environment of the firm.' Explain this statement and emphasise in your answer the major characteristics of strategic change, and the problems to be encountered by the firm committing itself to such change. (U.S.)

2. What would be the main headings in an annual marketing plan? Select one of these headings and show the detail with which it would be concerned, explaining how the content of your detailed section of the plan would be related to the whole. (I.M.)

3. While the marketing planner is the central figure in drawing up the annual product plan, other departments in the company will make important contributions to the final plan. Discuss. (U.S.)

4. Describe how a marketing audit might be conducted in a firm, and evaluate the contribution of such auditing to overall marketing control. (U.S.)

5. Assess the impact on marketing tactics and strategies of changes in roles within the family during the last 20 years. (I.M.)

6. Leading businessmen have been quoted as relying to a large extent on the regular submission and analysis of financial ratios from the trading

companies under their control. Why do you think they regard such measures of control as so important? (I.M.)

7. What is the function of a Marketing Plan and how does it relate to the Corporate Long-Range Plan of an organisation? (I.M.)

8. Explain the purpose and application of any six of the commonly used financial ratios relating to the operation of a business. (I.M.)

9. 'Every major industry was once a growth industry' (Theodore Levitt). Discuss. (U.S.)

10. 'Every major business enterprise requires a clear long-term marketing strategy in order to enable it to fulfil its obligations to its employees, shareholders and society.' Discuss. (U.S.)

11. Marketing planning begins with an analysis of a variety of factors including an internal audit of the firm's capabilities. What are the major factors to take into -account in such an internal audit? (U.S.)

12. What arguments might you use to persuade a business organisation of the need to develop strategic marketing plans? (U.S.)

13. For what reasons might you require a marketing audit to be carried out and what types of information would you expect to achieve from it? (I.M.)

14. Discuss the importance to a company of adequately defining what business it is in. (I.M.)

Note: no questions for Chapter 21.

Chapter 22

1. There continues to be emphasis on growth as the central corporate aim of most business organisations. Discuss the reasons for the importance of the growth concept, and consider the alternative of zero growth as a practical possibility. (U.S.)

2. What preconditions besides economic growth would you consider essential for the development of large-scale retailing? Provide illustrations of lack of development attributable to their absence. (U.S.)

3. How are the less developed countries assisted by the industrialised nations in pursuing economic development? (I.M.)

4. In what ways could the more widespread application of marketing techniques aid a country's economy? (I.M.)

5. In many industrialised and developing nations the number of households is rising much more rapidly than the corresponding increase in the population. Explain why this is happening. What are the consequences for marketers? (I.M.)

Chapter 23

1. Describe and evaluate the marketing techniques used to match supply and demand in one of the following:

  (a) the package holiday industry;
  (b) fast food restaurants.

2. Why are product positioning and differentiation such difficult concepts to operationalising in many service industries?
3. 'In most cases the everyday contact with customers is a more important part of marketing activities than advertising and mass communication' (Gronroos 1984, p.42). Provide a reasoned explanation of why 94.1 per cent of a randomly selected group of 219 service companies agreed with the above contention.
4. Describe why marketing activities in service companies are different from those carried out in manufacturing companies.
5. Evaluate the use of information technology (IT) in improving the service provision in ONE of the following services:

  (a) A major high street retailer of up-market clothing and interior design.
  (b) A national distribution company.
  (c) An international airline.

6. 'Managing supply and demand is the key task of the service manager' (Sasser 1976). Discuss this statement, and explain ways in which a marketing specialist could help service managers achieve this objective.
7. Describe and evaluate the marketing channels and delivery systems used by ONE of the following organisations:

  (a) A trans-Atlantic charter airline business.
  (b) An international firm of chartered accountants.
  (c) A UK-based package holiday company catering to the needs of young people.

8. 'Could marketing itself be 'myopic' in having failed to create relevant paradigms for the service sector?' (Shostack, 1977). Discuss this contention.
9. 'The internal marketing concept is the key to service marketing' (Gronroos 1981). Evaluate this concept and choose a service which might especially benefit from this approach, and indicate why.
10. How, and why, does the need to manage demand affect the marketing of services? Illustrate your answer as extensively as possible.
11. 'Deregulation and increased competition is changing the marketing environment of financial services.' Discuss this contention.
12. Evaluate the usefulness of having a different approach to marketing personal services from that used in marketing manufactured goods.
13. Describe how either a national clearing bank or large firm of management consultants could benefit from an awareness of service marketing theory.

Chapter 24

1. 'As the general rate of change in society accelerates, the economics of permanence are being replaced by the economics of impermanence'

(Toffler). Is there any evidence to suggest that the above statement is an accurate description of the way in which UK society is developing? What effects would such a change have upon marketing and, in particular, upon the marketing of consumer goods? (U.S.)

2. Write a critique of the concept of metamarketing, showing the extent to which you believe marketing ideals can legitimately be extended beyond business products and services. (U.S.)

3. It has been argued that a continued expansion of output will create intolerable ecological problems. Do market-oriented firms therefore perform a social disservice by encouraging more purchases? Give reasons for your answer. (U.S.)

4. A recent government publication described the main trends in the United Kingdom during the last decade. Identify these trends and comment on those of particular significance in marketing. (I.M.)

5. A major problem in the development of a consumer-oriented economy is defining the relative roles of government and business in ensuring consumer satisfaction. Evaluate the response of business to the consumerist challenge. (U.S.)

6. Advertising is often used to add subjective value to products (e.g. cosmetics, soft drinks). This practice is widely regarded as socially undesirable. Discuss this proposition. (U.S.)

7. Consumerism has arisen because management has been guilty of one-way communication with the buyer; it is not listening to what is being said in reply. Discuss. (U.S.)

8. Has consumerism become a casualty to inflation? (I.M.)

9. Consumer sovereignty is the myth of the contemporary market-place. Discuss the role of this concept in the development of a realistic consumerist philosophy. (U.S.)

10. Consumerism is a phenomenon of the post-war years, and is a fact of life for many companies. How is it likely to affect the work of:

    (a) the marketing department
    (b) the production department

    of a company marketing consumer durables? (I.M.)

11. What do you understand by the term 'social marketing'? What is the relationship between social marketing and consumerism?

12. Describe the factors leading to the growth of consumerism in the 1960s and 1970s and consider how adequately the present UK consumerist structure and philosophy meets the demands that arise from these factors. (U.S.)

13. Waste – in excess production of undesirable goods, in unnecessary packaging, in squandering precious resources – is an inevitable outcome of marketing freedom. Discuss, suggesting constraints and controls if you feel they are necessary. (U.S.)

14. Does the growing power of consumer groups mean that marketers have failed in their aim of meeting consumer needs? (I.M.)

15. As marketing manager of a major food manufacturer, you propose to give a talk to your department on the growth of the consumerist movement in the United Kingdom. Write notes for your talk, outlining what you consider to be the main reasons for the acceptance of the idea that consumers need protection, discussing also the role and activities of consumer bodies in this development. (C.A.M.)

16. How are marketing principles and techniques applied to non-profit-making activities in the public sector? Give examples. (I.M.)

17. You have just become promotions manager of a national charity concerned with disabled children. Up to now the charity's fund-raising has been very low-key, involving a discreet level of promotion on a relatively modest budget. On your appointment you have decided upon a radical change of policy, involving a full-blooded marketing approach to the problem of raising money. The attitude of the charity's committee is hostile, their view being that the application of product marketing techniques is wholly inappropriate to a charity. Write a report to your board justifying your viewpoint. (C.A.M.)

18. Describe the principal legislation currently in force which affects the sale of goods and services. (C.A.M.)

Supplementary reading list

It is clear that an introductory text can do no more than outline basic principles and provide an overview of the subject matter as a whole. The purpose of this reading list is to suggest sources which the author believes will prove useful in supplementing the material covered in this book. In turn, many of the references contain bibliographies, or cite other sources, which should prove useful in pursuing an in-depth study of a particular topic. Many of the sources cited have been 'carried over' from earlier editions and now appear to be dated. This is not believed to be the case – relatively few new books have been introduced which offer new perspectives or insights beyond those contained in what have come to be regarded as basic texts. However, the list is by no means exhaustive and students should consult the reading list published by the various examining bodies as well as those issued by their own tutors.

Magazines, periodicals, etc.

To keep abreast of current developments, and update factual data, as least some of the following publications should be consulted on a regular basis:

Admap
Advertiser's Weekly
European Business
European Journal of Marketing
Financial Times
Harvard Business Review
International Journal of Advertising
Journal of Marketing (USA)
Journal of Marketing Management
Journal of Marketing Research (USA)
Journal of the Market Research Society
Management Decision
Management Today
Sunday Times Business News
The Economist

■ General texts

Many general texts have appeared in several editions and students should seek to obtain the most recent.

Baker, Michael J., *et al.*, *Marketing Theory and Practice*, 2nd edn, London: Macmillan, 1983.

Baker, Michael J., *Marketing Strategy and Management*, London: Macmillan, 1985.

Baker, Michael J., *Macmillan Dictionary of Marketing and Advertising*, 2nd edn, London: Macmillan, 1990.

Baker, Michael J., *Research for Marketing*, London: Macmillan, 1991.

Baker, Michael J., (ed.) *The Marketing Book*, 2nd edn, London: Heinemann, 1991.

Bell, M., *Marketing: Concepts and Strategy*, 3rd edn, Boston: Houghton Mifflin, 1979.

Boyd, H. W. and Massey, W. F., *Marketing Management*, New York: Harcourt Brace & Jovanovich, 1972.

Cannon, T., *Basic Marketing*, 3rd edn, Cassell, 1990.

Davidson, J. H., *Offensive Marketing: or How to Make your Competitors Followers*, 2nd edn, Penguin, 1975.

Enis, B. and Cox, K. K., *Marketing Classics*, 3rd edn, Allyn & Bacon, 1988.

Kotler, P., *Principles of Marketing*, 2nd edn, Englewood Cliffs, N.J.: Prentice-Hall, 1986.

Kotler, P., *Marketing Management*, 6th edn, Englewood Cliffs, N.J.: Prentice-Hall, 1988.

Levitt, T., *Innovation in Marketing*, McGraw-Hill, 1962.

Levitt, T., *The Marketing Imagination*, New York: Free Press, 1983.

McCarthy, E. J. and Perreault, William D. Jr, *Basic Marketing*, 8th edn, Homewood, Ill.: Irwin, 1984.

Packard, Vance, *The Hidden Persuaders*, London: Penguin, 1957.

Ries, A. and Trout, J., *Marketing Warfare: Winning the Marketing War*, New York: McGraw-Hill, 1986.

Runyan, K. C., *The Practice of Marketing*, Columbus, Ohio: Charles Merrill, 1982.

Simmons, K., *Short Marketing Cases*, Oxford: Philip Allen, 1987.

■ 1   The marketing concept

Baker, Michael, J. *et al.*, *Marketing Theory and Practice*, 2nd edn, London: Macmillan, 1983.

Bartels, Robert, 'Development of Marketing Thought', in G. Schwartz (ed.), *Science in Marketing*, New York: Wiley, 1965.

Borden, Neil H., 'The Concept of the Marketing Mix', in Schwartz, G. (ed.), *Science in Marketing*, New York: Wiley, 1965.

Halbert, Michael, *The Meaning and Sources of Marketing Theory*, New York: McGraw-Hill, 1965.

Howard, John A., *Marketing: Executive and Buyer Behaviour*, New York: Columbia University Press, 1963.

Hunt, Shelby D., *Marketing Theory*, Homewood, Ill.: Irwin, 1983.

King, R. L., 'The Marketing Concept', in G. Schwartz (ed.), *Science in Marketing*, New York: Wiley, 1965.

Laczniack, G.R. and Murphy, P.E., *Marketing Ethics Guidelines for Managers*, Lexington, MA: Lexington Books, 1985.

Meadows, D. *et al.*, *The Limits to Growth*, London: Earth Island, 1972.

Robinson, P. J. and Luck, D. J., *Promotional Decision-Making, Practice and Theory*, New York: McGraw-Hill, 1964.

■ Articles

Kotler, P. and Levy, S. J., 'Broadening the Concept of Marketing', *Journal of Marketing*, vol. 33, January 1969.

Lipson, Harry A. and Reynolds, F. D., 'The Concept of the Marketing Mix: Its Development, Uses and Applications', *MSU Business Topics*, Winter 1970.

■ 2   Environmental Analysis

See General texts.

■ 3   Marketing strategy and management

Aaker, D. A., *Strategic Market Management*, New York: Wiley, 1984.

Day, George S., *Strategic Market Planning: The Pursuit of Competitive Advantage*, St Paul: West Publishing, 1984.

Day, George S., *Analysis for Strategic Market Decisions*, St Paul: West Publishing, 1986.

Greenley, G. E., *The Strategic and Operational Planning of Marketing*, New York: McGraw-Hill, 1986.

Weitz, B. A. *Strategic Marketing: Planning, Implementation and Control*, Kent Publishing, 1984.

■ Articles

Boxer, P. J. and Wensley, R., 'The Need for Middle Out Development of Marketing Strategy', *Journal of Management Studies*, vol. 23, no. 2, March 1986, pp. 189–204.

Day, George S. and Wensley, Robin, 'Marketing Theory with a Strategic Orientation', *Journal of Marketing*, vol. 47, Fall 1983, pp. 79–89.

Jacobson, Robert and Aaker, David A., 'Is Market Share All That It's Cracked Up to Be?', *Journal of Marketing*, vol. 49, Fall 1985, pp. 11–22.

Oliver, Gordon, 'Developing Marketing Strategy', in *Marketing Today*, Englewood Cliffs, N.J.: Prentice-Hall, 1986, Chapter 9.

■ 4   Market structure, conduct and performance

Hillebrandt, P. M. and Cannon, J., *The Modern Construction Firm*, London: Macmillan, 1990.

Pickering, John F., *Industrial Structure and Market Conduct*, London: Martin Robertson, 1974.

See also any introductory economic texts or introductory marketing texts.

■ 5   Demand and supply

Pickering, John F., *Industrial Structure and Market Conduct*, London: Martin Robertson, 1974.

Porter, Michael, *Competitive Strategy*, New York: Free Press, 1983.

Spencer, Milton H., *Managerial Economics*, 4th edn, Homewood, Ill.: Irwin, 1975.

■ 6   Consumer behaviour

Aaker, D. A. and Day, G. S. (eds), *Consumerism: Search for the Consumer Interest*, New York: Free Press, 1982.

Bem, D. I., *Beliefs, Attitudes and Human Affairs*, Monterey, CA: Brooks-Cole, 1970.

Bennet, P. and Kassarjian, H. H., *Consumer Behaviour*, Englewood Cliffs, N.J.: Prentice-Hall, 1972.

Chisnall, P. M., *Marketing: A Behavioural Analysis*, 2nd edn, New York: McGraw-Hill, 1985.

Clark, L. H. and Assael, H. (eds) *Consumer Behaviour*, vols 1 and 2, New York: University Press, 1978.

Engel, J. F., Blackwell, R. D. and Miniard, P. W., *Consumer Behaviour*, 5th edn, London: Dryden Press, 1986.

Foxall, G. R., *Consumer Behaviour: A Practical Guide*, London: Routledge, 1986.

Rachlin, H., *Introduction to Modern Behaviourism*, 2nd edn, London: Freeman, 1976.

Robertson, T. S., *Consumer Behaviour*, Glenview, Ill.: Scott Foresman, 1983.

Wallendorf, M. and Zaltman, G., *Readings in Consumer Behaviour*, New York: Wiley, 1979.

Warren, N. and Jahoda, M. (eds) *Attitudes*, Harmondsworth: Penguin Books, 1969.

Wilkie, W. L., *Consumer Behaviour*, New York: Wiley, 1990.

Worcester, R. M. and Downham, J., *The Consumer Market Research Handbook*, 3rd edn, London: McGraw-Hill, 1988.

■ 7 Organisational buying behaviour

Baily, P. J., *Purchasing and Supply Management*, 4th edn, London: Chapman & Hall, 1978.

Baily, P. J. and Farmer, D. H., *Purchasing Principles and Management*, 6th edn, London: Pitman, 1990.

Chisnall, P. M. *Strategic Industrial Marketing*, Englewood Cliffs, N.J.: Prentice-Hall, 1985.

Farmer, D. H., *Corporate Planning and Procurement*, London: Heinemann, 1975.

Hill, R. and Hillier, T. J., *Organisational Buying Behaviour*, London: Macmillan, 1977.

Hutt, M. D. and Speh, T. W., *Industrial Marketing Management*, 2nd edn, London: Dryden Press, 1985.

ISBA, *Business to Business: A Guide to Industrial Publicity*, London: ISBA, 1984.

Lee, L. and Dobler, D. W., *Purchasing and Materials Management*, 3rd edn, New York: McGraw-Hill, 1977.

Moriarty, R. T., *Industrial Buying Behaviour: Concepts, Issues, Applications*, Lexington, MA: Lexington Books, 1983.

Parkinson, S. T. and Baker, M. J., *Organisational Buying Behaviour*, London: Macmillan, 1986.

Reeder, R. R. and Brierty, E. G., *Industrial Marketing – Analysis, Planning and Control*, Englewood Cliffs, N.J.: Prentice-Hall, 1987.

Robinson, P. J., *Industrial Buying Behaviour*, London: Macmillan, 1967.

Stevens, J., *Measuring Purchasing Performance*, New York: Business Books, 1978.

Stevens, J. and Grant, J., *Purchasing/Marketing Interface*, London: Association of Business Programmes, 1975.

See also the *Journal of Purchasing and Supply Management*.

■ 8   Market segmentation

See General texts.

■ 9   Patterns of distribution

Baker, Michael J., *Marketing New Industrial Products*, London: Macmillan, 1975.

Ballon, Ronald H., *Basic Business Logistics*, Englewood Cliffs, N.J.: Prentice-Hall, 1989.

Buckley, A. and Swain, C., *Retail Developments in Great Britain*, London: Gower, 1979.

Christopher, Martin, *The Strategy of Distribution Management*, London: Heinemann, 1986.

Cox, R., *Retailing*, London: Macdonald & Evans, 1978.

Fisher, L. W., *Industrial Marketing*, 2nd edn, London: Business Books Macmillan, 1977.

Hill, R. W., *Marketing Technological Products to Industry*, Oxford: Pergamon Press, 1973.

Livesey, F., *The Distributive Trades*, London: Heinemann, 1979.

Randall, Geoffrey, *Marketing to the Retail Trade*, London: Heinemann, 1990.

Stern, L. W., El-Ansary, Adel J. and Brown, James R., *Management in Marketing Channels*, Englewood Cliffs, N.J.: Prentice-Hall, 1989.

West, Alan, *Managing Distribution and Change*, New York: Wiley, 1989.

■ Journals

> *Group Grocer*
> *International Journal of Physical Distribution and Materials Management*
> *Nielsen Reporter*
> *Retail Business*
> *Retailing and Distribution Management*

■ 10   Marketing research

Baker, M. J. and Hart, S., *Marketing and Competitive Success*, London: Philip Allen, 1989.

Chisnall, P., *Marketing Research*, 3rd edn, New York: McGraw-Hill, 1986.

Crimp, Margaret, *The Marketing Research Process*, 3rd edn, Englewood Cliffs, N.J.: Prentice-Hall, 1990.

Ehrenberg, A. S. C., *Data Reduction: Analysing and Interpreting Statistical Data*, New York: Wiley, 1975.

Enis, Ben M. and Broome, Charles L.. *Marketing Decisions: A Bayesian Approach*, Glasgow: International Textbooks, 1973.

Fitzroy, P. T., *Analytical Methods for Marketing Management*, New York: McGraw-Hill, 1976.

Green, Paul E. and Tull, Donald, *Research for Marketing Decisions*, Englewood Cliffs, N.J.: Prentice-Hall, 1978.

Hoinville, G., Jowell, R. and associates, *Survey Research Practice*, London: Heinemann, 1977.

Jain, Arun K. *et al.* (eds), *Marketing Research Applications and Problems*, New York: Wiley, London: Heinemann, 1972.

Luck, David J. and Rubin, Donald S., *Marketing Research*, 7th edn, Englewood Cliff, N.J.: Prentice-Hall, 1987.

Tull, D. S. and Hawkins, D. I., *Marketing Research: measurement and method*, 15th edn, West Drayton: Collier Macmillan, 1990.

■ 11 Product policy, planning and development

Baker, M. J., *Market Development*, Harmondsworth: Penguin, 1983.

Baker, M. J., *Marketing New Industrial Products*, London: Macmillan, 1975.

Baker, M. J. (ed.), *Industrial Innovation Technology Policy Diffusion*, London: Macmillan, 1979.

Baker, M. J. and McTavish, R., *Product Policy and Management*, London: Macmillan, 1976.

Bureau, J. R., *Brand Management*, London: Macmillan, 1981.

Carter, C. (ed.), *Industrial Policy and Innovation*, London: Heinemann, 1981.

Choffray, J. M. and Lilien, G. L., *Marketing Planning for New Industrial Products*, New York: Wiley, 1980.

Crawford, C. M., *New Products Management*, 2nd edn, Homewood, Ill.: Irwin, 1987.

Hisrich, R. D. and Peters, M. P., *Marketing Decisions for New and Mature Products*, Columbus, Ohio: Merrill, 1984.

Johne, Axel and Snelson, Patricia, *Successful Product Development*, Oxford: Blackwell, 1990.

Midgley, D. F., *Innovation and New Product Marketing*, London: Croom Helm, 1977.

Pessemier, E. A., *New Product Decisions: An Analytical Approach*, New York: McGraw-Hill, 1966.

Pessemier, E. A., *Product Management: Strategy and Organisation*, New York: Wiley, 1977.

Twiss, B. C., *Managing Technological Innovation*, 3rd edn, London: Pitman/Longman, 1986.

Wind, Yoram J., *Product Policy: Concepts, Methods and Strategy*, Addison-Wesley, 1982.

Rothwell, R. and Zegweld, W., *Reindustrialisation and Technology*, London: Pitman/Longman, 1985.

■ **Articles**

Constandse, William J. 'How to Launch New Products', *MSU Business Topics*, Winter 1971.
Horwood, William, 'Test Marketing on Trial', *Marketing*, July 1973.
Kline, Charles H., 'The Strategy of Product Policy', *Harvard Business Review*, July–August 1965.

■ 12   Packaging

Baker, Michael J., *Market Development*, Harmondsworth: Penguin, 1983.
Briston, J. G. and Veill, T. J., *Packaging Management*, London: Gower, 1972.
Kline, C. H. and Co. Inc., *Modern Packaging Encyclopeadia*, New York: McGraw-Hill, 1972.
Paine, F. A., *Fundamentals of Packaging*, London: Blackie & Son, 1962.
Pilditch, J. *The Silent Salesman*, London: Business Books, 1973.
Piner, S. H., *Modern Packaging Films*, London: Butterworth, 1967.

■ **Journals**

> *Packaging*
> *Packaging Directory*
> *Packaging Review*
> *Packaging Today*

■ 13   Pricing and price policy

Blackman, Jules, *Price Practices and Price Policies*, New York: Ronald Press, 1953.
Dean, Joel, *Managerial Economics*, Englewood Cliffs, N.J.: Prentice-Hall, 1951.
Gabor, A., *Pricing Principles and Practices*, London: Heinemann, 1977.
Marshall, A., *More Profitable Pricing*, New York: McGraw-Hill, 1980.
Winkler, John, *Pricing for Results*, London: Pan Books, 1984.
Price Commission Reports
Benke, R. L. and Edwards, J. D., 'Transfer Pricing Techniques and Uses', NAA, 1981.

▋ 14 Distribution policy and the selection of marketing channels

Baker, Michael J. *et al.*, *Marketing Theory and Practice*, 2nd edn, London: Macmillan, 1983.

Bucklin, Louis P., *A Theory of Distribution Channel Structure*, Institute of Business and Economic Research, Berkeley, CA: 1966.

Clewitt, Richard M. (ed.), *Marketing Channels for Manufactured Products*, Homewood, Ill.: Irwin, 1954.

Mallen, B., *Principles of Marketing Channel Management*, Lexington, MA: Lexington Books, 1977.

Stern, L. W. and El-Ansary, A. I., *Marketing Channels*, Englewood Cliffs, N.J.: Prentice-Hall, 1977.

Walker, B. J. and Haynes, J. B., *Marketing Channels and Institutions – Selected Readings*, Columbus, Ohio: Grid Press, 1978.

Waters, G. C., *Marketing Channels*, Santa Monica, CA: Goodyear, 1977.

See also texts for Chapter 9, Patterns of Distribution.

■ Articles

Bucklin, Louis P., 'A Theory of Channel Control', *Journal of Marketing*, vol. 37, January 1973, pp. 39–47.

Rosenberg, Larry J. and Stern, Louis W., 'Conflict Measurement in the Distribution Channel', *Journal of Marketing Research*, 8, November 1971.

■ Journals

European Journal of Physical Distribution
Journal of Marketing Management
Marketing
Retail and Distribution Management

■ 15 Marketing communications

Aaker, David A. and Myers, John G., *Advertising Management*, 3nd edn, Englewood Cliffs, N.J.: Prentice-Hall, 1990.

Baker, M. J. *et al.*, *Marketing Theory and Practice*, London: Macmillan, 1983, Chapter 6.

Baker, M. K., *The Marketing Book*, London, Heinemann, 1991, Chapter 19.

DeLoizier, M. Wayne, *The Marketing Communication Process*, New York: McGraw-Hill, 1976.

Dyer, Gillian, *Advertising as Communication*, London: Methuen, 1982.

Harris, Richard J. (ed.), *Information Processing Research in Advertising*, Hillsdale, NJ: Lawrence Erlbaum, 1983.

Hart, N., *Business to Business Advertising*, 3rd edn, London: Associated Business Programmes, 1984.

Jefkins, F., *Public Relations in Marketing Management*, London: Macmillan, 1985.

Percy, Larry and Rossiter, John R., *Advertising Strategy: A Communication Theory*, New York: Praeger, 1980.

Percy, Larry and Woodside, Arch W. (eds), *Advertising and Consumer Psychology*, Lexington, MA: Lexington Books, 1983.

■ 16   Advertising

Broadbent, S. (ed.), *Market Researchers Look at Advertising*, London: Sigmatext, 1980.

Broadbent, Simon and Jacobs, Brian, *Spending Advertising Money*, 4th edn, London: Business Books, 1984.

Corkindale, D. and Kennedy, Sherril, *Measuring the Effectiveness of Advertising*, London: Saxon House, 1975.

Davis, M., *The Effective Use of Advertising Media*, London: Business Books, 1981.

Glover, D., *The Sociology of the Mass Media*, Ormskirk: Causeway Press, 1984.

Hart, Norman, *Business to Business Advertising*, 3rd edn, Associated Business Press, 1984.

ISBA, *Choosing the Advertising Agency*, London: ISBA, 1990.

Jefkins, F., *Advertising Today*, 3rd edn, Glasgow: International Textbook Co., 1984.

Nevett, T. R., *Advertising in Britain: A History*, London: Heinemann, 1982.

Turner, E. S., *The Shocking History of Advertising*, Harmondsworth: Penguin, 1952.

Watson Dunn, S. and Barban, A. M., *Advertising: Its Role in Modern Marketing*, 5th edn, McGraw-Hill, 1982.

White, Roderick, *Advertising*, 2nd edn, New York: McGraw-Hill, 1988.

■ 17   Sales promotion

ISBA, *Guide to Sales Promotion*, London: ISBA, 1988.

Piper, J. (ed.), *Managing Sales Promotion*, London: Gower, 1980.

Quelch, John, *Sales Promotion Management*, Englewood Cliffs, N.J.: Prentice-Hall, 1989.

Spillard, Peter, *Sales Promotion: Its Place in Marketing Strategy*, 2nd edn, London: Business Publications, 1977.

Ward, J., *A Guide to Sales Promotion*, London: IPA, The Thomson Medals and Awards for Advertising Research, Thomson Organisation, 1969.

■ Articles

Hodgson, P., 'Sales Promotion Research: A Plea for More Research Investment', *Journal of the Market Research Society*, vol. 19, no. 1, January 1977.
Hodgson, P., 'What Happened to Sales Promotion Research?', *Marketing*, April 1977.

■ 18   Personal selling and merchandising

Bagozzi, R. P., *Developments from Behavioural and Decision Model Research*, Chicago: AMA/MSI Proceedings, 1979.
Cundiff, E. W. and Leonard, E. W., *Readings in Sales Management*, American Marketing Association, 1981.
Donaldson, Bill, *Sales Management Theory and Practice*, London: Macmillan, 1990.
Futrell, C., *Sales Management Behaviour, Practices and Cases*, London: Dryden Press, 1981.
Gillan, A., *The Principles and Practices of Personal Selling*, London: Heinemann, 1982.
Hartley, R. F., *Sales Management*, Boston: Houghton Mifflin, 1980.
Lancaster, G. and Jobber, D. *Sales Technique and Management*, 2nd edn, London: Pitman, 1990.
Ship, R. D., *Practical Selling*, Boston: Houghton Mifflin, 1980.
Stanton, W. J. and Buskirk, R. H., *Management of the Sales Force*, 5th edn, Homewood, Ill.: Irwin, 1978.
Still, R. R., Cundiff, G. W. and Govoni, N. A. P., *Sales Management: Decisions, Strategies and Cases*, Englewood Cliffs, N.J.: Prentice-Hall, 1987.
TACK, 'Salesman's Pay and Expenses', London: TACK, 1989.
Wilson, M., *Managing a Sales Force*, 2nd edn, London: Gower, 1983.

■ 19   The company: organising for marketing

Piercy, Nigel, *Marketing Organisation*, London: George Allen & Unwin, 1985.

■ 20   Planning for marketing

Abell, Derek F. and Hammond, John S., *Strategic Marketing Planning*, Englewood Cliffs, N.J.: Prentice-Hall, 1980.

Ackoff, R., *The Concept of Corporate Planning*, New York: Wiley, 1969.

Ansoff, H. I., *Corporate Strategy*, Harmondsworth: Penguin (Pelican), 1975.

Bureau, J. R., *Brand Management: Planning and Control*, London: Macmillan, 1981.

Kotler, P., *Marketing Management: Analysis, Planning and Control*, 6th edn, Englewood Cliffs, N.J.: Prentice-Hall, 1988.

Luck, D. *et al.*, *Marketing Strategy and Plans*, Englewood Cliffs, N.J.: Prentice-Hall, 1980.

Sizer, J., *An Insight into Management Accounting*, 2nd edn, Harmondsworth: Penguin, 1989.

Vause, R. and Woodward, N., *Finance for Managers*, 2nd edn, London: Macmillan, 1981.

■ 21   The written analysis of cases

Adler, Lee (ed.), *Plotting Marketing Strategy*, London: Business Books, 1968.

Easton, Geoff, *Learning From Case Studies*, London: Prentice-Hall International, 1982.

■ 22   Marketing in foreign environments

Albaum, G., Strandskov, J., Duers, E. and Dowd, L., *International Marketing and Export Management*, Reading, MA: Addison Wesley, 1989.

Branch, A. E., *Elements of Export Marketing and Management*, 2nd edn, London: Chapman & Hall, 1990.

Brooke, M. Z. and Remmers, H. L., *The Strategy of Multinational Enterprise*, 2nd edn, London: Pitman, 1978.

Cateora, P. R., *International Marketing*, 7th edn, Homewood, Ill.: Irwin, 1989.

Cundiff, E. W. and Hilger, M. T., *Marketing in the International Environment*, Englewood Cliffs, N.J.: Prentice-Hall, 1988.

Czinkota, M. and Ronkainen, I. K., *International Marketing*, 2nd edn, London: Dryden Press, 1990.

Deschampneufs, H., *Export for the Small Business*, London: Kogan Page, 1984.

Gilligan, C. and Hird, M., *International Marketing: Strategy and Management*, London: Croom Helm, 1986.

Jeannet, J. P. and Hennessey, H. D., *International Marketing Management: Strategies and Cases*, Boston: Houghton Mifflin, 1988.

Keegan, W. J., *Multinational Marketing Management*, 4th edn, Englewood Cliffs, N.J.: Prentice-Hall, 1988.

Onkviksit, S. and Shaw, J. J., *International Marketing*, Columbus Ohio: Merrill, 1989.

Paliwoda, S. J., *International Marketing*, London: Heinemann, 1986.

Piercy, N., *Export Strategy: Markets and Competition*, London: George Allen & Unwin, 1982.

Ricks, D., *Big Business Blunders*, Homewood, Ill.: Irwin, 1983.

Robock, S. H. and Simmonds, K., *International Business and Multinational Enterprises*, Homewood, Ill.: Irwin, 1983.

Root, F. R., *Entry Strategies for International Markets*, Lexington, MA: Lexington Books, 1987.

Rugman, A. and Lecraw, D., *International Business: Firm and Environment*, New York: McGraw-Hill, 1985.

Rutenberg, D. P., *Multinational Management*, Boston: Little, Brown, 1982.

Stapleton, J., *Elements of Export Marketing*, Cambridge: Woodhead-Faulkner, 1984.

Terpstra, V., *The Cultural Environment of International Business*, Cincinnati: South Western Publishing, 1983.

Terpstra, V., *International Marketing*, 4th edn, London: Dryden Press, 1987.

Young, S., Hamill, J. and Wheeler, C., *International Market Entry and Development: Strategy and Management*, Brighton: Wheatsheaf, 1989.

Whithead, G., *Elements of International Trade and Payments*, Cambridge: Woodhead-Faulkner, 1984.

■ Journals

British Business
Columbia Journal of World Business
Economist Intelligence Unit: Marketing in Europe
European Business
European Journal of Marketing
Export Times
Financial Times
The Economist

■ 23   The marketing of services

Bateson, J. E. G., *Managing Services Marketing*, London: Dryden Press, 1989.

Cowell, D., *The Marketing of Services*, London: Heinemann, 1985.

Eiglier, P., *Marketing Consumer Services: New Insights*, London: Marketing Science Institute, 1977

Giarini, O., *The Emerging Service Economy*, Geneva: World Services Forum, 1987.

Gronroos, C. *Strategic Marketing: Marketing in Service Industries*, Oxford: Chartwell-Bratt, 1985.

Lovelock, C., *Services Marketing*, Englewood Cliffs, N.J.: Prentice-Hall, 1984.

Normann, R., *Service Management: Strategy and Leadership in Service Business*, New York: John Wiley, 1987.
Rajan, A. *The Second Industrial Revolution*, London: Gower, 1987.

■ 24   Current issues and trends

Adamson, C., *Consumers in Business*, London: National Consumer Council, 1982.
Baker, M. J. (ed.), *Perspectives on Marketing*, New York: John Wiley, 1991.
Kotler, P., *Marketing for Non-Profit Organisations*, 2nd edn, Englewood Cliffs, N.J.: Prentice-Hall, 1982.

Index